A Grammar of Warlmanpa

A Grammar of Warlmanpa

As spoken by Bunny Naburula, Danny Cooper, Dick Foster, Donald Graham, Doris Kelly, Elizabeth Johnson, George Brown, Gladys Brown, Jack Walker, Jessie Cooper, Jimmy Newcastle, Julie Kelly, Lofty Japaljarri, Louie Martin, May Foster, Norah Graham, Penny Kelly, Penny Williams, Selina Grant, Susannah Nelson, Topsy Walker, Toprail Japaljarri and William Graham

MITCHELL BROWNE

ANU PRESS

ASIA-PACIFIC LINGUISTICS

ANU PRESS

Published by ANU Press
The Australian National University
Canberra ACT 2600, Australia
Email: anupress@anu.edu.au

Available to download for free at press.anu.edu.au

ISBN (print): 9781760466633
ISBN (online): 9781760466640

WorldCat (print): 1458062281
WorldCat (online): 1458062347

DOI: 10.22459/GW.2024

This title is published under a Creative Commons Attribution-NonCommercial-NoDerivatives 4.0 International (CC BY-NC-ND 4.0) licence.

The full licence terms are available at
creativecommons.org/licenses/by-nc-nd/4.0/legalcode

Cover design and layout by ANU Press.

Cover artwork: *Bush Peanut* by Penny Napaljarri Kelly,
© Penny Napaljarri Kelly/Copyright Agency, 2023.

This book is published under the aegis of the Asia-Pacific Linguistics editorial board of ANU Press.

This edition © 2024 ANU Press

Contents

List of illustrations	ix
Glossary	xvii
Acknowledgements	xxi
1. Introduction	1
1.1 Warlmanpa language and people	1
1.2 Methodology and aims of this grammar	17
1.3 Recordings	19
1.4 Grammar organisation	22
2. Phonetics and phonology	23
2.1 Phonemic inventory	23
2.2 Consonants	24
2.3 Vowels	34
2.4 Voicing	41
2.5 Phonotactics	42
2.6 Prosody	49
2.7 Vowel assimilation	55
2.8 Reduplication	59
3. Parts of speech	63
3.1 Nominals	65
3.2 Adverbs	81
3.3 Coverbs	81
3.4 Inflecting verbs	83
3.5 Auxiliary bases	84
3.6 Complementisers	86
3.7 Particles and interjections	86
3.8 Clitics	88
4. Nominals	91
4.1 Case morphology	95

	4.2 Adnominal case	124
	4.3 Number marking	129
	4.4 Derivational suffixes	137
	4.5 Demonstratives	146
	4.6 Ignoratives	153
	4.7 Further topics in nominals	162
5.	The auxiliary complex	171
	5.1 Internal structure	171
	5.2 Clausal positioning	172
	5.3 Auxiliary bases	175
	5.4 Bound pronouns	184
	5.5 =*nga* 'dubitative'	215
6.	Inflecting verbs	217
	6.1 The 'verb' word	218
	6.2 Inflecting verbs	220
	6.3 Direction and motion	264
	6.4 Directional and aspectual verb morphology	266
	6.5 Derivational morphology	275
	6.6 Further topics in verbs	288
7.	Coverbs	301
	7.1 Coverb morphology	303
	7.2 Coverb phonology	306
	7.3 Coverb syntax	308
	7.4 Coverb types	311
8.	Adverbs	319
	8.1 Manner adverbs	319
	8.2 Temporal adverbs	323
	8.3 Spatial adverbs	325
	8.4 Recognitional adverbs	327
9.	Particles, interjections and clitics	331
	9.1 Particles	331
	9.2 Interjections	337
	9.3 Doubly classified particles and interjections	340
	9.4 Clitics	342
10.	Grammatical relations	357
	10.1 Grammatical relations	357
	10.2 Verbal clauses	369

11.	Syntax of simple clauses	389
	11.1 Phrase structure and non-configurationality	390
	11.2 Copula constructions	399
	11.3 Verbless clauses	401
	11.4 Interrogative clauses	403
	11.5 Negation	408
	11.6 Secondary predicates	419
	11.7 Dislocation	426
12.	Syntax of complex clauses	431
	12.1 Complementisers	431
	12.2 Coordination	467
	12.3 Discourse relations between independent clauses	473
Appendix A: Inflecting verb finder list		477
	A.1 Class 1 verbs	480
	A.2 Class 2 verbs	486
	A.3 Class 3 verbs	501
	A.4 Class 4 verbs	507
	A.5 Class 5 verbs	508
Appendix B: Narrative collection		513
	B.1 Biography	513
	B.2 A boy and his dog	516
	B.3 Reminiscences of youth	518
	B.4 Palyupalyu dreaming story	525
Appendix C: Alternative verb analysis		531
Bibliography		535

List of illustrations

Figures

Figure 1.1 The Ngumpin-Yapa subgroup	2
Figure 1.2 Marriage preferences and father–child relations across subsections	10
Figure 1.3 Warlmanpa kinterms (male ego) in standard Aranda diagram	12
Figure 2.1 Spectrogram and intensity of *ngappa* 'water'	28
Figure 2.2 Spectrogram and intensity of *yapa* 'person'	28
Figure 2.3 Duration of bilabial stops, including long stops where the nominal root does not constitute the entire phonological word	31
Figure 2.4 Vowel ellipses of one speaker (DG) based on 677 tokens	34
Figure 2.5 Averaged realisations of short vowel allophones (categorised by phoneme) from one speaker (DG), based on 663 tokens	35
Figure 2.6 TextGrid and waveform of Example (41)	38
Figure 2.7 Formant data of three extra-long vowels	39
Figure 2.8 Formant tracking of the extra-lengthened /a/ vowel in Example (43)	40
Figure 2.9 Voicing of utterance-final vowels	41
Figure 2.10 Spectrogram of utterance-final voice creaking, spreading to the preceding consonant	42
Figure 2.11 Frequency of most common intra-morphemic consonant clusters	47
Figure 2.12 Pitch of declarative sentences and interrogative sentences	53
Figure 2.13 Pitch of polar question *pakarnun* 'did you kill it?'	54
Figure 2.14 Pitch contour of polar question *nyangujun ngayinya ngarnki* 'have you seen my partner?'	54
Figure 4.1 Configuration that prompted Example (306)	148

Figure 5.1 Temporal schema of Example (399), where *ka*- does not require coercion — 177

Figure 5.2 Temporal schema of Example (400), coercing *ka*- 'be' as a [+telic] event with habitual aspect — 178

Figure 6.1 Word-formation processes involved in a well-formed verb — 220

Figure 6.2 Temporal schema of Example (540) — 242

Figure 6.3 Temporal schema of Example (557) — 248

Figure 6.4 Temporal representation of the situations denoted in Example (624) — 272

Figure 6.5 Temporal schema of Example (625), a durative event with perfective aspect and event time as a proper subset of topic time — 273

Figure 6.6 Temporal schema of Example (626), a durative event with imperfective aspect and topic time as a subset of event time — 273

Figure 6.7 Summary of instantiated uses of the irrealis tense inflections (disregarding imperative moods) — 299

Figure 9.1 Temporal schema of the situations denoted in Example (804) — 346

Figure 9.2 Temporal schema of the situations denoted in Example (806b) — 347

Figure 11.1 Prosodic separation of afterthoughts from the other constituents in the clause — 428

Figure 12.1 Semantic hierarchy of suffixes related to *-ku* 'dative' — 464

Maps

Map 1.1 Map of Ngumpin-Yapa language areas and languages neighbouring Warlmanpa — 2

Map 1.2 Warlmanpa country and surrounding areas — 6

Plates

Plate 1.1 From left: Bonnie McLean, Penny Kelly Napaljarri, Mitch Browne and Susannah Nelson Nakamarra in Tennant Creek — 16

Plate 1.2 Susannah Nelson Nakamarra at Kajinpuru, just north of Banka Banka Station — 16

Tables

Table 1.1 Some areas where Warlmanpa people have lived in the past century	5
Table 1.2 Warlmanpa subsection names	9
Table 1.3 Warlpiri subsection names	9
Table 1.4 Subsection and preferred partners based on female subsection	11
Table 1.5 Distinctions in sibling kinterms	13
Table 1.6 Speakers referred to in this grammar	19
Table 1.7 Most commonly referred to collections in this grammar with corresponding year of collection	21
Table 1.8 Organisation of this grammar	22
Table 2.1 Phonemic consonant inventory in International Phonetic Alphabet with orthographic representation given in parentheses where they differ	24
Table 2.2 Vowel phonemes (with orthography given in parentheses where it differs from the International Phonetic Alphabet)	24
Table 2.3 Length of stops	27
Table 2.4 List of known geminate stops in Warlmanpa, with a corresponding Warumungu form, where known	29
Table 2.5 Palatal glide deletion	33
Table 2.6 Labiovelar glide deletion	33
Table 2.7 Root morpheme syllable length	43
Table 2.8 Segment frequency at word boundaries	45
Table 2.9 Consonant frequency across nominals, adverbs and coverbs	46
Table 2.10 Vowel frequency across nominals, adverbs and coverbs	46
Table 2.11 Frequency of consonant clusters in lexicon (phonemes sorted by frequency)	48
Table 2.12 Cluster types by frequency	48
Table 2.13 Summary of Warlmanpa vowel assimilation processes	55
Table 2.14 Reduplication of 'temporal' nominals and adverbs	60
Table 2.15 Reduplication of 'human' nominals	60
Table 2.16 Reduplication of directional nominals	60
Table 2.17 Reduplication of other nominals	61

Table 2.18 English/Kriol animal words borrowed in their reduplicated forms	61
Table 3.1 Summary of derivational suffixes that change the word class of the stem	64
Table 3.2 Free-person pronoun forms	76
Table 3.3 Forms of first and second-person free pronouns	77
Table 3.4 Particles and interjections in Warlmanpa	87
Table 4.1 Nominal suffixes in Warlmanpa	94
Table 4.2 Behaviour of different types of nominal morphology	95
Table 4.3 Prototypical case-marking patterns based on predicate valency	96
Table 4.4 Yankunytjatjara case endings	97
Table 4.5 Patterns of grammatical relation alignments across subsystems of Warlmanpa grammar	98
Table 4.6 Case allomorphy in Warlmanpa	102
Table 4.7 Instantiated interpretations of the dative suffix	106
Table 4.8 Composition of the aversive case in Warlpiri, Warlmanpa and Ngardi	119
Table 4.9 Nominal number marking	129
Table 4.10 Likely stages of borrowing -tarra from Mudburra	134
Table 4.11 Overview of Warlmanpa semblative forms and functions with corresponding Warlpiri cognate forms and functions	138
Table 4.12 Spatial proximity demonstratives inflected for most nominal cases	146
Table 4.13 The proximal demonstrative series in Warlmanpa, Bilinarra, Gurindji and Warlpiri	147
Table 4.14 Lexemes encoding knowledge categories	153
Table 4.15 Derived lexemes encoding knowledge categories	154
Table 4.16 Animacy distinctions in ignorative nominals in Warlmanpa, Warlpiri and Warumungu	155
Table 4.17 Standard possession suffixes across parts of speech	162
Table 4.18 Types of nominal possession	163
Table 4.19 Modes of expression of quantification in Warlmanpa	169
Table 5.1 Auxiliary complex template	172
Table 5.2 Auxiliary complex positioning	181

LIST OF ILLUSTRATIONS

Table 5.3 Form of bound pronouns	185
Table 5.4 Discontinuous subject and plural number marking involving =*lu* in bound pronouns	188
Table 5.5 Known bound pronoun combinations with two referents	196
Table 5.6 Bound pronoun template, with examples	198
Table 5.7 Distinguishing bound pronoun ordering constraints of 1PL.EXCL.NS + 2SG.S	199
Table 5.8 Examples of first-person subjects preceding all other material in the template	200
Table 5.9 Examples of object–subject ordering in the template	200
Table 5.10 Bound pronouns with =*lu* to mark plurality	201
Table 5.11 Examples of *lu* marking subject plurality	201
Table 5.12 Examples of null subject number marking	202
Table 5.13 Examples of reflexive and third-person oblique marking	202
Table 5.14 Examples of bound pronouns cross-referencing three referents	202
Table 5.15 Unpredicted form =*nyanun*	203
Table 5.16 Unpredicted form =*npalangu*	203
Table 5.17 Bound pronouns with *pala* marking dual number	204
Table 5.18 Abridged template approach with extended number slot allowing dual marking	204
Table 5.19 Bound pronouns pairs that mark non-subject status with *ngu*	205
Table 5.20 Possible history of the irregular form =*njarrangu*	207
Table 5.21 Imperative bound pronoun forms, identical to non-imperative third-person forms	207
Table 5.22 Cross-referencing of grammatical relations in the bound pronouns	212
Table 6.1 Structure of the verb word	218
Table 6.2 Example verb formations involving associated motion and inceptive derivations	219
Table 6.3 Inflections of verb classes	221
Table 6.4 Example correspondences between the infinitive form and the counterfactual form of verbs	222
Table 6.5 Example correspondences between the imperative form and the subjunctive form of verbs	222

Table 6.6 Class 1 verb forms	223
Table 6.7 Examples of Class 2 verb forms	224
Table 6.8 Class 3 verb forms, including Nash's (1979) division into two subclasses	224
Table 6.9 Class 4 verb forms	226
Table 6.10 Class 5a verb forms	226
Table 6.11 Forms of the augment by verb class and TAM inflection	227
Table 6.12 High vowel alternations in verb roots by class and inflection	229
Table 6.13 Summary of root vowel alternations	230
Table 6.14 Restrictions on -*NVrra* contraction for past inflections (augments omitted from the forms)	231
Table 6.15 Differences in the conditioning of the contraction process between inflections	232
Table 6.16 Imperative form allomorphy (with augment)	233
Table 6.17 Interspeaker variation of the imperative form for 1b verbs	236
Table 6.18 Form of the past-tense inflection by class	240
Table 6.19 Form of the present-tense inflection by class	242
Table 6.20 Form of the future inflection by verb class	245
Table 6.21 Form of the potential inflection by verb class	250
Table 6.22 Subjunctive form allomorphy	252
Table 6.23 Counterfactual inflection allomorphy	255
Table 6.24 Infinitive form allomorphy	257
Table 6.25 Morphologically conditioned allomorphy of the infinitive suffix (omitting augment)	257
Table 6.26 Verbal motion suffixes	266
Table 6.27 AM suffixes that produce a bound stem requiring further TAM morphology	276
Table 6.28 The interpretation of event structure in non-AM and AM constructions	277
Table 6.29 Permissible inflections following AM morphemes	278
Table 6.30 The interpretation of 'reference' time in inceptive and non-inceptive constructions	282

Table 6.31 Aktionsart of *-ja-* based on status of derived word	287
Table 6.32 Selected related languages sharing a verb suffix '*-rra*'	289
Table 6.33 Co-occurrences of AM stems with directional suffixes	290
Table 6.34 The use of *-ku* on finite verbs in Ngumpin-Yapa languages	294
Table 6.35 Distinguishing types of counterfactual constructions in Warlpiri and Warlmanpa	298
Table 7.1 Coverb exceptions to regular phonotactic constraints	306
Table 7.2 Examples of tight nexus coverbs	315
Table 8.1 Common temporal adverbs, divided by whether they relate to the day/night cycle	323
Table 8.2 Catalogue of spatial adverbs	325
Table 8.3 Nash's (1979) paradigm of cardinal directions	325
Table 9.1 Use of *kulanganta* in Warlpiri, Warlmanpa and Ngardi	334
Table 9.2 Summary of Warlmanpa clitics	342
Table 9.3 Clitics marking information status	353
Table 10.1 Criteria for distinguishing grammatical relations in Warlmanpa	358
Table 10.2 Morphosyntactic criteria for subjects	358
Table 10.3 Morphosyntactic criteria for objects	359
Table 10.4 Morphosyntactic criteria for indirect objects	360
Table 10.5 The distinctions between indirect objects, benefactive adjuncts and non-benefactive adjuncts	362
Table 10.6 Morphosyntactic criteria for external objects	363
Table 10.7 Morphosyntactic criteria for adjuncts	365
Table 10.8 Types of case frames selected for by predicates in Warlmanpa	369
Table 10.9 Marking of the argument in an intransitive clause	372
Table 10.10 Inflecting verbs with intransitive case frames	372
Table 10.11 Marking of arguments in a transitive clause	375
Table 10.12 Inflecting verbs that permit transitive patterns	375
Table 10.13 Marking of quasi-transitive arguments	378
Table 10.14 Marking of semi-transitive arguments	379
Table 10.15 Marking of conative arguments	381

Table 10.16 Marking of ditransitive arguments	383
Table 10.17 Marking of extended transitive arguments	386
Table 11.1 Extent of evidence for noun phrases based on four parameters from Louagie and Verstraete (2016)	397
Table 11.2 Negation strategies across speakers and clause types	409
Table 11.3 Strategies for prohibition in Warlmanpa compared with other Ngumpin-Yapa languages	415
Table 11.4 Truth value of the proposition denoted by types of secondary predicates relative to time of matrix event	424
Table 11.5 Encoded information by a depictive secondary predicate with temporal clitics	424
Table 12.1 Overview of Warlmanpa complementisers	435
Table 12.2 Cooperative truth conditions of kari when not combining with a counterfactual protasis	445
Table 12.3 Warlpiri cognates of Warlmanpa *nga=*	449
Table 12.4 Non-finite complementisers	452
Table 12.5 Shared forms between conjunctions and auxiliary bases	467
Table 12.6 Relations beyond the clause	474
Appendix Table A.1 Complete alphabetical verb list	477
Appendix Table C.1 Alternative verb root paradigm	531
Appendix Table C.2 Alternative verb inflection paradigm	532

Glossary

1	first person
2	second person
3	third person
ABS	absolutive
ALL	allative
ANOTHER	another
ASSOC	associated
AVER	aversive
AWAY	away
CAUSE	causative
CFACT	counterfactual
CONC	concurrent
CONJ	conjunction
CONT	continuous
DAT	dative
DENIZEN	denizen
DESIRE	desirous
DU	dual
DUB	dubitative
ELA	elative
ERG	ergative
EVIT	evitative
EXCL	exclusive
FOC	focus

FUT	future
GEN	genitive
HAB	habitual
IMP	imperative
IMPF	imperfective
INCL	inclusive
INF	infinitive
LIKE	like
LOC	locative
MOT	associated motion
NEG	negative
NMLZ	nominaliser
NOM	nomic
NS	non-subject
OBL	oblique
PAST	past
PERL	perlative
PL	plural
POST	posterior
POT	potential
PREP	preparative purposive
PRES	present
PRIV	privative
PROP	proprietive
RDP	reduplication
REFL	reflexive and/or reciprocal
REL	relative
RESIDE	resident
RESULT	resultative
S	subject
SEQ	sequential
SG	singular

SS	same subject
STILL	still
SUBJ	subjunctive
THEN	now/then
TOP	topic
TRANSL	translative
TWD	towards
WHEN	when
WITHOUT	without

Acknowledgements

I have benefited from the support of many wonderful and brilliant people during the writing of this book. This acknowledgements section understates my appreciation for everyone who has contributed to this project or otherwise supported me in any way.

First and foremost, I would like to thank the Warlmanpa people who welcomed me into their community and so patiently taught me what I know of their language (no matter how many times I misunderstood or mispronounced words). In particular, I am incredibly grateful to my language teachers Agnes Parker, Dick Foster, Doris Kelly, Gladys Brown, Julie Kelly, Penny Kelly, Penny Williams, Roseanna Foster, Selina Grant, Susannah Nelson and William Graham. Many of these people were also language teachers for David Nash. I would also like to thank the Warlmanpa-language teachers for Kenneth Hale and David Nash who have not already been mentioned, especially Aubrey Japanangka, Angus Riley, Bunny Nabarula, Donald Graham, George Brown, Hilda Johnson, Janet Napurrula, Jessie Cooper, Jimmy Newcastle, Lofty, Mary Kelly, May Foster, Norah Graham, Norma Foster and Peter Toprail. Without these people, this project would simply have been impossible.

I credit any of my remaining sanity to David Osgarby and Tom Ennever (fellow postgraduate Ngumpin-Yapa grammar writers). I will always cherish their friendship and support. Moreover, their ability to help me turn my incoherent thoughts into (somewhat coherent) grammatical analyses has been invaluable.

I am also extremely grateful to my PhD advisory team: Felicity Meakins, Mary Laughren and David Nash, who were always willing to read the chapters I sent off to them and respond with helpful feedback and suggestions. Felicity chose to accept me onto this project in the first place and has been so supportive of my work ever since. Mary provided valuable insights into my analyses, especially from the perspective of academic literature on Warlpiri, as well as generous amounts of relevant Warlpiri language data. David has paved the way for this research with the work he has done with Warlmanpa people. David was (and still is) incredibly patient and kind about putting up with my endless questions.

Alice Gaby and Harold Koch, as well as two anonymous reviewers, provided many insightful suggestions that have greatly improved the readability of this manuscript.

My first field trip to Tennant Creek was under the wings of David Nash, Jane Simpson and Samantha Disbray, who showed me how rewarding linguistic fieldwork can be, and they have continued to provide me with many insights throughout this project. I would also like to thank Ken Hale. I never met Ken, but the work he did with Warlmanpa people (and beyond) provided the foundations for this project.

In Tennant Creek, Barkly Regional Arts has been incredibly supportive of this project in so many aspects—in particular, I would like to thank Georges Bureau and Alan Murn. I am also grateful to the Charles Darwin University Tennant Creek Centre, which allowed me to use their space to work and record, and I am particularly grateful to Helen Hargraves. Papulu Apparr-kari Aboriginal Corporation has also been supportive of this project.

This project benefited from the financial support of the Australian Research Council, specifically via the Centre of Excellence for the Dynamics of Language (CoEDL; CE140100041), throughout my PhD candidature and a Post-Submission Scholarship, as well as via DP220102925. Additionally, I am grateful for financial support from the Australian Academy of the Humanities through the 2021 Publication Subsidy Scheme.

I have several absolutely delightful people to thank for their friendship, which made Brisbane a wonderful place to live: Amanda Hamilton-Hollaway, Claire Gourlay, Greg Dickson, Jayden Macklin-Cordes, Jacqui Cook, Janet Watts, Steffi Cook and Vivien Dunn.

Back in Perth, various friends have also provided me (virtual) company throughout my candidature, particularly James Allan, Theo Doraisamy, Paul Francis, Hugo Innes, Adrian Mennie, Sam Morgan and Sam Wilson.

I am forever grateful to Alexandra Miller, who has been a constant source of support. My family and, in particular, my parents, Fiona, Di, Adam and Luci, who have always supported me unconditionally.

1
Introduction

Warlmanpa is a Pama-Nyungan language of Australia presently spoken in Tennant Creek in the Northern Territory and surrounding country.[1] This book is a grammatical description of the language (and a revised version of my thesis: Browne [2021a]). This chapter contextualises the grammar. First, I discuss the Warlmanpa language and its people (§1.1). I then provide an overview of my methodology and aims (§1.2) and describe the recordings that are used in this grammar (§1.3). This chapter concludes with a summary of the structure of this grammar (§1.4).

1.1 Warlmanpa language and people

1.1.1 Warlmanpa language genetic affiliation

Warlmanpa country is located north-north-west of Tennant Creek in the Tanami Desert. Map 1.1 situates Warlmanpa relative to present-day towns and the locations of other languages. The term 'Warlmanpa' is used by speakers to refer to both the people and the language. Some speakers, particularly those more affiliated with Warlpiri, use the term 'Warnmanpa'.

---

[1] Aboriginal and Torres Strait Islander peoples should be aware that this book contains the images and names of people who have since passed away.

A GRAMMAR OF WARLMANPA

Map 1.1 Map of Ngumpin-Yapa language areas and languages neighbouring Warlmanpa
Cartography: Brenda Thornley, adapted from Meakins et al. (2023).

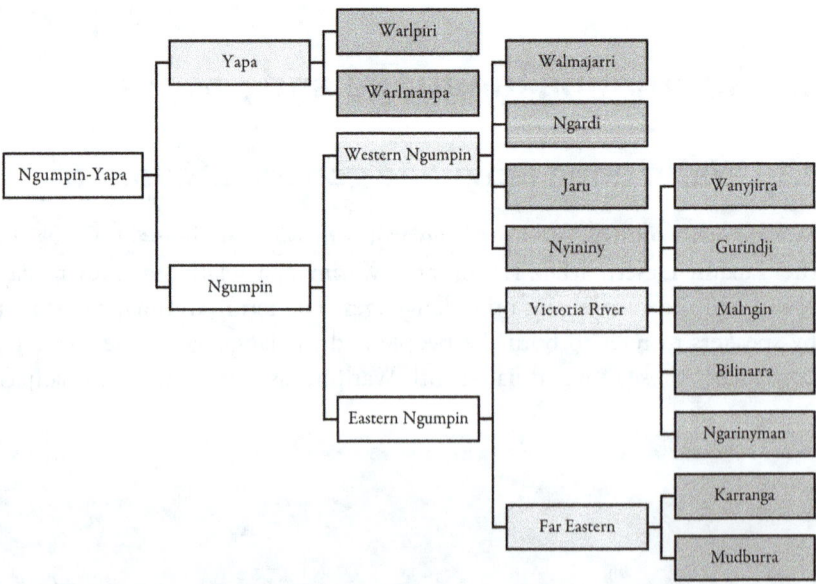

Figure 1.1 The Ngumpin-Yapa subgroup
Source: Adapted from Meakins et al. (2023).

Warlmanpa is a Ngumpin-Yapa language and the area in which it is spoken is bordered by several other Ngumpin-Yapa languages, as shown in Map 1.1. Warlpiri is found to the south-west, Gurindji to the west and Mudburra to the north. It also borders some non-Ngumpin-Yapa languages: Warumungu (Warumungic) to the south-east and Jingulu (Mirndi, non-Pama-Nyungan) to the north-east.[2]

The subgrouping of Ngumpin-Yapa languages is shown in Figure 1.1. Ngumpin-Yapa has two primary subgroupings: Yapa languages (Warlpiri and Warlmanpa) and Ngumpin languages. In the original classification of O'Grady et al. (1966: 39), Ngumpin ('Ngumbin') and Yapa ('Ngarga') did not form a single language family, rather both were analysed as subgroups of Pama-Nyungan. Laughren and McConvell (2004) demonstrate that Ngumpin and Yapa languages have several shared innovations, thus making Ngumpin-Yapa languages a subgroup of Pama-Nyungan (the Pama-Nyungan boundary is indicated by the dark line in Map 1.1). Furthermore, Laughren and McConvell reclassified Ngardi as a Ngumpin language based on morphological features found in it and Ngumpin but not in Yapa languages. Ngardi had previously been analysed as a Yapa ('Ngarga') language in O'Grady et al.'s classification. The present subgrouping of Warlpiri and Warlmanpa as the two Yapa languages is formally justified by a lexicostatistic analysis of cognates, demonstrated in Bowern and Atkinson (2012). Interestingly, this analysis also included Warumungu as a Ngumpin-Yapa language, as a sister to the Yapa branch (Bowern and Atkinson 2012: 835).

1.1.2 Warlmanpa people and language through time

Warlmanpa people have a close connection to Warlpiri and Warumungu people, as evidenced by the shared custody of places such as Pawurrinji, Miyikampi and Kanturrpa (ALC 1982a: 2) and the close similarity of subsection terms. The particularly strong connection between Warlmanpa and Warlpiri people is also demonstrated by Warumungu people often referring to Warlmanpa people as Warlpiri people (Nash 1992; Stanner 1979: 47). Indeed, Tindale lists 'Walmanba' as an alternative of Warlpiri. Conversely, Bell (2002: 7) groups Warlmanpa and Warumungu people together when describing the approximate population proportions of

---

2   Note I use a loose definition of 'borders', which is not intended to indicate discrete zones of land.

Alekarenge in 1976: 'Warlpiri constituted about 35 per cent of the Aboriginal population, Warumungu/Warlmanpa 20 per cent, Kaytej [Kaytetye] 10 per cent, Alyawarra [Alyawarr] 35 percent.'

This close connection has obscured the history of the Warlmanpa people in early sources (elaboration and further reasons are given by Nash [1992]). Before Capell (1952), who still considered 'Walmanba' a dialect of Warlpiri, there is sparse published material referencing the Warlmanpa language or people. A small number of sources refers to the name 'Wulmala', such as Spencer and Gillen (1904), who consider 'Warramunga' (Warumungu), 'Walpari' (Warlpiri) and 'Wulmala' three strongly connected groups. However, it is not clear that the term 'Wulmala' in fact refers to Warlmanpa people (see Nash 1992: 5); rather, it more likely refers to a group of Warlpiri people. Interestingly, Nash (1992) suggests that the Warlpiri people whom Spencer and Gillen met in Tennant Creek may have been speaking Warlmanpa.

Nash (1992: 7), via the Northern Territory Administration's 1957 Register of Wards, gives a preliminary distribution of people who identify as Warlmanpa. The most populated (recorded) location of Warlmanpa people was at Helen Springs Station (with four people), with others found at Banka Banka (one), Brunchilly (one), Renner Springs (two) and Montejinnie (two), although there is no information regarding when they came to be considered 'wards'.[3] However, Nash also notes that this distribution may not be accurate, as many people who identified as Warumungu could equally have identified as Warlmanpa.

Records of Warlmanpa became more frequent after Capell (1952), who treated Warlmanpa as a dialect of Warlpiri. The next known recording of Warlmanpa was collected by Ken Hale in 1959 or so. In 1966 Ken Hale and P. Chakravarti each recorded Warlmanpa in Tennant Creek, while David Nash began documenting Warlmanpa in 1977. Nash's (1979) grammatical preface (and accompanying vocabulary) is the most extensive prior study of the grammar (later studies include published analyses of subcomponents of the grammar, especially from a comparative perspective [Browne 2020a, 2021b; Browne et al. 2024]).[4] Several other sources have recorded and/or

---

3   A 'ward', specifically in the context of (European) Northern Territory laws at the time, refers to a person who 'is in need of special care', 'by reason of (a) his manner of living; (b) his inability, without assistance, adequately to manage his own affairs; (c) his standard of social habit and behaviour; and (d) his personal associations' (The Northern Territory of Australia 1977: 2312). People who were considered 'wards' were under the strict control of the director of welfare. In particular, the director controlled where the ward could live and 'placed the ward under the control or management of the person in charge of the conveyance, ship, or premises' (The Northern Territory of Australia 1977: 2314).
4   A comprehensive overview of references to Warlmanpa language is maintained by David Nash and is available online at: www0.anu.edu.au/linguistics/nash/aust/wpa/lx-ref.html.

published Warlmanpa language: in 1984, Adam Kendon recorded a few hours of Warlmanpa sign language, including a short video accompanied by a spoken narrative in Warlmanpa; a Warlmanpa biocultural knowledge book has been published (Nabarula et al. 2022); and, since 2002, the Central Land Council has recorded a number of videos of ecological knowledge in Warlmanpa.[5]

Table 1.1 Some areas where Warlmanpa people have lived in the past century[6]

Name	European name
Alekarenge	Warrabri, Ali Curung
Construction of the Warrabri (now Alekarenge) settlement began in 1955 as the Phillip Creek Mission was running out of useable water. All people who were considered wards living at Phillip Creek were moved to Alekarenge, in addition to Kaytetye and Alyawarr people from other areas. As a result, Warlmanpa, Warumungu, Warlpiri, Kaytetye and Alyawarr peoples came to occupy Kaytetye land. Living at Alekarenge (and other factors)—particularly for those removed from their land—has had an adverse effect (see, for example, the account of Bunny Naburula [CLC 2015: 357–58]).	
Jurnkkurakurr	Tennant Creek
Located on Warumungu land, Tennant Creek was 'claimed' as a telegraph station in 1872 and soon became a gold mining town. It was formally established as a permanent town in 1948 (Lea 1989; Nash 1997), two years after Aboriginal people were prohibited from living in the area. Many, if not most, Warlmanpa people presently live here. The name Jurnkkurakurr (Jurnkurakurra in Warlmanpa) refers specifically to a waterhole near the town.	
Kurlumirntini	Elliott
Mangarlawurru	—
Manuwangu	Muckaty
Mangkamarnta	Phillip Creek Mission
Also pronounced Mangkamarntangi, or Mangkamanta, the Phillip Creek Mission was established in 1945 (Nash 1997) by the Northern Territory Government to remove Aboriginal people from Tennant Creek (and surrounding areas), as Tennant Creek was 'declared a prohibited area for natives' (Carrington 1946: C4).	
Nyanya	Helen Springs Station
Parnkurr-parnkurr	Banka Banka Station
Banka Banka Station was established as a cattle station in the 1880s on Warumungu land. Warlmanpa and Warumungu moved to the station to work there. Many Warlmanpa speakers in Tennant Creek today were born and/or worked at Banka Banka Station (Nash 1997).	

---

5   These videos are currently available online at: www.clc.org.au/articles/info/indigenous-ecological-knowledge. See also: ictv.com.au/languages/group/146.
6   Unless otherwise stated, the source for all figures and tables is the author's own research.

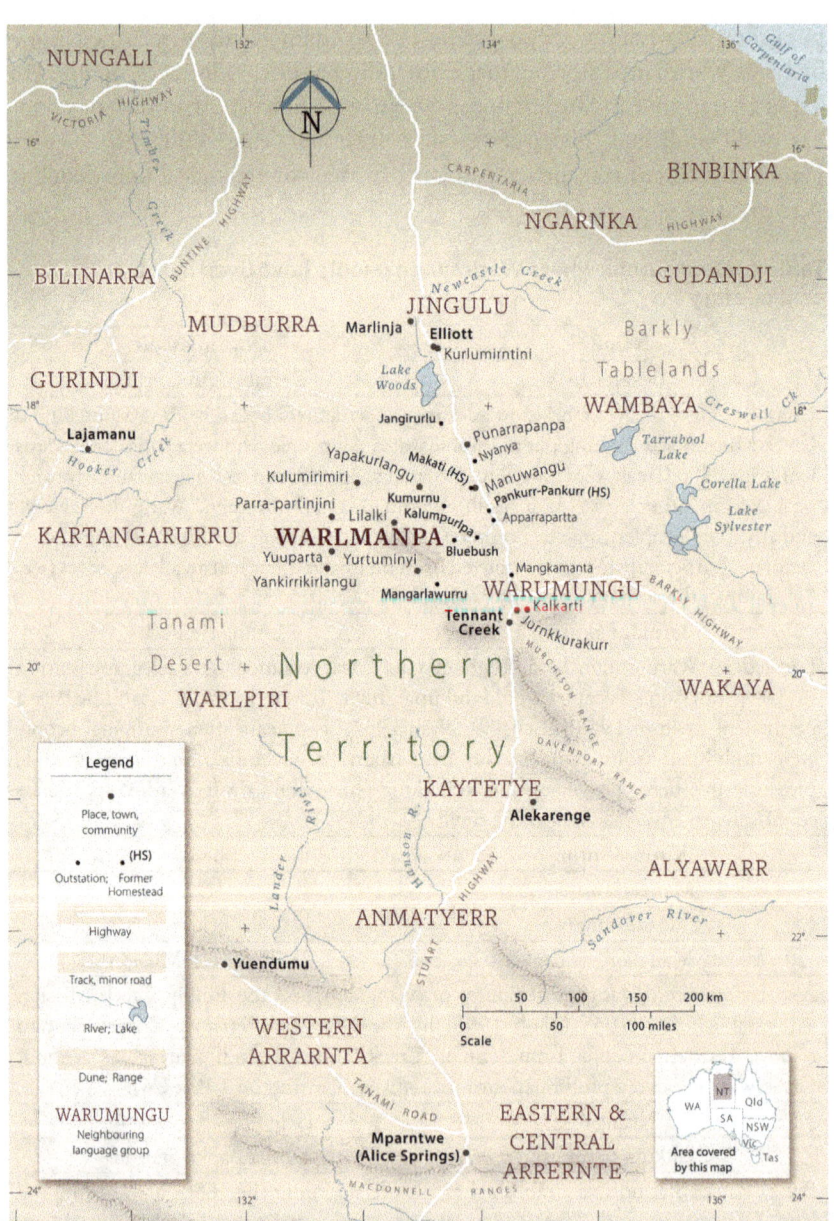

Map 1.2 Warlmanpa country and surrounding areas
Source: Brenda Thornley.

Table 1.1 provides an overview of some of the places where Warlmanpa people have lived since the late 1800s. In this table I make note of the traditional landowners for context, however, it should be read with caution, as the situation regarding land use and ownership is considerably more complex than what is conveyed here. Most names refer to sites on or near the European settlement or station and have been coopted to refer to the general area of European settlement. These locations are shown in Map 1.2. For more details of Warlmanpa places, the reader is directed to land claims (ALC 1982a, 1982b, 1997) and the analysis in Nash (1992).

Based on what we know of the history of the Warlmanpa people, Nash (1992: 11) notes:

> They have suffered this century as much as any neighbouring Aboriginal groups from disease and dispossession, but in one respect their history differs from the Warumungu, Jingili, Mudburra, Gurindji or Warlpiri: their institutionalised confinement has been away from the country of their language.

Turning to the present situation, an informal survey conducted by Papulu Appar-kari Aboriginal Corporation in 2014 lists 38 people who identify as Warlmanpa living in Tennant Creek. A small number of Warlmanpa people also live in Mparntwe (Alice Springs). I am not aware of any other locations where Warlmanpa people reside. Although the town of Tennant Creek is on Warumungu land, English and Wumpurrarni English are the present *lingua francas*. The primary school and high school curriculums are taught in English, although there are occasionally some Warumungu modules. Warlpiri (and numerous other traditional Australian languages) is spoken in Tennant Creek, however, this is to a lesser extent than English, Wumpurrarni English or Warumungu. Warlpiri is more commonly spoken presently in Yuendumu, Nyirrpi, Wirliyajarrayi (Willowra) and Lajamanu, and has seen sustained education programs largely designed and implemented by Warlpiri people (for an overview, see Disbray et al. [2020]; Browne and Napaljarri [2021]).

The language centre operating in Tennant Creek, Papulu Apparr-kari, aims to maintain and revitalise 16 languages—Warumungu, Warlpiri, Alyawarr, Kayetye, Warlmanpa, Wakaya, Mudburra, Wambaya, Jingulu, Kudanji, Ngarnga, Binbinga, Garrawa, Yanyuwa, Waanyi and Mara—in addition to providing numerous non-language services. For Warlmanpa, this has resulted in several illustrated picture books (including audiobooks) and mediation between linguists and the community (for example, hosting meetings). Warlmanpa is no longer used by speakers on a day-to-day basis and, to my knowledge, no children are acquiring the language.

1.1.3 Social organisation

1.1.3.1 Sociocentric kin terminology

The social organisation of Warlmanpa people is partly reflected in the subsection system, in which each person is assigned a subsection (or 'skin name') based on their parents' subsection. There are eight subsections, with a gender distinction for each. A person's subsection indicates preferred marriage partners and the types of relationships one has with people (depending on the relation between each person's subsection) and numerous other aspects of their life. In my experience, most Warlmanpa speakers in Tennant Creek do not use skin names on a daily basis. The Warlpiri forms are used more often, even in Warlmanpa recording sessions.[7] Despite this, the underlying system itself is used on a day-to-day basis but using Warlpiri terminology. Moreover, the social restrictions are still in place. For example, Dick Foster, who is Jangala, cannot directly work with (or talk to, etcetera) any Nakama women, because Nakama is *kurntanga* ('mother-in-law') to Jangala, so any trips or recording sessions with Jangala and a Nakama require (at least) a third party.

The Warlmanpa skin names are given in Table 1.2. The initial segment is historically a prefix—an apical nasal for females and a palatal stop for males (McConvell 1985)—however, it cannot be recognised as a synchronic prefix because there are some minor variations in the roots, for example, Jupula–Napula, where the vowel in the first syllable differs. The Warlpiri forms are given in Table 1.3 (and the system is discussed in further detail below), as they will be frequently used in examples throughout this grammar. The 'code' column represents the semi-patrimoieties (for example, a child of Japaja is Jungarra or Namurlpa). The subsection system is explained below.

---

7   For a personal anecdote, I was assigned a Warlpiri subsection, Japaljarri, despite only talking Warlmanpa (and English) with people (the assignment of a Warlpiri subsection, rather than a Warlmanpa subsection, was also likely based on my 'relation' to David Nash, who had been assigned a Warlpiri subsection).

Table 1.2 Warlmanpa subsection names

	Adult		Child[8]	
Code	Masculine	Feminine	Masculine	Feminine
A	Japaja	Napaja	Japalyi	Ngalyirri, Napalya
A	Jungurra	Namurlpa	Jukartayi	Napita
B	Japanangka	Napanangka	Janama	Namana
B	Japangarti	Napangarti	Japayarti	Ngampayarti
C	Jampijinpa	Nampijinpa	Jampilka	Nampija
C	Jangala	Nangala	Jangkali	Ngang(k)ala
D	Jakama	Nakama	Jakarra	Wajala
D	Jupula	Napula	Jula(ma)	Nampula

Source: Nash (1979).

Table 1.3 Warlpiri subsection names

	Adult		Child	
Code	Masculine	Feminine	Masculine	Feminine
A	Japaljarri	Napaljarri	Japalyi	Ngalyirri, Ngamalyi
A	Jungarrayi	Nungarrayi	Jukurtayi, Jukurdayi	Ngampukurlu
B	Japanangka	Napanangka	Janama	Ngamana
B	Japangarti	Napangardi	Japayardi, Jangari, Japangayi	Ngampayardi, Ngapayardi, Napangayi
C	Jampijinpa	Nampijinpa	Jampirlka	Ngampija, Ngampijakurdu
C	Jangala	Nangala	Jangkarli	Ngangkarla
D	Jakamarra	Nakamarra	Jakarra	Nakarra, Wajarla
D	Jupurrula	Napurrula	Jurlama	Ngapurru, Ngampurla

Source: Nash (2000b).

The preferred marriage partners and patrilines are given in Figure 1.2. The solid lines denote first-preference marriage partners (for example, a Jungarra should marry a Nangala) and the dashed lines denote the father–child relations between groups (thus, the father of any group can be read by following the dashed line to the corresponding male subsection). These are reciprocal, such that the father of Jangala (and Nangala) is Jampijinpa, and the father of Jampijinpa (and Nampijinpa) is Jangala. I am not familiar with non-first-preference marriages in Warlmanpa, though, in neighbouring groups, it is estimated that 90 per cent of Warlpiri marriages and 70 per cent

---

[8] See Koch and Simpson (2020) for a comparative analysis of children's skin names.

of Mudburra marriages are of first preference (based on ALC [1982b: 27]; for a visualisation of the Bilinarra system that includes second-preference marriages, see Meakins and Nordlinger [2014: 38]).

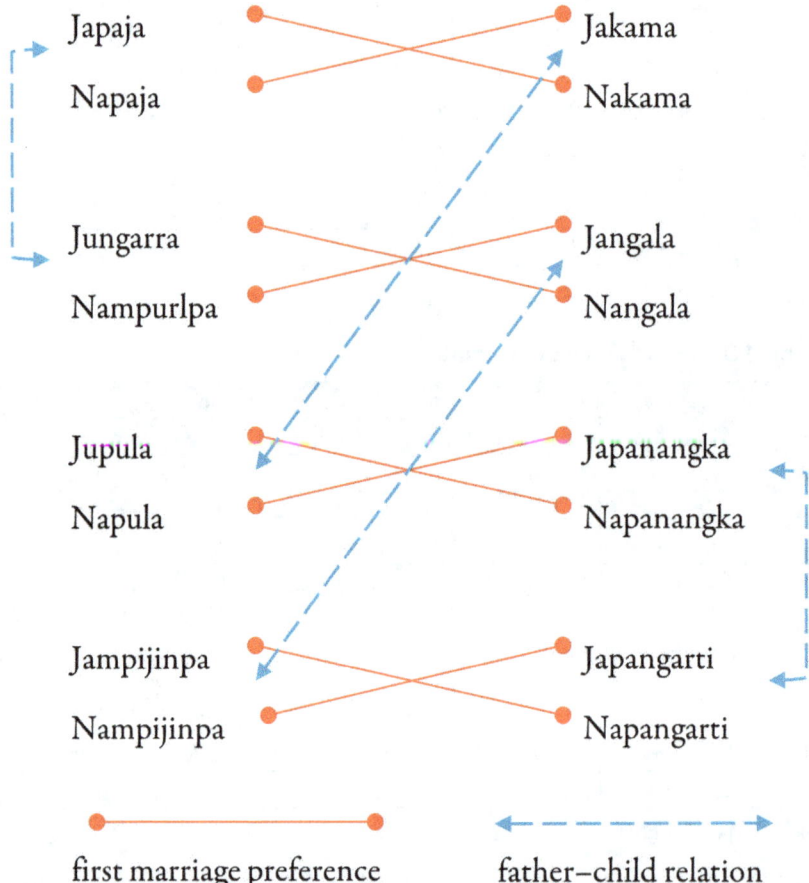

Figure 1.2 Marriage preferences and father–child relations across subsections

In general, a child's subsection is determined by the mother's subsection, shown in Table 1.4 (Nash 1980), though in some cases it can be assigned based on the father's subsection (there will only be a distinction in the case of non-first-preference marriages).

Table 1.4 Subsection and preferred partners based on female subsection

Female subsection	Preferred partner subsection	Subsection of children
Napaja	Jakama	Jupula, Napula
Nampurlpa	Jangala	Jampijinpa, Nampijinpa
Napanangka	Jupula	Jakama, Nakama
Napangarti	Jampijinpa	Jangala, Nangala
Nampijinpa	Japangarti	Japanangka, Napanangka
Nangala	Jungarra	Japaja, Napaja
Nakama	Japaja	Jungarra, Nampurlpa
Napula	Japanangka	Japangarti, Napangarti

1.1.3.2 Egocentric kin terminology

Kin terminology is shown in Figure 1.3.[9] It should be noted that there is interspeaker variation in terms, only some of which have been captured in this diagram. A major point of variation includes the historical kin-possession suffix *-na* 'my' freezing onto the root for parent terms *kirta* 'father', *ngarti* 'mother' and *kungurni* 'younger sibling'. Generally, for older speakers, *kirta-na* is morphologically complex, specifically referring to the speaker's father, and, for younger speakers, *kirtana* is morphologically simple, referring to anyone's father, with possessive pronouns able to specify the anchor—for example, *nyintinya* (2GEN) *kirtana* 'your father'. See §3.1.3 for further discussion.

The family relations are tightly interconnected with the subsection system: same-sex siblings (other than one's own; see Table 1.5) are referred to using the same kinterm (as they belong to the same subsection). For example, the term *kirta(na)* is used to refer to ego's father or any of ego's father's brothers (for an overview of similar systems in Australian languages, see Gaby and Singer [2014]).

---

9   Key for family trees: M = mother, F = father, Z = sister, B = brother, D = daughter, S = son, P = partner, − = younger, + = older.

A GRAMMAR OF WARLMANPA

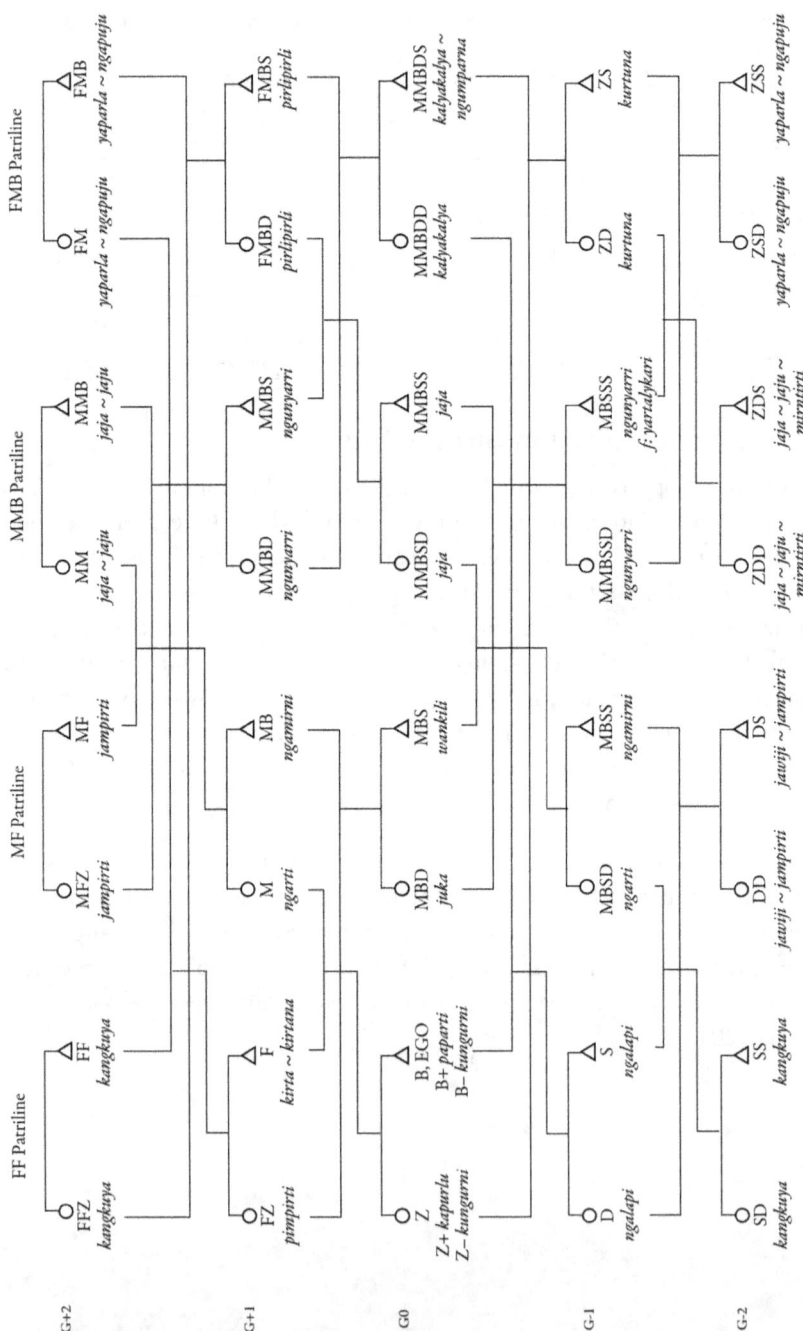

Figure 1.3 Warlmanpa kinterms (male ego) in standard Aranda diagram
Sources: Template, Mark Harvey; lexical information, David Nash with some variants added by Mitchell Browne.

1. INTRODUCTION

Warlmanpa makes a distinction between siblings of ego's subsection based on their relative age to ego (based on whether they are younger or older). A further distinction is made between genders, but only for older siblings, as shown in Table 1.5.

Table 1.5 Distinctions in sibling kinterms

	Younger	Older
Sister	*kungurni*	*kapurlu*
Brother		*paparti*

This distinction extends to parallel cousins (that is, mother's sister's children and father's brother's children), though not cross-cousins. For these cases, the distinction is based on the relative ages of the parents. For example, one's mother's younger sister's children are *kungurni*, and one's mother's older sister's children are *kapurlu* or *paparti*, regardless of their age relative to ego.

Moiety terms require fuller investigation; however, a number are included in Nash (2022). The term *kirta* 'father' can be used to refer to one's own patrimoiety and *kurtungurlu* refers to one's opposite patrimoiety. For members of the opposite matrimoiety, the term *jurtatja* is used.

In addition to kinterms that signal a relation between ego and kin, several terms refer to a relation between two people other than ego (that is, dyadic terms [Evans 2006])—for example, *makurntarlangu* 'mother-in-law and son-in-law pair' (Nash 2022). There are also terms to refer to a relation between three people—that is, tri relational kin terms (similar systems are found in numerous Australian languages [see Blythe 2018; Laughren 1982b: 73]), which are also referred to as triangular kin terms (Evans 2003). The terms listed in Nash (2022) are:

- *kapurlu-nginta*: pair of sisters
- *jarnimi-rlangu*: speaker's uncle paired with his mother, etcetera
- *japurn-nginta*: cross-cousin and their sister's child
- *ngarrjirn-*: addressed to cousin about cousin's mother's brother
- *panara-rlangu*: male ego's brother and father
- *wajimana-nginta*: ego's brother and wife's mother's brother
- *wapirranginta*: father–child pair where child is in same subsection as ego
- *yinkan-nginta*: siblings of different subsections of same section
- *yingarti*: addressed to cousin about cousin's mother.

McConvell (1982) presents a more complete system for Gurindji, which suggests that the Warlmanpa system may be more productive than understood here.

1.1.3.3 Patrilects

Each person also inherits a 'patrilect' from their father (referred to by speakers as *jaru*, which is also used to refer to languages, words, messages, and so on). Warlmanpa and Warumungu share patrilects. Patrilects are associated with Dreamings and a particular way of speaking, relating largely to voice quality (rather than lexical or morphological differences). See Nash (1990) for further discussion.

1.1.4 Speakers

Here I introduce some of the Warlmanpa speakers who have worked with David Nash, Ken Hale and/or myself. Note that for each speaker, I list languages that we know them to speak, but I have no doubt that some (or all) of these lists are non-exhaustive (and, furthermore, I have not distinguished which languages are their inherited languages and which are not).

Donald Graham (Jupurrula) was born about 1920, grew up on Helen Springs (approximately 150 kilometres north of Tennant Creek), later worked at Banka Banka (approximately 100 kilometres north of Tennant Creek) and then in Tennant Creek (Nash 1989). While in Tennant Creek in 1966, Donald met Ken Hale, where they recorded two hours of Warlmanpa. From 1977 until his death in 1989, Donald worked with David Nash on language recordings and land claims. Donald also worked with P. Chakravarti and Jane Simpson on Warumungu, and with numerous other researchers. Donald spent his last years at Kalumpurlpa, west of Banka Banka. Donald's languages were Warlmanpa, Warlpiri, Warumungu, Mudburra, Nyininy and Alyawarr. The reader is directed to Nash (1989) for further details of Donald's work.

Bunny Naburula (Napurrula) was born about 1930 at Kuwarta, on the Gosse River (approximately 40 kilometres east of Tennant Creek). Around the age of 12, she moved to Phillip Creek (approximately 50 kilometres north of Tennant Creek) and was later forced to move to Alekarenge, along with many others. The move to Alekarenge was to land that did not belong to Warlpiri, Warumungu or Warlmanpa people (Alekarenge is on

Kaytetye country) and was described by Bunny as a very negative experience (CLC 2015: 357–58). Bunny is perhaps best known for her activist work, campaigning against Muckaty Station being used as a nuclear waste facility (AAP 2014), among other campaigns (Tennant & District Times 2015; CLC 2015: 648–49), as well as work on land claims (ALC 1997). From 1978, Bunny worked with David Nash on recording Warlmanpa language. Bunny's languages were Warlmanpa, Warumungu, Warlpiri and Alyawarr.

Dick Foster (Jangala), born about 1940 at Powell Creek, worked at Jangkarti (Burke Station) from his early teen years and, after stints at various other stations, at Banka Banka Station for a number of years, where he received his first ever payment for his work (CLC 2015: 226–27). After Banka Banka, Dick worked as a bore mechanic in Helen Springs, then moved back to Banka Banka, before moving to Tennant Creek, where he lives now, working with Julalikari Housing (CLC 2015: 699). Dick has worked on several land claims, including the Muckaty claim for Warlmanpa (ALC 1997) and the Lurrnku Kunakiji claim for Warumungu (CLC 2015: 650). Dick's languages are Warlmanpa, Warumungu, Warlpiri and Mudburra.

Penny Kelly (Napaljarri) and **Susannah Nelson (Nakamarra)** are Barkly Arts Tartakula artists, both living in Tennant Creek. Penny and Susannah's languages are Warlmanpa, Warlpiri and Warumungu. Susannah has contributed to videos produced by the Central Land Council (CLC) promoting awareness of Aboriginal knowledge.[10]

Doris Kelly (Nakamarra) was born at Mangkamarntangi (Phillip Creek), before being moved to Alekarenge in 1956. She lived in many places around the Northern Territory, including Darwin, but settled in Tennant Creek when she started working with the CLC in 1994. She recently retired from the CLC. Doris was involved with the nuclear waste facility protests and regularly works with the CLC and researchers to help preserve Warlmanpa and Warumungu traditions. Her languages are Warlmanpa, Mudburra, Warumungu and Warlpiri, and she has also learnt Kaytetye and Alyawarr through living at Alekarenge.

---

10 These can be viewed online, at: ictv.com.au/video/item/6664 and ictv.com.au/video/item/1296.

Plate 1.1 From left: Bonnie McLean, Penny Kelly Napaljarri, Mitch Browne and Susannah Nelson Nakamarra in Tennant Creek
Source: ARC Centre of Excellence for the Dynamics of Language (2017: 121).

Plate 1.2 Susannah Nelson Nakamarra at Kajinpuru, just north of Banka Banka Station
Source: Mitch Browne.

1.2 Methodology and aims of this grammar

This grammar aims to be descriptive, avoiding being tightly bound in theoretical frameworks. However, a grammatical description is, by nature, an abstraction, so there must be some framework employed to present the analyses. This grammar is situated within the Dixonian tradition of Australian grammar writing (formalised as 'Basic Linguistic Theory' [Dixon 2009]). That is, carefully balancing being not too bound by theory (such that the description is readable regardless of theoretical background), while also utilising knowledge gained by linguistic theories to aptly describe the processes found and relating the Warlmanpa data to cross-linguistic categories.

There are several investigations of what makes a 'good grammar' (Rice 2005). The main problem is that there are numerous incompatible constraints, as well as more pragmatic constraints such as time and funding. Thus, a grammar must be focused. Evans (2008) provides an overview of a 'perfect grammar', which must appeal to every possible reader: structuralists, generativists, typologists, documentarists, sociolinguists, anthropologists—never mind beyond academia. There is essentially an infinite number of categories that would have to be accounted for in a 'perfect grammar' and, as such, (unfortunately) a single grammar cannot be universally satisfactory.

In writing this grammar, I have focused on appealing to the structuralist's ideals, for which Evans (2008: 1) stipulates four overarching concepts:

1. respect the 'distinctive genius' of the language
2. treat the grammar as a system—that is, examining consequences of interactions between rules
3. give language-internal justification for categories, labels, etcetera
4. embed the grammatical description in, and make it consistent with, the Boasian trilogy of grammar + texts + dictionary.[11]

---

11 I have not included a dictionary (though I have included a verb list in Appendix A). David Nash is preparing a dictionary, has previously distributed a vocabulary (Nash 1979) and last made limited copies of revised versions in 2018 (which were distributed to speakers in Alice Springs and Tennant Creek). Throughout this grammar, I refer to Nash (2022) for some lexical information, which is the most recent version of the vocabulary (an unpublished work in progress). A recent version is available (Nash 2018) from: catalog.paradisec.org.au/collections/DN1/items/Warlmanpa.

I have been concerned with making the analyses accountable, such that any future research should be readily able to propose competing analyses or extend hypotheses made throughout this book. To this end, I have attempted to make the data as readily available and transparent as I can. Each hypothesis is accompanied by numerous examples (where possible) and is linked to an utterance in the corpus.[12]

Furthermore, each example is glossed morpheme by morpheme. However, these interlinear glosses are not to be taken as perfectly accurate representations of the relationship between form and meaning, as Mosel notes:

> The meaning of words and larger units of grammatical analysis does not equal the sum of the meanings of their component parts, as interlinear glossing might suggest, but results from the interaction of the meaning of the construction as such and the meanings of its parts. *Thus interlinear glossing should only be seen as a tool to help the reader to understand examples*; and a useful tool indeed it is.
>
> (Mosel 2006: 50; emphasis added)

In other words, there is a constant tension in any grammatical analysis between glossing a morpheme consistently (but in so doing, the precise meaning in an utterance may be obscured) and glossing morphemes based on their function in a clause (but obscuring generalities across analysis). In this grammar, I have opted to label each morpheme with a single, consistent gloss. As noted, the upshot of this is that sometimes the meaning of a sentence will not be easily recoverable from the sum of its parts.

A further problem is the choice of the single gloss. To exemplify this problem, the word *mangku* can refer to grass plains, plains country, a lake or the sea (Nash 1979). An initial problem in glossing is whether to pick: 1) a gloss that captures every use (such as 'vast empty environment'), but of course, these glosses overgeneralise (not every 'vast empty environment' is a grass plain or a large body of water); or 2) one of the clearly identifiable senses (such as 'plains country'), in so doing, obscuring the translation when it is used to refer to the sea. In this grammar, I have attempted to utilise the gloss that refers to the most frequent or salient sense, though I acknowledge the inherently imperfect nature of glossing any morpheme (even the 'plains country' *sense* is not adequately captured by the *gloss* 'plains country').

---

12   However, it should not be assumed that all the utterances in this grammar reflect the culture of Warlmanpa people. Many examples are simply the result of the linguists eliciting hypothetical scenarios.

Last, there are cases where I have explicitly noted that I do not have a clear analysis of a process or construction. I believe it is important to include these cases, rather than omit them, so any future work or research on Warlmanpa is aware of any (known) shortcomings of my analysis.

1.3 Recordings

The data used in this grammar comprise approximately 30 hours of transcribed audio (with significantly more audio still requiring transcription). The corpora are divided into two categories—the 'heritage corpus' and the 'present corpus'—roughly reflecting two periods. The distinction between these two corpora is used to explain some of the variation across speakers cited in this grammar.

The speaker names referred to in this grammar (that is, this is a *non-exhaustive* list of speakers in the corpus) are given in Table 1.6. For the remainder of the grammar, these speakers will be referred to by their initials.

Table 1.6 Speakers referred to in this grammar

	Speaker initials	Speaker name (subsection)
Heritage corpus	BN	Bunny Nabarula (Napurrula)
	DC	Danny Cooper (Jampijinpa)
	DG	Donald Graham (Jupurrula)
	JC	Jessie Cooper (Napangarti)
	JJN	Jimmy Newcastle (Japaljarri)
	JW	Jack Walker (Jangala)
	LOF	Lofty (Japaljarri)
	LN	Louie Nakamarra
	MFN	May Foster (Napanangka)
	NG	Norah Graham (Napanangka)
	TWN	Topsy Walker Napanangka
Present corpus	DF	Dick Foster (Jangala)
	DK	Doris Kelly (Nakamarra)
	JK	Julie Kelly (Nakamarra)
	PK	Penny Kelly (Napaljarri)
	PW	Penny Williams (Nungarrayi)
	SN	Susannah Nelson (Nakamarra)

The referencing differs slightly according to whether the utterance is found in the heritage corpus or the present corpus.

Heritage corpus: code, speaker, time stamp, in which:

- code = Australian Institute of Aboriginal and Torres Strait Islander Studies (AIATSIS) call code, reduced slightly for readability ('HALE' reduced to 'H'; 'NASH' reduced to 'N')
- speaker = speaker's initials
- time stamp = beginning of utterance in the linked audio.

For example:

H_K01-505B,	**DG,**	**36:55 mins**
AIATSIS call code, where H is short for HALE	Speaker is Donald Graham	Utterance begins at 36 minutes, 55 seconds.

Present corpus: wrl-YYYYMMDD(-X), speaker, time stamp, in which:

- Y = year (four digits)
- M = month (two digits)
- D = day (two digits)
- X = session number (only used for days in which more than one recording was made)
- speaker = speaker's initials
- time stamp = beginning of utterance in the linked audio.

For example:

wrl-20190201,	**DK,**	**19:05 mins**
The recording was made on 1 February 2019.	Speaker is Doris Kelly.	Utterance begins at 19 minutes, 05 seconds.

Recordings in the present corpus that contain languages other than Warlmanpa have the appropriate ISO-639-3 code for the language(s)—for example, wrl-dmw-... means the recording includes Warlmanpa (wrl) and Mudburra (dmw) speech.

The next two sections provide overviews of the corpora: §1.3.1 details the heritage corpus and §1.3.2 details the present corpus.

1.3.1 Heritage corpus

The heritage corpus comprises language data provided by Warlmanpa speakers, recorded between 1959 and 2007 by Kenneth Hale and David Nash. The most common genres found in this corpus are elicitation and narratives. There are also some conversational data, however, much of this remains untranscribed, so its use in this grammar is limited. Elicitation in the heritage corpus is typically the linguist providing a prompt in Warlpiri, Warumungu or English (approximately in relative order of frequency, Warlpiri being the most common) and the Warlmanpa speaker providing their translation. Approximately 10 hours of language data have been transcribed from this corpus for use in this grammar. Most of the heritage corpus was transcribed by the linguist who recorded it (by hand) and, as part of this project, David Nash and I have linked the audio to a new electronic transcription in ELAN (Lausberg and Sloetjes 2009).

Table 1.7 gives a catalogue of the collections that have been used in this grammar and the (approximate) year that the data were collected. The language recordings were collected at various locations, usually within a few hundred kilometres of Tennant Creek, including Alekarenge (Warrabri), Elliott, Renner Springs, Morphett Creek and Tennant Creek itself (including at Kargaru camp).

Table 1.7 Most commonly referred to collections in this grammar with corresponding year of collection

Collection	Year collected (approx.)
HALE_K06	1959
HALE_K01	1966
NASH_D01	1977
NASH_D02	1978
NASH_D03	1979
NASH_D29	2004

1.3.2 Present corpus

The present corpus comprises language data collected since 2016 by David Nash and myself in Tennant Creek across six fieldtrips undertaken by me (totalling approximately seven months), on three of which I was accompanied by David Nash.[13] Further field trips were anticipated, however, they could

---

13 A few sessions were also recorded by the author with a Warlmanpa speaker, DK, who was visiting Moruya, in New South Wales.

not be undertaken due to Covid-19 travel restrictions imposed throughout 2020–21. The language data in the present corpus include elicited data (primarily elicited using English and some Warlpiri and Warumungu) and narratives. Time was also spent reviewing materials from the heritage data with speakers; this was usually not fully transcribed, as the main purpose was to tidy up and ensure the correctness of the heritage corpus transcriptions. Approximately 20 hours of language data have been transcribed (using ELAN) from this corpus for use in this grammar. Most of these recordings were in Tennant Creek at Barkly Arts, where some consultants worked, or at the Charles Darwin University Tennant Creek node. A small number of recordings took place on our trips out of town. The present corpus is being deposited with the Australian Institute of Aboriginal and Torres Strait Islander Studies (AIATSIS) and has been deposited to Paradisec (Browne 2016).

1.4 Grammar organisation

This grammar is organised according to a linguistic domain (Table 1.8). The smallest unit, sounds, is discussed first in Chapter 2. Word-level units are presented and analysed in Chapters 3 to 9 and clauses are discussed in Chapters 10 to 12.

Table 1.8 Organisation of this grammar

Domain	Chapter
Sounds	Chapter 2: Phonetics and phonology
Words	Chapter 3: Parts of speech
	Chapter 4: Nominals
	Chapter 5: The auxiliary complex
	Chapter 6: Inflecting verbs
	Chapter 7: Coverbs
	Chapter 8: Adverbs
	Chapter 9: Particles, interjections and clitics
Clauses	Chapter 10: Grammatical relations
	Chapter 11: Syntax of simple clauses
	Chapter 12: Syntax of complex clauses

There are three appendices. Appendix A provides a brief analysis of each inflecting verb. Appendix B is a collection of narratives. Appendix C has an alternative analysis of the morphological structure of inflecting verbs.

2
Phonetics and phonology

This chapter provides an overview of the phonetics and phonological processes in Warlmanpa. It discusses the phonemic inventory (§2.1), consonants (§2.2), vowels (§2.3), voicing (§2.4), phonotactics (§2.5), prosody (§2.6), vowel assimilation (§2.7) and reduplication (§2.8).

As much as was feasible, this chapter is based on quantitative instrumental data, rather than my own impressionistic observations. However, the data utilised were ultimately opportunistic (from the point of view of instrumental analysis)—including data collected on fieldwork that was not in a controlled environment, so some of the analyses may be impacted by the recording quality, background noise and other factors. The data comprise approximately 2,000 manually time-aligned segments, which utilised Praat's TextGrid function (Boersma 2001). The data were extracted from the TextGrids using scripts (Brato 2015; Kawahara 2010) that I adapted for use in this project. Many formant graphs are rendered using the phonR package (McCloy 2016) for RStudio (RStudio-Team 2020).

2.1 Phonemic inventory

Warlmanpa's phonemic inventory, given in Table 2.1, mostly corresponds closely to other Ngumpin-Yapa languages and more generally to a common Australian inventory. There are five places of articulation for stops and nasals, three for laterals and glides, and one alveolar tap. Warlmanpa makes a peripheral distinction (bilabial/velar) and an apical distinction (alveolar/postalveolar) but does not make a laminal distinction (having only a palatal series). The Warlmanpa phonemic system is notable for its stop length contrast. A stop length contrast is not evident in any other Ngumpin-Yapa language and is rare in Pama-Nyungan languages more generally (Dixon 2002: 605–15), however, a contrast is found in the neighbouring language Warumungu (Simpson 2017).

Table 2.1 Phonemic consonant inventory in International Phonetic Alphabet with orthographic representation given in parentheses where they differ

		Peripheral		Apical		Laminal
		Bilabial	Velar	Alveolar	Post-alveolar	Palatal
Stop	Singleton	p	k	t	ʈ (rt)	c (j)
	Geminate	pː (pp)	kː (kk)	tː (tt)	ʈː (rtt)	cː (jj)
Nasal		m	ŋ (ng)	n	ɳ (rn)	ɲ (ny)
Lateral				l	ɭ (rl)	ʎ (ly)
Tap				r (rr)		
Glide		w			ɻ (r)	j (y)

There are six vowel phonemes (a triangular system with a length distinction), shown in Table 2.2. Long vowels are very uncommon except in preverbs.

Table 2.2 Vowel phonemes (with orthography given in parentheses where it differs from the International Phonetic Alphabet)

	Front	Back
High	i, iː (ii)	u, uː (uu)
Low	a, aː (aa)	

2.2 Consonants

The discussion of consonants comprises establishing minimal pairs (§2.2.1) and analysis of major allophonic processes (§2.2.2).

2.2.1 Phonemic oppositions

2.2.1.1 Minimal pairs

The following (near) minimal sets establish the distinction between the coronal consonants (apical and laminal).

Coronal stops:

(1)   /kutu/   /kuʈu/   /yakucu/
      kutu   kurtu   yakuju
      'near'   'child'   'bag'

Coronal nasals:

(2)   /-wana/   /waṇa/   /waɲa/
      -wana   warna   wanya
      -PERL   'snake'   'emu feathers'

Coronal laterals:

(3)   /kala/   /kaḷa/   /kaʎaʈi/
      kala   karla-   kalyarti
      'but'   'spear'   'co-initiate'

And between the alveolar stop and alveolar tap:

(4)   /kutu/   /kuru/
      kutu   kurru
      'near'   'fire-saw'

The contrast between the peripheral stops is exemplified by the minimal pair in Example (5) and the contrast between the bilabial stop and the labiovelar glide is demonstrated in Example (6).

(5)   /paɲca/   /kaɲca/
      Panja   kanja
      'rib'   'close'

(6)   /paɲci/   /waɲci/
      panji   wanji
      'bauhinea tree'   'where'

The contrast between the peripheral nasals is demonstrated in (7).

(7)   /manta/   /ŋanta/
      ma-nta   nganta
      'get-IMP'   'supposedly'

25

A minimal between /r/ and /ɻ/, is given in (8).

(8)   /wiri/   /wiɻi/

       wirri   wiri
       'neck'   'big'

Some speakers in the present corpus exhibit free variation between the retroflex glide and alveolar tap. Specifically, for these speakers, /r/ is often realised as [ɻ]. Given that this variation is not evident in the heritage corpus, it is likely a recent development, indicative of a collapsing distinction between /ɻ/ and /r/.

2.2.1.2 Stop length

The analysis of phonemes in Warlmanpa is complicated by a potential stop length contrast, described in Nash (1979), where each stop has a 'lax' and 'tense' counterpart; however, this analysis has since been retracted, as reflected in the updated version of Nash (1979), which has withdrawn the 'tense' series (which was also followed in an earlier version of this manuscript [Browne 2021a]). The complication arises from: 1) the small number of vocabulary items with a geminate stop, and relatedly, 2) the lack of minimal pairs. Moreover, a stop length contrast is not analysed for any other Ngumpin-Yapa language. Near-minimal pairs for each place of articulation are given in (9)–(13).

(9)   /japa/   /ŋapːa/

       yapa   ngappa
       'person'   'water'

(10)   /mata/   /patːa/

       mata   patta
       'tired'   'hard'

(11)   /kuʈu/   /kuʈːa/

       kurtu   kurtta
       'child'   'skin'

(12)   /cacu/   /lacːu/

       jaju   lajju
       'grandmother'   'edible grub'

(13)   /ŋaka/   /lakːa/
       ngaka   *lakka*
       'soon'   'loosen'

Table 2.3 compares the duration of singleton and geminate stops for a given near-minimal pair. However, not all comparisons are ideal due to my overall preference to use words for which there were a satisfactory number of tokens and the low token count for geminates more generally (especially for the apical series, in which short /t/ and /tː/ are both very rare, so the 'apical' series in the table compares the length of /ʈ/ with that of /tː/). Each token was given in isolation (for example, during vocabulary elicitation) to avoid any length neutralisation processes due to morphology (as is found in Warumungu [Simpson and Heath 1982]).

Table 2.3 Length of stops

Stop	Singleton length ($\bar{x}$ seconds)	Geminate length ($\bar{x}$ seconds)	Differential (seconds)
Bilabial	0.074 (n = 19)	0.112 (n = 17)	0.038
Velar	0.027 (n = 6)	0.146 (n = 4)	0.119
Apical	0.038 (n = 11)	0.142 (n = 22)	0.104
Palatal	0.058 (n = 4)	0.130 (n = 6)	0.072

Beyond duration, the articulation of singleton and geminate stops differs in that the singleton stops can be lenited to continuants, whereas the geminate stops cannot (see §§2.2.2.1–2.2.2.2). Two spectrograms from the same speaker are compared in Figures 2.1 and 2.2, where the former involves a geminate stop and the latter involves a singleton stop. The spectrogram of the geminate stop demonstrates the clear burst of energy and the delay between the burst and voicing. The singleton stop is less defined on the spectrogram, reflecting a less audible burst. Due to the lack of constriction length in the short stop, the intensity of the sound never reaches lower than approximately 55 decibels (dB) throughout the articulation of /p/.

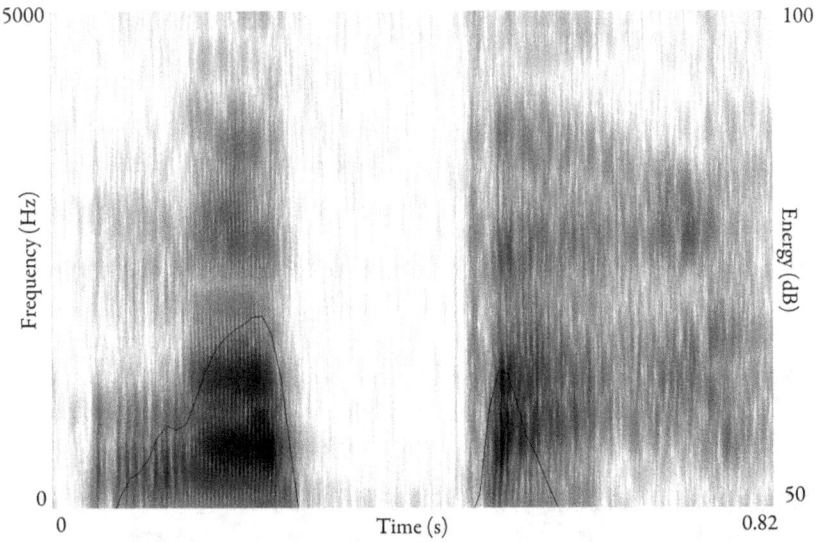

Figure 2.1 Spectrogram and intensity of *ngappa* 'water'
Source: wrl-230802-01, DK, 00:24 secs.

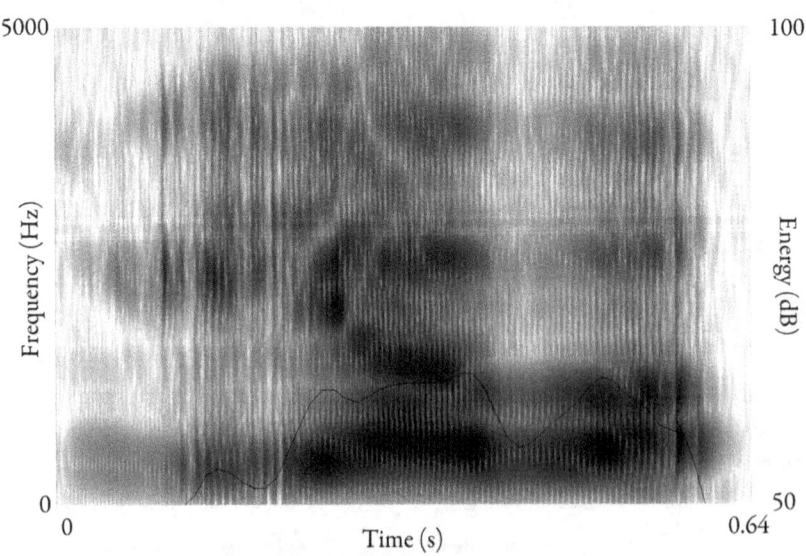

Figure 2.2 Spectrogram and intensity of *yapa* 'person'
Source: wrl-230806-01, DK, 03:44 mins.

As noted earlier, geminate stops are relatively uncommon in the lexicon; the known words with geminate stops (excluding placenames) are given in Table 2.4 (Warlmanpa lexical data from Nash [2022]; Warumungu lexical data from Disbray and Warumungu Speakers from the Tennant Creek Community [2005]; and Simpson 2023). Just under half (48 per cent) these words are shared with Warumungu, compared with an overall 25 per cent cognate density between the languages (Nash 2000a), suggesting that the extensive contact between Warlmanpa and Warumungu may have contributed to the development of a gemination contrast in Warlmanpa. However, a secondary collocation is that the geminate stops in Warlmanpa pattern almost identically to the stop series in Warlpiri in terms of duration (Bundgaard-Nielsen and O'Shannessy 2019), so the Warlmanpa singleton stops could reflect a historical lenition or shortening process becoming contrastive.

From this lexical list, some patterns are clear: geminate stops in Warlmanpa are found only between vowels and almost always in post-tonic position (post-tonic lengthening is evident but marginal in Warlpiri [Pentland and Laughren 2004]).

Table 2.4 List of known geminate stops in Warlmanpa, with a corresponding Warumungu form, where known

Place	Warlmanpa form	Shared form in Warumungu
Bilabial	*lappa* 'bone'	—
	ngappa 'water'	*ngappa* 'water'
	ngappala 'urine'	—
	ruppa 'empty'	—
	tuppa 'windbreak'	—
	wuppa 'ash'	*wuppa* 'ash'
Alveolar	*kitta* 'bare'	—
	kittapari 'plain'	—
	mayipatturla 'mountain devil'	*mayiparttula* 'mountain devil'
	patta 'hard'	*patta* 'hard ground'
	tattarr '(type of) bird'	*tattarr* '(type of) bird'
	witta 'small'	—
Post-alveolar	*kurtta* 'skin'	—
	kurttanyma 'knife'	—
	pirtta 'lump'	*pirtta* 'knob, lump, wart'
	pirttajangka 'pregnant'	—

Place	Warlmanpa form	Shared form in Warumungu
Palatal	*kujja* 'belongings of deceased'	*kujuwa~kujjuwa* 'ownerless, bereaved orphan'
	lajju 'edible grub'	—
	lijji 'dry'	*linjji* 'dry'
	majju (~*maju*) 'bad'	—
	wajjurra 'afternoon, yesterday'	*wanjjal* 'yesterday'
	wajjurrajurra 'afternoon'	—
	walarrpajji '(type of) tree'	*walarrapaji ~ walarrapajji* '(type of) tree'
	wijja 'farewell' (CV)	—
	wijji 'someone else's'	—
	wijjipalka 'troublemaker'	—
Velar	*jukku~jukku* 'pull (something) out' (CV)	—
	lakka 'loosen' (CV)	*lakka* 'open' (CV)
	likka 'sap'	*likkarr* 'red gum from trees'
	mukku 'all' (CV)	*mukku* 'all' (CV)
	pukka 'rotten'	*pukka* 'rotten'
	takka 'forearm'	*takka* 'hand, arm'
	yakkula 'ant bed'	*yakkula* 'ant bed'

2.2.2 Major allophonic processes

2.2.2.1 Geminate stop lenition

If a word with a geminate stop does not constitute the entire phonological word, the geminate stop is generally reduced to a singleton stop, especially in casual speech. For example, the stop in *ngappa* 'water' may be realised as [b] in words such as *ngappa-nga* 'water-LOC'. However, unlike the underlying singleton stops, the lenited geminate stops are rarely further reduced, and still typically have clear stop articulation.

This is demonstrated in Figure 2.3, where the '*pp-*' series represents the length of the stop in *ngappa* where the word either takes case or derivational morphology or hosts the auxiliary complex (the '*pp*' series represents articulations of the geminate stop and the '*p*' series represents articulations of the singleton stop). These durational data show that while the stop in *ngappa* may still optionally be lengthened (particularly evident in the max value of the series), its average duration is very similar to that of the short stop and, in fact, is marginally shorter, despite the higher upper limit.

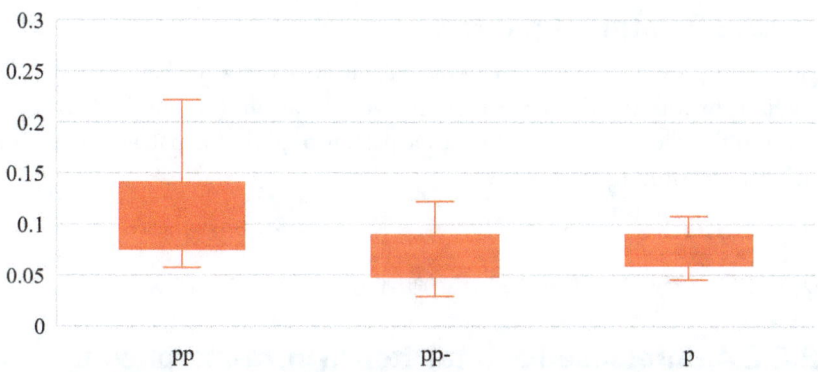

Figure 2.3 Duration of bilabial stops, including long stops where the nominal root does not constitute the entire phonological word

This is very similar to the process in Warumungu in which certain suffixes result in a singleton stop (Simpson 2017). For example, compare (14) and (15), where the Warumungu nominal root *nanttu* 'humpy' has a fortis stop, but when the ergative/locative suffix attaches, the stop is singleton (Warumungu [Simpson 2017: 714]).

(14)   *nanttu*   'humpy'
(15)   *nantu-ngku*   'humpy-ERG/LOC'

However, the lengthening process in Warumungu is much more productive, extending to nasals and laterals, as well as allowing geminates following consonants (rather than only between vowels, as in Warlmanpa), as evident in *nanttu* 'humpy'.

2.2.2.2 Singleton stop lenition

In casual speech, intervocalic singleton stops may be reduced, without a clear release. The singleton coronal stops are generally reduced to taps—that is, /t/ realised as [ɾ] and /ʈ/ realised as [ɽ]. The peripheral stops may be realised with (what is impressionistically) a weak fricated release, rather than plosive (this is also reported in Walmajarri [Hudson and Richards 1969: 174]). The palatal stop is rarely lenited (as is also the case in Ngardi [Ennever 2021: 59]). However, these lenition patterns remain to be systematically examined (for example, Ennever et al. 2017; Mansfield 2015).

2.2.2.3 Palatal offglides

Palatal stops and, to a lesser extent, palatal nasals tend to have an offglide when transitioning into a following vowel, as in (16) and (17). Less commonly, there is also sometimes a palatal onglide for palatal stops and nasals transitioning from a vowel.

(16) jaru   'language'   /caɹu/   [cʲeɹʊ] ~ [ɟʲeɹʊ]

(17) ngarrka-ja 'man-DU'   /ŋarkaca/ [ŋɐrgɐcʲɐ]

2.2.2.4 Unreleased palatal stop in intra-morphemic clusters

When the (singleton) palatal stop is the first member of an intra-morphemic stop + stop cluster, /c/ is not released, surfacing as [ɟ̚] ~ [c̚], with variable voicing, as in (18). When /c/ is the first member of an inter-morphemic stop + stop cluster, the release of /c/ may be coarticulated with the other stop, as in (19), or otherwise released normally.[1]

(18) yajka   'travelling' /jacka/   [jeɟ̚kɐ]

(19) kutij-karra! 'stand!'   /kutickara/ [kʊdɪc̚kɐra] ~ [kʊdɪc͡kɐra]

2.2.2.5 Glide deletion

The non-consonantal glides /w/ and /j/ are prone to deletion when occurring in the context of certain vowels: /i/ can trigger /j/-deletion and /a, u/ can trigger /w/-deletion.

The palatal glide /j/ can be deleted if /i/ is in its local environment. Conversely, the labiovelar glide can be deleted if /i/ is not in its local environment; however, neither process applies categorically. In the word-initial position, the glides are especially prone to deletion, though in this context, /a/ does not trigger /w/-deletion. The full combinations are given in Table 2.5 for the palatal glide and Table 2.6 for the labiovelar glide. The exact phonetic targets are usually conditioned by the local environment per the regular vowel allophony discussed in §2.3.

---

1 The only phonotactically permissible sequences of (potentially) inter-morphemic /c/ + stop clusters are coverb constructions. While there is morphosyntactic evidence that these clusters form a single word, it may be the case that for phonological processes, these are word boundaries, hence the difference in articulation between clearly intra-morphemic clusters and tenuous inter-morphemic clusters.

Table 2.5 Palatal glide deletion

/j/		V2		
		/a/	/i/	/u/
V1	/a/	[ɐjɐ]	[ɐi]	[ɐjʊ]
	/i/	[ɪɐ]	[iː]	*
	/u/	[ʊjɐ]	*	[ʊjʊ]

Note: Asterisks indicate an impermissible sequence.

Table 2.6 Labiovelar glide deletion

/w/		V2		
		/a/	/i/	/u/
V1	/a/	[ɐː]	[ɐwi]	[ɐʊ]
	/i/	[ɪwɐ]	[ɪwɪ]	*2
	/u/	[ʊɐ]	[ʊwi]	[uː]

Note: Asterisks indicate an impermissible sequence.

As shown in the tables, the deletion of glides results in phonetic VV sequences. Specifically, if the vowels are identical, the surface vowel is a long one, and if they are not, a phonetic diphthong arises. The phonetic diphthong is considered bimoraic, so (underlyingly) three-syllable words still take the allomorphs of case suffixes that attach to stems of more than two mora, such as *-rla*, rather than the allomorphs that attach to stems of two mora, as evidenced by *Pamayi* taking the locative case form *-rla* in (21).

(20) *Pam<u>ayi</u>* 'placename' /pamaji/ [pɐmɐi]

(21) *Pam<u>ayi</u>-rla* 'placename-LOC' /pamajila/ [pɐmɐiɭɐ]

Further examples of glide deletion are given in (22)–(25).

(22) *warn<u>a-w</u>arnu* 'snake-RSLT' /waɳawaɳu/ [wɔŋɐːɳʊ]

(23) *Jungarr<u>ayi</u>* 'skin name' /cuŋaraji/ [jʊŋɐrɐi]

(24) *t<u>uwu</u>* 'hot' /tuwu/ [tuː]

(25) *karl<u>i=yi</u>* 'boomerang-then' /kaʎiji/ [kɐʎiː]

One speaker, DK, deletes the palatal glide /j/ word initially in the demonstrative /jali/ 'that', articulated as [ɐli].

---

2   There is only a small number of words in the known lexicon with an *iwu* sequence, however, none is in my corpus to check the phonetic realisation of the vowel + glide + vowel sequence.

2.3 Vowels

There are three contrastive vowel qualities, /a/, /i/ and /u/, and a marginal length distinction (that is, /a:/, /i:/ and /u:/). The discussion of vowels includes an overview of the length distinction (§2.3.1), the allophony of each short vowel (§§2.3.1–2.3.4), a narrative device of extreme vowel lengthening (§2.3.5), while §2.3.5 summarises the section.

This section primarily draws on the acoustic data of one speaker's (DG) vowel formants, shown in Figure 2.4 (grouped by phoneme) and Figure 2.5 (grouped by analysed allophone). The allophones of /a/ share a significant amount of central overlap, demonstrating that the allophony is usually a tendency towards an articulatory target, which is impacted by speech rate, among other factors. In the chart, I have coded each vowel according to its 'articulatory target' based on its phonetic environment (under my analysis of the data), even in instances where it did not reach this target, allowing a more transparent and accurate reflection of the data, at the cost of emphasising the *maximal* distinction(s) between allophones. Despite this, the distance between average allophonic targets is comparable with other instrumental analyses of three-vowel systems (for example, Gooniyandi [McGregor 1990: 60]). Vowels in unstressed syllables may be reduced towards [ə], though this is quite infrequent.

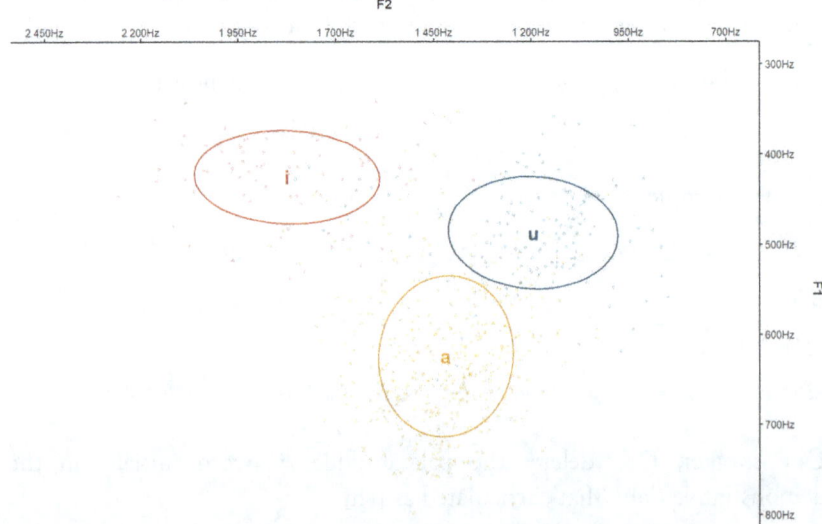

Figure 2.4 Vowel ellipses of one speaker (DG) based on 677 tokens

2. PHONETICS AND PHONOLOGY

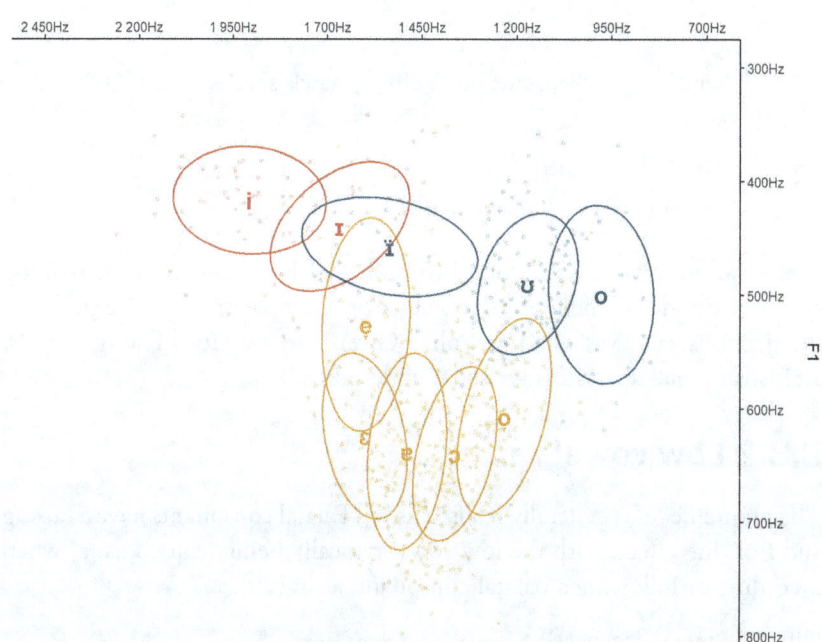

Figure 2.5 Averaged realisations of short vowel allophones (categorised by phoneme) from one speaker (DG), based on 663 tokens

These formant data also align very similarly with Butcher's (1994) findings for Warlpiri, which also has a three-vowel system, further reinforcing Butcher's finding that Australian languages realise vowel quality distinctions to a minimal extent in terms of acoustics (that is, a compact system with overlap between contrastive vowels).

2.3.1 Vowel length opposition

The vowel length contrast, like the stop length contrast, is marginal, in that long vowels in Warlmanpa are lexically infrequent.

Only the low vowel has a known minimal pair distinguishing length; the high vowels only have tenuous pairs, which serves to demonstrate that the vowel length cannot be predicted based on word length.

(26) /jala/   /jaːla/
      jala   *jaala*
      'now, soon' 'up and down'

(27) /puʈ/ /muːt/ see also: /mutpurpa/

purt *muut* *mutpurrpa*
'send' 'separate, break off' 'acacia species'

(28) /win/ /wiːt/

win *wiit*
'throw away' 'lift (someone) up'

Almost all long vowels are found in monosyllabic coverbs; the remaining few are found in uncommon nouns (for example, *tuurtpa* 'seagull') or interjections *yuu* 'yes!' and *yii* 'oh!'. Given the scarcity of long vowels, an instrumental analysis is yet to be undertaken.

2.3.2 Low vowel /a/

The phoneme /a/ is generally realised as [ɐ]. Palatal consonants have a raising and fronting effect, with the low vowel typically being realised as [ɛ] when preceding or following a palatal consonant, as in (29).

(29) *jaru* 'language' /caɭu/ [cʲɛɭʊ]

When the low vowel is in the environment of a peripheral consonant, especially bilabial consonants, the articulation is rounded and backed towards [ɔ], as in (30). The backing is particularly salient when following /w/.

(30) *warlu* 'fire, firewood' /waɭu/ [wɔɭʊ]

The effects on the articulation of /a/ are especially apparent when both adjacent consonants are of the same class (that is, both peripheral or both palatal), with the articulation sometimes reaching [e̞] for palatal consonants and [o̞] for peripheral consonants.

(31) *yanjarra* 'north' /jaɲcara/ [je̞ɲjɛrɐ]
(32) *wangani* 'dog' /waŋani/ [wo̞ŋɔni]

Conversely, when these two conditioning environments overlap—that is, when a low vowel is preceded by a palatal consonant and followed by a peripheral consonant, or vice versa—the vowel is realised centrally as [ɐ].

(33) *janganpa* 'possum' /caŋanpa/ [cʲɐŋɔnpɐ]

2.3.3 High front vowel /i/

Typical realisations of /i/ vary between [ɪ] and [i], with a tendency towards [ɪ] in most environments. When following a palatal nasal, palatal stop or alveolar lateral, it is typically raised and fronted to [i]. Word-final position also tends to be articulated as [i]. Examples are given in (34)–(36).

(34) *japirri* 'knife' /capiri/ [ɟʲɛbɪri]
(35) *lijji* 'dry' /licːi/ [licːʲi]
(36) *jirrima* /jirima/ [ɟʲirɪmɔ]

2.3.4 High back vowel /u/

The typical articulation of /u/ is [ʊ], as in (37).

(37) *wungu* 'together' /wuŋu/ [ʊŋʊ]

When flanked by peripheral consonants other than /w/, the vowel is backed to [o], as in (38), where the /u/ in the first syllable is flanked by velar stops.

(38) *kuku* 'wait' /kuku/ [gogʊ]

Palatal consonants have a significant fronting effect and cause the articulation to be unrounded. When preceded by a palatal stop or glide, or preceding any palatal consonant, the vowel realisation is typically [ɨ], as in (39) and (40).

(39) *julypu* 'sand, sandy country' /cuʎpu/ [ɟʲɨʎpʊ]
(40) *nyuntu* 'you' /ɲuntu/ [ɲʲɨntʊ]

2.3.5 Extra long vowels

In some cases, noted only in narratives, a vowel may become extra long. This lengthening is iconic in nature, signalling that the event has an extended duration (however, cf. Caudal and Mailhammer [2022], who demonstrate that a similar process in Iwaidja is more complex, beyond iconicity). In (41), the vowel in the bound pronoun =*lu* is lengthened to 1.18 seconds in duration—with the overall duration of the utterance being 2.36 seconds, so this single vowel comprises more than half of the utterance's overall duration, shown in Figure 2.6.

(41)   *Jitpi-nyi=lu::*   *ngu:layi.*
       run-FUT=3PLS.   finished
       They're going to run it [all day long].
       N_D02-007850, DG, 02:32 mins

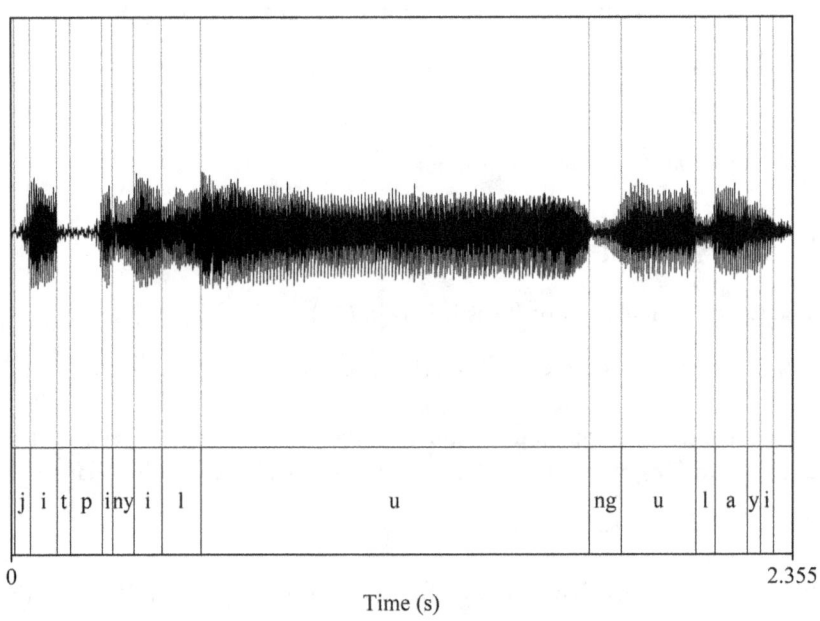

Figure 2.6 TextGrid and waveform of Example (41)

The phonetic realisation of an extra-long vowel bears very little, if any, correspondence to its non-extra-lengthened counterparts. In (41), the bound pronoun /lu/ is realised as [lɐɛ::]—that is, a diphthong that begins as a low vowel and transitions to a mid-front vowel. Yet, the extra long vowel in the bound pronoun /ṉalu/ in (42) is realised as a monophthong, [e]—that is, both underlying /u/ vowels become fronted as part of their lengthening.

(42)   *Pa-nangu-rnu=rnalu::*   *Latapa-ka.*
       go-PAST-TWD=1PL.EXCL.S   Latapa-ALL
       We went towards Ladabah.
       N_D09-013599, DG, 00:26 secs

2. PHONETICS AND PHONOLOGY

Interestingly, the extra long low vowel in (43) patterns much like the diphthong realisation of the extra long /u/ vowel in (42), despite being a phonemically different vowel. It is likely that this lengthening process neutralises the distinctions between vowels.

(43) *Pa-nangu-rra=rna*   *karlarra-purta::*   *nganayi-ka.*
     go-PAST-IMPF=1SG.S   west-FACING   whatsitcalled-ALL
     I went to the west to that place.
     N_D09-013599, DG, 00:59 secs

The formants of these three tokens of extra long vowels are given in Figure 2.7, demonstrating their unpredictability, particularly for the underlying /u/ vowel.

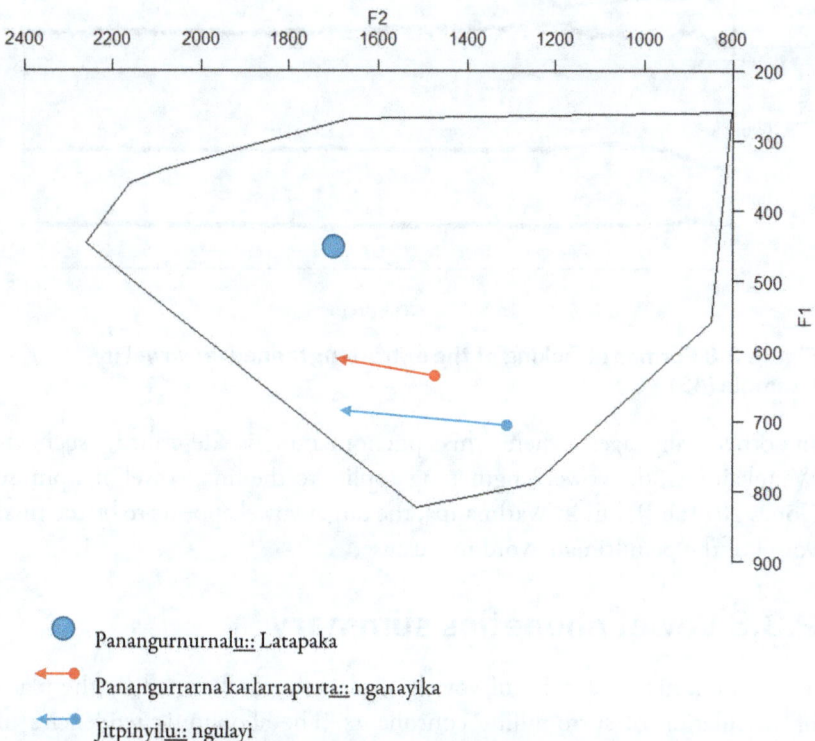

● Panangurnurnalu:: Latapaka
●—→ Panangurrarna karlarrapurta:: nganayika
●—→ Jitpinyilu:: ngulayi

Figure 2.7 Formant data of three extra-long vowels

Moreover, the transitions in the diphthongs take place over a short duration compared with the vowel. Figure 2.8 shows the formant values over the duration of the extra long /a/ vowel in (43); the rise in F2 happens towards the start of the vowel and over the duration of a normal-length vowel. The remaining duration is stable at this F2 value, rather than the diphthong transition occurring over the full duration of the vowel.

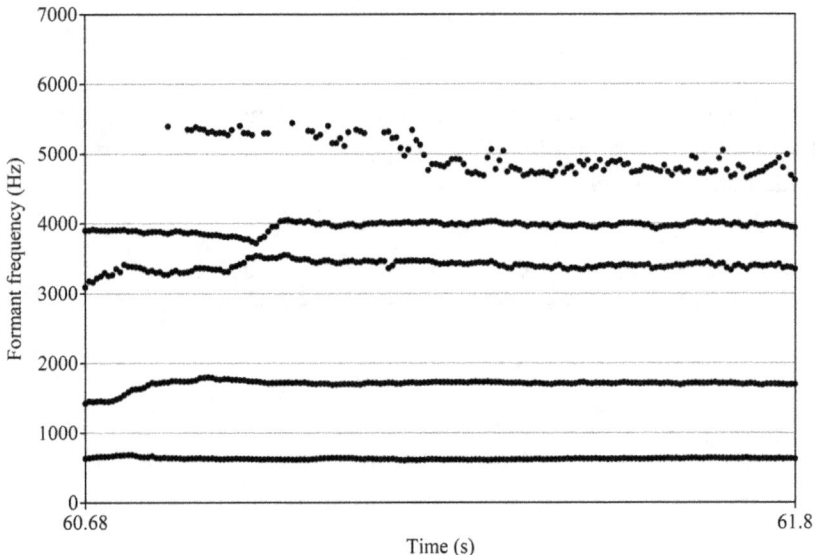

Figure 2.8 Formant tracking of the extra-lengthened /a/ vowel in Example (43)

In other languages where this phenomenon is described, such as Wangkajunga, the vowel lengthening applies to the final vowel of a phrase (Jones 2011: 48), but in Warlmanpa, the target vowel appears to be the final vowel of the penultimate word in a clause.

2.3.6 Vowel phonetics summary

The allophonic tendencies of vowels are largely conditioned by the place of articulation of surrounding consonants. The allophonic tendencies of vowels can be summarised as follows:

1. Peripheral consonants tend to have a backing effect, except for /i/. Peripheral consonants have a raising effect on /a/ and a lowering effect on /u/.

2. Palatal consonants have a fronting and raising effect.
3. Word position does not appear to impact the realisation of vowels, except in the case of /i/, which is raised and fronted in word-final position.

2.4 Voicing

Continuant consonants /w, y, ɻ, l, ḻ, ʎ and r/ are always fully voiced. Geminate stops are always unvoiced. Other occlusive consonants are typically voiced but can become unvoiced in certain conditions. The singleton stops may be unvoiced as part of clusters (especially stop + stop clusters). Nasals and vowels are underlyingly voiced but may be affected by a process of utterance-final devoicing.

In utterance-final position, vowels may be completely or partially unvoiced. Figure 2.9 shows the proportions of vowel realisations in utterance-final position across a sample of 89 tokens (64 tokens of /a/, 16 of /u/ and nine of /i/). Vowels that were voiced for 80 per cent or more of the duration were categorised as 'voiced', vowels that had no voicing (0 per cent voicing for the duration) for the duration were categorised as 'unvoiced', with the remainder of vowels categorised as 'creaky'. The high back vowel /u/ is least likely to be fully voiced and by far the most likely to be completely unvoiced. Conversely, /i/ is most likely to be fully voiced and there are no completely unvoiced instances.

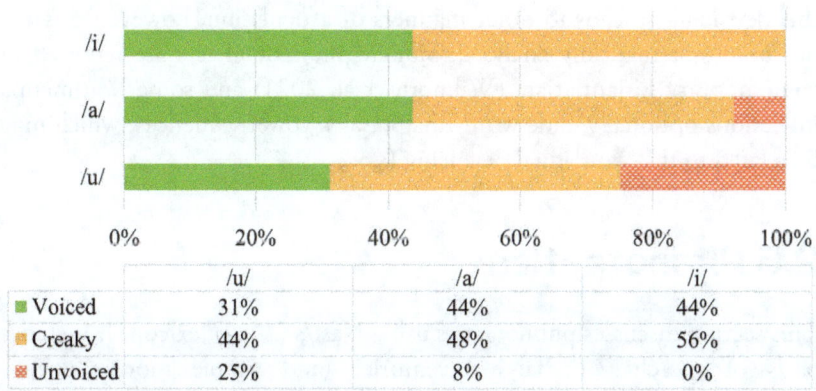

Figure 2.9 Voicing of utterance-final vowels

There are no noted conditioning factors: no segment or class of segments preceding the vowel predicts its voicing. However, in some cases, the creaky or unvoiced feature also spreads to the preceding nasal: 30 per cent of vowels that were at least partially unvoiced also had a partially unvoiced nasal preceding them. To exemplify, Figure 2.10 shows a spectrogram extract of *yamaka panama* from the phrase given in (44).

(44)   *Ngampurrpa=rna   ka-nya   nga=rna   **yama-ka   pa-nama.***
       desire=1SG.S   be-PRES   PURP=1SG.S   **shade-ALL   go-POT**
       I want to go to the shade.
       H_K01-505B, DG, 25:55 mins

The utterance-final /ma/ can be compared with the /ma/ within *yamaka*. The glottal pulses of utterance-final /ma/ are much further apart and the intensity rapidly decreases.

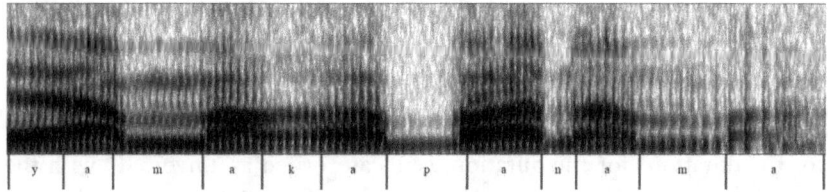

Figure 2.10 Spectrogram of utterance-final voice creaking, spreading to the preceding consonant

If the unvoiced or creaky nasal is part of a nasal + nasal cluster, both nasals share the unvoiced or creaky feature. There is no available evidence that this devoicing spreads to other manners of articulation, however, this has not been systematically analysed. Similar phonetic effects are reported in contemporary Pitjantjatjara (Wilmoth et al. 2021) and some Warlmanpa inflections optionally elide word-final nasal + vowel sequences, which may be related to this word-final devoicing (§6.2.2.2.2.1).

2.5 Phonotactics

This section discusses phonotactics using Nash's (2022) lexicon. It includes parts of speech with large inventories (and simple morphology)—specifically nominals, coverbs and adverbs—for 1,358 monomorphemic tokens (1,071 nominals, 203 coverbs and 84 adverbs). Inflecting verbs were excluded due to their low inventory size (there are 46 known verb roots) and issues regarding morpheme boundaries. However, it is worth noting that no known inflecting verbs violate any phonotactic rules and pattern very similarly to nominals.

2.5.1 Syllable structure

There are four syllable types:

i. V
ii. CV
iii. CVC
iv. CVCC

Syllable types (ii) and (iii) are the most common and are found in all word classes. Syllable type (i) is restricted to word-initial position in some placenames (for example, Apparrapartta) and two nominals: *ali*, a variant of *yali* 'that' used by one speaker and *amiki-amiku* '(native) pine tree'. Syllable type (iv) is only found in a coverb, *warlk* 'bark'—a variant form of *warlku*.

2.5.2 Root morphemes length

Known roots in Warlmanpa range from one to eight syllables, with the mode number of syllables being three (represented in Table 2.7). The only word classes that can be one syllable are coverbs and the auxiliary (a highly morphologically complex template; see discussion in Chapter 5). Most coverbs are two syllables long and most nominals and adverbs are three syllables long.

Table 2.7 Root morpheme syllable length

Syllable length	Proportion of lexicon	Nominals/adverbs	Coverbs
1	3.1%	0.0%	20.6%
2	27.8%	21.9%	61.3%
3	35.4%	39.5%	12.3%
4	26.7%	30.5%	5.4%
5	5.4%	6.2%	0.5%
6	1.4%	1.6%	0.0%
7	0.1%	0.1%	0.0%
8	0.1%	0.1%	0.0%

2.5.3 Word-position constraints

Word boundary frequencies, with vowels included, are given in Table 2.8. The distribution of consonants is given in Table 2.9 and the distribution of vowels in Table 2.10. Generally, words are consonant-initial and vowel-final.

All consonants are found word-medially. Geminate stops are restricted to this position: they are not found word-initially, word-finally or in clusters.[3] Most other consonants can be found in multiple word positions, specifically word-medially and word-initially and/or word-finally.

Most consonants that can be found in the coda position of a syllable can occur word-finally, except /m/, which is relatively common in coda positions but not found word-finally. However, it should be noted that of the 167 word-final consonants in the sample, 148 are found in coverbs. Unlike Warlpiri (Nash 1986: 175), in Warlmanpa there is no synchronic epenthesis process that prohibits consonant-final words. This is exemplified in (45) with the coverb *tij* clearly expressed at the end of the utterance, with no epenthetic syllable to avoid the word-final palatal stop.

(45) Kurtu=ma   ka-ngu-rra   ***tij.***
      child=TOP   be-PAST-IMPF   overnight_camp
      The child camped overnight.
      K_003, BN, 01:29 mins

Word-initially, the contrast between the alveolar and postalveolar series is neutralised (rendered as the alveolar series in this sample), as in most Australian languages (Fletcher and Butcher 2014: 103). The palatal lateral and alveolar tap are not found word-initially, as in other Ngumpin-Yapa languages (Ennever 2021; Meakins and McConvell 2021; Nash 1986: 79; Meakins and Nordlinger 2014: 59; Tsunoda 1981a: 36; Hudson 1978: 6; Senge 2015: 80).

---

3   Thus, an alternative analysis is that geminate stops are consonant clusters, which is why they are only found word-medially and cannot occur in clusters.

Table 2.8 Segment frequency at word boundaries

Segment	Word-initial	Word-final
pː	0	0
p	213	1
m	135	0
w	222	0
kː	0	0
k	203	18
ŋ	99	4
tː	0	0
t	81	7
n	28	14
l	59	11
r	0	20
ʈː	0	0
ʈ	0	12
ɳ	0	5
ɭ	0	21
ɺ	2	3
cː	0	0
c	161	21
ɲ	20	8
ʎ	0	22
j	133	0
aː	2	542
a	2	542
iː	0	1
i	0	400
uː	0	0
u	0	247

Table 2.9 Consonant frequency across nominals, adverbs and coverbs

Consonants	Word-initial	Word-medial			Word-final
		Onset (intervocalic)	Coda (cluster)	Onset (cluster)	
pː	0	7	0	0	0
p	213	148	0	244	1
m	135	87	53	30	0
w	222	115	0	31	0
kː	0	7	0	0	0
k	203	184	4	184	18
ŋ	99	93	56	13	4
tː	0	6	0	0	0
t	81	49	14	44	7
n	28	101	114	0	14
l	59	148	72	1	11
r	0	217	78	0	20
ʈː	0	4	0	0	0
ʈ	0	177	4	60	12
ɳ	0	65	87	0	5
ɭ	0	168	74	0	21
ɻ	2	208	0	0	3
cː	0	10	0	0	0
c	161	150	18	108	21
ɲ	20	36	111	0	8
ʎ	0	56	31	0	22
j	133	75	0	1	0

Table 2.10 Vowel frequency across nominals, adverbs and coverbs

Vowels	Word-initial	Word-medial	Word-final
aː	0	10	1
a	2	2,002	542
iː	0	11	1
i	0	1,220	400
uː	0	6	0
u	0	938	247

2.5.4 Intra-morphemic consonant clusters

Intra-morphemic consonant clusters are restricted to two consonants. The most common clusters are shown in Figure 2.11 and all permissible clusters are counted in Table 2.11.

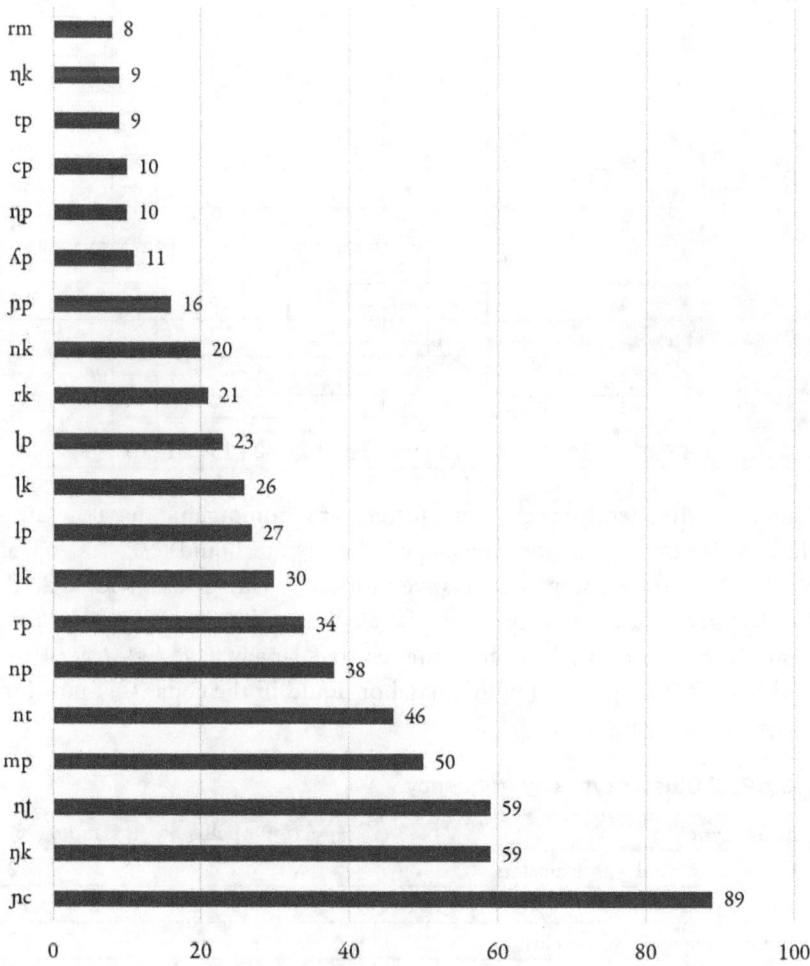

Figure 2.11 Frequency of most common intra-morphemic consonant clusters

A GRAMMAR OF WARLMANPA

Table 2.11 Frequency of consonant clusters in lexicon (phonemes sorted by frequency)

		Onset (C2)										Total
		p	k	c	ʈ	t	w	m	ŋ	l	j	
Coda (C1)	n	40	20	—	—	44	—	6	4	—	—	114
	ɲ	15	1	90	—	—	2	2	1	—	—	111
	ɳ	10	10	—	60	—	—	3	4	—	—	87
	r	38	21	4	—	—	3	10	2	—	—	78
	ɭ	25	33	3	—	—	7	4	2	—	—	74
	l	28	33	—	—	—	8	3	—	—	—	72
	ŋ	—	56	—	—	—	—	—	—	—	—	56
	m	53	—	—	—	—	—	—	—	—	—	53
	ʎ	12	6	2	—	—	9	1	—	1	—	31
	c	12	4	—	—	—	1	—	—	—	1	18
	t	9	—	5	—	—	—	—	—	—	—	14
	ʈ	1	—	2	—	—	—	1	—	—	—	4
	k	1	—	2	—	—	1	—	—	—	—	4
	Total	244	184	108	60	44	31	30	13	1	1	

The most frequently occurring clusters are homorganic nasal + stop clusters. Beyond this, most consonant clusters are liquids (/l, ɭ, ʎ, r/) or nasals followed by a stop. The relative proportions are given in Table 2.12. As these generalisations suggest, almost all clusters have a stop in the onset position (89 per cent). The remaining clusters largely have /w/, /m/ or /ŋ/ in the onset (C2) position with a nasal or liquid in the coda (C1) position (10 per cent of clusters).

Table 2.12 Cluster types by frequency

Cluster type	Proportion of clusters in sample (%)
Homorganic nasal + stop clusters	42
Liquid + stop clusters	29
Heterorganic nasal + stop clusters	13
Other cluster types	16

Consonant clusters are not found word-initially or word-finally, except *warlk*, which is a variant of *warlku* 'bark'.

2.5.5 Inter-morphemic clusters

Inter-morphemic clusters in Warlmanpa are unrestricted, in that the only restrictions are based on the morphological combinatorial possibilities. In general, no accommodations are made to account for any impermissible clusters across morpheme boundaries for Warlmanpa words. English borrowings that are stop-final, such as *Tennant Creek*, are subject to vowel epenthesis when hosting the clitic =*lku* (see §2.5.6).

Most lexemes that historically may have ended in a consonant cluster received a (historical) epenthetic *pa* that prevented dispreferred complex clusters. While this epenthesis process is no longer synchronically active, the epenthetic form has fused with the lexemes.

2.5.6 English borrowings

Borrowings from English generally conform to the phonemic generalisations discussed throughout this chapter. However, they are occasionally exceptional regarding their phonotactics—for example, *kultringk* 'cool drink' has a tri-segmental cluster and a word-final consonant cluster.

In rare cases, loan words that end in consonants receive an epenthetic low vowel if there would otherwise be a dispreferred three-consonant cluster. For example, the placename 'Tennant Creek' when hosting =*lku* 'now, then' receives an epenthetic /a/ vowel to avoid a */klk/ cluster—that is, *Tennant Creek-a=lku* /tenənt kɹiːkɐlku/. Interestingly, the complex cluster /nt kɹ/ is not reduced (including the audible release of both stops). Clearly, further research is required to formalise which three-consonant clusters are dispreferred and the integration of English borrowings into the grammar.

2.6 Prosody

In this section, I briefly describe several observations pertaining to the prosody of Warlmanpa—in particular, stress assignment (which largely follows Nash 1979) and the interaction between question clauses and pitch.

2.6.1 Stress

The basic patterns of stress in Warlmanpa are: a) disyllabic morphemes (including roots) receive stress on their initial syllable; b) adjacent syllables cannot both be stressed; and c) word-final syllables cannot be stressed.

To account for these facts (and some minor caveats), I present an analysis of stress, largely following analyses of Warlpiri (Pentland and Laughren 2004; Nash 1986). Stress assignment is determined by the position of the syllable in the phonological and prosodic word. Syllables are assigned to feet, where each disyllable in a prosodic word constitutes a well-formed foot, from first to last (or, from the perspective of the writing convention, left to right).[4] Any remaining unassigned syllables are then linked to the same foot as the preceding syllable. A strong–weak pattern is assigned to all nodes (first to last), in which the left-most branch of each constituent is 'strong' and all other daughter nodes are 'weak'.

This is exemplified (right) for *minija* 'cat', where the final syllable, *ja*, would be unassigned to a foot (based on feet being assigned first to last), so it links to the same foot as the preceding syllable. The first syllable is assigned 'strong', as it is the left-most syllable in the foot and all other syllables are 'weak'.

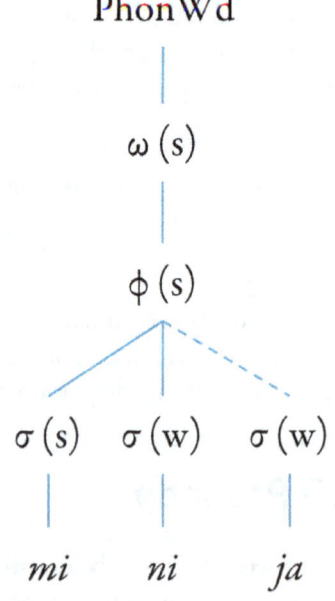

---

4   I have not investigated whether this is sensitive to mora count, rather than syllable count, due to the low frequency of long vowels.

A syllable that does not have any weak branches up to the phonological word receives primary stress (this is always, and only, the initial syllable of a phonological word, with a single known exception: *mayi'patturla*); all other strong syllables receive secondary stress. For example, the four-syllable word *Jampijinpa* (a skin name) forms two feet, (*'Jampi*)(*jinpa*), as shown (right).

The analysis so far has focused on single prosodic words. A point of interest, common to other Ngumpin-Yapa languages (Ennever 2021; Hale 1977), is that morphemes (suffixes and clitics) that comprise two or more syllables constitute a new prosodic word (in contrast to monosyllabic affixes, which do not). A stem, its affixes and any clitics always form a phonological word (as analysed for Warlpiri [Pentland and Laughren 2004]).

Thus, when trisyllabic stems such as *maliki* take a monosyllabic suffix, the third syllable is assigned to a well-formed foot along with the suffix, as shown to the right for *'mali͵ku-rlu* 'dog-ERG', resulting in secondary stress on the third syllable.

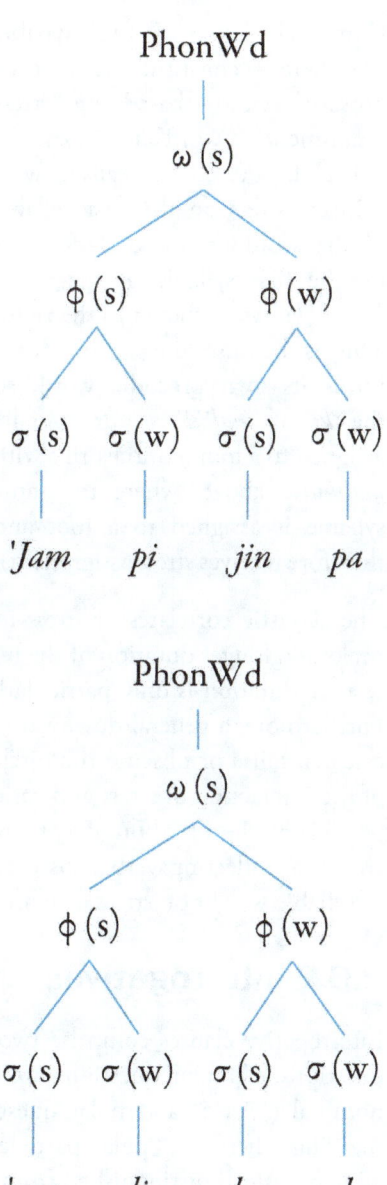

Conversely, as multisyllabic morphemes constitute their own prosodic word (based on stress assignment), a word such as *maliki-kuma* 'dog-AVER' is realised with primary stress on the first syllable of the word and secondary stress on the first syllable of the suffix ˈ*maliki*ˌ*kuma*, as shown to the right. This is because the suffix *-kuma* forms its own prosodic word, so the *ki* of *maliki* is not initially assigned to a foot (contrast this with *malikurlu* above, where the same syllable is assigned to a foot and therefore receives stress assignment).

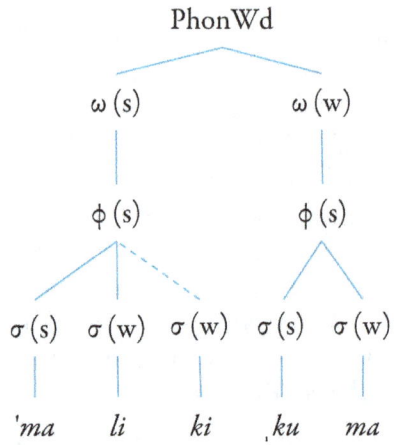

The acoustic correlates of stress in Warlmanpa are pitch peaks, intensity peaks and longer duration of the nucleus of a stressed syllable; however, the relative duration is only particularly salient during single-word elicitation. Furthermore, a general downward trend of pitch throughout an utterance can neutralise or obscure the pitch peaks. Further investigation is needed of the interaction of stress and various phenomena, such as inflecting verbs (especially where the boundary between 'root' and 'inflection' is ambiguous), coverb + inflecting verb constructions, compound words and the effect of syllable weight on stress assignment.

2.6.2 Interrogatives

Interrogative clauses comprise two subtypes: content questions and polar questions. Content questions are obligatorily marked with an ignorative nominal (§3.1.5) and polar questions typically lack special grammatical marking (there is a 'polar particle' used once in the corpus; see §9.1.6) and are instead distinguished from declarative clauses only based on pitch. See §11.4 for further details of the morphosyntax and semantics of these clause types.

Content questions are associated with a general falling intonation pattern across the utterance, particularly on the last syllable. This is distinguished from declarative clauses, which tend to have a pitch peak on the final syllable.

For example, Figure 2.12 gives the pitch tracks for the utterances in (50) and (51). The declarative utterance has a clear utterance-final rising intonation, whereas the interrogative has an utterance-final falling intonation.

(50) *Wantiyi-na   pa-nangu-rnu*
      PF-1GEN   go-PAST-TWD
      My wife's father came.
      N_D03-007868, BN, 32:38 mins

(51) *Ngana   pa-nangu-rnu?*
      who   go-PAST-TWD
      Who came?
      N_D03-007868, BN, 32:35 mins

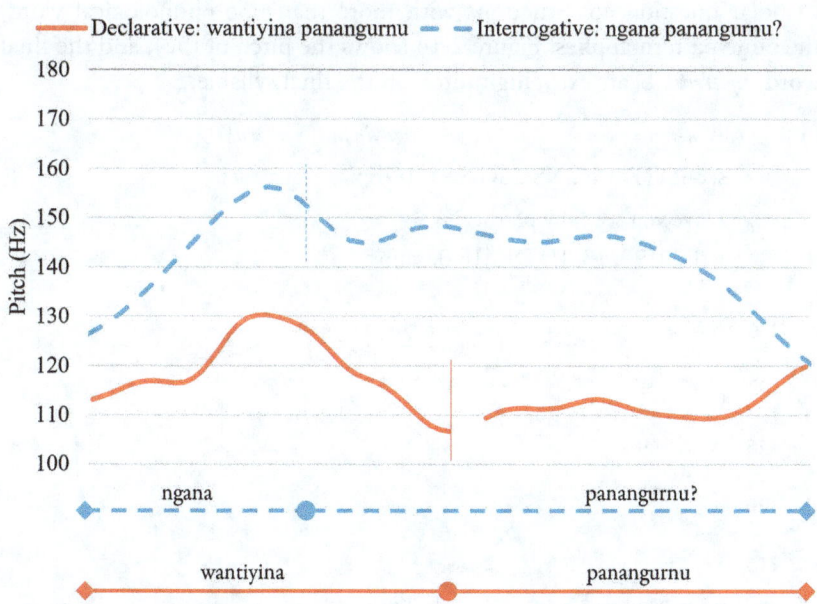

Figure 2.12 Pitch of declarative sentences and interrogative sentences

Polar questions, on the other hand, exhibit markedly high pitch on the final syllable of the utterance. For example, in Figure 2.13, the polar question construction is a single word with three syllables: the first two syllables are both low pitch, with F0 peaking at approximately 170 Hertz. In the third (and final) syllable, F0 is nearly 240 Hertz—notably higher than the previous syllables.

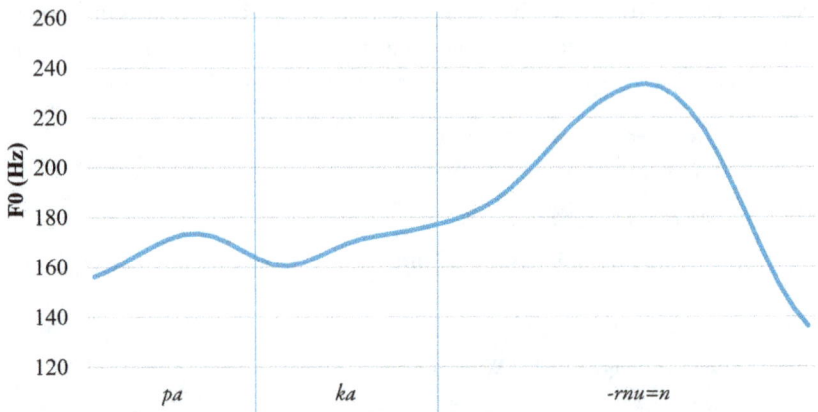

Figure 2.13 Pitch of polar question *pakarnun* 'did you kill it?'

In polar question constructions with more than one phonological word, the same pattern applies. Figure 2.14 shows the pitch of (52), and the final word, *ngarnki*, bears extra high pitch on the final syllable.

(52) Nya-ngu=ju-n   ngayinya   ngarnki
      see-PAST=1SG.NS-2SG.S   1GEN   partner
      Have you seen my partner?
      wrl-20190213-01, DK, 16:02 mins

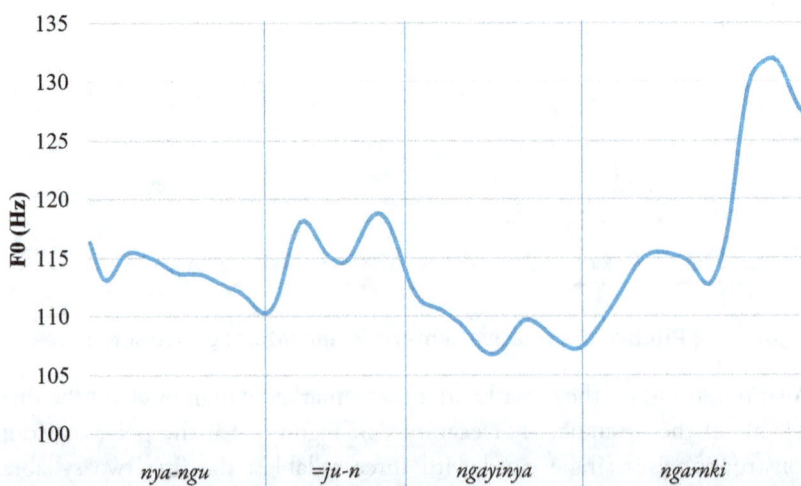

Figure 2.14 Pitch contour of polar question *nyangujun ngayinya ngarnki* 'have you seen my partner?'

2.7 Vowel assimilation

Vowel harmony is not productive across the grammar of Warlmanpa, however, there is evidence for three synchronically active processes.

One of these three processes is obligatory: a high front vowel may also trigger regressive vowel assimilation (most commonly, the clitics =*yi* 'still' or =*yijala* 'also'). This assimilation process is always triggered, given the appropriate environment, however, the triggering environment is relatively rare (these clitics are infrequently used, compared with the ergative suffix, for example). This assimilation process spreads leftward and is only blocked by /k/, a low vowel or a word boundary. This is discussed in §2.7.1.1.

The other two processes are optional. First, a high front vowel may trigger long-range progressive assimilation, however, this is extremely rare. This is discussed in §2.7.1.2. The other optional assimilation process involves regressive assimilation triggered by a high back vowel (most triggered by the ergative suffix -*ngu*/-*rlu*), which may assimilate a stem-final //i// to /u/. While the triggering environment is extremely common (that is, the ergative suffix attaching to a stem ending in a high front vowel), this process only applies sporadically. This process is discussed in §2.7.1.3.

All assimilation triggered by a high front vowel is long range, whereas assimilation triggered by a high back vowel has a local range and the productivity of the assimilation process is inversely correlated to the frequency of the appropriate triggering environment. This is summarised in Table 2.13.

Table 2.13 Summary of Warlmanpa vowel assimilation processes

Triggering vowel	Direction	Iterative	Productivity	Frequency of triggering environment	Section
//i//	Regressive	Yes	Obligatory	Low	§2.7.1.1
//i//	Progressive	Yes	Very low	High	§2.7.1.2
//u//	Regressive	No	Low	High	§2.7.1.3

The assimilation processes discussed in this section pertain primarily to nominals. Inflecting verbs have their own distinct morphophonological processes, which are discussed in §6.2.2.2, after the verb inflections have been introduced (as the inflections are the triggers of the morphophonological processes).

2.7.1 High front vowel regressive assimilation

The only obligatory vowel assimilation process in Warlmanpa is regressive assimilation of //i// when it follows //j//. The only known context for this to occur is the clitic =*yi* 'still' or =*yijala* 'also' attaching to a word ending in //u//. Unlike the other assimilation processes in Warlmanpa, this assimilation is seemingly obligatory. Examples are given in (53)–(55). The assimilation spreads leftward and is blocked by velar stops, as in (54), though interestingly, it is not blocked by velar nasals, as exemplified in (55).

(53) *Ngarrka-ngu* *tartu-ngu=nganpa-lu* *nya-nganya* *tartu=yijala*
man-ERG many-ERG=1.EXCL.PL.NS-3PL.S see-PRES many=also

//ŋarka-ŋu taʈu-ŋu=ŋanpa-lu ɲa-ŋaɲa taʈu=jicala//

/ŋarkaŋu taʈuŋuŋanpalu ɲaŋaɲa taʈijicala/

That mob of men is looking at us mob as well.
H_K01-505B, DG, 51:19 mins

(54) *Ku**ku**=yi=rna* *nga-rninya*
wait=STILL=1SG.S eat-PRES

//k**u**ku=ji=ɳa ŋa-ɳiɲa//

/k**u**kijiɲa ŋa-ɳiɲa/

Wait, I'm still eating!
wrl-20180615-02, DK, 19:15 mins

(55) *Jinta=yi=lu* *wawirri* *la-rnu* *tartu-ngu=yi*
one=STILL=3PL.S kangaroo shoot-PAST many-ERG=STILL

//cinta=ji=lu wawiri la-ɳu taʈ**u**-ŋ**u**=ji//

/cintajilu wawiri laɳu taʈiŋiji/

Only that mob shot a kangaroo.
wrl-20191208-02, DK, 03:36 mins

2.7.2 High front vowel progressive assimilation

In rare cases, a high vowel in the root spreads the [+front] feature to any following high vowels, blocked only by a low vowel /a/, a bilabial stop /p/, a peripheral glide /w/ or a phonological word boundary—a process also found in Warlpiri (see Nash 1986: 86). In the case of (56), the word boundary prevents the vowel harmony spreading rightwards to the verb, however, it still spreads across the clitic boundary, just like the regressive assimilation. It is not clear what triggers this assimilation and it is highly sporadic.

(56) **Lani=lku=ju**   jutpu-ngu
      //lani=lku=cu//   cutpu-ŋu//
      /lanilkici/   cutuŋu/
      afraid=THEN=1SG.NS   run-PAST
      Then it ran, afraid of me.
      wrl-20180528-03, JK, 18:02 mins

(57) Ngayu=lpa   wa-nganya   karnta-ku   **yali-ku**
      //ŋaju=lpa   wa-ŋaɲa   kaɳʈa-ku   **jali-ku**//
      /ŋajulpa   waɲaɲa   kaɳʈaku   **jaliki**/
      1=1PL.INCL.S   speak-PRES   woman-DAT   that-DAT
      We're speaking to that woman.
      wrl-20190117, SN, 10:20 mins

(58) **Jarrawarti=ju**   karta   pu-ngu
      //carawaʈi=cu//   kaʈa   puŋu//
      /carawaʈici/   kaʈa   puŋu/
      thigh=1SG.NS   spear   act_on-PAST
      He speared me in the thigh.
      H_K06-004555, LOF, 35:04 mins

2.7.3 High back vowel regressive assimilation

The ergative allomorph -*rlu* causes some stems ending in //i// to become /u/, as in (59). This process is not noted for the ergative allomorph -*ngu*.

(59) Mali**ki**-**rlu**   nga=ngu=nga   pi-nya
      //mali**ki**-**ɭu**//   ŋa=ŋu=ŋa   pi-ɲa//
      /mali**ku**ɭu/   ŋaŋuŋa   piɲa/
      dog-ERG   POST=2SG.NS=DUB   act_on-POT
      Careful, that dog might bite you!
      H_K01-505B, DG, 02:16 mins

(60) Yarri-r**lu**=ju   paka-rnu
      that-ERG=1SG.NS   hit-PAST
      ⫽jari-⌊**u**=ju   paka-ɳu⫽
      /jar**u**⌊**u**ju   pakaɳu/
      That [one] hit me.
      H_K01-505B, DG, 11:34 mins

This assimilation is sporadic, in that it does not always trigger in the appropriate phonetic environment—for example, not all cases of *maliki-rlu* trigger assimilation. It also appears to be local: unlike other types of assimilation exhibited in Warlmanpa, there is no evidence this spreads further than one adjacent vowel. For example, in (61), the nominal *japirri* 'knife' is inflected with the ergative case *-rlu*, which triggers the vowel assimilation of the final vowel in *japirri*, however, this does not spread to the penultimate vowel of the root, even though this is a high vowel.

(61) Kuyu=rna   kuma-nmi   japirri-rlu
      meat=1SG.S   cut-FUT   knife-ERG
      ⫽kuju=na   kuma-nmi   jap**i**ri-⌊**u**⫽
      ⫽kujuɳa   kumanmi   jap**i**r**u**⌊**u**⫽
      I'll cut the meat with a knife.
      H_K01-505B, DG, 42:23 mins

Interestingly, in Warlpiri, a similar process occurs, yielding quite different surface forms. In Warlpiri, the most pervasive vowel harmony spreads rightward, so the stem *maliki* 'dog' taking the ergative inflection *-rlu* spreads the ⫽i⫽ of the stem rightward, causing the ergative to be a high front vowel, *maliki̲rli* (Nash 1986; Harvey and Baker 2005). This form can be contrasted with the Warlmanpa form *maliku̲rlu*. Both languages have the same underlying forms for both morphs and both forms are subject to vowel assimilation/harmony, but in Warlmanpa the frontness feature spreads leftward and in Warlpiri it spreads rightward, resulting in rather different surface forms. The next two sections discuss some regressive vowel assimilation processes in Warlmanpa (structurally like this process just described for Warlpiri), however, regressive assimilation processes in Warlmanpa are vastly less productive than those in Warlpiri.

2.8 Reduplication

Reduplication is not a productive process in Warlmanpa; however, there are several temporal and human nominals that have a simplex form with a corresponding reduplicated form. The reduplicated temporal nominals have either a 'specific' or a 'generic' meaning in relation to their simplex form. A 'specific' meaning refers to a temporal reference that falls within a subset or specific point within the temporal range denoted by the simplex form. For example, *yakarlu-yakarlu* 'before dawn' refers to a specific subset of a time of 'night', denoted by the simplex form *yakarlu*. Conversely, a 'generic' meaning refers to a reduplicated form with a broader meaning than its simplex form; this correspondence is only noted between *jala* 'now' and *jalajala* 'nowadays'.

The reduplication of 'human' nominals is more straightforward: a small set of nominals with human referents can be reduplicated to specify a plural number.

Temporal nominals (with temporal adverbs for completeness) are given in Table 2.14 and human nominals are given in Table 2.15. In both tables, several simplex forms are given that lack a corresponding reduplicated form, where one might expect a corresponding form in a more productive reduplication system. For example, there is a reduplicated form of *karnta* 'woman', *karntakarnta* 'women', but no reduplicated form of *ngarrka* 'man'. Conversely, there is a reduplicated form of *pulka* 'old man', *pulkapulka* 'old men', but no reduplicated form of *japaka* 'old woman'.

There are some other nominals that appear to be reduplicated, but there is no synchronic reason to suggest that they are; the semantic relation between forms is often historical/cultural.

One last point of interest regarding reduplicated forms in Warlmanpa is that some English/Kriol borrowings referring to animal terms are only found as (seemingly) reduplicated forms but may refer to singular referents. These reduplicated forms were likely borrowed in as frozen forms, especially given the lack of corresponding simplex forms in other nearby languages (Kaytetye [Turpin and Ross 2012: 621] and Warumungu [Simpson and Heath 1982: 25]).

Table 2.14 Reduplication of 'temporal' nominals and adverbs

Word class	Simplex form		Reduplicated form		Reduplication type	Semantic relation
Adverb	jala	'now, today, soon'	jala-jala	'nowadays'	Full	Generic
Adverb	jalangu	'now, today, soon'	jalangu-jalangu	'nowadays'	Full	Generic
Adverb	larrpa	'before'	larrpa-larrpa	'long ago'	Full	Generic
Adverb	jawarti	'morning, tomorrow'	jawarti-jawarti	'early in morning'	Full	Specific
Nominal	parra	'daytime'	parra-parra	'daybreak'	Full	Specific
Adverb	wajjurra	'afternoon, yesterday'	wajurra-jurra	'afternoon'	Partial (right-to-left)	Specific
Nominal	yakarlu	'night'	yakarlu-yakarlu	'before dawn'	Full	Specific
Adverb	ngaka	'soon'	—	—	—	—
Nominal	yakarla	'yesterday evening'	—	—	—	—

Table 2.15 Reduplication of 'human' nominals[5]

Simplex form		Reduplicated form		Reduplication type	Semantic relation
kurtu	'child'	kurtu-kurtu	'children'	Full	Plural
karnta	'woman'	karnta-karnta	'women'	Full	Plural
ngarrka	'man'	—	—	—	—
pulka	'old man'	pulka-pulka	'old men'	Full	Plural
japaka	'old woman'	—	—	—	—
yapa	'person'	yapa-yapa	'people'	Full	Plural

Table 2.16 Reduplication of directional nominals

Simplex form		Reduplicated form		Reduplication type
kakarrija	'in the east'	kakarrija-kakarrija	'on the east side'	Full
karlija	'in the west'	karlija-karlija	'on the west side'	Full
kurlija	'in the south'	kurlija-kurlija	'on the south side'	Full

---

5   Note that *witta* 'small' and *wiri* 'big' (and their reduplicated forms) seem to have primarily human reference, though they have been included in Table 2.14 because they do not exclusively refer to human referents.

2. PHONETICS AND PHONOLOGY

Simplex form		Reduplicated form		Reduplication type
yantija	'in the north'	yantija-yantija	'on the north side'	Full
kuya	'thus'	kuyarni-kuyarni	'from both sides'	Other

Table 2.17 Reduplication of other nominals

Simplex form		Reduplicated form		Reduplication type	Semantic relation
japangarti	male subsection	japangarti-japangarti	'cricket (insect)'	Full	Cultural
japurla	'boy'	Japurla-japurla	'Laughing Boys Dreaming'	Full	Cultural
jarulpa	'rock shelter'	jaru-jarulpa	'rock shelters'	Partial (left-to-right)	Plural
wini	'burnt country'	wini-wini	'extensive burnt country'	Full	Plural
witta	'small'	witta-witta	'small ones/bits'	Full	Plural
wiri	'big'	wiri-wiri	'big ones'	Full	Plural
lurrija	'quickly'	lurrija-lurrija	'quickly'	Full	?
manya	'soft'	manya-manya	'soft'	Full	?
palya	'wax'	palya-palya	'sticky'	Full	Quality of simplex
wirinkirri	'yellow ochre'	wirinkirri-wirinkirri	'yellow'	Full	Quality of simplex
kantu	'under'	kantu-kantu	'hidden'	Full	Quality of simplex
ngamari	'mistletoe tree'	ngamari-ngamari	'tree bearing lots of ngamari'	Full	Plural
—	—	ngapala-ngapala	'insect species'	—	—
kunjuru	'smoke'	kunjuru-kunjuru	'grey, smoke colour'	Full	Quality of simplex

Table 2.18 English/Kriol animal words borrowed in their reduplicated forms

Simplex form	Reduplicated form	
—	juku-juku	'chicken'
—	puni-puni	'pony'
—	kapi-kapi	'calf'
—	piki-piki	'pig'

3
Parts of speech

The parts of speech in Warlmanpa are nominals, adverbs, free pronouns, coverbs, inflecting verbs, auxiliary bases, particles and clitics. Of these classes, nominals are the only truly open class—evidenced best by the regularity of English borrowings as nominals (which may then undergo derivation to other parts of speech). In Ngumpin languages, the borrowing of English verbs as coverbs is common (Meakins 2010; McConvell 2009), but this is not the case in Warlmanpa (nor is it the case in Warlpiri).

Evidence for parts of speech primarily comes from morphological characteristics, as well as some syntactic characteristics, although it will become apparent that some parts of speech are more similar than others (for example, nominals and free pronouns share the ability to take dative case marking). Furthermore, most parts of speech have several subcategories that behave slightly differently to other members of the category. The following is a summary of the characteristics of Warlmanpa parts of speech:

- **Nominals (§3.1):** Nominals are the only part of speech that are obligatorily marked for case in the appropriate grammatical relations (this contrasts primarily with adverbs, which may optionally take ergative marking).
- **Adverbs (§3.2):** Adverbs optionally agree in case with the subject (this contrasts primarily with nominals, which are obligatorily marked, and with particles, which can never inflect for case); most adverbs can be categorised into one of two groups that have further defining criteria.
- **Coverbs (§3.3):** Coverbs are never inflected and must always co-occur with an inflecting verb.

- **Inflecting verbs (§3.4):** Inflecting verbs obligatorily take one inflectional affix from a set of affixes unique to this class. They can never precede an auxiliary base.
- **Auxiliary bases (§3.5):** Auxiliary bases are a small set of words that host bound pronouns (§5.4). They occur in first or second position in a clause and always precede an inflecting verb (although there can be intervening constituents).
- **Complementisers (§3.6):** Complementisers indicate the relationship a subordinate clause has with its matrix clause.
- **Particles (§3.7):** Particles never inflect and can occur anywhere in a clause.
- **Clitics (§3.8):** Clitics do not meet the requirements for wordhood (that is, many clitics are monosyllabic) but are always prosodically attached to a word.

There is very little word-class-changing morphology. The known class-changing morphology is given in Table 3.1.

Table 3.1 Summary of derivational suffixes that change the word class of the stem

↓ Input	Output →	Nominal	Inflecting verb
Nominal		Derivational suffixes	-ja- 'become'; -ma- 'cause'
Coverb		-wari (not productive)	
Inflecting verb		-nja- forms an infinitive	Associated motion; inceptive

Most derivational morphology derives a nominal from another part of speech, and each derivational process has caveats. First, the coverb → nominal suffix -wari is unproductive, restricted to only a small set of coverbs (§7.1). The inflecting verb → nominal suffix forms an infinitive (§6.2.3.8), which obligatorily takes a complementising suffix (nominals can take complementising suffixes and many complementising suffixes also function as case suffixes in other contexts; see §12.1.2). This infinitive cannot take other nominal morphology. Finally, the nominal → inflecting verb constructions could equally be treated as complex verb constructions, though the inchoative -ja- must attach to a nominal host, so the most consistent analysis is to treat this paradigm as a derivational morphology paradigm. These derivations are discussed in further detail in §6.5.2.

3.1 Nominals

Nominals are by far the largest part of speech and are the main topic of Chapter 4. Nominals have a wide range of possible denotations: from simple entities such as *maliki* 'dog' to event-like references such as *kili* 'fight'. Nominals are formally defined by their ability to take case marking and other morphology restricted to nominals (subject to some semantic restrictions).

Generally, nominals can function as arguments, modifiers and even as matrix and secondary predicates, as exemplified in (62)–(65).[1] Note that Warlmanpa is a hybrid head and dependent-marking language, so while nominals can function as arguments, taking case marking as appropriate (that is, 'dependent marking'), there is also 'head marking' in that grammatical relations are marked on the auxiliary complex (see the discussion of bound pronouns in §5.4). Strictly speaking, this is not head-marking, as defined in Nichols (1986), as the marking is not on the inflecting verb; rather, it is in a fixed position in the clause. In any case, nominals are not the only part of speech that represent arguments.[2]

(62) *Maliki* wa-nu.
 ARGUMENT
 dog wall-PAST
 The dog fell.
 H_K01-505B, DG, 02:06 mins

---

1 Note that in §11.6.2, I argue against making a distinction between 'secondary predicate' and 'nominal modifiers'.
2 There is also some disagreement about which part of speech represents the 'true' arguments in languages that have both head and dependent marking. There are three core analyses (with finer arguments to be found within each): 1) the nominals (or the case markers that attach to nominals) constitute the arguments (Simpson 1991; Legate 2002); 2) the bound pronouns constitute the arguments (Speas 1990; Baker 2001); and 3) phonologically null elements constitute the arguments (Baker 1991, 1996b; Jelinek 1984; Pensalfini 2004). In this grammar, I do not treat any single grammatical element as comprising argument-hood. Instead, evidence for arguments comes from a multifactorial approach, including, but not limited to, both nominals and pronominals (in the spirit of Witzlack-Makarevich 2019). As such, the labels 'modifier' and 'argument' in (62)–(65) are tenuous (presented only as a starting point for further discussion). I discuss these properties of nominals in more detail in §11.1.4.2 and, in particular, Note 2 in Chapter 11.

(63) <u>Ngarrka-ngu</u>=ju   <u>wiri-ngu</u>   nya-ngu.
     ARGUMENT   MODIFIER
     man-ERG=1SG.NS   big-ERG   see-PAST
     The big man saw me.
     H_K01-506A, DG, 52:30 mins

(64) <u>Ali</u>=nya   <u>karnanganja</u>   <u>wiri</u>   <u>yawirri-piya</u>!
     MODIFIER   ARGUMENT   MATRIX PREDICATE   MODIFIER
     that=FOC   emu   big   kangaroo-LIKE
     That emu is big, like a kangaroo!
     wrl-20200220, DK, 33:40 mins

(65) <u>Ngayu</u>=ma=rna   kuma-nmi   <u>kuyu</u>   <u>wittawitta-karta</u>.
     ARGUMENT   ARGUMENT   SECONDARY PREDICATE
     1=TOP=1SG.S   cut-FUT   meat   small-TRANSL
     I'll cut the meat into small bits.
     wrl-20191208-01, DK, 36:46 mins

Relatedly, nominals allow 'indefinite', 'definite' or 'secondary predicate' readings, as demonstrated for Warlpiri (Bittner and Hale 1995) and exemplified for Warlmanpa in (66).

(66) Wawirri=rna   nya-nganya.
     kangaroo=1SG.S   see-PRES
     I see a kangaroo.   [indefinite]
     I see the kangaroo.   [definite]
     I see it, which is a kangaroo.   [predicative]
     H_K01-505B, DG, 17:18 mins
     (Adapted from research on Warlpiri by Bittner and Hale [1995: 95].)

This is discussed further in §11.6.2.

Most nominals belong to a group that I refer to as 'general nominals'. These nominals are obligatorily marked for case (under the relevant conditions), as discussed in §4.1, can take the derivational morphology listed in §4.2 and may be derived into inflecting verbs by -ja- 'become' or -ma- 'cause to be', as discussed in §6.5.2.

3. PARTS OF SPEECH

Nominals are the only word class in Warlmanpa that allows loan-word integration, with borrowed nominals taking appropriate case marking, as in (67) and (68).

(67) *[naef]-ngu=lu*   *piya-nnya.*
      knife-ERG=3PL.S   cut-PRES
      They cut it with a knife.
      H_K06-004548: 24, JW, 02:38 mins

(68) *[pædək]-ka=rla*   *ya-nu-rra.*
      paddock-ALL=3.OBL   put-PAST-IMPF
      He used to build fences for him.
      N_D29-023128, MFN, 04:35 mins

The integration of loan words as nominals allows derivation into verbs, as in (69), where the nominal *work* is derived into an inflecting verb with *-ja-* 'inchoative' (see §6.5.2.1 for the semantic effect of this derivation).[3]

(69) *Nyuntu-jarra=li*   *[wɜːk]-ja-nya.*
      2-DU=1DU.INCL.S   **work**-INCH-PRES
      You'll work with me/we'll work together.
      wrl-20200224, DK, 30:37 mins

There are some sets of nominals that do not behave exactly like 'general' nominals, warranting further explanation. These are:

- action nominals (§3.1.1)
- number nominals (§3.1.2)
- kinship nominals (§3.1.3)
- demonstratives (§3.1.4)
- ignoratives (§3.1.5)
- infinitives (§3.1.6)
- placenames (§3.1.7)
- free pronouns (§3.1.8).

---

3 For some speakers, the English word *work* has been integrated as /warikŋali/—that is, with what appears to be a suffix, *-ngali*, though I have been unable to trace its origin or any synchronic meaning.

I do not distinguish between a subgrouping of 'general nominals' and 'adjectivals' because I do not believe a clear demarcation could be established, though preliminary criteria would likely include:

- compatibility with the verbalisers *-ja-* and *-ma-* (with adjectivals more likely to be compatible with the verbalisers)
- the relative frequency in which it is used as a predicate (intuitively, prototypical general nominals would almost never be used as predicates and adjectival nominals would frequently be used as predicates).

However, I have not yet investigated this in detail and I believe these would be relative frequencies, rather than any clear-cut distinction.

3.1.1 Action nominals

Action nominals are distinguished from general nominals by their inability to function as arguments; rather, they function only as predicates—either matrix or secondary. Action nominals are common in Ngumpin-Yapa languages (as is the use of the term). Syntactically and semantically similar subclasses in other languages have been referred to as 'predicate nominals' or 'predicate adjectives', typically minimally comprising words that refer to psychological states, especially related to knowledge (for example, Kuuk Thaayorre [Gaby 2017] and Kayardild [Evans 1995]).

Action nominals are grammatically distinct from the 'adverb' part of speech, as evidenced by action nominals obligatorily agreeing in case with the nominal of which they are predicative, whereas adverbs can appear unmarked.

Action nominals as matrix predicates:

(70) *Kayi=n*   *pa-nami-rni*   *pina,*   *ngayu=ma=rna*   ***jarta***.
      WHEN=2SG.S   go-FUT-TWD   return   1=TOP=1SG.S   **sleep**
      When you return, I will be asleep.
      wrl-20190201, DK, 32:06 mins

(71) ***Pina**=rna.*
      know=1SG.S
      I know.
      H_K01-506A, DG, 31:33 mins

Action nominals as secondary predicates:

(72) Maliki-rlu   kurtu   kapu-ngunya,   **wajili**-rlu   kapu-ngunya.
      dog-ERG   child   chase-PRES,   **fast**-ERG   chase-PRES
      The dog is chasing the child, it's chasing her.
      H_K01-505B, DG, 02:31 mins

(73) Minija-purta   pala=lu   kapu-ngunya,   jinta-ngu   might be
      cat-FACING   HAB=3PL.S   chase-PRES   one-ERG
      ngarrka-ngu-purta   kapu-ngunya   **wirlinyu**-rlu=ma.
      man-ERG-FACING   chase-PRES   **day_trip**-ERG=TOP
      They chase cats, might be one man who chases them [on] hunting trips.
      H_K06-004548: 26, JW, 02:52 mins

When functioning as secondary predicates, action nominals may be construed as non-subject referents, as in (74), where the action nominal *jarta* 'sleep' is modifying the dative-marked nominal *yawirri* 'kangaroo'.

(74) Yali=ma   Japanangka=ma   pa-nyinga   yawirri-ku   **jarta**-ka.
      that=TOP   Japanangka=TOP   go-PATH   kangaroo-DAT   **sleep**-ALL
      Japanangka is going for the kangaroo [which is] **sleeping**.
      wrl-20180616-01, DK, 08:38 mins

3.1.2 Number nominals

There are two number nominals: *jinta* 'one' and *jirrima* 'two', with other numerals built from compounding these two. They take case as appropriate, like general nominals, as exemplified in (75)–(77).

(75) **Jinta**-ngu   marta-nnya   mukarti   wiri.
      one-ERG   have-PRES   hat   big
      One grabbed a big hat.
      H_K01-505B, DG, 01:01:56 hrs

(76) **Jinta**-ngu=ju   paka-rnu.
      one-ERG=1SG.NS hit-PAST
      One hit me.
      H_K01-506A, DG, 28:18 mins

(77) Wa-nganya=lu   Warlmanpa   Warumungu   **jinta**-nga=yi.
      speak-PRES=3PL.S   Warlmanpa   Warumungu   **one**-LOC=STILL
      The Warlmanpa and Warumungu are speaking **as one still**.
      N_D02-007841, BN, 13:28 mins

Number nominals are distinct from other nominals in their ability to form phonological compounds. The compounds are additive, so, for example, the compounding of *jirrima-jirrima* 'two-two' denotes a set of four, as in (78).

(78) **Jirrima-jirrima**=lpa   ka-nya   ngayu.
      two-two=1PL.INCL.S   sit-PRES   1
      We **four** are sitting.
      N_D01-007836, JJN, 20:09 mins

Evidence for phonological compounding comes from case marking: the polysyllabic-stem allomorph of the ergative case is used (§4.1.1.3 discusses ergative allomorphs), as in (79). If the two number nominals did not form a compound, the disyllabic allomorph *-ngu* would be used and each word would be marked for case.

(79) [Jirrima-jinta]-**rlu**=rna-jana-lu   jirrima-jinta   ngarrka   nya-nganya.
      two-one-ERG=1EXCL.S-3PL.NS-S.PL   two-one   man   see-PRES
      We three were looking at those three men.
      H_K01-505B, DG, 55:21 mins

Interestingly, however, when combining with the dative suffix to indicate a duration, each number nominal must be individually marked (which is a coordination strategy; see §12.2), as in (80).

(80) Ngappa   wa-nu   parra-ku=ma   **jirrima-ku**   **jinta-ku.**
      water   fall-PAST   sun-DAT=TOP   **two-DAT**   **one-DAT**
      It rained for three days.
      wrl-20200221, DK, 32:25 mins

Like nominals generally, number nominals are not grammatically required (unlike the bound pronouns that obligatorily encode number for sentient referents). Other nominals are lexically unspecified for number (with number being obligatorily encoded in the bound pronouns for animates). See §4.7.3 for further discussion of quantification.

3.1.3 Kinship nominals

Kinship nominals have several unique suffixes, mostly pertaining to a relation the kin referent has with a discourse participant: *-na* 'first-person possessive', *-jupu* 'second-person possessive', *-nyanu* 'third-person possessive' and *nginta ~ -rlangu* 'reciprocal pair'. These suffixes are rare in the corpus; (81)–(84) provide examples of *-na*, *-jupu* and *-nyanu*, although the other morpheme, *-nginta ~ -rlangu*, has been found only in isolated vocabulary elicitation (for example, *kapurlunginta* 'pair of sisters'). As shown in (81)–(83), these kinship suffixes always attach to the root, before other nominal suffixes.

(81) **Ngamirni-na-rlu**=ju karli yu-ngu.
 uncle-MY-ERG=1SG.NS boomerang give-PAST
 My uncle gave me the boomerang.
 H_K01-505B, DG, 37:35 mins

(82) Kari=rna-rla ngayu ngayinya-ku **paparti-na-ku** yi-nja-jila
 COND=1SG.S-DAT 1 1.GEN-DAT **B+-MY-DAT** give-INF-PRIV
 money. paka-nmi=ju.
 hit-FUT=1SG.NS
 If I hadn't given money to my brother, he would have hit me.
 N_D02-007842, BN, 52:23 mins

(83) **Ngati-nyanu-rlu** **kirta-nyanu-rlu**=pala ka-ngu-rra.
 mother-THEIR-ERG **father-THEIR-ERG**=3DU.S take-PAST-IMPF
 Their mother and father were taking her.
 K_003, BN, 00:03 secs[4]

(84) **Makarri-jupu**=ma[5] wartarti=lku ka-nya.
 spouse-YOUR=TOP painted_up=THEN be-PRES
 Your husband is now all painted up for ceremony.
 N_D03-007868, BN, 19:50 mins

---

4 This utterance is from Adam Kendon's recording deposited with AIATSIS (KENDON_A001).
5 The word *makarri*, more specifically, is when the speaker is in the same alternative generation as the addressee and referent (David Nash, p.c.).

For younger speakers, these suffixes are not used productively. Most interestingly, the kinship nominals appear to have frozen in the form X*na*, the historically first-person form (suggesting that historically kinship nominals were bound roots). This is particularly evident where the nominal is part of a possession construction, as in (85), where *kirtana* (traditionally *kirta-na* 'father-MY') is modified by a third-person genitive pronoun, meaning 'his/her father'.

(85) **Nyaninya kirtana** partu-nga wirlinyi.
3GEN **father** leave-PAST.IMPF hunting
His father left on a hunting trip.
wrl-20190213-01, DK, 15:24 mins

Thus, for younger speakers, it seems kinship nominals are not distinct from general nominals.

3.1.4 Demonstratives

Demonstratives are a closed subclass of nominals referring to proximity and/or discourse anaphora. The roots are *yimpa* 'this', *yarri* 'that', *yali* 'that removed' and *nyanungu* 'the aforementioned'. The proximal demonstrative *yimpa* has a suppletive root *mi-* ~ *mu-* for inflected forms (for example, *murlu* 'this ERG').

Demonstratives are considered a subclass of nominals because, like nominals, they obligatorily inflect for case. However, demonstratives are distinct from other nominals in their inability to function as predicates, and they take the polysyllabic-stem allomorph of case suffixes (although of course this is only a distinguishing factor for the disyllabic roots).

Demonstratives are discussed in further detail in §4.5.

3.1.5 Ignoratives

Ignoratives relate to a knowledge domain—usually as part of an interrogative construction, though they can also be used as indefinites (typically only in embedded contexts, such as negation). For example, consider the following pair: in (86), *ngana* functions as an interrogative, resulting in the meaning 'who', and in (87), *ngana* is under the scope of *kula* 'negative', resulting in the meaning 'nobody' (rather than 'who did not …').

(86) ***Ngana**=n*   *purtu-ka-nya?*
      who=2SG.S   listen-be-PRES
      Who did you hear?
      H_K01-505B, DG, 36:55 mins

(87) ***Kula**=rna*   ***ngana***   *purtu-ka-ngu.*
      NEG=1SG.S   **who**   listen-be-PAST
      I didn't hear anybody/anything.
      H_K01-505B, DG, 42:35 mins

The five ignorative nominal roots are *ngana* 'who, what', *nyapa* 'how', *nyangurla* 'when', *wanji* 'where' and *nyayanga ~ nyajangu* 'how many'. These nominals inflect and take derivational morphology, like general nominals, except they take the polysyllabic-stem allomorph of case suffixes. Ignorative nominals are discussed in further detail in §4.6.

3.1.6 Infinitives

Infinitives are nominals that are derived from an inflecting verb taking the infinitive inflection (§6.2.3.8). They are bound stems that function as the main predicate of a non-finite subordinate clause.[6] An infinitive is obligatorily marked with a complementising suffix (§12.1.2), which indicates the relation between the subordinate clause and the matrix clause.

Infinitives are classified as nominals due to their ability to take case, as in (89), where the allative case is functioning as a complementising suffix or as agreement after some complementising suffixes, as in (88), where the infinitive takes the ergative case to indicate agreement with the ergative subject of the matrix clause (which in this case does not surface).

(88) ***Yina-nga-rninja-karra-rlu***   *karta-pu-ngunya*   *karli.*
      sing-eat-INF-SS-ERG   spear-act_on-PRES   boomerang
      The singing one is trimming their boomerang.
      H_K01-505B, DG, 36:15 mins

---

6   Much like matrix clauses, non-finite subordinate clauses can have true nominal predicates in lieu of an infinitive.

In (89), the infinitive *jitinjaka* has the internal structure of a verb root, *jiti-* 'run', taking the infinitive suffix *-nja-*, deriving an infinitive. The infinitive is then obligatorily marked with a complementising suffix—in this case, the allative is used to indicate simultaneous tense and that the object of the matrix clause is the subject of the infinitive. This structure is reflected in (90).

(89)   *Ngarrka-ngu*   *nya-ngu*   *karnta*   ***jiti-nja-ka.***
        man-ERG   see-PAST   woman   **run-INF-ALL**
        The man saw the woman running.
        wrl-20190201, DK, 19:05 mins

(90)   *jiti-*   *nja-*   *ka*
        run-   INF-   ALL
        Verb root   Infinitive suffix   Complementising suffix

Unlike other nominals, however, infinitives cannot take derivational morphology and their arguments are dependent on the matrix clause, depending on the complementising suffix (these criteria are among those discussed in Nordlinger 2002). In terms of morphosyntax, infinitives behave extremely similar to action nominals (§3.1.1). Unlike action nominals, infinitives can never be a matrix predicate (by their very nature).

3.1.7 Placenames

Placenames, unlike other nominals, exhibit high amounts of variation regarding whether they can be marked with locative case and, if so, whether it takes the short-stem allomorph (generally used for disyllabic stems) or the long-stem allomorph (generally used for stems with three or more syllables).

In (89), *Pamayi* 'Powell Creek' takes the long-stem allomorph *-rla*, as is expected for a nominal stem with three syllables.

(91)   *Pamayi-ngurlu*   *kala=rnalu*   *ka-ngu-rra,*   **Pamayi-rla::**
        Powell Creek-ELA   HAB=1PL.EXCL.S   be-PAST-IMPF   **Powell Creek-LOC**
        kala=rnalu   *parti-nja-na*   *Marlinja-ka=lku.*
        HAB=1PL.EXCL.S   leave-MOT-PRES   Marlinja-ALL=THEN
        We'd leave Powell Creek, we'd stay at Powell Creek and then we'd leave for Marlinja.
        N_D29-023128, MFN, 02:42 mins

However, in (92), *Mangka Mantangi* takes the disyllabic allomorph *-nga*, despite being unambiguously more than two syllables.

(92) *Ngayu=ma=rna*   *palka-ja-ngu*   ***Mangka Mantangi-nga.***
      1=TOP=1SG.S   exist-INCH-PAST   **Mangka Mantangi-LOC**
      I was born in Mangka Mantangi.
      wrl-20190208, DK, 01:59 mins

Further to unexpected allomorphy, Warlmanpa also (although rarely) allows placenames to be morphologically unmarked when functioning as spatial coincidences, as in (93).

(93) *Kala=rnalu*   *tiij-wa-nja-na,*   *Punarrapan.*
      HAB=1PL.EXCL.S   overnight_camp-fall-MOT-PRES   Punarrapan
      We would stay overnight at Punarrapan.
      N_D29-023128, MFN, 02:32 mins

A last point of interest is the status of placename loan words, as in (94), where 'Tennant Creek' is marked with the locative and, conceivably, the speaker only considers the right edge of the compound word, hence the short-stem allomorph *-nga*. This contrasts with number nominals, in which the entire compound word conditions the syllable-counting allomorphy (a number compound ending in a disyllabic word still takes the long-stem allomorphs).

(94) *Jala=ma=rna*   *ka-nya*   ***Tennant Creek-nga***   *tarnngayi.*
      now=TOP=1SG.S   be-PRES   **Tennant Creek-LOC**   eternal
      Now I live in Tennant Creek permanently.
      wrl-20190208, DK, 26:14 mins

3.1.8 Free pronouns

Free pronouns distinguish person (first, second and third person, with no clusivity distinction). Each person value has a 'general' form, a 'genitive' form and a 'derivational base' form. The genitive series is used to encode possession, the derivational bases are used to allow certain cases to mark the pronoun (but do not encode possession) and the general series is used elsewhere. Free pronouns are unspecified for number. The free pronoun paradigm is given in Table 3.2. Notably, the genitive and derivational base forms are syncretic.

Table 3.2 Free-person pronoun forms

Person	General	Derivational base	Genitive
1	ngayu	ngayinya	ngayinya
2	nyuntu	nyintinya	nyintinya
3	nyantu	nyaninya	nyaninya

The 'general' series can only take a small set of nominal suffixes, whereas the 'genitive' series patterns morphologically identically to general nominals. An example of the general series is given in (95) and the genitive series in (96).

(95)   ***Ngayu***   kula=rna   nga-rnu   yarnunju.
        1   NEG=1SG.S   eat-PAST   food
        It was me who didn't eat the food.
        wrl-20200219, DK, 41:05 mins

(96)   ***Ngayinya***   ngapuju   wa-nganya   Warlmanpa   Mudburra.
        1GEN   FaMo   speak-PRES
        My father's mother speaks Warlmanpa and Mudburra.
        wrl-20200224, DK, 04:44 mins

For most spatial cases to mark the general pronouns, the derivational base must be used (specifically spatial case, even in subordinating function). Despite having the same forms as the genitive pronouns, the derivational bases do not encode possession. This is best exemplified when the free pronoun is in a subordinate clause, so it must exhibit case agreement with the infinitive verb, as in (97). In this pair of utterances, a. is the Ken Hale prompt in Warlpiri, which demonstrates that Warlpiri free pronouns allow case marking directly, and b. is DG's Warlmanpa translation of the prompt, in which the free pronoun surfaces in its derived form to allow the stem to agree in case with the infinitive verb marked with the allative.

(97)   a.   Witta=rna   nya-ngu   [***nyuntu-kurra***   pangi-rninja-kurra].
            small=1SG.S   see-PAST   2-ALL   spear-INF-ALL
            I saw the small one spear **you**.
            (Warlpiri, H_K01-505B, Ken Hale prompt, 32:36 mins)
      b.   Witta=rna   nya-ngu   [***nyintinya-ka***   karta-pi-nji-ka].
            small=1SG.S   see-PAST   2-ALL   spear-act_on-INF-ALL
            I saw the small one spear **you**.
            H_K01-505B, DG, 32:41 mins

3. PARTS OF SPEECH

The documented forms of free pronouns are given in Table 3.3 for first and second person (the third-person free pronoun appears to follow the same paradigmatic patterns but is significantly less well documented).

Table 3.3 Forms of first and second-person free pronouns[7]

Case	First person		Second person	
	[–genitive]	[+genitive]	[–genitive]	[+genitive]
Absolutive	*ngayu*	*ngayinya*	*nyuntu*	*nyintinya*
Ergative	*ngayu*	*ngayinyarlu*	*nyuntu*	*nyintinyarlu*
Dative	*ngayuku*	*ngayinyaku*	*nyuntuku*	*nyintinyaku*
Locative	*ngayinyarla*		*nyintinyarla*	
Allative	*ngayinyaka*		*nyintinyaka*	
Elative	*ngayungurlu*	*ngayinyangurlu*	*nyuntungurlu*	*nyintinyangurlu*
Preparative	*ngayinyakapina*		*nyintinyakapina*	
Aversive	*ngayukuma*	*ngayinyakuma*	*nyuntukuma*	*nyintinyakuma*
Lacking	*ngayujila*	*ngayinyajila*	*nyuntujila*	*nyintinyajila*

The general free pronoun roots are discussed in further detail in §3.1.8.1 and the genitive pronoun stems are discussed in §3.1.8.2.

3.1.8.1 Free pronoun forms

There are two freely occurring independent pronouns: *ngayu* for first person and *nyuntu* for second person. There is also a rare third-person pronoun, *nyantu*.[8]

The free pronouns do not inflect for core case other than dative case, so the form of free pronouns is the same regardless of whether it is the transitive subject, intransitive subject or object, as demonstrated in examples (98)–(100), in contrast to nominals that exhibit an absolutive/ergative alignment.

---

7   Some combinations of general free pronouns and derivational suffixes have been rejected on my fieldwork, such as **ngayu-kupa* '1-DESIRE', *ngayu-wangu* '1-PRIV' and **ngayu-parna* '1-PROP'. Unfortunately, it is not clear whether using the genitive base—that is, *ngayinyakupa*—would be an acceptable alternative without encoding [+genitive].

8   The free pronoun forms *ngayu, nyuntu* and *nyantu* historically derive from ergative forms (Blake 1987b).

Intransitive subject (S):

(98) ***Ngayu**=rna   wa-ngami.*
1=1SG.S   speak-FUT
I will speak.
H_K01-505B, DG, 01:38 mins

Transitive subject (A):

(99) ***Ngayu**=rna   karnta   nya-nganya.*
1=1SG.S   woman   see-PRES
I see the woman.
H_K01-505B, DG, 17:41 mins

Object (O/P):

(100) *Wawirri-rlu=ju   **Ngayu**   nya-nganya.*
kangaroo-ERG=1SG.NS   **1**   see-PRES
The kangaroo sees me.
H_K01-505B, DG, 17:25 mins

The free pronouns are also unspecified for number, as exemplified in (101), in which the free pronoun *ngayu* has a plural referent (evidenced by the bound pronouns, which obligatorily distinguish singular/dual/plural; here the =*lu* in the bound pronoun is cross-referencing a plural subject).

(101) ***Ngayu**=rna-ngu-**lu**   ngarra   paka-nmi   nyuntu   jinta.*
1=1.EXCL.S-2SG.NS-S.PL   pot   hit-FUT   2   one
We might hit you.
H_K01-506A, DG, 41:03 mins

While they are unspecified for number and do not obligatorily take number marking, they can optionally take number suffixes. When taking number marking, the pronoun is derived into a nominal and, as such, it takes case marking if appropriate, as in (102), where the free pronoun *ngayu* is marked for dual number with -*jarra*, which derives a nominal. Because this derived nominal is the subject of a transitive clause, it takes ergative case.

(102) **Ngayu-jarra-rlu**   kuyu=ja   kupa-rnu.
1-DUAL-ERG   meat=1DU.EXCL.S   cook-PAST
We two cooked the meat.
wrl-20190213-02, DK, 14:59 mins

There is also limited evidence of a plural form of the second-person pronoun, presented in (103) and (104), which has the *nyuntu* stem with a suffix *-manta*.[9] There is no evidence of this occurring with the first or third-person pronouns.

(103) Ngayu=rna-nyangu-lu   nya-nganya   **nyuntu-manta.**
1=1.S-2PL.NS-PL.S   see-PRES   **2-RPL**
We are looking at you mob.
H_K01-505B, DG, 52:39 mins

(104) Ngarrka-ngu=nyangu   nyanganya   **nyuntu-manta.**
man-ERG=2PL.NS   see-PRES   **2-RPL**
The man is looking at you mob.
H_K01-505B, DG, 59:01 mins

This suffix is also found on demonstratives, to a limited extent (see §4.3.2.3). I suggest *-manta* may have been more productive historically but has since been replaced with *-tarra* 'plural' in §4.3.2.1.

3.1.8.2 Genitive pronoun forms

Genitive pronouns encode possession. The genitive pronouns are transparently built off the general pronoun form with a suffix *-nya*, with all high vowels in the pronoun root being fronted and the /t/ deleted in the third-person pronoun. The three genitive pronouns are demonstrated in (105)–(107).

(105) Wanji-la   karli   **ngayinya?**
where-LOC   boomerang   **1.GEN**
Where is my boomerang?
H_K01-505B, DG, 29:25 mins

---

9 The 2AUG.S (that is, referring to three or more second-person referents) bound pronoun in Gurindji is *=nta* (Meakins and McConvell 2021), which may be related to this suffix.

(106) Wanji=ngu   karli   **nyintinya**=ma?
      where=2SG.NS   boomerang   2.GEN=TOP
      Where is your boomerang?
      H_K01-505B, DG, 29:30 mins

(107) Wanji-la   karli   **nyaninya**?
      where-LOC   boomerang   3.GEN
      Where is his boomerang?
      H_K01-505B, DG, 29:38 mins

One speaker deletes the /t/ in the second-person genitive (so for this speaker all genitive pronouns have an identical phonotactic template, *NV.CV.nya*).

(108) **Nyininya**-rlu   ngartina-rlu   kupa-nnya   yarnunju.
      2.GEN-ERG   mother-ERG   cook-PRES   food
      Your mother is cooking food.
      wrl-20190213-01, DK, 14:26 mins

I treat the genitive forms as portmanteau forms, as a compositional analysis would require a synchronic analysis of why the alveolar stop is kept (for most speakers) when transforming the second-person *nyuntu* into *nyintinya* but not between *nyantu* and *nyaninya*, as well as a series of vowel alternations triggered by a possessive *-nya* suffix.

The genitive pronouns are nominals in all respects, including taking regular case suffixes where appropriate, contrasting with the free pronouns. For example, in (109), the genitive pronoun *ngayinya* 'my' is indicating possession of the ergative subject *maliki* 'dog', so the genitive pronoun takes ergative case.

(109) Maliki-rlu   **ngayinya-rlu**   kapi=ngu   pi-nyi.
      dog-ERG   **1.GEN-ERG**   FUT=2SG.NS   act_on-FUT
      My dog will bite you.
      H_K01-505B, DG, 27:52 mins

When encoding possession, the genitive pronoun almost always occurs preceding the possessum, as in (110), though as this example shows, the auxiliary complex (a second-position phenomenon) can intervene. This is one of the few instances in Warlmanpa of what appears to be a definite preference for ordering between words, though it is not without exceptions, as exemplified in (105)–(107) and (109), where the possessum precedes the genitive pronoun. Furthermore, the genitive pronoun must be adjacent to the possessum, regardless of the ordering between them (other than the auxiliary complex, which can intervene).

(110) ***Ngayinya-ku=rna-rla***   ***ngartina-ku***   *wayi-nnya.*
1.GEN-DAT=1SG.S-DAT   mother-DAT   search-PRES
I'm searching for my mother.
wrl-20190117, SN, 13:27 mins

The pattern of a 'dative' or 'genitive' free pronoun form serving as the base for other inflections (especially semantic case) is found in some Ngumpin-Yapa languages—specifically, Bilinarra, Gurindji and Mudburra (Meakins and Nordlinger 2014: 218; Meakins and McConvell 2021; Osgarby 2018: 257). Furthermore, similar processes are also found in several non-Ngumpin-Yapa languages to the north, including Garrwa (Mushin 2013: 86–89) and Wambaya (Nordlinger 1998: 127–28), as well as in Warumungu to the south (Simpson and Heath 1982: 30–31).

3.2 Adverbs

The prototypical semantic contribution of an adverb to a clause is to qualify an event, in terms of manner, time and space. Adverbs can never function as arguments. There are three subcategories of adverbs: manner adverbs, temporal adverbs and spatial adverbs. Each set has a restricted compatibility with case suffixes: manner adverbs can only take ergative, temporal adverbs can only take dative and spatial adverbs only take elative, though these adverbs also have a unique paradigm to encode directionality. Adverbs (manner adverbs, in particular) are the topic of Chapter 8.

3.3 Coverbs

Coverbs (also referred to as 'preverbs' or 'uninflecting verbs' in other grammars) are uninflected words that occur adjacent to an inflecting verb. They generally modify the situation denoted by the inflecting verb. Coverbs are the topic of Chapter 7. This section provides the basis on which coverbs are distinguished from other parts of speech.

Coverbs always require an inflecting verb in the clause, although there are rare cases of coverbs occurring as afterthoughts (§11.7.2). There are two classes of coverbs, distinguished only by whether the coverb can host derivational morphology and/or clitics. Coverbs that can host derivational morphology and/or clitics are classed as 'loose nexus' and those that are unable to are classed as 'tight nexus'—both of which fall under the 'bound continuous' category in Schultze-Berndt's (2000) typology. There is only one derivational suffix that can attach to coverbs, *wari* 'NMLZ', which derives the coverb into a nominal. For example, in (111), *-wari* attaches to *kiit*, a coverb meaning 'broken', thus *kiit* is classified as a loose nexus coverb. As the coverb is derived into a nominal, it can function as the primary predicate of a matrix clause (unlike coverbs without derivation).

(111)   *Ali=nya*   *jurlaka*   **kiit-wari**   *panja.*
        that=FOC   bird   **break-NMLZ**   Wing
        That bird has a broken wing.
        wrl-20191208-01, DK, 04:59 mins

An example of a clitic attaching to a coverb is given in (112), in which the clitic *=lku* is hosted by the loose nexus coverb *pina* 'return'.

(112)   *Ngurra-ka*   **pina=lku**   *pa-nnya.*
        camp-ALL   **return=THEN**   go-PRES
        Now he's returning to camp.
        H_K06-004547, JW, 28:02 mins

Coverbs can also be semantically categorised as adverbial or predicational. Adverbial coverbs specify a manner of the situation denoted by the inflecting verb or denote a specific subtype of the predicate (most inflecting verbs have vague semantics). Predicational coverbs contribute the full semantics to the predication of the clause and, essentially, the function of the inflecting verb in these cases is to take the tense, aspect and mood (TAM) marking since coverbs cannot. Unlike the distinction between 'tight nexus' and 'loose nexus', there is no morphosyntactic distinction between these two subclasses.

3.4 Inflecting verbs

Inflecting verbs are a closed class of at least 45 bound roots (a complete list of identified roots is given in Appendix A). This is far fewer than Warlpiri, which has upwards of 115 inflecting verbs (Nash 1982: 168; 1986), and Ngardi, which has 88 (Ennever 2018: 35). On the other hand, Warlmanpa has more inflecting verbs than do languages to its north, such as Bilinarra, which has 23 (Meakins and Nordlinger 2014: 89). In terms of inflecting verb counts, Warlmanpa patterns much like Gurindji, Wanyjirra and Jaru, which have 34, 38 and 40 inflecting verbs, respectively (Meakins et al. 2013; Senge 2015: 113; Tsunoda 1981a: 76).

All inflecting verbs are bound roots and obligatorily take one TAM inflection (§6.2.2.2.2)—imperative, past, present, future, potential, subjunctive, counterfactual, infinitive (note that the infinitive derives a verb into an infinitive, which is a subclass of nominals)—or allow a derivation of associated motion or the inceptive. The inflecting verbs are categorised into five main subclasses, based on the form of the TAM inflections, with a small number of further subclasses (§6.2.1).

At least 25 inflecting verbs combine with at least two distinct coverbs (generally no more than one coverb in each clause), six inflecting verbs have only been identified with one coverb and 15 inflecting verbs have been found not in combination with any coverbs. In isolation, most inflecting verbs encode broad or non-specific semantics. For example, the inflecting verb *paka-* 'strike' can have several interpretations based on context, including 'chop', as in (113); 'kill', as in (114); or 'hit', either physically, as in (115), or metaphorically, as in (116).

(113) *Karli=rna   paka-nmi.*
boomerang=1SG.S   strike-FUT
I will trim a boomerang.
H_K01-505B, DG, 10:25 mins

(114) *Paka-rnu=n?*
strike-PAST=2SG.S
Did you kill him/it?
H_K06-004555, LOF, 55:09 mins

(115) Jinta-ngu=ju   paka-rnu.
      one-ERG=1SG.NS   strike-PAST
      One [person] hit me.
      H_K01-506A, DG, 28:18 mins

(116) Kulykulypa-rlu   ngayu=ju   paka-nnya.
      fever-ERG   1=1SG.NS   hit-PRES
      I have a cold [lit.: the fever is hitting me].
      wrl-20180614-02, DK, 03:32 mins

Inflecting verbs are the main topic of Chapter 6.

3.5 Auxiliary bases

Auxiliary bases are part of the 'auxiliary complex' (Chapter 5), which is a templatic phonological word.

(117)
Slot 1	Slot 2	Slot 3
Auxiliary base	**Bound pronouns**	**Auxiliary clitic**
kala 'apprehensive'	(§5.4)	(§5.5)
kala 'habitual'		
kapi 'future'		
nga 'future'		
pala 'continuous'		
(§5.3)		

An example of the auxiliary complex with each template slot filled is given in (118).

(118)
Auxiliary base	Bound pronouns	Auxiliary clitic	
[Nga	=*ngu*	=*nga]*ω	*pi-nya*
FUT	=2SG.NS	=DUB	act_on-POT

It might bite you!
H_K01-506A, DG, 46:38 mins

The auxiliary base is the only word class other than interjections that can surface as a monosyllabic phonological word, as in (119), where the auxiliary base *nga* 'future' has no overt bound pronouns (the third singular subject bound pronoun is phonologically null).

(119)	*Karnu-ngu=nyanu*	*partakurru-ma-nnya*	*ngurra*
	poor_thing-ERG=RR	good-CAUSE-PRES	camp
	Kayi	**nga**	*kurtu~kurtu*	*marta-nmi.*
	WHEN	FUT	child-PL	have-FUT

The poor thing is fixing the nest for when she has children.
wrl-20191207-02, DK, 23:56 mins

Auxiliary bases are generally not grammatically obligatory (for example, the future auxiliary *nga=* is not used in every clause referring to future time). In clauses with no auxiliary bases, the auxiliary complex generally encliticises to the first word in a clause (see §5.2 for a more thorough analysis). There are five auxiliary bases in Warlmanpa: *kala* 'apprehensive', *kala* 'habitual', *kapi* 'future', *nga* 'future' and *pala* 'continuous'.[10] *Kala* in both functions and *nga* 'future' are productive, though *kapi* 'future' seems to be a Warlpiri borrowing and is only used by one speaker, and *pala* 'continuous' is not well instantiated. The functions of each auxiliary are discussed in §5.3. Auxiliary bases are distinguished from particles by several syntactic differences:

1. there can only be one auxiliary base in a clause (there can be multiple particles)
2. where auxiliary bases occur, they obligatorily host the bound pronouns and auxiliary clitics (unlike particles)
3. auxiliary bases occur in first or second position within a clause, while particles can occur anywhere in a clause
4. auxiliary bases cannot occur in subordinate clauses (whether finite or non-finite; though [119] above provides the single exception to this), whereas particles can occur in finite subordinate clauses
5. an inflecting verb cannot precede an auxiliary base (inflecting verbs can precede particles).

---

10 Nash's (1979) analysis of Warlmanpa posits a null auxiliary with a range of meanings, including 'past', 'present', 'future', 'potential', 'counterfactual' and 'imperative'. I do not follow this analysis, as this would make the analysis of the bound pronoun encliticisation more difficult and attributes a semantic load to a null unit that can be fully accounted for by the verbal inflections. The analysis of a null auxiliary base may in part be motivated by most other Ngumpin-Yapa languages having a 'default' auxiliary base. This default auxiliary base covers approximately the same range of meanings as Nash's 'null' base—for example, in Gurindji, the auxiliary base *ngu-* 'catalyst' is 'used for most assertions about states and events, whether past, present, or future indicative' (McConvell 1996b: 94).

3.6 Complementisers

Complementisers (§12.1) relate a subordinate clause to its matrix clause. All complementisers with word status in Warlmanpa relate finite clauses (§12.1.1); non-finite subordinate clauses are related to matrix clauses by morphology (§12.1.2). There are four finite complementisers in Warlmanpa: *ngula* 'relative clause' (§12.1.1.1), *kari* 'logical conditional' (§12.1.1.2), *kayi* 'temporal conditional' (§12.1.1.3) and *nga* 'purposive' (§12.1.1.4).

Most complementisers occur clause-initially (in the subordinate clause they head), although the complementisers can occasionally occur in the second position (much like an auxiliary), preceded by a nominal. Regardless of whether the complementiser surfaces in the first or second position, it obligatorily hosts the bound pronouns of the subordinate clause; relatedly, auxiliary bases are not permitted in subordinate clauses (that is, both complementisers and auxiliary bases appear to fill the same slot of the auxiliary complex). Examples of complementisers are given in (120) and (121) and are discussed further in §12.1.1.

(120) *[Ali-ngu=nya* **ngula** *karta-pu-ngunya] yarnunju=lpangu kupa-nmi.*
that-ERG=FOC REL spear-act_on-PRES food=1PL.INCL.NS cook-FUT
He, the man digging, will cook food for us.
wrl-20180616-01, DK, 14:46 mins

(121) *[Karnta-panyji* **kari**=*lu jitpi-nyi] nga=lu=nga wa-nma.*
woman-PAUC COND=3PL.S run-FUT POST=3PL.S=DUB fall-POT
If the women run, they might fall.
H_K01-505B, DG, 15:07 mins

3.7 Particles and interjections

Particles and interjections represent two distinct word classes, though there are some words that are doubly classified as both a particle and an interjection. Both are uninflected words, distinguished primarily by their ability or inability to form a complete utterance in isolation. Particles are integrated into a clause, whereas interjections are not. This is best evidenced by particles being able to host the bound pronouns—that is, filling slot (1) in the auxiliary complex—whereas interjections are obligatorily dislocated from the clause, unable to host bound pronouns. There are several lexemes that can be neatly categorised as either a particle or an interjection based on this criterion. There are four lexemes that constitute a complete utterance in isolation and, in other contexts, are integrated into a clause (hosting the bound pronouns, specifically) and, as such, are analysed as doubly classified lexemes.[11] A list of particles and interjections (including doubly classified lexemes) is given in Table 3.4.

Table 3.4 Particles and interjections in Warlmanpa

Part of speech	Form	Gloss
Particles	*jupu*	'just because'
	kala	'or'
	kapi	'and'
	kirli	'leave it, let it'
	kulanganta	'mistakenly'
	marta[a]	'maybe'
	murra[a]	'don't know'
	nganta	'supposedly'
	ngarra	'might, maybe'
	ngayi	'oh, really, is that so'
	numu[12]	'no, not'
	puta	'incompletely'
	wayi	POLARQ
Interjections	*kaya*	'watch out!'
	kari[a]	'don't know'
	kirri[a]	'hey!'
	wiyarrpa[a]	'sorry'
	yaya	'yes'
	yii[a]	'oh!?'
	yuu, yuwayi	'yes'

---

11 The lack of a clear distinction between interjections and particles is not uncommon in Ngumpin-Yapa languages. An alternative analysis is to allow the word class of 'interjections' to be integrated into the clause (taken up, for example, by Meakins and Nordlinger 2014: 96), however, the analysis presented here allows a distinction between interjections that can be integrated and those that cannot.
12 This is a borrowing from Kriol, originally from English 'no more' (Sandefur 1986: 70). It is fully integrated into Warlmanpa syntax and is even able to host the bound pronouns.

Part of speech	Form	Gloss
Doubly classified	*walku*	'nothing, NEG'
	ngulayi	'okay, finished, PERF'
	warta	'surprise, for no reason'
	kuku	'wait'

Note: [a] Taken from Nash (2022), not instantiated in the transcribed corpus.

Particles are discussed further in §9.1, interjections in §9.2 and doubly classified lexemes in §9.3. Two particles, *kapi* 'and' and *kala* 'but', form a subclass of coordinating particles (henceforth 'coordinators'), which are discussed in §12.2.

3.8 Clitics

Clitics, discussed further in §9.4, are phonologically dependent lexemes that prosodically attach to words—in particular, nominals, adverbs, free pronouns, inflecting verbs and particles. Clitics rarely attach to coverbs and do not attach to auxiliary bases, complementisers or interjections. Clitics always attach outside any inflection or derivation; only clitics can attach to another clitic. The auxiliary complex may attach to the outside of a clitic, as in (122c.).[13] Clitics generally specify semantic or pragmatic information about their host in some way—for example, the clitic =*ma* 'topic' marks its host as given content, as in (122), in which *jurlaka* 'birds' are introduced in a. and, in c., the demonstrative *nyanungu* 'aforementioned' referring to the same birds is marked with =*ma*.

---

13 Within the auxiliary complex is a slot labelled 'auxiliary clitic', which occurs after the bound pronouns. I do not view this as a 'clitic' part of speech, given that it cannot occur elsewhere in the clause. Rather, I view the auxiliary complex as a word that encliticises to a word if a certain slot within the auxiliary complex is not filled.

(122) a. **Jurlaka**=*lu-rla* wirriri nya-ngu-rra yipakarli-ku.
bird=3PL.S-DAT in_a_circle see-PAST-IMPF lizard-DAT
The birds were looking around for lizards.

b. *Wangani-rlu* *wirriri~wirriri* *wirri* *ya-nu-rra,*
dog-ERG in_a_circle-RDP chase put-PAST-IMPF

c. **Nyanungu**=***ma***=*lu* *putjanarra* *partu-ngu-rra.*
aforementioned=TOP=3PL.S cause_to_scatter leave-PAST-AWAY
The dog was chasing the birds, but they would fly away.
wrl-20190207-01, DK, 50:02 mins

Some clitics, such as =*lku* 'now, then' and =*wiyi* 'first, before', can have scope over the proposition denoted by the clause when the clitic occurs in second position—that is, immediately preceding the auxiliary complex. For example, in (123), =*lku* is hosted by the nominal *maani* 'money' but does not modify *maani*; instead, it has scope over the proposition, to temporally locate it relative to the subordinate clause.

(123) *Kari*=*ju-n* *wa-nganjakurla,* <u>*money*=***lku***=*rna-ngu*</u> *yi-njakurla.*
COND=1SG.NS-2SG.S speak-CFACT money=THEN=1SG.S-2SG.NS give-CFACT
If you were to talk to me **then** I would give you money.
H_K01-506A: DG, 04:00 mins

The clitics identified in Warlmanpa are =*lku* 'now, then' (§9.4.1), =*yijala* 'also' (§9.4.2), =*yi* 'still' (§9.4.3), =*ma* 'topic' (§9.4.4), =*nya* 'focus' (§9.4.5) and =*wiyi* 'first, before' (§9.4.7).

4
Nominals

The class of nominals in Warlmanpa prototypically refers to entities or attributes (of entities). Nominals express grammatical relations but are grammatically optional. In fact, clauses with all arguments expressed are rare in natural speech. Nominals are distinct from other word classes in that:

- they are obligatorily case marked (bearing in mind absolutive case is null and is not explicitly glossed)
- many nominals can act as predicates, arguments and modifiers
- they form the only open word class.

See §3.1 for further explicit comparison of criteria across word classes. The general template for a nominal word in Warlmanpa is a root, followed by optional derivational suffix(es), an optional number suffix, an optional adnominal suffix, and then an obligatory case or complementiser suffix (bearing in mind the absolutive case is phonologically null):

0   root
1   (derivational suffix)
2   (number suffix)
3   (adnominal suffix)
4   (complementiser$_1$)
5   case/complementiser$_2$.

I am not aware of any instances in the corpus where there are more than two slots filled. For example, there are no cases of a nominal with two derivational suffixes.

There is a large overlap in the case and complementiser suffix systems—a phenomenon common to many Australian languages (Simpson 1988; Austin 1981; Dench and Evans 1988). Furthermore, some adnominal and derivational suffixes can also function as complementisers; in this case, they still occur in the 'adnominal' or 'derivational' slot in the template, so they will agree in case where applicable.

Only two complementising suffixes (*-karra* and *-pa-*) can fill the complementiser$_1$ slot and only the ergative case is known to fill the case slot in these instances. All other complementising suffixes occur in the final slot as complementiser$_2$. See §12.1.2 for a discussion of complementising suffixes. There is no known 'case stacking' in Warlmanpa—that is, there is no occurrence of more than one case on a nominal. Agreement processes are not available to nominals that are introduced by their own case to relate them to the clause.

Clitics (specifically discourse clitics, discussed in §9.4, or the bound pronouns, discussed in §5.3.6) can attach to well-formed nominals, although this is essentially true of any word class.

Some examples of ordering are presented below. There are no tokens in the corpus of a nominal with more than two suffixes (likely a restriction due to the corpus, rather than the language). Example (124) shows a number suffix preceding an adnominal suffix, (125) shows a derivational suffix preceding a case suffix, (126) shows a number suffix preceding a case suffix and (127) shows a derivational suffix preceding an adnominal suffix.

Number suffix prior to adnominal suffix:

(124) *Yapa* *witta* *partu-nga* *wirlinyi* **wangani-jarra-parna.**
person small leave-PAST.AWAY hunting **dog-DU-PROP**
The child left hunting **with two dogs**.
wrl-20200220, DK, 02:21 mins

Derivational suffix prior to adnominal suffix:

(125) *Karli-ku=ju-rla* **yapa-kanyanu-rlu** *wayi-nnya.*
boomerang-DAT=1SG.NS-3.OBL **person-ANOTHER-ERG** search-PRES
Someone else is looking for the boomerang for me.
H_K01-505B, DG, 01:00:28 hrs

Number suffix prior to adnominal suffix:

(126) **Ngayinya-jarra-rlu** **wangani-jarra-rlu** ngapij-nya-nya=pala yawirri.

1GEN-DU-ERG **dog**-DU-ERG smell-look-POT=3DU.S kangaroo

My two dogs might smell a kangaroo.
wrl-20180608-01, DK, 23:58 mins

Derivational suffix prior to adnominal suffix:

(127) Ngayinya ngalapi ka-nya wang– **wangani-kanyanu-parna.**

1GEN child be-PRES **dog**-ANOTHER-PROP

My child is with another dog.
wrl-20200221, DK, 27:21 mins

Case suffixes are discussed in §4.1. Case suffixes can be further grouped into 'core case' and 'semantic case'. The distinction is based purely on whether the case is selected for by the predicate (grammatical relations are discussed in §10.1)—excluding uses of the case to indicate agreement. Those selected by predicates (namely, the absolutive, ergative and dative) are core cases, while the remainder are non-core cases (for example, the locative, allative, aversive and others). Two suffixes can function as either core or semantic cases:[1] the dative suffix, which can mark indirect objects as well as adjuncts (for example, purposives); and the allative suffix, which can marginally be selected by a single predicate (see §10.2.7) and otherwise marks adjuncts.

Number suffixes are discussed in §4.4.7, as well as number marking more generally in Warlmanpa.

Derivational suffixes, discussed in §4.2, derive a new nominal, which then allows further number, adnominal or case marking.

Table 4.1 provides a summary of all known nominal suffixes in Warlmanpa and Table 4.2 details their interactions with the larger grammatical system of the language.

---

1 There are uses of the ergative and absolutive that are non-core, though I believe these are better viewed as case agreement, distinct from case application.

After presenting the nominal morphology system throughout §4.1 and §4.2, the discussion turns to other types of nominals: demonstratives are discussed in §4.5 and ignoratives in §4.6. The chapter concludes with four morphosyntactic topics highly relevant to nominals: possessive constructions (§4.7.1), comparative constructions (§4.7.2) and quantification (§4.7.3).

Table 4.1 Nominal suffixes in Warlmanpa

Suffix type		Suffix gloss	Allomorphs	Section	Nash (1979) gloss
Case	Core case	Absolutive	∅	§4.1.2	—
		Ergative	-ngu, -rlu	§4.1.3	Ergative
	Semantic case	Dative*	-ku	§4.1.4	Dative
		Locative*	-nga, -rla	§4.1.5	Locative
		Allative*	-ka	§4.1.6	Allative
		Elative	-ngurlu	§4.1.7	Elative
		Perlative	-wana	§4.1.8	Perlative
		Aversive*	-kuma	§4.1.9	Admonitive
		Preparative	-kapina	§4.1.10	Preparative purposive
		Desiderative*	-kupa	§4.1.11	Desiderative
		Translative	-karta	§4.1.12	—
		Concurrent	-puru	§4.1.13	—
Adnominal		Privative*	-wangu	§4.2.1	Negative
		Without*	-jila	§4.2.2	Lacking
		Genitive	-kurla	§4.2.3	Genitive, having
		Proprietive	-parna	§4.2.4	Having
Number				§4.3	
Derivational		Like	-nganja, -piya	§4.4.1	Like
		Source*	-warnu	§4.4.2	Resultative
		Another	-kanyanu	§4.4.3	Another
		Resident	-wartingi	§4.4.4	Native of
		Denizen	-ngarnarra	§4.4.5	Denizen of
		Associative	-palka	§4.4.6	Associated with
		Nomic	-ni	§4.4.7	Nomic

Note: Suffixes marked with an asterisk also have a complementising function.

Table 4.2 Behaviour of different types of nominal morphology

		Can be required by predicate	Can be referenced in bound pronouns	Allows further morphology
Core case	Absolutive	✓	✓	—
	Ergative	✓	✓	✗
	Dative	✓	✓	✗
Semantic case	Locative	✗	✗	✗
	Allative	~	~	✗
	Elative	✗	✗	✗
	Aversive	✗	✗	✗
	Privative	✗	✗	✗
	Desiderative	✗	✗	✗
	Translative*	✗	✗	?
	Perlative*	✗	✗	?
	Preparative*	✗	✗	?
	Concurrent*	✗	✗	?
Derivational and adnominal suffixes	Privative	✗	✗	?
	Without	✗	✗	✓
	Belonging	✗	✗	✓
	Having	✗	✗	✓
	Like	✗	✗	✓
	Source	✗	✗	✓
	Another	✗	✗	✓
	Resident of	✗	✗	✓
	Denizen*	✗	✗	✓
	Associated*	✗	✗	?

Note: * These suffixes are extremely infrequent in the corpus and have proven difficult to elicit, so their categorisation is tentative.

4.1 Case morphology

Core case morphology for nominals in Warlmanpa aligns to an ergative-absolutive system. In most circumstances, the core case marking exhibited by Warlmanpa nominals in verbal clauses is as given in Table 4.3 (though, of course, there are variations to be found; see §10.2 for a more detailed investigation).

Table 4.3 Prototypical case-marking patterns based on predicate valency

Predicate valency	Cases
1 (intransitive)	Absolutive
2 (transitive)	Ergative-absolutive
3 (ditransitive)	Ergative-absolutive-dative

In addition to core case, nominals exhibit several other cases, which I refer to as 'semantic case': dative (recall that the dative can function as either a core or a semantic case), locative, allative, elative, perlative, aversive, preparative purposive, source, desiderative, translative and concurrent. These semantic cases behave similarly to core case, in that they do not allow any further suffixing, however, they are differentiated by the inability of the case-marked nominal to be cross-referenced by the bound pronouns—except one predicate, *ya-* 'put', which requires an allative-marked argument (the argument status being evidenced by its registration in the bound pronouns; §10.2.7).

Before the case morphemes are introduced in further detail, there are three preliminary sections that situate the discussion of case: the notion of 'split ergativity' (§4.1.1.1), the functions of case more generally (§4.1.1.2) and recurring allomorphic patterns (§4.1.1.3). Each case suffix is then presented in §§4.1.2–4.1.13.

4.1.1 Preliminaries to an analysis of case morphemes

4.1.1.1 Split ergativity

Before turning to the individual cases, a brief foray into a discussion of 'split ergativity' is warranted. Some Australian languages exhibit a split within the nominal system, in which one set of nominals distinguishes different grammatical relations. For example, Yankunytjatjara common nouns distinguish A (transitive subject) from S (intransitive subject) and O (object), both of which share the same unmarked form (an ergative-absolutive alignment) (Goddard 1982: 179). Within the same word class, anaphoric pronouns distinguish O from A and S (a nominative–absolutive alignment). As such, the nominal system in Yankunytjatjara is analysed as exhibiting a split in the pattern of surface marking, warranting an analysis of three core cases to mark nominals.

Table 4.4 Yankunytjatjara case endings

Syntactic role		Common nouns	Proper nouns, kin names	Pronouns, anaphoric
A	ERG	-*ngku*	-*lu*	∅
S	NOM	∅	-*nya*	∅
O	ACC	∅	-*nya*	-*nya*

Source: Adapted from Goddard (1982: 179).

In Warlmanpa, no such split within the nominal system is found. All nominals mark S and O in identical fashion, in opposition to A—evidence for a classic ergative case-marking system. There is no nominal that distinguishes O from A and S. Perhaps the closest paradigm is that of the free pronouns that do not distinguish A, S or O, which does not call for a separate case system (a neutral system, using terminology from Comrie [1978: 332]); they are simply unmarked for core case—and recall from §3.1.7 that I analyse free pronouns as a distinct word class.

Interestingly, much like other Ngumpin-Yapa languages, the bound pronouns and some other syntactic processes instead pattern according to a nominative-accusative system. However, this does not constitute a split, because the bound pronoun paradigm is a separate system to nominals (Blake 1987a; Nordlinger 2014; Ennever 2021). They are just as separate as the various syntactic processes that group different sets, such as the bound pronouns and some complementisers, which pattern according to a nominative-accusative alignment. For example, the complementiser -*karra* (§12.1.2.1) indicates that the subject of its predicate is that of the subject of the main predicate (in other words, a 'same-subject' marker), regardless of transitivity, thus patterning according to a nominative-accusative system. Conversely, the complementiser -*pa*- (§12.1.2.7) also indicates that the subject of its predicate is that of the subject of the main predicate, but it can only be used if the subject of the main predicate is a transitive subject, thus patterning according to an ergative-absolutive system. So, Warlmanpa grammar as a whole exhibits various subsystems behaving in different ways, as exemplified in Table 4.5.

Table 4.5 Patterns of grammatical relation alignments across subsystems of Warlmanpa grammar

Grammatical subsystem		A	S	O
Nominal case marking				
Free pronouns				
Bound pronouns				
Reflexivisation				
Complementisers (exemplars)	-*karra*			
	-*pa*			

Note: Shaded cells represent identical marking of the grammatical relation.

Nothing is gained from analysing the nominal case-marking system in Warlmanpa as a split system (unlike languages such as Yankunytjatjara). This is consistent with findings that languages that have an ergative-absolutive morphological system rarely have entirely ergative-absolutive grammars (Comrie 1978; Moravcsik 1978; Silverstein 1976), and this is especially true of Australian languages (Nordlinger 2014: 219–24).[2]

4.1.1.2 Functions of case

I analyse four uses of case in Warlmanpa: relational, adnominal, referential and complementising (following the terminology of Dench and Evans 1988).

Relational uses of a case signal a relation between a predicate and the case-marked nominal. For example, in (128), the inflecting verb *kupa-* 'cook' requires an ergative subject and the nominal *Nampijinpa* is marked with the ergative, which allows the interpretation that it is the subject of the predicate.

(128)   **Nampijinpa-rlu**   *kupa-rnu-rra*   *yarnununju.*
        Nampijinpa-ERG   cook-PAST-IMPF   veg_food
        Nampijinpa was cooking food.
        wrl-20200224, DK, 36:22 mins

---

2   Bilinarra is analysed as a split-ergative language and, as such, nominals are analysed as distinguishing ergative (which is overtly marked) from nominative and accusative, which are both unmarked in the nominal case system (Meakins and Nordlinger 2014: 112–14). See also Legate (2002) for a detailed analysis of case in Warlpiri.

The relational function covers both 'core' case (case required by a predicate), as in (128), and 'non-core' case (case not required by a predicate), as in (129), where the predicate does not require an elative-marked constituent.

(129) *Kurtu   wa-nu   **yiwirti-ngurlu**.*
       child   fall-PAST   **tree-ELA**
       The child fell **from the tree**.
       H_K01-505B, DG, 31:23 mins

The adnominal function of case specifies a semantic relation between two nominals. For example, in (130), the privative case *-wangu* relates its host, *jarta* 'sleep', to *wangani* 'dog'.

(130) ***Jarta-wangu*** *ali=nya*   *wangani*   *warlku*   *wa-nganyu-rra.*
       sleep-PRIV   that=FOC   dog   bark   speak-PAST-IMPF
       The sleepless dog was barking.
       wrl-20190206, DK, 35:25 mins

Adnominal case marking is rare in the corpus, though there is a small set of 'adnominal suffixes', which I do not treat as 'case' for morphological reasons (see §4.2 for a discussion).

Referential case marking 'involves the marking of some NP [noun phrase] or adverb in agreement with some other (usually core) NP in the same clause' (Dench and Evans 1988: 13)—that is, secondary predication. This is exemplified for Warlmanpa in (131), where *karli* 'boomerang' is marked with ergative case (thereby construing it with the subject of the transitive predicate) and the bound pronoun registers a (first-person singular) subject, so *karlingu* is interpreted as expressing the instrument with which the event was performed by the subject.

(131) ***Karli-ngu**=rna*   *la-nmi.*
       boomerang-ERG=1SG.S   shoot-FUT
       I'll hit it **with a boomerang**.
       H_K01-506A, DG, 38:27 mins.

The main distinction between adnominal and referential functions for Dench and Evans (1988: 13) is whether the related nominals form an NP constituent and, in §11.1.4, I argue against an analysis of NPs in Warlmanpa. As such, whether there is a distinction between adnominal case and referential case functions in Warlmanpa is tentative. Notably, Dench and Evans (1988: 14) include Warlpiri as an example of a language in which 'there may be no good formal tests which distinguish referential agreement from adnominal agreement'.

Finally, in their complementising function, some case forms may be used to mark subordinate clauses (specifically, marking the syntactic relation between the subordinate clause and the matrix clause). The complementising function of case is discussed further in §12.1.2.

(132)   *Pa-nama=li*   *nya-nja-ku*   *papulu-ku.*
        go-FUT.AWAY=1DU.INCL.S see-INF-DAT   house-DAT
        Let's go to see the house.
        wrl-20190213-01, DK, 17:53 mins

4.1.1.3 Multiple case marking

Australian languages are well known for their case-marking patterns, in which a single nominal can be marked with multiple case morphemes (Dench and Evans 1988). For example, in the Warlpiri sentence given in (133), the nominal *ngurra* 'camp' has an argument-taking locative case, *-ngka* (to mark *ngurra* as being a space in which an entity or event is located), and an attributive ergative case, *-rlu* (to mark *ngurra-ngka* as being construed as the unexpressed subject of the predicate—that is, where the subject is located).

(133)   *Nga-rnu=lpa*   *yangka*   **ngurra-ngka-rlu.**
        eat-PST=PST   ANAPH   **camp-LOC-ERG**
        He was eating in camp yesterday.
        (Warlpiri [Simpson 2005: 80])

In many Ngumpin-Yapa languages, multiple case marking is restricted to a small set of combinations, such as a complementising case (which can be contrasted with Ngardi, in which there are many instantiated combinations of case stacking [Ennever 2021]). For example, in (134), an example from Warlpiri, the nominal *parraja* takes the locative case to indicate spatial containment (a relational usage of case) and the dative case to indicate syntactic relatedness to the indirect object *kurdu-ku* 'child-DAT' (an adnominal function of case). Similar, though not identical, processes are found in Bilinarra (Meakins and Nordlinger 2014: 100–2) and Gurindji (Meakins and McConvell 2021).

(134) Karnta-ngku ka=rla kurdu-ku miyi yi-nyi parraja-rla-ku.
woman-ERG PRES=3DAT child-DAT food give-NPST coolamon-LOC-DAT

The woman is giving food to the baby who is in the coolamon.
(Simpson 1991: 206)

Combinations of any case, including locative, ergative and/or dative, are not found in Warlmanpa (instead Warlmanpa seems to prefer using finite relative clauses; see §12.1.1.1). A nominal in Warlmanpa can have only one case suffix and there are clear rules dictating which case types take priority over others. Case operating with a relational function will always take priority over case with adnominal or referential functions.

For example, in (135), the nominal *pamarrpa* 'rock' modifies *karli* 'boomerang', which is dative marked. *Karli* is dative marked and, despite *pamarrpa* modifying this dative-marked constituent, it does not receive the dative case, because it is blocked by the application of the locative case functioning as an argument-taking predicate.[3]

(135) *Wayi-rnu-rra=rla* **karli-ku** **pamarrpa-rla**
search-PAST-IMPF=3.OBL **boomerang-DAT** **rock-LOC**
kankarlija.
on_top

He was searching for a boomerang which was on top of a rock.
wrl-20191207-02, DK, 36:09 mins

4.1.1.4 Allomorphy conditioned by syllable count

Only two case morphemes are subject to allomorphy in Warlmanpa, both of which exhibit the same basic pattern: the consonant in the suffix is a velar nasal if attached to a disyllabic stem and a retroflex lateral occurs elsewhere—a pattern common to Ngumpin-Yapa languages (Ennever 2018: 93; Hale 1982; Tsunoda 1981a: 55; Meakins and Nordlinger 2014: 114; McConvell 1996b). The allomorphs are presented in Table 4.6.

---

3   This structure is ambiguous and, indeed, the locative could be functioning as a relational case, modifying the event rather than an argument of the predicate. In this case, based on discussion with the speaker and the strangeness of '#he was searching on a rock for a boomerang', I am reasonably confident the intended interpretation is that *pamarrparla* is construed of *karliku*, however, most examples of this structure are ambiguous.

Table 4.6 Case allomorphy in Warlmanpa

	Two-syllable stem	Elsewhere
Ergative	*-ngu*	*-rlu*
Locative	*-nga*	*-rla*

To exemplify, when the ergative attaches to *ngarrka* 'man', the allomorph is *-ngu* because the stem is two syllables (136), but when *ngarrka* has a dual marker, *-ja*, the allomorph is *-rlu* because the stem is three syllables (137).

(136)　**Ngarrka-ngu**=*jangu*　　*nya-nganya*　　*ngayu.*
　　　　man-ERG=1DU.EXC.O　　see-PRES　　　　1
　　　　The man sees us.
　　　　H_K01-505B, DG, 48:55 mins

(137)　**Ngarrka-ja-rlu**=*ju-pala*　　　*nya-nganya.*
　　　　man-DUAL-ERG=1SG.NS-3DU.S　　see-PRES
　　　　The two men see me.
　　　　H_K01-505B, DG, 48:40 mins

Some demonstratives and ignoratives take the lateral allomorphs, regardless of their syllable count (this is discussed in further detail in the sections discussing these nominals: §4.5 for demonstratives and §4.6 for ignoratives), as in (138).

(138)　**Mu-rlu**=*ju*　　*pamarrpa-rlu*　　*nama-nnya.*
　　　　this-ERG=1SG.NS　stone-ERG　　　　weigh_down-PRES
　　　　This stone is weighing me down.
　　　　H_K01-506A, DG, 30:31 mins

(139)　**Ngana-rlu**=*ngu*　　*paka-rnu?*
　　　　who-ERG=2SG.NS　　hit-PAST
　　　　Who hit you?
　　　　H_K01-505B, DG, 11:28 mins

Unlike most Ngumpin languages, in which there is allomorphy conditioned by the stem-final consonant, there does not appear to be conditioning specific to consonant-final stems in Warlmanpa (Meakins and McConvell 2021; Meakins and Nordlinger 2014: 112–16; Senge 2015: 169; Osgarby 2018: 248; Ennever 2018: 80; Tsunoda 1981a: 55). The lack of allomorphs in Warlmanpa is highly likely due to the lack of consonant-final nominal stems. In (140), the English word *knife* [naef] takes ergative case but, despite ending in a labiodental fricative, the form of the ergative remains *-ngu*.

(140)   **Knife-ngu**=lu   piya-nya,   or   mayingka-rlu=lu   tiirltiirl-kuma-nnya.
        knife-ERG=3PL.S   break-PRES   axe-ERG=3PL.S   split-cut-PRES
        They cut it with a knife or they cut it with an axe.
        H_K06-004548, JW, 02:38 mins

4.1.2 Absolutive

The absolutive case is phonologically unmarked. In most situations, the absolutive case is used for subjects (of intransitive predicates), objects (see §10.1 and §10.2 for more detail) and any modifying nominals construed as an absolutive head (unless the modifying nominal is introduced by its own non-core case).

(141)   **Karnta**   wa-nganya   kutij-ka-nja-karra.
        woman.ABS   speak-PRES   stand-be-INF-SS
        The woman [who is] standing is speaking.
        wrl-20190206, DK, 07:07 mins

(142)   **Wawirri**=rna   karla-rnu   wantarli-ka.
        kangaroo.ABS=1SG.S spear-PAST   across-ALL
        I speared the kangaroo going across.
        N_D02-007842, BN, 45:58 mins

(143)   Ali-ngu=nya   ngarrka-ngu   **kuyu**=rla   yu-ngu   kurtu-ku.
        that-ERG=FOC   man=ERG   **meat.ABS**=3.OBL give-PAST   child-DAT
        That man gave meat to the child.
        wrl-20190211-02, DK, 09:06 mins

(144)   Jinta-ngu   marta-nnya   **mukarti**   **wiri.**
        one-ERG   have-PRES   **hat.ABS**   **big.ABS**
        [That] one has a big hat.
        H_K01-505B, DG, 01:01:53 hrs

Note that outside this subsection, the ABS component of unmarked nominals is not included in the gloss.

4.1.3 Ergative

The prototypical role of the ergative case *-ngu/-rlu* is to mark the subject of transitive or ditransitive clauses (§10.2 discusses exactly which constructions require an ergative-marked subject). The form of the ergative suffix is *-ngu* for disyllabic roots, as in (147), and *-rlu* elsewhere, as in (145). There are no animacy restrictions on the use of the ergative, as evidenced in (147), where *parra* 'sun' is marked for ergative.

(145) **Maliku-rlu**   *kala=ngu*   *pi-nyi.*
     dog-ERG   APPR=2SG.NS   bite-FUT
     Careful, the dog will bite you!
     wrl-20180531-02, DF, 37:05 mins

(146) **Ali-ngu**=*nya*   **warungka-rlu**   *paka-nya=nyanu.*
     that-ERG=FOC   **crazy-ERG**   hit-PRES=RR
     That crazy person is hitting themself.
     wrl-20190213-02, DK, 25:22 mins

(147) **Parra-ngu**=*ju*   *milpa*   *ji-nnya,*   *kapakapa*   *ma-nnya=ju,*
     sun-ERG=1SG.NS   eye   burn-PRES   hinder   do-PRES=1SG.NS
     kula=rna   *kari=ma*   *nya-nganya.*
     NEG=1SG.S   far=TOP   see-PRES
     The sun is burning my eye, hindering me, I can't see far.
     N_D02-009887, DG, 03:01 mins

(148) **Kulykulypa-rlu**   *ngayu=ju*   *paka-nnya.*
     fever-ERG   1=1SG.NS   hit-PRES
     I have a cold [lit.: a fever is hitting me].
     wrl-20180614-02, DK, 03:32 mins

Other nominals modifying an ergative constituent will also generally host the ergative suffix to mark concordance (unless the modifier requires its own case; see §4.1.1.3 for discussion of case concordance). Many ergative modifiers bear the thematic role of instrument. The lack of differentiation between agent and instrument is not unusual in Australia (Dixon 1980: 304) and is theoretically predicted since the semantic roles of agents, instruments and causes often are not grammatically distinguished (Santorini and Kroch 2007). Examples of ergative-marked nominals functioning as instruments are given in (149)–(151).

(149) *Kuyu   kuma-nnya   karnta-ngu   **japirri-parna-rlu.***
    meat   cut-PRES   woman-ERG   **knife-PROP-ERG**
    The woman is cutting the meat with her knife.
    wrl-20190201, DK, 05:39 mins

(150) ***Yiwirtu-rlu**=ju   paka-rnu.*
    stick-ERG=1SG.NS   hit-PAST
    He hit me with a stick/the stick hit me.
    N_D03-007868, BN, 05:42 mins

(151) *Nga=rna-ngu   yiwirti-rlu   karta   pi-nyi   **ngayinya-kurla-rlu***
    POST=1SG.S-2SG.NS   spear-ERG   pierce   act_on-FUT   **1GEN-GEN-ERG**
    kirtana-kurla-rlu.
    father-GEN-ERG
    I will stab you with my father's spear.
    H_K01-506A, DG, 49:56 mins

I view these cases as a type of secondary predicate (analysed in §11.6.2). Instruments may additionally be marked with the adnominal suffix *-parna* 'proprietive' (§4.2.4), especially if the instrument is possessed by the agent. The ergative is never used as an instrumental in intransitive clauses, supporting the secondary predicate analysis—that is, the ergative here is a referential rather than a relational use. The equivalent construction in intransitive clauses is to use *-parna* 'proprietive' (§4.2.4), which can be used in ergative contexts as well.

Some adverbs may optionally agree in case with an ergative subject, as in (152) and (153). Given its apparent optionality (cf. [154]), I am uncertain of the semantic effect of this use of the ergative (and whether the lack of ergative reflects clausal scope).

(152) ***Lurrija-lurrija-rlu**   warlu   jarrajarra   ma-nta*
    quickly-RDP-ERG   fire   flame   get-IMP
    Build a fire quickly!
    H_K01-506B, DG, 08:39 mins

(153) *Warlu=ju   ma-nta   **lurrija-rlu.***
    fire=1SG.NS   get-IMP   **quick-IMP**
    Get firewood quickly!
    H_K01-506B, DG, 08:32 mins

(154) Kuyu   yarri=nya   **lurrija~lurrija**   kuma-ka.
      meat   that=FOC   quickly~RDP   cut-IMP
      Cut that meat quickly!
      H_K01-506B, DG, 08:47 mins

Other than adverbs such as in the examples above, Warlmanpa does not exhibit optional ergative marking (Chappell and Verstraete 2019). While the nominals themselves are optionally expressed, if a nominal surfaces that is expected to have ergative marking, it will obligatorily be ergative-marked (that is, a subject of a transitive predicate or any nominals construed of a transitive subject).

4.1.4 Dative

The dative case *-ku* is unique in that it can function as either a core case (selected for by the predicate) or a non-core case (not selected for by the predicate). As shown in Table 4.7, the uses of the suffix vary with regards to whether they are selected for by the predicate and/or whether they are cross-referenced by the bound pronouns.

Table 4.7 Instantiated interpretations of the dative suffix

	Semantic interpretation	Selected for by predicate	Cross-referenced by bound pronouns
Core case	Indirect object	✓	✓
Non-core case	External object	~	✓
	Purposive	✗	✗
	Duration	✗	✗

(i) Indirect object

In its core-case use, the dative suffix marks indirect objects, as exemplified in (155) and (156). Indirect objects are discussed in §10.1.3.

(155) Warlmanpa=rla   wa-ngka   **yarru-ku=nya**.
      Warlmanpa=3.OBL   speak-IMP   **that-DAT=FOC**
      Speak Warlmanpa to that one!
      H_K01-505B, DG, 16:26 mins

(156) *Maliki-rlu=rla* **kuyu-ku** *wayi-nnya.*
dog-ERG=3.OBL **meat-DAT** search-PRES
The dog is searching for meat.
H_K01-505B, DG, 07:51 mins

(ii) External object

The dative suffix can also mark external objects. External objects can be introduced via an applicative rule, which signals a benefactive, malefactive or possessor relation (the interpretation is dependent on context); or via certain preverbs (Browne 2021b). The external object grammatical relation is detailed in §10.1.4. Examples of external objects introduced via applicatives are given in (157)–(159) and of external objects introduced via coverbs in (160) and (161).

External object introduced via applicative rule:

(157) *Yarnunju=rla* **kurtu-ku** *kupa-nnya.*
veg_food=3.OBL **child-DAT** cook-PRES
He's cooking food for the child. (Benefactive)
wrl-20190205, DK, 14:22 mins

(158) *Ngayu=ma=rna-rla* *pa-nyinga,* *ngappa=rna-rla* *ma-nmi*
1=TOP=1SG.S-**3.OBL** go-PATH water=1SG.S-**3.OBL** get-FUT

wangani-ku *pirraku.*[4]
dog-DAT thirsty
I'm going for him, I'll get water for the thirsty dog. (Benefactive)
wrl-20190205, DK, 40:32 mins

(159) *Murtika=rla* **Japangka-ku** *maju-ja-ngu* *yimpa.*
car=3SG.OBL **Japanangka-DAT** bad-INCH-PAST this
This car broke on Japanangka. (Malefactive)
This car of Japanangka's broke. (Possessive)
N_D02-007841, BN, 25:56 mins

---

4 As this example stands, it is difficult to explain why *pirraku* does not receive dative marking (that is, *pirraku-ku*) to indicate case concordance with *wangani-ku* 'dog-DAT'. As far as I am aware, *pirra* is not a nominal in Warlmanpa, so this cannot be explained as being *pirra-ku* (unless the speaker has analysed it as such).

External object introduced via coverb:

(160) *Japanangka=**jana** <u>yirrkin</u> pa-nangu **kurtu~kurtu-ku** ngurra-ka.*
Japanangka=3PL.NS with go-PAST child~PL-DAT camp-ALL
Japanangka went with the kids to camp.
N_D02-007842, BN, 01:12 mins

(161) *Yiwirti=**rla** yimpa **yarnunjuku-ku** <u>yirrkin</u> kurtij-ka-nya.*
tree=3.OBL this food-DAT with stand-be-PRES
This tree is standing with food [on it].
N_D02-007842, BN, 01:33 mins

(iii) Purposive

Purposives are semantically similar to benefactives. However, purposives and benefactives can be distinguished on semantic and morphosyntactic grounds. In general, purposive interpretations benefit the agent (that is, the dative-marked constituent refers to something that will benefit the agent), whereas benefactive interpretations benefit someone other than the agent (and, in these cases, the dative-marked constituent refers to the beneficiary). The distinguishing morphosyntactic feature is that beneficiaries are cross-referenced in the bound pronouns and purposives are not. In (162), the only available interpretation is the purposive, as *yarnunju* 'food' cannot benefit from the action. In (163), similarly, the only available interpretation is the purposive (that is, where the agent benefits), because the object of purpose *nyuntu* '2' is not cross-referenced by the bound pronouns, so cannot be interpreted as a beneficiary.

(162) *Ngayu=rna pa-nyinga, ngayu=rna pa-nyinga **yarnunju-ku** ngurra-ka.*
1=1SG.S go-PATH 1=1SG.S go-PATH food-DAT camp-ALL
I'll go, I'll go to camp for food.
wrl-20191207-02, DK, 18:14 mins

(163) Yumpa=nya=ma pa-nnya jawarti=ma Warrabri-ka=lku **nyuntu-ku**=lku.
this=FOC=TOP go-PRES tomorrow=TOP Warrabri-ALL=THEN **2-DAT**=THEN

He's going to Warrabri tomorrow to fetch you.
H_K01-506A, DG, 33:15 mins

The purposive interpretation is clearly the basis of *-ku* as a subordinator (see §12.1.2.6), as shown in (164). In most cases, it is difficult (or impossible) to distinguish (if they should be at all).

(164) Pa-nama=rna **la-nja-ku** **yawirri-ku.**
go-FUT.AWAY=1SG.S **shoot-INF-DAT** **kangaroo-DAT**

I'll go off to hunt kangaroo.
wrl-20190201, DK, 40:59 mins

(iv) Duration

The dative case can also denote the duration of an event. In these constructions, the dative case attaches to the temporal nominal, and *ngurra* 'camp' or *parra* 'sun', functioning as a duration (seemingly, the number of nights) for the temporal nominal to quantify.

(165) Mirla=yi=li ka-mi **jirrima-ku** **ngurra-ku.**
this.LOC=STILL=1DU.INCL.S be-FUT **two-DAT** **camp-DAT**

We'll just stay here for two days.
wrl-20191207-02, DK, 08:45 mins

(166) **Jirrima-ku** **ngurra-ku**=n tij ka-mi.
two-DAT **camp-DAT**=2SG.S overnight_camp be-FUT

You'll stay for two nights in camp.
wrl-20191207-01, DK, 02:16 mins

(167) Tij **ngurra-ku** **jinta-ku** kala=rnalu earlypala
overnight_camp **camp-DAT** **one-DAT** HAB=1PL.EXCL.S early

parti-nja-nu-rnu munga-nga=yi.
leave-MOT-PAST-TWD shelter-LOC=STILL

We would stay in the shelter for one night and leave early in the morning.
N_D29-023128, MFN, 02:20 mins

(168) *Ngappa wa-nu* **parra-ku=ma** *jirrima-ku jinta-ku.*
water fall-PAST **sun-DAT=TOP** two-DAT one-DAT
It rained for three days.
wrl-20200221, DK, 32:25 mins

Unlike some other Ngumpin-Yapa languages, the dative is not used for animate goals, as exemplified for Bilinarra in (169). In Warlmanpa, the equivalent construction (dative marking on an animate adjunct) could only be interpreted as a benefactive or purposive construction, depending on whether the referent was cross-referenced in the bound pronouns. Warlmanpa marks animate goals with the allative case, as exemplified in §4.1.6.

(169) *Ngayi=ma=rna=rla=nga ya-n.gu* **janggarni-wu gardiba-wu.**
1MIN=TOP=1MIN. go-POT **big-DAT whitefella-DAT**
S=3OBL=DUB
I might have to go back to my boss.
(Bilinarra [Meakins and Nordlinger 2014: 132])

4.1.5 Locative

The locative case *-nga*/*-rla* denotes the time or space in which an entity is located at the reference time. The form is *-nga* for disyllabic roots and *-rla* elsewhere.

(170) **Ngayinya-rla papulu-rla** *ka-nya.*
1.GEN-LOC **house-LOC** sit-PRES
He is **at my house**.
H_K01-506A, DG, 54:42 mins

(171) **Ngappa-nga**=*rna jarrawarti-jarra kangkurr ka-ngu-rra.*
water-LOC=1SG.S thigh-DU submerge be-PAST-IMPF
My legs were floating **in the water**.
N_D02-007842, BN, 11:07 mins

The locative includes perlative uses, translated as 'along', as the perlative suffix is rarely used (see §4.1.8), as exemplified in (172).

(172) Ngayu=ma=rna   pa-nyinga   **mirla=nya**   **partakurru-rla**
       1=TOP=1SG.S   go-PATH   **this.LOC=FOC** **good-LOC**
       wantarri-rla.
       road-LOC
       I'm going along this good road.
       wrl-20200221, DK, 00:47 secs

As noted in §3.1.7, the free pronouns may host the locative, but they surface in their genitive form (a regular process for the locative and allative in which no genitive semantics is encoded by the different form).

(173) Witta   ka-nya   **nyintinya-rla**.
       small   be-PRES   **2-LOC**
       The child is sitting **on you**.
       H_K01-505B, DG, 32:53 mins

As exemplified in (174), the locative-marked nominal can be construed of a particular participant in the event, rather than denoting the location of the event more generally. Due to the lack of case stacking, in many cases, the scope of a locative-marked constituent is ambiguous.

(174) Wayi-rnu-rra=rla   **karli-ku**   **pamarrpa-rla** kankarlija.
       search-PAST-IMPF=3.OBL   **boomerang-DAT**   **rock-LOC**   on_top.
       He was searching for the boomerang [which was] on top of the rock.
       ('He was searching on the rock/hill for the boomerang' is also an acceptable reading of this sentence, though the established context of this utterance prohibits this reading.)
       wrl-20191207-02, DK, 36:09 mins

Subordinate clauses with a copula predicate and locative modifier can be used as a periphrastic alternative (see §12.1.1.1), as in (175).

(175) Wayi-nnya=rla   karli-ku   ngula   ka-nya   kankarlija
       search-PRES=3.OBL   boomerang-DAT   REL   be-PRES   on_top
       pamarrpa-rla.
       rock-LOC
       He's searching for a boomerang which is on top of the rock.
       wrl-20191207-02, DK, 36:46 mins

In addition to locating entities in space, the locative can locate entities in various states. Most commonly, these are states locating entities in time, as in (176) and (177), but other states are used, as in (178) and (179).

(176) **Munga-nga**=rna   jarta   ka-nya.
      night-LOC=1SG.S   sleep   be-PRES
      I sleep at night.
      H_K01-506A, DG, 28:06 mins

(177) Wanjila=n   **parra-nga**=ma   pa-nanga?
      where.LOC=2SG.S   **sun-LOC**=TOP   go-PAST.IMPF
      Where were you going during the day?
      wrl-20191207-01, DK, 05:10 mins

(178) **Wila-nga**=pala   ka-nya.
      play-LOC=3DU.S   be-PRES
      Those two are playing [lit.: two are at playing].
      H_K06-004547, JW, 31:34 mins

(179) Ali-ngurlu=ma=rna   pina   ka-ngu   Mangalawurru-ka=lku
      that-ELA=TOP=1SG.S   return   take-PAST   Mangalawurru-ALL-THEN
      witta-nga.
      small-LOC
      I brought him back to Mangalawurru when he was small.
      wrl-20190208, DK, 17:50 mins

In contemporary Warlpiri, -*ngka* is the only locative suffix used, with -*rla* falling out of use in its locative function, only retaining its use as a complementiser (Mary Laughren, p.c.).

Ngumpin-Yapa languages exhibit some variation with regards to marking accompaniment, although generally the locative case is somehow involved, either directly or as a formative. For example, the locative is used in Bilinarra (Meakins and Nordlinger 2014: 127) and Ngardi (Ennever 2018: 96). Warlpiri can use a comitative suffix (parasitic to the locative case [Hale 1982]) to signal accompaniment. In Warlmanpa, it is not clear whether a locative-marked constituent can be interpreted as accompaniment. A possible instance is provided in (180), where *ngartina* 'mother' is locative marked, though it is possible that this refers to the mother's location, without the mother necessarily also participating in the event. Accompaniment is more regularly encoded by *-parna* (§4.2.4) or the coverb *yirrkin* 'with', which selects for a dative-marked constituent denoting accompaniment (briefly discussed in §4.1.4).

(180) *Witta-ngu   yapa-ngu   nga-rnu-rra   yarnunju   **ngartina-rla.***
      small-ERG   person-ERG   eat-PAST-IMPF   food   **mother-LOC**
      The child is eating food with/on [her] mother.
      wrl-20191208-02, DK, 26:49 mins

A subordinator, *-rla* 'prior', may be related (likely diachronically rather than synchronically, based on the lack of allomorphy) to the locative case (see §12.1.2.4 for discussion).

4.1.6 Allative

The allative case *-ka* is used to denote the endpoint (that is, the goal) of a motion event. As with the ergative, there is no apparent animacy distinction: the allative can be used equally with inanimate referents and animate referents.

(181) ***Ngurra-ka**=rna   pa-nnya.*
      camp-ALL=1SG.S   go-PRES
      I'm going home.
      H_K01-505B, DG, 08:40 mins

(182) ***Ngayinya-ka**   jutu-ngu-rnu.*
      1GEN-ALL   run-PAST-TWD
      He ran towards me.
      wrl-20180528-03, DK, 13:22 mins

(183) ***Papulu-ka**=rna   purlun-ya-nmi   ngappa-warnu   kinja-nji-ngarnu.*
      house-ALL=1SG.S enter-go-FUT   water-SOURCE   wet-INF-SOURCE
      I'm going into the house because of the rain wetting [me].
      H_K01-505B, DG, 35:49 mins

(184) *Ngayu=ma=rna   pa-nanga   **pulka-ka.***
      1=TOP=1SG.S   go-PAST.AWAY   **old_man-ALL**
      I went to the old man.
      wrl-20200219, DK, 05:56 mins

(185) *Purlin-ya-nya*   *kantija*   **blanket-ka**.
enter-go-PRES   underneath   **blanket-ALL**
He's getting underneath the blanket.
N_D28-2003.1, JK, 14:56 mins

A placename referring to a goal always inflects for the allative, as in (186). This contrasts with the locative, which is seemingly optional for placenames. Spatial adverbs do not take the allative, as shown in (187).

(186) *Ali-ngurlu=ma*   *ngayu=ma=jarra*   *kangkuya-jarra*   *partu-nga*
that-ELA=TOP   1=TOP=DUAL   old_man-DUAL   leave-PAST.AWAY
Darwin-ka=*lku*
Darwin-ALL=THEN
Then me and the old man moved to Darwin.
wrl-20190211-01, DK, 03:22 mins

(187) **Yanjarra(*-ka)**=*rna*   *pa-nnya*.
north(*-ALL)=1SG.S   go-PRES
I'm going north.
H_K01-505B, DG, 01:02:14 hrs

The allative suffix also functions as a complementising suffix, indicating that the subject of its clause is a non-subject argument or modifier of the matrix clause (see §12.1.2.1).

(188) *Nya-ngu=ju-n*   **partakurru-ma-nji-ka.**
see-PAST=1SG.NS=2SG.S   **good-CAUSE-INF-ALL**
You saw me **fixing it**.
N_D03-007868, BN, 40:57 mins

The allative form *-ka* seems to be cognate to the allative form found in some Ngumpin-Yapa languages *-(ng)kurra* (Osgarby 2018: 248; Nash 1986: 31; Meakins and McConvell 2021; Meakins and Nordlinger 2014: 114; Ennever 2021), where Warlmanpa has reduced many VrrV sequences to V, hence the synchronic form *-ka*. Alternatively, it may be related to the locative form *-ka* in Gurindji and Bilinarra, which is synchronically derived from *-ngka* after nasal cluster dissimilation (Meakins and Nordlinger 2014; Meakins and McConvell 2021).

4.1.7 Elative

The elative case *-ngurlu* marks the origin (or source) of an event. In the prototypical case, this is the origin point of a motion event (*-warnu* seems to be preferred for 'metaphoric' or causal sources; §4.4.2), regardless of whether the source is a contained space, as in (189), or not, as in (190) (that is, there is no elative/ablative distinction). Further examples are given in (191) and (192).

(189)   Wari   palyal   partu-ngu   **ngulya-ngurlu.**
         snake   emerge   rise-PAST   **hole-ELA**
         The snake came out of the hole.
         wrl-20191207-02, DK, 33:11 mins

(190)   ***Pankupanku-ngurlu****=rnalu*   *partu-nga,*   *Purnarrapanpa-ka.*
         Banka Banka-ELA=1PL.EXCL.S   leave-PAST.AWAY   Renner Springs-ALL
         We left Banka Banka, to Renner Springs.
         N_D02-007850, DG, 00:38 secs

(191)   ***Yiwirti-ngurlu***   *ngula=rna*   *wanu*   *warlapirti=rna*   *tarlurr-wa-nu.*
         tree-ELA   REL=1SG.S   fall-PAST   shin=1SG.S   break-FALL-PAST
         My shin broke when I fell from the tree.
         H_K01-505B, DG, 44:58 mins

(192)   *Yapa=nya*   *witta*   *ka-ngu*   *hospital-ka*   *ngula*   ***pirnti-ngurlu***   *wa-nu.*
         child=FOC   small   carry-PAST   hospital-ALL   REL   **tree_top-ELA**   fall-PAST
         He took the child to the hospital when she fell out of the treetop.
         N_D02-007842, BN, 45:02 mins

The elative is also compatible with non-motion events, such as indicating the orientation of an event participant, as in (193), or the source of an event, as in (194) and (195).

(193)   *Wangani-rlu*   ***pamarrpa-ngurlu***   *nya-nganya.*
         dog-ERG   **hill-ELA**   see-PRES
         The dog is looking from the hill.
         wrl-20191207-01, DK, 08:54 mins

(194) Purtu   ka-ngu=n   **Jungarrayi-ngurlu**=ma.
      hear   be-PAST=2SG.S   **Jungarrayi-ELA**=TOP
      Have you heard from Jungarrayi?
      wrl-20180609-01, DK, 00:18 secs

(195) Karli=ma=lu   pilka-ma-nnya   **yiwirti-ngurlu.**
      boomerang=TOP=3PL.S   make-CAUSE-PRES   **tree-ELA**
      They make boomerangs out of trees.
      wrl-20200219, DK, 26:03 mins

The demonstrative *yali* can take the elative (or source) suffix to denote a narrative time jump, similar to the English 'after that' (in the terminology of Schiffrin [1996], this demarcates a linguistic episode in the narrative). For example, in (196), the first two clauses describe a sequence of events. The third clause happens sometime later, overtly marked by *yalingurlu* to indicate the passing of time.

(196) i.   *Sho̱w-ma-nu-rra=lpa-jana-lu*   ngurra-wana   yanjarra
           show-CAUSE-PAST-IMPF=1INCL.S-3PL.NS-S.PL camp-PERL   north

           kakarra.
           east.
           We showed them around camp, north and east.

      ii. Kurlarra=lpa   pa-nangu   nyanungu.
           south=1PL.INCL.S   go-PAST   aforementioned
           We went to that place.

      iii. **Yali-ngurlu**=lpa   pa-nangu-rnu.
           that-ELA=1PL.INCL.S   go-PAST-TWD
           After that, we headed back.
           N_D01-007840A, DG, 00:36 secs

Unlike other spatial cases (the locative and allative), the elative suffix may attach to spatial adverbs, as in (197) and (198), and does not require a frozen form of the free pronouns, as exemplified in (199).

(197) **Kakarra-ngurlu**=rna   pa-nti-nya.
      east-ELA=1SG.S   go-TWD-PRES
      I'm coming from the east.
      H_K01-505B, DG, 01:02:59 hrs

(198) **Kankarlarra-ngurlu**=lu   kiya-rnu-rnu   karrarlarla.
      above-ELA=3PL.S   throw-PAST-TWD   spear
      They threw their spears from above.
      wrl-20190213-01, DK, 34:26 mins

(199) Ngayu=rna   marta-nnya   kuyu   **nyuntu-ngurlu.**
      1=1SG.S   have-PRES   meat   **2-ELA**
      I have the meat from you.
      wrl-20200219, DK, 13:30 mins

The form *-ngu(r)lu* is shared by all Ngumpin-Yapa languages as an ablative/elative case (Ennever 2021; Meakins and McConvell 2021; Meakins and Nordlinger 2014: 138–39; Nash 1986: 31; Osgarby 2018: 31; Tsunoda 1981a: 248). I retain the label 'elative' following Nash (1979).

4.1.8 Perlative

The perlative case *-wana* is used to indicate motion through or along a referent, as in (200)–(202).

(200) **Wirliya-wana**=yi=lu-rla   purtangirli=yi   pa-nnya.
      tracks-PERL=STILL=3PL.S-3.OBL behind=STILL   go-PRES
      Still along the tracks they are going behind for it.
      H_K06-004548, JW, 02:03 mins

(201) Show-ma-nu-rra=lpa-jana-lu   **ngurra-wana**   yanjarra
      show-DO-PAST-IMPF=1EXCL.S-3PL.NS-S.PL **camp-PERL**   north
      kakarra.
      east
      We showed them around camp, north and east.
      N_D01-007840A, JN, 00:35 secs

(202) *Yali=nya   painting=ma   ngur— nguru   **ngayinya-wana**.*
       this=FOC   painting=TOP   country   **1-PERL**
       This is a painting of around my district.
       N_D_20071010, SN, 00:32 secs

As in Bilinarra and Gurindji (Meakins and Nordlinger 2014: 143), the perlative is very rare in Warlmanpa. Typically, the locative case is used for these functions. Moreover, uses of the perlative case are outright rejected by some speakers. In the following exchange, I begin to formulate a sentence starting with *wilpa-wana=rna* 'creek-PERL=1SG.S'. After I hesitate on an appropriate verb form, JK completes my sentence with *pananga* 'go-PAST. IMPF'—that is, 'I was going along/around the creek', implying she accepts the use of *-wana*. However, DK immediately interjects to qualify that the suffix is a 'Warlpiri' form. Note that *pananga* is not a Warlpiri form, so JK could not have been thinking I was eliciting Warlpiri.

(203) **MB**   Could I say *wilpawanarna*   [...
       JK   [*pananga*.
       DK   no::, not *wana*,
              that's Warlpiri's word.
              (wrl-20180528-03, 1:04 mins)

Instead, DK uses the locative for translational motion along or through referents, as exemplified in (204).

(204) *Wajurra=ma=rna   pa-nangu-rra   **wilpa-nga**.*
       yesterday=TOP=1SG.S   go-PAST-IMPF   **creek-LOC**
       Yesterday I was walking along the creek.
       wrl-20180614-01, DK, 18:05 mins

Given the scarcity of the perlative in the corpus it is difficult to make any claims about its variation or status. However, there is some usage of *-wana* in both the 'heritage' corpus and the 'present' corpus, which may suggest that its low frequency is not a recent change.

4.1.9 Aversive

The aversive case *-kuma* marks a referent as something or someone 1) that is undesired and 2) whose negative effects are avoidable or can be mitigated. The referents are construed with and situated within an implicit and negatively evaluated event, as in (205), where *ngappa* 'water' is marked with aversive case, signifying an event of (undesired) rain, and in (206), where *wangani* 'dog' is marked, signifying that any conceivable event associated with this dog would be undesired.

(205) [**Ngappa-kuma**]=rna   mulpunga   purluny   ya-n.
 water-AVER=1SG.S   Shelter   enter   go-FUT
 For fear of the rain, I will enter the shelter.
 H_K01-506A, DG, 39:08 mins

(206) Kurtu   lamarta-ka   ayi=nya   [**wangani-kuma**].
 child   hold-IMP   that=FOC   **dog**-AVER
 Hold the child, for fear of the dog.
 wrl-20190205, DK, 58:34 mins

Dixon (2002: 171) notes that apprehensive meaning in many Australian languages is encoded as a special sense of a particular case suffix or encoded isomorphically as an increment to another case. The aversive in Warlmanpa follows the latter pattern, as its form is transparently built off the dative suffix *-ku* with an increment, *-ma* (this increment is phonologically identical to the topic clitic =*ma* but is unlikely to be related). Interestingly, both components are synchronically used in other Ngumpin-Yapa languages: the Warlpiri aversive case is also built off the dative suffix *-ku*, except its increment is *-jaku* (where *jaku* has no function on its own in Warlpiri). In Ngardi (Ennever 2018: 83), the increment is *-marra* (which is cognate with the Warlmanpa increment *ma* based on a regular VrrV > V sound correspondence), except the Ngardi base is the locative, not the dative, so follows the same widespread pattern observed in Western Desert languages (the apprehension systems of Ngumpin-Yapa languages, including Warlmanpa, are discussed in greater detail in Browne et al. 2024; and apprehension systems of other Australian languages are overviewed in Zester 2010). This is summarised in Table 4.8.

Table 4.8 Composition of the aversive case in Warlpiri, Warlmanpa and Ngardi

Language	Base	Increment
Warlpiri	-ku	-jaku
Warlmanpa	-ku	-ma
Ngardi	-ngka	-marra

Finite clause-level apprehension is encoded via an auxiliary base *nga=* combining with the auxiliary clitic *=nga* (see §5.4.3). However, *-kuma* can also behave as a non-finite complementiser, as discussed in §12.1.2.7.

4.1.10 Preparative purposive

The preparative purposive case *-kapina* seems to be an alternative to the allative case (and is parasitic to the allative case *-ka*), specifically for events that are not completed or are yet to begin, where *-kapina* indicates the intended goal of motion. The *pina* component may be related to *pina* 'return'. Examples of incomplete events are provided in (207)–(209), where the goal is marked with *-kapina*; (210) is an example of an event that was about to begin; and the use of *-kapina* in (211) is to indicate that the child chased the dog in the direction of the camp (marked with the preparative purposive), without committing to either participant actually making it into camp. Warlpiri has a suffix *-kungarnti* 'preparative purposive' that appears to have the same function (Nash 1986: 32); *-ngkawu* in Gurindji appears to have a similar function as well (Meakins and McConvell 2021). The Warlmanpa form differs from the Warlpiri form in both the 'base' (which appears to be the dative *-ku* in Warlpiri and the allative *-ka* in Warlmanpa) and the parasitic form (which is *pina* in Warlmanpa and *ngarnti* in Warlpiri). The Gurindji form appears to be *-ngka-wu* LOC-DAT, historically.

(207)   *Ngappa=nyanu*   *ka-nyinga*   **ngurra-kapina.**
water=RR   take-PATH   **camp-PREP**
She's carrying water for herself towards camp.
H_K06-004547, JW, 29:42 mins

(208)   *Wawirri=rna*   *karla-rnu,*   *nganjina-nganjinaka,*   **ngayinya-kapina,**
kangaroo=1SG.S   spear-PAST   RDP-towards_speaker   **1-PREP**
nganjinaka-rla.
towards_speaker-LOC
I speared a kangaroo coming towards me.
N_D02-007842, BN, 45:35 mins

(209)   *Pina=rna*   *ka-nganya*   **ngurra-kapina.**
return=1SG.S   take-PRES   **home-PREP**
I'm taking him back home.
wrl-20200219, DK, 30:50 mins

(210) **Ngurra-kapina**=rna pa-nyinga wirliya.
 camp-PREP=1SG.S go-PATH foot
 I'm about to walk home.
 wrl-20180614-02, DK, 13:18 mins

(211) Kurtu-ngu wirri yarnu maliki **ngurra-kapina**.
 child-ERG chase put-PAST dog **camp**-PREP
 The child chased the dog towards camp.
 wrl-20190201, DK, 11:46 mins

4.1.11 Desiderative

The desiderative case *-kupa* is offered by Warlmanpa speakers as the translation of Warlpiri *-ku-purda* 'desiderative purposive'. The referent of a desiderative marked nominal is one desired by the agent of the clause and expected to be obtained as a result of the main clausal event. It is formally parasitic to the dative suffix and its function is a subset of that of the dative suffix. The desired referent can be an entity, as in (212)–(214), or an event (in its complementising function), as discussed in §12.1.2.10.

(212) Kurtu lu-ngunya **ngampurlu-kupa**.
 child cry-PRES **milk**-DESIRE
 The child is crying for milk.
 H_K01-505B, DG, 47:47 mins

(213) Ngayu=ma=rna pa-nnya **kuyu-kupa**.
 1=TOP=1SG.S go-PRES **meat**-DESIRE
 I'm going for meat.
 H_K01-505B, DG, 47:57 mins

(214) Ngayu=rna pa-nangu-rnu **yarnunju-kupa**.
 1=1SG.S go-PAST-TWD **food**-DESIRE
 I came for food.
 N_D02-009887, DG, 24:31 mins

In Warlpiri, the cognate suffix *-kupurda* 'desiderative' does allow further suffixation, as in (215). There are no examples of *-kupa* in Warlmanpa occurring with a transitive predicate, so the classification of *-kupa* as a case morpheme is tentative (if the nominal with *-kupa* can also take ergative suffix, for example, it would be reclassified as a derivational suffix).

(215) | *Kaarr-paka-rni* | *ka=ju* | *warrarda* | *jurlpu-ngku*
frustrate-hit-NPAST | PRES=1SG.NS | frequently | bird-ERG

mangarri-kipurda-rlu.
veg_food-DESID-ERG

The bird is always bothering me for my food.
(Warlpiri [Laughren et al. 2022: 162–63])

4.1.12 Translative

The suffix *-karta* ascribes a quality as being a result of the event indicated by the main predicate (in other words, *-karta* marks a resultative secondary predicate).

For example, in (216), the main predicate refers to an event of cutting and the nominal *witta-witta* 'small-PL' (construed of the object *kuyu* 'meat') is marked with *-karta* to indicate that the object enters a state of small pieces because of the cutting. Further examples are given in (217) and (218).

(216) | *Ngayu=ma=rna* | *kuma-nmi* | *kuyu* | **wittawitta-karta.**
1=TOP=1SG.S | cut-FUT | meat | **small-TRANSL**

I'll cut the meat into small pieces.
wrl-20191208-01, DK, 36:46 mins

(217) | *Ngayu=ma=rna* | *pangu-rnu* | *ngulya* | **lawunpa-karta.**
1=TOP=1SG.S | dig-PAST | hole | **wide-TRANSL**

I dug a wide hole [that is, I dug a hole, causing it to be wide].
wrl-20200220, DK, 20:21 mins

(218) | *Kupa-ka* | *kuyu* | *kula* | **lijji-karta.**
cook-IMP | meat | NEG | **dry-TRANS**

Cook the meat, not too dry.
wrl-20180610-01, DK, 05:41 mins

The three examples given above are the only clear uses of *-karta* in the corpora. Furthermore, as discussed in §11.6, there are resultative secondary predicates that are not marked with *-karta*.

This suffix is shared with Warlpiri (*-karda*) and Ngardi (*-karra*) (Laughren et al. 2022; Ennever 2021). Unlike *-karra* in Ngardi, Warlmanpa *-karta* does not necessarily express the telic point of the action; rather, Warlmanpa *-karta* encodes a resultative state that may or may not have been the telic point.

Resultative secondary predicates are not obligatorily marked with -*karta*, as exemplified in (219), where the resultative state *pirtaku* 'satiated' is not marked with -*karra*. Particularly given the rarity of -*karta* in the corpus, it is not clear what is signalled by the use or non-use of -*karta* in these contexts.

(219)   *Yarnunju*   *nga-rnu*   **pirtaku**.
           food   eat-PAST   **satiated**
           He ate [until he was] full.
           wrl-20200219, DK, 23:15 mins

There is a suffix, -*karra* (and various allomorphs), in many Ngumpin languages that signals an iterative/continuative action (for Gurindji, Meakins and McConvell 2021; for Bilinarra, Meakins and Nordlinger 2014: 342; for Wanyjirra, Senge 2015: 433–34; for Jaru, Tsunoda 1981a: 241–42), which may be related, though the historical relation is only tentative given that these are disjointed sets of languages in terms of the function of -*karra*.

4.1.13 Concurrent

A nominal referring to a situation can be marked with -*puru* to indicate the situation is concurrent with that of the main predicate. In particular, -*puru* seems to be restricted to nominals representing weather or atmospheric states, although the suffix is infrequently used. Examples are given in (220)–(222).

(220)   *Ngarrka=lu*   *ka-nya*   *papulu-rla*   **ngappa-puru.**
           man=3PL.S   be-PRES   house-LOC   **rain-CONC**
           The men are sitting in the house **during the rain**.
           N_D02-007842, BN, 41:52 mins

(221)   *Karntakarnta-rlu=lu*   *ngurlu*   *jama-nnya*   **ngappa-puru**
           women-ERG=3PL.S   seeds   grind-PRES   **water-CONC**
           The women are grinding seeds **during the rain**.
           N_D02-007842, BN, 42:39 mins

(222)   *Yeah,*   '*wa-nganya=rna-ngu*   **yukurtu-puru**',   *partakurru*.
                        speak-PRES=1SG.S-2SG.NS   **smoke-CONC**   good
           Yeah, 'I'm talking to you **during the smoke**', good.
           (Said of prompt.)
           wrl-20191209, DK, 07:42 mins

In some cases, *-puru* is rejected on weather nominals. For example, *-puru* was rejected in the following utterance, with DK preferring the locative:

(223) *Karntakarnta-rlu=lu   jama-nnya   ngurlu   { **pirtiya-rla.**
      women-ERG=3PL.S   grind-PRES   seed   **cold-LOC**
                                                       pirtiya-puru.
                                                       cold-CONC }

The women are grinding seeds **in the cold/*during the cold**.
wrl-20191208-01, DK, 28:56 mins

The cognate suffix in Warlpiri is far more productive, even attaching to non-finite verbs to indicate simultaneity, as in (224). The suffix is also found in Wangkajunga, attaching to nominals to denote a season exhibiting features of the nominal stem (Jones 2011: 71–72). Furthermore, in some Ngayarda languages including Nyiyaparli, a suffix *-puru* 'attaches to an entity that is obscuring something or someone' (Battin 2019: 36).

(224) *Wiri-wiri   ka=lu   nyina   kurdu-kurdu   **manyu-karri-nja-puru.***
      big-big   PRES=3PL.S   sit.NPAST   child-child   **play-stand-INF-TEMPCOMP**

The grownups are sitting while the children **are playing**.
(Warlpiri, adapted from Simpson [1991: 106])

4.2 Adnominal case

Warlmanpa exhibits four adnominal suffixes: *-wangu* 'privative' (§4.2.1), *-jila* 'without' (§4.2.2), *-kurla* 'genitive' (§4.2.3) and *-parna* 'proprietive' (§4.2.4). Adnominal suffixes are characterised by their high productivity, adnominal function and morphological position immediately preceding case suffixes. There are no examples of two adnominal suffixes co-occurring (with each other). Adnominal suffixes bear morphological and semantic similarities to Blake's (1987a: 31–32, 81–86) 'pre-case' and to Simpson's (1991) 'derivational case' (also used by Ennever 2021). I use the term 'adnominal suffix' following other analyses of Ngumpin-Yapa languages (Meakins and Nordlinger 2014; Meakins and McConvell 2021; McConvell 1996b).

However, it should be noted that this is not an uncontroversial position: an alternative analysis would categorise these suffixes as case and subsequently explore an analysis of multiple case marking (à la Dench and Evans 1988), which would be compatible with the analysed functions of case discussed in §4.1.1.2. The two reasons I have not followed this analysis are: first, treating them as a separate class is typologically established in Ngumpin-Yapa grammars; and second, this analysis clearly reflects a morphosyntactic distinction, in that these suffixes may co-occur with case suffixes (in contrast to case suffixes, which cannot co-occur with other case suffixes). These arguments are clearly situated in the descriptive perspective of this work, to maximise the contrasts and establish similarities with related languages; however, a formal morphological treatment may better regard them as case suffixes, without the proliferation of extra categories exhibited by my analysis.

4.2.1 -wangu 'privative'

The privative suffix *-wangu* marks an entity as not existing, as in (225), or a situation as not eventuating, as in (226) (or an entity/situation being absent as far as discourse is concerned).

(225) | *Wajurrajurra=pala* | *pina* | *pa-nangu* | *nyaninya-parna* | *yiwirti-parna* |
| --- | --- | --- | --- | --- |
| afternoon=3DU.S | return | go-PAST | 3.GEN-PROP | stick-PROP |

kapi	*Wangani-parna*	*ngurra-ka=lku*	***yipakarli-wangu.***
CONJ	dog-PROP	home-ALL=THEN	**lizard-PRIV**

In the afternoon the child with his dog and spear went home, without any lizards.
wrl-20190207-01, DK, 57:55 mins

(226) | ***Jarta-wangu*** | *ali=nya* | *wangani* | *warlku* | *wa-nganyu-rra.* |
| --- | --- | --- | --- | --- |
| **sleep-PRIV** | that=FOC | dog | bark | speak-PAST-IMPF |

The sleepless dog was barking.
wrl-20190206, DK, 35:25 mins

Interestingly, the extremely semantically similar adnominal suffix *-jila* also expresses a privative meaning.

4.2.2 -*jila* 'without'

The adnominal suffix -*jila* marks an entity as being lacking or missing, as in (227).

(227) *Nyuntu=ma=n   yarti   ka-mi   ngayu-jila.*
      2=TOP=2SG.S   stay_in_camp   be-FUT   1-WITHOUT
      You'll stay in camp **without me**.
      wrl-20200224, DK, 28:12 mins

Like other adnominal case, -*jila* can be followed by case suffixes, as in (228) and (229).

(228) *Ngarrka-ngu=ma   kula   la-njakurla   kuyu=ma   makiti-jila-rlu.*
      man-ERG=TOP   NEG   shoot-CFACT   meat=TOP   gun-WITHOUT-ERG
      The man **lacking a gun** couldn't have shot the kangaroo.
      N_D02-007842, BN, 55:58 mins

(229) *Wayi-nya=rla   ngayinya-ku   wangani-ku   pijara-jila-ku.*
      search-PRES=3.OBL   1GEN-DAT   dog-DAT   ear-WITHOUT-DAT
      I'm looking for my **earless** dog.
      wrl-20200220, DK, 16:47 mins

Potentially cognate suffixes seem to further encode a 'detrimental' component to the lacking—for example, -*jirrija* in Ngardi denotes some referent as lacking to someone's detriment, which itself may be a borrowing from Western Desert languages (Ennever 2018: 125). However, it is not clear whether this is encoded by -*jila* in Warlmanpa.

This suffix can also be used as a subordinator (which is prototypically a feature of case in Warlmanpa), as exemplified in (230) and discussed further in §12.1.2.7.

(230) *Kuyu   kapi=rna-rla   yi-nyi,   nga-rninja-jila-ku.*
      meat   FUT=1SG.S-3.OBL   give-FUT   eat-INF-WITHOUT-DAT
      I'll give meat to the **hungry** [one].
      H_K01-506B: 66, DG, 06:54 mins

The difference between *-wangu* and *-jila* is not clear. Both are used to mark non-existent entities, non-eventuated situations and negative imperatives (including by the same speaker). There are also no clear sociolinguistic differences: speakers generally use both suffixes. This clearly remains an area for future research.

4.2.3 *-kurla* 'genitive'

The genitive suffix *-kurla* denotes the owner of the entity being construed. For example, in (231), the allative-marked nominal *ngulya-ka* 'hole-ALL' is modified by *karlawurru-kurla-ka* 'goanna-GEN-ALL' to indicate that the hole belongs to a goanna. Further examples are given in (232) and (233).

(231) Ali=nya   wari   purluny-wanu   **karlawurru-kurla-ka**   ngulya-ka.
      that=FOC snake   enter-fall-PAST   **goanna-GEN-ALL**   hole-ALL
      That snake went into the goanna's hole.
      wrl-20200219, DK, 01:21:09 hrs

(232) **Kilipanji-kurla-rla**=rna   ka-nya.
      police-GEN-LOC=1SG.S   be-PRES
      I'm at the police station.
      H_K01-506A, DG, 33:38 mins

(233) Yarti   ya-ka-pa=ju   **Doug-kurla-rla.**
      leave   put-IMP-AWAY=1SG.NS   **Doug-GEN-LOC**
      Leave me at 'Doug's Place' [a shop in town called 'Doug's Place'].
      wrl-20180614-02, DK, 17:49 mins

Warlpiri has a genitive suffix *-kurlangu* (Simpson 1988: 208) that may be cognate with this form. It is also likely that these suffixes are parasitic (perhaps historically) to the dative case *-ku* (which can be used for possession, as discussed in §4.1.4).

This suffix can also be used on genitive-marked pronouns, as in (234), where the possessive phrase *ngayinya kirta* 'my father' is marked with *-kurla* to indicate the subject, *yiwirti* 'spear', belongs to the speaker's father.

(234) Yumpa=nya=ma   yiwirti,   **ngayinya-kurla**   **kirta-kurla.**
      this=FOC=TOP   stick   **1GEN-GEN**   **father-GEN**
      This spear is my father's.
      H_K01-506A, DG, 49:44 mins

4.2.4 -*parna* 'proprietive'

The suffix -*parna* marks an entity that accompanies the entity being modified. Typically, this is accompaniment in space and time, as in (235), where *wangani-parna* 'dog-PROP' relates to the subject *Jungarrayi* to indicate that during the event denoted by the clause, *Jungarrayi* was accompanied by a *wangani*. Note that this does not encode participation in the event (though neither does it exclude the possibility). In (236), the accompaniment is more metaphorical.

(235)   *Jungarrayi=ma*   **wangani-parna**   *pa-nangu*   *wawirri-ku.*
Jungarrayi=TOP   **dog-PROP**   go-PROP   kangaroo-DAT
Jungarrayi went with his dog for kangaroos.
wrl-20180609-01, DK, 24:34 mins

(236)   **Kulykulypa-parna**=*lku=rna.*
fever-PROP=NOW=1SG.S
I have a cold.
H_K06-004555, LOF, 39:53 mins

It can also be used to denote an instrument, as in (237), or something that is characteristic of an entity, as in (238) (both these meanings are born of the general accompaniment meaning).

(237)   *Ngarrka-ngu*   *la-nu*   *yawirri*   **karli-parna-rlu.**
man-ERG   shoot-PAST   kangaroo   **boomerang-PROP-ERG**
The man shot the kangaroo with his boomerang.
wrl-20180610-01, DK, 01:06 mins

(238)   *Nganayi,*   **ngampurlu-parna**   *kala=rnalu*   *ka-nja-nu-rnu*
DUMMY   **milk-PROP**   HAB=1PL.EXCL.S   take-MOT-PAST-TWD
kala=rnalu   *yard-ka*   *ya-rnu-rra.*
HAB=1PL.EXCL.S   yard-ALL   put-PAST-IMPF
We used to bring the, what-you-call-it, the one with milk, we used to take it and put it in the yard.
N_D29-023128, MFN, 06:57 mins

As part of the accompaniment, the entity marked by -*parna* is often possessed by the entity to which it is relating (this appears to be used as a pseudo-possession construction, in contrast to other possession constructions that encode a possessor–possessum relationship; cf. §4.7.1).

(239) *Ngayu=ma=rna*   *ka-ngu-rra*   **jirrima-jinta-parna.**
       1=TOP=1SG.S   be-PAST-IMPF   **two-one-PROP**
       I was living there with [my] two children.
       wrl-20190208, DK, 21:43 mins

(240) *Ngayu=ma=rna*   *jinta-parna*   **wangani-parna.**
       1=TOP=1SG.S   one-PROP   **dog-PROP**
       I'm with [my] one dog.
       wrl-20200221, DK, 25:03 mins

Eastern Warlpiri has a cognate form, *-parnta* (Laughren et al. 2022). This form is not found in any Ngumpin languages.

4.3 Number marking

Number marking in Warlmanpa is rather heterogeneous: some number values have an associated nominal, some number values have suffixes (each number value that has a suffix then has multiple suffixes) and some nominals can be reduplicated to indicate their plurality, in lieu of a number suffix. The strategies are listed in Table 4.9.[5] All number suffixes are derivational and form a general nominal, regardless of the word class of the root. It should be noted that both strategies in this table are optional and not mutually exclusive.

Table 4.9 Nominal number marking

	Morphological exponent	Nominal(s)
General	—	—
Singular	—	*jinta*
Dual	*-ja(rra), -jima* 'dual'	*jirrima*
Plural	*-panji* 'paucal' *-tarra* 'plural' (some speakers) *-manta* 'plural' (demonstratives and free pronouns) Reduplication 'plural' (some human-referring nominals)	*jirrima-jinta* 'three' *jirrima-jirrima* 'four' *tartu* 'many'

---

5 Note that this discussion primarily pertains to count nouns. While the distinction between count nouns and mass nouns is not well understood in (this analysis of) Warlmanpa, my understanding is that mass nouns cannot take number suffixes but may be construed with a number nominal to force a count reading.

Each of the wide range of strategies to mark number using nominals is optional. Number marking is only obligatory for the bound pronouns (see §5.4). In this regard, any nominal unmarked for number is 'general' (in the sense of Corbett 2000: 9–18), not necessarily singular. The optionality of number marking on nominals is exemplified in (241), in which the bound pronoun coreferences the men with plural marking, but the nominal *yapa* does not exhibit number marking.

(241)   *Wanji*=***jana***   *papulu*   ***yapa-kurla.***
        where=**3PL.NS**   house   **man-**GEN
        Where is the men's house?
        H_K01-505B, DG, 01:04:03 hrs

The number suffixes can co-occur with the cardinal numerals, as in (242), where the nominal *jirrima* 'two' is marked for dual by the *-ja* 'dual' suffix.

(242)   *Nyuntu*=*npala*   ***jirrima-ja***   *ka-nya.*
        2=2DU.S   **two-**DUAL   sit-PRES
        You two are sitting.
        N_D01-007836: 053, JJN, 15:24 mins

The discussion of number marking in this section pertains primarily to the morphological exponents of number: dual marking is discussed in §4.3.1 and plural marking in §4.3.2. Within plural marking, *-tarra* (a suffix likely borrowed from Mudburra) is discussed in §4.3.2.1, *-panji* (a rarely used paucal suffix) in §4.3.2.2, *-manta* (a rarely used plural suffix restricted to demonstratives and free pronouns) in §4.3.2.1 and, finally, in §4.3.2.4 reduplication, which is common but restricted to a small set of nominals that refer to human entities.

Number suffixes in Warlmanpa cannot clearly be categorised as either derivational or inflectional. Like inflectional morphology, number suffixes have a predictable (or grammatical) meaning (Janda 2010) and show agreement when used. Unlike inflectional morphology, number suffixes are entirely optional (Stump 2015) and, like derivational morphology, number suffixes occur preceding other derivational morphology (with inflectional morphology occurring on the outside of the stem). Furthermore, number suffixes change the word class of the stem—deriving general nominals from free pronouns and demonstratives. However, Haspelmath (1996) argues against the notion that inflectional morphology cannot change the word class of its stem.

Quantification more generally (that is, across other parts of speech) is discussed in §4.7.3.

4.3.1 -ja(rra), -jima 'dual'

The dual suffix has several allomorphs. The most common are *-jarra* and *-ja*.

4.3.1.1 -jarra

(243) *Ngayu=rna-palangu* **ngarrka-jarra** *nya-nganya.*
1-1SG.S-3DU.NS **man-DU** see-PRES
I am looking at the **two men**.
H_K01-505B, DG, 52:52 mins

(244) *Ngayu=rna-palangu* *wa-nganya* **muku-jarra-ku.**
1-1SG.S-3DU.NS speak-PRES **this-DU-DAT**
I am speaking to **these two**.
H_K01-506A, DG, 06:36 mins

(245) **Ngayinya-jarra** **minija-jarra** *jirrima=pala.*
1GEN-DUAL **cat-DU** two=3DU.S
The two cats are mine.
wrl-20170328-01, SN, 06:50 mins

4.3.1.2 -ja

(246) **Maliki-ja-rlu**=*ju-pala* *pu-ngu.*
dog-DUAL-ERG=1SG.NS-3DU.S act_on-PAST
The two dogs bit me.
H_K01-505B, DG, 05:20 mins

(247) *Wanyjila=pala* **kurtu-ja** **nyintinya-ja.**
where=3DU.S **child-DU** **2GEN-DU**
Where are **your two children**?
H_K01-505B, DG, 29:59 mins

It is not clear what conditions the choice between *-ja* and *-jarra* (although *VrrV > V* appears to have been a historical sound change in Warlmanpa, this variation possibly reflects an ongoing change or remnants of where the sound change ceased diffusing).

There also appears to be a restricted dual suffix, *-jima*, as shown in (248), though this is the only example of *-jima* in the corpus.

(248)   **Karnta-jima**   *kari=pala*   *jitpi-nyi*   *nga=pala=nga*   *wa-nma.*
      woman-DU   COND=3DU.S   run-FUT   ADM=3DU.S=ADM   fall-POT
      The two women might fall over if they run.
      H_K01-505B, DG, 15:16 mins

The dual suffix derives a general nominal, regardless of the stem's part of speech. For example, the free pronouns *ngayu* and *nyuntu* do not inflect for core case (§3.1.7). Number suffixes derive a new nominal, which must then be inflected for case (where appropriate), as exemplified in (249).

(249)   **Ngayu-jarra-rlu**   *kuyu=ja*   *kupa-rnu.*
      1-DU-ERG   meat=1DU.EXCL.S   cook-PAST
      We two cooked the meat.
      wrl-20190213-02, DK, 14:59 mins

The demonstratives undergo a similar process when affixed with number suffixes. The proximal demonstrative series 'this' undergoes suppletion when inflected for case. Its unmarked form is *yimpa* 'this', but the dative form is *muku* 'this.DAT', which is analysed as a portmanteau (see §4.5 for a more detailed analysis). When *muku* hosts a number suffix, it becomes a general nominal, so must still host a dative suffix (that is, derivations derive morphosyntactically opaque nominals), despite the root being the dative form of the demonstrative, as in (250) and (251).

(250)   *Ngayu=rna-palangu*   *wa-nganya*   **muku-jarra-ku**
      1=1SG.S-3DU.NS   speak-PRES   **this.DAT-DU-DAT**
      I'm speaking to those two.
      H_K01-506A, DG, 06:36 mins

(251)   *Wanji=palangu*   *maliki*   **muku-jarra-ku**=ma?
      where=3DU.NS   dog   **this.DAT-DU-DAT**=TOP
      Where is the dog for these two?
      H_K01-506A, DG, 02:45 mins

4.3.2 Plural

Like dual suffixes, the plural expression (either the plural suffix or the word *tartu* 'many') of a referent is not grammatically obligatory within the nominals system (unlike the bound pronouns, where number marking is obligatory; see §5.4). The most common method is to use the nominal *tartu*, which is also found in Mudburra (Osgarby 2018).

(252) **Yapa** kala=lu **tartu** ka-ngu-rra.
person HAB=3PL.S **many** be-PAST-IMPF
Lots of people used to stay.
N_D29-023128, MFN, 01:56 mins

(253) **Ngarrka-ngu**=ju-lu **tartu-ngu** nya-nganya.
man-ERG=1SG.NS-3PL.S **many-ERG** see-PRES
Lots of men are looking at me.
H_K01-505B, DG, 48:47 mins

(254) **Tartu-ngu**=lu nya-ngu.
many-ERG=3PL.S see-PAST
They saw him.
N_D03-007868, BN, 18:45 mins

There are a few rare morphological ways to encode plurality: *-tarra*, *-panji*, *-manta* and reduplication, which are now discussed in turn.

4.3.2.1 *-tarra* 'plural'

Present-day speakers may use *-tarra* to indicate plurality, as exemplified in (255) and (256).

(255) **Jurlaka-tarra**=lu nga-rninya.
bird-PL=3PL.S eat-PRES
Lots of birds are eating.
wrl-20170321-02, SN, 16:44 mins

(256) *Pawarrayi*=lu **ngarrka-tarra**=ma partu-nga la-nja-ku kuyu-ku.
all=3PL.S **man-PLUR**=TOP leave-PAST. shoot- meat-DAT
AWAY INF-DAT
All the men left to hunt game.
wrl-20191208-01, DK, 40:40 mins

This suffix is not found in the heritage corpus, although it is productive in the present corpus and in Mudburra (Osgarby 2018: 249). The recent use of *-tarra* in Warlmanpa likely reflects a recent borrowing (all speakers who use *-tarra* also speak Mudburra). Interestingly, in Mudburra, *-tarra* cannot attach to free pronouns other than third person (that is, first person and second person have special number suffixes, similar to the system in the Warlmanpa heritage corpus), however, in Warlmanpa there is evidence *-tarra* can attach to free pronouns.

(257)   *Nyuntu=nganpa-n*   *wayi-rnu-rra*   **ngayu-tarra-ku.**
        2=1PL.EXCL-2SG.S   search-PAST-IMPF   1-PLUR-DAT
        You were looking for us mob.
        wrl-20191208-01, DK, 17:49 mins

This may reflect a two-step change in Warlmanpa. In the heritage material, there is no generic plural suffix, except for free pronouns and demonstratives (§4.3.2.3). It is likely *-tarra* began to be used on some nominals in Warlmanpa, while not using it on free pronouns, given that: a) there already existed a plural suffix for this purpose in Warlmanpa, and b) it is not used on the free pronouns in Mudburra. However, as the suffix increased in usage in Warlmanpa, it was integrated alongside the dual suffix, being used on free pronouns and nominals. This change is represented in Table 4.10.

Table 4.10 Likely stages of borrowing -tarra from Mudburra

	T1 >	T2 >	T3
	Heritage system		**Present system**
Nominal plural suffix	—	*-tarra*	*-tarra*
Free pronoun suffix	*-manta*	*-manta*	*-tarra*

4.3.2.2 -*panji* 'paucal'

The paucal suffix *-panji* denotes a small set of referents, minimally three (evidenced by the plural agreement in the bound pronouns), however, it is unclear how much higher than three would be acceptable using *-panji*. It does not appear to be used by any present speakers and in the heritage materials it is offered as the translation of Warlpiri *-patu*, which denotes 'definite plural, lesser plural' (Nash 1986: 24).

(258) **Karnta-panji** kari=lu jitpi-nyi nga=lu=nga wa-nma.
woman-PAUC COND=3PL.S run-FUT POST=3PL.S=DUB fall-POT
If the few women run, they might fall.
H_K01-505B: DG, DG, 15:04 mins

(259) **Ngarrka-panji**-rlu=ju-lu nya-nganya.
man-PAUC-ERG=1SG.NS-3PL.S see-PRES
Those men are looking at me.
N_D01-007836, JJN, 22:43 mins

(260) Ngarrka-ngu=nganpa nya-nganya **ngayu-panji**.
man-ERG=1PL.EXCL.NS see-PRES **1**-PAUC
The man is looking at us few.
N_D01-007836: 100, JJN, 23:23 mins

(261) **Nyuntu-panji**-rlu=ju-nkulu nya-nganya ngayu.
2-PAUC-ERG=1SG.NS-2PL.S see-PRES 1
You few men are looking at me.
N_D01-007836: 140, JJN, 30:52 mins

4.3.2.3 -*manta* 'restricted plural'

The restricted plural suffix *-manta* is restricted to demonstratives and free pronouns and, furthermore, is used only by speakers in the heritage corpus.

(262) Ngayu=rna-jana wa-nganya **muku-manta**-ku.
1=1SG.S-3PL.NS speak-PRES **this**-RPL-DAT
I'm speaking to this mob.
H_K01-506A, DG, 06:44 mins

(263) Wanyji=jana maliki **muku-manta**-ku=ma.
where=3PL.NS dog **this**-RPL-DAT=TOP
Where are the dogs for them?
H_K01-506A, DG, 02:37 mins

(264) Ngarrka-ngu=nyangu nya-nganya **nyuntu-manta**.
man-ERG=2PL.NS see-PRES **2**-RPL
The man is looking at you mob.
H_K01-505B, DG, 59:01 mins

(265) Ngayu   kapi=rna-jana   wanga   **yarri-manta-ku.**
      1   FUT=1SG.S-3PL.NS   talk[FUT] **that-RPL-DAT**
      I will talk to that mob.
      H_K01-506A, DG, 07:16 mins

Younger speakers seem to avoid the use of *-manta*—for example, the free pronoun in (266) has *-tarra* 'plural' instead. There are no tokens of *-manta* 'RPL' in the present corpus.

(266) Nyuntu=nganpa-n   wayi-rnu-rra   **ngayu-tarra-ku.**
      2=1PL.EXCL.NS-2SG.S   search-PAST-IMPF   **1-PL-DAT**
      You were looking for us mob.
      wrl-20191208-01, DK, 17:49 mins

4.3.2.4 Reduplication

Nominal reduplication indicates plurality and only productively occurs with nominals referring to human entities. Reduplication as a more general process in Warlmanpa is discussed in §2.8.

(267) **Pulka~pulka**=lu   yama-nga   ka-nya.
      old_man~PLUR=3PL.S   shade-LOC   sit-PRES
      The old men are sitting in the shade.
      H_K01-505B, DG, 41:37 mins

(268) Ngayu=rna purtu-ka-nya ngula=lu **witta~wtita**=wiyi ka-ngu-rra.
      1=1SG.S   listen-be-PRES REL=3PL.S **small~PLUR**=STILL be-PAST-IMPF
      I remember back when they were small.
      N_D02-007842, BN, 34:14 mins

(269) Kantukantu=lpa   **yapa~yapa**   ka-nji-nmi.
      hide=1INC.PL.S   **person~PLUR**   be-INC-FUT
      We people have to start hiding ourselves.
      N_D02-007844, BN, 26:18 mins

4.4 Derivational suffixes

There are many similarities between 'case' and 'derivational' morphology in Ngumpin-Yapa languages (Simpson [1991: 58] also notes difficulties in classifying Warlpiri suffixes into coherent groups). The distinction between 'case morphology' and 'derivational suffixes' is based on morphological rather than semantic grounds—specifically the relative ordering between suffixes. Derivational suffixes are those that occur closest to the nominal root. Each known derivational suffix is now discussed in turn.

4.4.1 -Nginja, -nganja, -nganjarri, -kanjarri, -piya 'like'

There are several related suffixes sharing a central meaning of 'like' that are difficult to tease apart. Three of the forms demonstrate a clear lenition scale: *-kanjarri ~ -nganjarri ~ -nganja*, and somehow related is *-nginja*, although it is not clear what triggers the vowel change. Additionally, there is one form, *-piya*, which is phonologically unrelated. Both these sets have cognates in Warlpiri: *-kanjarri/-kanjayi* (subsequently lenited in Warlmanpa in most cases) is a suffix denoting a distance and *-piya* denotes a similarity. The meaning of the *-kanjarri set in Warlmanpa has generalised to a semblative much like *-piya*, although the *-nganjarri* and *-kanjarri* forms can still be used to denote a spatial resemblance. Due to the difficulties in clearly delimiting the transition between *-kanjarri* (used specially for spatial distances)[6] and *-nganja* (used as a general semblative), I have tentatively opted to treat them under a single gloss, 'LIKE'. I use the gloss 'LIKE$_2$' for *-piya*, as its form is clearly unrelated, so I am unable to ascertain a meaningful difference.[7] This discussion is summarised in Table 4.11 and examples follow in (270)–(282). As shown in the table, two of the forms, *-kanjarri* and *-nganja*, are found only once in the corpus and *-nganjarri* is used by only one speaker in the corpus. It is unclear whether this reflects a lack of use by other speakers or poverty of data.

---

6   There is only one example of *-kanjarri* in the corpus, so it is possible this was an accidental use of the Warlpiri form. The other forms (*-nganjarri*, *-nganja*, *-nginja*) are far more common.
7   Doris Kelly has told me that *-piya* is the Warlpiri form and *-nganjarri* (etcetera) are the Warlmanpa forms.

Table 4.11 Overview of Warlmanpa semblative forms and functions with corresponding Warlpiri cognate forms and functions

Warlmanpa form	Warlmanpa function(s)	Approximate frequency	Warlpiri cognate	Warlpiri cognate function
-nginja	General semblative (not clearly used for spatial distance)	Common	-kanjarri	Semblative restricted to spatial distance
-nganja		Rare (1)		
-nganjarri	Semblative used for spatial and non-spatial distance	Common (though tokens from only one speaker)		
-kanjarri	Semblative restricted to spatial distance (though limited tokens)	Rare (1)		
-piya	General semblative	Common	-piya	General semblative

4.4.1.1 -nginja

(270) *Kuya-nginja=ma:* '*yarnunju=ma ma-nja-ku nga-rninja-ku*'.
thus-LIKE=TOP vegetable=TOP take-INF-DAT eat-INF-DAT
Like this: 'vegetables are for taking and eating'.
wrl-20160908-01, SN, 04:05 mins

(271) *Karli-nginja kirtily ka-nya.*
boomerang-LIKE bendy be-PRES
It's bendy like a boomerang.
wrl-20190213-01, DK, 20:34 mins

(272) *Nyapa-nginja=n marta-nnya?*
how-LIKE=2SG.S hold-PRES
What kind do you have?
wrl-20200219, DK, 02:43 mins

4.4.1.2 -nganja

(273) *Papulanyi-nganja=rnalu ka-nya*
white_person-LIKE=1PL.EXCL.S be-PRES
We are like white people.
H_K01-506A, DG, 35:48 mins

4.4.1.3 -nganjarri

(274) Ali-nganjarri   kiya-ka!
       that-LIKE₁   throw-IMP
       Throw it that far! (Speaker translation)
       wrl-20200220, DK, 31:08 mins

(275) Nyuntu-   nya-ngu,   kala   yangka.
       nganjarri=rna-ngu
       2-LIKE=1SG.S-2SG.NS   see-PAST   but   another
       I saw someone like you, but it was someone else.
       wrl-20200224, DK, 21:29 mins

(276) Jilij-ka-nganya: 'Nya-ngu=ju-n   ngayinya   wangani   yumpa-nganjarri?'
       ask-take-PRES   see-PAST=1SG.   1GEN   dog   this-LIKE
                              NS-2SG.S
       One asks: 'Have you seen my dog like this one?'
       wrl-20200224, DK, 24:44 mins

4.4.1.4 -kanjarri

(277) Ali-kanjarri=lu   ka-ngu-rra.
       that-LIKE=3PL.S   be-PAST-IMPF
       They're sitting that far away.
       wrl-20200220, DK, 29:59 mins

4.4.1.5 -piya

(278) Nyapa-piya=n   ma-nmi?
       how-LIKE₂=2SG.S   get-FUT
       What type will you get?
       wrl-20200219, DK, 02:20 mins

(279) Warlmanpa-piya=rna   wa-nganya.
       Warlmanpa-LIKE₂=1SG.S speak-PRES
       I speak like a Warlmanpa.
       H_K01-506A, DG, 32:18 mins

(280) *Lulykurlulyku-piya*   *ka-nya*   *ngurrawaji=ma.*
rose_ringed_parakeet-LIKE₂   be-PRES   budgerigar=TOP
The budgerigar bird is like the rose ringed parakeet.
H_K01-506A, DG, 32:18 mins

(281) *Yawirri-piya*   *purlpaj*   *nga-rninya.*
kangaroo-LIKE₂   jump   eat-PRES
He's jumping like a kangaroo.
(Or: the kangaroo-like [thing] is jumping.)
wrl-20191208-02, DK, 26:01 mins

(282) *Ali=nya*   *yapa*   *witta*   *kirtana-piya=yi.*
that=FOC   person   small   father-LIKE₂=STILL
That child is just like his father.
wrl-20191208-02, DK, 24:25 mins

4.4.2 -*warnu* 'source'

A nominal marked with -*warnu* indicates a cause that has impacted the entity with which it is construed. For example, in (283), the subject is said to be tired, with -*warnu* marking the nominal referring to the event that caused the tiredness (*yajka-warnu* 'from travelling'). Further examples are given in (284)–(286).

(283) *Palapala=rna*   *ka-nya*   **yajka-warnu.**
tired=1SG.S   be-PRES   **travel-SOURCE**
I'm tired from travelling.
H_K01-505B, DG, 28:09 mins

(284) *Jirrmirinypa=rna*   *jut-pungunya*   **parra-warnu.**
sweat=1SG.S   run-PRES   **sun-SOURCE**
I'm sweating from the sun.
H_K01-505B, DG, 39:07 mins

(285) *Kuyu*   *nga-rnu*   *ngarrkangu*   **wirliya-warnu-rlu.**
meat   eat-PAST   man-ERG   **foot-SOURCE-ERG**
The man ate the meat [he got] from walking.
N_D02-007842, BN, 45:20 mins

(286) Yina   nga-nmi=lpa   **lijinpa-warnu.**
      sing   eat-FUT=1PL.INC.S   **ill-SOURCE**

We're singing from illness [translated by speaker as 'for health'].
Nash fieldnotes, 08/09/1981, TWN.[8]

Like the elative case *-ngurlu*, *-warnu* can attach to *(y)ali* 'that' to indicate a progression of time in a narrative, as in (287). Notably, Nash (1986: 31) describes the Warlpiri suffix of the same form as an 'elative of source'.

(287) a. *Witta*   *yapa-ngu*   *nya-ngu*   *wangani-parna-rlu.*
         small   child-ERG   see-PAST   dog-PROP-ERG
         A child with her dog saw [a kangaroo].

      b. ***Ali-warnu**=ma* *yangka=lku=lu*   *payangka*   *kapu-ngu.*
         that-SOURCE=TOP another=THEN=3PL.S intercept   chase-PAST
         After that, then they found another kangaroo.
         wrl-20200220, DK, 04:39 mins

Interestingly, *-warnu* exhibits allomorphy based on the word class of its host: nominals take *-warnu*, whereas infinitive verb forms (that is, infinitives) take *-ngarnu* (see §12.1.2.3), despite infinitive verbs being essentially nominals in most other regards. The form *-warnu* is shared with Warlpiri and Mudburra, neither of which language has an allomorph *-ngarnu* (Laughren et al. 2022; Osgarby 2018: 215). Gurindji and Bilinarra have a suffix, *-nginyi*, that performs a similar function (Meakins and McConvell 2021; Meakins and Nordlinger 2014: 139–43).

4.4.3 *-kanyanu* 'another'

Attaching the suffix *-kanyanu* to a nominal denotes that this nominal refers to an entity or entities that increase a previously established set. For example, in (288), the speaker had already discussed her firstborn son, and *jirrima* 'two' hosts *-kanyanu* 'another', which denotes these two sons are in addition to the previously introduced son.

---

8 The notes provide the translation: 'They're singing from health.'

(288) | *Ngula=ja* | *pina* | *pa-nangu* | *Alekarengi-ka*
REL=1DU.EXCL.S | return | go-PAST | Alekarenge-ALL
martu-rnu=rna | | *kurtu* | *jirrima-kanyanu=lku.*
have-PAST=1SG.S | | child | TWO-ANOTHER=THEN

I had two more sons when we returned to Alekarenge.
wrl-20190211-01, DK, 06:00 mins

Further examples are given in (289)–(291).

(289) *Wajurra-kanyanu=rnalu* *pa-nangu.*
yesterday-ANOTHER=1PL.EXCL.S go-PAST
We went the day before yesterday.
wrl-20190131-03, DK, 01:10 mins

(290) *Karli-ku=ju-rla* *yapa-kanyanu-rlu* *wayi-nnya.*
boomerang-DAT=1SG.NS-DAT person-ANOTHER-ERG search-PRES
Another person is looking for a boomerang for me.
H_K01-505B, DG, 01:00:28 hrs

(291) *Nguru-kanyanu-rla* *yirrarra-ja-nnya.*
country-ANOTHER-LOC lonely-INCH-PRES
I'm feeling lonely in another country.
N_D02-007842, BN, 33:41 mins

Narratives may begin with *parra-kanyanu* 'sun-ANOTHER', which seems to be a frozen form referring to 'one day' (that is, some irrelevant day: literally 'another sun'), as in (292).

(292) | *Parra-kanyanu* | *wirlinyi* | *partu-nga* | *kurtu* | *wangani-parna*
SUN-OTHER | hunting | leave-PAST.AWAY | child | dog-PROP
wayi-nja-ku | *yipakarli-ku* | *kapi* | *jurlaka-ku.*
search-INF-DAT | lizard-DAT | CONJ | bird-DAT

One day he went away hunting with a dog, to search for lizards or birds.
wrl-20190207-01, DK, 42:31 mins

4.4.4 -wartingi 'resident of'

The suffix *-wartingi* attaches to nominals denoting locations that are the residence of the entity being construed at the time. It allows both location names, as in (293) and (294), and natural habitats, as in (295).

(293) *Ngayu=ma=rna* **Brisbane-wartingi.**
1=TOP=1SG.S **Brisbane-RESIDE**
I'm a Brisbane-ite.
wrl-20190213-01, DK, 24:17 mins

(294) **Tennant Creek-wartingi-rlu**=*ju-rla* *wayi-rnu-rra.*
Tennant Creek-RESIDE-ERG=1SG.NS-3.OBL search-PAST-IMPF
The Tennant Creek-ian was looking for me for someone.
wrl-20200219, DK, 49:13 mins

(295) *Jalajirrpa=ma=lu* **lamanpa-wartingi.**
white_cockatoo=TOP=3PL.S **hollow-RESIDE**
White cockatoos live in tree hollows.
(Lit.: white cockatoos are hollow-residers.)
wrl-20200219, DK, 01:28:16 hrs

In Warlpiri, the suffix *-wartingki* performs the same function, but can also be used to denote habitual activities, as in (296), suggesting *-wartingi* in Warlmanpa may have a broader usage than what is found in the corpus.

(296) *Karnta-ngku* *ka=lu-nyanu* **yawulyu-wardingki-patu-rlu** *palka*
woman-ERG PRES=3PL.S-RR **ceremony-RESIDE-PL-ERG** body
wari-rni *yinirnti-kirli-rli* *wirnti-nja-ku-ngarnti-rli.*
tie-NPST bean_tree-PROP-ERG dance-INF-DAT-PREP-ERG
Women who are involved in ceremonies drape strings of *yinirnti* beans around their bodies before dancing.
(Warlpiri [Laughren et al. 2022: 1127])

4.4.5 -ngarnarra 'denizen'

There are only two instances of *-ngarnarra* in the corpus, which are given in (298). Based on these examples, the use of the suffix appears to translate as 'one who lives at X'. This is like the derivational suffix *-wartingi* (§4.4.4), and the distinction is likely that *-ngarnarra* is used for habitats or permanent dwellers, whereas *-wartingi* refers only to a place of residence at a particular time. Examples are given in (297) and (298).

(297) *Bu̱sẖ-ngarnarra-tarra. wi̱ld̠ o̱ne̱-tarra=rna-jana ya-rnu-rra.*
Bush-DENIZEN-PL   wild_one-PL=1SG.S-3PL.NS   put-PAST-IMPF
Lots of the bush residents. I put [painted] lots of wild ones.
N_D_20071010, SN, 01:06 mins

(298) *Yurtuminyi-ngarnarra, puwarrijpa ngula ka-ngu-rra Yurtuminyi-rla.*
place-DENIZEN   dreaming   rel   be-PAST-IMPF   place-LOC
He lives in Yurtuminyi, the dreaming is for him who lives at Yurtuminyi.
N_D09-013557, DG, 00:48 secs

The form *-ngarnarra* was not recognised by my consultants during fieldwork and only *-wartingi* was used. This suffix may reflect a borrowing from Mudburra or Warlpiri: both languages have *-ngarna ~ -nganarra*. While in Mudburra it is not clear what conditions the variation (see Osgarby 2018: 248), the Warlpiri forms are conditioned by the number of entities residing in the habitat, where *-ngarnarra* is reserved for multiple entities—that is, a plural form (Laughren et al. 2022). In Ngardi (Ennever 2018), similar forms are found: one form, *nga(r)na*, relates an entity to a place (in particular, ecological zones) and another form, *-wardingki*, relates an entity to a geographical area (such as a town). Gurindji and Bilinarra also have the form *-ngarna*, which is an associative suffix (Meakins and McConvell 2021; Meakins and Nordlinger 2014) that is likely related to Warlmanpa's *-ngarnarra*. This is one of the only suffixes that seems not to have undergone the VrrV > V sound change in Warlmanpa.

4.4.6 *-palka* 'associative'

The suffix *-palka* indicates a quality strongly associated with the entity of which it is being construed. It is translated by Warlmanpa speakers for Warlpiri *-panu* 'excessively' and is very rarely used in the corpus. Examples are given in (299)–(301).

(299) *Marrimarri   kili-palka.*
cheeky   fight-ASSOC
Cheeky ones are fighters.
H_K06-004555, LOF, 59:30 mins

(300) *Yumpa-manta=lu   ka-nya   Jupula-palka=yi.*
      this-RPL=3PL.S   be-PRES   Jupula-ASSOC=STILL
      These ones are associated with only Jupulas.
      H_K01-506A, DG, 06:22 mins

(301) *Maliki   yimpa,   kuyu-palka.*
      dog   this   meat-ASSOC
      This dog, he's a hunter.
      H_K01-506B, DG, 07:34 mins

4.4.7 *-ni* 'nomic'

A nominaliser, *-ni*, suffixes to an infinitive that indicates that an entity habitually performs the action denoted by the infinitive. Examples are given in (302) and (303).

(302) *Kupa-nja-ni.*
      cook-INF-NOM
      He's a cook.
      N_D03-007868, BN, 29:17 mins

(303) *Maliki   kapi=rna   la-nmi   pi-nji-ni.*
      dog   FUT=1SG.S   hit-FUT   bite-INF-NOM
      I will hit the bitey dog.
      H_K01-505B, DG, 27:19 mins

The object of a nomic infinitive may have the dative suffix, as exemplified in (304) and (305), though not necessarily (see [1,187] and [1,230]).

(304) *Maliki   nga=rna   purt   pi-nyi   **kuyu-ku   nga-rninji-ni.***
      dog   POST=1SG.S   send   act_on-FUT meat-DAT   eat-INF-NOM
      I will hunt away the dog who eats a lot of meat.
      H_K01-505B, DG, 34:23 mins

(305) *Ngayinya   kirta-na   **kuyu-ku   paka-nji-ni.***
      1.GEN   father-MY   meat-DAT   hit-INF-NOM
      My father kills a lot of game.
      H_K01-506B, DG, 07:17 mins

This suffix is only present in the heritage corpus and appears to not be used by present-day speakers. Gurindji has a nominaliser, *-ny-*, creating nominals from nominals and coverbs with a general semantic correspondence of association (Meakins and McConvell 2021), which may be related to this nominaliser (this suffix is also found in Bilinarra, though seemingly only attaching to demonstratives and coverbs [Meakins and Nordlinger 2014: 174–75]).

4.5 Demonstratives

Warlmanpa has seven demonstratives. *Yimpa* 'this', *yarri* 'that' and *yali* 'that (removed)' are primarily related to spatial proximity (§4.5.1); *yayi* 'the' relates to definiteness (§4.5.2); *nyanungu* 'the aforementioned' relates to discourse proximity (§4.5.3); *nyamu* 'that time' relates to temporal location (§8.4.1); and *kuya* 'thus' relates to a manner of doing (§8.4.1).

The spatial proximity demonstratives are given in Table 4.12, along with their inflections for the most common nominal cases. The inflectional possibilities of the other demonstratives are less well documented.

Table 4.12 Spatial proximity demonstratives inflected for most nominal cases

	Proximal	Distal	Distal (removed)
Abs	yimpa ~ yumpa	yarri	yali
Erg	murlu	yarrirlu	yalirlu
Dat	muku	yarriku	yaliku
Gen	mukurla	yarrikurla	yalikurla
Loc	mirla(yi)	yarrirla	yalirla ~ yalinga
All	muka	yarrika*	yalika
Ela	mungkurlu	yarring(k)urlu*	yalingurlu

Note: * predicted forms

As can be seen, *yimpa* has suppletion in any non-absolutive context; the root becomes *mu-/mi-*. All the demonstratives take the polysyllabic-stem allomorph of cases (that is, the ergative form of *yarri* is *yarrirlu*, rather than *yarringu). Interestingly, while the proximal series generally reflects the synchronic nominal suffixes, the elative form is *mungkurlu* with a nasal + stop cluster, whereas for other nominals the elative suffix is *-ngurlu*, without a stop. *Nyanungu* 'the aforementioned' also inflects for case, though this is less clear for *nyamu* 'that time' and *kuya* 'thus'; there is no evidence these can inflect, although there are insufficient data to be certain. *Kuya* can, however, take two suffixes otherwise restricted to cardinals: *kuyarni* 'towards speaker' and *kuyapurta* 'away from speaker' (*-rni* and *-purta* are discussed in §8.3). Note also that while they are not represented in the table, many of the high vowels in the demonstrative roots are particularly prone to vowel harmony processes (§2.7.1.1).

The suppletive forms are interesting from a historical perspective: demonstrative suppletion is not found in Warlpiri, whereas Bilinarra and Gurindji also have a suppletive root *murlu-/murla-* for the proximal series, except the uninflected lexeme is *nyawa*—clearly unrelated to the uninflected form *yimpa* in Warlmanpa (Meakins and McConvell 2021; Meakins and Nordlinger 2014: 170). This suggests that the root *murlu* was reanalysed in Warlmanpa as *mu-rlu*, given *-rlu* is an ergative allomorph. The paradigm of the proximal series in each language is given in Table 4.13.

Table 4.13 The proximal demonstrative series in Warlmanpa, Bilinarra, Gurindji and Warlpiri

	Warlmanpa	Bilinarra	Gurindji	Warlpiri
Absolutive[9]	*yimpa ~ yumpa*	*nyawa*	*nyawa*	*nyampu*
Ergative	*mu-rlu*	*murlu-lu*	*murlu-ngku*	*nyampu-rlu*
Dative	*mu-ku*	*murlu-wu*	*murlu-wu*	*nyampu-ku*
Locative	*mi-rla*	*murla-la*	*murla-ngka*	*nyampu-rla*
Allative	*mu-ka*	*murla-nggurra*	*murla-ngkurra*	*nyampu-kurra*
Elative/ablative	*mu-ngkurlu*	*murla-ngurlu*	*murla-ngurlu*	*nyampu-ngurlu*

4.5.1 Spatial proximity demonstratives *yimpa*, *yarri* and *yali*

The demonstratives *yimpa*, *yarri* and *yali* primarily refer to the spatial proximity of the speaker. *Yimpa* is used for close proximity, *yarri* for mid-proximity and *yali* for removed proximity.

To exemplify, two objects (pens) were placed on a table between the speaker and the addressee—one that was close to the speaker and one that was close to the addressee, as depicted in Figure 4.1. As given in (306), the object more proximal to the speaker was translated as *yumpanya* and the object less proximal to the speaker was translated as *alinya*. Notably, neither pen was known to either interlocutor before the prompt, so recognition/discourse status is unlikely to be a conditioning factor in this prompt.

---

9 Analysed as the nominative and accusative series in Bilinarra and Gurindji.

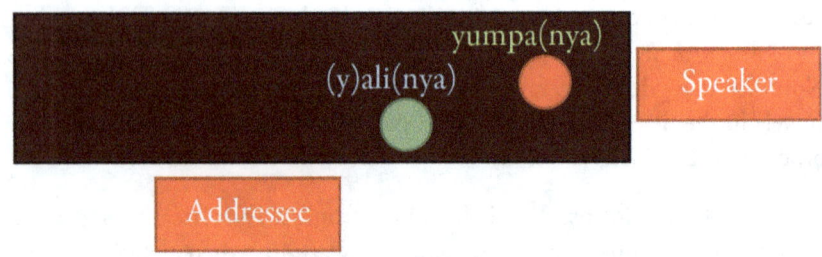

Figure 4.1 Configuration that prompted Example (306)

(306) *This one's* **yumpa=nya,** *and that's* **ali=nya.**
 this=FOC that=FOC
 This one is '*yumpanya*' and that is '*alinya*'.
 wrl-20190213-01, DK, 19:25 mins

For DK, and sporadically for some other speakers, the initial /j/ of *yali* (and other /j/-initial demonstratives) does not surface (this may be an influence from Warumungu, in which the demonstrative root is *ala/alu/ali*).

In Nash (1979), *yimpa* is glossed as 'this', *yarri* as 'that' and *yali* as 'that (removed)'. Examples of each of the demonstratives are given below. As the examples show, demonstratives are loci of the prominence marker =*nya* (§9.4.5). Note that in the glosses here, I indicate a morpheme boundary between the suppletive room *mu/mi-* and the case form, though elsewhere in the grammar these are treated as portmanteau forms, mainly due to: 1) the case forms being the polysyllabic-stem forms, which is not predicted from the 'synchronic' analysis of the allomorphy; and 2) the unexpected form of the proximal elative *mungkurlu*, as noted earlier.

4.5.1.1 Yimpa 'this' (proximal)

(307) *Pamarrpa* **yumpa** *rampaku.*
 rock **this** light
 This rock is light.
 H_K01-506A, DG, 30:38 mins

(308) **Mu-rlu**=*nya* *wangani-rlu* *yilyi-ngu* *nga-rnu.*
 this-ERG=FOC dog-ERG greedy-ERG eat-PAST
 This greedy dog ate [it].
 wrl-20200219, DK, 01:15:39 hrs

(309) **Mi-rla**=yi=li ka-mi jirrima-ku ngurra-ku.
this-LOC=STILL=1DU.INCL.S be-FUT two-DAT camp-DAT
We'll stay here for two days.
wrl-20191207-02, DK, 08:35 mins

(310) Pawarrayi=lpa parti-ma **mu-ngkurlu**=ma.
completely=1PL.INCL.S leave-FUT.AWAY **this**-ELA=TOP
We all should get out from here.
N_D02-007842, BN, 04:18 mins

4.5.1.2 *Yarri* 'that' (distal)

(311) Warlmanpa=rla wa-ngka **yarru-ku**=nya.
Warlmanpa=3.OBL speak-IMP **that**-DAT=FOC
Speak Warlmanpa to that one!
H_K01-505B, DG, 16:26 mins

(312) Ngarrka=rla wa-nganyu karnta-ku 'Kula **yarri**=nya
man=3.OBL speak-PAST woman-DAT NEG **that**=FOC
yapa-ngu nga-rnu-rra.'
child-ERG eat-PAST-IMPF
A man said to a woman, 'The child wasn't eating that.'
N_D02-007842, BN, 53:54 mins

(313) Kaya Jakamarra, **yarri**=nya kanja=ngu warna!
watch_out Jakamarra **that**=FOC close=2SG.NS snake
Watch out Jakamarra, that snake is beside you!
N_D02-007841, BN, 03:53 mins

4.5.1.3 *Yali* 'that' (distal, removed)

(314) Yulu **yali**=ma tuyu-ka-nya.
dust **that**=TOP waft-be-PRES
That dust is blowing around.
H_K06-004547, JW, 32:06 mins

(315) Ka-rra **yali-rla.**
be-IMP **that**-LOC
Stand there!
wrl-20190123, SN, 20:32 mins

(316) *Kula*   **ali-nga**=*nya*   *warlu-nga*   *kutij*   *ka-rra*.
NEG   **that-LOC**=FOC   fire-LOC   stand   be-IMP
Don't stand in that fire!
wrl-20180610-01, DK, 14:12 mins

(317) *Ngayu*=*ma*=*rna-rla*   *lani-ja-nya*   **ali-ku**=*nya*   *wangani-ku*.
1=TOP=1SG.S-3.OBL   afraid-INCH-PRES   **that-DAT**=FOC   dog-DAT
I'm afraid of that dog.
wrl-20200221, DK, 36:12 mins

The distal series *yarri* seems to have fallen out of use with younger speakers, with the distinction collapsing to *yimpa* 'this' and *yali* 'that'. Conversely, *yali* is rarely used in the heritage corpus. Three paradigms are given below (focusing on the uninflected and locative forms), representing instantiated uses by various speakers in the corpus. They may be seen as a change over time: at T1, there was a binary distinction between *yimpa* and *yarri*. A third demonstrative, *yali*, seems to have been introduced at T2, which became associated with locatives (*yarrirla* fell out of use). For speakers today, *yarri* does not seem to be available, so the paradigm has returned to a binary distinction, now between *yimpa* and *yali*.

T1 (DG paradigm):

Absolutive	Locative
yimpa	*mirla(yi)*
yarri	*yarrirla*

T2 (BN, MFN paradigm):

Absolutive	Locative
yimpa	*mirla(yi)*
yarri	*yarrirla*
yali	**yalirla**

T3 (DK, SN paradigm):

Absolutive	Locative
yimpa	*mirla(yi)*
yarri	
yali	*yalirla(yi)*

Finally, the spatial proximity demonstratives, when inflected for the locative, may have =*yi* attached. It is possible this =*yi* performs the same function as the usual clitic =*yi* 'still, only', which restricts a situation—typically to a point in time or to a number of participants (§9.4.3)—and is perhaps translatable as 'right here' for *mirlayi* and 'right there' for *yalirlayi*. Examples of locative-marked demonstratives with =*yi* are given in (319)–(321).

(319) **Mirla=yi**=rna ka-nya.
this.LOC=STILL=1SG.S be-PRES
I'm sitting right here.
H_K01-505B, DG, 05:41 mins

(320) **Mirla=yi**=li ka-mi jirrima-ku ngurra-ku.
this.LOC=STILL=1DU.INCL.S be-FUT two-DAT camp-DAT
We'll stay right here for two days.
wrl-20191207-02, DK, 08:35 mins

(321) *Ali*=ma kurlarra **ali-rla=yi** ka-nya.
that=TOP south **that-**LOC=STILL be-PRES
That one's living right in the south.
wrl-20190212-02, DK, 08:21mins

4.5.2 Yayi 'the'

The demonstrative *yayi* refers to a definite entity (or definite set of entities) known to the interlocutors. *Yayi* is offered as a translation of Warlpiri *yangka* 'that evocative, the one you know about'. Examples are given in (322)–(324).

(322) *Ngana=lu* ka-nya **ayi**=nya=ma?
who=3PL.S be-PRES **the**=FOC=TOP
Who's the mob sitting?
N_D01-007836: 074, JJN, 18:29 mins

(323) *Kula* **yayi**=nya karli kiya-ka!
NEG **the**=FOC boomerang throw-IMP
Don't throw the boomerang!
wrl-20180610-01, DK, 02:23 mins

(324) Ngulayi **yayi**=nya timpak kiya-rnu.
  PERF **the**=FOC full throw-PAST
  He has filled the [container].
  wrl-20190205, DK, 30:12 mins

4.5.3 *Nyanungu* 'aforementioned'

The demonstrative *nyanungu* refers to an established discourse referent, as exemplified in (325), in which the *nyanungu* in clause c. refers to the birds, introduced with the nominal *jurlaka* in clause a.

(325) a. ***Jurlaka**-rlu=lu-rla*   *wiriri*   *nya-ngu-rra*   *yipakarli-ku.*
  bird-ERG=3PL.S-3.OBL   in_a_circle   see-PAST-IMPF   lizard-DAT
  The birds were circling looking for lizards.

     b. *Wangani-rlu*   *wirriri~wirriri*   *wirri*   *ya-nu-rra,*
  dog-ERG   in_a_circle~RDP   chase   put-PAST-IMPF
  The dog was chasing them around.

     c. ***Nyanungu**=ma=lu*   *putjanarra*   *partu-ngu-rra.*
  aforementioned=TOP=3PL.S   cause_to_scatter   leave-PAST-AWAY
  But **those [birds]** would fly away.
  wrl-20190207-01, DK, 52:05 mins

Semantically, *nyanungu* functions much like a third-person pronoun, as it can only refer to animate referents, and, in Warlpiri, the third-person pronoun is *nyanungu*. However, *nyanungu* in Warlmanpa patterns differently to free pronouns. Namely, free pronouns do not inflect for the ergative case (§3.1.7), whereas *nyanungu* can take the ergative, as in (326), demonstrating its status as demonstrative rather than pronoun. Additionally, *nyanungu* has no 'genitive' form like the free pronouns do. *Nyanungu* is also found in Warlpiri, in which it is glossed as 'the, that aforementioned, the former' (Nash 1986: 216).

(326) ***Nyanungu-rlu***   *ma-ntarla.*
  aforementioned-ERG   get-IRR
  That one should get it.
  H_K01-506A, DG, 01:01:21 hrs

Nyanungu can also take dative case, as in (327) and (328), though there is no evidence of it taking any other suffixes.

(327) *Ngayu=rna-rla   wa-nganya   **nyanungu-ku.***
      1=1SG.S-DAT   speak-PRES   **aforementioned-DAT**
      I am speaking to him.
      H_K01-506A, DG, 01:59 mins

(328) *Ngayu=rna-rla   yu-ngu   **nyanungu-ku.***
      1=1SG.S-3.OBL   give-PAST   **aforementioned-DAT**
      I gave it to that one.
      N_D02-007841, BN, 09:53 mins

4.6 Ignoratives

Ignoratives in Warlmanpa are a closed class set of nominals that refer to a knowledge category (following Mushin 1995). In most situations, these words function as interrogatives, though in some contexts, particularly embedded contexts, they can be used as indefinite pronouns (sets of this type in other Ngumpin-Yapa languages have also been referred to as ignoratives [for example, Ennever 2021; Meakins and McConvell 2021]). Table 4.14 gives the five roots corresponding to knowledge categories and Table 4.15 gives the list of identified derivations corresponding to further knowledge categories. Interrogatives take nominal suffixes (including case) where appropriate, except that the long-stem allomorph of the ergative and locative is used, rather than the disyllabic-stem allomorph. This section introduces the ignorative lexemes and §11.4.1 discusses interrogative constructions.

Table 4.14 Lexemes encoding knowledge categories

Form	Knowledge category	Gloss
ngana(rla)	THING	who, what
nyapa	MANNER	how
nyangurla	TIME	when
wanji(la)	PLACE	where
nyayanga	QUANTITY	how many

Table 4.15 Derived lexemes encoding knowledge categories

Base knowledge category	Form	Derived meaning	Gloss
THING	ngana-ku	REASON	what-DAT
	ngana-ngurlu	CAUSE	what-ELA
	ngana-warnu	CAUSE	what-SOURCE
MANNER	nyapa-piya	TYPE	how-LIKE
	nyapa-purta	DIRECTION	how-FACING
PLACE	wanji-ngurlu	FROM PLACE	where-ELA
	wanji-ka	TO PLACE	where-ALL

4.6.1 *Ngana* 'who, what'

The ignorative *ngana* refers to some entity that can be animate, as in (329), or inanimate, as in (330).

(329) *Ngana   yali=ma   kurtuj   ka-nya?*
       what   that=TOP   stand   sit-PRES
       Who is that standing?
       H_K06-004555, LOF, 45:29 mins

(330) *Ngana   kapi=n   jawarti=ma   partakurru-ma-n?*
       what   FUT=2SG.S   tomorrow=TOP   good-CAUSE-FUT
       What will you make tomorrow?
       H_K01-505B, DG, 24:03 mins

(331) *Yali=ma   ngana   ka-nya?*
       that=TOP   what   sit-PRES
       Who is that sitting?
       H_K06-004555, LOF, 45:42 mins

(332) *Ngana-rlu   win   kiya-rnu?*
       what-ERG   throw away   throw-PAST
       Who threw it?
       H_K06-004555, LOF, 52:26 mins

In Warlpiri, a contrast is made between *ngana ~ nyana* 'who' and *nyiya ~ nyayi* 'what' (Nash 1986: 235), whereas *ngana* in Warlmanpa collapses this animacy distinction, only using *ngana* for these functions. Similar distinctions are found in most Ngumpin languages, including Bilinarra, Gurindji, Mudburra, Ngardi and Wanyjirra (Ennever 2021; Meakins and

McConvell 2021; Meakins and Nordlinger 2014: 187–92; Osgarby 2018: 252; Senge 2015: 241–48). Like Warlmanpa, Warumungu does not make an animacy distinction, using *nyayi* for both 'who' and 'what' (Simpson and Heath 1982: 32). The contrast between Warlmanpa, Warlpiri and Warumungu paradigms is shown in Table 4.16.

Table 4.16 Animacy distinctions in ignorative nominals in Warlmanpa, Warlpiri and Warumungu

		Warlmanpa	Warlpiri	Warumungu
[+sentient]	'who'	ngana	ngana ~ nyana	nyayi
[−sentient]	'what'		nyiya ~ nyayi	

Other knowledge categories can be derived using *ngana* as the root: a dative suffix can query a purpose, as in (333), and an elative or source suffix can query a cause, as in (334) and (335). It should be noted that the distinction between the use of the elative or source suffix in this context is not well understood.

Purpose:

(333) **Ngana-ku**=n   lu-ngunya?
      what-DAT=2SG.S   cry-PRES
      Why are you crying?
      (That is, for what reason are you crying?)
      H_K06-004555, LOF, 57:53 mins

Reason:

(334) **Ngana-ngurlu**=n   ka-nya   lanpa?
      what-ELA=2SG.S   be-PRES   awake
      Why are you awake?
      (That is, what caused you to be awake?)
      wrl-20200219, DK, 1:04:01 hrs

(335) **Ngana-warnu**=n   lani-ja-nya?
      what-SOURCE=2SG.S afraid-INCH-PRES
      Why are you afraid?
      (That is, what has resulted in you being afraid?)
      H_K01-506A, DG, 22:52 hrs

Additionally, the form *ngana* seems to be the (historical) root of the 'dummy word' *nganayi* 'whatsit'.

(336) **Nganayi**, jalajirrpa=ma=lu ka-nya lamanpa-rla.
whatsit white_cockatoo=TOP=3PL.S be-PRES tree-LOC
Whatsit, those white cockatoos live in trees.
wrl-20200219, DK, 1:26:36 hrs

Ngana allows a suffix, *-japa*, which is not found on any other lexeme to my knowledge. The suffix encodes an indefinite use of *ngana*, as in (337)–(340), and occurs following the ergative case in (340), which is unlike usual derivational morphology that otherwise occurs before case.[10]

(337) Warlmanpa-rlu=rnalu nga-nya: 'nyiya kurrkurr wa-nganya
Warlmanpa-ERG=1PL.EXCL tell-PRES what owl speak-PRES
yulu=rla pangi-nya, **ngana-japa** ngarra pali-mi'.
ground=3.OBL dig-PRES **what-INDF** POT die-FUT
We'll tell it in Warlmanpa: that owl is saying he's digging [a grave] in the ground for someone, someone will die.
wrl-201609194-02, DF, 28:29 mins

(338) Ngayu=ma=rna jinjirla paka-rnu **ngana-japa**=ju wa-nganya.
1=TOP=1SG.S sneeze hit-PAST **what-INDF**=1SG.NS speak-PRES
I sneezed, someone must be talking about me.
wrl-20180614-02, DK, 02:42 mins

(339) **Ngana-japa**=rna parrparta nya-nganya.
what-INDF=1SG.S far_away see-PRES
I can see someone far away.
wrl-20180616-01, DK, 03:14.20 hrs

---

10 In Warlpiri, the same form is analysed as a clitic (Laughren et al. 2022), though in Warlpiri *=japa* can attach to a wide range of nominal types, unlike in Warlmanpa, where it appears to be restricted to ignorative nominals (and possibly just *ngana*). Analysing *=japa* as a clitic in Warlmanpa would explain why the ergative case occurs on the inside of *=japa*, though I am not aware of any other clitics in Warlmanpa that are restricted to a particular word. More data are needed for a clear analysis. Derivational morphology occurring outside case morphology in Ngumpin-Yapa languages is extremely rare, though there are some isolated cases, such as *-p* in Gurindji and Bilinarra, which derives a coverb from a nominal that occurs following the ergative case (Meakins and McConvell 2021). The freezing of a clitic to an ignorative form has been noted cross-linguistically (Haspelmath 1993), which may explain the difference in productivity between Warlmanpa and Warlpiri.

(340)   *Kurtu*   *ngarra*   **ngana-rlu-japa**   *wali*   *ma-nu.*
child   POT   **what-ERG-INDF**   trip   do-PAST
Something must have tripped up the child.
wrl-20190205, DK, 21:11 mins

4.6.2 *Nyapa* 'how'

Nyapa refers to manner and is generally translated as 'how'. This can be the manner of a particular event, as in (341), or a manner of being, as in (342). Further examples are given in (343)–(345).

(341)   ***Nyapa=ngu***   *wa-nganyu?*
how=2SG.NS   speak-PAST
How did he speak to you?
(That is, what did he say to you?)
H_K01-505B, DG, 01:01:02 hrs

(342)   ***Nyapa-rla=n***   *ka-nya?*
how-LOC=2SG.S   be-PRES
How are you?[11]
H_K01-505B, DG, 05:36 mins

(343)   ***Nyapa=n***   *pa-na?*   *Wirliya=n*   *pana,*   or   *mutika-rla=n*   *pa-na?*
how=2SG.S   go-FUT   foot=2SG.S   go-FUT   car-LOC=2SG.S   go-FUT
How will you go? Will you go on foot? Or will you go in a car?
H_K01-505B, DG, 42:56 mins

(344)   ***Nyapa=rna***   *pa-nama*   *ngurra-ka?*
how=1SG.S   go-FUT.AWAY   camp-ALL
How will I get home?
wrl-20200219, DK, 45:23 mins

(345)   *Yurt-nga-nnya=rna-ngu*   ***nyapa-ku***   *wa-nganja-ku*
show-tell-PRES=1SG.S-2SG.NS   **how-DAT**   speak-INF-DAT
I'll show you how to speak.
wrl-20191207-02, DK, 01:48 mins

---

11   States construed as manner often take locative marking. For example, *wilangapala kanya* 'the two are playing' can be translated literally as 'the two are at play' (H_K06-004547, JW, 31:34 mins).

Nyapa can also be derived to denote at least two other knowledge categories: *nyapa-piya* queries a type, as in (346), and *nyapa-purta* queries a direction, as in (347).

Type:

(346)   ***Nyapa-piya**=n*   *ma-nmi?*
       how-LIKE$_2$=2SG.S   get-FUT
       What kind will you get?
       wrl-20200219, DK, 02:20 mins

Direction:

(347)   ***Nyapa-purta***   *wantarri*   *Kalumpurlpangurlu*   *ka-nyinga*
       how-FACING   road   Kalumpurlpa-ELA   be-PATH
       Mangalawurru-ka?
       Mangalawurru-ALL
       Which direction is the road from Kalumpurlpa to Mangalawurru?
       wrl-20200221, DK, 22:16 mins

Interestingly, *nyapa* can be reduplicated (a process not evident for any other ignorative), in which it queries a pluractional event, as in (348).

(348)   ***Nyapa~nyapa**=n*   *kuma-nya?*
       how~RDP=2SG.S   cut-PRES
       How are you cutting it?
       wrl-20200219, DK, 43:08 mins

4.6.3 *Nyangurla* 'when'

Nyangurla queries time, although it is rarely found in the corpus: there are no examples of *nyangurla* as an indefinite 'sometime', nor any case-marked examples. Examples of *nyangurla* querying the time of future events are given in (349) and (350).

(349)   ***Nyangurla***   *kapi=n*   *pa-nami?*
       when   FUT=2SG.S   go-FUT
       When are you going?
       H_K01-505B, DG, 40:25 mins

(350) ***Nyangurla**=rna*   *ngayu=ma*   *parti-ma?*
       when=1SG.S   1=TOP   leave-FUT.AWAY
       When should I leave?
       wrl-20191207-02, DK, 10:36 mins

For durative events, the assumed queried time is the beginning of the event, although this can be made explicit with the inceptive verb inflection, as in (351), or the cessation time of an event can be targeted, too, using *pawarrayi-ja-* 'finish' as the matrix predicate, as in (352).

(351) ***Nyangurla**=n*   *nga-rninji-nmi?*
       when=2SG.S   eat-INC-FUT
       When will you start eating?
       wrl-20190211-02, DK, 04:01 mins

(352) ***Nyangurla**=n*   *pawarrayi-ja-mi*   *partakurru-ma-nja-ku?*
       when=2SG.S   complete-INCH-FUT   good-CAUSE-INF-DAT
       When will you finish fixing it?
       wrl-20200221, DK, 32:56 mins

4.6.4 Wanji 'where'

Wanji queries a location, either of an event or of some entity(ies).

(353) ***Wanji***   *janyungu*   *ngula=rna-ngu*   *yu-ngu?*
       where   tobacco   REL=1SG.S-2SG.NS   give-PAST
       Where is the tobacco that I gave you?
       H_K01-505B, DG, 39:16 mins

(354) ***Wanji**=jana*   *maliki*   *muku-manta-ku=ma?*
       where=3PL.NS   dog   this.DAT-RPL-DAT=TOP
       Where is the dog for them?
       H_K01-506A, DG, 02:37 mins

When used to query a static location, *wanji* almost always surfaces as *wanjila*, seemingly *wanji-la* 'where-LOC' except that the locative suffix has alveolar place of articulation rather than postalveolar, and it is used even when the locative suffix is not expected (see §11.4.1 for further details). For example, the goal of *pa-* 'go' events is marked with allative case in declarative clauses (even if the event is completed and the subject referent is no longer moving at reference time), yet in (355), the locative form of *wanji* is used to query the endpoint of a *pa-* event.

(355)   ***Wanjila***   *ngarra*   ***pa-nama***
        where.LOC   POT   **go-POT**
        I wonder where he's gone.
        wrl-20191209, DK, 03:58 mins

However, when not querying a container (that is, when the referent is not at the endpoint), *wanji* can take spatial suffixes to denote a path to (allative) or from (elative) a location, as in (356).

(356)   *Pa-nyinga-rni=n*   ***wanji-ka?***
        go-PATH-TWD=2SG.S   **where-ALL**
        Where are you going to?
        wrl-20190131-01, DK, 04:38 mins

(357)   ***Wanji-ngurlu****=n*   *pa-nangu-rnu?*
        where-ELA=2SG.S   go-PAST-TWD
        Where did you come here from?
        wrl-20200219, DK, 32:15 mins

Wanjila appears to have a suffix, *-nti*, not clearly found on any other lexeme. Its function is unknown; I have tentatively glossed it as an emphatic 'on earth'. It may be related to the irregular associated motion towards deictic centre allomorph used by some speakers on *pa-* 'go', which surfaces as *pantinya* (expected: *panjinya*).

(358)   *Jilij*   *ka-ngka*   ***wanjila-nti***   *pa-nama!*
        ask   take-IMP   **where-ON_EARTH**   go-POT
        Ask him where he is going!
        H_K06-004555, LOF, 45:08 mins

In addition to its spatial sense, *wanji* can be used to query a particular member of a set, as in (359)—a polysemy also shared by Warlpiri *nyarrpara* (Nash 1986: 235).

(359)   ***Wanji-rlu***   *wangani-rlu*   *ma-nu?*
        where-ERG   dog-ERG   get-PAST
        Which dog got it?
        wrl-20200219, DK, 41:57 mins

4.6.5 Nyayanga~nyajangu 'how many'

Nyayanga~nyajangu is a cardinal ignorative, cognate with Warlpiri *nyajangu*. It refers to a quantity of countable entities. As exemplified in (361), the lexeme takes ergative marking where appropriate, though there are no other noted suffixes that can attach, nor any indefinite usages.

Nyayanga:

(361)   ***Nyayanga**=n*   *marta-nnya?*
         how_many=2SG.S   have-PRES
         How many do you have?
         H_K01-506A, DG, 28:45 mins

(362)   ***Nyayanga**-rlu=lu-ngu*   *paka-rnu?*
         how_many-ERG=3PL.S-2SG.NS   hit-PAST
         How many people hit you?
         H_K01-506A, DG, 28:52 mins

(363)   ***Nyayanga***   *yarru-rlu=nya*   *ngarrka-ngu*   *marta-nnya*   *yiwirti?*
         how_many   that-ERG=FOC   man-ERG   have-PRES   stick
         How many spears does that man have?
         H_K01-506A, DG, 50:51 mins

Nyajangu:

(364)   ***Nyajangu**=n*   *karli*   *marta-nnya?*
         how_many=2SG.S   boomerang   have-PRES
         How many boomerangs do you have?
         wrl-20191208-01, DK, 00:21 secs

(365)   ***Nyajangu**=n*   *kurtukurtu*   *marta-nnya?*
         how_many=2SG.S   children   have-PRES
         How many children do you have?
         wrl-20191208-01, DK, 00:54 secs

4.7 Further topics in nominals

This section concludes the nominals chapter by discussing three topics highly relevant to nominals: strategies of encoding possession are discussed in §4.7.1, comparative constructions in §4.7.2 and quantification in §4.7.3.

4.7.1 Possession

Warlmanpa has several strategies to encode possession. Lexically, possession can be encoded with the predicate *marta-* 'have', which denotes a possessive relationship between the subject (marked with ergative case) and the object (marked with absolute case), as in (365) and (366).

(365) *Karli=rna   marta-nnya.*
        boomerang=1SG.S   have-PRES
        I have a boomerang.
        H_K01-505B, DG, 28:54 mins

(366) *Jinta-ngu   marta-nnya   mukarti   wiri.*
        one-ERG   have-PRES   hat   big
        [That] one has a big hat.
        H_K01-505B, DG, 01:01:56 hrs

Other possessive strategies are morphological. There is a restricted set of kinship suffixes (discussed further in §3.1.3), although these appear to not be productive; a genitive form of each free pronoun (discussed further in §3.1.8.2); while regular nominals have a further number of morphological strategies, primarily *-ku* 'dative' and *-kurla* 'genitive'. These strategies are summarised in Table 4.17.

Table 4.17 Standard possession suffixes across parts of speech

Person	1	2	3
Kinship (§3.1.3)	*-na*	*-jupu*	*-nyanu*
Free pronouns (§3.1.8.2)		*-nya*	
Nominal (alienable)		*-ku, -kurla*	

The remainder of this section details two subtypes of nominal possession: alienable (§4.7.1.1) and inalienable (§4.7.1.2). Alienable possession involves a possessor, which is either a genitive pronoun or a nominal taking *-kurla* 'genitive', and the entire possessive phrase is cross-referenced by a bound pronoun. Inalienable possession requires a possessor in the same case as the possessum, and it is the possessor who is cross-referenced by a bound pronoun. These strategies are summarised in Table 4.18, and discussed in turn.[12]

Table 4.18 Types of nominal possession

Type	Morphological exponent(s)	Bound pronoun registration
Alienable (§4.7.1.1)	Genitive pronouns, -kurla 'genitive', possessor agrees in case with possessum	Possessor phrase
Inalienable (§4.7.1.2)	Possessum agrees in case with possessor	Possessor

4.7.1.1 Alienable possession

In alienable possession constructions, the possessum is unmarked for possession and the possessor will agree in case with the possessum, as exemplified in (367), where the genitive pronoun and the possessum are both marked for ergative case. These two nominals constitute a 'possessor phrase'. Unlike other types of nominal expressions, nominals constituting an alienable possession construction are never discontinuous (though, like other nominal expressions, they can be separated by the auxiliary complex; see §11.1.4 for discussion of the status of noun phrases). The entire possessor phrase is cross-referenced by a bound pronoun. Alienable possession is typically used for ownership that is not inherent.

An example is given in (367). The possessum is *wangani-jarra* 'dog-DUAL', which takes the ergative case as it is the subject of a transitive predicate. The possessor, *ngayinya* 'first-person genitive', thus undergoes agreement,

---

[12] The status of 'possessor dissension' or 'oblique possession' in which the possessor is marked for dative (or genitive, in the case of free pronouns) case and cross-referenced with a bound pronoun is uncertain in Warlmanpa. Given its occurrence in Ngumpin languages (Meakins and Nordlinger 2017; Bond et al. 2019), it is likely present in Warlmanpa as well. However, there are no clear cases in the corpus. One possible example is (i) below, in which the possessor phrase is overtly marked with a genitive pronoun *nyintinya* (2GEN) and the possessor is cross-referenced with the reflexive bound pronoun =*nyanu*. Alternatively, this may be a benefactive construction (that is, 'for yourself').

(i) *Ma-nta=nyanu   nyintinya   ngumpana.*
    get-IMP=RR   2GEN   husband
    Get your husband [to you]!
    wrl-20200219, DK, 57:01 mins

See also example (106) as a possible example of possessor dissension.

taking *-jarra-rlu* '-DUAL-ERG' to indicate its relation to the possessum. The phrase 'my two dogs' is then cross-referenced by the third-person dual-subject bound pronoun =*pala*. Further examples are given in (368)–(371).

(367) **Ngayinya-jarra-rlu wangani-jarra-rlu** kapi-nyanya=**pala**
1.GEN-DUAL-ERG **dog**-DUAL-ERG follow-MOT.AWAY=**3DU.S**
yawirri.
kangaroo
My two dogs are following the kangaroo.
wrl-20180608-01, DK, 23:58 mins

(368) Wanji **maliki** yarru-kurla?
where **dog** that-GEN
Where is that one's dog?
H_K01-505B, DG, 01:03:36 hrs

(369) B̰ut kula=rna-jana ngayu=ma **nyaninya jaru** purtu
NEG=1SG.S-3PL.NS 1=TOP **3.GEN language** listen
ka-ngu-rra.
be-PAST-IMPF
But I wasn't listening to their language.
N_D02-007844, BN, 26:04 mins

(370) Nya-ngu=n **maliki ngayinya?**
see-PAST=2SG.S **dog** 1.GEN
Did you see my dog?
wrl-20170328-01, SN, 15:20 mins

(371) **Ngayinya-rla papulu-rla** ka-nya.
1GEN-LOC **house**-LOC be-PRES
He is at my house.
H_K01-506A, DG, 54:42 mins

4.7.1.2 Inalienable possession

In inalienable possession, the possessor is unmarked and cross-referenced by a bound pronoun in the appropriate grammatical relation. This construction is used when the two units cannot conceivably be separated or are somehow inherent to each other (Chappell and McGregor 1996). The availability of this construction is common across many Australian languages, usually minimally extending to body parts (Dixon 1980: 293) and sometimes extending to other concepts, such as names, as in Ngardi (Ennever 2021), as well as shadows and reflections (Meakins and McConvell 2021). The only examples of inalienable possession in Warlmanpa correspond to body parts. The possessor is the 'syntactically active' constituent (in the terminology of Hale [1981: 334]), in that the possessum is a secondary predicate of the possessor (see §11.6.2), which is best evidenced by the possessor being cross-referenced by the bound pronouns, unlike in alienable possession.[13] Examples are given in (372)–(374). Note that (373) has two instances of inalienable possession: *kurtungu* 'child' is the possessor of *takkangu* 'hand' (with no overt cross-referencing with a bound pronoun because it is third-person singular) and first-person singular (no overt pronoun, but cross-referenced by =*ju* in the bound pronouns) is the possessor of *milpa* 'eye'.

(372) **Wangani-rlu**   *lirra-ngu*   pu-ngu
      dog-ERG   **teeth-ERG** act_on-PAST
      The dog's teeth bit him.
      wrl-20180605-01, DK, 05:17 mins

(373) **Kurtu-ngu**=*ju*   kala-rnu   *milpa*   **takka-ngu.**
      child-ERG=1SG.NS spear-PAST   eye   **hand-ERG**
      The child's hand poked my eye.
      N_D02-007842, BN, 12:48 mins

(374) **Walu**=*rna*   maju-ja-nya.
      head=1SG.S   bad-INCH-PRES
      My head hurts.
      H_K01-506A, DG, 09:03 mins

4.7.2 Comparatives

Like many Australian languages, Warlmanpa does not have degree arguments. Comparative constructions arise through two strategies: antonyms and dative-marked modifiers. Bowler (2016) presents a further number of strategies available in Warlpiri, which are likely available in Warlmanpa, though this remains a question for future research.

---

13 In Warlpiri, this can also be seen by the possessor being eligible for argument control of non-finite complementisers; this is likely the case for Warlmanpa as well, but there is no evidence to be certain.

4.7.2.1 Antonyms

The use of antonymic gradable predicates allows an ordering between entities. For example, in (375), there are two nominal gradable predicates: *kirrirti* 'tall' and *parlka* 'short', each with a different argument, which allows a logical ordering between the two entities in terms of height.

(375) Jakamarra=ma   kirrirti   Japanangka   parlka.
       Jakamarra=TOP   tall   Japanangka   short

Prompt: Jakamarra is taller than Japanangka.
Literal: Jakamarra is tall, Japanangka is short.
N_D02-009883, DG, 06:37 mins

Similarly, (376) presents an example of referents mapped onto positions in space (relative to a goal).

(376) Yumpa   kampangarli-ka   yimpa   warnangantajarra   yimpa
       this   ahead-ALL   this   middle   this
       purtangarli-ka.
       behind-ALL

Prompt: This horse runs faster than that horse, and that horse runs faster than the third one.
Literal: This one is (going) ahead, this one is in the middle, this one is (going) behind.
N_D02-009883, DG, 07:38 mins

These constructions allow a relative ordering between entities; they do not presuppose that one entity objectively has a given attribute, despite the 'literal' translations given above. That is, (375) is not intended to convey that 'Japanangka is (definitively) short', rather, it conveys that Japanangka is lower on the gradable scale of 'tallness' than Jakamarra, by virtue of the explicit comparison.[14]

---

14 To be slightly more technical, this construction sets up a comparison class, containing only the entities being compared, so, for example, the predicate *kirrirti* 'tall' will only be applicable to one entity and *parlka* 'short' to the other. This has no bearing on whether the entities being compared could be said to be 'generally' tall or short. Outside this construction, these same predicates use comparisons of other relevant members of a set—for example, *Jakamarra kirrirti* 'Jakamarra is tall [compared with other relevantly similar people]' (Bowler 2016: 3; M. Browne 2020a: 237–38).

4.7.2.2 Dative-marked modifiers

Some predicates can take dative modifiers for comparative constructions, which indicate that the subject of the gradable predicate exhibits it to a greater degree than the dative-marked referent. Each example in the corpus additionally includes an antonymic predicate, hence this strategy appears to be a subtype of the 'antonymic' strategy discussed above. For example, in (378), the predicate *kirrirti* 'tall' takes *jinta* 'one' (in context: 'one of the two children') as its subject, to indicate that this child exhibits a greater degree of *kirrirti* to the dative-marked constituent (only cross-referenced by the oblique series of bound pronouns); this is contrasted with *parlka* 'short' immediately after, which also has an oblique referent.

(377)   *Waka-nnya=**rla**   kampangali-ka   Japanangka=ma;*
         climb-PRES=**3.OBL** ahead-ALL   skin=TOP

   *Jakamarra=ma=**rla**   purtangarli   waka-nnya.*
   skin=TOP=**3.OBL**   behind   climb-PRES

   Prompt: Japanangka climbed up further than Jakamarra.
   Translation: Japanangka is climbing **ahead of Jakamarra**; Jakamarra is climbing **behind Japanangka**.
   N_D02-009883, DG, 08:05 mins

(378)   *Witta-ja   yapa-ja,   jinta=**rla**   kirrirti, jinta=ma=**rla** parlka.*
         small-DU   person-DU   one=**3.OBL**   **tall**   one=TOP=**3.OBL** **short**

   Two children, one is **tall to/for the other**, the other is **short to/for him**.
   N_D02-009883, DG, 08:32 mins

Using dative arguments in comparative constructions is also available in Warlpiri, except the dative-marked nominals in Warlpiri do not appear to be cross-referenced by the bound pronouns, although this may be because there is no verbal predicate in the Warlpiri example.[15]

---

15 Bowler (2016) notes the clitic *=juku* 'still' may also contribute to the comparative reading. This clitic is not evident in Warlmanpa (in most circumstances, the clitic *=yi* in Warlmanpa, §9.4.3, seems to be equivalent to Warlpiri *=juku*, though perhaps not in this usage).

(379) *Napaljarri=ji*   *ngula=ju*   **kirrirdi=jiki**,   **Nakamarra-ku**=*ju*.
Napaljarri=TOP   that=TOP   **tall**=STILL   **Nakamarra**-DAT=TOP
Prompt: Napaljarri is taller than Nakamarra.
Translation: That Napaljarri is tall for/to Nakamarra.
(Warlpiri: Bowler 2016: 11)

See Bowler (2016: 12) for a formal denotation of *-ku* in this function in Warlpiri.

4.7.3 Quantification

Quantification of entities in Warlmanpa is conveyed by a heterogeneous group of constructions. Most ways of encoding quantity make a primary distinction between singular and non-singular. Number suffixes (§4.4.7) can distinguish between dual, paucal and plural (though the paucal and plural are rare). The lack of a number suffix on a nominal does not encode a singular referent, rather it encodes an unspecified non-zero number. The exhaustive list of non-derived number nominals is *walku* 'nothing', *jinta* 'one' and *jirrima* 'two'. *Jinta* and *jirrima* can be compounded to derive a compositional compound (for example, *jirrima-jinta* refers to a set of three); impressionistically this system seems to refer to up to sets of five. As discussed in §2.8, a small set of nominals (particularly those referring to humans) can reduplicate to refer to plural sets. Bound pronouns (§5.4), which cross-reference arguments, have a distinct series for singular, dual and plural. Unlike the other methods of conveying quantity, bound pronouns are obligatory (at least for animate entities). Quantifier coverbs either refer to a full set or individuate each member of the set. The quantification strategies are overviewed in Table 4.19.[16] This system is very similar to that found in Warlpiri (see Bowler 2017).

---

16   Note that the zero number constructions—that is, grammatical negation—are obligatory (in contrast to the non-zero constructions, which are not obligatory). Negation is discussed in more detail in §11.5.

Table 4.19 Modes of expression of quantification in Warlmanpa

		Distinctions made in category	Obligatoriness
Nominals	Number suffixes on nominals	Zero (*-wangu, -jila*)	Obligatory
		Dual (*-jal-jarra*) Paucal (*-panji*; rare) Plural (*-manta, -tarra*; both rare)	Not obligatory
	Number nominals	Zero (*walku*)	Obligatory
		One (*jinta*) Two (*jirrima*) Three (*jinta-jirrima*) (etc.) Several (*yukarti*) Many (*tartu*)	Not obligatory
Particles/ clitics	Bound pronouns	Singular series Dual series Plural series	Obligatory for animate arguments
Coverbs/ adverbs	Quantifiers	*larlkirlarlki-* 'separately, each' *mukku* 'all' *pawarrayi* 'all, completely'	Not obligatory

Some quantified entities are exemplified below, which highlight the interaction between the different parts of speech. In (380), the nominal *ngarrka* 'man' takes the plural suffix *-tarra* to signal at least three men participated in the event, and similarly, the obligatory bound pronoun *=lu* also indicates that the subject set contains at least three entities. The quantifier *larlkirlarlki* 'separately' indicates that each member of the subject set performed the event individually. In this case, it means that each *ngarrka* shot a kangaroo (rather than a generic event in which at least one member of the set participated).

(380)   ***Ngarrka-tarra*-rlu**   ***larlkirlarlki***   *la-rnu=**lu***   *wawirri*.
        man-PL-ERG   **seperately**   shoot-PAST=**3PL.S**   kangaroo
        Each of the men shot a kangaroo.
        [Every x: MAN(x)] [A y: KANGAROO(y)] SHOOT(x, y)
        wrl-20191208-02, DK, 02:08 mins

As such, this sentence encodes that every man in the contextually determined group shot a kangaroo (and, since the bound pronouns register a third-person singular object, that just one kangaroo was shot). The use of *larlkirlarlki* here can be contrasted with (381): there is a number nominal, *jinta*, construed of the *wawirri* 'kangaroo', and *jinta* hosts the restrictive clitic *=yi*—that is, 'just one', which forces a different scopal reading, meaning there is one kangaroo and the members of the subject set shot this kangaroo (reflected in the formalisations beneath the translations). Moreover, the absence of *larlkirlarlki* leaves as ambiguous the quantity of members of the set who participated. The proposition is true regardless of whether it was one member of the set who shot a kangaroo, multiple members or all members.

(381) **Jinta-yi=lu**   wawirri   la-rnu   **tarti-ngi=yi.**
      one-STILL=3PL.S kangaroo shoot-PAST   **many-ERG=STILL**
      The mob shot just one kangaroo.
      [A y: KANGAROO(y)] [A/Some/Every x: MAN(x)] SHOOT(x, y)
      wrl-20191208-02, DK, 03:36 mins

The other quantifier coverbs and adverbs seem to relate more to the completeness of the event than to quantifying a set of participants (*larlkirlarlki* conceptualises the event as a series of distinct events, one for each agent). For example, the adverb *pawarrayi* 'completely' focuses on the completed event. In (382), *pawarrayi* conveys the event as a completed event of every member of the set leaving (rather than focusing on the fact that each participant left).

(382) Pawarrayi=lu   partu-nga   Warumungu   muju.
      completely=3PL.S   leave-PAST.IMPF   Warumungu   also
      All of them left, even the Warumungu people.
      wrl-20200221, DK, 08:57 mins

Semantically, it may seem tempting to consider *pawarrayi* as quantifying the set of participants, though it seems more appropriate to analyse *pawarrayi* as a modifier of the event, specifically signalling an exhaustive or completed event. This analysis can be applied to (383), in which *pawarrayi* signals that each of the spears was broken—that is, the event of 'breaking spears' was exhaustive (rather than the alternative analysis, in which *pawarrayi* quantifies sets but each use is ambiguous about whether it is quantifying the subject or object set). Note also in this example *ngarrka* 'man' is entirely unspecified for number: there is no overt *tartu* 'many' nominal or number suffixes. The plural subject is only encoded by the bound pronoun.

(383) **Ngarrka-ngu=lu**   karrarlarla   kiitkiit   piya-rnu   **pawarrayi.**
      man-ERG=3PL.S   spear   break   break-PAST   **completely**
      The men completely broke the spears.
      wrl-20191208-01, DK, 39:50 mins

5

The auxiliary complex

The auxiliary complex in Warlmanpa, as in many Ngumpin-Yapa languages, is a complex locus of grammatical information. Its internal structure is templatic, with three slots: an auxiliary base, bound pronouns and a slot for an 'auxiliary clitic', =*nga*. The auxiliary base typically encodes TAM information, particularly either habituality or epistemic modality. The bound pronouns are themselves a complex locus of information on grammatical relations. The auxiliary clitic encodes epistemic possibility and can combine with a small number of auxiliary bases to generate apprehensional meanings. Each finite clause has one auxiliary complex. The internal structure of the auxiliary complex is discussed in §5.1, the placement of the auxiliary complex in a clause in §5.2, the auxiliary bases in §5.3, the bound pronouns in §5.4 and the auxiliary clitic in §5.5.

5.1 Internal structure

In Warlmanpa, the 'auxiliary complex' registers the person and number information of event participants and TAM information. The template is given in Table 5.1.

The auxiliary bases typically contribute TAM information (§5.3). The bound pronouns register person and number of event participants (§5.4). Finally, there is a single auxiliary clitic that expresses uncertainty in the proposition expressed by the clause (§5.4.3). The auxiliary base and auxiliary clitic slots are not obligatorily filled, whereas the bound pronouns are obligatory in verbal clauses (however, third-person singular subjects and objects are phonologically null).

Table 5.1 Auxiliary complex template

Slot 1	Slot 2	Slot 3
Auxiliary base	Bound pronouns	Auxiliary clitic
§5.3	§5.4	§5.5
kala 'apprehensive' *kala* 'habitual' *kapi* 'future' *nga* 'posterior' *pala* 'continuous'		=*nga* 'dubitative'

An auxiliary with every template slot filled is given in (384): there is an auxiliary base, *kala*, a bound pronoun, =*rna*, and the auxiliary clitic, =*nga*.

(384)   **Kala=rna=nga**   *wa-nmi.*
        APPR=1SG.S=DUB   fall-FUT
        Lest I fall.
        wrl-mud-20180606-02, DK, 42:53 mins

5.2 Clausal positioning

If there is an overt auxiliary base, the auxiliary complex may occur in first position, as in (384) and (386), or second position, as in (385) (see also §11.1.4.1 for examples of the auxiliary preceding complex constituents). If there is no overt auxiliary base, the auxiliary complex (that is, the bound pronouns, the auxiliary clitic or both) will typically encliticise to the first constituent in the clause, as in (387), where =*rna* '1SG' encliticises to the first word in the clause, *ngurra-ka* 'camp-ALL'. Neither the bound pronouns nor the auxiliary clitic can ever occur clause-initially. See §5.3.6 for more detailed discussion of types of hosts for the auxiliary complex when there is no overt auxiliary base.

(385)   *Papulu-ka*   **kapi=rna**   *purlun*   *ya-nmi.*
        house-ALL   FUT=1SG.S   enter   go-FUT
        I will go into the house.
        H_K01-506A, DG, 20:30 mins

(386)   **Kapi=rna**   *ngayu*   *jitpi-nyi.*
        FUT=1SG.S   1   run-FUT
        I will run.
        H_K01-505B, DG, 03:41 mins

(387) *Ngurra-ka=**rna** pa-nangu.*
       camp-ALL=**1SG.S** go-PAST
       I went to camp.
       H_K01-505B, DG, 09:07 mins

Second position is common for auxiliaries across the Ngumpin-Yapa languages, although there is some variation usually attributed to information structure (Osgarby 2018: 98–100; Meakins and Nordlinger 2014: 255–62). Most analyses are based on Simpson's (2007: 420) analysis of Warlpiri, in which she argues that the auxiliary signals a transition from 'prominent' information (topic, focus and/or contrast) to less 'prominent' information, although she (p. 424) is clear that 'much of what I have written here is tentative and requires serious investigation of the Warlpiri corpus'.

This analysis can be cautiously applied to examples from Warlmanpa narratives. Examples (388)–(390) are consecutive utterances by a speaker detailing some events from her life. In (388), the free pronoun is found in the first position: it is not new information, as the story has been about her, and the first-person pronoun is still prominent—further evidenced by it hosting the clitic *=ma* 'topic' (§9.4.4). The inflecting verb *parti-* 'leave' is new information and is placed immediately following the transition slot of the clause (where the auxiliary is found, here comprising only a bound pronoun, *=rnalu* '1PL.EXCL.s'), which is in line with Simpson's analysis.

Prominence	Prominent	Transition	Less prominent →	
Newness	Less new		New	Not specified →
(388)	*Ngayu=ma*	*=rnalu*	*partu-ngu-rnu*	*Mangkamarnta-ngirli*
	1=TOP	=1PL.EXCL	leave-PAST-HITH	Phillip Creek Mission-ELA
	ngurra-ka	*Warrabri-ka*		
	camp-ALL	Warrabri-ALL		
	We moved from Phillip Creek to Warrabri.			
	wrl-20190211-01, DK, 00:27 secs			

Turning to (389), again the first constituent, *jala* 'now', hosts a topic marker, reinforcing its prominence. The likely explanation for it being in the 'less new' slot is that the speaker is aware that the addressee knows that this location has a different name *now*, but the name itself, 'Alekarenge', comes later in the clause rather than here because it is not prominent enough, whereas *jala* creates a contrastive state suitable for prominence.

Prominence	Prominent	Transition	Less prominent →		
Newness	Less new		New	Transition	Not specified
(389)	*Jala=ma*	*=lu*	*yirti*	*ma-nnya*	*'Alekarenge'=lku*
	now=TOP	=3PL.S	name	get-PRES	Alekarenge=THEN

Now they call it Alekarenge.
wrl-20190211-01, DK, 02:03mins

Finally, (390) has a very similar structure to (388), with the first-person pronoun in the first slot hosting the *=ma* clitic and the inflecting verb immediately following the transition slot.

Prominence	Prominent	Transition	Less prominent →		
Newness	Less new		Transition	Not specified →	
(390)	*Ngayu=ma*	*=rna*	*pa-nangu-rra*	*school-ka*	*Alekarengei-rla*
	1=TOP	=1SG.S	go-PAST-IMPF	school-ALL	Alekarenge-LOC

I went to school in Alekarenge.
wrl-20190208, DK, 01:59 mins

Beyond discourse, there is a clear syntactic restriction: the auxiliary base in Warlmanpa cannot come after an inflecting verb. For example, the constituent order in (384) cannot be swapped, as this would result in the inflecting verb preceding the auxiliary base *kala*.

(384) *Wa-nmi   kala=rna=nga.
       fall-FUT   APPR=1SG.S=DUB

However, if there is no auxiliary base (see §5.3.6 for discussion of the auxiliary complex without an auxiliary base), the auxiliary can be hosted by an inflecting verb, as in (391). Thus, the syntactic restriction is only for the word class 'auxiliary base', rather than the auxiliary complex as a whole unit.

(391) **La-nmi=rna-ngu**   *karli-ngu*   *murlu.*
       shoot-FUT=1SG.S-2SG.NS   boomerang-ERG   this.ERG

I'll hit you with this boomerang.
H_K01-505B, DG, 29:12 mins

This differs from Warlpiri, in which, under certain conditions, an inflecting verb can precede the auxiliary base, as in (392).

(392) | *Warru-**pu**-ngu* | ***kala**=lu* | *kuyu* | *yapa-patu-rlu.*
around-**kill**-PAST | PAST=3PL.S | animal | person-PL-ERG

The people used to kill animals all over.
(Warlpiri [Laughren 2002: 92])

To summarise the placement of the auxiliary complex in Warlmanpa:

- The auxiliary complex cannot precede inflecting verbs, except where the auxiliary complex encliticises to the verb.
- If there is no auxiliary base, the auxiliary cannot occur clause-initially.
- The auxiliary complex typically occurs after the first constituent in a finite clause and this first constituent is usually given prominent information.

5.3 Auxiliary bases

5.3.1 *Kala* 'apprehensive'

Kala can be used when the proposition expressed by the clause is considered by the speaker to be both undesirable (for the event participants) and avoidable.

(393) | *Ngayu=ma=rna* | *pa-nyinga* | *ngurra-ka* | ***kala**=nga* | *yakarlu-rla-ja-nmi.*
1=TOP=1SG.S | go-PRES.AWAY | home-ALL | APPR=DUB | night-LOC-INCH-FUT

I'm going home, lest it gets dark.
wrl-20180615-02, DK, 24:42 mins

Morphemes with similar meanings are found in many Australian languages, with a wide range of labels (see also Browne et al. 2024; Zester 2010); here I use 'apprehensive'. The form *kala* is shared with Warlpiri, in which the auxiliary base is *kalaka*, which is labelled 'admonitive' by Nash (1986: 60), although Laughren (1999: 7) labels it more generally as 'potential'. Some speakers use the form *kalaka* in Warlmanpa sentences, as in (394), though this is particularly rare.

(394) **Kalaka**=n wa-nmi.
APPR=2SG.S fall-FUT
You'll fall! (You're liable to fall, and this is undesirable for you.)
wrl-mud-20180606-02, DF, 40:52 mins

Clauses with this auxiliary often co-occur with another clause that denotes how the undesirable event can be avoided, as in (393) and (395), although this is not required, as in (394) and (396).

(395) Kula=jana pa-nka-pa, **kala**=ngu-lu pi-nyi.
NEG=3PL.NS go-IMP-AWAY APPR=2SG.NS-3PL.S act_on-FUT
Don't go near them, lest they bite you!
wrl-20180605-01, DK, 10:37 mins

(396) **Kala**=ju piya-nma.
APPR=1SG.O break-POT
He might bite me!
wrl-20180601-01, DK, 25:26 mins

Some speakers use the auxiliary base *nga=* in concert with the auxiliary clitic *=nga* for apprehensive situations, instead of *kala*. Browne et al. (2024) discuss apprehension constructions in more detail for Ngumpin-Yapa languages, including Warlmanpa.

5.3.2 *Kala* 'habitual'

The auxiliary base *kala* encodes habitual aspect, as in (397) and (398)—that is, a situation as being a characteristic feature of an extended period (Comrie 1976: 29). *Kala* is only found with verbs inflected for PAST tense.

(397) Larrparlarrpa **kala**=lu pa-nangu-rra wirlinyi kala=lu
old_times HAB=3PL.S go-PAST-IMPF hunting HAB=3PL.S
payang-kapu-ngu-rra.
find-chase-PAST-IMPF
In the olden days, they used to go hunting, they used to go tracking.
wrl-20160908-01, SN, 02:01 mins

(398) **Kala**=lu   parti-nja-na   work-ku,   ngayu
       HAB=3PL.S   leave-MOT-PAST.AWAY   work-DAT   1
       kala=rnalu   ka-ngu.
       HAB=1PL.EXCL.S   be-PAST
       They would leave for work, and we would stay [home].
       N_D29-023128, MFN, 05:58 mins

Habitual aspect refers to an indefinite number of topic times, rather than one topic time, and 'topic time ⊂ situation time' is true for each topic time (Klein 1994: 48). For telic events, the event is iterated. For non-telic events, the event is protracted indefinitely beyond topic time. The use of *kala* coerces a telic event, regardless of the normal interpretation of the situation denoted by the predicate. This can be contrasted with habitual readings of events without *kala*: in (400), the main predicate, *kangurra* 'be', refers to a continuous state that is true for several indefinite topic times, whereas the use of *kala* (399) forces an indefinite number of bounded events of staying. These are represented with temporal schemas in Figure 5.2 and Figure 5.3, respectively.

(399) Ngayu=ma=rna   **ka-ngu-rra**   Mangkamantangi-rla.
       1=TOP=1SG.S   **be-PAST-IMPF**   Mangkamantangi-LOC
       I lived in Mangkamantangi.
       (There was one protracted state of 'staying'.)
       wrl-20190213-01, DK, 20:26 mins

(400) Kala=rna   ngurra-nga   ka-ngu   young one.
       HAB=1SG.S   **camp-LOC**   be-PAST
       I used to stay at home.
       (There were an indefinite number of bounded 'staying' events.)
       N_D18-013596, LN, 18:03 mins

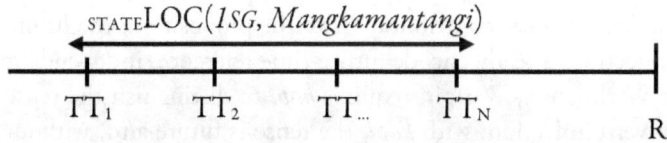

Figure 5.1 Temporal schema of Example (399), where *ka-* does not require coercion

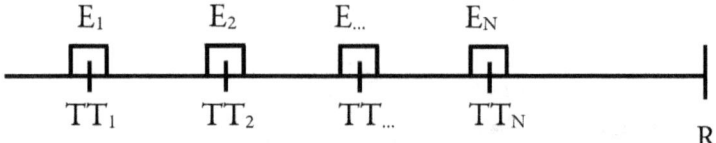

Figure 5.2 Temporal schema of Example (400), coercing *ka-* 'be' as a [+telic] event with habitual aspect

There are no instances of *kala* in the corpus occurring with any verb inflection other than PAST. Notably, *kala* is also the form of the apprehensive auxiliary base, which only occurs with future and potential verb inflections.

5.3.3 *Kapi* 'future'

Kapi encodes future-time reference. It only co-occurs with the future and potential inflections and is only used by one speaker (DG). Examples are given in (401)–(403).

(401) Ngayu   **kapi**=rna-rla   wa-nga   yarri-ku=nya.
      1   FUT=1SG.S-DAT   speak-FUT   that-DAT-FOC
      I will speak to that one.
      H_K01-506A, DG, 06:58 mins

(402) Ngappa   **kapi**   jawarti   wa-nmi.
      water   FUT   tomorrow   fall-FUT
      It will rain tomorrow.
      H_K01-505B, DG, 01:27 mins

(403) Jurnpurnpu   **kapi**=rna   ma-nma.
      tobacco   FUT=1SG.S   get-POT
      I will get tobacco.
      H_K01-505B, DG, 31:39 mins

It is unclear what its semantic contribution is to the proposition: the future and potential inflections already encode future-time reference, independent of *kapi*. Unlike Warlmanpa, Warlpiri requires *kapi* to distinguish the tense of the non-past verb inflection: with *kapi*, the tense is future and, without *kapi*, the tense is generally present. It appears that with the (apparent) innovation in Warlmanpa of the future/potential inflections, *kapi* has fallen out of use. Alternatively, it may be a Warlpiri code switch to accommodate the Walpiri prompts that included *kapi*. One further alternative analysis is that DG interpreted it as the conjunction *kapi* (§12.2.1).

5.3.4 *Nga* 'posterior'

Similar to *kapi*, *nga=* is used to encode future-time reference, as in (404) and (405).

(404)   *Ngulayi,*   *na*   *nga=rna*   *pa-nami*   *ngurra-ka=lku.*
         okay   now   POST=1SG.S   go-FUT   home-ALL=THEN
         Okay, I will go home.
         wrl-20180615-02, DK, 00:38 secs

(405)   *Nga=rna-ngu*   *yiwirti-rlu*   *karta*   *pi-nyi*   *ngayinya-kurla-rlu*
         POST=1SG.S-2SG.NS   spear-ERG   spear   act_on-FUT   1GEN-GEN-ERG

         kirtana-kurla-rlu.
         father-GEN-ERG
         I'll spear you with my father's spear.
         H_K01-506A, DG, 49:56 mins

This auxiliary base is the only known word that can surface as a monosyllabic word without a coda, as in (406). It descends historically from **ngarra* 'FUTURE' (Browne 2020b).

(406)   *Karnu-ngu=nyanu*   *partakurru-ma-nnya*   *ngurra*
         poor_thing-ERG=RR   good-CAUSE-PRES   camp
         kayi   **nga**   *kurtu~kurtu*   *marta-nmi.*
         WHEN   POST   child-PL   have-FUT
         The poor thing is fixing it for when she has children.
         wrl-20191207-02, DK, 23:56 mins

When co-occurring with the auxiliary clitic *=nga*, the meaning shifts from a neutral-connotation future event to a future event that is undesired. This is discussed further in §5.4.3.

When occurring in apposition to another clause, *nga=* often has the meaning 'so', as in (407) and (408), where the *nga=* clause occurs because of the other apposed clause. In §12.1.1.4, this is analysed as a homophonous complementiser.

(407) | *Pingka* | *wa-ngka,* | *nga=rna* | *purtu* | *ka-mi.*
| slowly | speak-IMP | PURP=1SG.S | understand | be-FUT

Speak slowly, so I can understand.
H_K01-506A, DG, 32:12 mins

(408) | *Ngayu=ma=rna* | *wayi-nnya* | *ngayinya-ku* | *wangani-ku,*
| 1=TOP=1SG.S | search-PRES | 1GEN-DAT | dog-DAT

nga=rna-rla *yarnunju* *yi-nyi.*
PURP=1SG.S-3.OBL food give-FUT

I'm looking for my dog, so I can give him food.
wrl-20190131-02, DK, 11:57 mins

5.3.5 *Pala* 'continuous'

Pala appears to be an alternant form of *kala* 'habitual', though this is based on a small number of data, as *pala* is used very infrequently. Examples are given in (409) and (410).

(409) | *Wawirri* | *pala=rnalu* | *kapu-ngu-rra.*
| kangaroo | CONT=1.EXCL.PL.S | chase-PAST-CONT

We all used to chase kangaroos.
H_K06-004548, JW, 01:54 mins

(410) | *Yanja-rna-purta* | *pala=lu* | *wa-nganya* | *Warnmanpa=ma*
| north-FROM-FACING | CONT=3PL.S | speak-PRES | Warlmanpa=TOP

jaru=ma.
talk=TOP

Those people in the north speak Warlmanpa.
H_K06-004548: 03, JW, 01:01 mins

In his fieldnotes, Ken Hale suggests this is a 'past usit[ative] aux[iliary]' (H_K06-004548 notes, p. 3), likely based on correspondence with Warlpiri *kala* 'usitative' (and see discussion of *kala* in Warlmanpa in §5.3.1). A similar form is found in Mudburra—*abala* 'relative complementiser' (Osgarby 2018: 210)—though this does not appear to be related to Warlmanpa *pala*, based on the meaning correspondence.

One speaker, DK, when asked what *pala* meant, said it means 'while', and used it as such, as shown in (411)–(413).

(411) *Kuyu nga-nja pala=rna ngappa nguka-nnya.*
Meat eat-IMP CONT=1SG.S water drink-PRES
Eat the meat while I drink the water.
wrl-20190201, DK, 21:55 mins

(412) *Warlaku=n nya-ngu pala=rna wirli ya-rnu-rra.*
dog=2SG.S see-PAST CONT=1SG.S chase put-PAST-IMPF
You saw the dog while I was chasing it around.
wrl-20191207-01, DK, 31:07 mins

(413) *Kantu purlun yanta ngappa pala wa-nmi!*
under enter go-IMP water CONT fall-FUT
Get inside while it's raining!
wrl-20191208-01, DK, 25:38 mins

In this usage, it appears *pala* is a complementiser, although it is not clear whether this should be treated the same as the uses of *pala* in the heritage corpus.

5.3.6 Non-auxiliary bases

If there is no auxiliary base, the remainder of the auxiliary complex (that is, the bound pronouns and the clitic *=nga* 'possibility') encliticises to a non-auxiliary base. In these cases, the host is determined by a hierarchy, as shown in Table 5.2.

Table 5.2 Auxiliary complex positioning

Preference	Host
Highest	Auxiliary base
	Complementiser (§12.1.1)
	ngarra 'POT' (§9.1.1)
	kula 'NEG' (§11.5.1.1)
Lowest	Initial constituent of clause or inflecting verb

If the clause is a subordinate finite clause with a complementiser, the complementiser obligatorily hosts the bound pronouns, regardless of the complementiser's position within the clause, as demonstrated in (414) and (415), where the complementiser is clause-initial in the former and clause-second in the latter, yet the auxiliary attaches to the complementiser in each.

(414) **Kari=ju**   wangani-rlu   nya-nyi,   kula   warlku- wa-ngami
      COND=1SG.NS   dog-ERG   see-FUT   NEG   bark-speak-FUT
      If the dog sees me, it won't bark.
      wrl-20180601-01, DK, 24:30 mins

(415) Witta   **ngula=rna**   ka-ngu-rra   yarri=ma=rna   Warlmanpa
      small   REL=1SG.S   be-PAST-IMPF   that=TOP=1SG.S   Warlmanpa
      wa-nganyu-rra.
      speak-PAST-IMPF
      I was speaking Warlmanpa while I was small.
      H_K01-505B, DG, 44:36 mins

For clauses without a complementiser or an auxiliary base, *ngarra* 'maybe' and *kula* 'NEG' (if used in the clause) can host the auxiliary complex. With context, this is unsurprising: *ngarra* in Warlpiri is considered a fully fledged auxiliary base and complementiser (Laughren et al. 2022), explaining the similarities in Warlmanpa in regard to hosting auxiliaries (although it has diverged in terms of syntax otherwise; see §9.1.1). *Kula* on the other hand is obligatorily first or second position (typically first) and, since the auxiliary base prefers to attach to the first constituent, it collocates frequently with the auxiliary, such that even when *kula* is not clause-initial, it still hosts the auxiliary, as in (416) and (417).

(416) Walku   **kula=rna**   paka-rnu.
      nothing   NEG=1SG.S   hit-PAST
      No, I didn't hit him.
      H_K01-505B, DG, 10:46 mins

(417) Murnma   **kula=rna**   nya-ngu.
      do_not_know   NEG=1SG.S   see-PAST
      I don't think I saw him.
      H_K01-506A, DG, 41:43 mins

While *kula* and *ngarra* clearly both attract the auxiliary, *ngarra* demonstrates a higher priority if the two co-occur within a clause, as in (418).

(418) Maliki-rlu   **kula**   **ngarra=jana**   pi-nya.
      dog-ERG   NEG   POT=3PL.NS   act_on-POT
      The dog might not bite them.
      N_D03-007868: BN, 34:10 mins

If there is no complementiser, *ngarra* or *kula*, the auxiliary will generally attach to the first constituent in the clause, as in (419).

(419)   **Tartu=lu**   *wa-nganya*   *Warlmanpa.*
         many=3PL.S   speak-PRES   Warlmanpa
         They all speak Warlmanpa.
         H_K01-505B, DG, 43:25 mins

This is often used as evidence for NPs, in that the auxiliary can be hosted by a phrasal constituent, as in (420).

(420)   *[Ngarrka*   *jinta]*$_{NP?}$**=rnalu**   *nya-nganga*   *jirrima-jinta-rlu.*
         man   one=**1PL.EXCL.S**   see-PRES   two-one-ERG
         We three are looking at one man.
         H_K01-505B, DG, 54:20 mins

However, the auxiliary can also be hosted by the first constituent within a phrase, as in (421). This, and the existence of NPs more generally, is discussed in further detail in §11.1.4.1.

(421)   *[Ngarrka-ngu=***ju**   *wiri-ngu]*$_{NP?}$ *nya-ngu.*
         man-ERG=**1SG.NS**   big-ERG   see-PAST
         The big man looked at me.
         H_K01-506A, DG, 52:30 mins

Similarly, whether an auxiliary can intervene between an inflecting verb and a coverb is used as a diagnostic of the categorisation of the coverb (see §7.3). Some coverbs are syntactically bound to the inflecting verb and must occur immediately preceding it, which prevents the bound pronoun (or any other constituent) from intervening, as in (422).

(422)   *[Purtu*   *kanya]*$_{VP}$**=rna**   *tarnnga=yi.*
         remember   be-PRES=**1SG.S**   always=STILL
         I still always remember.
         N_D02-007844, BN, 27:51 mins

There are exceptions to the auxiliary occurring after the first constituent. In some cases, where there is no overt auxiliary base, the pronoun complex may attach to the inflecting verb, regardless of its syntactic position (especially in imperative constructions [McConvell 2010]), as exemplified in (423)–(426).[1]

---

[1] McConvell (1980, 1996a) describes the encliticisation of the bound pronouns on inflecting verbs in Bilinarra as a 'topic switch' process.

(423) *Yali=nya=ma   wangani   pa-nji-nya=**ju**   ngayu-ku.*
      that=FOC=TOP   dog   go-TWD.MOT-PRES=**1SG.NS**   1-DAT
      That dog is coming towards me.
      wrl-20180614-01, DK, 34:30 mins

(424) *Wirri-wirri   kutij-ka-nya=**lu**.*
      boy-PL   stand-BE-PRES=**3PL.S**
      The boys are standing.
      N_DAT2003-8, JK, 55:59 mins

(425) *Ngappa   ka-ngka-rti=**ji**.*
      water   carry-IMP-TWD=**1SG.NS**
      Bring the water here to me.
      wrl-20190123, SN, 02:07 mins

(426) *Ngayinya-rlu   paparti-rlu   wayi-rnu-rra=**ngu-rla**.*
      1GEN-ERG   senior_brother-ERG   search-PAST-IMPF=**2SG.NS-DAT**
      My older brother is looking for you.
      wrl-20190213-01, DK, 12:05 mins

Notably, in all recorded cases where this occurs, the inflecting verb itself occurs after the first constituent in the clause, suggesting that in clauses without an auxiliary, the inflecting verb may be attracted to second position to host the auxiliary.

5.4 Bound pronouns

The bound pronominal systems of Ngumpin-Yapa languages have been extremely well documented and studied (Ennever 2018: 246–302; Osgarby 2018: 96–143; Meakins and Nordlinger 2014: 222–69; McConvell 1996a: 56–60; Tsunoda 1981b: 124–62; Hudson 1978: 56–76; Senge 2015: 303–60; Nash 1986: 59, 1996; Hale 1973; Simpson and Withgott 1986), particularly due to their complexity and combinatorial properties. Warlmanpa has two series of bound pronouns: 'subjects', corresponding to the subject grammatical relation, and 'non-subjects', corresponding to all other grammatical relations other than 'adjuncts' (grammatical relations are discussed in §10.1). Unlike other Ngumpin-Yapa languages, only a very restricted set of adjuncts can be registered by the bound pronouns (for an overview, see Browne et al. 2024: 13).

5. THE AUXILIARY COMPLEX

Basic forms of bound pronouns and their participant features are given in Table 5.3, although it should be noted that forms may differ when more than one series is marked within a single auxiliary complex (§5.4.2). The bound pronouns distinguish first, second and third person, with a clusivity distinction in the first person (inclusive includes the addressee, exclusive excludes the addressee). In each person category, there is also a distinction between singular, dual and plural. Additionally, there is a form for a reflexive non-subject, regardless of person and number, and an oblique form, =*rla*, used for third singular or mass noun INDIRECT OBJECTS and third singular BENEFACTIVE ADJUNCTS.[2]

Table 5.3 Form of bound pronouns

	Subject	Non-subject
1SG	=*rna*	=*ju*
1DU.EXCL	=*ja(rra)*	=*jangu*
1DU.INCL	=*li*	=*ngali*
1PL.EXCL	=*rnalu*	=*nganpa*
1PL.INCL	=*lpa(lu)*	=*lpangu*
2SG	=*n(ku)*	=*ngu*
2DU	=*npala*	=*ngupala*
2PL	=*nkulu*	=*nyangu*
(3)SG	∅	∅
(3)DU	=*pala*	=*palangu*
(3)PL	=*lu*	=*jana*
REFL/RECP	–	=*nyanu*
OBLIQUE	–	=*rla*

Note that the forms of the bound pronouns bear very little resemblance to the free pronouns *ngayu* 'first person' and *nyuntu* 'second person', unlike some Ngumpin languages (Ngardi [Ennever 2018: 249] and Bilinarra [Meakins and Nordlinger 2014: 230]). The first-person singular non-subject form =*ju* is likely historically derived from *ngayu*, the first-person pronoun (which is cognate with *ngaju* in Warlpiri).

---

2 Given this distinction made in third-person singular, where the object form is phonologically null and the oblique form is =*rla*, some analyses of Ngumpin-Yapa languages instead recognise three series. In these analyses, the object and oblique series are syncretic in every person/number combination except third-person singular (for Warlpiri, Nash [1986: 59]; for Ngardi, Ennever [2021]).

The remainder of the bound pronoun discussion is organised as follows. Form alternations are discussed in §5.4.1. The combinatorial forms of bound pronouns are given in §5.4.2. These sections culminate in a synchronic analysis of the bound pronoun forms (that is, attempting to recognise the bound pronouns as morphologically complex units) in §5.4.3. Finally, the types of entities and arguments that can be cross-referenced by the bound pronouns are discussed in §5.4.4.

5.4.1 Form alternations

This section overviews the different allomorphic forms of bound pronouns. The allomorphy can be categorised according to whether there is clear conditioning (§5.4.1.1) or the allomorphs seem to be in free variation (§5.4.1.2).

5.4.1.1 Form alternations conditioned by bound pronoun combinations

There are two changes in form invariably conditioned by the bound pronoun appearing in combination with another overt (that is, non-third singular) bound pronoun: =*n* 2SG.S surfacing as =*nku*; and =*lpa* 1PL.INC.S surfacing as =*lpa...lu*.

The second-person singular subject is =*n*, except the form =*nku* is used when preceding =*rla* DAT, as in (427).

(427)   *Ngana-ku=**n-ku**-rla*   *wayi-nnya.*
        what-DAT=2SG.S-EP-DAT   search-PRES
        What are you searching for?
        H_K01-505B, DG, 07:37 mins

If analysed as morphologically complex (see §5.4.3), the second-person plural subject =*nkulu* exhibits the same allomorphy—that is, the *n* denotes second-person subject, the *lu* denotes the subject is plural and the *ku* is an epenthetic portion to avoid [–continuant][+continuant] clusters.[3] The only other known context in which the second-person singular-subject bound pronoun precedes a consonant is when it precedes the auxiliary clitic =*nga* 'potential', which does not trigger the epenthetic form, as in (428).

---

[3] I am grateful to an anonymous reviewer for suggesting this constraint.

(428) Kari=n   kari=ma   pa-njakurla   nga=**n=nga**   palapala-ja-ma.
       COND=2SG.S far=TOP   go-CFACT   POST=**2SG.S**=DUB   tired-INCH-POT

If you were to go far, you might become tired.
H_K01-506A, DG, 04:59 mins

This epenthetic portion *ku* is also evident in the Warlpiri bound pronoun paradigm—although interestingly, it is more productive in Warlmanpa. In Warlpiri, *ku* is also in the plural form of the second-person plural subject =*nku=lu*, but for the singular and dual forms, the epenthetic portion is *pa* instead—that is, =*npa* '2SG.S' and =*npa-pala* '2DU.S' (Nash 1986: 59). More widely, many Ngumpin languages also have an epenthesised form =*nku* for second-person singular when combining with the third singular oblique =*rla*: Walmajarri (Hudson 1978: 71; though it seems to be optional), Ngardi (Ennever 2018: 288), Jaru (Tsunoda 1981a: 128), Wanyjirra (Senge 2015: 347), Mudburra (Osgarby 2018: 137) and Gurindji (McConvell 1996b: 60).[4]

The other bound pronoun with synchronic variation is the first-person inclusive plural =*lpa*, which in combination with other bound pronouns is discontinuous, realised as =*lpa-...-lu*. This is exemplified in (429), where the third-person plural non-subject pronoun attaches after *lpa* and then *lu* attaches at the right edge.[5]

(429) Pa-nama=**lpa**-jana-**lu**.
      go-POT=1.INCL.S-3PL.NS-PL.S

We'll go for them.
wrl-20190205, DK, 48:23 mins

Interestingly, a similar process is found with the first-person exclusive subject plural =*rnalu*, except unlike =*lpa*, =*rnalu* requires its *lu* plural marking even in isolation (retaining the distinction between =*rna* as the singular form and =*rnalu* as the plural form).

---

[4] Furthermore, the Warumungu form for second-person singular combining with third-person oblique is =*nga-kku*, though in this case the -*kku* is marking the oblique argument, rather than being an epenthetic portion (Simpson 2002: 83–84).

[5] Person and number separation in complex pronouns are common across Ngumpin-Yapa languages, though the systems vary across the languages (Meakins et al. 2023).

A GRAMMAR OF WARLMANPA

Table 5.4 Discontinuous subject and plural number marking involving =lu in bound pronouns

	Isolation	Combination
=rnalu	=rnalu	=rna...lu
=lpa(lu)	=lpa	=lpa...lu

In §5.4.3, the *lu* portion is analysed as a plural subject marker.

5.4.1.2 Forms in free variation

At least one speaker optionally uses =*ji* instead of =*ju* for the first-person singular non-subject, as in (430)–(432), whereas (433) provides the only known example of this speaker using =*ju*.

(430)   *Walu=ji   paka-ka!*
        head=1SG.NS   hit-IMP
        Hit me in the head!
        H_K06-004555, LOF, 29:07 mins

(431)   *Jarrawarti=ji   karta   pu-ngu!*
        thigh=1SG.NS   spear   hit-PAST
        He speared me in the thigh.
        H_K06-004555, LOF, 35:04 mins

(432)   *Purtu   ka-rra=ji!*
        listen   sit-IMP=1SG.NS
        Listen to me!
        H_K06-004555, LOF, 42:36 mins

(433)   *Yu-ngka-rti=ju!*
        give-IMP-HITH=1SG.NS
        Give it to me!
        H_K06-004555, LOF, 52:50 mins

This variation is particularly interesting as the first-person non-subject bound pronoun in most Ngumpin languages is =*yi* (for example, Bilinarra, Gurindji, Mudburra, Ngardi, Wanyjirra and Jaru). In Warlpiri, the underlying form is analysed as =*ju*, but progressive vowel assimilation can trigger a =*ji* form. However, the use of =*ji* in Warlmanpa cannot be attributed to vowel assimilation—best evidenced in (430), where the final vowel of the host is /u/, yet the bound pronoun form is =*ji*. Instead, =*ji* in Warlmanpa may be a retention of a historical form that then lenited to =*yi* in Ngumpin languages.

In some cases, the form -*jarra* is used in the bound pronouns to mark the preceding bound pronoun as having dual reference (corresponding to the nominal dual suffix -*jarra*; §4.3.1). For example, the first-person singular subject =*rna* can refer to a dual subject in the form =*rnajarra*, as in (434).

(434) *Ngayu=ma=**rna-jarra*** *kangkuya-jarra partu-nga* *Darwin-ka=lku.*
1=TOP=**1SG.S-DU** old_man-DU leave-PAST.AWAY Darwin-ALL=THEN

Then the old man and I left to Darwin.
wrl-20190211-01, DK, 03:44 mins

It is also worth noting that the use of -*jarra* on the nominal *kangkuya* 'old man' is unexpected, as usually this refers to two entities of the nominal (in this case, two old men), but this use appears to be more akin to an inclusive construction (Singer 2001), in which it denotes two members, at least one of whom is a *kangkuya*.

Similarly, the first-person exclusive dual subject =*ja* can be realised as =*jarra*, as in (435).

(435) *Ngayu-jarra-rlu* *ali-ku=nya* *karnta-ku* *kuyu=**jarra-rla***
1-DU-ERG that-DAT=FOC woman-DAT meat=**1DU.EXCL.S-3.OBL**
kupa-rnu.
cook-PAST

We two cooked meat for that woman.
wrl-20190213-02, DK, 12:23 mins

Note for this utterance, there is no possible way to construe the =*jarra* as a dual suffix attaching to the *kuyu* 'meat' nominal because: 1) *kuyu* is a mass noun and cannot be quantified to an exact integer; and 2) the subject has an overt nominal *ngayu-jarra-rlu*, meaning the first-person dual subject must be cross-referenced in the bound pronouns, and =*jarra* is the only feasible unit doing this (additionally, the =*jarra* precedes the -*rla* third singular dative bound pronoun). In sum, the most common form corresponding to

1DU.EXCL is =*ja*, however, there is free variation between this form, =*jarra* and =*rnajarra*. Interestingly, *jarra* is still used in Eastern Warlpiri, as part of the first-person dual exclusive pronoun =*rlujarra* (Nash 1996).

Finally, the first-person reflexive alternates between =*rna-ju*, as in (436)–(438), and =*rna-nyanu*, as in (439)–(443).[6] The reflexive form for all other bound pronoun series is =*nyanu*, with first-person singular being exceptional in allowing the typical non-subject form =*ju* to be the reflexive form, as in (436).

Direct objects:

(436) *Kala=**rna-ju**   paka-nmi.*
       APPR=1SG.S-1SG.NS   hit-FUT
       I might hit myself.
       wrl-mud-20180606-02, DK, 30:53 mins

(437) *Ngayu=**rna-ju**   piya-rnu.*
       1=1SG.S-1SG.NS   cut-PAST
       I cut myself.
       wrl-20170327-01-1, SN, 07:26 mins

(438) *Nga=**rna-ju**   paka-nmi.*
       POST=1SG.S-1SG.S   hit-FUT
       I'll hit myself.
       H_K01-506A, DG, 45:11 mins

For most speakers, the =*rna-nyanu* form is restricted to clauses where the first-person singular non-subject is occupying a syntactic role other than object; this includes external objects (as benefactives), indirect objects and inalienably possessed objects, as exemplified in (439)–(442).

External objects:

(439) *Kuku=**rna-nyanu**   karta-pi-nyi.*
       wait=1SG.S-RR   spear-act_on-FUT
       Wait while I trim it for myself.
       H_K01-506A, DG, 57:58 mins

---

6   Strictly speaking, this is more akin to lexical choice than allomorphy.

(440)   *Kuyu=lku=**rna-nyanu***   *kupa-rnu-rra*   *yama-nga=ma.*
meat=THEN=1SG.S-RR   cook-PAST-IMPF   shade-LOC=TOP
Then I was cooking meat in the shade for myself.
N_D02-007850, DG, 00:42 secs

Indirect objects:

(441)   *Yumpa=**rna-nyanu***   *turru-ma-nu-rra*   *ngayu=ma.*
this=1SG.S-RR   tell-do-PAST-IMPF   1=TOP
I would tell this story to myself.
N_D18-013596, LN, 18:16 mins

Inalienably possessed objects:

(442)   *Takka=**rna-nyanu***   *karta*   *pu-ngunya.*
arm=1SG.S-RR   spear   act_on-PRES
I am cutting myself in the arm.
H_K01-505B, DG, 33:16 mins

One speaker appears to use *-nyanu* as a (direct) object, in (443). It is possible that the conditioned variation has been lost to free variation.

(443)   *Kala=**rna-nyanu***   *piya-nmi.*
APPR=1SG.S-RR   cut-FUT
I might cut myself [accidentally].
wrl-mud-20180606-02, DF, 31:10 mins

In Warlpiri, =*nyanu* cannot be used for the first-person singular, nor in imperatives if the number is singular (Simpson 1991: 167). Neither of these conditions holds in Warlmanpa, as demonstrated above for first-person singular and as demonstrated in §5.4.3.4 for imperatives. However, Ngumpin languages share similarities with the Warlmanpa patterning—for example, the Bilinarra first-person singular reflexive bound pronoun is also conditioned by the role of the non-subject (Meakins and Nordlinger 2014: 236–38). The direct objects use the reflexive bound pronoun, as in (444), and elsewhere the non-subject bound pronoun is used, as in (445)—that is, while the conditioning environment is the same as Warlmanpa, the bound pronouns pattern in reverse.

(444) *Nyawa=ma=rna=**nyunu**   ba-ni   ngarlaga-la=ma   ngayi=rni*
       this=TOP=1MIN.S=RR   hit-PST   head-LOC=TOP   1MIN=ONLY
       wardan-jawung.
       hand-PROP
       I hit myself on the head with my own hand. (Direct object)
       (Bilinarra [Meakins and Nordlinger 2014: 383])

(445) *Nyila=ma   birrga=rna=**yi**   ma-n.gu   burdurn.*
       that=TOP   make=1MIN.S=1MIN.O   do-POT   wind_break
       I'll build myself a house. (Benefactive)
       (Bilinarra [Meakins and Nordlinger 2014: 236])

5.4.2 Bound pronoun combinations

The bound pronoun combination paradigm demonstrates the complexities of the system. The paradigm itself is given in §5.4.2.2, although first a preliminary discussion of dual neutralisation, in §5.4.2.1, is required to interpret the paradigm. The next section, §5.4.3, presents an analysis that attempts to capture the discontinuous exponents of the same referent and varied constituent order (which is constrained by both a person hierarchy and a grammatical role hierarchy).

5.4.2.1 Dual neutralisation

In any combination of two non-singular referents, the bound pronouns will cross-reference both referents with a plural form—termed 'dual neutralisation' (Simpson 1991: 423), which is a phenomenon also found in Eastern Warlpiri and Warumungu (Hale 1973: 330), as well as Eastern Ngumpin languages such as Gurindji (Meakins and McConvell 2021) and Bilinarra (Meakins and Nordlinger 2014). This contrasts with 'dual replacement', which blocks two dual pronouns co-occurring, but one can still co-occur with a plural pronoun. Dual replacement is found in Jaru (Tsunoda 1981a: 133–34), Wanyjirra (Senge 2015: 341–46) and Ngardi (Ennever 2018: 292–93), as well as Western Warlpiri (with slightly different details [Hale 1973]).

5. THE AUXILIARY COMPLEX

To exemplify, in (446), the object reference is dual, which is made explicit by the unmarked quantifier *jirrama* 'two'. Yet, the bound pronoun form for the object is *=nyangu*, which is the plural form. The subject bound pronoun is *=rnalu*—also a plural form—though due to the nature of dual neutralisation, this could be cross-referencing either dual or plural subjects (recall from §3.1.7 that free pronouns are inherently unmarked for number, so the free pronoun *ngayu* does not distinguish number).

Plural subject + dual object:

(446) *Ngayu=**rna-nyangu-lu***   *nya-nganya*   ***nyuntu***   *jirrama.*
1=**1.S-2PL.NS-PL.S**   see-PRES   **2**   **two**
We see you two.
H_K01-505B, DG, 52:30 mins

Similarly, in (447), the subject is overtly marked as dual by nominal suffixes *-jarra*, but because the object is plural, both sets of bound pronouns use the plural forms.

Dual subject + plural object:

(447) ***Ngarrka-jarra-rlu***   *jirrama-jarra-rlu=**lpangu-lu***   *nya-nganya.*
man-DU-ERG   two-DU-ERG=**1**PL.EXCL.NS-**3PL.S**   see-PRES
The two men can see us.
H_K01-505B, DG, 50:26 mins

In (448), both the subject and the object are explicitly dual: the subject free pronoun takes the dual suffix and the object has the quantifier *jirrama*, but the bound pronoun forms are both plural (despite neither referent having plural reference).

Dual subject + dual object:

(448) ***Nyuntu-jarra-rlu***   *ngarrka=**jana-nkulu***   *jirrama*   *nya-nganya.*
2-DU-ERG   man=**3PL.NS-2PL.S**   **two**   see-PRES
You two can see two men.
H_K01-505B, DG, 57:48 mins

There is one speaker of Warlmanpa noted in the heritage corpus who appears not to exhibit (complete) dual neutralisation, which may be indicative of a dialectal split akin to Eastern/Western Warlpiri. For example, in (449), there are two clear bound pronouns: *=jangu*, which refers to a first-person dual object, and *=lu*, which refers to a third-person plural subject.

(449) *Ngarrka-panji-rlu=jangu-lu*   *nya-nganya*   *nyuntu-jarra.*
       man-PAUC-ERG=1DU.EXC.O-3PL.S   see-PRES   2-DUAL
       They're looking at us two.
       N_D01-007836, JJN, 34:45 mins

Unfortunately, there are not enough data to ascertain the conditioning behind this process; if this speaker exhibits dual replacement, the expectation is that dual subject and dual object pronouns in combination with each other will be prohibited (and at least one bound pronoun will be 'replaced' with a plural version). However, cases for this speaker where there are two overt dual referents are unclear. For example, in (450), there is an overt dual subject (*ngayujarrarlu* 'we two') and an overt dual object (*ngarrkajarra* 'two men'), yet the bound pronouns seem to register only the first-person dual subject.

(450) *Ngayu-jarra-rlu=ja*   *nya-nganya*   *ngarrka-jarra.*
       1-DU-ERG=1DU.EXCL.S   see-PRES   man-DU
       We see two men.
       N_D01-007836: 125, JJN, 27:30 mins

One possible analysis is that the third-person dual subject is replaced in the bound pronouns with a third-person singular subject, which is phonologically null. This is motivated by the surface data, though it is unclear why this would be the case, given all other dual-replacement processes replace the dual with a plural, rather than a singular. Alternatively, where there is competition between two dual pronouns, it is possible that one of the pronouns will simply be deleted, likely according to the same hierarchy that conditions which dual pronoun is replaced in Western Warlpiri's dual-replacement process: first person > second person > third person (where the lowest member of the hierarchy is replaced). This is in line with the first-person bound pronoun being maintained in (450) and the third-person pronoun not being maintained.

One final note on dual neutralisation is that reflexive/reciprocal constructions are not subject to dual neutralisation, which is evidence that =*nyanu*, the reflexive/reciprocal bound pronoun, does not inherently encode number (or person). For example, in (451), the subject bound pronoun is =*pala*, which encodes third-person dual, and the non-subject bound pronoun is =*nyanu*, indicating the event is reciprocal between the dual referents, but =*pala* is not replaced with plural =*lu*.

(451)   *Wa-nganya=pala-nyanu.*

speak-PRES=3DU.S-RR

Those two are speaking to each other.

wrl-20190117, SN, 02:55 mins

5.4.2.2 Combinatorial forms

The complete set of known combinations of two bound pronouns is given in Table 5.5. Some combinations are not known, particularly different combinations of first-person subjects with first-person objects of different clusivity and number.

A question mark indicates there is no instantiated use of the combination in the transcribed corpus. Empty shaded cells are subject to dual neutralisation. A hyphen indicates that the REFL non-subject form should be referred to. Multiple forms in a cell indicate variation, with the topmost form being the more common one.

Table 5.5 Known bound pronoun combinations with two referents

Subject ↓	Non-subject												
	1SG.NS	1DU.EXCL.NS	1DU.INCL.NS	1PL.EXCL.NS	1PL.INCL.NS	2SG.NS	2DU.NS	2PL.NS	3SG.O	3.OBL	3DU.NS	3PL.NS	REFL
1SG.S	-	?	?	?	?	rnangu	rnangupala	rnanyangu	rna	rnarla	rnapalangu	rnajana	rnaju / rnanyanu
1DU.EXCL.S	?	-	?	?	?	jangu			ja / rnajarra	jarla / jarrarla			janyanu
1DU.INCL.S	?		-			?			li	lirla			linyanu
1PL.EXCL.S	rnajulu			-		rnangulu		rnanyangulu / rnanjarrangulu	rna	rnalurla		rnajanalu	rnalanyanu
1PL.INCL.S	?			?	-	lpangulu		?	lpa	lparla		lpajanalu	lpanyanu
2SG.S	jun	jangun / nmajangu	?	nganpan	?	-	?	?	n	nkurla	npalangu	janan	nyanun
2DU.S	junpala					?	-		npala	npalarla			npalanyanu
2PL.S	nkunjulu / junkulu			nganpankulu	?	?		-	nkulu	nkulurla		janankulu	nkulunyanu
3SG.S	ju	jangu	ngali	nganpa	lpangu	ngu	ngupala	nyangu	∅	rla	palangu	jana	nyanu
3DU.S	jupala					ngupala			pala	palarla	-		palanyanu
3PL.S	julu			nganpalu	lpangulu	ngulu		nyangulu	lu	lurla		janalu	lunyanu

5.4.3 A synchronic account of the forms

This section presents a synchronic analysis of the bound pronoun forms, based on the known bound pronoun combination forms presented in the preceding section. Most of the section utilises a templatic approach (§5.4.3.1), the remainder discusses some patterns not resolved by the template: other recurring forms of meaning (§5.4.3.2) and irregular forms of bound pronoun combinations (§5.4.3.3).

5.4.3.1 A templatic approach

With the variations (§5.4.1, §5.4.3.4) and combinations (§5.4.2) presented, I now provide an analysis of the bound pronouns that aims to predict: 1) the forms of the bound pronouns, and 2) the order of constituents in the bound pronouns. Many Ngumpin-Yapa bound pronoun systems are treated as templatic (Osgarby 2018: 121; Meakins and Nordlinger 2014: 243; Simpson and Withgott 1986), which clearly interact with multiple levels of grammar: the lexicon, phonology, morphology and syntax. Templatic approaches are particularly fruitful for the analysis of bound pronouns of Ngumpin-Yapa languages, due to their lack of clear morphological or syntactic heads, zero morphs and discontinuous exponence—all of which motivate a templatic approach (the concepts of templatic approaches as they apply to Australian languages are neatly established in Nordlinger 2010).

However, templatic approaches are difficult to reconcile with the subject/object inversion noted in some first-person bound pronoun combination categories (Osgarby 2018: 123; McConvell 1996b: 59), the precise details of which naturally vary across these languages. This will be discussed in further detail for Warlmanpa after first presenting the template.

The template is given in Table 5.6, accompanied by numerous examples of how the template applies to known combinations of bound pronouns (and the two known examples for which the template incorrectly predicts the form). In general, the template suggests a preference for first person to precede non–first person, and objects to precede subjects that precede the specialised forms =*nyanu* 'REFL' and =*rla* '3.OBL'.

Table 5.6 Bound pronoun template, with examples

Surface form	1P subject	Non-subject	Non-1P subject	Subject number	Reflexive	Oblique
=rnaju 1SG.S + 1SG.EXCL.NS	rna 1EXCL.S	ju 1SG.EXCL.NS		∅ S.SG		
=rnangulu 1PL.EXCL.S + 2SG.NS	rna 1EXCL.S	ngu 2SG.NS		lu S.PL		
=jangu 1DU.EXCL.S + 2SG.NS	ja 1DU.EXCL.S	ngu 2SG.NS				
=ngupala 3DU.S + 2SG.NS		ngu 2SG.NS	pala 3DU.S			
=janalu 3PL.S + 3PL.NS		jana 3PL.NS	∅ 3.S	lu S.PL		
=janan 3PL.NS + 2SG.S		jana 3PL.NS	n 2.S	∅ S.SG		
=janankulu 2PL.S + 3PL.NS		jana 3PL.NS	nku 2.S	lu S.PL		
=jun 2SG.S + 1SG.EXCL.NS		ju 1SG.EXCL.NS	n 2.S	∅ S.SG		
=lpajanalu 1PL.INCL.S + 3PL.NS	lpa 1INCL.S	jana 3PL.NS		lu S.PL		
=lurla 3PL.S + 3.OBL			∅ 3.S	lu S.PL		rla 3OBL
=npalanyanu 2DU.S + REFL			npala 2DU.S		nyanu REFL	
=rnangulurla 1PL.EXCL.S + 2SG.NS + 3.OBL	rna 1EXCL.S	ngu 2SG.NS		lu S.PL		rla 3OBL
=nyanurla REFL + 3.OBL					nyanu REFL	rla OBL
=nyanun 2SG.S + REFL			*n 2.S	∅ S.SG	nyanu REF	
=npalangu 2SG.S + 3DU.NS		*palangu 3DU.S	n 2.S			

5. THE AUXILIARY COMPLEX

In Warlmanpa and Mudburra, unlike other Ngumpin-Yapa languages, all first-person bound pronouns precede all other bound pronouns. In other Ngumpin-Yapa languages, this rule applies only to the first-person singular pronouns. This rule is exemplified in Table 5.7 for the combination of second-person singular subject with first-person plural exclusive non-subject: in Warlmanpa and Mudburra, the first-person exponent =*nganpa*/=*nganda* must precede any other material—in this case, =*n*, which denotes the second-person referent.[7] Conversely, in Ngardi, Bilinarra and Warlpiri, the subject precedes the object, despite the object being first person in this combination (of course, this is not to say that the bound pronouns in these languages are always in S-O order; they each have their own complex structures and analyses).

Table 5.7 Distinguishing bound pronoun ordering constraints of 1PL.EXCL.NS + 2SG.S

Language	First surface constituent	Second surface constituent	Order
Warlmanpa =*nganpan*	=*nganpa* 1PL.EXCL.NS	-*n* 2SG.S	1-2
Mudburra =*ngandan*	=*nganda* 1PL.EXCL.NS	-*n* 2SG.S	1-2
Ngardi =*nkunganpa*	=*nku* 2SG.S	-*nganpa* 1PL.EXCL.NS	S-O
Bilinarra =*nngandiba*	=*n* 2MIN.S	-*ngandiba* 1AUG.EXCL.O	S-O
Warlpiri =*npanganpa*	=*npa* 2SG.S	-*nganpa* 1PL.EXCL.NS	S-O
Wanyjirra =*nngandiba*	=*n* 2SG.S	-*ngandiba* 1PL.EXCL.NS	S-O

Osgarby (2018) incorporates this phenomenon into a templatic approach by stipulating a basic subject–object order and introducing a subject/non-subject transposition of certain combinations; however, the scope of this transposition accounts for other phenomena in the Mudburra bound pronoun paradigms that are not evident in Warlmanpa. Instead, I opt to introduce a special slot at the left-most position in the template,

---

7   This may also first appear to be phonologically motivated—that is, perhaps Warlmanpa and Mudburra instead represent languages that allow consonant-final bound pronoun complexes, whereas the other languages represent languages that do not permit consonant-final bound pronoun complexes. However, other examples demonstrate that it is not just phonologically motivated—for example, =*nganpa* '1PL.EXCL.NS' and =*lu* '3PL.S' also put the first-person referent before the subject pronoun, as in =*nganpalu*.

which requires a first-person pronoun (if one exists in the combination). Specifically, the left-most slot is restricted to first-person subjects, as the second slot is for objects of any person reference (which will be covered shortly). Thus, for the combination of =*rna* '1SG.EXCL.S' and =*ju* '1SG.EXCL. NS', the form is =*rnaju*, as explicated in (i) in the template examples, with further examples provided in (ii) and (iii).

Table 5.8 Examples of first-person subjects preceding all other material in the template

	Surface form	1P Subject	Object	(...)	Subject number	(...)
(i)	=*rnaju* 1SG.S + 1SG.EXCL.NS	*rna* 1.EXCL.S	*ju* 1SG.EXCL.NS		∅ S.SG	
(ii)	=*rnangulu* 1PL.EXCL.S + 2SG.NS	*rna* 1.EXCL.S	*ngu* 2SG.NS		*lu* S.PL	
(iii)	=jangu 1DU.EXCL.S + 2SG.NS	*ja* 1DU.EXCL.S	*ngu* 2SG.NS			

Interestingly, then, despite the preference for subject–object order for first-person combinations, there is overwhelming evidence for the basic order of object–subject, with first-person subjects providing the systematic exception. For example, the combination of =*jana* '3PL.NS' and =*n* '2PL.S' puts the non-subject form first, as in (vi), as well as further examples in (iv) and (v).[8]

Table 5.9 Examples of object–subject ordering in the template

	Surface form	(...)	Object	Non-1P subject	Subject number	(...)
(iv)	=*ngupala* 3DU.S + 2SG.NS		*ngu* 2SG.NS	*pala* 3DU.S	∅ S.SG	
(v)	=*janalu* 3PL.S + 3PL.NS		*jana* 3PL.NS	∅ 3.S	*lu* S.PL	
(vi)	=*janan* 3PL.NS + 2SG.S		*jana* 3PL.NS	*n* 2.S	∅ S.SG	

---

8   This contrasts with Jaru in which the second person should precede the third person, resulting in an unexpected cluster: the combination of =*n* '2SG.S' and =*yanu* '3PL.NS' results in fortition of the palatal glide to a stop—that is, =*njanu*, to accommodate the prohibited */n.j/ cluster (Tsunoda 1981a: 131).

5. THE AUXILIARY COMPLEX

Following the non-first-person-subject slot is a 'subject number' slot, which synchronically is only active for =*lu*, which marks a plural subject, as shown in Table 5.10.

Table 5.10 Bound pronouns with =*lu* to mark plurality

Pronoun reference	Pronoun form
1EXCL.S	=*rnalu*
1INCL.S	=*lpalu* (the =*lu* portion only arises in combinations)
2PL.S	=*nkulu*
3PL.S	=*lu*

Subject pronouns mark plurality with =*lu*, of which a smaller subset may be discontinuous with the plural marker. The second-person plural =*nkulu* has no environment in which =*nku* and =*lu* could be discontinuous, as the =*nku* would fill the subject slot, which is immediately preceding the subject number slot.[9] The third-person plural is compositionally analogous, except that the third-person subject is phonologically null. However, person and number marking in the first-person subjects will be discontinuous if there is also a non-subject pronoun, as in (ii) and (ix), with (v) providing an example of a third-person plural subject and (vii) providing an example of a second-person plural subject.

Table 5.11 Examples of *lu* marking subject plurality

	Surface form	1P subject	Object	Non-1P subject	Subject number	(...)
(ii)	=*rnangulu* 1PL.EXCL.S + 2SG.NS	*rna* 1.EXCL.S	*ngu* 2SG.NS		*lu* S.PL	
(v)	=*janalu* 3PL.S + 3PL.NS		*jana* 3PL.NS	∅ 3.S	*lu* S.PL	
(vii)	=*janankulu* 2PL.S + 3PL.NS		*jana* 3PL.NS	*nku* 2.S	*lu* S.PL	
(ix)	=*lpajanalu* 1PL.INCL.S + 3PL.NS	*lpa* 1INCL.S	*jana* 3PL.NS		*lu* S.PL	

This also motivates treating null number marking as singular for the pronouns that have =*lu* available, as in (i) and (vi).

---

9 I assume that the alternation between =*n* and =*nku* (that is, the epenthetic) is resolved via a phonological rule external to this template.

Table 5.12 Examples of null subject number marking

	Surface form	1P subject	Object	Non-1P subject	Subject number
(i)	=rnaju 1SG.S + 1SG.EXCL.NS	rna 1.EXCL.S	ju 1SG.EXCL.NS		∅ S.SG
(vi)	=janan 3PL.NS + 2SG.S		jana 3PL.NS	n 2.S	∅ S.SG

The two right-most slots in the template are reserved for the reflexive/reciprocal pronoun =*nyanu* and the third-person singular oblique =*rla*, as in (x) and (xi), respectively. When =*nyanu* and =*rla* co-occur, the reflexive occurs first, followed by =*rla*, as in (xii).

Table 5.13 Examples of reflexive and third-person oblique marking

	Surface form	(…)	Non-1P subject	Subject number	Reflexive	Oblique
(x)	=lurla 3PL.S + 3.OBL		∅ 3.S	lu S.PL		rla 3OBL
(xi)	=npalanyanu 2DU.S + REFL		npala 2DU.S		nyanu REFL	
(xii)	=nyanurla REFL + 3.OBL				nyanu REFL	rla 3.OBL

The logical maximum of filled slots (with overt exponents) in this template is four (given that there are two subject slots, only one could be filled), which correspond to three grammatical relations. This maximal template is exemplified in (xiii) by =*rnangulurla* '1PL.EXCL.S + 2SG.NS + 3.OBL', which cross-references three referents. The only empty slot is the non-first-person-subject slot, because the first-person-subject slot is filled instead. The only other known bound pronoun combination cross-referencing three referents is (xii), =*rnangurla* '1SG.S + 2SG.NS + 3.OBL', which is the same except with singular-subject number (formally null).

Table 5.14 Examples of bound pronouns cross-referencing three referents

	Surface form	1P subject	Object	Subject number	Oblique
(xii)	=rnangurla 1PL.EXCL.S + 2SG.NS + 3.OBL	rna 1.EXCL.S	ngu 2SG.NS		rla 3OBL
(xiii)	=rnangulurla 1PL.EXCL.S + 2SG.NS + 3.OBL	rna 1.EXCL.S	ngu 2SG.NS	lu S.PL	rla 3OBL

5. THE AUXILIARY COMPLEX

There are two bound pronoun combinations that do not fit this template. First, the second-person reflexive *=nyanun* is incorrectly predicted as **=nnyanu*, as explicated in (xiv). In all other combinations, *=nyanu* occurs after the other subject and object bound pronouns. This does not seem to be phonologically motivated, since *nny* clusters are permitted in Warlmanpa and the second-person singular utilises an epenthetic *ku*, which otherwise avoids prohibited clusters (for example, *=nku-lu*), while still allowing the templatic ordering (rather than reordering and violating the template).

Table 5.15 Unpredicted form =nyanun

	Surface form	(…)	Non-1P subject	Subject number	Reflexive
(xiv)	=nyanun 2SG.S + REFL		*n 2.S	∅ S.SG	nyanu REF

Second, the combination of the second-person singular subject *=n* and third-person dual non-subject *=palangu* is incorrectly predicted as **=palangun*, on the basis of all other non-first-person-subject combinations being ordered as O-S, whereas the actual form is *=npalangu*—that is, S-O.

Table 5.16 Unpredicted form =npalangu

	Surface form	(…)	Object	Non-1P subject	(…)
(xv)	=npalangu 2SG.S + 3DU.NS		*palangu 3DU.NS	*n 2.S	

Interestingly, both these exceptions involve the second-person singular subject *=n*: in one case, it follows a bound pronoun that otherwise follows all other person/number forms; and in the other, *=n* precedes a bound pronoun that otherwise precedes all other non-first-person forms.

In summary, the template presented for bound pronouns seems to reflect two hierarchies:

- first person > non–first person
- object > subject > oblique and reciprocal/reflexive.

The template also necessitates the discontinuous expression of certain subjects and their number reference.

An alternative analysis is given in Browne (2021a: 520–24), in a constraint hierarchy model, deviating from the standard templating approach of describing bound pronouns in Ngumpin-Yapa languages.

5.4.3.2 Other recurring patterns of meaning

There are two recurring forms that may be ascribed a meaning/function, which are not explicitly analysed in the template.

First, there is the recurrence of the form *pala* in the non-first-person dual bound pronouns, shown in Table 5.17.

Table 5.17 Bound pronouns with *pala* marking dual number

	Subject	Non-subject
2DU	=npala	=ngupala
3DU	=pala	=palangu

Feasibly, the template could have recognised *pala* as marking dual number, except the only number slot in the template is for subject number, whereas *pala* clearly marks dual regardless of grammatical relation. Even so, the correct forms can mostly be predicted by extending the number slot to allow *pala* to mark dual (and then one would need to posit some kind of rule that links *pala* to the appropriate grammatical relation, now that the slot is no longer specified for subject), as demonstrated in Table 5.18. However, (xix) leaves the form *ngu* unaccounted for, which is the second recurring form of meaning.

Table 5.18 Abridged template approach with extended number slot allowing dual marking

	Surface form	Object	Non-1P subject	Number	?
(xvi)	=npala 2DU.S		n 2.S	pala S.DU	
(xvii)	=ngupala 2DU.NS	ngu 2.NS		pala NS.DU	
(xviii)	=pala 3DU.S		∅ 3.S	pala S.DU	
(xix)	=palangu 3DU.NS	∅ 3.S		pala S.DU	ngu

Leaving the discussion of *pala* aside for now, *ngu* recurs across three subject–object bound pronoun pairs as an identifier of the non-subject bound pronoun, shown in Table 5.19.[10]

---

10 The same form, =*ngu*, also refers to second-person objects, however, this is homophony, rather than bearing a relation to the *ngu* marked here.

5. THE AUXILIARY COMPLEX

Table 5.19 Bound pronouns pairs that mark non-subject status with *ngu*

	Subject	Non-subject
1DU.EXCL	=ja	=jangu
1PL.INCL	=lpa(lu)	=lpangu
3DU	=pala	=palangu

Based on this, a maximally compositional template could also include an 'object marker' slot, which would be used to indicate that the next-left exponent refers to an object, thus (xix) could be broken down as:

	Surface form	Object	Number	Object marker
(xix)	=palangu 3DU.NS	∅ 3.S	pala S.DU	ngu

However, I do not believe incorporating *pala* into the number slot or introducing an object marker slot is fruitful for the templatic analysis. While *pala* could feasibly be incorporated without the introduction of an extra slot, this leaves the form *=palangu* as an exception to the template approach (that is, the separation of *pala* as a number marker necessitates the addition of a slot for *ngu* or treating *palangu* as a variant of *pala* used only for 3DU.NS). Furthermore, the *pala* and *ngu* portions are never separated from the rest of the forms given in Table 5.10 and Table 5.18, even in combination with other bound pronouns. The motivation for the number slot was due to the possibility of *lu* marking plural subject and being discontinuous from the remainder of the subject marker, which is not true of *pala* or *ngu*. Thus, in a templatic approach, nothing is gained by separating these forms.

5.4.3.3 Irregular forms

There are several 'irregular' bound pronoun combinations that warrant further discussion.

=nmajangu:

The form *=nmajangu* was used once in the corpus, as shown in (452), in which it refers to a second-person singular subject (*=n*) and a first-person dual exclusive non-subject (*=jangu*). The same form was used in the single repetition of this sentence.

(452)   Kala=nma-jangu   paka-nmi.
        APPR=2SG.S-1DU.EXCL.NS   hit-FUT
        You might hit us two.
        wrl-20190213-02, DK, 02:04 mins

This irregular form is not predicted by the template discussed in §5.4.3 for two reasons. First, the template predicts that the first-person exponent should be on the left edge of the bound pronouns, whereas here the first-person exponent is on the right edge. Second, the =*n* 2SG.S pronoun appears to take an epenthetic portion *ma*, but it is not clear why *ma* should be the epenthetic form, given the only noted epenthetic forms in the bound pronoun system are *ku* and *pa*. It is possibly a process of nasal assimilation—the synchronic form in Warlpiri is =*npa-jarrangku*, which, if taken to be the conservative historical form, can be accounted for by means of regular historical deletion processes in Warlmanpa and assimilation of /np/ to /nm/.

=*rnajarra*:

As discussed earlier, this form is used to refer to first-person dual exclusive, in (453) and in two repetitions of this same sentence.

(453)   *Ngayu=ma=**rna-jarra**   kangkuya-jarra   partu-nga*
        1=TOP=1EXCL.S-DUAL   old_man-DU   leave-PAST.AWAY
        Darwin-ka=lku.
        Darwin-ALL=THEN
        Then the old man and I left to Darwin.
        wrl-20190211-01, DK, 03:44 mins

This bound pronoun form, =*rnajarra*, appears to be a compositional reanalysis: =*rna* is the first-person exclusive, unmarked for number, and -*jarra* is used in a small number of bound pronoun combinations, however, none of them refers to dual referents. This is not the case in Eastern Warlpiri, in which =*rlujarra* marks a first-person dual exclusive subject, so these *jarra* portions are likely historically from the same source.

=*rnan.jarrangulu*:

This form, exemplified in (454), is particularly interesting as it may reflect the historical form of the second-person plural non-subject form, which is synchronically (typically) =*nyangu*.

(454)   *Ngayu=rna-**n.jarrangu**-lu*   *nya-nganya-rra*   *tartu-ngu.*
        1=1.S-2PL.NS-S.PL   see-PRES-IMPF   many-ERG
        We are looking at you mob.
        N_D01-007836, JJN, 26:05 mins

This could be seen as the historical form, with the modern form =*nyangu* being the result of two sound changes: *ara* > *a* and *nc* > *ɲ*. The former is a well-established change, though the latter involves both assimilation and lenition and is not established with sound correspondences, making it somewhat less plausible.

Table 5.20 Possible history of the irregular form =*njarrangu*

Older form	*n.jarrangu*
arra > *a*	*njangu*
nc > *ɲc* > *ɲ*	*nyangu*
Modern form	*nyangu*

5.4.3.4 Imperative clauses

In imperative constructions, the subject is only marked for number; there is no overt realisation of second person in the bound pronouns. The dual subject pronoun =*pala* and plural subject pronoun =*lu* only specify number, and the person value is inferred from context: in imperative clauses, the subject is second person and otherwise (for example, declarative clauses), the subject is third person, which is reflected in Table 5.21.

Table 5.21 Imperative bound pronoun forms, identical to non-imperative third-person forms

	Clause type:	Imperative	Non-imperative
Subject person (inferred from clause type):		2nd person	3rd person
Subject number	Singular	∅	∅
	Dual	=*pala*	=*pala*
	Plural	=*lu*	=*lu*

Thus, in singular-subject imperatives, there is no overt subject bound pronoun, as in (455) and (456).

(455)   *Ngutungutu   ya-ka!*
          Carefully   place-IMP
          Place it carefully!
          N_D03-007868, BN, 12:09 mins

(456)   *Kuku=ju   kutij-ka-rra!*
          Wait=1SG.NS   stand-be-IMP
          Stand there waiting for me!
          Wrl-20180615-02, DK, 19:46 mins

When the imperative subject is dual, the dual pronoun =*pala* is used, and when the imperative subject is plural, the plural pronoun =*lu* is used, as in (457) and (458), respectively.

(457) Kula=**pala**-nyanu   paka-ka!
       NEG=DU.S-RR   hit-IMP
       Don't you two hit each other!
       Wrl-20200220, DK, 21:22 mins

(458) Numu=**lu**-rla   yu-ngka!
       No_more=PL.S-3.OBL   give-IMP
       You all should stop giving it to him!
       H_K01-506A, DG, 01:00:59 hrs

The non-subject bound pronouns are unchanged, as exemplified in (458) with the =*rla* indirect object, (459) with the =*jana* indirect object, (460) with the =*ju* (direct) object and (461) with the =*nyanu* reflexive benefactive. Also demonstrated by (461) is that the reflexive form =*nyanu* can occur in imperatives with singular-subject reference, unlike Warlpiri (Simpson 1991: 167).

(459) Warlu=**jana**   yu-ngka   ngarrka-panyji-ku.
       Fire=3PL.NS   give-IMP   man-PAUC-DAT
       Give the firewood to the few men.
       H_K01-505B, DG, 39:59 mins

(460) Nya-ngka=**ju**!
       See-IMP=1SG.NS
       Look at me!
       H_K01-506A, DG, 59:25 mins

(461) Tajpaka=**nyanu**   tingkirr   pu-ngka.
       Properly=RR   tie   act_on-IMP
       Tie it up properly for yourself.
       N_D03-007868, BN, 11:39 mins

While the second-person-subject bound pronoun =*n* is prohibited in imperative constructions, the free pronoun may still be used, as in (462).

(462) *Nyuntu,   wa-ngka!*
       2   speak-IMP
       You, speak!
       H_K01-505B, DG, 01:51 mins

5.4.4 Topics in participant registration

While §5.4.2 and §5.4.3 demonstrate the combinatorial possibilities of bound pronouns, there are several factors that condition whether a referent will be registered in the bound pronoun complex. These involve animacy effects (§5.4.4.1), competition between two oblique bound pronouns (§5.4.4.2) and two object bound pronouns (§5.4.4.3).

5.4.4.1 Animacy effects

The bound pronouns obligatorily cross-reference animate referents, so long as their grammatical relation is cross-referenced by the bound pronouns (§10.1). This includes humans, as in (463), and some animals, such as birds (465), wallabies (466), kangaroos (466) and lizards (467).

(463) ***Kurtu-kurtu=lu***   *lu-ngunya.*
       Child-PL=3PL.S   cry-PRES
       The children are crying.
       H_K01-505B, DG, 30:23 mins

(464) ***Maliki-panyji-rlu=ju-lu***   *pu-ngu!*
       Dog-PAUC-ERG=1SG.NS-3PL.S   act_on-PAST
       The few dogs bit **me**!
       H_K01-505B, DG, 05:25 mins

(465) ***Jurlaka*=*ma=lu***   *kunturru-rla.*
       Bird=TOP=**3PL.S**   sky-LOC
       The birds are in the sky.
       Wrl-20190212-02, DK, 14:42 mins

(466) ***Yukulyarri***   ***wawirri*=*rna-palangu***   *karta-pu-ngu.*
       Wallaby   **kangaroo=1SG.S-3DU.NS**   spear-act_on-PAST
       I speared **a wallaby** and **a kangaroo**.
       H_K01-505B, DG, 46:22 mins

(467) **Jurlaka-rlu=lu-rla**   wirriri-nya-ngu-rra   **yipakarli-ku**.
Bird-ERG=3PL.S-3.OBL   in_a_circle-see-PAST-IMPF   lizard-DAT
The birds were looking for **a lizard**.
Wrl-20190207-01, DK, 51:07 mins

Interestingly, the set of animate referents includes eggs, as in (468).[11] However, the set does not extend to insects, bugs, etcetera, as exemplified in (469), where *pingirri* 'ant' is not cross-referenced. Examples of clear non-animates are given in (470) and (471), where *pamarrpa* 'hill' and *yiwirti* 'tree/spear' are construed with a plural nominal *tartu* but are not cross-referenced by a bound pronoun.

(468)   Nama-nnya   **mula=jana**   kayi=lu   kurtukurtu   palyalpalyal
weigh_down-PRES   **egg=3PL.NS**   WHEN=3PL.NS   children   emerge

parti.
Leave.FUT
He's sitting on the eggs until they hatch as children.
Wrl-20191207-02, DK, 27:52 mins

(469)   Jarrawarti-rla   kanya,   pirtij-pirtij   jutpu-ngunya   **pingirri**.
Thigh-LOC   be-PRES   climb-RDP   run-PRES   **ant**
They're on his thigh, **the ants** are climbing up his thigh.
N_D02-007842, BN, 17:16 mins

(470)   **Tartu**   pamarrpa   ka-nya.
Many   hill   be-PRES
There are lots of hills.
Wrl-20190121, PK, 43:10 mins

(471)   **Tartu**=rna   yiwirti   marta-nnya.
Many=1SG.S   tree   have-PRES
I have many spears.
H_K01-506A, DG, 50:43 mins

---

11 Alternatively, this may be an example of inalienable possession, where the (unborn) birds contained within the eggs possess their egg, and the bound pronoun is in fact cross-referencing the birds, rather than the eggs.

5. THE AUXILIARY COMPLEX

The exception to the animacy restriction is that indirect objects and external objects are cross-referenced, regardless of animacy (grammatical relations are discussed in §10.1). For example, in (472), the indirect object of the predicate is *karliku* 'for a boomerang', which is cross-referenced with the oblique pronoun =*rla*.

(472)   *Ngayu=rna-**rla**   **karli-ku**   wayi-nnya.*
        1=1SG.S-**3.OBL**   **boomerang-DAT**   search-PRES
        I'm searching for a boomerang.
        H_K01-505B, DG, 18:07 mins

Mass nouns are cross-referenced with =*rla* in (473)–(475), whereas (count) plural referents receive plural cross-referencing with the non-subject series instead, as in (476), where *wangani-ku* 'dog-DAT' is cross-referenced by =*jana*, indicating a plural referent.

Mass nouns (indirect object), cross-referenced with =*rla*:

(473)   ***Kuyu-ku**=rna-**rla**   wayi-nnya.*
        Meat-DAT=1SG.S-**3.OBL**   search-PRES
        I'm searching for meat.
        H_K01-505B, DG, 07:43 mins

(474)   *Karnta-ngu=**rla**   **ngappa-ku**   wayi-nnya.*
        Woman-ERG=**3.OBL**   **water-DAT**   search-PRES
        The woman is searching for water.
        H_K01-505B, DG, 08:05 mins

Mass nouns (external object), cross-referenced with =*rla*:

(475)   *Yiwirti=rna-**rla**   yirrkin   paka-rnu   **ngurlu-ku**.*
        Tree=1SG.S-**3.OBL**   with   chop-PAST   **seed-DAT**
        I chopped the tree with seeds on it.
        N_D02-007842, BN, 02:38 mins

Count nouns (indirect object), cross-referenced according to number:

(476)   *Yangka=ma=**jana**=lu   karntakarntarlu   yu-ngu   **wangani-ku**.*
        Another=TOP=**3PL.NS**-3PL.S   woman~PL-ERG   give-PAST   **dog-DAT**
        The women gave a bit more food **to the dogs**.
        Wrl-20191208-02, DK, 04:39 mins

Note that this is particular to the grammatical role of indirect object rather than the dative case marking. Other types of dative-marked constituents are not cross-referenced, as in (477), where *ngappaku* 'for the water' is a purposive adjunct, so it is not marked, unlike *ngappaku* above, where it is functioning as an indirect object of *wayi-* 'search for'.

(477)   **Ngappa-ku**=*lu*   *pa-nanga.*
        Water-DAT=3PL.S   go-PAST.AWAY
        They're going for water.
        Wrl-20180605-01, DK, 52:58 mins

The summary of animacy effects is given in Table 5.22. Animates have three series of distinct bound pronouns (subject, object, oblique) that are marked for number as appropriate. Inanimates are only registered in the indirect object grammatical role, and only by =*rla*, regardless of number (where =*rla* is reserved for singular animates).

Table 5.22 Cross-referencing of grammatical relations in the bound pronouns

Grammatical relation	Animate	Non-animate
Subject	Subject series	Not registered
Object	Object series	Not registered
Indirect object External object	Object series Oblique =*rla* if 3SG.S	Oblique =*rla* if mass noun or 3SG.S (No data on non-sentient IO count nouns)
Adjuncts	Not registered	Not registered

The environment may seemingly be cross-referenced with an =*rla* (3SG oblique series), as in (478), particularly in relation to rain and storms. A similar phenomenon is found in Warlpiri, as in (479), however, this is not well understood in either language.

(478)   *Ngappa-ngu*=**rla**   *talan*   *ma-nu-rnu.*
        water-ERG=**3.OBL**   lightning   get-PAST-TWD
        There was lightning coming.
        wrl-20190201, DK, 56:04 mins

(479)   *Puululu*   *ka*=**rla**   *ka-nyi-rni.*
        bring_rain   PRES=**3.OBL**   bring-NPAST-TWD
        It's bringing the rain with it.
        (Warlpiri [Laughren et al. 2022: 758])

5.4.4.2 Double dative

Two dative-marked constituents can be cross-referenced by the bound pronouns, but only if one referent is third-person singular (*=rla* 3.OBL) and the other is any other non-subject form. This is due to the templatic nature of the bound pronouns as analysed in §5.4.3.1: *=rla* occupies a slot in the template that can only be filled by *=rla* or *nyanu* 'REFL', and similarly, the other non-subject pronouns occupy a slot that can only be filled by one pronoun.

An example of two dative event participants being cross-referenced in the bound pronouns is given in (480), where the bound pronoun *=ngu* 2SG.NS cross-references the overt free pronoun *nyuntu-ku* 'for you', and the *=rla* 3.OBL cross-references a benefactive adjunct. This combination of two dative arguments being cross-referenced is permitted because *=ngu* and *=rla* fill different slots in the template.

(480) *Wayi-rnu-rra=rna-ngu-rla* *nyuntu-ku.*
search-PAST-IMPF=1SG.S-2SG.NS-3.OBL 2-DAT
I was searching for you for him.
wrl-20190213-01, DK, 10:14 mins

However, when both dative-marked constituents are singular and third person, only one non-subject bound pronoun is permitted, as exemplified in (481), where there is an indirect object that is singular (*karliku*) and a benefactive adjunct (*yapakanyanuku*) that is also singular. Under normal conditions, both constituents would be cross-referenced in the bound pronouns by *=rla*, but there is only one *=rla* used (and it is ambiguous which constituent is being cross-referenced).

(481) **Karli-ku**=rna-**rla** *wayi-nnya* **yapa-kanyanu-ku**.
boomerang-DAT=1SG.S-3.OBL search-PRES **man-OTHER-DAT**
I'm searching for a boomerang for another man.
H_K01-505B, DG, 01:00:43 hrs

This contrasts with Warlpiri, which has a specific form, *=rlajinta*, when two third-person singular dative arguments would be cross-referenced in the bound pronouns.

(482) *Karli-rlangu-ku*   *kajika=**rla-jinta***   *liji-yirra-rni*
boomerang-TOO-DAT   POT=**3DAT-3DAT**   covet-NPST
yangka   *ngarrka-kariyinyanu-ku.*
the   man-OTH.SELF-DAT

He might covet the boomerang, for example, of another man.
(Warlpiri [Simpson 1991: 183])

5.4.4.3 Constraints against multiple non-subject bound pronouns

Different types of objects may be subject to competition—in particular, objects and the reflexive bound pronoun *=nyanu* seem to be incompatible. To exemplify, the utterance in (483) includes a reflexive pronoun to signify the relationship between the addressee and her husband (that is, husband to/for addressee). The same utterance with a first-person benefactive adjunct uses the *=ju* bound pronoun instead of combining *=ju* and *=nyanu* into a complex form (for example, **=ju-nyanu*).

(483) *Ma-nta=nyanu*   *nyintinya*   *ngumpana.*
get-IMP=RR   2GEN   husband
Get your husband [to you]!
wrl-20200219, DK, 57:01 mins

(484) *Ma-nta=ju*   *nyintinya*   *ngumpana.*
get-IMP=1SG.NS   2GEN   husband
Get your husband for me!
wrl-20200219, DK, 57:47 mins

This may indicate that *=nyanu* and another object bound pronoun are incompatible with each other, where *=nyanu* has the lowest priority. There are no instances in the corpus of *=nyanu* co-occurring with an object bound pronoun. However, *=nyanu* cannot be considered to fill the 'non-subject' slot of the template, as it follows subject bound pronouns, whereas the non-subject slot of the template precedes subject bound pronouns—best exemplified by (xi) in the template: *=npala-nyanu* '2DU.S-RR'. Attributing *=nyanu* to the non-subject slot would incorrectly predict **=nyanu-npala*.

Further research is needed for other cases of competition between non-singular non-subject bound pronouns in Warlmanpa. Based on other Pama-Nyungan languages with bound pronouns, the expected pattern would be for the indirect objects to be expressed and objects to be unexpressed (Ennever and Browne 2023).

5.5 =nga 'dubitative'

The right-most slot of the auxiliary complex is reserved for the clitic =*nga*, as in (485), where there is an auxiliary base *nga* 'posterior', a bound pronoun =*ju* '1SG.NS', followed by the dubitative clitic =*nga*.

(485)   **Nga=ju=nga**   *pi-nya*   *maliku-rlu*   *majju-ng.u!*
POST=1SG.NS=DUB   act_on-POT   dog-ERG   bad-ERG
Careful, the bad dog might bite you!
N_1977-11-23, DG, 14:23 mins

This clitic cannot occur in any other position in a clause, nor can any other clitic follow the bound pronouns. It typically encodes epistemic possibility, as in (486).

(486)   *Kari=**nga***   *jutu-nga,*   *ngarra*   *wirli*   *ya-nnya*   *karlawurru.*
far=DUB   run-PAST.AWAY   might   hunt   go-PRES   goanna
He might have run off, he might be hunting goannas.
wrl-20180610-01, DK, 22:25 mins

When co-occurring with the auxiliary base *nga=* 'FUT', the resulting construction has an apprehensional meaning, serving as a warning of an undesired event, as in (487).

(487)   *Ngarrka-ngu*   **nga**=*ngu*=**nga**   *karta-pi-nya.*
man-ERG   POST=2SG.NS=DUB   spear-act_on-POT
[Careful,] the man might spear you.
H_K01-505B, DG, 19:51 mins

This construction is particularly common with apposed clauses denoting a way to avoid an undesired event, as in (488), where the clause containing *nga=...=nga* denotes an undesired event (not having food cooked) and the clause to its left denotes a way to avoid the undesired event (going home). This is particularly interesting as the apprehensional has scope over a negative-polarity event—that is, the event *not* occurring is seen as detrimental.

(488) Ngurra-ka=rna   pina   pa-na,   kula   **nga=ju=nga**
      camp-ALL=1SG.S   return   go-POT   NEG   **POST=1SG.NS=DUB**
      yarnunju   ji-nnya.
      vegetable_food   burn-PRES
      I should return home, **lest** he not cook food for me.
      N_D03-007868, BN, 36:57 mins

These apprehensional constructions are discussed in further detail in Browne et al. (2024).

Finally, =*nga* seems to be able to attenuate claims (akin to English 'maybe'), as in (489).

(489) Wittuwittu=rnulu=nga   ngayu,   but   ngayu-jarra=ma=ja,
      small=1EXC.S=DUB   1   1-DU=TOP=1DU.EXCL,
      little bit   wiri,   yumpa=ma   witta   one.
                             big,   this=TOP   small
      Maybe we were all small, but us two were a bit bigger, this one was small.
      N_D29-023128, BN, 5:34 mins

This clitic is also found in Bilinarra, in which it may also attach to inflecting verbs, in addition to the right edge of the auxiliary complex (Meakins and Nordlinger 2014: 306–8).

6

Inflecting verbs

This chapter discusses the morphology and semantics of the 'verb' and 'coverb' parts of speech in Warlmanpa. The chapter begins by defining the 'verb' word, proposing an essentially templatic structure of the word (§6.1), though a more detailed analysis demonstrates a more hierarchical structure. Verb classes are then introduced (§6.2), with a brief overview of how 'augments' (somewhat akin to 'class markers') complicate the analysis of verb morphology, in §6.2.2.1, and an analysis of the morphophonological process relevant to root-final high vowels in §6.2.2.2. The form and function of the TAM inflections are then discussed (§6.2.2.2.2.1). This is followed by analyses of additional inflectional morphology (§6.2.3.10)— specifically directional motion (§6.4.1) and the imperfective aspect suffix (§6.4.2). The final topic pertaining to inflecting verbs is derivational morphology (§6.5). This includes analysis of derivational morphology affecting verb roots (§6.5.1) to derive complex verbs including associated motion (§6.5.1.1), inceptives (§6.5.1.2) and verb reduplication (§6.5.1.3). The derivational morphology of verbs from nominals is discussed in §6.5.2. The chapter concludes by discussing some inflections that warrant further analysis and comparison with other inflections: the relationship between the 'imperfective' and the 'away' suffix is discussed in §6.6.1, the relationship between the directional suffixes and the associated motion derivations is discussed in §6.6.2 and the relationships between the four non-imperative irrealis inflections are examined in §6.6.3.

6.1 The 'verb' word

The basic verb word template is represented in Table 6.1 (henceforth, I will refer to 'inflecting verbs' as just 'verbs').[1]

Table 6.1 Structure of the verb word

(i)	(ii)	(iii)	(iv)
Root	-AUG	-TAM	-DIR **or** -ASP
Obligatory	Conditioned	Obligatory	Optional
	(§6.2.2.1)	(§6.2.2.2.2.1)	(§6.4.1, §6.4.2)

As shown in the template, the components of a well-formed verb word are minimally a verb root and a TAM inflection suffixed to the root, as in (490).

(490)　Witta　**ka**$_{ROOT}$**-nya**$_{TAM}$.
　　　 small　**be-PRES**
　　　 It is small.
　　　 H_K01-505B, DG, 32:20 mins

Some combinations of roots and the TAM inflection require an augment, as in (491). The present-tense inflection cannot immediately attach to the root *nga-* 'eat', as this specific combination requires an augment, *-rni*. Augments are discussed in §6.2.2.1.

(491)　Kuyu　**nga**$_{ROOT}$**-rni**$_{AUG}$**-nya**$_{TAM}$.
　　　 meat　**eat-AUG-PRES**
　　　 He's eating meat.
　　　 H_K01-505B, DG, 32:20 mins

Either a directional or an aspectual suffix may attach to the verb stem, as in (492) and (493). There are no tokens of a directional and aspectual suffixing co-occurring. Directional suffixes are discussed in §6.4.1 and the aspectual suffix is discussed in §6.4.2. Example (492) also shows a clitic attaching to a verb word: as discussed in §9.1.6, clitics can attach to all well-formed words, so are not considered part of the verb 'word'.

---

[1]　Despite presenting the verb word as a 'flat' template for readability, I view the structure of the verb word to be hierarchical, following Laughren's (2010: 181) analysis of Warlpiri verbs, as shown in Table 6.2.

6. INFLECTING VERBS

(492)   *Pa$_{ROOT}$-na$_{AUG}$-ngu$_{TAM}$-rnu$_{DIR}$=lu.*
go-AUG-PAST-TWD=3PL.S
They came here.
wrl-20170321-02, SN, 01:35 mins

(493)   *Kala=lu*   **kupa$_{ROOT}$-rnu$_{TAM}$-rra$_{ASP}$.**
HAB=3PL.S   cook-PAST-IMPF
They used to cook it.
wrl-20160908-01, SN, 02:18 mins

Two constructions allow the derivation of a verb stem, which is treated as a 'root' in the word structure given above. The associated motion (§6.2.3.9) and inceptive (§6.5.1.2) derivational suffixes (with an augment where appropriate) form a stem, which then undergoes the regular word-formation processes a bare verb 'root' would undergo. Examples of this formation are given in Table 6.2 based on the same verb root, *nga-* 'eat'. These are analysed as derivational because: 1) the constructions change the verb class of the root to a unique class not found for any lexical roots; and 2) the constructions require inflectional TAM marking on the outside of the derived stem.

Table 6.2 Example verb formations involving associated motion and inceptive derivations

	Associated motion	Inceptive	Explanation
(i)	*nga* eat	*nga* eat	Verb root *nga-* 'eat'.
(ii)	*nga-rni* eat-AUG	*nga-rni* eat-AUG	Verb root hosts V4 INF augment to allow derivational suffix.
(i)'	[*nga-rni*]-**nya** eat-AUG-MOT	[*nga-rni*]-**nji** eat-AUG-INC	Stem hosts derivational suffix, forming a bound verb stem that is considered equal to a verb 'root', hence required to host TAM.
(ii)'	[*nga-rni*]-[*nya-n*] eat-AUG-MOT-AUG	[*nga-rni*]-[*nji-n*] eat-AUG-INC-AUG	Stem hosts augment to allow Class 5b PRES inflection.
(iii)'	[[[*nga-rni*]-[*nya-n*]]-**nya**] eat-AUG-MOT-AUG-PRES	[[[*nga-rni*]-[*nji-n*]]-**nya**] eat-AUG-INC-AUG-PRES	Stem hosts PRES inflection, is now a well-formed word.

This derivational process may be seen as semi-cyclical (given that once a verb has been derived through an associated motion or inceptive suffix, it cannot then undergo a further derivation), as visually depicted in Figure 6.1.

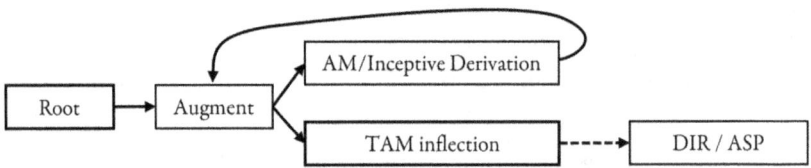

Figure 6.1 Word-formation processes involved in a well-formed verb

Note also that stage (ii) of the process exemplified in Table 6.2 highlights the value of synchronically maintaining 'augments'; this avoids having to redundantly specify an augment or unpredictable shared form for each of the four derivational processes for each class.

6.2 Inflecting verbs

Warlmanpa has 45 documented inflecting verbs, which can be classified into five major classes. These classes are determined by the forms of the inflections a particular verb requires (particularly the imperative form). A full list of inflecting verbs and lexical aspects of the well-documented inflecting verbs is provided in Appendix A.

The verbal inflections (including augments) are given in Table 6.3. A full stop represents the boundary between the augment and the inflection. Not included in this table are the two path inflections: *-nyinga* (§6.2.3.9) and -POT-*ma* (§6.2.3.10), which are only currently instantiated with a small number of inflecting verbs.

6. INFLECTING VERBS

Table 6.3 Inflections of verb classes

Members	1a	1b	1c	1d	2	3	4	5a	5b
	1	2	2	2	27	7	1	3	
IMPERATIVE	-ng.ka	-ng.ka	-n.ka	-rra	-ka	-ng.ka	-n.ja	-n.ta	-rra
PAST	-nga.nyu	-ngu	-na.ngu	-ngu	-rnu	-ngu	-rnu	-nu	-nu
FUTURE	-nga.mi	-mi	-na.mi	-mi	-n.mi	-nyi	-n.mi	-n.mi	-n.mi
POTENTIAL	-nga.ma	-ma	-na.ma	-ma	-n.ma	-nya	-n.ma	-n.ma	—
PRESENT	-nga.nya	-ngu.nya	-n.nya	-nya	-n.nya	-ngu.nya	-rni.nya	-n.nya	-n.nya
INFINITIVE	-nga.nja	-nja	-nja	-nja	-nja	-nja	-rni.nja	-nja	—
INCEPTIVE	-nga-nji-	-nji-	-nji-	-nji-*	-nji-	-nji-	-rni.nji-	-nji-	—
COUNTERFACTUAL	-nga.njakurla	-njakurla	-njakurla	-njakurla	-njakurla	-njakurla	-rni.njakurla	-njakurla	—
SUBJUNCTIVE	-ng.karla*	-ng.karla*	-n.ka.rla	-rrarla*	-karla	-ng.karla	-n.jarla	-n.tarla	—
MOTION	-nga-nja-	-nja-	-nja-	-nja-	-nja-	-nja-	-rni.nja-	-nja-	—
MOTION.AWAY	-nga-nya-	-nya-	-nya-	-nya-	-nya-	-nya-	-rni.nya-	-nya-	—
MOTION.TWD	-nga-nji-	-nji-	-nji-	-nji-	-nji-	-nji-	-rni.nji-	-nji-	—

Note: *Expected form, but not found in the transcribed corpus. A full stop represents the division between the inflection (bolded) and the augment.

Two of the inflections can be seen as 'built' off another inflection: the counterfactual suffix is formally a verb inflected for the infinitive form of the verb + *kurla*. Similarly, the subjunctive form of a verb is formally the imperative form of the verb + *rla*. This is particularly salient given the wide range of surface forms of the imperative: *-ka*, *-rra*, *-ta* and *-ja*. Some examples are given in Table 6.4 of the correspondence between infinitive and counterfactual forms of verbs, and in Table 6.5 of correspondences between imperative and subjunctive forms of verbs.

Table 6.4 Example correspondences between the infinitive form and the counterfactual form of verbs

Infinitive form	Counterfactual form
wa-nganja	wa-nganja*kurla*
speak-INF	speak-CFACT
nga-rninja	nga-rninja*kurla*
eat-INF	eat-CFACT
yi-nja	yi-nja*kurla*
give-INF	give-CFACT

Table 6.5 Example correspondences between the imperative form and the subjunctive form of verbs

Imperative form	Subjunctive form
ma-nta	ma-nta*rla*
get-IMP	get-SUBJ
-nga-nja	nga-nja*rla*
eat-IMP	eat-SUBJ
pa-nka	pa-nka*rla*
go-IMP	go-SUBJ

No features of the inner 'inflection' are kept. That is, the counterfactual form of a verb (which is built off the non-finite form of a verb) is not in any way synchronically non-finite, and the subjunctive form of a verb (which is built off the imperative form of a verb) is not in any way imperative.

In his analysis of Latin verb inflections, Matthews (1972: 85–86) has labelled this process 'parasitic formation'—a term also utilised by Koch (2014: 158), who demonstrates that this is a common process for verbs in Australian languages. In some Ngumpin-Yapa languages, the imperative form of a verb allows the same increment, *rla*, for a 'hortative' meaning (Jones et al. 2019: 40; McConvell 1980: 90; Meakins and Nordlinger 2014: 303). I do not follow this analysis for Warlmanpa because the function of the subjunctive form has a wide range of meanings (see §6.2.3.6).

6.2.1 Verb classes

This section provides the classes for Warlmanpa verbs. While some of these classes may not be strongly motivated within Warlmanpa, they are maintained on comparative grounds, allowing accessible comparison with other descriptions of Ngumpin-Yapa languages.

The paradigms given throughout this section give the 'maximal' form—that is, where there is variation between forms, the variation always takes the form of C* ~ ∅, so the paradigms in this section give the C* version and the variation is discussed in the section of the particular inflection. For example, the 'leave' verb exhibits interspeaker variation between the imperative forms *partungka* and *partuka*, where the variation is *ng* ~ ∅, so in this section the form is given as *partungka* and the variation is discussed in the 'imperatives' section.

6.2.1.1 Class 1

Class 1 is one of the two classes that require division into 'subconjugations' (the other being Class 5), due to their irregularity (importantly, however, all subconjugations except 1a have at least two members). The paradigm for each verb in this class is given in Table 6.5. Forms that are not found in the corpus are given with an asterisk following, to indicate I have analogically derived this form.

Table 6.6 Class 1 verb forms

		Imperative	Past	Future	Potential	Present	Infinitive
a	'speak'	wangka	wanganyu	wangami	wangama	wanganya	wanganja-
b	'die'	palungka	palungu	palimi	palima*	palungunya	palinja-*
	'leave'	partungka	partungu	partimi	partima	partungunya	partinja-*
c	'go'	panka	panangu	panami	panama	pannya	panja-
	'burn'	jinka*	jinangu	jinami	jinama*	jinnya	jinja-*
d	'be, sit'	karra	kangu	kami	kama	kanya	kanja-
	INCH	—²	-jangu	-jami	-jama	-janya	-janja-

---

2 While the imperative form of the inchoative is semantically incongruous, the subjunctive inflection is an incremental *-rla* to the imperative form of a verb (§6.2.3.6.1), which for the inchoative is *-jarrarla*, allowing us to posit *-*jarra* as the imperative form.

6.2.1.2 Class 2

Class 2 is by far the most populous verb class, with 25 documented verbs. Most are transitive, though there is a small number of intransitive verbs in this class. Table 6.7 provides the paradigm for five example verbs.

Table 6.7 Examples of Class 2 verb forms

	Imperative	Past	Future	Potential	Present	Infinitive
'throw'	*kiyaka*	*kiyarnu*	*kiyanmi*	*kiyanma*	*kiyannya*	*kiyanja-*
'cut'	*kumaka*	*kumarnu*	*Kumanmi*	*kumanma*	*kumannya*	*kumanja-*
'hit'	*pakaka*	*Pakarnu*	*pakanmi*	*pakanma*	*pakannya*	*pakanja-*
'search'	*wayika*	*wayurnu*	*wayinmi*	*wayinma*	*wayinnya*	*wayinja-*
'put'	*yaka*	*yarnu*	*yanmi*	*yanma*	*yannya*	*yanja-*

6.2.1.3 Class 3

Class 3 comprises seven documented inflecting verbs. Nash (1979) divides this class into two subclasses, which are primarily based on the different present-tense morphology—for example, *nya-ngany*a 'see-PRES' compared with *lu-ngunya* 'cry-PRES'—and whether the root is subject to any vowel alternations. I have opted to treat the class without any subclasses, as the vowel in the present-tense inflection can be predicted based on the rightmost vowel specified for the verb root; and, as discussed in §6.2.2.2, morphophonological rules are already utilised to predict the phonemic vowel forms of this class (and others) without requiring lexical subclassing. Table 6.8 gives the paradigm for all Class 3 verbs and includes Nash's (1979) subclassing for reference—indicated by the horizontal line separating *ka-* 'take' and *nya-* 'see' from the other Class 3 verbs.

Table 6.8 Class 3 verb forms, including Nash's (1979) division into two subclasses

	Imperative	Past	Future	Potential	Present	Infinitive
'take'	*kangka*	*kangu*	*kanyi*	*kanya*	*kanganya*	*kanja-*
'see'	*nyangka*	*nyangu*	*nyanyi*	*nyanya*	*nyanganya*	*nyanja-*
'cry'	*lungka**	*lungu*	*linyi*	*linya*	*lungunya*	*linja-*
'act on'	*pungka*	*pungu*	*pinyi*	*pinya*	*pungunya*	*pinja-*
'chase'	*kapungka*	*kapungu*	*kapinyi*	*kapinya**	*kapungunya*	*kapinja-*
'run'	*jutpungka*	*jutpungu*	*jitpinyi*	*jitpinya*	*jutpungunya*	*jitpinja-*
'give'	*yungka*	*yungu*	*yinyi*	*yinya**	*yungunya*	*yinja-*

The forms for 'chase' and 'run' are seemingly historically formed from the root for *pu-* 'act on':

(494)   *pu-ngka*   act_on-IMP
    ka   *pu-ngka*   chase-IMP
    jut   *pu-ngka*   run-IMP

I have treated these as three synchronically distinct inflecting verbs, following Nash (1979, 2022), however, a potential alternative analysis is to treat *ka* and *jut* as coverbs that only combine with *pu-ngka*. The evidence for treating both as simplex rather than complex verbs is phonological, although different for both cases. Including *ka* as a coverb would create a phonotactically exceptional coverb, as all other coverbs are minimally CVC. The evidence for *jutpu-ngka* is that it can be shown to be phonologically one word: the vowel in *jut* is subjected to the expected alternations predicted for verb roots in this class. For example, in the future inflection, the vowel is high front—that is, *jitpinyi*. If *jut* were a coverb, it would not undergo these alternations. When coverbs combine with *pu-ngka-*, their vowels are not subjected to this alternation, as exemplified in (495) with the coverb *purt* 'send', which retains its back vowel when the verb is in its future inflection form.

(495)   *Jilij-ka-ngka*   *nga=ju*   *ngayu-ku*   *muju*
    ask-take-IMP   POST=1SG.S   1-DAT   also
    purt-pi-nyi!
    send-act_on-FUT
    Ask him to send it to me!
    N_D02-009887, DG, 10:22 mins

Furthermore, *jutpu-ngka* has a different case frame to *pu-ngka* (this is not perfect evidence, however, as some coverbs do change the argument structure of their inflecting verb):

(496)   *jutpu-ngka*   ABS runs
(497)   *pu-ngka*   ERG acts on ABS

6.2.1.4 Class 4

Class 4 has just one member, 'to eat' (or, more generally, 'to ingest'). Ngumpin languages have one other member of this class, however, Yapa languages do not (Laughren and McConvell 2004: 169).[3]

Table 6.9 Class 4 verb forms

	Imperative	Past	Future	Potential	Present	Infinitive
'eat'	nganja	ngarnu	nganmi	nganma	ngarninya	ngarninja-

6.2.1.5 Class 5

Class 5 has two free verbs and two verbs that require either a nominal host (*-ma-nta* 'CAUSE') or a coverb (*ya-nta* 'go'). Inceptive and motion formatives also form a root belonging to Class 5, however, the imperative suffix for these derived forms is *-rra*, hence the motivation for subcategorising Class 5 verbs. The non-derived verbs belong to Class 5a (in which the imperative form is *-nta*), whereas the inceptive and motion-derived verbs belong to Class 5b. I have not included any derived verbs in Table 6.10 as they are not fully productive (see §6.5.1.1 and §6.5.1.2).

Table 6.10 Class 5a verb forms

	Imperative	Past	Future	Potential	Present	Infinitive
'get'	manta	manu	manmi	manma	mannya	manja-
cause	-manta	-manu	-manmi	-manma	-mannya	-manja-
'fall'	wanta	wanu	wanmi	wanma	wannya	wanja-
'go'	-yanta	-yanu	-yanmi	-yanma	-yannya	-yanja-

6.2.2 Root and augment processes

6.2.2.1 Augments

The categorisation of the five classes is somewhat complicated by 'augments'—a phenomenon like 'conjugation markers' in other languages. Augments are lexically specified for certain verb + inflection combinations. The augment occurs between the verb root and its inflection and does not have any apparent semantic function. The forms of the augments are given in Table 6.11.

---

3   Analyses of Warlpiri do find a second sense of *nga-* 'eat' to account for the coverbs that combine with it to create a motion meaning (Nash 1986: 246).

6. INFLECTING VERBS

Table 6.11 Forms of the augment by verb class and TAM inflection

Class	Imperative, subjunctive	Past	Future, potential	Present	Infinitive, associated motion, inceptive, counterfactual
1a	–	a	a	a	a
1b	ng	–	–	ngu	–
1c	n	na	na	n	–
1d	–	–	–	–	–
2	–	n	n	n	–
3	ng	–	–	ngu	–
4	n	–	n	rni	rni
5	n	–	n	n	–

Historically, the augments appear to be markers of imperfectivity. For example, in Gurindji, seemingly cognate forms are still used productively:

(498)   yuwa-ni   put-PAST   'he went'

(499)   yuwa-na-ni   put-IMPF-PAST   'he was putting it'
        (Gurindji [Meakins and McConvell 2021])

So, in Gurindji, the presence or absence of these markers signals an aspectual contrast.[4] This is not the case in Warlmanpa, as the presence or absence of these markers is grammatically conditioned: the augment cannot be 'removed' to signal a meaning difference; the removal of an augment where it is required is always ungrammatical:

(500)   *pa-ngu   go-PAST

(501)   pa-na-ngu   go-AUG-PAST   'he put it'

In Warlmanpa, augments must be treated as a separate component in a formal account of verb inflection forms due to their unpredictability and involvement in some derivational processes. From a synchronic perspective, augments can be considered morphologically conditioned allomorphy— conditioned by a combination of the verb root and the inflectional suffix, though there is debate in other Australian languages with similar phenomena about the locus of this allomorphy. To maintain minimally a bound root and a bound TAM inflection, there are three solutions to

---

[4]   It should be noted that even in languages in which this contrast is productive, it does not necessarily reflect the whole paradigm. For example, in Gurindji, the aspectual distinctions in the future-tense forms of this verb are not so analogical: compare *yuwarru* 'will put it' and *yuwanangku* 'will be putting it' (Meakins and McConvell 2021), where the future inflection form changes based on whether *na* is used.

incorporate 'augments'—as allomorphs: 1) of the root, 2) of the inflection, or 3) of an underlying null (sub)morpheme for every verb. I assume (3), as per the verb word template introduced at the beginning of this chapter; however, as discussed in Ennever (2021), all these solutions are problematic. For the sake of clarity when glossing examples, I include the augment as part of the following inflection, in line with other grammatical descriptions of Ngumpin-Yapa languages. However, see Appendix C for an alternative analysis.

Augments exhibit a small number of synchronic processes: the infinitive augment is required before the associated motion or inceptive suffixes can attach (see §6.2.3.9), even though the infinitive *suffix* itself does not attach to the stem. Furthermore, there is also some variation in which the augment is retained but the inflection is elided (§6.2.3.4.1)—that is, by maintaining augments in a synchronic analysis, another morphological process is neatly captured at the correct boundary.

6.2.2.2 Verbal morphophonology

There are two morphophonological processes that apply to inflecting verbs: first, verb roots with high vowels undergo several alternations (§6.2.2.2.1); and second, the imperfective suffix *-rra* and away suffix *-rra* both trigger contraction on certain verb inflections (§6.2.2.2.2).

6.2.2.2.1 High vowels in verb roots

Lexical verb roots containing high vowels in Warlmanpa cannot be adequately described phonemically without positing a level of morphophonological representation that allows for the derivation of /i/ and /u/ phonemes across different phonological and morphological (verb class membership) environments.

Verb roots with high vowels are morphophonemically specified with the features [+high, +front]—that is, //i//. Appendix A explicitly labels which of the known verbs are subject to this alternation, although it is entirely predictable: any verb root that has a final high vowel will be subject to these alternations, and any high vowels to the left of this vowel will also be affected, unless blocked by a low vowel. Specifically, these vowels undergo a morphophonological process that derives /u/ in certain combinations of verb class and inflection forms, otherwise they are processed phonemically as /i/. The alternations are as given in Table 6.12.

6. INFLECTING VERBS

Table 6.12 High vowel alternations in verb roots by class and inflection

	1a	1b	1c	1d	2	3	4	5
IMP		u			i	u		
PAST		u			u	u		
FUT		i			i	i		
POT		i			i	i		
PRES		u			i	u		
INC		i			i	i		
CFACT		i			i	i		
IRR		u			i	u		
MOT		i			i	i		
MOT.AWAY		i			i	i		
MOT.TWD		i			i	i		
INF		i			i	i		

As indicated earlier, this process does not apply to high vowels with an intervening low vowel in the verb root—for example, the high vowel in *kuma-* 'cut' is not subject to these alternations due to the intervening low vowel. Where there are multiple high vowels without an intervening low vowel, such as in *jutpu-ngka* 'run', each vowel is subject to the same alternation, thus, the future form of 'run' (V3) is *jitpi-nyi*.

Not all vowel alternations can be straightforwardly predicted in a single phonological or morphophonological rule, however, there are patterns for certain classes. Any inflection in Class 1b beginning with a velar consonant conditions the high vowel to be /u/. Class 2–only high vowels alternate to /u/ for the past-tense inflection, which could be considered triggered by either 1) the retroflex consonant, as the alternation of 1b is conditioned by the consonant, or 2) the /u/ vowel in the inflection, which is a more typical trigger of vowel alternations in related languages, especially Warlpiri (see Nash 1986: 84). For Class 3, the high vowel(s) in the root is specified as /u/ when the inflection begins with a velar consonant. This conditioning is summarised in Table 6.13 and is particularly interesting as it is both lexical (the process differs across classes) and phonological (there is a clear phonological environment within each class that predicts the patterns).

Table 6.13 Summary of root vowel alternations

Root vowel	Class 1b	Class 2	Class 3
/u/	_ [+dorsal]	_Cu	_ [+dorsal]
/i/	Elsewhere	Elsewhere	Elsewhere

The derived phonemes undergo the expected phonemic allophony discussed in §2.3.

6.2.2.2.2 Verb inflection + -rra contraction

The imperfective suffix and the away suffix are homophonous, sharing the form -*rra* (see §6.6.1). When either of these suffixes attaches to an inflecting verb that ends in a high vowel (for example, -*ngu* or -*rnu* PAST inflections, -*nmi* or -*mi* FUTURE inflections), the resulting word may contract, keeping the nasal of the inflected form and the vowel of the imperfective/away suffix, as represented in (502).

(502)   *NVrra* contraction

$$\| C_{[+\text{NASAL}]} V_{[+\text{HIGH}]} \text{ra} \| \rightarrow /Ca/$$

However, the processes are distinct for these two inflections: the contraction of the past inflection is discussed in §6.2.2.2.2.1 and the contraction of the future inflection in §6.2.2.2.2.2. Notably, historically in Warlmanpa, VrrV sequences were reduced to V, which is exactly the process resulting in these contractions, but differing in the degree of completion.

6.2.2.2.2.1 Past-tense contraction

The past-tense contraction involves the sequence -*Nu-rra* contracting to -*Na*. Some examples of the contraction applying are given in (503)–(505). All past-tense contractions are optional.

(503)   ⫽ṉu-ra⫽ → /ṉa/

Kitchen-nga	kala	work-ja-ngu,	yarnunju	kala=jana
kitchen-LOC	HAB	work-INCH-PAST	food	HAB=3PL.NS

kupa-**rna**	papulanyi-ku	yapa-ku.
cook-PAST.IMPF	white_people-DAT	aboriginal_person-DAT

She used to work in the kitchen, cooking food for all of us white people and Aboriginal people.
N_D29-023128, MFN, 04:42 mins

(504) //ŋu-ra// → /ŋa/

      Wajurra=ma=rna   ngurra-ka   partu-**nga**.

      yesterday=TOP=1SG.S home-ALL   leave-PAST.AWAY

      I left [here] towards home yesterday.

      wrl-20180614-02, DK, 13:35 mins

(505) Ngurra-ka=rna   pana-**nga**.

      camp-ALL=1SG.S   go-PAST.AWAY

      I went home.

      wrl-20180614-02, DK, 11:48 mins

For the past inflection, this contraction cannot apply when the resulting word would be disyllabic. For example, *ka-ngu-rra* 'be-PAST-IMPF' could not be contracted to *ka-nga 'be-PAST.IMPF', since the resulting word comprises only two syllables.

Second, there are certain classes of verbs that appear to prohibit past-tense contraction—namely, Class 1a (comprising one verb: *wa-* 'talk', in the past imperfective *wa-nganyu-rra*); and Class 3, which contains predominantly monosyllabic roots, however, even the disyllabic roots *kapi-* 'chase' and *jitpi-* 'run' do not undergo the contraction.

These restrictions are summarised in Table 6.14.

Table 6.14 Restrictions on -*NVrra* contraction for past inflections (augments omitted from the forms)

Class	Past inflection	Contractible	Notes
1a	-*nyu*	No	
1b	-*ngu*	Yes	
1c		Yes	
1d		No	Would result in surface disyllabic word.
2	-*rnu*	Yes	Only on disyllabic roots.
3	-*ngu*	No	
4	-*rnu*	No	Would result in surface disyllabic word.
5a	-*nu*	No	
5b			

6.2.2.2.2.2 Future-tense contraction

The future-tense contraction involves the sequence *-Ni-rra* contracting to *-Na*. Some examples of the contraction applying are given in (506) and (507).

(506) //nmi-ra// → /nma/

Karli=rna   kiya-**nma.**
boomerang=1SG.S   throw-FUT.AWAY
I'll throw the boomerang away.
H_K01-506A, DG, 01:03:54 hrs

(507) //ɲi-ra// → /ɲa/

Ngaka=rnalu   ngurrurla   pi-**nya.**
soon=1PL.EXCL.S   return_home   act_on-FUT.AWAY
We'll go home soon.
H_K01-506A, DG, 52:06 mins

On the surface, this process is formally identical to the past-tense contraction. However, there are several significant points of difference. First, the future-tense contraction is obligatory—that is, there are no noted sequences of, for example, **kiya-nmi-rra* 'throw-FUT.AWAY'. Additionally, there are no clear cases of FUT.IMPF forms in the corpus, only FUT.AWAY.

This results in the future inflection with *-rra* being formally identical to the potential inflection. In turn, this collapses a phonological distinction between the POTENTIAL inflection and FUTURE.AWAY forms (the semantic/analytical consequences of which are discussed further in §6.6.3.1).

Second, the future-tense contraction operates regardless of syllable count (even if the resulting word is disyllabic) and regardless of the verb class. These differences are summarised in Table 6.15.

Table 6.15 Differences in the conditioning of the contraction process between inflections

	Past inflection	Future inflection
Obligatory	No	Yes
Syllabic constraints	Yes	No
Class constraints	Yes	No

6.2.3 TAM inflections

Each verb TAM inflection is now discussed. Each verb word must contain exactly one TAM inflection to be well formed. Inflections that denote a temporal reference are discussed in terms of reference time (in the sense of Reichenbach 1947), rather than speech time, as the 'tense' inflections in Warlmanpa are sensitive to the deictic centre. This is prototypically speech time, though there are cases where it is not—most notably, in represented speech (see Browne 2019).

Note that I tend to only discuss positive polarity uses of each inflection in this section; negative polarity is discussed in §11.5.1.

6.2.3.1 Imperative

6.2.3.1.1 Form

The imperative suffix is *-ka*, except for a small number of verbs. Class 4 has the form *-ja*, Class 5 is *-ta* and Class 1 has two verbs that have *-rra* (which are categorised as Class 1d). Inceptive and associated motion constructions also derive a verb that takes *-rra* as its imperative inflection form. Most classes that have an imperative inflection *-ka* have an augment, (N(V)), in which N is a nasal and V is a vowel.

Table 6.16 Imperative form allomorphy (with augment)

Class	Underlying morpheme	Allomorphs			Process/conditioning
1a	-ngka	-ngka			
1b	-ngka	-ngka	~	-ka	Interspeaker variation
1c	-nka	-n.ka			
1d	-rra	-rra			
2	-ka	-ka	~	∅	Lexically conditioned
3	-ngka	-ngka	~	-ka	*-ka* in disyllabic verb roots
4	-nja	-nja			
5a	-nta	-nta			
5b	-rra	-rra			

Class 3 has no augment if the verb root is disyllabic.

Disyllabic root, no augment (-*ka*):

(508)   *Jutu-**ka**-pa!*
        run-IMP-away
        Run away!
        wrl-20180618-01, DK, 07:17 mins

(509)   *Kapu-**ka**-rti*   *Kalkinipurta!*
        chase-IMP-TWD   towards_speaker
        Drag it this way!
        H_K06-004555, LOF, 53:32 mins

Monosyllabic root, has augment (-*ngka*):

(510)   *Tajpaka=nyanu*   *tingkirr*   *pu-**ngka**!*
        properly=RR   tie   act_on-IMP
        Tie it properly!
        N_D03-007868, BN, 11:39 mins

(511)   *Karli=ju*   *yu-**ngka***   *ngula=n*   *partakurru*   *ma-nu!*
        boomerang=1SG.NS   give-IMP   REL=2SG.S   make   do-PAST
        Give me the boomerang that you made!
        H_K01-505B, DG, 23:51 mins

Note that (510) includes a coverb construction, suggesting that the phonological conditioning is restricted to the verb root (that is, the coverb is not considered part of the 'verb word').

This variation is restricted to Class 3. For example, the imperative suffix for Class 2 is -*ka*, regardless of the syllable count of the verb root:

(512)   *Karli-ngu*   *la-**ka**!*
        boomerang-ERG   shoot-IMP
        Shoot it with a boomerang!
        H_K01-506A, DG, 38:33 mins

In Class 2, the verb root *paka-* optionally surfaces without an overt imperative suffix, as exemplified in (513), where the imperative suffix is overt, and in (514), where it is not.

6. INFLECTING VERBS

(513) *Yali-ngu=nya   ngarrka-ngu   wa-nganya=ju   'yiwirti   paka-**ka**!*.
that-ERG=FOC   man-ERG   speak-PRES=1SG.NS   tree   hit-IMP

That man is saying to me 'cut the tree!'.
wrl-20190201, DK, 34:22 mins

(514) *Maliki   yurt   paka-∅   nga=ngu=nga   pi-nya!*
dog   hunt_away   hit-IMP   POST=2SG.NS=DUB   bite-POT

Hunt that dog away, in case he bites you!
N_D02-009887, DG, 11:42 mins

Ken Hale elicited a sentence from Donald Graham, given in (515), which is repeated with and without the overt -*ka*.

(515) *Yapa   witta   **paka(-ka)**!*
person   small   **hit(-IMP)**

Hit the child!
H_K01-506A, DG, 47:19 mins

The verb root *waka-* 'climb' can also surface without an imperative inflection.

(516) *Pirtij   **Waka!***
climb   **climb.IMP**

Climb up!
H_K06-004555, LOF, 47:34 mins

These verbs may be in the process of reanalysis, in which the root is monosyllabic, hence for these speakers, the morphological composition of (516) may be better reflected in (516)*.

(516)* *Pirtij   **wa-ka!***
upwards   **climb-IMP**

Climb up!
H_K06-004555, LOF, 47:34 mins

Interestingly, Hale explicitly notes this variation is not possible with *nguka-* 'drink' (H_K01-506A, 47:27 mins), despite *ngu-ka* being an analogical reanalysis. It is not clear why this variation is not permissible for *nguka-* 'drink', so for now I consider this *ka-Ø* variation restricted to *paka-* 'hit' and *waka-* 'climb'.

Moreover, this variation is not found in younger speakers, only in the heritage corpus. All speakers in the present corpus have the overt imperative inflection for these two verbs (that is, *wakaka* and *pakaka*).

Finally, V1b has *ng~ngk*, which is subject to interspeaker variation (but is consistent intraspeaker).[5] A clear contrast is shown in (517) and (518)—the same utterance spoken by different speakers—in which PK uses *-ngka* and DG uses *-ka*. The form is given for six speakers in Table 6.17.

Table 6.17 Interspeaker variation of the imperative form for 1b verbs

Speaker	V1b IMP suffix
DK	-ngka
PK	-ngka
SN	-ngka
BN	-ngka
LOF	-ka
DG	-ka

(517)   *Kutij   partu-ngka!*
          stand   rise-IMP
          Stand up!
          wrl-20170825-01, PK, 06:51 mins

(518)   *Kutij   partu-ka!*
          stand   rise-IMP
          Stand up!
          H_K01-506A, DG, 18:46 mins

---

5   Note that an analysis that suggests that some speakers have reclassified the Class 1b verbs to Class 2 (where the imperative form is *-ka*) is untenable, as the past tense for the Class 1b verbs still corresponds to the rest of the Class 1b paradigm. For example, the past tense for 'leave' is *partungu* for all speakers, whereas if some speakers had reanalysed the verb as a Class 2, the expected past-tense form would be **parturnu*.

6.2.3.1.2 Function

The function of the imperative inflection is to express a command that some action should be undertaken by the addressee(s). This inflection is the strongest form of directive in Warlmanpa, contrasting with other constructions instantiating directives that are more 'desiderative' (for the future inflection, see §6.2.3.4.2, for the potential inflection, §6.2.3.5.2 and, for the subjunctive inflection, §6.2.3.6.2). The imperative inflection in Warlmanpa is prototypically used for orders and can also be used for requests and recommendations (in the sense of Aikhenvald 2010: 198–99). Examples are given in (519)–(524).

(519) *Ngulya* **pangi-ka!**
ground **dig-IMP**
Dig the ground!
H_K01-506A, DG, 24:06 mins

(520) *Jinta-ku=lku* *wa-***ngka,** *nga=rna-ngu* *purtu* *ka-mi.*
one-DAT=THEN speak-IMP POST=1SG.S-2SG.NS hear be-FUT
Say it once more so I can hear you.
wrl-20191207-01, DK, 56:45 mins

(521) *Nya-***ngka**=*rla* *kuyapurta,* *ngayu=rna-rla* *kuyapurta* *nya-nyi.*
see-IMP=3.OBL this_way 1=1SG.S-DAT this_way see-FUT
Look this way for her, and I'll look this way for her.
wrl-20190123, SN, 28:43 mins

(522) *Purtu* *ka-***rra** *jaru* *ngula=rna* *wa-nganya!*
listen be-IMP language REL=1SG.S speak-PRES
Listen to the language that I'm speaking!
H_K01-505B, DG, 37:46 mins

(523) *Tajpaka=nyanu* *tingkirr* *pu-***ngka!**
tight=RR tie act_on-IMP
Tie it up tightly!
N_D03-007868, BN, 11:39 mins

(524) *Kuku=ju* *kutij* *ka-***rra!**
wait=1SG.NS stand be-IMP
Stand there waiting for me!
wrl-20180615-02, DK, 19:46 mins

The Warlmanpa speakers with whom I worked do not have any clear authority hierarchy among one another, so it is difficult to ascertain whether the imperative encodes authority (that is, whether there are any circumstances in which it would be inappropriate based on the relationship between the speaker and the addressee). Based on elicitations with speakers, the imperative suffix seems appropriate regardless of the relative authority between the speaker and the addressee. This is exemplified in (525), where the prompt was for a child addressing a parent, and in (526), where the prompt was for a parent addressing a child, although it should be noted these are both hypothetical elicited situations.

(525) *Ngappa=rla*   *yu-ngka!*
water=3.OBL   give-IMP
Give water to him! (Child addressing parent.)
wrl-20190123, SN, 00:57 secs

(526) *Ngappa=rla*   *yu-ngka*   *witta-ku!*
water=3.OBL   give-IMP   child-DAT
Give water to the child! (Parent addressing child.)
wrl-20190123, SN, 04:34 mins

The subject bound pronoun marker is unmarked for person,[6] as in all described Ngumpin-Yapa languages (Meakins and Nordlinger 2014: 302; Hudson 1978: 80; Tsunoda 1981a: 133; Osgarby 2018: 139; Ennever 2018: 250; Hale 1973: 326–27), although there are slightly different accounts of this phenomena. Imperatives presuppose a second-person subject, and then the bound pronoun only marks number, hence the lack of an overt 2SG.S marker on any of the previous examples despite the subject being 2SG.S, and a plural subject is marked with the bound pronoun *=lu* (typically the 3PL.S pronoun, where the third-person component is inferred, rather than encoded as part of *=lu*). For example, (527) and (528) both have 2PL as their subject, but the form of the pronouns differs: *=lu* in the imperative clause and *=nkulu* in the non-imperative clause. This is discussed further in §5.4.3.4.

---

6   More specifically, the bound pronouns in the following examples are just number markers, unspecified for person, which is second person by default in imperative constructions.

6. INFLECTING VERBS

(527) *Karli=lku=lpangu-**lu***   *Paka!*
boomerang=THEN=1PL.INCL.NS-S.PL   cut.IMP
You mob, trim a boomerang for us all!
H_K01-506A, DG, 57:34 mins

(528) *Ngana-ku=**nkulu**-rla*   *wa-nganyu-rra?*
what-DAT=2PL.S-DAT   speak-PAST-IMPF
What were you mob talking for?
H_K01-505B, DG, 19:02 mins

The imperative inflection can be used by some younger speakers in conjunction with *kula*—the clausal negator for a negative imperative—as in (529).

(529) ***Kula***   *yayi=nya*   *karli*   *kiya-**ka**!*
NEG   that=FOC   boomerang   throw-IMP
Don't throw that boomerang!
wrl-20180610-01, DK, 02:23 mins

For most speakers, this construction is ungrammatical. Other younger speakers use the (positive polarity) finite predicate *ka-rra* 'be-IMP' clause in combination with a subordinate privative clause, prohibiting the addressee(s) from undertaking the event denoted in the subordinate clause, as in (530).

(530) *Ka-**rra***   *pa-nja-**wangu**!*
be-IMP   go-INF-PRIV
Don't go! (Lit.: 'Be without going!')
wrl-20190123, SN, 09:59 mins

For older speakers, the imperative inflection is not used for prohibition at all. Instead, they use *-wangu* in an insubordinate clause (see §11.5.2 for discussion of negative imperatives).

6.2.3.2 Past

6.2.3.2.1 Form

The past-tense inflection is *Nu* in every class, with only V1a and V1c having augments (which take the form *-Na*). There is no noted variation in the corpus.

Table 6.18 Form of the past-tense inflection by class

Class	Underlying morpheme	Allomorphs
V1a	-nganyu	-nganyu
V1b	-ngu	-ngu
V1c	-nangu	-nangu
V1d	-ngu	-ngu
V2	-rnu	-rnu
V3	-ngu	-ngu
V4	-rnu	-rnu
V5	-nu	-nu

6.2.3.2.2 Function

The past-tense inflection locates the event time before some reference time (typically speech time). Examples of the past inflection are given in (531)–(533).

(531)   **Nya-ngu**=n   maliki   ngayinya?
         see-PAST=2SG.S   dog   1GEN
         Did you see my dog?
         wrl-20170328-01, SN, 15:20 mins

(532)   Ngarrka=nganpa   missionary=lku   **pa-nangu**-rnu.
         man=1EXL.PL.NS   missionary=THEN   **go-PAST**-TWD
         The missionary came to us.
         N_D02-007844, BN, 27:14 mins

(533)   Wawirri=rna   **karla-rnu**   wantarli-ka.
         kangaroo=1SG.S   **spear-PAST**   across-ALL
         I speared a kangaroo going across.
         N_D02-007842, BN, 45:58 mins

The past inflection regularly combines with the directional suffixes (§6.4.1), as in (534) and (535), and the imperfective suffix (§6.4.2), as in (535).

(534)   Mu-ka=nya=rna   **pa-nangu-rnu**   wa-nganja-ka.
         this-ALL=FOC=1SG.S   **go-PAST-TWD**   speak-INF-DAT
         I came here to talk.
         H_K01-505B, DG, 34:14 mins

(535) | Wangani-rlu | wirriri~wirriri | wirri | **ya-nu-rra,**
dog-ERG | in_a_circle-RDP | chase | **put-PAST-IMPF**

nyanungu=ma=lu | *putjanarra* | **partu-ngu-rra.**
aforementioned=TOP=3PL.S | cause_to_scatter | **leave-PAST-AWAY**

The dog was going around chasing the birds, but they would fly away.
wrl-20190207-01, DK, 52:05 mins

There are no grammatical remoteness distinctions, so the past tense can describe recent events and events long in the past. Remoteness distinctions can be made periphrastically, typically by using an adverb: *larrpa* 'already, short time ago' for recent past, as in (536) and (537), or *larrpalarrpa* 'long time ago' for remote past, as in (538) and (539).

Recent past:

(536) **Larrpa**=*rna* | *yarnunyju* | **nga-rnu.**
before=1SG.S | food | **eat-PAST**
I've already eaten food.
H_K01-506A, DG, 27:52 mins

(537) **Larrpa**=*jangu* | **nya-ngu.**
before=1DU.INCL.O | **see-PAST**
He just saw us.
wrl-20180609-01, DK, 06:56 mins

Distant past:

(538) *Ngayu=rna-ngu* | *wa-nganya* | **larrpalarrpa** | *ngula=rnalu*
1=1SG.S-2SG.NS | speak-PRES | **long_ago** | REL=1PL.EXCL.S

pa-nangu-*rra* | *wijara-ku.*
go-PAST-IMPF | yam-DAT
I'm telling you that we used to go for yams.
N_D02-007842, BN, 34:57 mins

(539) **Larrparlarrpa** | *kala=lu* | **pa-nangu**-*rra* | *wirlinyi,* | *kala=lu*
long_ago | HAB=3PL.S | **go-PAST-IMPF** | hunting | HAB=3PL.S

payang | **kapu-ngu-rra.**
find | **chase-PAST-IMPF**
Long ago, they used to go hunting, finding [the ngurtila trees].
wrl-20160908-01: 08, SN, 02:01 mins

An example of the past inflection being sensitive to the deictic centre (that is, relative tense) is given in (540), in which the temporal reference of the subordinate clause with the past inflection is prior to that of the future-marked matrix clause (which establishes reference time as the matrix predicate), but both are posterior to speech time, as represented in Figure 6.2.

(540)   Ngayu=ma=rna—   [kayi=rna   ngayu   ***pa-nangu***   *wirlinyi*
        1=TOP=1SG.S   WHEN=1SG.S   1   **go**-PAST   hunting

        yarnunju-ku   *paka-nja-ku]*   *ngarra=rna* *kupa-nmi.*
        food-DAT   hit-INF-DAT   might=1SG.S   cook-FUT

        I—once I have gone hunting for food, I should cook.
        wrl-20190206, DK, 25:53 mins

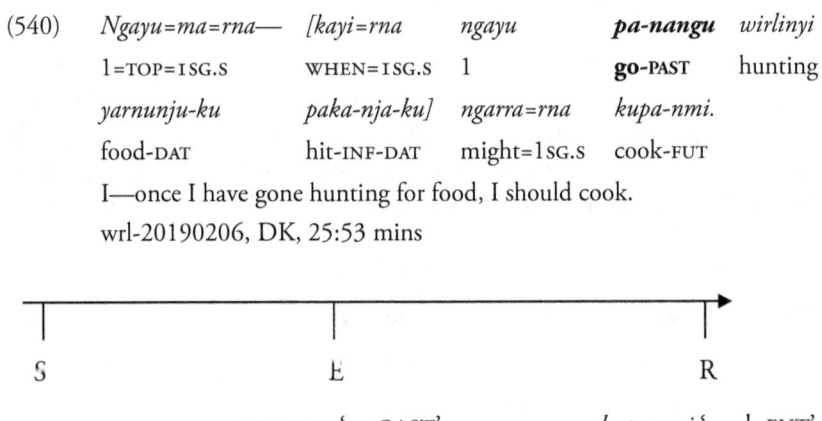

pa-nangu 'go-PAST'   *kupanmi* 'cook-FUT'

Figure 6.2 Temporal schema of Example (540)

6.2.3.3 Present

6.2.3.3.1 Form

The forms of the present inflection are given for each verb class in Table 6.19.

Table 6.19 Form of the present-tense inflection by class

Class	Underlying morpheme	Allomorphs	Process/conditioning
V1a	-nganya	-nganya	
V1b	-ngunya	-ngunya	
V1c	-nnya	-nnya	
V1d	-nya	-nya	
V2	-nnya	-nnya	
V3	-ngVnya	-nganya, -ngunya	Selected by preceding vowel
V4	-rninya	-rninya	
V5	-nnya	-nnya	

There is no known variation in the corpus for the present inflection, other than for Class 3, in which the vowel of the inflection is selected based on the preceding vowel in the root: if it is a low vowel, the allomorph is *-nganya-*, and if it is a high vowel, the allomorph is *-ngunya*. This is related to a more general morphophonological process discussed in §6.2.2.2.

Browne (2017) discusses the phonetics of the *-nnya* and *-nya* contrast, which suggests the phonotactically rare sequence *-n.ny* is due to historical reduction of a disyllabic sequence, *-NVnya*, and that the contrast between *-nnya* and *-nya* may be neutralising to *-nya* for present-day speakers. This is further supported by the forms found in other languages, such as *-nanya* being the Class 5 present inflection in Warlpiri (Nash 1986: 40), which corresponds to *-nnya* in Warlmanpa.

When co-occurring with associated motion suffixes (§6.2.3.9), the palatal nasal often surfaces as an alveolar nasal, as in (541).[7]

(541) *Kari=rnalu   ka-ngu-rra,   kala=rnalu   ngurrurla   parti-nja-**na**.*
       FAR=1PL.EXCL.S   be-PAST-IMPF   HAB=1PL.   return   leave-MOT-PRES
                                           EXCL.S

We used to stay far away, and then we'd be coming back.
N_D29-023128, MFN, 01:48 mins

6.2.3.3.2 Function

The present inflection typically refers to a situation overlapping with the reference time, as in (542)–(544).

(542) *Ngana=n   **kupa-nnya**?*
       what=2SG.S   cook-PRES

What are you cooking?
wrl-20190211-02, DK, 13:14 mins

(543) *Ngarrka   **wa-nganya**   kantu   ngula   papulu-rla   **ka-nya**.*
       man   speak-PRES   under   REL   house-LOC   be-PRES

The man sitting in the house is speaking.
N_D02-007842, BN, 37:42 mins

---

7 It is possible that this *na* form is a reflex of the imperfective *-na* found in many Ngumpin languages.

(544)   *Jala=ma=rna*   **ka-nya**   *Tennant Creek-nga*   *tarnnga=yi.*
        now=TOP=1SG.S   be-PRES   Tennant Creek-LOC   permanent=STILL
        Nowadays I live only in Tennant Creek.
        wrl-20190208, DK, 26:14 mins

It has a general non-past meaning and can be used for future reference when the temporal information can be recovered—for example, in (545), where there is a temporal nominal, *jawarti*, that specifies the temporal reference (this function of the present inflection is only noted with *partu-* 'leave' and *pa-* 'go').

(545)   **Partu-ngunya**=*li*   *jawarti*   *yimpa-ja.*
        leave-PRES=1DU.EXCL.S   tomorrow   this-DU
        We two are going to leave tomorrow.
        N_D03-007868, BN, 25:38 mins

Examples such as (545) could alternatively be considered as desire/intention at the time of reference, specifically of the agent of the event, as in (546).

(546)   *Yumpa=nya=ma=ngu*   **pa-nnya**   *jawarti=ma*   *warrabri-ka=lku*
        this=FOC=TOP=2SG.NS   go-PRES   tomorrow=TOP   Warrabri-ALL=THEN
        nyuntu-ku=lku.
        2-DAT=THEN
        This one is going to Warrabri tomorrow for you.
        H_K01-506A, DG, 33:15 mins

The present inflection can be used to describe situations that are conceptualised as being always true (or perhaps habitual, though there are too few examples to be certain), as in (547), though these types of statements are more common without an overt verb (cf. §11.3).

(547)   *Wumpurr*   **ka-nya.**
        black   be-PRES
        [The *kumulajpurru* bird] is black.
        wrl-20160914-02, SN, 01:45 mins

Finally, the present inflection can be used as a 'historical present', as in (548). In these cases, the temporal reference is prior to speech time, as the reference time (that is, the time with which the speaker is concerned) is in the past.

(548) *Ngayu=ma=rna-jana* **wa-nganya-rra** *'kula=lpangu*
1=TOP=1SG.S-3PL.NS **speak-PRES-IMPF** NEG=1INC.PL.NS

ngana-ngurlu *la-nmi'.*
what-ELA shoot-FUT

I'm telling them, 'they won't shoot us without reason' [lit.: 'from anything'].

N_D02-007844, BN, 26:42 mins

6.2.3.4 Future

6.2.3.4.1 Form

The forms of the future inflection are given in Table 6.20.

Table 6.20 Form of the future inflection by verb class

Class	Underlying morpheme	Allomorphs	Process/conditioning
V1a	*-ngami*	*-ngami, -nga*	Optional; restricted to one speaker
V1b	*-mi*	*-mi,* ∅	Optional; restricted to one speaker
V1c	*-nami*	*-nami, -na*	Optional for some speakers
V1d	*-mi*	*-mi*	
V2	*-nmi*	*-nmi, -n*	Optional for disyllabic roots for one speaker
V3	*-nyi*	*-nyi*	
V4	*-nmi*	*-nmi*	
V5	*-nmi*	*-nmi, -n*	Optional for disyllabic roots for one speaker

For most speakers, the future inflection exhibits no variation in the transcribed corpus. The only instantiated variation is the deletion of *-mi* to ∅, which is only permitted on disyllabic roots. In all cases, the augment, if there is one, is retained, including when it results in a consonant-final word, as in (550), where the verb form is *kupa-n* (with the *mi* deleted from *kupanmi*)—and compare this with the full *-nmi* form in (549).

(549) *Kuyu=lu* ***kupa-nmi.***
meat=3PL.S **cook-FUT**

They'll cook meat.

wrl-20190213-02, DK, 15:53 mins

(550) | *Wawirri=rna* | **kupa-n** | *ngula=n* | *karta* | *pu-ngu.*
kangaroo=1SG.S | **cook-FUT** | REL=2SG.S | spear | act_on-PAST
I'll cook the kangaroo that you speared.
H_K01-505B, DG, 21:56 mins

Interestingly, as the variation only applies to disyllabic stems, the process cannot apply to the set of roots in V5, but the variation does surface in words that are derived into Class 5 verbs, such as the inceptive. This can be seen in (551) and (552), where the verb root is monosyllabic, but due to derivational suffixes forming a disyllabic stem, the elision is permitted. In (552) both verbs are derived Class 5b stems, yet the *nya-* 'see' verb only has the augment *-n*, contrasting with the *nga-* 'eat' verb, which has the full form, *-nmi*.

(551) *Ngana=n* *karta* **pi-nji-n?**
what=2SG.S spear **kill-INC-FUT**
What will you go and spear?
H_K01-506A, DG, 01:05:08 hrs

(552) *Nganayi-rla=lku* *mirla* *karlarra-purta* *kari=lpa-jana-lu*
dummy-LOC=THEN that.LOC west-FACING far=1.INC.DU.S-3PL.NS-S.PL

nya-nji-n *timana* *ngula* *purn* **nga-rninji-nmi.**
see-INC-FUT horse REL jump **eat-MOT-FUT**
We're going to go, whatsit, westward, and see those horses who jump around.
N_D02-007850, DG, 03:37 mins

There is only one token in the transcribed corpus of a speaker other than DG exhibiting this variation, which is given in (553), where the future form of 'go' is *pana* rather than the typical *panami* (where *-na* is an augment).

(553) *Ngurra-ka=rna* *pina* **pa-na** *kula* *nga=ju=nga* *ji-nnya!*
camp-ALL return **go-FUT** NEG POT=1SG.NS=FUT burn-PRES
I'll go back home, or else he might not cook tucker for me!
N_D03-007868, BN, 36:57 mins

When the future-inflected verb is marked with *-rra* 'away' or 'imperfective', the resulting form is best treated as a portmanteau. The final /i/ of the future inflection is replaced with an /a/, as in (554), where the future form *panami* combining with the away suffix *-rra* results in the form *panama*.

(554)   *Kula=rna*   *ngayu=ma*   *pa-**nama**,*   *ngayu=ma=rna*   *ka-mi*   *yarti.*
       NEG=1SG.S   1=TOP   go-FUT.AWAY   1=TOP=1SG.S   be-FUT   stay
       I won't go away, I'll stay.
       wrl-20180616-01, DK, 25:03 mins

The phonology of this process is discussed in §6.2.2.2.2, and the implications of this process are further addressed in §6.6.3.1.

6.2.3.4.2 Function

The function of the future inflection is to locate some situation posterior to reference time and expresses the speaker's commitment that the situation will occur unless some unforeseen circumstances intervene (compare with the POTENTIAL inflection, which also locates a situation posterior to reference time but is agnostic about the speaker's commitment, as discussed in §6.2.3.5.2). This is exemplified in (555), where the speaker is committing to an event that has not yet taken place.

(555)   *Jawarti=rna-ngu*   ***ka-nyi**-rni.*
       tomorrow=1SG.S-2SG.NS   **take**-FUT-TWD
       I will bring you [some] tomorrow.
       wrl-20180531-02, DF, 17:17 mins

The use of the future inflection in (556) signals that the event of 'act on' (in this case, 'biting') will happen if the speaker goes near the dogs and, through the combination of the *kala* auxiliary base (§5.3.1) with the future inflection, the speaker also signals that this event will not transpire if the speaker's warning is heeded.

(556)   *Kula=lu-rla*   *pa-nka-pa*   *tartu,*   *kala=ngu-lu*   ***pi-nyi***
       NEG=3PL.S-DAT   go-IMP-AWAY   many   APPR=2SG.NS-3PL.S   **act_on**-FUT
       tartu!
       many
       Don't go near the dogs, lest they bite you!
       wrl-20180605-01, DK, 09:16 mins

There are some instances of the future inflection co-occurring with past events that were expected but did not transpire. For example, in (557), the use of the future inflection signals that the event of 'become night on X' would have happened if the referent had not left. The avoided event is located posterior to reference time (which is the time of leaving), hence the use of the future inflection, as depicted in Figure 6.3. This contrasts with the use of the counterfactual inflection (§6.2.3.7.2), which is used for temporal reference anterior to reference time.

(557)   *Nakamarra   pa-nanga   kala=rla=nga   **yakarlu-rla-ja-nmi.***
        Nakamarra   go-PAST.AWAY   APPR=3.OBL=DUB   **night-LOC-INCH-FUT**
        Nakamarra left, lest it become night on her.
        wrl-20180615-02, DK, 25:56 mins

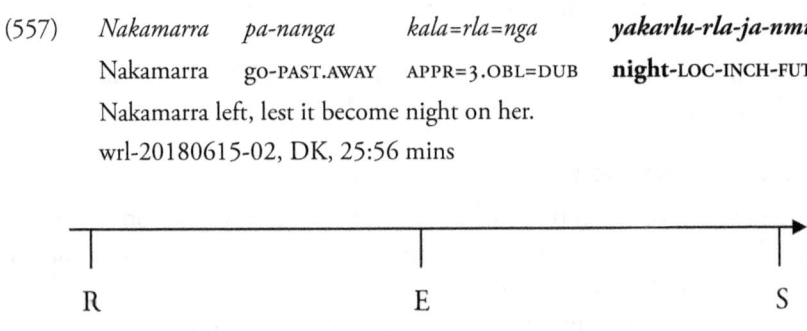

panangu 'left'   *yakarlurlajanmi* 'become night'

Figure 6.3 Temporal schema of Example (557)

The future inflection can also be used for directives/requests, as in (558)–(560). This is likely a polite alternative to the imperative verb form, communicating an ideal possible world posterior to reference time that the addressee has the ability or authority to realise, which can then be inferred as a polite request. These are interpreted as optatives—that is, wishes from the perspective of the speaker.

(558)   *Wa-ngka=rla   kurtu-ku   **pa-nami-rni!***
        speak-IMP=3.OBL   child-DAT   **go-FUT-TWD**
        Tell the child to come here!
        H_K01-505B, DG, 25:36 mins

(559)   *Kuku=yi=rna   **nga-nmi**,   kala=rna   Japaja   pa-nami-rni!*
        wait=STILL=1SG.S   **eat-FUT**   APPR=1SG.S   Japaja   go-FUT-TWD
        Let me eat, lest Japaja come here [before I finish eating]![8]
        wrl-20180615-02, DK, 21:48 mins

---

8   I am not sure how the first-person bound pronoun fits into the second clause.

(560) *Wangani=li* **ka-nyi** *muju?*
dog=1DU.INCL.S **take-FUT** too
Can we take the dog with us, too?
(Lit.: We'll bring the dog with us, too.)
wrl-20190213-01, DK, 02:52 mins

There is possible counterevidence to the 'commitment' analysis of the future inflection, as the inflection can be used in clauses with the particle *ngarra* 'potential', as in (561), where both clauses have the particle *ngarra* and a verb with the future inflection.

(561) *Kula* **ngarra**=*lpa* **pa-nami**, **ngarra**=*lpa* *yarti* **ka-mi.**
NEG POT=1PL.EXCL.S **go-FUT** POT=1PL.EXCL.S stay **be-FUT**
We might not go, we might stay.
wrl-20190131-01, DK, 22:05 mins

(562) *Ngayu=rna-ngu-lu* **ngarra** **paka-nmi** *nyuntu* *jinta.*
1=1.EXCL.S-2SG.NS-S.PL POT **hit-FUT** 2 one
We might hit you.
H_K01-506A, DG, 41:03 mins

In §9.1.1, I argue that the use of *ngarra* here serves to explicitly cast doubt on the likelihood of the state of affairs that would allow the situation denoted by the verb to occur, which is compatible with the current analysis of the future inflection.

6.2.3.5 Potential
6.2.3.5.1 Form

The potential inflection is formally identical to the future inflection for each class, except the vowel is /a/ instead of /i/. In §6.2.3.4.1, the future inflection is analysed as exhibiting variation essentially between *-mi* ~ ∅, following Nash (1979). However, since the future and potential inflections are identical other than the final vowel, it is possible that the potential inflection is subject to the same variation and these cases of elision are being misanalysed as future forms. I have opted to preserve Nash's analysis: the main functional distinction between the two inflections is that the future encodes a speaker's commitment to a situation occurring whereas the potential inflection does not, and all the tokens of the elided forms in the transcribed corpus appear to be compatible with the narrower future reading. The forms of the potential inflection suffixes are given in Table 6.21, assuming the variation is restricted to the future inflection.

Table 6.21 Form of the potential inflection by verb class

Class	Underlying morpheme	Allomorphs
V1a	-ngama	-ngama
V1b	-nama	-nama
V1c	-nama	-nama
V1d	-ma	-ma
V2	-nma	-nma
V3	-nya	-nya
V4	-nma	-nma
V5	-nma	-nma

Interestingly, the Class 3 potential inflection is identical to the past inflection in Ngumpin languages (Ennever 2018: 320; Meakins and Nordlinger 2014: 272; Meakins and McConvell 2021; Osgarby 2018: 36; Senge 2015: 401; Tsunoda 1981b: 77).

6.2.3.5.2 Function

The function of the potential inflection is to refer to an event posterior to reference time. Unlike the future inflection, the potential inflection does not encode a speaker's commitment as to whether the situation will occur. But because the future inflection does commit to the situation occurring, by implicature, the potential inflection tends to be used mostly for situations that are uncertain in some way. This uncertainty is usually epistemic possibility, where the uncertainty pertains to the actualisation of the event.

In (563), the speaker uses the potential inflection to encode that the event of 'child falls' occurs posterior to reference time and the use of the auxiliary clitic =nga explicitly encodes that the event is a possibility (and context supplies the epistemic modality). Further examples of the potential inflection with =nga explicitly specifying possibility are given in (564)–(566). Note that the combination of the clitic =nga 'dubitative' with the auxiliary base nga= 'posterior' signals an apprehensive construction (§5.5), whereas some speakers prefer to use the auxiliary base kala for this construction (§5.3.1).

6. INFLECTING VERBS

(563) *Kurtu   yali=nya   yirri   kapu-ka   kala=**nga**   wa-**nma**!*
child   that=FOC   watch_over   chase-IMP   APPR=DUB   fall-POT
Watch the child, in case she falls!
wrl-20190205, DK, 56:51 mins

(564) *Maliki-rlu   nga=ngu=**nga**   pi-**nya**!*
dog-ERG   POST=2SG.NS=DUB   bite-POT
The dog might bite you!
H_K01-505B, DG, 02:16 mins

(565) *Kula=jana=**nga**   nya-**nya**.*
NEG=3PL.NS=DUB   see-POT
He might not see them.
N_D03-007868, BN, 36:14 mins

(566) *Ngurra-ka=rna   pina   pa-na   nga=ju=**nga**   parra*
home-ALL=1SG.S   return   go-FUT   POST=1SG.NS=DUB   sun
*purlun   ya-**nma**.*
disappear   go-POT
I'll go back home lest it gets dark.
H_K01-505B, DG, 40:09 mins

Uses of the potential inflection without the =*nga* clitic vary, with most uses subsumed under prototypical 'potential' functions—that is, where the event is uncertain, as in (567), for desires, as in (568), or events that are expected, as in (570). It is rare within the transcribed corpus for the potential inflection to occur without some modal auxiliary or adverb that specifies the type of modality (for example, *kalaka* 'apprehensive', *ngarra* 'potential, =*nga* 'potential') or in an interrogative construction.

Uncertain events:

(567) *Kari-nya-nyi   yapa   pa-nama,   ngulya-ka   kalaka   wa-**nma**!*
fail-see-FUT   child   go-FUT.AWAY   ground-ALL   APPR   fall-POT
He isn't watching where the child is going, she might fall onto the ground!
N_D02-007842, BN, 52:46 mins

251

Desires:

(568) *Wanjila=rna-ngu   ya-nma?*
where=1SG.S-2SG.NS   put-POT
Where should I drop you off?
(Lit.: Where will I put you?)
wrl-20180614-02, DK, 17:32 mins

(569) *Pa-nama=li   muju?*
go-POT=1DU.INCL.S   Too
Can we both go?
wrl-20190213-01, DK, 00:27 secs

Expected events:

(570) *Kuku=rna   wila-ngu   ka-nya   wilpa-ka   wangani.*
wait=1SG.S   fun-ERG   carry-POT   creek-ALL   dog
Wait, I'll just take the dog to the creek for fun [9]
wrl-20180614-01, DK, 20:10 mins

6.2.3.6 Subjunctive

6.2.3.6.1 Form

The subjunctive inflection is parasitic, forming as an increment *rla* to the imperative form of a verb. The paradigm is currently incomplete and requires further examination (particularly where the imperative inflection exhibits allomorphy).

Table 6.22 Subjunctive form allomorphy

Class	Underlying morpheme	Allomorphs
V1a	*-ngkarla**	
V1b	*-ngkarla**	
V1c	*-nkarla*	*-nkarla*
V1d	*-rrarla**	
V2	*-karla*	*-karla*
V3	*-ngkarla*	*-ngkarla*
V4	*-njarla*	*-njarla*
V5	*-ntarla*	*-ntarla*

---

9 True instances of the POTENTIAL inflection marking verbs that represent events that are 'expected to happen' are rare and, in fact, most (including this example) may be better analysed as FUT.AWAY (compare with §6.6.3.1).

6.2.3.6.2 Function

The subjunctive inflection encodes that there is some relevant possible world in which the proposition contained by the clause is true, but that it is false in the real world.

This morpheme has also been labelled 'irrealis' in previous analyses of Warlmanpa (for example, Nash 1979), however, there are valid criticisms of the label 'irrealis' to refer to a grammatical morpheme (particularly Bybee 1998), which are particularly relevant in Warlmanpa as there are three other verb inflections that encode an irrealis mood (future, potential, counterfactual) that have distinct functions to this inflection (the set of inflections denoting irrealis modalities is further discussed in §6.6.3).

I have opted for the label 'subjunctive', as the morpheme in Warlmanpa shares much semantic space with analyses of 'subjunctive' morphemes in other languages (for example, for Latin, Lakoff 1968: 182–89; and for a typological perspective, see Palmer 2001). This also follows Osgarby's (2018: 39) analysis of Mudburra.

The most common use of the subjunctive inflection is to encode unactualised events, where the event occurred in some relevant possible world. A typical 'relevant world' is one in which the event would have happened if not for some intervening factor (for discussion of what it means to be a relevant world, see Kearns 2011: 88–92; McCawley 1993: Ch. 12). This use is exemplified in (571)–(573).

(571) *Wajurra*=rna   paka-**karla**,   kirli=rna   win   ya-rnu.
       yesterday=1SG.S   hit-SUBJ   leave_it=1SG.S   separate   put-PAST
       Yesterday I should have hit him, but I left him alone.
       wrl-mud-20180606-02, DF, 04:06 mins

(572) *La-**karla**=ja-rla*   palka-parna-rlu   makiti-parna-rlu.
       shoot-SUBJ=1DU.EXCL.DAT   apparent-PROP-ERG   gun-PROP-ERG
       We would have shot at the kangaroo if we had had a gun.
       N_D02-007842, BN, 56:08 mins

(573)	*Kari=rna*	*karrarlarla*	*marta-**karla***	*yarri=ma=rna=nga*	*wawirri*
COND=1SG.S	spear	have-SUBJ	that=TOP=1SG.S=DUB	kangaroo

karta	*pu-**ngkarla**.*
spear	act_on-SUBJ

If I had a spear, I might have speared the kangaroo.
H_K01-506A, DG, 03:32 mins

Examples (571)–(573) also demonstrate an implicature of the subjunctive inflection: the event has past-time reference. This implicature arises through the non-use of the future and potential inflections that encode future-time reference, however, the uses of the subjunctive inflection discussed below obtain non-past temporal reference (and see §6.6.3 for further discussion of the relationship between the irrealis inflections). Temporal reference of the subjunctive inflection depends on whether the proposition has the ability to become true (which itself is obtained from context): in the examples above, the proposition is necessarily false, so the events are interpreted with past reference, and in examples (574)–(577) (where the implicature is not available due to context), the proposition may yet become true, so they obtain non-past reference.

The use of the subjunctive can be interpreted as a directive where the addressee can cause the proposition to be true, as in (574) and (575), in which the addressee has the power to allow the event to happen. These are interpreted as deontic necessities (that is, social obligations), unlike directive uses of the FUTURE inflection, which are optative.

(574)	*Kirli=rla*	*yu-**ngkarla**!*
leave_it=3.OBL	give-SUBJ

Let him give it to him! (Ken Hale translation)
H_K01-506A, DG, 01:01:10 hrs

(575)	*Jaru=ma=nku-rla*	*turru*	*ma-**ntarla***	*pulka*	*Mack.*
story=TOP=2SG.S-DAT	tell	get-IRR	old_man

You should tell him the story, old man Mack.
H_K01-506A, DG, 33:13 mins

Deontic necessities can also be said of participants other than the addressee, as in (576) and (577).

(576) *Japanangka-rlu   karta   pu-**ngkarla**,   kala   walku.*
Japanangka-ERG   spear   act_on-SUBJ   but   NEG
Japanangka should be digging, but he's not.
wrl-20180616-01, DK, 19:56 mins

(577) *Nyanungu-rlu   ma-**ntarla**.*
aforementioned-ERG   get-SUBJ
He should get it. (Ken Hale translation)
H_K01-506A, DG, 01:01:21 hrs

6.2.3.7 Counterfactual

6.2.3.7.1 Form

The counterfactual inflection is another parasitic inflection, formed through an increment, *kurla*, to the infinitive form of a verb (with the low vowel allomorph—that is, *-nja-*).

Table 6.23 Counterfactual inflection allomorphy

Class	Underlying morpheme	Allomorphs
V1a	-nganjakurla	-nganjakurla
V1b	-njakurla*	
V1c	-njakurla	-njakurla
V1d	-njakurla	-njakurla
V2	-njakurla	-njakurla
V3	-njakurla	-njakurla
V4	-rninjakurla	-rninjakurla
V5	-njakurla	-njakurla

6.2.3.7.2 Function

The counterfactual inflection conveys that the situation denoted by the verb has not occurred at the reference time, but there are possible worlds in which it occurs.

The counterfactual inflection is almost always part of a conditional construction, in which the protasis clause obligatorily has the conditional complementiser *kari* (§12.1.1.1.5). This construction, labelled a future-less-vivid counterfactual, is discussed further in §6.6.3.2 and essentially encodes that the protasis and apodosis are presently false (that is, future-time reference) and implies that the protasis is unlikely to become true, but if it were to become true, so too would the apodosis.

(578) **Kari**=n   kuyu   nga-**rninjakurla**,   nga=n=nga
      COND=2SG.S   meat   eat-CFACT,   POST=2SG.S=DUB

      murrumurru-ja-ma.
      sick-become-POT

      If you were to eat the meat, you might become sick.
      (In all worlds where 'you eat the meat' is true, 'you might become sick' is true.)
      H_K01-506A, DG, 04:42 mins

(579) Yapa   **kari**   wa-**njakurla**,   nga=nga   li-nya.
      child   COND   fall-CFACT   POST=DUB   howl-POT

      Were the child to fall, she might cry.
      (In all worlds where 'child falls' is true, 'she might cry' is true.)
      H_K01-506A, DG, 05:10 mins

The verb in both clauses can take a counterfactual inflection. In these cases, the complementiser *kari* distinguishes the protasis from the apodosis, as in (580), where the left clause is marked as the subordinate (protasis) clause with *kari* 'COND'.

(580) **Kari**=ju-n   wa-**nganjakurla**,   maani=lku=rna-ngu
      COND=1SG.NS-2SG.NS   talk-CFACT   money=THEN=1SG.S-2SG.NS

      yi-**njakurla**.
      give-CFACT

      If you were to talk to me then I would give you money.
      (In all worlds where 'you talk to me' is true, 'I give you money' is true.)
      H_K01-506A, DG, 04:00 mins

Tokens of the counterfactual inflection in constructions without a subordinate *kari* clause convey that there is some unactualised event, but there are relevant possible worlds in which the event occurred. Specific instantiations of this are deontic necessity, as in (581), or inability, as in (582). As (581) suggests, the temporal reference of the counterfactual is not necessarily future (without a *kari* clause) and can indicate past events, though this appears to be rare.

(581) Wirlinyi=n   pa-**njakurla**.
      hunting=2SG.S   go-CFACT

      You should have gone hunting.
      N_D02-009887, DG, 26:15 mins

(582) *Ngarrka-ngu=ma   kula   la-njakurla   kuyu=ma,   lamanpa-jila-rlu.*
man-ERG=TOP   NEG   shoot-CFACT   meat=TOP   gun-WITHOUT-ERG
The man can't shoot a kangaroo, [he is] without a gun.
N_D02-007842, BN, 55:58 mins

6.2.3.8 Infinitive

6.2.3.8.1 Form

The forms for each verb class are given in Table 6.24. The infinitive suffix is underlyingly a homorganic palatal nasal + stop cluster with an unspecified vowel: //ɲcV//, with two verb classes having a syllabic augment. There is morphologically conditioned allomorphy, /ɲca/ ~ /ɲci/, depending on the following morpheme (the infinitive inflection forms a bound stem, so there is obligatorily a following morpheme), given in Table 6.25. There are no clear phonological or semantic correlations to explain the allomorphy, hence its under-specification.

Table 6.24 Infinitive form allomorphy

Class	Underlying morpheme	Allomorphs
V1a	*-ngVnja-*	*-nganja-, -nganji-*
V1b	*-njV-*	*-nja-, -nji-*
V1c	*-njV-*	*-nja-, -nji-*
V1d	*-njV-*	*-nja-, -nji-*
V2	*-njV-*	*-nja-, -nji-*
V3	*-njV-*	*-nja-, -nji-*
V4	*-rninjV-*	*-rninja-, -rninji-*
V5	*-njV-*	*-nja-, -nji-*

Table 6.25 Morphologically conditioned allomorphy of the infinitive suffix (omitting augment)

Following suffix	Gloss	Infinitive allomorph
-jila	WITHOUT	*-nja-*
-karra	SS	*-nja-*
-ku	DAT	*-nja-*
-kuma	AVER	*-nja-*
-kupa	DES	*-nja-*
-wangu	PRIV	*-nja-*
-ni	NOM	*-nji-*
-ngarnu	RESULT	*-nji-*
-ka	ALL	*-nji- ~ -nja-*
-rla	PRIOR	*-nji- ~ -nja-*

In Warlpiri, the infinitive form is always *-nja-* (though the stem to which it attaches is parasitic on the non-past inflection for certain conjugations [Nash 1986: 41]). However, in both languages there is a derivational suffix, *-nji-* (an inceptive in both languages; additionally an associated motion marker in Warlmanpa), which is likely somehow related to the Warlmanpa infinitive allomorph *-nji-* (for further analysis of *-nja-* and *-nji-* in Warlpiri, see also Laughren 2010), though it is not clear what changes would result in the morphologically conditioned allomorphy exhibited by the infinitive suffix.[10]

6.2.3.8.2 Function

The infinitive form of a verb allows it to take a complementising suffix (see Table 6.25; the morphosyntax thereof is discussed in §12.1.2). The infinitive suffix can be seen as derivational morphology to derive a nominal from a verb, which is typically the main predicate of a non-finite clause, though there are some rare cases of a verb formed with the infinitive suffix acting as the predicate of a finite clause (restricted to negative imperatives, as discussed below). Through a cross-linguistic study of this process in Australian languages, Nordlinger (2002) argues against labelling this process 'nominalisation', as the derived form is not a typical 'noun'. Indeed, in Warlmanpa, I consider the derived form 'nominal', however, it is unlike any other non-derived nominal class. In §3.1.6, I analyse non-finite verb forms in Warlmanpa as 'infinitives'—a subclass of the nominal category. Many nominal suffixes can have case functions or complementising functions: a typical nominal allows either function in different contexts, however, an infinitive verb only allows the 'complementising' function of the suffix.

Examples of verbs formed with the infinitive suffix are given in (583)–(586). In these examples, the verb is the main predicate of the non-finite subordinate clause, with the relation to the matrix clause encoded through the following suffix.

---

10 The infinitive suffix *-nja-* is also cognate with the infinitive suffix in Arandic languages. Additionally, Koch (2020) analyses numerous aspect and associated motion constructions in Arandic languages as being historically derived from non-finite verb forms—a very similar process to what seems to have happened in Warlpiri and Warlmanpa.

6. INFLECTING VERBS

(583) *Ngarrka*   *wa-nganya*   **ka-nja-karra.**
man   speak-PRES   **be-INF-SS**
The sitting man is talking.
N_D02-007842, BN, 36:53 mins

(584) *Karnta=rna*   *purtu-ka-ngu*   **wa-nganji-ka.**
woman=1SG.S   listen-be-PAST   **speak-INF-ALL**
I'm listening to the woman speaking.
H_K01-505B, DG, 09:47 mins

(585) **Paka-nja-wangu**   *winja-ka*   *yarri=nya=ma*   *karli!*
hit-INF-PRIV   leave_alone-IMP   that=FOC=TOP   boomerang
Don't strike [with it], leave the boomerang alone!
H_K01-505B, DG, 11:04 mins

(586) *Wawirri=rna*   *nya-ngu*   *yama-ka*   **ka-nji-ka.**
kangaroo=1SG.S   see-PAST   shade-ALL   **be-INF-ALL**
I saw the kangaroo sitting in the shade.
H_K01-505B, DG, 21:11 mins

The counterfactual form of a verb is parasitic (that is, a formal increment but not semantically/syntactically compositional), formed by the infinitive form of a verb + *kurla*:

(587) *Kari=n*   *pirraku-ja-rrarla=ma,*   *nga=rna-ngu=nga*   *ngappa*
COND=2SG.S   thirsty-INCH-IRR=TOP   POST=1SG.S-2SG.NS=DUB   water
yi-njakurla.
give-CFACT
If you were to become thirsty, I would give you water.
H_K01-506A, DG, 07:28 mins

An example of an infinitive verb acting as a predicate of a (finite) matrix clause is given in (588). This seems to be restricted to the two privative suffixes: *-jila* (§11.5.2.2) and *-wangu* (§11.5.2.1). It is possible these are parasitic, like the counterfactual inflection, given their apparent finiteness, however, these privative suffixes are also found marking nominals in non-finite clauses, suggesting they are synchronically decompositional.

(588) *Nga-rninja-wangu!*
eat-INF-PRIV
Don't eat it!
H_K06-004555, LOF, 38:26 mins

6.2.3.9 Path

The inflection *-nyinga* encodes an event as having a path with a specified endpoint, as exemplified in (589) and (590). This suffix has only been found with five verbs: *pa-* 'go', *ma-* 'get', *purlun-wa-* 'fall', *ka-* 'be' and *ka-* 'take'.

(589) **Purluny-wa-nyinga**=rna   ngappa-kuma.
enter-fall-PATH=1SG.S   water-AVERSE
I'm going to go inside to avoid the rain.
wrl-20230731-01, DK, 06:55 mins

(590) Nyapa-purta   wantarri   Kalumpurlpangurlu   **ka-nyinga**
how-FACING   road   Kalumpurlpa-ELA   **be-PATH**
Mangalawurru-ka?
Mangalawurru-ALL
Which direction is the road from Kalumpurlpa to Mangalawurru?
wrl-20200221, DK, 22:16 mins

As shown in this example, when combining with stative predicates, the state is distributed along a path and has present temporal reference. When combining with dynamic predicates, the event is interpreted to involve motion along the path, with the event actualising at the endpoint of the path (that is, GO&X). In these cases, the temporal interpretation is that the motion has begun (and is ongoing) at the time of speaking, as in (591), or will begin imminently, as in (592) and (593), where the endpoint is marked with *-kapina* 'preparative purposive' (§4.1.10).

(591) *Ali=ma*   *pa-nyinga*   *wangani-ka.*
that=TOP   go-PATH   dog-ALL
He's walking towards that dog.
wrl-20180614-01, DK, 33:52 mins

(592) *Ngurra-kapina=rna*   *pa-nyinga*   *wirliya.*
home-PREP=1SG.S   go-PATH   walk
I'm about to walk home.
wrl-20180614-02, DK, 13:18 mins

(593) *Ngappa=nyanu*   *ka-nyinga*   *ngurra-kapina.*
water=RR   take-PATH   camp-PREP
She's about to take water to camp for herself.
H_K06-004547, JW, 29:42 mins

Because the spatial deictic centre is set to the goal, the 'towards' suffix is used on the verb when encoding direction (compare this with the other motion suffixes that are speaker-centric):

(594) *Wanji-ka=n*   *pa-**nyinga-rni**?*
where-ALL=2SG.S   go-PATH-HITH
Where are you going to?
wrl-20190131-01, DK, 04:28 mins

While path suffixes are semantically related to the associated motion paradigm (§6.5.1.1), the path suffixes are not classified as associated motion markers for several reasons.

First, the associated motion markers derive a bound stem, which requires a TAM inflection. As seen in the examples in this section, a root inflected with *-nyinga* is a well-formed word and cannot take further inflection.

Second, unlike the associated motion markers, the spatial deictic centre is set to the location of the goal (placing emphasis on the goal rather than the event itself). Thus, the event almost always takes an allative-marked nominal expression—the common surface form of a spatial goal.

There is no clear cognate suffix of *-nyinga* in nearby languages, however, it bears semantic similarities to the path auxiliary system in Kaytetye (Panther and Harvey 2020), in which the system of path auxiliaries is particularly elaborate—though the Warlmanpa form, *-nyinga*, does not appear to be phonologically related to any of the Kaytetye path auxiliary forms. The form *-nyinga* may be a heavily reduced form of *-nji-ngu-rra* (-MOT.TWD-PAST-AWAY/IMPF), where the palatal stop was deleted and the *-ngurra* form reduced to *-nga*—that is, *njingurra* > *nyingurra* > *nyinga*. Both are indeed evident sound changes in Warlmanpa, however, this being the source seems unlikely for several reasons:

1. The associated motion markers in the language are inherently imperfective so it is unlikely that *-rra* would correspond to the IMPF marker, and, if the *-rra* was instead an away suffix, that seems incompatible with the *-nji-* motion marker that encodes motion towards the deictic centre.
2. The synchronic function is a present and not a past tense, so *-ngu* 'PAST' is unlikely to be part of the source.
3. The associated motion suffixes derive a Class 5b verb, which would have *-nu* as its past form, not *-ngu*.

6.2.3.10 Path away

The 'path away' inflection takes the form of the POTENTIAL form of the verb followed by *-mu*. It encodes that an event is distributed along a path away from the deictic centre (in contrast to the 'path' suffix, *-nyinga*, which seems to encode paths towards the deictic centre or otherwise unspecified directionality), with present temporal reference. In most cases, the event involves motion (this suffix predominantly co-occurs with *pa-* 'go'), in which the motion occurs along the path, as in (595) and (596).

(595)   a.   *Kurdu*   *ka*   *papulu-kurra*   *ya-ni.*
                child   PRES   house-ALL   go-NPST
                The child is going to the house.
                H_K01-505B, Ken Hale, 40:55 mins
                (Warlpiri prompt)

       b.   *Kurtu*   *papulu-ka*   *pa-**namama**.*
                child   house-ALL   go-PATH.AWAY
                The child is going to the house.
                H_K01-505B, DG, 40:58 mins
                (Given Warlmanpa translation of a.)

(596) a. *Nyayil   api-rranta*
       when   go-PATH.AWAY
       When is he/she/it going away [from speaker]?
       H_K01-506A, Ken Hale, 01:02:07 hrs
       (Warumungu prompt)

   b. *Ngana   yarri   **pa-namama.***
      who   that   **go-PATH.AWAY**
      Who is that one setting off?
      H_K01-505B, DG, 01:02:08 hrs
      (Given Warlmanpa translation of a.)[11]

For predicates lacking encoded motion, the 'path away' suffix refers to the spatial distribution of the subject in relation to the deictic centre, as in (597).

(597) a. *Wanyantta   yuwaji   ngunjjirranta?*
       where   road   lie.PRES.AWAY
       Which way does the road go?
       H_K01-506A, DG, 01:04:51 hrs
       (Warumungu prompt)

   b. *Wanyjila   warntarri   **ka-mama?***
      where   road   **be-PATH.AWAY**
      Which way does the road go?
      H_K01-506A, DG, 01:04:54 hrs
      (Given Warlmanpa translation of a.)

Further examples are given in (598)–(602), which also demonstrate the widespread usage of this inflection across speakers.

(598) *Pulka-ka=pala   **pa-namama**   ngurra-ka.*
      old_man-ALL=3DU.S   **go-PATH.AWAY**   camp-ALL
      The two of them are going to the old man.
      H_K01-505B, DG, 41:51 mins

---

11 There may have been a misunderstanding between the prompt and the translation, given that type of question change (from 'when' to 'who').

(599) *Pa-namama*   *yangarlu=nyanu*   **wa-ngamama.**
go-PATH.AWAY   alone=REFL   **speak-PATH.AWAY**

The two of them are going along talking to each other alone.
H_K01-506A, DG, 01:02:18 hrs

(600) *Ngurra-ka=lku=rna*   **pa-namama.**
camp-ALL=THEN=1SG.S   **go-PATH.AWAY**

I'm going to camp now.
H_K06-004555, LOF, 46:26 mins

(601) *Kula=ja*   *partu-ngunya*   *jawarti=ma*   *ka-nya=ja*
NEG=1DU.EXCL.S   leave-PRES   tomorrow=TOP   be-PRES=1DU.EXCL.S

yarti,   *or you say*   *kula=ja*   **parti-mama.**
stay_in_camp   NEG=1DU.EXCL.S   **leave-PATH.AWAY**

'We aren't leaving tomorrow, we'll stay in camp'—or you say 'we aren't leaving'.
N_D03-007868, BN, 26:30 mins

(602) *Karu-ngurlu*   *ngula=lu*   *buṣh-nga* — *buṣh-wana*   *ka-***mama.**
west-ELA   REL=3PL.S   bush-LOC   bush-PERL   be-**PATH.AWAY**

As for the ones [horses] from the west, they live around the bushes away [from us].
N_D20071010, SN, 01:37 mins

6.3 Direction and motion

Direction and motion in Warlmanpa can be encoded at three points in the inflecting verb. These can be catalogued according to their proximity to the verb root. Because they occupy different morphological positions (and different grammatical status), they are discussed in detail in different sections throughout this chapter. This section serves to present a brief unified analysis of direction and motion encoding in Warlmanpa.

First, associated motion can be expressed via derivational suffixes that attach directly to the verb root (and any augment, if relevant). These associated motion suffixes add motion to an event and derive a Class 5b verb stem that still requires a TAM suffix to be a well-formed word. An example is given in (603). These derivational associated motion suffixes are discussed in §6.5.1.1.

(603) *Kuyu-ku   pa-nji-nya.*
       meat-DAT   go-MOT.TWD-PRES
       It's coming here for meat.
       wrl-20160914-02, SN, 11:43 mins

Second, there are two TAM suffixes that appear to be portmanteau morphemes encoding paths. The inflection *-nyinga* encodes motion towards a goal along a path. An example is given in (604). This suffix is discussed in §6.2.3.9. The suffix -POT-*ma* encodes a motion away from an origin along a path, as discussed in §6.2.3.10.

(604) *Ngayu=ma=rna   pa-nyinga,   ali-rla   nga=rna-rla   turru-ma-nmi.*
       1=TOP=1SG.S   go-PATH   that-LOC   PURP=1SG.S-   tell-do-FUT
                                               3SG.OBL
       I'm going there so I can tell him a story.
       wrl-20190205, DK, 37:21 mins

Finally, a directional suffix may attach to a well-formed verb word (that is, one inflected for TAM), as exemplified in (605). Unlike the other expressions of motion/directionality, these suffixes do not necessarily encode movement; they may alternatively express directionality. These directional suffixes are discussed in §6.4.1.

(605) *Muka=nya=rna   pa-nangu-rnu   wa-nganja-ku.*
       this.ALL=FOC=1SG.S   go-PAST-TWD   speak-INF-DAT
       I'm coming to talk.
       H_K01-505B, DG, 34:14 mins

The associated motion and directional suffixes can co-occur with one another, as shown in (606). However, the TAM suffixes *-nyinga* and -POT-*ma* are not documented co-occurring with associated motion or directional suffixes.

(606) *Maliki   jitpi-nja-nu-rnu.*
       dog   run-MOT-PAST-TWD
       The dog is running here.
       H_K01-505B, DG, 23:19 mins

As noted by an anonymous reviewer, the proximity to the root appears to correlate with the combinatorial possibilities of the expression of motion/directionality. The associated motion suffixes, which attach closest to the root, are restricted to simultaneous motion and a restricted set of TAM suffixes, and are incompatible with stative predicates. The TAM suffix *-nyinga* is restricted to present or future temporal aspect and can combine with stative predicates. Finally, there appear to be few semantic restrictions on the directional suffixes *-rni/-rnu* 'towards' and *-rra* 'away', and these suffixes combine with a range of predicates. However, further research is required to properly compare the combinatorial properties of all expressions of direction and motion.

6.4 Directional and aspectual verb morphology

This section discusses the morphology applicable to well-formed verb words. This includes the directional suffixes (§6.4.1) that make a binary distinction between 'towards' (§6.4.1.1) and 'away' (§6.4.1.2). The imperfective suffix is also discussed (§6.4.2). Note that all suffixes discussed in this section are mutually exclusive: a well-formed verb maximally hosts one of the suffixes discussed in this section—that is, an inflecting verb can host just one directional suffix or the imperfective aspect suffix.

6.4.1 Directional motion

The directional paradigm is given in Table 6.26. There is some allomorphy: there is a distinct form when attaching to imperative inflected verbs, as well as vowel alternations of *-rni* 'towards' based on the preceding vowel. The 'towards' suffix is discussed in §6.4.1.1 and the 'away' suffix is discussed in §6.4.1.2. The relation between directional motion and associated motion is discussed in §6.6.2.

Table 6.26 Verbal motion suffixes

	Imperative	Non-imperative
towards, centripetal	*-rti*	*-rni, -rnu*
away, centrifugal	*-pa*	*-rra*

The directional suffixes signal various spatial relations: these include the direction of a motion event, as in (607) and (608), the posture of a non-motion event, as in (609), and the direction of motion associated with a non-motion event, as in (610) and (611).

Direction of motion event:

(607) *Kula   ngarra=rna   pa-nami-rni   ngurra-ka.*
NEG   POT=1SG.S   go-FUT-TWD   camp-ALL
I might not come back home.
wrl-20190201, DK, 36:46 mins

(608) *Pa-nangu-rnu=rna-ngu.*
go-PAST-TWD=1SG.S-2SG.NS
I came for you.
H_K01-505B, DG, 34:08 mins

Posture of non-motion event:

(609) *Ngarrka-ngu=ju   nya-ngu-rnu.*
man-ERG=1SG.NS   see-PAST-TWD
The man looked towards me.
H_K01-506A, DG, 01:04:21 hrs

Motion associated with non-motion event:

(610) *Ngappa-ngurlu=rla   kanja   talan   ma-nu-rnu.*
water-ELA=3.OBL   close   lightning   get-PAST-TWD
Lightning came out from the clouds.
wrl-20190201, DK, 55:45 mins

(611) *Kankarlarra-ngurlu=lu   kiya-rnu-rnu   karrarlarla.*
above-ELA=3PLS.   throw-PAST-TWD   spear
They threw spears here from above.
wrl-20190213-01, DK, 34:26 mins

The distinction between motion associated with non-motion events and associated motion constructions (as discussed in §6.5.1.1) is not clear, particularly when the two co-occur—though see §6.6.2 for some tentative discussion.

The motion appears to be strictly related to the speaker, rather than the deictic centre. For example, in (612), the 'towards' suffix is used on a 'leave' verb with motion ending where the speaker was presently speaking. The likely cognate suffixes in Mudburra are also shown to encode motion (Osgarby 2021).

(612) *Yali-ngurlu=ma partu-ngu-rnu=rnalu Tennant Creek-ka=lku.*
that-ELA=TOP leave-PAST-TWD=1PL.EXCL.S Tennant Creek-ALL=THEN
We left there to Tennant Creek.
wrl-20190208, DK, 24:35 mins

6.4.1.1 -rni 'towards'

The 'towards' suffix attaches to finite inflecting verbs to indicate motion towards the speaker. The form of the suffix depends on the final vowel of the stem to which it is attaching. When the stem to which *-rni* is attaching ends with the high back vowel *u*, the suffix form is *-rnu*, and elsewhere it is *-rni*.

-rnu following high back vowels:

(613) *Pana-ngu-rnu=ju-npala nya-nja-kupa.*
go-PAST-HITH=1SG.NS-2DU.S see-INF-DESIRE
You two came wanting to see me.
H_K01-506A, DG, 56:49 mins

-rni elsewhere:

(614) *Ngampulka=rna ka-nya kula nya-nganya-rni.*
desire=1SG.S be-PRES neg see-PRES-HITH
I want to see him, but I can't.
N_D03-007868, BN, 33:25 mins

(615) *Nya-ngu=rla kapi=n ngurrurla pi-nyi-rni.*
see-PAST=3.OBL FUT=2SG.S return act_on-FUT-HITH
On seeing him, you will have returned.
H_K01-505B, DG, 48:02 mins

6. INFLECTING VERBS

This form is found in many other Ngumpin-Yapa languages as a suffix indicating motion towards the speaker or deictic centre (Meakins and Nordlinger 2014: 308; Osgarby 2018: 63–64; Ennever 2018: 320; Tsunoda 1981a: 208; Senge 2015: 426). Interestingly, it is not found in Gurindji (Meakins and McConvell 2021).

In imperative constructions, the allomorph is *-rti*. All imperative suffixes end in /a/, and there is no known morphology that can intervene between the imperative suffix and the directional suffix, thus, there is no appropriate environment to test whether this allomorph is also subject to the same morphophonological alternations as the non-imperative allomorphs. Examples of the imperative allomorph are given in (616) and (617).

(616) *Karli=ju   kiya-ka-**rti**!*
boomerang=1SG.NS   throw-IMP-HITH
Throw the boomerang to me!
H_K01-506A, DG, 01:04:01 hrs

(617) *Yu-ngka-**rti**=ju!*
give-IMP-HITH=1SG.NS
Give it to me!
H_K06-004555, LOF, 52:49 mins

6.4.1.2 *-rra* 'away'

The suffix *-rra* 'away' signals motion away from the deictic centre. It is homophonous with the imperfective suffix *-rra*, as discussed in §6.4.2. It is often difficult to distinguish without context and, in §6.6.1, I discuss whether these suffixes would be better analysed as one polysemous morpheme. Examples of the *-rra* signalling directionality are given in (618) and (619).

(618) *Yimpa   Japanangka   jaru-kupa   pa-nangu-rra.*
this   Japanangka   language-DESIRE   go-PAST-AWAY
This Japanangka went away for language.
H_K01-506A, DG, 33:10 mins

(619) *Mirla=nya=lu   partu-ngu-rra   kurlarra.*
this.LOC=FOC=3PL.S   leave-PAST-AWAY   south
They left off to the south.
N_D02-007850, DG, 06:06 mins

As with the 'towards' suffix, there is an imperative allomorph of the away suffix, *-pa*, as exemplified in (620)–(622).

(620) *Ngurra-ka   pa-nka-pa!*
home-ALL   go-IMP-AWAY
Go home!
H_K01-506A, DG, 53:22 mins

(621) *Kiya-ka-pa!*
throw-IMP-AWAY
Throw it away!
H_K01-506A, DG, 01:03:38 hrs

(622) *Wirliny   kapu-ka-pa!*
follow   chase-IMP-AWAY
Follow him!
H_K06-004555, LOF, 48:14 mins

The same form (*-rra*) is found in several Ngumpin-Yapa languages, as either an imperfective suffix or an away suffix. It is a directional suffix in Warlpiri, Mudburra, Ngardi and marginally in Wanyjirra (Nash 1986; Osgarby 2018; Senge 2015: 427; Ennever 2021). It is an imperfective suffix in Bilinarra and Ngarinyman (Meakins and Nordlinger 2014: 272). The connection between *-rra* as a marker of imperfectivity and/or directionality is discussed further in §6.6.1.

As with the *-rra* IMPF suffix, the *-rra* AWAY suffix combining with tense inflections ending in high vowels can cause the final vowel of the inflection and the *rr* of the away suffix to delete, as in (623), in which *-mi-rra* contracts to *-ma* (this morphophonological process is discussed further in §6.2.2.2.2; the resulting collapse of the phonological distinction between the potential inflection and the FUTURE.AWAY form is discussed further in §6.6.3.1).

(623) *Nyangurla=n   parti-**ma**?*
when=2SG.S   leave-FUT.AWAY
When are you leaving?
H_K01-506A, DG, 49:07 mins

6.4.2 -rra 'imperfective'

Verbs may take a *-rra* suffix to indicate imperfective aspect, which can be subclassified into habitual and continuous aspects (Comrie 1976).

Imperfective aspect (as denoted by *-rra*) in Warlmanpa is formally defined as topic time being a proper subset of situation time—that is, 'topic time ⊂ situation time', following Klein's (1994) conceptualisation of describing aspect. I follow Klein's (1994: 4) definition of topic time as 'the time span to which the speaker's claim on this occasion is confined', which is distinct from reference time.

By implicature, then, unmarked perfective aspect in Warlmanpa is 'situation time ⊆ topic time'. This distinction can be exemplified with (624), which involves two clauses: the first is unmarked for aspect and taken to be perfective aspect, and the second clause is overtly marked for imperfective aspect. The temporal reference of the first clause is situated within that of the second clause.

(624) *Wiri-ja-ngu=rnalu*   1945   *school-ka=lku=rnalu*
       big-INCH-PAST=1PL.S   school-ALL=THEN=1PL.S

   *pa-nangu-**rra***   *tartu*   *kurtukurtu.*
   go-PAST-IMPF   many   children

   [When] we became big in 1945, we children were all going to school.
   N_D02-007844, BN, 28:28 mins

In this utterance, there are two situations: a change of state (conceptualised as a punctual event) and a (habitual) state of 'going to school'. The topic time is assigned to the change of state, as it frames the temporal perspective, so in this case, situation time and topic time entirely overlap, which is considered perfective aspect (hence the definition of perfective aspect in Warlmanpa earlier as 'situation time ⊆ topic time' rather than 'situation time ⊂ topic time'). The habitual state of going to school is marked with *-rra* to denote that this situation has a wider temporal scope than the topic time that situates it—that is, the participants were in this state prior to becoming big and after becoming big.

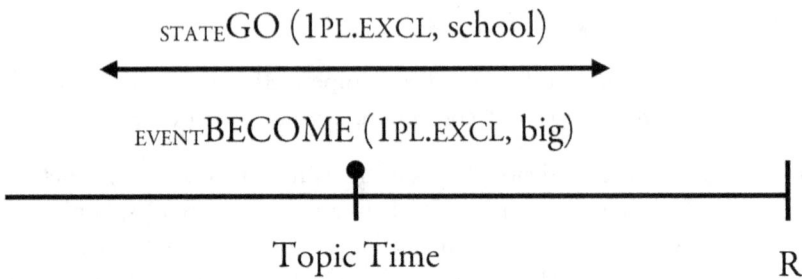

Figure 6.4 Temporal representation of the situations denoted in Example (624)

In a typical interpretation of a situation with perfective aspect, the topic time is established by the verb inflection and is underspecified without lexical content or some shared knowledge to believe otherwise. For example, the PAST inflection is defined as 'locating an event time before reference [typically speech] time', which places topic time as any time before reference time, and the situation is located somewhere within that topic time. Similarly, the future inflection places topic time anywhere after reference time. Naturally, there are several temporal adverbs that can be used to further specify topic time (§8.2) or 'framing' events, as in (624).

A contrast between perfective and non-perfective conceptualisations of the same situation is given in (625) and (626), which differ only in the occurrence of -*rra*. In (625), the utterance without -*rra*, the topic time remains unspecified, the only specification coming from the past inflection that stipulates 'prior to reference time'. This gives rise to a perfective reading, in which the situation time is a subset of the topic time. Conversely, in (626), the use of -*rra* specifies topic time at a particular point as a subset of the situation time, giving rise to an imperfective reading.

(625)   *Kuyu   nga-rnu.*
        meat   eat-PAST
        He ate the meat.
        H_K01-506A, DG, 47:57 mins

(626)   *Kuyu   nga-rnu-rra.*
        meat   eat-PAST-IMPF
        He was eating the meat.
        H_K01-505B, DG, 18:22 mins

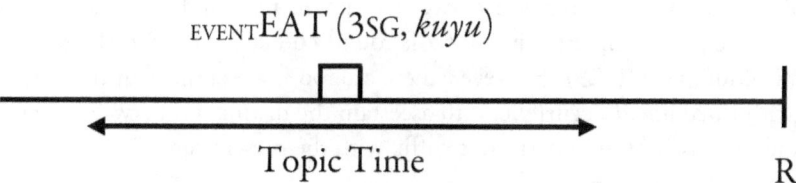

Figure 6.5 Temporal schema of Example (625), a durative event with perfective aspect and event time as a proper subset of topic time

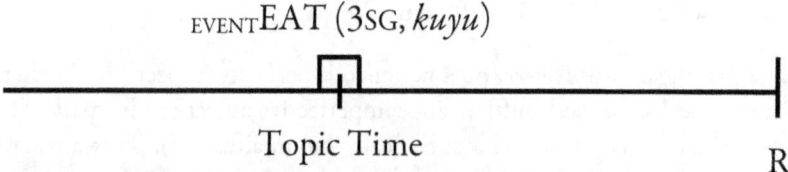

Figure 6.6 Temporal schema of Example (626), a durative event with imperfective aspect and topic time as a subset of event time

Thus far, the discussion of *-rra* has focused on continuous aspect, which frames a unitary topic time within some situation. The use of *-rra* does not explicitly distinguish between habitual and continuous aspects and can be used equally for both. Habitual aspect is discussed in detail for the habitual auxiliary base *kala* (§5.3.2), though a clause can be marked as habitual with *-rra*:

(627)   *Wirliya=rnalu*   **pa-nangu-rra.**
        foot=1PL.EXCL   go-PAST-IMPF
        We would go by foot.
        N_D29-023128, MFN, 01:35 mins

(628)   *Kurtu*   **ka-ngu-rra**   *Kunayungku-rla*   *nyaninya-parna*   *panpiya-parna.*
        child   be-PAST-IMPF   Kunayungku-LOC   3GEN-PROP   family-PROP
        A child used to live at Kunayungku with his family.
        wrl-20190207-01, DK, 41:44 mins

The imperfective suffix is clearly found co-occurring with the past and subjunctive inflections. Based on this analysis, Warlmanpa can be said to have compositional tense and aspect marking for the past and future inflections: these obligatory verb inflections specify the relation between reference time and situation time (that is, tense), and the use or non-use of -*rra* specifies the relation between situation time and topic time (that is, aspect). The imperfective suffix is found co-occurring with the present inflection, as in (629). However, there are too few examples in the corpus (with three noted occurrences) to ascertain the distinction between the use and non-use of the imperfective suffix with the present tense.

(629)   *Yarnunju=rna*   *nga-rninya-rra.*
        food=1SG.S   eat-PRES-IMPF
        I'm eating food.
        wrl-20190201, DK, 43:14 mins

Note that the non-use of -*rra* does not encode perfective aspect (that is, there is no -∅ 'perfective' verb suffix), since imperfective aspect can be marked by the auxiliary *kala* (which is a specifically habitual aspect). This auxiliary does not require the co-occurrence of -*rra* (though they may co-occur). For example, the use of the 'habitual' auxiliary, as in (630), encodes imperfective aspect without an overt -*rra* suffix

(630)   *Yangka*   **kala**=*lu*   *work-ja-ngu.*
        other   HAB=3PL.S   work-INCH-PAST
        Others used to work.
        N_D29-023128, MFN, 03:12 mins

The 'be' verb *ka-* with past imperfective is highly lexicalised as referring to living at a location, as in (631).

(631)   *Ngula=rna*   *mi-rla*   **ka-ngu-rra**   *yarri=ma=rna*
        COMP=1SG.S   this-LOC   **be-PAST-IMPF**   that=TOP=1SG.S
        ngarrka   *ma-nu-rra.*
        know   get-PAST-IMPF
        I used to know that one when I was living here.
        H_K01-506A, DG, 31:25 mins

The suffix form of -*rra* in Warlmanpa is ambiguous between 'away' and 'imperfective' and the two cannot co-occur, suggesting they may be better analysed as one polysemous suffix (this is discussed further in §6.6.1).

6.5 Derivational morphology

This section discusses derivational morphology pertaining to inflecting verbs. An analysis is presented in §6.5.1 of derivation affecting verb roots to derive semantically complex inflecting verbs, including associated motion (§6.5.1.1), inceptives (§6.5.1.2) and verb reduplication (§6.5.1.3), though verb reduplication does not seem to be a synchronically active process. Section 6.5.2 analyses deriving inflecting verbs from other parts of speech (typically nominals): *-ja-* 'inchoative' (§6.5.2.1) and *-ma-* 'cause' (§6.5.2.2).

6.5.1 V → V derivation

6.5.1.1 Associated motion

Verb roots can be derived with a suffix that encodes concurrent movement with the situation to which the root refers—that is, 'associated motion' (AM). These roots require the same augment and vowel alternations as for their infinitive form, before allowing the motion suffix to attach. Note that this does not involve the infinitive inflection *-nja-/-nji-* itself, just the same augment that is used for the infinitive form of the verb and vowel alternations also found on the infinitive form of the verb. This bound stem then requires an imperative, past, present, future or potential inflection to attach (AM suffixes in Mudburra also allow only a subset of the TAM inflections [Osgarby 2018: 62]).

To exemplify the 'infinitive form augment' (augments are discussed in §6.2.2.1), the root *nga-* 'eat' has an augment, *rni*, for its infinitive form, hence *nga-rni-nji-nu* 'eat-AUG-MOT.TWD-PAST' is decomposed as in (632).

(632) | *Nga* | *-rni* | *-nji* | *-nu* |
|---|---|---|---|
| root | augment | motion suffix | TAM suffix |
| eat | | MOT.TWD | PAST |

Turning to the high vowel alternation, this is exemplified in (633), where the verb root *pi-* is specified to have a front high vowel in the infinitive form, unlike some other inflections, which require it to surface with a high back vowel. High vowel specifications are discussed in §6.2.2.2.

(633) *Pi*   -*nji*   -*nu*
       root   motion suffix   TAM suffix
       act_on   MOT.TWD   PAST

The motion suffixes are given in Table 6.27, exemplified with the PRESENT inflection.

Table 6.27 AM suffixes that produce a bound stem requiring further TAM morphology

Direction of motion	Form		Example
Unspecified or 'around'	-*nja*-	*li-nja-nya*	he's going around crying
Towards deictic centre	-*nji*-	*li-nji-nya*	he's coming crying
Away from deictic centre	-*nya*-	*li-nya-nya*	he's going away crying

The AM constructions combine with all event types except for states (event types as per Moens and Steedman 1988; Vendler 1957), as exemplified in (634)–(636).

(634)   **Process (activity)**

   Warlu   *ji-nji-nya.*
   fire   burn-MOT.TWD-PRES
   The fire is burning this way.
   wrl-20170321, SN, 07:13 mins

(635)   **Culmination (achievement)**

   Lamarta-nji-nya   *yiwirti.*
   catch-MOT.TWD-PRES   stick
   He's catching the sticks [being thrown at him], coming here.
   wrl-20180614-02, DK, 09:48 mins

(636)   **Point (semelfactive)**

   Jinjirla=n   *paka-nya-nya.*
   sneeze=2SG.S   hit-MOT.AWAY-PRES
   You're sneezing, going away from me.
   wrl-20180614-02, DK, 05:34 mins

Non-durative events are interpreted as repeated events for the duration of the motion, as modelled in Table 6.28. For example, in (635), the verb root is 'catch', which refers to a non-durative event of catching; however, when combining with a motion suffix, the forced interpretation is that this event repeated for the duration of the movement, rather than a single event that happened during the motion. States (such as 'know') appear to be unable to combine with AM constructions.

Table 6.28 The interpretation of event structure in non-AM and AM constructions

Event type	Interpretation of event structure	
	Non-associated-motion	Associated motion
[+durative] Activities; Accomplishments	E	Motion / E
[–durative] Achievements; Semelfactives	E	Motion / E E E E E E E

The AM construction is restricted to simultaneous movement. A movement preceding or following an event requires a separate predicate that encodes movement, as exemplified in (637)–(639).

(637)   ***Pa-nka-pa   yarnunju   kupa-nmi!***
    go-IMP-AWAY   veg_food   **cook-**FUT
    Go and cook some food!
    (The cooking involves no encoded motion.)
    wrl-20180615-02, DK, 04:42 mins

(638)   ***Pa-nyinga**=pala   **paka-nja-ku.***
    go-PRES.AWAY=3DU.S   **hit-**INF-DAT
    Those two are going away to hit him.
    (The hitting involves no encoded motion.)
    wrl-mud-20180606-02, DK, 26:27 mins

(639)   ***Parti-nyanya**=rnalu   **paka-nja-ku.***
    leave-PRES.AWAY=1PL.EXCL.S   **hit-**INF-DAT
    We're leaving to go fight.
    (The fight involves no encoded motion.)
    wrl-mud-20180606-02, DK, 37:24 mins

Furthermore, the AM has nominative patterning, in that the movement can only be predicated of the subject (whether the verb root is intransitive or transitive) and never encodes motion of an object or other argument. This is a common feature of AM constructions (Guillaume 2016: 91).

As noted earlier, the AM markers do not derive a fully productive verb stem. They derive a Class 5b stem (§6.2.1.5), which has a defective paradigm, in terms of combinations with verb inflections, as shown in Table 6.29. The 'motion' *-nja-* and 'motion towards' *-nji-* are productive and can combine with the imperative, present, past and future inflections. The 'motion away' suffix, *-nja-*, has been found to combine only with the present inflection.

Table 6.29 Permissible inflections following AM morphemes

AM morpheme	IMP -rra	PRES -nya	PAST -nu	FUT -nmi
-nja- 'motion'	✓	✓	✓	✓
-nji- 'motion towards'	✓	✓	✓	✓
-nyu- 'motion away'		✓		

A final general point before discussing each of the associated morpheme suffixes in detail: there appears to be a palatal dissimilation process pertinent to AM verbs taking the present inflection. The present inflection is typically *-nya* but may be realised with an alveolar nasal when occurring after any of the associated motion markers—for example, *wanganjanya* 'go while speaking' may be realised as *wanganjana*. When providing examples, I have attempted to record the variant I perceived for each utterance.

AM in Ngumpin-Yapa (and Australian languages more generally) has been a topic of recent interest. Laughren (2010) demonstrates the distinction between inceptives and AM in Warlpiri, showing the two constructions can co-occur within the same verbal complex (whereas in Warlmanpa the inceptive construction is homophonous with an AM construction and the two cannot co-occur). In Warlpiri, the AM component does not seem to strictly encode a direction (direction can still be specified with a suffix, as in Warlmanpa), unlike the Warlmanpa AM paradigm, in which *-nji-* and *-nya-* do encode directionality in addition to motion. Ennever (2021) analyses the Ngardi AM system, which makes a distinction between motion prior to the event and motion following the event, as well as tracing a diachronic path for the paradigm with reference to the Warlpiri forms. Osgarby (2021) provides an account of Mudburra, which utilises the suffixes *-rru* 'away' and *-rni* 'towards' (with various allomorphs) following the verb inflection to encode motion, unlike the systems of Warlmanpa, Warlpiri and Ngardi, in which the AM component precedes the verb inflection (with the post-inflection suffixes tending to be directional or aspectual). Koch (2021) provides an areal perspective of AM in Pama-Nyungan languages, including the Ngumpin-Yapa languages Warlmanpa, Warlpiri and Mudburra.

6.5.1.1.1 -*nja*- MOT

For underspecified paths, -*nja*- may be used, as in (640) and (641), where the event may take place over a path that is neither strictly 'away' nor 'towards' (that is, unspecified for directionality), which is here translated as 'around (the area)'.

(640) *Ngulya pangi-**nja**-rra!*
ground dig-MOT-IMP
Dig around the area!
wrl-20180601-01, DK, 27:20 mins

(641) *Wilpa-nga=rna pa-**nja**-na.*
creek-LOC=1SG.S go-MOT-PRES
I'm walking around the creek.
wrl-20180528-03, DK, 01:45 mins

While -*nja*- does not encode a particular direction, it can freely combine the 'towards' directional morphology (§6.4.1), as in (642) and (643). There are no tokens of -*nja*- co-occurring with the -*rra* 'imperfective' or 'away'.

(642) *Kala=rna-jana kurtukurtu ka-**nja**-nu-**rnu** school-ku=ma*
HAB=1SG.S-3PL.NS children take-MOT-PAST-TWD school-DAT=TOP
Warrego Mine-ka.
Warrego Mine-ALL
I used to bring the children to Warrego Mine for school.
wrl-20190208, DK, 20:03 mins

(643) *Maliki jitpi-**nja**-nu-**rnu**.*
dog run-MOT-PAST-TWD
The dog was running towards [me].
H_K01-505B, DG, 23:19 mins

As well as allowing 'around' and 'towards' interpretations, this construction allows 'away' interpretations, as exemplified in (644), in which the speaker provides a translation between an English sentence and a Warlmanpa predicate.

(644) When he's walking away from you, he's eating along, that's   *nga-rninja-nya.*

                                                              eat-MOT-PRES

wrl-20180601-01, DK, 03:21 mins

6.5.1.1.2 -nji- MOT.TWD

The suffix *-nji-* is used to encode motion towards the deictic centre, as in (645)–(648). This construction is homophonous with the inceptive construction (§6.5.1.2).

(645) *Warna=ngu   kanja   pa-**nji**-nya,   kaya   nga=ngu=nga*
       snake=2SG.NS   close   go-MOT.TWD-PRES   watch_out   POST=2SG. NS=DUB

pi-nyi!
bite-FUT

That snake is coming towards you—watch out, lest it bite you!
N_D02-007841, JC, 05:08 mins

(646) *Ngarrka-ngu   nga-**rninji**-nya.*
       man-ERG   eat-MOT.TWD-PRES
The man is eating coming towards me.
wrl-20180528-03, JK, 25:20 mins

(647) *Wartayi=n   wa-**nganji**-nmi.*
       continuously=2SG.S   speak-MOT.TWD-FUT
You'll always be talking while coming here.
(Speaker translation: 'You talk too much!')
N_D03-007868, BN, 21:29 mins

(648) *Kuyu-ku   pa-**nji**-nya.*
       meat-DAT   go-MOT.TWD-PRES
He's coming for meat.
wrl-20160914-02, SN, 11:43 mins

6. INFLECTING VERBS

For one speaker, DG, the form is -nti-, only for pa- 'go':

(649)   *Yiwirti-parna*   *yarri*   *pa-**nti**-nya.*
        spear-PROP   that   go-HITH-PRES
        That one with the spear is coming.
        H_K01-506A, DG, 01:03:26 hrs

6.5.1.1.3 -nya- MOT.AWAY

The suffix *-nya* attaching to a verb root (with its infinitive augment) denotes motion away from the deictic centre as part of the event denoted by the verb root. This analysis has been explicitly supported by speakers during elicitation sessions, as in (650) and (651).

(650)   '*Yali=ma*   *jitpi-nya-nya*   *kuyapurta*,' that means him going that way.
        that=TOP   run-MOT.AWAY-PRES   away
        wrl-20180531-02, DF, 03:15 mins

(651)   '*Nga-rninya-nya*'   means he's going off.
        eat-MOT.AWAY-PRES
        wrl-20180601-01, JK, 02:56 mins

Further examples of *-nya* are given in (652) and (653). Example (653) can be contrasted with (641), repeated below, which is identical other than the subject of the predicate (irrelevant to the discussion here) and the motion suffix: in (641), the motion suffix is *-nja*, which is unspecified motion, hence may be interpreted as 'around the creek' or 'along the creek', whereas *-nya* 'MOT.AWAY' can only be interpreted with the motion along/through the creek away from the speaker.

Specified motion direction with *-nya-*:

(652)   *Jalangu*   *jakarr*   *pi-nya-na=lku.*
        now   cover_up   act_on-MOT.AWAY-PRES=THEN
        Now [the moon] is covering up [the sun] [in a direction moving away from speaker].
        N_D09-013557, DG, 01:13 mins

(653)   *Pa-nya-nya*   *wilpa-nga.*
        go-MOT.AWAY-PRES   creek-LOC
        He's walking at/along the creek [away from me].
        wrl-20180614-01, DK, 03:43 mins

Unspecified motion direction with *-nja-*:

(641) *Wilpa-nga=rna pa-**nja-na.***
creek-LOC=1SG.S go-MOT-PRES
I'm walking around the creek.
wrl-20180528-03, DK, 01:45 mins

There are no noted tokens of MOT.AWAY occurring with a TAM suffix other than present. It is unclear whether this is a grammatical restriction or a lack of data.

6.5.1.2 Inceptives

Inceptives are formed by a verb root with its infinitive augment hosting *-nji-*, which forms a Class 5b stem (just as with the AM constructions), requiring a TAM inflection. The usage of the inceptive construction places the reference time at the beginning of some event (rather than it being placed 'during' the event), as modelled in Table 6.30. The relation to speech time is resolved by the TAM suffix. This form is homophonous with the MOT.TWD construction (§6.5.1.1.2).

Table 6.30 The interpretation of 'reference' time in inceptive and non-inceptive constructions

Construction type	Event and reference time interpretation
Inceptive: Reference time specifically at beginning of event	Reference / Event / Time
Non-inceptive: Reference time not specifically set at a point in the event, general reference	Reference Time / Event / Time

Examples of the inceptive are given in (654)–(656).

(654) *Nga=rna-ngu-lu*   turru   ma-**nji**-nmi   jaru.
POST=1S-2SG.NS-S.PL.EXCL   tell   get-INC-FUT   message
We're going to start telling a story for you.
N_D29-023128, MFN, 01:15 mins

(655) *Jaru-ku=rna-ngu*   purt   pu-ngu-nya
message-PURP=1SG.S-2SG.NS   send   act_on-AUG-PRES
nyuntu=lku=rla   turru   ma-**nji**-rra.
2=THEN=3.OBL   tell   get-INC-IMP
I'm sending you this message, then you can start telling him.
H_K01-506A, DG, 33:40 mins

(656) *Kula=lu-nyanu*   *pi-**nji**-rra!*
NEG=PL.S-RR   act_on-INC-IMP
Don't start hitting each other!
wrl-20180610-01, DK, 19:22 mins

6.5.1.3 Verb reduplication

There appears to be extremely rare verb reduplication, examples of which are given in (657) and (658). In both cases, it appears to be the go verb *pa-* being reduplicated, with the augment *-na* forming the reduplicated stem *pana~pana*. Interestingly, there is no clear TAM marking on this reduplicated form. Its semantic effect is unclear: it appears to refer to a pluractional event, though more tokens would be needed for a clearer analysis.

(657) *Kala=lpangu*   *la-nma*   *kayi=lpa*   *kita-nga=ma*   *pana~pana,*
HAB=1INC.PL.NS   shoot-POT   if=1INC.PL.S   bare-LOC=TOP   go-RDP

wartawarta-rla=lpa   **pana~pana**   *kantu*   *yimirna-rla.*
scrub-LOC=1INC.PL.S   **go-RDP**   under   scrub-LOC
They might shoot us if we go about in the open, we'll go about in the scrub.
N_D02-007844, BN, 27:05 mins

(658) *Wurtaja=lpa*   **pana~pana.**
properly=1PL.INCL.S   **go-RDP**
We gotta walk around properly.
N_D03-007868, BN, 14:23 mins

I do not believe verb reduplication is a synchronically productive process, however, I include this discussion for completeness and as stimulus for further research.

The reduplicated forms found in the corpus may specifically refer to future temporal reference, as DK seems to offer *panapana* as an alternative to *panjinmi* 'will be coming', as shown in (659), where the utterance seems to restart after 'or'.

(659)   *Ngayu=ma=rna*   *pa-nji-nmi,*   *or.*   ***pana~pana**=rna*   *kayi=rna*
       1=TOP=1SG.S   go-MOT.   **go~RDP**=1SG.S   WHEN=1SG.S
                                TWD-FUT

       palapala-ja-mi.
       tired-INCH-FUT
       I'll come, or, I'll come when I become tired.
       wrl-20190201, DK, 44:09 mins

There is no evidence that other inflecting verbs can be reduplicated, though inflecting verb reduplication is a core component of Mudburra grammar (Osgarby 2018), which might be an influence here, as well as Warlpiri (Nash 1986). Relatedly, coverbs exhibit reduplication, though the semantic effect is presently unknown (see §7.2).

6.5.2 N → V derivation

Verbs can be derived from nominals using *-ja-* 'become X' and *-ma-* 'cause X'. The derived verb is intransitive if derived using *-ja-* and transitive if derived using *-ma-*, which is contrasted below using the same nominal, *palka* 'present, apparent'. In (660), the derivational suffix is *-ma-*, which requires an agent (subject) causing the existence of a theme (object), whereas in (661), the derivational suffix is *-ja*, which requires only a theme (subject). The prototypical case frames for the derived verbs are:

     X-*ja-rra*   ABS becomes X   §6.5.2.1
     X-*ma-nta*   ERG causes ABS to X   §6.5.2.2

(660)   *Ngayu=ma=rna*   ***palka-ma-nu***   *kurtu=lku.*
       1=TOP=1SG.S   **present-CAUS-PAST**   child=THEN
       I had a child there [lit.: I caused a child to exist].
       wrl-20190211-01, DK, 03:02 mins

(661) *Ngula=ja*   *ka-ngu-rra*   *Darwin-nga*   *kurtu=lku*
REL=1DU.EXCL.S   be-PAST-IMPF   Darwin-LOC   child=THEN
palka-ja-ngu,   *karnta.*
present-INCH-PAST   woman

While we were living in Darwin a child was born, a girl.

wrl-20190211-01, DK, 05:18 mins

The same derivational paradigm is found in Warlpiri, where *-jarri-* is the inchoative and *-ma-* is the causative (Laughren 2010).

The nominals hosting these derivational suffixes lose their nominal status, as evidenced by the lack of complementising suffixes in non-finite clauses, as in (662), where the complementising suffix attaches to the nominalised verb (rather than the nominal root).

(662) *Nya-ngu=ju-n*   *karli-ka*   **partakurru-ma-nji-ka.**
see-PAST=1SG.NS-2SG.S   boomerang-ALL   **good-CAUS-INF-ALL**

You saw me fixing the boomerang.
(Lit.: You saw me causing the boomerang to be good.)

H_K01-505B, DG, 24:11 mins

Ignorative nominals can be derived into verbs, as in (663), though temporal adverbs and free pronouns cannot be derived into verbs.

(663) **Nyapa-ja-ngu-**rra=n?
how-INCH-PAST-IMPF=2SG.S

What have you been doing?

wrl-20170327-1, PK, 01:17 mins

6.5.2.1 *-ja-rra* 'inchoative'

The suffix *-ja* derives a verb stem of Class 1d.[12] This verb denotes some change of state to its subject, where the state is the denotation of the nominal root. Examples are given in (664)–(666).

---

12 However, it should be noted that there are no tokens in the corpus of a verb derived using *-ja-* with the imperative inflection. This is likely due to *-ja-* deriving stative verbs denoting some attribute of a referent, and such verbs are not grammatical in English imperative constructions either: '*Be(come) born/rotten/red/etc.'!

(664) Yali-warnu=nya=ma **pawurra-ja-nmi,** ngayu=ma=lpa parti-ma=lku.
that-RSLT=FOC=TOP **finish-INCH-FUT** 1=TOP=1DU.INCL.S leave-POT=THEN
After that when they've finished, we'll leave.
N_D02-007850, DG, 02:36 mins

(665) **Pirraku-ja-nya**=rna ngappa-ku.
thirsty-INCH-PRES=1SG.S water-DAT
I've become thirsty for water.
H_K01-506A, DG, 48:43 mins

(666) Kuyu **puka-ja-ngu.**
meat **rotten-INCH-PAST**
The meat became rotten.
H_K01-506A, DG, 16:39 mins

This derivation is also regularly used for English verbs, as in (667) and (668), and the same process is found in Warlpiri (Meakins and O'Shannessy 2012; Bavin and Shopen 1985).

(667) **Learn-ja-ngu**-rra=rnalu papulanyi way, partakurru.
learn-INCH-PAST-IMPF=1PL.EXCL.S white_people good
We learnt white people's way, well.
N_D02-007844, BN, 28:41 mins

(668) Ngula=rna wiri-ja-ngu **marry-ja-ngu**=lku=rna.
REL=1SG.S big-INCH-PAST **marry-INCH-PAST**=THEN=1SG.S
When I was older, I got married.
wrl-20190208, DK, 06:25 mins

Due to the lack of overt nominals, it is difficult to tell whether these transitive English verbs are being treated in Warlmanpa as transitive or intransitive—that is, semantically, 'learning' and 'marrying' are perhaps expected to be transitive verbs, however, there is no strong evidence to suggest the valency of these derived verbs in these examples.

6. INFLECTING VERBS

When deriving English words, it loses its [+telic] and [–durative] semantics, which is particularly evident in its ability to co-occur with the habitual auxiliary base to indicate a regularly ongoing activity (rather than a regularly incepting state), as in (669). In all uses of -*ja*-, the event is [+dynamic]. The aktionsart of -*ja*- is shown in Table 6.31.

(669)   *Ngayinya   ngamini   **kala   work-ja-ngu**=pala,   jirrima=yi.*
        1GEN   uncle   HAB   work-INCH-PAST=3DU.S   two=STILL

      My uncles used to work, the two [of them].[13]

      N_D29-023128, MFN, 03:15 mins

Table 6.31 Aktionsart of -*ja*- based on status of derived word

	Durative	Telic	Dynamic
Non-loans	–	+	+
Loans	±	±	+

6.5.2.2 -*ma-nta* 'causative'

The suffix -*ma*- forms a transitive verb belonging to Class 5a from a nominal. It is formally identical to the verb root *ma*- 'get, take'. Examples are given in (670)–(672). Unlike -*ja*-, the derived predicate is obligatorily transitive.

(670)   *Ngayu=rna   kirlka-ma-ni   murtika,   kula=rna   pa-nami.*[14]
      1=1SG.S   clean-CAUSE-FUT   car   NEG=1SG.S   go-FUT

      I have to clean the car, I can't go.

      wrl-20190213-01, DK, 32:01 mins

(671)   *Japaja-rlu   maliki   kari~kari-ma-nu.*
      Japaja-ERG   dog   far~RDP-CAUSE-PAST

      Japaja chased the dog far away.

      (Lit.: Japaja caused the dog to be far away.)

      N_D02-007841, BN, 07:37 mins

---

13 Interestingly, the bound pronoun =*pala* attaches to the inflecting verb here, rather than the auxiliary *kala*.

14 The bilabial nasal is dropped by the speaker here (*kirlka-manmi* is expected), which resembles the Warlpiri form. However, the remainder of the sentence is clearly Warlmanpa (best evidenced by the free pronoun *ngayu*, rather than *ngaju* in Warlpiri).

(672)   *Karli=rna-ngu*   *maju-ma-nu.*
        boomerang=1SG.S-2SG.NS   bad-CAUSE-PAST
        I spoiled the boomerang on you.
        (Lit.: I caused the boomerang to be bad on you.)
        N_D02-007841, BN, 27:32 mins

As with *-ja-*, which can incorporate nonce borrowings (particularly English verbs) into intransitive verbs, *-ma-* can incorporate non-Warlmanpa words into transitive verbs:

(673)   *Numu=ju-n*   *kari-ja-nya,*   *nga=rna-ngu*   *kutu*   **p̲uj̲u-ma-nmi.**
        NEG=1SG.NS-2SG.S   far-INCH-PRES   POST=1SG.S-2SG.NS   close   **push-CAUSE-FUT**
        If you don't get away from me, I'll push you.
        wrl-20170905-02, PW, 00:44 secs

6.6 Further topics in verbs

This section discusses relationships between related verb suffixes (phonologically or semantically) that warrant further analysis: first, the relationship between the imperfective and away suffix is discussed, particularly whether they are best analysed as two homophonous morphemes or a single polysemous morpheme (§6.6.1). Second, I discuss the co-occurrences of the AM constructions with directional suffixes (§6.6.2). Finally, I turn to the four irrealis TAM inflections and, in particular, attempt to highlight what distinguishes them from each other (§6.6.3).

6.6.1 The relationship between the imperfective suffix and the away suffix

There are several reasons the imperfective suffix (§6.4.2) and the away suffix (§6.4.1.2) may be better analysed as a single morpheme. First, they cannot co-occur. Second, they seem to trigger the same morphophonological processes to the verb stem that hosts them (§6.2.2.2.2). I opt to treat them separately in this grammar, largely following Nash (1979, 2022). The function can often be discerned through context (not always available to the reader of this grammar for practical reasons), thus making the gloss maximally descriptive (furthermore, it seems preferable to gloss them as though they are indeed distinct, rather than collapse a possible distinction, if in doubt).

The origin of *-rra* is unclear. However, interestingly, Bilinarra has an imperfective suffix *-rra*, which is restricted to past tense (Meakins and Nordlinger 2014: 295), and Warlpiri and Ngardi have an away suffix *-rra* (Nash 1986: 62; Ennever 2021). This is shown in Table 6.32, contrasted with Warlmanpa.

Table 6.32 Selected related languages sharing a verb suffix '-rra'

Verb inflection function	Bilinarra	Warlpiri	Warlmanpa
Away	(no V infl.)	*-rra*	*-rra*
Imperfective	*-rra*	(no V infl.)	

Cross-linguistically, it is common for a form with a spatial meaning to extend into the temporal domain, particularly GO/COME verbs becoming FUTURE (Bybee et al. 1994: 267–68). More generally, Traugott and Dasher (2004: 86) note the extensive cross-linguistic evidence of SPACE > TIME remappings. If *-rra* is inherited from the common ancestor of these languages, it is possible that these languages represent the three stages of the change. Warlpiri and Ngardi are the most conservative, Warlmanpa still exhibits polysemy and Bilinarra has fully undergone the change:

T_1 *-rra* 'away'   Warlpiri and Ngardi   p   (SPACE)
T_2 *-rra* 'away', 'imperfective'   Warlmanpa   p ~ q   (SPACE & TIME)
T_3 *-rra* 'imperfective'   Bilinarra   q   (TIME)

If this is indeed how *-rra* is related in these languages, this is further evidence for analysing *-rra* in Warlmanpa as a polysemous morpheme, where the meanings are related by metaphor. Therefore, I opt to gloss the morpheme as 'imperfective' or 'away' depending on my analysis of its function in that instantiation, but analytically it seems more likely to be a single morpheme. It is also worth noting that *-rra* in Warumungu is a future/imperative verb inflection (Simpson 2002: 50), as well as the imperative form for Class 1d and 5b verbs in Warlmanpa.

6.6.2 The relationship between AM and directional suffixes

Both the AM and the directional suffix paradigms are not fully productive, as discussed in their respective sections. Some further paradigmatic issues arise in that the AM suffixes and directional suffixes can co-occur, albeit rarely. These combinations are given in Table 6.33. The AM suffixes that encode a path (-*nji*- 'MOT.TWD' and -*nya*- 'MOT.AWAY') do not allow any directional suffixes. The unspecified path suffix -*nja*- allows the path to be specified with certain inflections (see Table 6.33), however, there is no clear regularity: -*rni* 'towards' can co-occur with present and past inflections and -*rra* 'away' can co-occur only with the future inflection.

Table 6.33 Co-occurrences of AM stems with directional suffixes

	Directional suffix	IMP	PRES	PAST	FUT
-*nja*- 'motion'	-*rni* 'towards'	–	✓	✓	–
	-*rra* 'away'	–	–	–	✓
-*nji*- 'motion towards'	-*rni* 'towards'	–	–		–
	-*rra* 'away'	–	–		–
-*nya*- 'motion away'	-*rni* 'towards'			–	
	-*rra* 'away'			–	

Note: Empty cells indicate a general incompatibility between the inflection and the AM marker, hence a directional suffix would not be expected regardless.

This defective paradigm is somewhat expected: the directional suffixes co-occurring with the AM suffixes that encode a path would be over-specifying a path. From a genealogical perspective, descriptions of the AM systems of Ngumpin languages also exhibit idiosyncratic and restricted combinations—if combinations are permissible at all. For example, Mudburra has one AM paradigm with no separate directional paradigm (Osgarby 2018, 2021).

6.6.3 On the relationship and distinctions between the irrealis verb inflections

Warlmanpa has five verb inflections that refer to unactualised (that is, irrealis) situations: imperative (§6.2.3.1.2), future (§6.2.3.4.2), potential (§6.2.3.5.2), subjunctive (§6.2.3.6.2) and counterfactual (§6.2.3.7.2). This section attempts to clarify the semantic distinctions (and overlap) between these inflections. First, I discuss the distinctions between the future-time reference inflections: the future and the potential (§6.6.3.1). Second,

I discuss the distinctions between the non-future-time reference inflections: the subjunctive and counterfactual (§6.6.3.2). An overall summary of the (non-imperative) distinctions is given in §6.6.3.3.

6.6.3.1 Future-time reference inflections

6.6.3.1.1 On the phonological distinction between FUTURE and POTENTIAL inflections

In §6.2.2.2.2, I posit a productive general morphophonological contraction rule that causes the FUTURE inflection with a suffix -*rra* 'away' or 'imperfective' to surface with the form as the POTENTIAL inflection (for example, -*nyi-rra* surfaces as -*nya*, where the potential form for the same verb would also be -*nya*). Two questions naturally arise:

1. What evidence is there this contraction rule applies to the future inflection, if all surface forms could be analysed as POTENTIAL forms?
2. Conversely, could all instances of the POTENTIAL inflection in fact be FUTURE.AWAY or FUTURE.IMPERFECTIVE?

With regards to (1), the clearest evidence comes from the elicitation from Ken Hale. Example (674) is an extract from a dialogue between Ken Hale, who prompts using Warumungu, and Donald Graham, who gives a Warlmanpa translation. In b., the Warlmanpa speaker translates Warumungu *appi-jji-rra* 'here-become-FUT' with *pa-nama-rni*—that is, the 'go' verb with the expected 'future' inflection and the towards suffix. Yet, in c. and d., the only difference in the Warumungu prompt is that the inchoative -*jji(rr)* 'become' is hosted by 'away' instead. In this case, DG gives a coverb, *ngurrurla* 'return home', with the inflecting verb suffix taking the form -*nya*. While this could be interpreted as a potential inflection, the Warumungu prompt in c. suggests a better analysis is to consider it the future inflection with the away suffix, which underwent contraction (likely historical, such that the synchronic form is a portmanteau, unlike the past inflection where the variation is still synchronically active).[15]

---

15 My thanks to Jane Simpson and David Nash (p.c.) for providing glosses for these Warumungu prompts. I have slightly simplified c. for readability, in which the exact gloss given for the verb is: 'this.way.away.from.addressee-become-ImmedFut', where the TAM inflection may also be interpreted as 'future centrifugal'.

(674) a. *Akkil*   *arnkun*   **appi**-*jji*-**rra.**
soon   1PL.EXCL.S   **here**-become-FUT
We'll come soon.
(Warumungu [Ken Hale prompt, H_K01-506A: 51:56 mins])

b. *Ngaka=rnalu*   *pa-**nami**-rni.*
soon=1PL.EXCL.S   go-FUT-TWD
We'll come soon. (Given translation of a.)
H_K01-506, DG, 51:59 mins

c. *Akkil*   *arnkun*   **purtakijji**-*jirr*-**ikal.**
soon   1PL.EXCL.S   **away**-become-FUT
We'll go away soon.
(Warumungu [Ken Hale prompt, H_K01-506A: 52:03 mins])

d. *Ngaka=rnalu*   *ngurrurla*   *pi-**nya.***
soon=1PL.EXCL.S   return_home   act on-FUT.AWAY
We'll return home soon. (Given translation of c.)
H_K01-506A, DG, 52:06 mins

Furthermore, this analysis explains the apparent asymmetry, where the future inflection could host a 'towards' suffix, but not an away suffix.

However, this results in some cases where it is not clear whether the form is a potential inflection or the future + away form, as in (675).[16]

(675) *Kula*   *ngappa*   *wa-nmi,*   *wirliya=rna*   *pa-**nama.***
NEG   water   fall-FUT   foot=1SG.S   go-POT/FUT.AWAY
It won't rain, I will/might go [away] by foot.
wrl-20190201, DK, 29:31 mins

With regards to (2.), there are several utterances that would seem semantically incompatible with a direction marker or imperfective aspect marker, so the more likely analysis is that the verbs have the potential inflection:

---

16 Furthermore, for DK, I am not aware of any cases of a 'POT' form signalling possibility (without an accompanying particle *ngarra* 'might'), so it is possible there has been a language-internal reanalysis, where the so-labelled 'POT' forms are indeed all FUT.IMPF or FUT.AWAY.

(676) *Nga=nyanu-n=nga* *kuma-**nma**!*
POST=RR-2SG.S=DUB cut-POT
Careful, you might cut yourself!
#Careful, you might cut yourself away [from you]!
H_K01-505B, DG, 38:14 mins

(677) *Nya-**nya**=jana=nga.*
see-POT=3PL.NS=DUB
He might see them.
#He might see them [away from him].
N_D03-007868, BN, 34:33 mins

6.6.3.1.2 On the semantic distinction between the future and potential inflection

There are cases such as (678) where there was no uncertainty about the event, yet the potential inflection was used. These cases represent the shared semantic space between the future and potential inflections under the present analysis.

(678) *Pa-nama=rna* *ngappa=rna-ngu* *ma-nma.*
go-POT=1SG.S water=1SG.S-2SG.NS get-POT
I can/will go and get you water.
wrl-20180614-01, DK, 00:17 secs

Further evidence of the shared semantic space between the two inflections can be found in responses to Warlpiri elicitations. To express a future event in Warlpiri, speakers use an auxiliary base *kapi* 'FUT' with the non-past inflection on the verb, with no grammatical distinction between whether a speaker expresses commitment to the situation. Warlpiri sentences using *kapi* + NPAST can be translated into Warlmanpa using the future or potential inflection interchangeably, as shown in the contrasts between the b. sentences of (679) and (680). Despite the Warlpiri elicitation in both cases exhibiting a combination of *kapi* + NPAST, the Warlmanpa speaker uses the future inflection in (679)b and the potential inflection in (680)b.

(679) a. *Warlu* **kapi**=rna *ma-**ni**.*
firewood FUT=1SG.S get-NPAST
I will get the firewood.
(Warlpiri [Ken Hale prompt: H_K01-505B, 8:16 mins])

b. *Warlu=rna ma-**nmi**.*
firewood=1SG.S get-FUT
I will get the firewood.
(Given Warlmanpa translation of a.)
H_K01-505B, DG, 08:22 mins

(680) a. *Kurdu* **kapi**=rna *ma-**ni** ngula ka yula-mi.*
child FUT=1SG.S get-NPAST REL PRES cry-NPAST
I will get the child who is crying.
(Warlpiri [Ken Hale prompt: H_K01-505B, 26:58 mins])

b. *Kurtu=rna ma-**nma** ngula lu-ngunya.*
child=1SG.S get-POT REL cry-PRES
I will get the child who is crying.
(Given Warlmanpa translation of a.)
H_K01-505B, DG, 27:01 mins

Warlmanpa is exceptional in the Ngumpin-Yapa subgroup in having five verb inflections that signal unactualised situations (future, potential, counterfactual, subjunctive and imperative). Also, interestingly, despite this preponderance of non-actualised inflections, Warlmanpa lacks the future/potential verb inflection *-ku* found in all other Ngumpin-Yapa languages (as listed in Table 6.34).

Table 6.34 The use of *-ku* on finite verbs in Ngumpin-Yapa languages

Language	Label	Reference work
Warlmanpa	—	
Warlpiri	Immediate future	(Nash 1986: 40)
Bilinarra	Potential	(Meakins and Nordlinger 2014: 291)
Gurindji	Potential	(Meakins and McConvell 2021)
Ngardi	Potential	(Ennever 2018: 320)
Mudburra	Potential	(Osgarby 2018: 52–55)
Wanyjirra	Future	(Senge 2015: 411)
Jaru	Purposive	(Tsunoda 1981a: 84)
Walmajarri	Future	(Hudson 1978: 79)

6.6.3.2 On the semantic distinction between the counterfactual and the subjunctive inflections

In irrealis contexts it is rather difficult to predict the use of the counterfactual over the subjunctive, and vice versa. In syntactically positive-polarity clauses (that is, clauses without *kula*), the two seem to overlap, both conveying some event that could or should have occurred but did not. In syntactically negative-polarity clauses (that is, clauses with *kula*), the counterfactual conveys some inability to perform an event (that is, non-past temporal reference), whereas the subjunctive encodes some situation that could not or should not have happened (that is, past temporal reference).

One further difference between the two inflections appears to be in conditional constructions, where they form counterfactual statements, seemingly to distinguish between two types of counterfactual constructions, which can be compared with Warlpiri, which does not formally distinguish these types. In the following examples, the same Warlpiri construction (in terms of auxiliaries and verb inflections) is translated into Warlmanpa by the same speaker, differing only by the use of the verb inflection. The Warlpiri prompts in the a. sentences of (681) and (682) have a subordinate clause with the *kaji* 'conditional' auxiliary and the irrealis verb inflection and the matrix clause with the *kajika* 'potential' auxiliary and the non-past verb inflection. This combination of auxiliaries and verb inflections is ambiguous between a 'future-less-vivid' (FLV) counterfactual and a 'present' counterfactual (Legate 2003). An FLV counterfactual is said by Iatridou (2000: 231–32, 234) to imply that the proposition of the clause is unlikely to become true,[17] whereas a present counterfactual serves to assert that both the protasis and the apodosis are false at the present time and are often interpreted as general truths at any given time.[18] Cross-linguistically, it is common for FLVs and present counterfactuals to be formally identical (Iatridou 2000: 251). The interesting thing here is that the Warlmanpa translations of the two Warlpiri prompts differ by the use of tense inflections, as shown in the b. sentences of (681) and (682).

---

17   Or, to be more precise, as Iatridou (2000: 234) words it: '[T]he actual world is more likely to become a *~p* world than a *p* world.'
18   For example, consider Lewis's (1973) classic example: 'If kangaroos had no tails they would topple over.' This is a present counterfactual for which the speaker is asserting present time reference, but it would generally be interpreted as true at any time (given similar enough circumstances to the present time).

Warlpiri [*kaji* COND + *Carla* IRR] *kajika* POT + *Ni* NPAST:

(681) a. ***Kaji****=lpa=npa*   *nyampurla*   *nyina-**karla***   ***kajika****=rna-ngku*
    COND=IMPF=2SG.S   this-LOC   sit-IRR   POT=1SG.S-2SG.NS

*pi-**nyi***!

hit-NPAST

If you were to sit there, I might hit you!

(Warlpiri [Ken Hale prompt: H_K01-506A, 05:32 mins])

Warlmanpa [*kari* COND + *njakurla* CFACT] *nga=...=nga* LEST + *nma* POT:

b. ***Kari****=n*   *mirla*   *ka-**njakurla**,*   ***nga****=rna-ngu=**nga***
    COND=2SG.S   this.LOC   sit-CFACT   POST=1SG.S-2SG.NS=DUB

*paka-**nma***!

hit-POT

If you were to sit there, I might hit you!

H_K01-506A, DG, 05:36 mins

Warlpiri [*kaji* COND + *Carla* IRR] *kajika* POT + *Ni* NPAST:

(682) a. *Kaji=lpa=rna*   *wurnturu*   *ya-ntarla*   *ngula=ju*   *kajika=rna*
    COND=IMPF=2SG.S   far   go-IRR   REL=1SG.NS   POT=1SG.S

mata-jarri!

tired-INCH.NPAST

If I were to go far, I would become tired!

(Warlpiri [Ken Hale prompt: H_K01-506A, 03:41 mins])

Warlmanpa [*kari* COND + *Carla* SUBJ] *nga=...=nga* LEST + *Carla* SUBJ:

b. *Kari=rna*   *kari=ma*   *pa-nkarla,*   *nga=rna=nga*
    COND=1SG.S   far=TOP   go-SUBJ   POST=1SG.S=DUB

palapala-ja-rrarla.

tired-INCH-SUBJ

If I were to go far, I might become tired.

H_K01-506A, DG, 03:46 mins

The main semantic difference between the two clauses is that the first, (681), is temporally bound to an immediate future-time reference: it is clearly not true at the present time reference; the protasis is unlikely to matter to the speaker in the distant future. The second, (682), is a more general truth: it is true at the time of utterance and the temporal scope would extend to include any time (more formally, an irrealis aorist). That is, at any given time, if the speaker were to go far, they would become tired. Based on these interpretations, (681) should be seen as an FLV counterfactual and (682) as a present (possibly even generic) counterfactual, which appear to be grammatically distinguished in Warlmanpa through the use of the inflection in the matrix clause: a potential inflection encodes an FLV counterfactual and an irrealis inflection encodes a present counterfactual. This is in line with the current analysis of the potential inflection (as discussed in §6.2.3.5.2), with obligatory reference to future time.

The counterfactual inflection in Warlmanpa can also be used in the matrix clause of an FLV construction, as in (683), in variation with the potential inflection, as in (684). It is presently unclear what the semantic implication of the variance is.

(683) *Kari=ju-n*   *wa-nganjakurla,*   *money=**lku**=rna-ngu*
       COND=1SG.NS-2SG.S   speak-CFACT   money=THEN=1SG.S-2SG.NS
       yi-njakurla.
       give-CFACT
       If you were to talk to me, **then** I would give you money.
       H_K01-506A, DG, 04:00 mins

(684) a. *Kaji=lpa=npa*   *wurnturu* *ya-ntarla* *kajika=npa* *mata-jarri.*
           COND=IMPF=2SG.S   far   go-IRR   POT=2SG.S   tired-INCH.
                                                                        NPAST
           If you were to go far, you might get tired.
           (Warlpiri [Ken Hale prompt: H_K01-506A, 04:51 mins])

       b. *Kari=n*   *kari=ma*   *pa-njakurla*   *nga=n=nga*
           COND=2SG.S   far=TOP   go-CFACT   POST=2SG.S=DUB
           palapala-ja-ma.
           tired-INCH-POT
           If you were to go far, you might become tired.
           H_K01-506A, DG, 04:56 mins

A GRAMMAR OF WARLMANPA

This discussion is summarised in Table 6.35, which lists the counterfactual constructions found in Warlpiri and Warlmanpa with a corresponding counterfactual type. Note that at the beginning of this section, both the counterfactual and the subjunctive inflections were described as denoting situations with past tense (as in 'X should have Ved'), yet in counterfactual constructions this past-tense reference is lost: the use of morphemes that otherwise have past-time reference is common for counterfactuals (von Prince 2019; Romero 2014).

Table 6.35 Distinguishing types of counterfactual constructions in Warlpiri and Warlmanpa

		Subordinate	Matrix		CF type
	Auxiliary	Verb inflection	Auxiliary[19]	Verb inflection	
Warlpiri	*kaji=lpa* COND=IMPF	*-Carla* -IRR	*kajika* POT	*-Ni* NPAST	FLV/ Pres
	kaji= COND	*-Carla* -IRR	*kapi/ngarra* FUT	*Curla* -IRR	Past
Warlmanpa	*kari* COND	*-njakurla* -CFACT	*nga=…=nga* POST=…=DUB	*-nmal-njakurla* -POT/-CFACT	FLV
	kari COND	*-Carla* -IRR	*nga=…=nga* POST=…=DUB	*-Carla* -IRR	Pres

6.6.3.3 Summary of irrealis inflections

The discussion of the semantics of the irrealis inflections is summarised in Figure 6.7, which highlights the overlap in the denotation of the inflections. The irrealis inflections can essentially be divided into future (potential and future) and non-future (subjunctive and counterfactual), though the non-future inflections are recruited for use in counterfactual constructions regardless of temporal reference (a cross-linguistically common phenomenon; see §6.6.3.2). The future inflection is used for expected future-time situations (§6.2.3.4.2), which are a subset of functions of the potential inflection (§6.2.3.5.2), which encompasses any future-time situation regardless of the speaker's stance on certainty. This results in the implicature that the event is uncertain, given the option to use the future for

---

19 Further analysis is needed of the contribution of the auxiliary in the finite clause to the type of counterfactual construction. In Warlpiri, it seems *kajika* POT is the expected auxiliary in FLV and present counterfactuals, but past counterfactuals are seen with *kapi* FUT, *ngarra* FUT, but not *kajika* POT. In Warlmanpa, I am not aware of any counterfactual constructions without *nga=…nga* FUT.POT in the matrix clause.

6. INFLECTING VERBS

certain events instead. The counterfactual inflection near-exclusively occurs in counterfactual constructions (hence the gloss), though in non-conditional clauses it can be used to denote a situation that did not happen, typically due to inability of some kind (§6.2.3.7.2). The subjunctive (§6.2.3.6.2) may be used in counterfactual constructions for present counterfactuals and in non-conditionals to denote situations that did not happen but that the speaker believes should or was likely to happen. All the irrealis modalities except for the counterfactual can be used for directive force (though only the imperative inflection *encodes* this; the rest are by implicature).

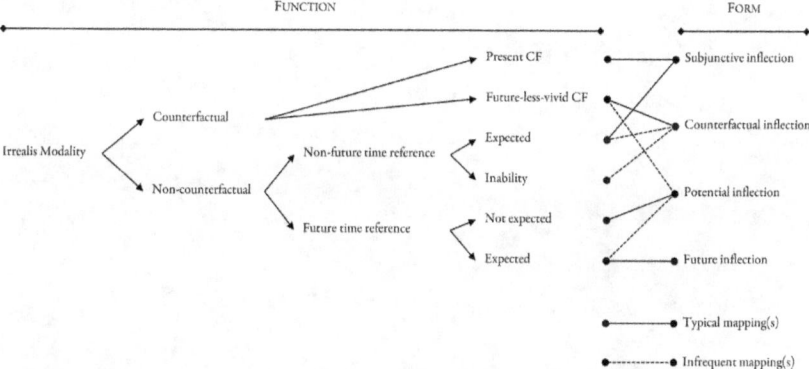

Figure 6.7 Summary of instantiated uses of the irrealis tense inflections (disregarding imperative moods)

7

Coverbs

The prototypical function of a coverb in Warlmanpa is to form a syntactic constituent with an inflecting verb that results in a complex predicate comprising multiple predicational elements. For example, the coverb *kutuj* 'stand' can combine with *parti-* 'leave, rise' to mean 'stand up', as exemplified in (685) and (686), with *wa-* 'speak' to mean 'speak standing', and numerous other possible combinations.

Simple predicate, *parti-* 'leave, rise':

(685) *Ngura   parra   **parti-mi,**   ngayu=ma=rna   jarta   wa-nmi.*
      country   sun   **leave-FUT**   1=TOP=1SG.S   sleep   fall-FUT
      [When] the sun **rises**, I will be asleep.
      wrl-20180528-03, DK, 05:20 mins

Complex predicate, *parti-* 'leave, rise' + *kutij* 'stand':

(686) *Kurtu   ayi=nya   **kutij-partu-ngu**   ngula   wali-ma-nu*
      child   that=FOC   **stand-leave-PAST**   REL   trip-CAUSE-PAST
      jantapa-rlu.
      ant_bed-ERG
      That child, who tripped over the ant bed, **stood up**.
      wrl-20190205, DK, 25:58 mins

Coverbs (also referred to as 'preverbs' in other languages) are found in Ngumpin-Lapa languages, including Warlpiri (Nash 1982; Laughren 2010), Mudburra (Osgarby 2018), Bilinarra (Meakins and Nordlinger 2014), Gurindji (Meakins and McConvell 2021), Ngardi (Ennever 2021) and

Wanyjirra (Senge 2015). Coverbs (a more accurate label would be 'complex verb constructions') are found in many Western Desert languages, as well as non-Pama-Nyungan languages north of Warlmanpa, however, other Pama-Nyungan languages with complex predicates involving coverbs are rare (see, for example, the complex verb area analysed in Schultze-Berndt 2000). See Osgarby and Bowern (2023) for an overview of complex predication in Australian languages.

I will not dwell on the formal semantic composition of complex verb constructions in this grammar. For formal analysis of complex predicates, see Butt (1998) and, for analyses focused particularly on Australian languages, see Schultze-Berndt (2000) and Baker and Harvey (2010). Additionally, Laughren (2010) provides a detailed analysis of complex predicates in Warlpiri, much of which is applicable to Warlmanpa, and Browne (2021b) presents a formal account of a subclass of coverbs in Warlmanpa and Warlpiri, specifically 'external object coverbs' (§10.1.4.2).

Interestingly, while coverbs seem a rich class for synchronic loan-word integration in other Ngumpin-Yapa languages (Meakins and Nordlinger 2014: 91; Meakins 2010), and further north (for example, Jaminjung [Schultze-Berndt 2008]), this does not appear to be the case in Warlmanpa (at least synchronically); rather it appears that only nominals form an 'open class'.

Coverbs are phonotactically distinct from the other major word classes in Warlmanpa: unlike other word classes, coverbs do not need to be disyllabic and commonly end in consonants. The word status of coverbs requires further investigation. While coverbs usually precede the inflecting verb (suggesting a possible compound), some coverbs may follow the inflecting verb or occur as afterthoughts to a clause. As such, I tentatively assume that coverbs do have word status.

One final point of interest of coverbs is that in 'Mali' language (a register used for a mother-in-law relation), there is a restricted set of coverbs that should be used instead of the semantically equivalent inflecting verb. For example, (687) provides the usual way of asking where the addressee is going and (688) asks the same question, but the addressee is *Mali* to the speaker, using *pu-ngunya* 'act on' as a generic verb, and a coverb, *miti*, to specify the lexical semantics of the situation.

(687) *Wanjila=n   pa-nnya?*
where=2SG.S   go-PRES
Where are you going?
H_K01-505B, DG, 08:35 mins

(688) *Wanjila=n*   **miti**   *pu-ngunya?*
where=2SG.S   **go**   act_on-PRES
Where are you going?
(Man addressing his *Mali*.)
H_K01-506B, DG, 05:43 mins

The remainder of this chapter is as follows. First, the morphology (§7.1), phonology (§7.2) and syntax (§7.3) are discussed, and then three subclasses of coverbs are discussed in further detail in §7.4.

7.1 Coverb morphology

Coverb morphology is very restricted. No coverbs may take inflectional morphology. This is most apparent in non-finite subordinate clauses, where every word obligatorily hosts a complementising suffix (see §12.1.2), except coverbs. Examples of coverbs occurring in non-finite subordinate clauses are given in (689)–(691) and contrasting examples of adverbs in the same context are given in (692) and (693). Furthermore, the adverb in (693) surfaces in a non-finite clause *without* an inflecting verb, which is prohibited for coverbs.

Coverbs in non-finite subordinate clauses:

(689) *Purtu   ka-nya=n   ngarrka   [**yina**   nga-rninji-ka].*
listen   be-PRES=2SG.S   man   **sing**   eat-INF-ALL
You're listening to the man [singing].
H_K01-506A, DG, 17:08 mins

(690) *Maliki=rna   purtu   ka-ngu   [**warlku**   wa-nganji-ka].*
dog=1SG.S   hear   be-PAST   **bark**   speak-INF-ALL
I heard the dog [barking].
H_K01-505B, DG, 10:20 mins

303

(691) Karnta   wanganya   [**kutij**   ka-nja-karra].
      woman   speak-PRES **stand**   be-INF-SS
      The woman is speaking [standing].
      wrl-20190206, DK, 07:07 mins

Adverbs in non-finite subordinate clauses:

(692) Purt   pu-ngu=rna   Jinarinji-ka   ngayinya ngalapi [puliki-ku
      send   act_on-PAST=1SG.S   Jinarinji-ALL   1GEN   son   bull-DAT
      ka-nja-ku   **ngurrurla-ku**].
      take-INF-DAT   **return-DAT**
      I sent my son to Jinarinji [to bring back a bullock].
      N_D02-009887, DG, 07:10 mins

(693) Wawirri=rna   karla-rnu   [**wantari-ka**].
      kangaroo=1SG.S   spear-PAST   **across-ALL**
      I speared a kangaroo [going across].
      N_D02-007842, BN, 45:58 mins

This is particularly distinct from other Ngumpin-Yapa languages, in which coverbs can be the main predicate of non-finite subordinate clauses without an inflecting verb (Meakins and Nordlinger 2014: 425–32; Meakins and McConvell 2021; Osgarby 2018: 219–20; Ennever 2021; Senge 2015: 612).

While all coverbs prohibit inflectional morphology, loose nexus coverbs (§7.4.1) allow derivational morphology and some clitics. The single derivational suffix that can attach to coverbs is *-wari*, which may derive parts of nominals with 1) a synonymous meaning, as in (694); 2) a semantically narrowed meaning, as in (695); or 3) a metaphorical extension, as in (696).

(694) CV   *wirtikily*   'bend'
      N   *wirtikily-wari*   'bent'
(695) CV   *timirl*   'gap'
      N   *timirl-wari*   'narrow gap'
(696) CV   *purntuny*   'bump'
      N   *purntuny-wari*   'prominent'

7. COVERBS

This suffix has cognates throughout Ngumpin-Yapa languages (and in Jaminjung [Schultze-Berndt 2003: 153]). In Bilinarra and Gurindji, *-bari* (with *-wari* as an allomorph) derives an adjectival nominal from adverbs and coverbs, in that it describes attributes of the entity denoted by the root (Meakins and Nordlinger 2014: 341; Meakins and McConvell 2021). Similarly, the Mudburra suffix *-bari* is described as an adjectival nominal suffix (Osgarby 2018: 248).

Note that *-wari* is not a specialised coverb → nominal suffix, as it can also derive nominals from other nominals, as in (697) and (698).

(697)	N	*jilyi*	'dust'
	N	*jilyi-wari*	'dust cloud'
(698)	N	*ngawirirri*	'circular'
	N	*ngawirirri-wari*	'circular'

It is presently unclear whether this should be treated as a synchronic suffix at all due to its low productivity. However, the suffix may have been more productive historically, as evidenced by several forms ending in *wari* with no equivalent counterpart lacking *-wari*, such as *tarrawarlwari* 'white' and *tiikwari* 'red'. Moreover, *tiikwari* 'red' is the only intra-morphemic /kw/ cluster in the recorded lexicon (if analysed as monomorphemic).

Unlike tight nexus coverbs, loose nexus coverbs (like adverbs) may host clitics, as in (699).

Loose nexus coverb *yarta* 'again' hosting a clitic:

(699)   *Yali-ngu=nya=ju*   *paka-rnu*   **yarta=yijala.**
         that-ERG=FOC=1SG.NS   hit-PAST   **again=ALSO**
         That one hit me again.
         wrl-20190131-01, DK, 16:47 mins

The last morphological process evident for coverbs is that loose nexus coverbs may be derived into inflecting verbs, as in (700), and in fact some coverbs only co-occur with *-ja-* 'INCH' (that is, there are no instances of these coverbs without hosting *-ja-*).

(700)   ***Kapakapa-ja-nnya.***
         hindrance-INCH-PRES
         He is hindered.
         N_D02-009887, DG, 00:26 secs

7.2 Coverb phonology

Coverbs may also have anomalous phonotactics compared with other word classes, including adverbs (attributed to coverbs being borrowings from non-Pama-Nyungan languages [McConvell 2009]). General phonotactic rules for other word classes include being minimally disyllabic, having no long vowels and a strong dispreference for word-final consonants—but coverbs may infringe any (or multiples) of these rules, as exemplified in Table 7.1.

Table 7.1 Coverb exceptions to regular phonotactic constraints

Regular phonotactic constraint	Example coverb
No word-final consonants	*jalal* 'lifted'
Minimally disyllabic words	*maly* 'spread'
No long vowels	*kiit* 'broken'

Coverbs often have simplex and reduplicated forms. The semantic effect of reduplication is unclear, as reduplication is rare in the transcribed corpus. An example pair of a simplex and a reduplicated form of a coverb is given in (701) and (702), where both denote durative states. The simplex form is temporally bound to the time of rain and the reduplicated form is for a specific duration.

Simplex, *yarti*:

(701) Kayi   ngappa   wa-nmi,   yali=ma=rna   **yarti**   ka-mi.
      WHEN   water   fall-FUT   that=TOP=1SG.S   **stay**   be-FUT
      When it rains, I'll stay [at home].
      wrl-20190201, DK, 29:45 mins

Reduplicated, *yartiyarti*:

(702) Ngayu=ma=rna   **yarti~yarti**   ka-ngu.
      1=TOP=1SG.S   **stay~RDP**   be-PAST
      I stayed [at home]. (In reference to what the speaker did the previous evening.)
      wrl-20180614-02, DK, 11:24 mins

The noted types of reduplication include full reduplication, as in (703), or partial reduplication in which only the onset and nucleus of the second syllable are reduplicated, as in (705). In this example, the simplex version is *jilij* and the reduplicated form reduplicates the onset of the second syllable /l/, and the nucleus /i/, but not the coda /c/, thus *jil<u>ij</u> – jil<u>ili</u>j*. These patterns are also found in other Ngumpin-Yapa languages and are typically attributed to encoding the plurality of event participants (Meakins and Nordlinger 2014: 346; Meakins and McConvell 2021; Senge 2015: 430–31; Ennever 2021; Osgarby 2018: 13), though this appears to not be the case in Warlmanpa; examples (702) and (705) involve reduplication of a coverb, yet each has only singular event participants. Reduplication may relate to pluractionality of the event, however, this requires further investigation.

(703)   *Mayingka-rlu*   **tiirl-tiirl**   *kuma-nnya.*
        knife-ERG   split-RDP   cut-PRES
        The knife cuts it.
        H_K06-004548, JW, 02:38 mins

Simplex coverb, *jilij*:

(704)   *Jilij*   *ka-ngka,*   *wanjila*   *pa-nnya!*
        ask   take-IMP   where   go-PRES
        Ask him where he's going!
        H_K01-506A, DG, 18:30 mins

Reduplicated coverb, *jililij*:

(705)   *Kari=ngu*   *jawarti=ma*   **jililij**   *ka-nji-nmi,*   *yi=ngu*
        COND=2SG.NS   tomorrow=TOP   ask   take-INC-POT   purp=2sg.ns
        jutpu-ngunya   *nyuntu=lku*   *wanji.*
        run-PRES   2=THEN   where
        When he starts asking you tomorrow, he can go to you [for the story].
        H_K01-506A, DG, 33:42 mins

7.3 Coverb syntax

Coverbs can occur in two positions in a clause: as part of a predicational phrase (PredP) or on the right periphery of a clause.

The structure of a predicational phrase in Warlmanpa is given in (706). The 'core' predicational elements are an optional external object coverb, followed by an optional tight nexus coverb, followed by an obligatory inflecting verb. These three elements form a single syntactic constituent and occur in this strict linear order. There may be one loose nexus coverb preceding this constituent or, rarely, immediately following it.

(706)   PredP → (Coverb)   [(Coverb)   (Coverb)   Inflecting
                                                                verb]PRED

                 Loose nexus   External object Tight nexus   Predicate

This structure essentially follows the complex predicate structure described for Wagiman (Krauße and Harvey 2021). The primary structural difference is that Warlmanpa has a small set of 'external object' coverbs that may co-occur with other predicational coverbs. The other differences are basically descriptive: first, the modificational position here is included within the PredP (this is purely for descriptive simplicity). Second, the modificational position can be filled by an adverb in the Wagiman structure. While adverbs can of course modify a predication in Warlmanpa, I have not included them in the structure of the PredP here because adverbs are unrestricted in where they can occur in a sentence, whereas coverbs (other than those occurring on the right periphery) are restricted to these positions, defined in relation to the position of the inflecting verb. Third, I have adopted the terminology used to describe similar coverbs in Ngumpin-Yapa languages: the labels 'tight' and 'loose' nexus coverbs come from McConvell (1996b) and this distinction (with some minor structural and terminological differences) is common to other Ngumpin-Yapa languages (Meakins and McConvell 2021; Meakins and Nordlinger 2014; Ennever 2021; Osgarby 2018; Senge 2015; Tsunoda 1981a). The term 'external object' coverb comes from Simpson (1991) and, to my knowledge, these coverbs are not evident in any Ngumpin languages, being found only in Warlpiri and Warlmanpa.

There are no examples of each slot of PredP being filled; the maximal number of coverbs found in a single clause in the corpus is two.

An example of a loose and tight nexus coverb co-occurring is given in (707). This utterance contains two clauses, in the second of which the predication comprises two elements: the inflecting verb *kanya* 'be' and a stance coverb, *kutij*, which specifies the configuration of the subject. The loose nexus coverb *kangkurr* 'submerge' specifies that the event occurs underwater.

(707) *Ngappa-nga   kangkurr   [wa-nya],   **kangkurr   [kutij   ka-nya]**.*
      water-LOC   submerge   fall-PRES   **submerge   stand   be-PRES**
      He's bathing in the water, he's standing submerged.
      wrl-20170321-02, SN, 06:27 mins

An example of external object and tight nexus coverbs co-occurring is given in (708): *yirrkin* 'with' is an external object coverb and *karta* 'spear' is a tight nexus coverb.

(708) *Yulu=rna   [yirrkin   karta   pi-nyi]   kirtana-parna-rlu.*
      ground=1SG.S with   spear   act_on-FUT   father-PROP-ERG
      I'm digging the ground with my father.
      wrl-20200225, DK, 25:22 mins

There are no examples of a loose nexus coverb co-occurring with an external object coverb. The justification for treating them distinctly is that the external object coverbs are clearly part of the core predicational constituent, whereas the loose nexus coverbs are not.

First, loose nexus coverbs can occur following the predicational complex, whereas external object coverbs cannot. An example of a coverb following the inflecting verb is given in (709).

(709) *Yayi=nya=ma   ka-nja-nu   warnanganta,   [nga-   wirrpiny.*
                                                      rnu-rra]
      that=FOC=TOP   take-MOT-PAST   between   **eat-PAST-   completely**
                                                      IMPF
      He took that one halfway, eating it all.
      K_003, BN, 00:30 secs

Second, the bound pronoun complex may intervene between a loose nexus coverb and the predicational complex, whereas the bound pronoun complex may not intervene between an external object coverb and the rest of the predicational complex. Compare the bound pronoun placement when there is a loose nexus coverb, as in (710), and when there is an external object coverb, as in (711). In the case of the modificational coverb *yarta* 'again', the bound pronoun intervenes between the coverb and the predicational complex, whereas in the case of the external object coverb *yirrkin* 'with', the bound pronoun follows the predicational complex (since the coverb and inflecting verb are treated as a single syntactic constituent).

(710) **Yarta=yijala=rla** [wulyurr ya-ka]!
again=ALSO=3.OBL pour put-IMP
Pour some more for him!
wrl-20191208-02, DK, 21:35 mins

(711) *[Yirrkin* **ka-nya]=rna** *ngapuju-parna.*
with **be-PRES=1SG.S** FM-PROP
I'm with my grandmother.
wrl-20200225, DK, 15:43 mins

Third, on a semantic level, external objects can augment the argument structure of the predicate, whereas loose nexus coverbs are adverbial. This is discussed further in §7.4.

A concluding note on the structure of predicational phrases is that there is one construction that allows loose nexus coverbs to occupy the tight nexus position. Specifically, loose nexus coverbs may occupy the tight nexus slot only when combining with *ka-* 'be'. In this context, the combination forms a syntactic unit, as evidenced by the bound pronouns attaching after the inflecting verb, shown in (712).

(712) **Kutij ka-nya=rna** *parra-nga.*
stand be-PRES=1SG.S sun-LOC
I am standing in the sun.
wrl-20190205, DK, 27:15 mins

As noted earlier, outside the predicational phrase, coverbs may only appear on the right periphery of a clause. Right dislocation is a relatively common syntactic process applicable to numerous parts of speech, not just coverbs (see §11.7.2).

(713) *Pungarrapan-nga   kala=rnalu   pa-nja-nu-rnu*
Renner_Springs-LOC   HAB=1PL.EXCL.S   go-MOT-PAST-TWD
tij   —   ***takarltakarl.***
camp_overnight   **going_past**
We would camp at Renner Springs—right through.
N_D29-023128, MFN, 02:09 mins

7.4 Coverb types

The structure of a predicational phrase, as introduced in §7.3, highlighted three classes of coverbs: loose nexus (§7.4.1), tight nexus (§7.4.2) and external object (§7.4.3). It should be noted that clear demarcation of coverbs into categories has proven difficult in grammatical descriptions thus far (Ennever 2021: 426). In this analysis, I have attempted a largely syntactic categorisation, based on the relative ordering between co-occurring coverbs and whether the bound pronouns can intervene between constituents. However, the drawback of this approach is fuzzy semantic boundaries between the categories.

7.4.1 Loose nexus coverbs

Loose nexus coverbs are those found on the periphery of the predicational phrase, either before the inflecting verb (and any other coverbs) or following the inflecting verb.

All loose nexus coverbs are adverbial modifiers—that is, the core predication is not altered and there is still only one predicational element in the verbal complex. The modificational coverb specifies some manner of the core event. For example, the coverb *pirtijpirtij* 'upward' can combine with the inflecting verb *jitpi-* 'run' to specify that the direction of the running is upward, as in (714), in which ants are running up someone's leg.

(714) *Jarrawarti-rla   ka-nya,   pirtij~pirtij   jutpu-ngunya   pingirri.*
thigh-LOC   be-PRES   upward~RDP   run-PRES   ant
[The ants] are on his thigh, they're running up [his leg].
N_D02-007842, BN, 17:16 mins

Most loose nexus coverbs can combine with numerous inflecting verbs. For example, the coverb *kutuj* 'stand' combines with *wa-* 'speak' to mean 'speak standing'; with *purtu-ka-* 'listen' to mean 'stand listening'; with *parti-* 'rise' to mean 'stand up'; and so on.

Only loose nexus coverbs may host clitics (including the pronominal clitics). Example (715) shows the loose nexus coverb *yartiyarti* hosting the clitic *=lku* 'then'.

(715)   **Yartiyarti=lku**$_{MOD}$ *ka-mi*$_{PRED}$ *ngurra-nga*.
       stay_in_camp=THEN   be-FUT   camp-LOC
       He'll be staying in camp then.
       wrl-20180614-02, DK, 12:08 mins

Unlike some Ngumpin languages (for example, Ngardi [Ennever 2021: 434]), it appears loose nexus coverbs cannot function as the main predicate of a clause. To function as a main predicate, coverbs in Warlmanpa must first be derived into nominals since nominals can function as main predicates.

(716)   *Ali=nya*   *jurlaka*   **kiit-wari**   *panja*.
       that=FOC   bird   **break-NMLZ**   wing
       That bird has a broken wing.
       wrl-20191208-01, DK, 04:59 mins

There is one known counterexample to loose nexus coverbs being adverbial: the combination *wirriri* 'circle' is generally compositional in its combinations—combining with *wa-* 'speak' means 'speak in a circle', combining with *pa-* 'go' means 'go on a curved path', and so on. However, its combination with *ya-* 'put' seems to alter the argument structure of *ya-*. In isolation, *ya-* is ditransitive: an agent moves a theme to a location. This location can be cross-referenced—indicative of its argument status. However, in *ya-* combining with *wirriri*, the resulting combination is transitive: an agent chases a patient in circles. This is particularly interesting, as tight nexus coverbs combining with *ya-* 'put' may also invoke a specific transitive 'chase' sense. Clearly, these interactions warrant further analysis.

7.4.2 Tight nexus coverbs

Tight nexus coverbs are found immediately preceding the inflecting verb. Unlike loose nexus coverbs, all of which are adverbial, tight nexus coverbs vary in their contribution to the predicate structure. Tight nexus coverbs may be adverbial or predicational.

However, even the adverbial tight nexus coverbs are not straightforwardly compositional. For example, consider the tight nexus coverb *wuruly* 'conceal' and three exemplar combinations, which do appear to be compositional:

	jutpu-	Agent_ABS **runs**	exemplified in (717)
wuruly	*jutpu-*	Agent_ERG **runs (out of sight)**	exemplified in (718)
	kiya-	Agent_ERG **throws** Theme_ABS	
wuruly	*kiya-*	Agent_ERG **throws** Theme_ABS **(out of sight)**	
	ka-	Agent_ERG **moves** Theme_ABS to Goal_ALL	
wuruly	*ka-*	Agent_ERG **moves** Theme_ABS to Goal_ALL **(out of sight)**	

(717) *Maliki   jutpu-ngunya.*
       dog   run-PRES
       The dog is running.
       H_K01-505B, DG, 02:39 mins

(718) *Wawirri=rna-palangu   nya-ngu   jirrama,   wuruly   jutpu-ngu=pala.*
       kangaroo=1SG.S-3DU.NS   see-PAST   two   conceal   run-PAST=3DU.S
       I saw two kangaroos, they ran out of sight.
       H_K01-506A, DG, 55:20 mins

In each combination, *wuruly* specifies that the event has a resultative state of the theme being out of sight.

However, when *wuruly* combines with *nya-* 'see, perceive', the semantic relation is slightly less straightforward. In this combination, the theme is placed outside some other participant's line of sight.[1] Critically, this participant is treated as a core argument.

---

[1] Note that I discuss some coverbs as 'changing' the inherent argument structure of the inflecting verb, though this is shorthand to explain that the combination of some coverbs with some inflecting verbs tends to have different surface arguments than what normally surfaces with just the inflecting verb. Further research is needed into how the argument structure and semantics of predicates can be manipulated and whether they are inherently required by the combination at all.

	nya-	Agent<small>ERG</small> sees Theme<small>ABS</small>
wuruly	*nya-*	Agent<small>ERG</small> places Theme<small>ABS</small> **(out of sight)** for Experiencer<small>DAT</small>

(719) ***Nya-nyi****=rna-ngu.*

see-FUT=1SG.S-2SG.NS

I'll see you.

H_K06-004555, LOF, 41:13 mins

(720) *Jawarti=rna-ngu* **wuruly** ***nya-nyi****-rni.*

tomorrow=1SG.S-2SG.NS **conceal** see-FUT-TWD

Tomorrow I will come and hide the meat from you.

wrl-20180531-01, DF, 16:52 mins

For tight nexus coverbs that are predicational, the resulting predication is usually entirely dependent on the coverb. As an example, consider the contrast between *kiya-* 'throw' in isolation and in a complex predicate with a non-compositional coverb, as given in (721) and (722). In (721), *kiya-* is a transitive predicate meaning 'throw'; (722) shows the complex predicate *wijja-kiya-* 'farewell'.

(721) *Ngarrka-ngu=ju* *karli* ***kiya-nmi****-rni.*

man-ERG=1SG.NS boomerang **throw-FUT-TWD**

The man will throw a boomerang at me.

H_K01-506A, DG, 01:04:06 hrs

(722) *Ngarrka=rla* *wa-nganyu* *karnta-ku* ***wijja-kiya****-rnu.*

man=3SG.OBL speak-PAST woman-DAT **farewell-throw-PAST**

The man spoke to the woman before [he] left her.

N_D02-007842, BN, 50:14 mins

In this combination, it is not clear what the inflecting verb *kiya-* 'throw' contributes to the event structure.

Exemplar tight nexus coverb combinations in which the coverb contributes the event structure of the predication are catalogued in Table 7.2 (data from Nash 2022).

Table 7.2 Examples of tight nexus coverbs

Coverb	Coverb gloss	Combining inflecting verb
nyaru	'howl'	*karla-* 'spear'
ngart	'breathe'	*kiya-* 'throw'
wijja	'farewell'	
jirti	'stalk'	*nga-* 'eat'
purlpaj	'jump'	
purn	'jump'	
purt	'jump, boil, flush'	
yina	'sing'	
marntiwa	'hover'	*pi-* 'act on'
purt	'send'	
yurrpulu	'whistle'	
wirri	'chase'	*ya-* 'send'
nungkurr	'believe'	*wa-* 'fall'
pirlirl	'twinkle'	
marlal	'twinkle'	*wa-* 'speak'

It is cross-linguistically common for inflecting verbs to contribute minimal event structure information, instead contributing largely TAM or light predicational information (Baker and Harvey 2010; Bowern 2014); and indeed, some tight nexus coverbs in Warlmanpa can even have independent argument structure (that is, seemingly overriding the argument structure of the inflecting verb).

There are coverbs that result in a combination requiring fewer arguments than the inflecting verb would otherwise. For example, *ya-* 'send' is ditransitive, requiring an agent moving a theme to a goal; however, when combining with the coverb *wirri*, the resulting argument structure is transitive. Moreover, *wirri ya-* selects a patient (that is, an affected animate participant), rather than a theme (that is, an affected inanimate participant).[2] In both cases, the theme or patient undergoes a (forced) change of location.

	ya-	Agent_ERG **moves** Theme_ABS to GoalALL
wirri	*ya-*	Agent_ERG **chases** Patient_ABS

---

[2] However, this should not be taken as a significant issue, since many theories of thematic roles collapse the distinction between theme and patient (Dowty 1989 provides a good overview of the problem).

Examples of *ya-* 'put' are given in (723) and (724) and an example of *wirri ya-* 'chase' is given in (725).

(723) *Ngarrka-ngu   karli   **ya-nnya**   yulu-ka.*
      man-ERG   boomerang   **put-PRES**   ground-ALL
      The man is putting the boomerang on the ground.
      H_K01-505B, DG, 40:43 mins

(724) *Jakamarra-rlu=nyanu   **ya-rnu**   pirntija   kurlarta   yulu-ka.*
      Jakamarra-ERG=RR   **put-PAST**   beside   spear   ground-ALL
      Jakamarra put the spear on the ground beside himself.
      N_D02-007841, BN, 08:26 mins

(725) *Maliki-rlu=ju   **wirri**   **ya-nnya.***
      dog-ERG=1SG.NS   **chase**   **put-PRES**
      The dog is chasing me.
      H_K06-004555, LOF, 48:49 mins

Conversely, there are also coverbs that require more arguments than the combining inflecting verb. For example, *pi-* 'act on' is transitive, but the combination *purt pi-* 'send' is ditransitive:

    pi-   Agent_{ERG} **acts on** Patient_{ABS}
purt *pi-*   Agent_{ERG} **sends** Patient_{ABS} **to** Goal/Purpose_{DAT}

An example of *purt pi-* 'send' is given in (726).

(726) *Ngayu=rna   purt   pu-ngu   wangani   wirlinyi-ku   pa-nja-ku.*
      1=1SG.S   send   act_on-PAST   dog   hunting-DAT   go-INF-DAT
      I sent the dog to go hunting.
      wrl-20190211-02, DK, 10:51 mins

There are also cases of *purt pu-* 'send' allowing an absolutive-marked theme, as exemplified by *jaru* 'message' in (727).

(727) *Japanangka-rlu=ju   jaru   **purt**   **pu-ngu**-rnu   nya-nja-ku.*
      Japanangka-ERG=1SG.NS   message   **send**   **act_on-PAST-**TWD   see-INF-DAT
      Japanangka_{Agent} sent me_{Patient} a message_{Theme} to see him_{Goal}.
      N_D02-009887, DG, 08:28 mins

These interactions between coverbs and argument structures suggest that these constructions may not be 'true' complex predicates, if indeed the inflecting verb only contributes TAM. More research is needed in this regard.

Another interesting property of tight nexus coverbs is that a number of motion coverbs combine with *nga-* 'eat'. Motion coverbs combining with the 'eat' verb are also evident in Warlpiri. The analysis of this phenomenon in Warlpiri involves the inclusion of a homophonous inflecting verb to account for the coverb combinations. In Warlpiri, the form is *ngarri-* 'eat', which in isolation conveys a transitive eating event. Nash (1986: 246) and other authors additionally analyse a homophonous verb, *ngarri-*, in Warlpiri glossed as 'move', which only occurs in combination with preverbs.

I resist this analysis for two reasons. First, given that I already allow coverbs to contain the exhaustive predicational semantics (based on other clear examples, as catalogued), this analysis would (somewhat artificially) inflate the number of inflecting verbs in Warlmanpa. Second, not all coverbs combining with *nga-* convey movement, such as the 'boil' sense of *purt-*. So, in these cases, the coverb would still be non-compositional despite the proliferation of inflecting verbs (alternatively, a semantically vacuous homophonous inflecting verb could be analysed to account for these). Nonetheless, this is clearly a fruitful topic for formal analyses of the lexicon and complex predicates.

A further point of interest regarding *nga-* 'eat' is that it can combine with the coverb *yina* 'sing' to indicate the subject singing, as in (728). Unlike most of the other coverbs combining with *nga-*, *yina* is transitive (taking an ergative subject). *Nga-* 'eat' combining with a 'sing' coverb does not seem to be observed elsewhere. In fact, the coverb *yina* seems to historically derive from an inflecting verb, which is synchronically productive in Warlpiri as *yunpa-* (Nash 1986: 246), though it is not clear what process would cause *yunpa-* to change word class to coverb, nor is it clear why *-nga-* would be the combining inflecting verb.

(728) *Ali-ngu=nya* *jurlaka-rlu* **yina-nga-rninya** *pirnti-nga.*
that-ERG=FOC bird-ERG **sing-eat-PRES** tree_top-LOC
That bird on top of the tree is singing.
wrl-20191208-01, DK, 08:31 mins

7.4.3 External object coverbs

There are two known external object coverbs: *yirrkin* 'with' and *jurnta* 'away'. *Yirrkin* functions to introduce an entity who is involved in the event, regardless of their contribution. *Jurnta* specifies motion away from an origin point.

(729)   *Janyungu=**ju***   ***jurnta***   *mirni-ma-nu.*
       tobacco=1SG.NS   **away**   unperceived_location-CAUSE-PAST
       Someone relocated my tobacco **away from me**.
       N_D02-007841, BN, 30:05 mins

These introduced entities, if expressed, are external objects (§10.1.4)—a grammatical relation found in Warlpiri and Warlmanpa (Browne 2021b). They may also be unspecified.

External object coverbs occur preceding any tight nexus coverb but cannot host clitics (including the bound pronouns) and cannot occur following the inflecting verb, nor can they occur as right-dislocated constituents.

8
Adverbs

This chapter presents a categorisation of adverbs based primarily on their inflectional possibilities. Manner adverbs (§8.1) are those that may take case in its attributive function (that is, agreement), but do not do so obligatorily (unlike nominals). Temporal adverbs (§8.2) cannot take any case other than dative case to signal a duration. Spatial adverbs (§8.3) have a unique paradigm, though they may also take the nominal elative case. Recognitional adverbs (§8.4) can take a restricted set of the suffixes found in the spatial adverbs paradigm.

8.1 Manner adverbs

Manner adverbs optionally agree in case with the subject of a clause, although this is only transparent when the subject is ergative marked. An example is given in (730), in which *lurrijalurrija* 'quickly' takes ergative case, agreeing with the subject nominal *karnta* 'woman'.

(730)   **Karnta-ngu**   **ali-rlu**=*nya*   **lurrijalurrija-rlu**   *piya-nnya.*
       woman-ERG   **that-**ERG=FOC   **quickly-**ERG   cut-PRES
       That woman is quickly cutting it.
       wrl-20180605-01, DK, 19:06 mins

Adverbs can take case, though different types of adverbs allow different cases. Manner adverbs can take ergative case, as they pertain to manner rather than framing (orienting) the proposition to some space or time. For example, *wirlinyi* 'hunting' specifies a manner of the event denoted by the inflecting verb, as in (732), where it specifies the manner of *kapungunya* 'chasing', so it hosts an ergative suffix, indicating it is the ergative subject who is 'hunting'. Conversely, temporal adverbs such as *jawarti* 'tomorrow' frame the event rather than specify how it is carried out, so it cannot be said to pertain to the subject of the clause and never receives core-case marking—as exemplified in (733) with a transitive verb.[1] However, it is clear that there are coverb-like adverbs (in this regard), as there are apparent counterexamples. For example, in (734), the adverb *pawarrayi* 'all' does not receive ergative marking, though it does host the auxiliary complex. There are no instances of adverbs taking non-core case. Furthermore, even the adverbs that can receive ergative marking in transitive clauses are not always inflected for ergative case in these constructions: compare (731), where *lurrija* takes ergative case, with (735), where it does not, despite both clauses being transitive.

Adverbs in transitive clauses with ergative suffixes:

(731)   *Warlu=ju*   *ma-nta*   ***lurrija-rlu!***
         fire=1SG.NS   do-IMP   **quickly-ERG**
         Make a fire for me, quickly!
         H_K01-506B, DG, 08:32 mins

(732)   *Kapu-ngunya*   ***wirlinyu-rlu=ma.***
         chase-PRES   **hunting-ERG=TOP**
         He's hunting it.
         H_K06-004548, JW, 02:58 mins

Adverbs in transitive clauses without ergative suffixes:

(733)   ***Jawarti=rna***   *paka-nmi.*
         tomorrow=1SG.S   hit-FUT
         I'll hit it tomorrow.
         H_K01-505B, DG, 10:51 mins

(734)   ***Pawarrayi=lu***   *wirrpin*   *nguka-rnu.*
         all=3PL.S   completely   drink-PAST
         They all drank [it] completely.
         N_D02-007842, BN, 05:28 mins

---

1   Modern analyses of English tend to treat words such as *tomorrow* and *today* as pronouns (which can act as adverbials), as they can function as the subject or object of a clause (Pullum and Huddleston 2002: 564). However, the same cannot be said for Warlmanpa: *jawarti* 'tomorrow' and *jala* 'now' cannot instantiate a core grammatical relation of the verb, hence their classification as adverbs.

(735) *Kuyu*   *yarri=nya*   ***lurrija~lurrija***   *kuma-ka!*
       meat   that=FOC   **quickly~RDP**   cut-IMP
       Cut that meat quickly!
       H_K01-506B, DG, 08:47 mins

The semantic effect of the use or non-use of ergative marking is unclear. Intuitively, case agreement is likely to be indicative of a subject-orientated use of an adverb—that is, the difference between 'Louisa rudely answered Patricia', which is subject orientated, and 'Louisa answered Patricia rudely', which is manner orientated (see McConnell-Ginet 1982: 156)—which is best evidenced by adverbs only being able to agree in case with subjects (and not other case-marked constituents—for example, dative-marked indirect objects). Optional ergative agreement of adverbs is also noted in Ngardi (Ennever 2021; Meakins and McConvell 2021; Meakins and Nordlinger 2014: 91), whereas in Warlpiri the adverb must agree with the argument of which it is predicated (Simpson 1991: 125–26).

Some manner adverbs in Warlmanpa are semantically similar to 'manner nominals' in Warlpiri. For example, in Warlpiri, *kilji* 'fast' is classified as a manner nominal and, in Warlmanpa, *lurrija* 'quickly' is classified as an adverb.[2] In Warlpiri, manner nominals must either agree in case with the nominal they are modifying or constitute part of the noun phrase along with the head noun (Simpson 1983: 245–47).[3] This is quite distinct from Warlmanpa, in which *lurrija* (an adverb) can be unmarked in a transitive clause:

(736) *Kuyu*   *yarri=nya*   ***lurrija~lurrija***   *kuma-ka!*
       meat   that=FOC   **quickly~RDP**   cut-IMP
       Cut the meat quickly!
       H_K01-506B: 78, DG, 08:47 mins

---

2 Interestingly, some other manner nominals in Warlpiri correspond to coverbs in Warlmanpa—that is, words that are highly integrated with the inflecting verb and can never inflect for case—a stark contrast to nominals, which must agree in case. For example, Warlmanpa's *wuruly* 'secretly' is a coverb corresponding to the manner nominal *wurulypa* in Warlpiri.
3 An exponent/evidence of noun phrases in Warlpiri is the ability for only the right-most word in the phrase to be case marked. This is not the case in Warlmanpa, so unmarked adverbs in Warlmanpa cannot be said to form an NP based on being unmarked.

Other manner adverbs in Warlmanpa include *larlkirlarlki* 'separate', *ngutungutu* 'properly', *pingka* 'slowly', *wajili* 'chasing', *warlnga* 'partly', *wirlinyi* 'hunting' and *wintaru* 'loudly', which are exemplified in (737)–(740).

(737) *Ngarrka-tarra-rlu* **larlkirlarlki** *la-rnu=lu* *wawirri.*
man-PL-ERG **separate** shoot-PAST=3PL.S kangaroo
Each of the men shot a kangaroo.
wrl-20191208-02, DK, 02:08 mins

(738) **Ngutungutu** *wa-ngka=ju!*
properly speak-IMP=1SG.NS
Speak to me properly!
N_D03-007868, BN, 08:54 mins

(739) **Pingka** *pa-nka* *wa-nja-kuma.*
slowly go-IMP fall-INF-AVERSE
Go slowly, lest you fall.
H_K01-505B, DG, 43:41 mins

(740) *Maliki-rlu* *kurtu* *kapu-ngunya,* **wajilu-rlu** *kapu-ngunya.*
dog-ERG child chase-PRES **run_in_pursuit-ERG** chase-PRES
The dog is chasing the child, it's chasing after her.
H_K01-505B, DG, 02:31 mins

While adverbs only optionally take case marking to agree with nominals in finite clauses (in particular, only ergative), they obligatorily take case suffixes when they are in a non-finite subordinate clause (see §12.1.2), as exemplified in (741) and (742), in which the adverbs are part of the purposive subordinate clause, so the adverbs take dative case as agreement. Adverbs other than manner adverbs in subordinate clauses are not well attested, so I am unsure whether this extends to other types of adverbs.

(741) *Ngarrka=ma=nya* *pa-nanga* *lamanpa-ku* *ma-nja-ku*
man=TOP=FOC go-PAST.IMPF gun-DAT get-INF-DAT
[**wirlinyi-ku** *pa-nja-ku].*
hunting-DAT go-INF-DAT
The man went to get his gun to go hunting.
wrl-20190205, DK, 53:28 mins

(742)   *Ngarrka*   *kutij-partu-ngu*   *[wa-nganja-ku*   **wintaru-ku]**.
            man   stand-leave-PAST   speak-INF-DAT   **loud-DAT**
            The man stood up in order to speak loudly.
            N_D02-007842, BN, 49:11 mins

8.2 Temporal adverbs

Some adverbs modify the temporal reference of the event they modify. Unlike other adverbs, there is no evidence these temporal nominals can take case agreement morphology (for example, manner adverbs can take ergative case). In contrast, temporal adverbs, as well as corresponding adverbs in Warlpiri, can take locative case. Temporal adverbs can be further subcategorised as: 1) those specifying time in relation to the diurnal cycle; and 2) those referring to some temporal distance.

Table 8.1 Common temporal adverbs, divided by whether they relate to the day/night cycle

Related to diurnal cycle		Temporal distance/sequence	
jawarti	'morning, tomorrow'	*larrpa*	'before'
wajjurra	'yesterday'	*ngaka*	'soon'
		jala ~ jalangu[4]	'now, today, soon'
		purtanga	'later'

Adverbs are not the only word class that can refer to the diurnal cycle: there are nominals such as *yakarlu* 'night' that clearly relate to the semantic domain, despite being distinct word classes. The status of *yakarlu* as a nominal is evidenced by its ability to inflect for locative case, as in (743). While temporal adverbs cannot take case in Warlmanpa, they can still host clitics, as shown in (744), where the adverb *wajjurra* 'yesterday' hosts the topic marker *=ma*.

---

4   *Jalangu* appears to be a frozen form, rather than a synchronic root with case marking, as it can be used in intransitive contexts (where ergative case marking is not expected). Also, interestingly, it would seem *jala~jalangu* has both day/night cycle and temporal distance uses.

(743) Pukaj-wanu=rna   **yakarlu-rla**   kankarlarra-ngurlu.
       from_on_top-fall-PAST=1SG.S **night-LOC**   above-ELA
       I fell out from high up in the night.
       wrl-20191208-01, DK, 07:16 mins

(744) Wanjila=n   ka-ngu   **wajurra=ma?**
       where=2SG.S   be-PAST   **yesterday=TOP**
       Where were you yesterday?
       wrl-20170905-02, PW, 04:48 mins

While unable to host case agreement morphology (unlike other adverbs), temporal adverbs can host the dative suffix to indicate the duration of an event:

(745) **Jawarti~jawarti-ku**=lpa-jana-lu   ka-ngurra.
       tomorrow~RDP-DAT=1.INCL.S-3PL.NS-S.PL be-PAST-IMPF
       We stayed with/for them until the morning.
       N_D01-007840A, JJN, 00:45 secs

Most temporal adverbs have reduplicated and simplex forms, although there is no clear semantic difference (this is examined in more detail in §2.8).

To conclude the discussion of temporal adverbs, there is an interesting interaction between a temporal adverb and TAM marking: *larrpa* 'before', when hosting the clitic =*yi* 'still', often has an anterior present function, which places the consequences of some past event in the present—formally modelled as encoding that the event time precedes both the reference point and speech time (which coincide). For example, the sentence in (746) can be a response to someone offering another food: the event of eating happened in the past, but the consequences (that is, that the speaker does not want more food) are relevant at the time of speech (a particle, *ngulayi*, has a similar grammatical function; see §9.3.2).

(746) Yarnunju=ma=rna   **larrpa=yi**   nga-rnu.
       veg_food=TOP=1SG.S   **before=STILL**   eat-PAST
       I've already eaten food.
       wrl-20180615-02, DK, 17:31 mins

(747) Milkari-ja-ngu=n   **larrpa=yi.**
       blind-INCH-PAST=2SG.S   **before=STILL**
       You already became blind.
       H_K06-004547, JW, 30:34 mins

8.3 Spatial adverbs

Spatial adverbs can be further subdivided into cardinal directions and spatial paths, though this division is purely a semantic one and does not reflect any morphosyntactic differences.

Table 8.2 Catalogue of spatial adverbs

Cardinal directions	Spatial paths or positions
yanjarra 'north'	*kankarlarra* 'up, above'
kurlarra 'south'	*kanja* 'close'
kakarra 'east'	*kanjarra* 'down, below'
karlarra 'west'	*kantu* 'inside'
	kalkirni 'towards speaker'

Spatial adverbs have a unique paradigm, which is given in Table 8.3, from Nash (1979).

Table 8.3 Nash's (1979) paradigm of cardinal directions

Basic form	English	'In the —, across the —'	'From the —'
yanjarra	'north'	*yantija*	*yanjarni*
kurlarra	'south'	*kurlija*	*kurlarni*
kakarra	'east'	*kakarrija*	*kakarni*
karlarra	'west'	*karlija*	*karlarni*
kankarlarra	'up', etc	*kankarlija*	*kankarlarni*
kanjarra	'down', etc.	*kantija*	—
kantu	'long way down/inside'	—	—

While not fully morphologically predictable, the general pattern for spatial adverbs is:

Xrra	↔	Xija	↔	Xrni
base form		in/across		from

Interestingly, *-rni* is a 'towards' suffix on inflecting verbs (and note the form *kalkirni* 'towards speaker'), despite having an elative meaning with spatial adverbs. In combination with other suffixes, such as *-purta* '(to)wards' (discussed below), the 'from' series has a hither meaning—

for example, *yajna-rni-purta* north-FROM-TOWARD 'this way from the north' (for analogous structures in Warlpiri, see also Laughren 1978: Examples [16] and [17]).[5]

Like other adverbs, spatial adverbs are unable to take locative or allative marking, as demonstrated in (748)–(751).

(748)   *Ngayu=ma=rna*   *pa-nangu*   **kakarra(*-ka).**
        1=TOP=1SG.S   go-PAST   **east(*-ALL)**
        I went east.
        wrl-20190212-02, DK, 17:32 mins

(749)   *Ali=ma*   **yanjarra(*-rla)**   *ka-nya.*
        that=TOP   **north(*-LOC)**   be-PRES
        That one's living in the north.
        wrl-20190212-02, DK, 06:39 mins

(750)   *Pa-nama=li*   **kantu(*-ka).**
        go-FUT.AWAY=1PL.INCL   **under(*-ALL)**
        We're going into the tunnel.
        wrl-20191207-02, DK, 31:55 mins

(751)   *Papulu-rla*   **kantu(*-nga)**   *ka-nya.*
        house-LOC   **under(-LOC)**   be-PRES
        He's inside the house.
        H_K01-506A, DG, 54:15 mins

Interestingly, they can still take the elative suffix for movement away from a point, as in (752) and (753).

(752)   *Pukaj*   *wa-nu=rna*   *yakarlu-rla*   **kankarlarra-ngurlu.**
        fall_out   fall-PAST=1SG.S   night-LOC   **above-ELA**
        I fell out last night from up high.
        wrl-20191208-01, DK, 07:16 mins

(753)   **Yanjarra-ngurlu**=*rna*   *pa-nti-nya.*
        north-ELA=1SG.S   go-TWD-PRES
        I'm coming from the north.
        H_K01-505B, DG, 01:02:19 hrs

---

5   My thanks to David Nash for pointing this out to me.

A further point of interest is that *kantu* with the elative suffix systematically means 'lying down':

(754) Yiwirti-rla   **kantu-ngurlu**   ka-nya.
       tree-LOC   **under-ELA**   be-PRES
       He's lying under the tree.
       H_K01-506A, DG, 54:06 mins

(755) Ngayu=rna   **kantu-ngurlu**   ka-ngu-rra.
       1=1SG.S   **under-ELA**   be-PAST-IMPF
       I was lying down.
       wrl-20191208-03, DK, 04:49 mins

Finally, spatial adverbs can take *-purta*, which Nash (1979) glosses as 'towards, facing'.

(756) Nganayi-rla=lku,   mirla   **karlarra-purta** kayi=lpa-jana-lu
       dummy-LOC=THEN   this.LOC   **west-FACING**   when=1.INCL.S-3PL.
                                                           NS-S.PL

       nya-nji-n   timana,   ngula=jana   purn-nga-rninji-nmi.
       see-INC-FUT   horse   REL=3PL.NS   jump-eat-INC-FUT
       Out here on the west side, when we see those horses who will start jumping for them.
       N_D02-007850, DG, 03:37 mins

(757) **Kalkini-purta**   wa-nganji-nya.
       speaker-FACING   speak-MOT.TWD-PRES
       He's coming this way speaking.
       wrl-20180614-01, DK, 28:13 mins

This suffix is primarily found on spatial adverbs, though it also regularly appears on *kuya* 'thus', a recognitional adverb; *nyapa* 'how' (a demonstrative), which derives a directional ignorative, *nyapapurta* 'what direction'; and, in some rare cases, regular nominals.

8.4 Recognitional adverbs

I analyse two 'recognitional adverbs' in Warlmanpa that refer to discourse information. Specifically, *nyamu* (§8.4.1) refers to a discourse-salient time and *kuya* (§8.4.2) refers to manner (of doing events).

These have been reclassified from Nash's (1979) analysis, in which *nyamu* and *kuya* were categorised as demonstratives. My reclassification is primarily due to their inability to inflect for case, whereas demonstratives obligatorily inflect for case (§4.5). Additionally, *kuya* allows suffixes that are otherwise associated with adverbs, as discussed in detail in §8.4.2.

8.4.1 *Nyamu* 'that time'

The demonstrative *nyamu* refers to a time, rather than an entity (unlike other demonstratives). There are only two instances in the corpus, with *nyamu* bearing no inflection in either example. The two examples are given in (758) and (759).

(758)   *Pa-nanga=li,*   ***nyamu**=ma=li*   *pa-nanga.*
go-PAST.IMPF=1DU.INCL.S   **that_time**=TOP=1DU.INCL.S   go-PAST.IMPF
[I'll tell you about] that time we went around, going around.
N_D01-007840A, JJN, 00:17 secs

(759)   *No not 'jala=n*   *nya-ngu',*   ***'nyamu**=n*   *larrpa*   *nya-ngu*
now=2SG.S   see-PAST   **that_time**=2SG.S   earlier   see-PAST
ngula=lpa   *pa-nanga*   *wuppa-ku'.*
REL=1PL.INCL.S   go-PAST.IMPF   ash-DAT
No, not 'now you saw it', [say:] 'you saw it that time earlier when we were going for ash'.
wrl-20200224, DK, 10:15 mins

In Bilinarra and Gurindji, *nyamu* is a complementiser (Meakins and Nordlinger 2014; McConvell 1996b; Meakins and McConvell 2021). In these languages, it is a general relativiser that often translates as 'when' (also 'who', 'that', 'which', etcetera). Based on the presumed cognacy with the Warlmanpa form, McConvell (2006) highlights a regular grammaticalisation path of demonstratives to complementisers in Ngumpin-Yapa languages, suggesting the demonstrative use of *nyamu*, as in Warlmanpa, is the historically conservative use. Its status as an adverb in Warlmanpa (rather than a complementiser as in Bilinarra and Gurindji) is clearly based on (759). In this example, there are two finite clauses—one headed by *ngula*, the relative complementiser that heads finite subordinate clauses (§12.1.1.1), so the other (which contains *nyamu*) must be the matrix clause.

8.4.2 *Kuya* 'thus'

The adverb *kuya* specifies a manner of performing an action, including similar event structure, as in (760), manner of speech, as in (761), and direction, as in (762) and (763). As (762) and (763) also demonstrate, *kuya* allows suffixes associated with spatial adverbs: *-rni* 'towards' and *-purta* 'facing' are otherwise only found on cardinals and some ignoratives.

(760) **Kuya**=nyanu   pulka~pulka-rlu   turru-ma-nu-rra   larrpalarrpa.
      thus=RR   old_man-RDP-ERG   tell-do-PAST-IMPF   long_time_ago
      The old men were telling themselves stories **like this** a long time ago.[6]
      N_D02-007850, DG, 05:56 mins

(761) *No,*   **kuya**   wa-ngka: 'walku   kula=rna   pana-nga.'
            thus   speak-IMP   nothing   NEG=1SG.S   go-PAST.AWAY
      No, say it **like this**: 'I didn't go out.'
      wrl-20180614-02, DK, 11:20 mins

(762) **Kuya-rni**=rna   pa-nanga.
      thus-TWD=1SG.S   go-PAST.IMPF
      I was coming this way.
      wrl-20191207-01, DK, 06:01 mins

(763) *Yali*=ma   jitpi-nya-nya   **kuya-purta**,   *that means*
      that=TOP   run-MOT.AWAY-PRES   **thus**-FACING
      him going that way.
      That one's running away.
      wrl-20180531-02, DF, 03:15 mins

This demonstrative has several likely cognates that are complementisers: *kuya* in Bilinarra (Meakins and Nordlinger 2014: 170), *kuja* in Western Warlpiri and *kuja~kuwa* in Jaru (Tsunoda 1981a: 165–71). As with *nyamu* discussed earlier, McConvell (2006) again analyses the demonstrative use (as in Warlmanpa) as being the conservative use.

---

[6] It is not clear why there is no subject plural bound pronoun =*lu* in this example, given that the subject is plural (encoded by the reduplicated form of *pulka* 'old man').

9

Particles, interjections and clitics

This chapter discusses particles, interjections and clitics. Particles and interjections are uninflected words; they meet the prosodic requirements of word status—that is, they are at least bimoraic—whereas clitics do not necessarily meet this criterion. Clitics require a host. Particles and interjections are distinguished from each other based on whether the word can form a complete utterance: interjections can, but particles cannot (Ameka 1992). However, there are several words that function as both an interjection and a particle. Clitics are distinguished from the particles and interjections by their dependence on a host. Particles are discussed in §9.1, interjections in §9.2, doubly classified particles and interjections in §9.3, and clitics in §9.4.

9.1 Particles

Particles are grammatical words contributing to event semantics, typically with aspect or modality information. They are almost always in the 'auxiliary' position (that is, the second position in a clause), however, there are some instances where they occur after the auxiliary complex:

(764) *Ngayu=**rna-ngu-lu**   **ngarra**   paka-nmi   nyuntu   jinta.*
       1=1EXCL.S-2SG.NS-S.PL   **might**   hit-FUT   2   one
       We might hit you while you're alone.
       H_K01-506A, DG, 41:03 mins

In addition to being syntactically similar to auxiliary bases, particles are also semantically similar to auxiliary bases (in that they typically specify tense, aspect or mood information) and, in some cases, there is little distinction.[1] The primary distinction is that auxiliary bases obligatorily host the bound pronouns, whereas particles do not. This section covers the following particles: *kirli* 'let/leave it be' (§9.1.1); *kulanganta* 'deontic correction' (§9.1.2); *nganta* 'supposedly' (§9.1.3); *ngarra* 'might' (§9.1.4); *puta* 'incompletely' (§9.1.5); and *wayi* 'polar question' (§9.1.6).

9.1.1 *Kirli* 'let (it be), leave (it be)'

Kirli conveys a directive to allow something to happen. While the inflecting verb in the clause does not inflect for imperative mood (rather, the TAM marking specifies the temporal reference), the use of *kirli* seems to come with directive illocutionary force, for the addressee(s) to allow an event to happen (the event is expected to occur unless the addressee intervenes).

(765)   **Kirli**   *ji-nami!*
         let   burn-FUT
         Let it burn! (Speaker translation)
         wrl-20190131-01, DK, 24:54 mins

(766)   **Kirli**   *ka-mi!*
         let   be-FUT
         Leave him be!
         H_K01-506A, DG, 21:38 mins

This particle is also found in the Hansen River[2] dialect of Warlpiri (Laughren et al. 2022).

9.1.2 *Kulanganta* 'deontic correction'

Kulanganta is used to indicate that this event should have occurred, based on evidence gained after the situation. For example, in (767), the speaker reports that they travelled east, but now they know that they should have travelled south.

---

[1] In Warlpiri, propositional particles can be postposed to a constituent to indicate their scope over this constituent (Laughren 1982a: 133). I am not aware of this being the case in Warlmanpa. In Warlmanpa, particles seem to occur either in the auxiliary position (that is, second position or, less commonly, first position) or immediately after the auxiliary.

[2] Mainly spoken now at Alekarenge.

(767) Ngayu=ma=rna   pa-nangu   kakarra,   **kulanganta**=rna
      1=TOP=1SG.S   go-PAST   east   CORRECT=1SG.S
      pa-nkarla-rra   kurlarra-purta.
      go-SUBJ-IMPF   south-FACING

[I] went east, instead of *kurlarra* [south]. (Speaker translation)

I went east, not south like I should have. (Author translation)

wrl-20190212-02, DK, 18:48 mins

There are two points of interest regarding *kulanganta*.

First, there is an issue of whether it should be treated compositionally, comprising the negative particle *kula* (§11.5.1.1) and the particle *nganta* 'supposedly' (§9.1.3). However, it does not seem to hold up synchronically: the information for *nganta* 'supposedly' is obligatorily from a secondary source, whereas the information leading the speaker to use *kulanganta* can be gained first hand (for example, after travelling east and discerning that it was the wrong direction).

Second, this particle is related to *kulanganta* in Warlpiri (Laughren 1982a: 148–50) and Ngardi (Ennever 2021). However, in Warlpiri and Ngardi, *kulanganta* is used to negate a *false* proposition that was believed to be true. For example, in (768), the Warlpiri use of *kulanganta* indicates that the proposition 'he is staying put' was thought to be true, but now the speaker knows it is false. As shown above, the use of *kulanganta* in Warlmanpa indicates a proposition that is false but ought to have occurred based on new evidence.

(768) **Kulanganta**=lpa   yantarli   nyina-ja.   Kala   lawa.
      CFACT_BELIEF=IMPF   stay   be-PAST   but   nothing

It was thought that he was staying put. But no [he wasn't there].

(Warlpiri [Laughren et al. 2022: 264])

In all languages' uses of *kulanganta*, it indicates that the proposition is false at speech time. The differences are that Ngardi and Warlpiri use *kulanganta* to encode that the event was thought to be true, while Warlmanpa uses *kulanganta* to indicate that the proposition ought to be true—summarised in Table 9.1. As far as I can tell, the 'ought' pertains to deontic rather than epistemic necessity, however, further examples are needed to be certain.

Table 9.1 Use of *kulanganta* in Warlpiri, Warlmanpa and Ngardi

Kulanganta	Belief at event time	Belief at speech time
Ngardi, Warlpiri	True	False
Warlmanpa	False	False (but now known it ought to be true)

9.1.3 *Nganta* 'supposedly'

Nganta is a marker of evidentiality—specifically, it indicates that some information comes from a source other than the speaker. For example, in (769), at the time of speaking, the speaker lived in Elliott, a town approximately 250 kilometres north of Tennant Creek (and the conversation was taking place in Elliott). The speaker, talking about two people, makes the claim that they live in Tennant Creek. However, the speaker uses *nganta* to indicate that this information is reported, rather than claiming that they have firsthand evidence of it being true.

(769)   Yimpa=nya   **nganta**=pala   ka-nya   Tennant Creek-nga=ma.
        this=FOC   **supposedly**=3DU.S   be-PRES   Tennant Creek-LOC=TOP
        Those two supposedly live in Tennant Creek.
        N_D_1977-11-22, DC, 00:39 secs

Nganta is also attested with extremely similar functions in Warlpiri (Laughren 1982a: 137–41), Ngardi (Ennever 2021) and Gurindji (Meakins and McConvell 2021).

9.1.4 *Ngarra* 'might'

Ngarra indicates epistemic uncertainty. Unlike the auxiliary clitic =*nga* (which is restricted to future temporal reference), *ngarra* is compatible with any tense (past, present or future). It can have scope over the clause, indicating the proposition is uncertain, as in (770)–(772); or it may have scope over a certain participant in the situation, which indicates that the general event is occurring and it may be the case that the *ngarra*-modified referent is participating in the event, as in (773).

(770) **Ngarra**=lpangu ngapij nya-ngu ngula wuruly jutu-ngu.
POT=1PL.INC.O smell see-PAST REL run_away run-PAST

He [the dog] who ran away might have smelled us.

(That is, he has smelled something, it might have been us that he smelled.)

wrl-20180609-01, DK, 08:31 mins

(771) Ngayu=ma=rna jinjirla paka-rnu. **ngarra**=rna
1=TOP=1SG.S sneeze hit-PAST POT=1SG.S

Kulykulypa marta-nnya!
fever have-PRES

I sneezed, I might have a fever!

wrl-20180614-02, DK, 03:25 mins

(772) Ngana-ku **ngarra**=rla warlku wa-nganya.
what-DAT POT=3.OBL bark speak-PRES

Who might that dog be barking at?

wrl-20180615-02, DK, 08:36 mins

(773) Yali=ma **ngarra** Japaja nga-nnya.
that=TOP POT Japaja scold-PRES

That [dog] might be barking at Japaja.

(The dog is barking, it might be Japaja whom he is barking at.)

wrl-20180615-02, DK, 10:46 mins

Ngarra is well attested across the Ngumpin-Yapa subgroup—with some variation in its form (for example, *ngaja* in Bilinarra and Gurindji [Meakins and Nordlinger 2014: 419–20; McConvell 1996b: 93–94]), meaning (ranging from a general irrealis modality marker to a specific apprehensional marker [see Browne et al. 2024]) and word class (either a particle, as in Ngardi [Ennever 2021], or a complementiser, as in Bilinarra [Meakins and Nordlinger 2014: 419–20]).

9.1.5 *Puta* 'incompletely'

I have been unable to confidently analyse *puta*. Its core meaning (following Nash 1979, 2022) seems to be 'incompletely' or 'not all'. For example, in (774), the imperative *nganja* 'eat it!' is modified by *puta* to denote the speaker is offering part of the food, but not the entirety.

(774) **Puta** nga-nja=ju.
   incompletely eat-IMP=1SG.NS
   Eat a little bit on me.
   N_D03-007868, BN, 10:49 mins

In (775), the imperative *wanganjirra* 'start speaking' is modified by *puta* to indicate only some talking should be done (with context supplying the further derived meaning of 'don't talk too much!').

(775) **Puta** wa-nganji-rra!
   incompletely speak-INC-IMP
   Don't talk too much!
   N_D03-007868, BN, 10:40 mins

Interestingly, when combined with situations that cannot be done partially, the resulting illocutionary force is a negative imperative, which follows from the 'not all' meaning; if an event cannot be done partially then the only value that is compatible with 'not all' is 'none'.

(776) **Puta** ya-ka!
   incompletely put-IMP
   Don't put it down!
   H_K06-004555, LOF, 52:07 mins

In non-imperative contexts (of which there are two tokens in the corpus), it seems to denote an activity that the subject referent wishes to cease (but with little or no control over the activity), based on the speaker translations of (777) and (778), however, more tokens are needed for a more accurate analysis.

(777) **Puta** wa-nganji-na.
   incompletely speak-INC-PRES
   He's talking too much [speaker translation].
   wrl-20180531-02, DF, 04:01 mins

(778) **Puta**=rna-rla wa-nganyu.
   incompletely=1SG.S-3.OBL speak-PAST
   I didn't want to listen to him [speaker translation].
   (Possibly literally closer to: I didn't want to continue speaking to him.)
   wrl-20180531-02, DF, 05:06 mins

9.1.6 *Wayi* 'polar question'

Wayi introduces a polar question, although there is only one instance in the corpus. It is also not clear whether there is a distinction between polar questions introduced by *wayi*, as in (779), and polar questions without an overt polarity particle (as discussed in §11.4.2).

(779)   *Wayi=nkulu*   *win-kiya-karla?*
           POLAR=2PL.S   chuck-throw-IRR
           Did you mob throw it?
           H_K06-004555, LOF, 52:39 mins

While *wayi* is seemingly rare in Warlmanpa, the same particle is much more common in other Ngumpin-Yapa languages, such as Bilinarra (Meakins and Nordlinger 2014: 305–6) and Gurindji (McConvell 1996b: 95–96; Meakins and McConvell 2021). In Gurindji, *wayi* can also function as an irrealis marker.

9.2 Interjections

Interjections that do not also function as particles are rare. These are *kaya* 'watch out' (§9.2.1), *yuwayi* 'yes' (§9.2.2) and *yaya* 'yes really' (§9.2.3). Interjections are commonly followed with an extended clause, although they can also constitute a perfectly well-formed clause in isolation.

9.2.1 *Kaya* 'watch out'

Kaya serves as a warning to the addressee(s) about an imminent threat. Examples are given in (780) and (781).

(780)   **Kaya**   *Jakamarra,*   *yarri=nya*   *kanja=ngu*   *warna!*
           watch_out   Jakamarra   that=FOC   close=2SG.NS   snake
           Watch out Jakamarra, that snake is beside you!
           N_D02-007841, BN, 03:53 mins

(781) Warna-ngu   kanja   pa-nji-nya,   **kaya,**   nga=ngu=nga
       snake-ERG   close   go-MOT.TWD-PRES   **watch_out**   POST=2SG.
                                                             NS=DUB

pi-nyi!

act_on-FUT

A snake is coming close, watch out, it might bite you!

N_D02-007841, JC, 05:08 mins

9.2.2 Yuwayi 'yes'

Yuwayi is used to affirm the truth or correctness of an utterance. Prototypically, a speaker says *yuwayi* to affirm something said by another discourse participant, rather than self-affirming or emphasising the truth of their own claims. Two examples are given below of interactions between the researcher and a Warlmanpa speaker.

In (782), MFN is telling a story about her childhood and says that her parents (and their parents) used to work in *mangkkurunga* country, which has an unexpected form.[3] In response, David Nash (DN) attempts to confirm the pronunciation, to which MFN replies '*Yuwayi, yuwayi, mangkunga*', with the expected Warlmanpa form. DN repeats the form again in agreement, to which MFN replies '*yuwayi*' and elaborates.

(782) MFN: Pulkapulka=ma   like way down   kala=lu   work-ja-ngu-
                                                           rra,

              old_men=TOP   HAB=3PL.S   work-INCH-
                                                           PAST-IMPF

              true,   mangkkuru-nga.

                      plains_country-LOC

       The old men used to work far away, true, out in black soil country.

       DN: 'mangkkuru-ka'?

---

3 Specifically, the root *mangkkuru* appears to be the Warumungu form for plains country, as the expected Warlmanpa form is *mangku*. However, the locative suffix form *-nga* is not expected for two reasons: first, if the root is indeed the Warumungu form, the expected Warumungu locative form is *-jja*; and second, while *-nga* is a form of the locative in Warlmanpa, it is restricted to disyllabic roots, when *mangkkuru* has three syllables, so the allomorph *-rla* is expected to be used. Interestingly, the expected Warlmanpa root *mangku* would take the *-nga* allomorph of the locative, so it seems that MFN used the Warumungu form of the root and the appropriate Warlmanpa suffix for the Warlmanpa root.

9. PARTICLES, INTERJECTIONS AND CLITICS

MFN:	***Yuwayi,***	***yuwayi,***	mangku-nga.
	yes	**yes**	plains_country-LOC

Yes, 'mangkunga'.

DN: 'Mangku-nga'.

MFN:	*Yuwayi,*	*kala=lu*	w̪ork̪-ja-nga,	b̪ore-nga.
	yes	HAB=3PL.S	work-INCH-PAST.IMPF	bore-LOC

Yes, they worked at the bore [there].

N_D29-023128, MFN, 06:12 mins

In (783), I am investigating the truth conditions of *kapi* 'and', and am attempting to elaborate on the discussion with DK. I ask whether it is acceptable to say '*yuwayi*' to a question involving *kapi* when only one part of the conjunction is true, to which DK confirms, stating '*yuwayi, jintayi*' would be an acceptable response to the question, and elaborates with a more complete response.

(783) MB: Maybe, so you asked that, and maybe the person has seen just me, would they say '*yuwayi*' or would they say '*yuwayi*' to that if they've

MB: [just seen me]

DK: *[ya,* ***yuwayi,*** *jinta=yi].*

yes one=STILL

jinta=yi=rna	*nya-ngu*	*Japaja.*
one=STILL=1SG.S	see-PAST	Japaja

Yes, yes, only one. I only saw Japaja.

wrl-20191209, DK, 03:16 mins

9.2.3 *Yaya* 'yes really'

Yaya emphasises the truthfulness of a claim made by the speaker (in contrast, *yuwayi* more commonly affirms the truthfulness of a claim made by another speaker). There are only two instances in the corpus:

(784) ***Yaya!*** *La-rnu=rna-jana-lu.*

yes_really shoot-PAST=1.S-3PL.NS-S.PL

Yes! We shot them.

(Ken Hale prompt)

H_K01-506A, DG, 55:34 mins

(785) **Yaya,**   kankarlarra   jat   wa-nya=rla!
       yes_really on_top   cover   fall-PRES=3.OBL
       Yes, it's really covering it up!
       N_D09-013557, DG, 00:26 secs

9.3 Doubly classified particles and interjections

Some words can function as a fully independent clause (that is, interjections) and be integrated into a clause (that is, particles). These are doubly classified as particles and interjections: *walku* (§11.5.1.2), *ngulayi* 'okay/PERF' (§9.3.2) and *kuku* 'wait' (§9.3.3).

9.3.1 *Walku* 'no, nothing'

Walku is discussed in §11.5.1.2.

9.3.2 *Ngulayi* 'okay', 'PERF'

As a particle, *ngulayi* indicates that the event denoted by the clause has either already occurred (when occurring with past-tense inflections, as in [786]) or begun before the utterance and is ongoing (when occurring with present-tense inflections, as in [787]). In both cases, *ngulayi* also signals that the consequences of the situation are relevant at speech time. The resulting meaning is like that of the English 'present perfect' construction, hence its label, PERF.

(786) ***Ngulayi*=rna**   karta   pu-ngu.
       PERF=1SG.S   spear   act_on-PAST
       I have speared it.
       H_K01-506A, DG, 58:03 mins

(787) ***Ngulayi*=rna-rla**   yarnunju=ma   marta-nnya.
       PERF=1SG.S-DAT   vegetables=TOP   hold-PRES
       I have vegetables for him [and am still holding them now].
       wrl-20180608-01, DK, 06:48 mins

As an interjection, *ngulayi* typically translates as 'finished' or 'all right' and is used especially at the end of conversations or meetings, as in (788).

9. PARTICLES, INTERJECTIONS AND CLITICS

(788) **Ngulayi,** *walku=lku.*
Okay NEG=THEN
Okay, finished, nothing now.
wrl-20170321-02, SN, 22:14 mins

Warumungu has a particle, *kamarnta*, which also performs both these functions (Jane Simpson, p.c.). Interestingly, in Warlpiri, *ngulajuku* is found with a similar function (though lacking the grammatical perfective function). *Ngulajuku* is analysed (implicitly throughout Laughren et al. 2022) as formally compositional: *ngula* 'that' and *=juku* 'still' (*ngula* in Warlmanpa is a complementiser; see §12.1.1.1). Similarly, in Warlmanpa, *ngulayi* could be analysed as *ngula* 'that' and *=yi* 'still'—morphemically analogous to the Warlpiri form. I opt against this analysis as I am unable to explain how the two synchronic meanings could combine for a 'completive' meaning. However, there is clearly some relation between the meanings of *ngula* 'that, who' and *=juku/=yi* 'still' in these languages.

9.3.3 Kuku 'wait'

When used with future-time reference, *kuku* expresses a desire of the subject for the post-state of the matrix event (rather than a desire for the event itself).

(789) **Kuku**=rna wirliya jawu-wa-nmi.
wait=1SG.S foot cool_down-fall-FUT
I'm waiting for my foot to cool off.
H_K01-506A, DG, 02:54 mins

(790) **Kuku** ka-rra kayi=rna pa-nama yarnunju-ku ma-nja-ku.
wait sit-IMP WHEN=1SG.S go-POT vegetables-DAT get-INF-DAT
Wait here while I go to get vegetables [that is, I'll return with food].
wrl-20190201, DK, 25:26 mins

Like some other particles in Warlmanpa, *kuku* can be used as an interjection, as evidenced in the corpus by its lack of integration into the clause— specifically, it does not host the bound pronouns (whereas it does in [789], in its particle use) and the interjection use is prosodically detached from other clauses, as indicated by the comma. Examples of the interjection uses of *kuku* are given in (791) and (792).

(791) **Kuku,** kupa-nya=rna kuyu.
 wait cook-PRES=1SG.S meat
 Wait, I'm cooking meat.
 wrl-20190131-01, DK, 07:57 mins

(792) *I forget now.* **Kuku.** Ngarlpirinpa! Ngarlpirinpa!
 wait bush_cucumber bush_cucumber
 I forget now. Wait. Bush cucumber! Bush cucumber!
 wrl-20160914-02, DF, 39:48 mins

9.4 Clitics

Clitics always attach on the right edge of a well-formed word. The only constituent that can attach on the right edge of a clitic is another discourse clitic or the bound pronoun clitics. Some clitics do not occur in the corpus with another clitic; these are =*wiyi* 'first', =*yijala* 'also' and =*yi* 'still'. Each of the remaining three clitics, =*lku* 'then', =*nya* 'focus' and =*ma* 'topic', can co-occur with each other (although there are no cases where all three are hosted by a single constituent). The relative ordering between these three is =*lku*=*nya*=*ma*.

Clitics vary with regards to the type of host with which they are compatible: =*lku*, =*yijala* and =*yi* can be attached to any part of speech (other than the auxiliary complex), whereas the information structure clitics =*ma* and =*nya* must attach to lexemes denoting definite entities, which means they can only occur on nominals. Finally, =*wiyi* can only attach to nominals that denote states. A summary of clitics is given in Table 9.2.

Table 9.2 Summary of Warlmanpa clitics

Form	Gloss	Compatible host types	Likely cognate found in
=*lku*	'then'	Unrestricted	Warlpiri Ngardi (seems to have broadened)
=*yijala*	'also'	Unrestricted	Warlpiri
=*yi*	'still'	Unrestricted	Warlpiri (restricted to verbs)
=*ma*	'topic'	Nominals	Ngardi Wanyjirra Mudburra Bilinarra (also found on coverbs) Gurindji (also found on coverbs)

9. PARTICLES, INTERJECTIONS AND CLITICS

Form	Gloss	Compatible host types	Likely cognate found in
=nya	'focus'	Nominals	Warlpiri Ngardi (rare) Mudburra (restricted to questions)
=wiyi	'first'	Nominals	Warlpiri (also found on verbs)

Each clitic is now discussed in turn: =*lku* 'then' in §9.4.1, =*yijala* 'also' in §9.4.2, =*yi* 'still' in §9.4.3, =*ma* 'topic' in §9.4.4, =*nya* 'focus' in §9.4.5 and =*wiyi* 'first, before' in §9.4.7. A brief interlude takes place in §9.4.6, where I discuss the co-occurrences of the topic and focus clitics.

9.4.1 =*lku* 'then'

The clitic =*lku* locates a situation in the consequent state of some other situation (Browne 2020a), translated into English as 'now' or 'then' following a line of research of similar clitics/particles cross-linguistically (Ritz and Schultze-Berndt 2015; Ritz et al. 2012; Lee and Choi 2009). This analysis is exemplified in (793), in which the adverb *lani* 'afraid' hosts =*lku*, which denotes that the state of being afraid began after the prior event (the spearing event, in this case).[4]

(793) Wawirri=rna   karta pu-ngu   kapi lani=**lku**   jutu-ngu.
       kangaroo=1SG.S   spear   act_on-PAST   and   afraid=THEN   run-PAST
       I speared the kangaroo, and then afraid, it ran off.
       wrl-20180528-03, DK, 18:59 min

When the clitic has clausal scope, it occurs in the second position (immediately preceding the bound pronouns), as in (794) and (795). If the second position is occupied by a non-referring constituent (that is, an auxiliary or particle), it may instead attach to the primary predicate (typically an inflecting verb) to have equivalent scope. The clitic may also occur on secondary predicates (discussed further in §11.6.2). When occurring on a secondary predicate, it encodes that the situation denoted by the secondary predicate was not occurring until at least the situation denoted by the main predicate started, as in (796) and (797).

---

4 The notion of consequent state used here follows Ritz and Schultze-Berndt's (2015: 14) formalisation of the clitic =*biyang* in Jaminjung, which in turn follows Moens and Steedman's (1988: 16) definition in which some situation causes a change in the world and the speaker considers the consequences of this change to be 'contingently related to other events that are under discussion'.

Wide scope =*lku* (second position and/or on the main predicate):

(794) *Kipirrij wa-nu=**lku**, kuya-purta-kanyanu=**lku** pa-nangu.*
turn_around fall-PAST=THEN thus-FACING-ANOTHER=THEN go-PAST

Then he turned around, [and] **then** he went the other way.
wrl-20200225, DK, 30:36 mins

(795) *Tarnnga=yi=rna ka-nya, pulkapulka-rlu=ju winja-rnu,*
long_time=STILL=1SG.S be-PRES old_men-ERG=1SG.NS leave_at-PAST

*ngayu=**lku**=rna ka-nya nguru-nga mirlayi=nya.*
1=THEN=1SG.S be-PRES country-LOC this.LOC=FOC

I've lived here a long time, the old men left me here, [so] **now** I live in this country.
N_D18-013596, LN, 17:51 mins

Narrow scope =*lku* (on a secondary predicate):

(796) *Ngapij nya-nya **kari-ngu=lku** ngarra.*
smell see-POT **far-ERG=THEN** maybe

He might be smelling, far away now, maybe.
wrl-20180610-01, DK, 23:01 mins

(797) *Pa-nja-na=rna ngurra-ka **pina=lku**.*
go-MOT-PRES=1SG.S camp-ALL **return=THEN**

I'll go to camp then return.
H_K01-506B, DG, 02:27 mins

Note that when occurring with present temporal reference, =*lku* is translated as 'now', as in (798), although this reflects a quirk of English, rather than a distinct meaning in Warlmanpa (see Ritz and Schultze-Berndt 2015: 14; Browne 2020a).

(798) *Makarri-jupu=ma wartarti=**lku** ka-nya.*
partner-YOUR=DEF painted=THEN be-PRES

Your partner is all painted up **now**/*then [and wasn't before].
N_D03-007868, BN, 19:50 mins

9.4.2 =yijala 'also'

The clitic *=yijala* encodes that the expression or proposition to which it relates also pertains to another set of referents (at least one argument must be coreferential between the *=yijala* expression and the other set). For example, in (799), there are two overt propositions, HIT(*ngarrka*, 1SG) and HIT(*ngarrka*, 2SG), and the clitic *=yijala* attaches to the inflecting verb pertaining to the second proposition to indicate that this is essentially a repetition of the previous proposition (just with a different object, in this case).

(799) *Ngarrka-ngu   ngula=ju   paka-rnu,   nga=ngu=nga*
man-ERG   REL=1SG.NS   hit-PAST   POST=2SG.NS=DUB
paka-nma=yijala.
hit-POT=ALSO
The man who hit me might hit you too.
H_K01-506B, DG, 08:22 mins

(800) *Ngarrka-ngu   tartu-ngu=nganpa-lu   nya-nganya   **tartu=yijala.***
man-ERG   many-ERG=1.EXCL.PL.NS-3PL.S   see-PRES   **many=ALSO**
That mob of men is looking at us mob as well.
H_K01-505B, DG, 51:19 mins

For one speaker, *=yijala* seems to have fused with the coverb *yarta* 'again'; there are no cases where this speaker uses *=yijala* on any other stem. The use of *yartayijala* still only denotes one further event (rather than a repeated instance of an already iterated event, which might be expected from a purely compositional semantics), as exemplified in (801)–(803).

(801) ***Yarta=yijala**=ju   yu-ngka-rti!*
again=ALSO=1SG.NS   give-IMP-TWD
Give some here to me as well!
wrl-20191208-02, DK, 20:24 mins

(802) *Ali-ngu=nya=ju   paka-rnu   **yarta=yijala.***
that-ERG=FOC=1SG.NS   hit-PAST   **again=ALSO**
That one hit me as well.
wrl-20190131-01, DK, 16:47 mins

(803) **Yarta=yijala**=rla   wulyurr   ya-ka!
      again=ALSO=3.OBL   pour   put-IMP
      Pour some more for him!
      wrl-20191208-02, DK, 21:35 mins

9.4.3 =yi 'still'

The clitic =*yi* has two functions: when attaching to constituents that denote states, =*yi* indicates that the state is ongoing posterior and anterior to reference time. Typically, this is speech time, as in (804) and (805), and as reflected in Figure 9.1.

(804) Warlu=ma   **ji-nnya=yi.**
      fire=TOP   **burn-PRES=STILL**
      The fire is still burning.
      wrl-20190207-01, DK, 08:10 mins

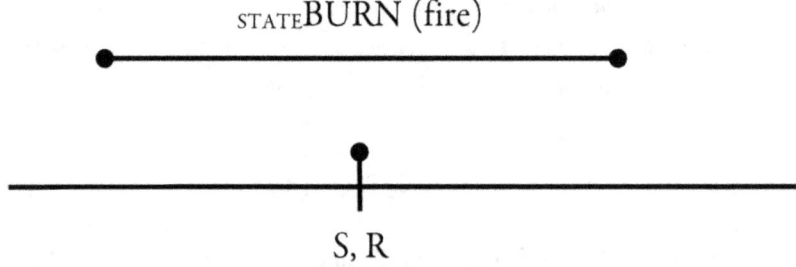

Figure 9.1 Temporal schema of the situations denoted in Example (804)

(805) Yapa-tarra=lu   **wiri=yi**   ka-nya.
      person-PL=3PL.S   **big=STILL**   be-PRES
      Still big mob of people here.
      wrl-20170321-02, SN, 10:42 mins

In (806)b, reference time has been established in the discourse as an earlier point in time. The =*yi* attaching to *witta* 'small' indicates that the speaker was small anterior and posterior to this point in time, as reflected in Figure 9.2.

(806) a. *Kula   jala,   larrpa.*
         NEG   now   before
         Not now, before.

  b. *Ngayu=ma=rna   **witta=yi**   pa-nangu-rra.*
     1=TOP=1SG.S   **small=STILL** go-PAST-IMPF
     I was going while [I was] still small.
     N_D02-007850, DG, 06:24 mins

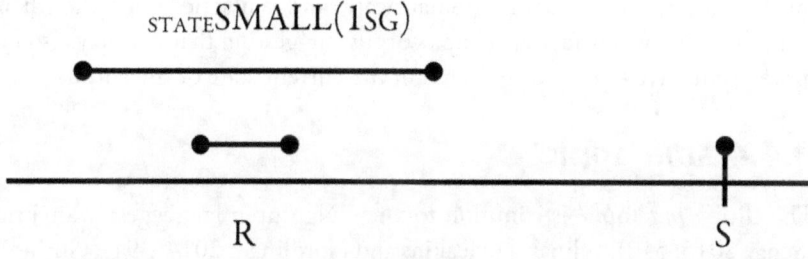

Figure 9.2 Temporal schema of the situations denoted in Example (806b)

Second, *=yi* can restrict a situation. This use has only been found on numeral nominals *jinta* 'one' and *jirrima* 'two', which restrict several participants in an event, as in (807)–(810).

(807) ***Jinta=yi***   *pa-nami-rni   kula   lawunpa.*
      one=STILL   go-FUT-TWD   NEG   wide
      Only one of you can come, [the car] isn't wide [enough].
      wrl-20180609-01, DK, 15:00 mins

(808) ***Jinta=yi***   *Jungarrayi   wa-nganya.*
      one=STILL   Jungarrayi   speak-PRES
      Only Jungarrayi is speaking.
      wrl-20191207-02, DK, 21:48 mins

(809) *Paka-nmi=rna-ngupala*   ***jirrima=yi.***
      hit-FUT=1SG.S-2DU.NS   **two=STILL**
      I am going to kill only you two.
      H_K06-004555, LOF, 54:17 mins

(810) **Not**   '*kurtu-ku-ku*',   '*kurtuku*',   **jinta=yi.**
                   'child-DAT-DAT'   'child-DAT'   **one=STILL**
Not '*kurtukuku*', '*kurtuku*', just one [*ku*].
wrl-20190211-02, DK, 10:13 mins

These two functions are also found of =*rni* in Gurindji (McConvell 1983) and of =*juku* in Warlpiri (Laughren et al. 2022), among other functions of =*rni* and =*juku*. In particular, the restrictive function of these clitics in these languages appears to be considerably more productive, attaching to a much wider range of lexemes (semantically and syntactically), rather than just nominals, as in the Warlmanpa corpus, suggesting that =*yi* may also be more productive—just not reflected in the current state of the corpus.

9.4.4 =ma 'topic'

The clitic =*ma* 'topic' is common to a few Ngumpin languages: Wanyjirra (Senge 2015: 512), Bilinarra (Meakins and Nordlinger 2014: 391), Gurindji (McConvell 1996b: 98–99; Meakins and McConvell 2021) and Mudburra (Osgarby 2018: 181–84). In each of these languages, it is described as a topic marker and Osgarby (2018: 183–84) notes that in Mudburra it also seems to function as a definiteness marker (the link between topic-hood, definiteness and specificity is cross-linguistically established [Givon 1978; Rochemont 2019]). I similarly analyse =*ma* in Warlmanpa as a clitic that primarily pertains to referent-tracking—specifically, that =*ma* encodes that its host denotes hearer-old information (that is, shared knowledge) that is salient to the discourse. Consider the narrative extract given in (811).

(811) a. ***Jurlaka*=*lu-rla***   *wirriri*   *nya-ngu-rra*   *yipakarli-ku.*
       bird=3PL.S-DAT   in_a_circle   see-PAST-IMPF   lizard-DAT
       The birds were looking around for lizards.

     b. ***Wangani-rlu***   *wirriri~wirriri*   *wirri*   *ya-nu-rra,*
       dog-ERG   in_a_circle~RDP   chase   put-PAST-IMPF
       The dog was running around chasing them,

     c. ***Nyanungu*=*ma*=*lu***   *putjanarra*   *partu-ngu-rra.*
       aforementioned=TOP=3PL.S   cause_to_scatter   leave-PAST-AWAY
       But these [birds] flew away.

d. **Wangani-rlu=ma**   *lamarta-rnu*   *yipakarli,*   *nga-rnu=lku.*
   dog-ERG=TOP   catch-PAST   lizard   eat-PAST=THEN
   The dog caught a lizard then ate it.
   wrl-20190207-01, DK, 50:02 mins

In a., *jurlaka* 'bird' is used to introduce a new referent to the narrative: a group of birds, which are said to be searching for lizards. In b., *wangani* 'dog' is used to describe a simultaneous action by an event participant—the dog was mentioned earlier in the narrative but had fallen out of focus. In c., which is after a. and b., the birds are the subject again (after being omitted from b.), and the speaker refers to the birds with the demonstrative *nyanungu* 'aforementioned', which hosts the clitic *=ma*. Here, the clitic appears to be functioning to reinforce that these are the same birds mentioned earlier—and, in line with Meakins and Nordlinger's (2014: 393) analysis of *=ma* in Bilinarra, it appears to be providing a contrastive topic reading, given that the previous clause had been establishing what the *wangani* 'dog' was doing while these birds were looking for lizards. Similarly, in d., the topic again switches back to the *wangani* 'dog', so this nominal is marked by *=ma*.

Almost all tokens of *=ma* in Warlmanpa attach to demonstratives, as in (812) and (813); free pronouns, as in (814)–(816); and names, as in (817) and (818)—all of which are classic examples of parts of speech that refer to accessible information (Ariel 1988). In other words, the information referred to by the *=ma*-marked constituent is always hearer-old (in the sense of Birner 2012: 217–19; see also Prince 1981), even if it is not discourse-old information, which suggests *=ma* pertains more to (perceived) hearer status than discourse status.

Demonstratives:

(812) **Ali=ma**   *pa-nyanya*   *nguka-nya-nya.*
      that=TOP   go-MOT.AWAY   drink-MOT.AWAY-PRES
      That one's going away drinking.
      wrl-20180614-01, DK, 32:12 mins

(813) *Kari=rna*   *karrarlarla*   *marta-karla*   **yarri=ma**=*rna=nga*
      COND=1SG.S   spear   have-IRR   **that=TOP**=1SG.S=DUB
      wawirri   *karta-pu-ngkarla.*
      kangaroo   spear-act_on-IRR
      If I had a spear, I would spear that kangaroo.
      H_K01-506A, DG, 03:32 mins

Free pronouns:

(814) **Ngayu=ma**=rna   pa-nama   kari.
1=TOP=1SG.S   go-FUT.AWAY   far
I'll go far away.
H_K01-505B, DG, 45:59 mins

(815) Kula=rna   **ngayu=ma**   pa-nama,   ngayu=ma=rna   ka-mi   yarti.
NEG=1SG.S   **1**=TOP   go-FUT.AWAY   1=TOP=1SG.S   be-FUT   stay
I won't go, I'll stay.
wrl-20180616-01, DK, 25:03 mins

(816) **Nyuntu=ma**=n   ka-mi   yarti   Tennant Creek-nga.
2=TOP=2SG.S   be-FUT   stay   Tennant Creek-LOC
You'll stay in Tennant Creek.
wrl-20200224, DK, 27:32 mins

Names:

(816) **Jungarrayi=ma**   partu-nga   wirlinyi   yawirri-ku.
Jungarrayi=TOP   leave-PAST.AWAY   hunting   kangaroo-DAT
Jungarrayi left to hunt kangaroos.
wrl-20180609-01, DK, 23:45 mins

(817) **Warlpiri=ma**=lu   Alekarengei-rla.
Warlpiri=TOP=3PL.S   Alekarengei-LOC
The Warlpiri mob are in Alekarenge.
wrl-20190213-01, DK, 23:36 mins

The analysis that =*ma* indicates hearer-old information is reinforced by the ability of =*ma* to attach to ignoratives, which are presupposed by the speaker to be old information for the interlocutor (hence why the question is cooperative), even though the referent is new (and definitionally unknown) information to the *speaker*. In this construction, =*ma* attaches to either the ignorative nominal itself, as in (819), or another nominal pertaining to the question under discussion, as in (820) and (821).

(819) ***Ngana=ma?***
       what=TOP
       What was that? ['Huh?']
       wrl-20200224, DK, 04:18 mins

(820) ***Ngana**=n*   ***jaru=ma***   *wa-nganya?*
       what=2SG.S **language**=TOP   speak-PRES
       What language are you speaking?
       H_K01-505B, DG, 16:08 mins

(821) ***Ngana***   ***yali=ma***   *kurtuj*   *ka-nya?*
       what   **that**=TOP   stand   sit-PRES
       Who's that standing?
       H_K06-004555, LOF, 45:29 mins

It is also worth noting that the constituent hosting =*ma* almost always occurs as the left-most available syntactic position (blocked only by lexemes that are elsewhere noted to be obligatorily clause-initial, such as *kula* 'negative' and ignoratives). Simpson (2007) finds that the least new information in Warlpiri clauses tends to occur on the left edge of clauses, in line with this analysis of =*ma*. Simpson's analysis is explained in further detail and taken up for Warlmanpa in §5.2.

9.4.5 =nya 'focus'

The clitic =*nya* indicates discourse-new and prominent information. This can be best seen in the question–answer pair given in (822), in which I asked for a generic word for 'bird'. DK responded with the word *jurlaka*, which hosted the clitic (overtly marking it as the new information for me, since I would not have asked had I known/remembered the word), and nested it within an example clause.

(822) MB: Is there a word for any kind of bird?
       DK: *Ye̞a̞ḥ,*   ***jurlaka=nya,***   *ka-nya*   *ngurra-nga.*
                       bird=FOC   be-PRES   camp-LOC
            Yeah, '*jurlaka*'. It is sitting in the nest.
            wrl-20191207-02, DK, 26:48 mins

A further example is given in (823), in which the speaker alerts the interlocutor to the cup being likely to spill, where the nominal *jawurra* 'cup' hosts the focus clitic.

(823)   *Lamarta-ka* **jawurra=nya** kala=nga ngappa walikwalik-wa-nmi.
        hold-IMP   **cup=FOC**   APPR=DUB water   overflow-fall-FUT
        Hold the cup, lest it spill!
        wrl-20190205, DK, 34:01 mins

This clitic is extremely common on demonstratives, as exemplified in (824)–(827).

(824)   **Muka=nya**=rna pa-nangu-rnu.
        this.ALL=FOC=1SG.S   go-PAST-TWD
        I came to here.
        H_K01-505B, DG, 23:06 mins

(825)   *Ngayu=ma-rna* *pa-nyinga* **mirla=nya** partakurru-   wantarri-rla.
                                                 rla
        1=TOP=1SG.S   go-PATH   **this.LOC=FOC** good-LOC   road-LOC
        I'm going along this good road.
        wrl-20200221, DK, 00:47 secs

(826)   **Yumpa=nya** ngappa kari=n   nguka-nmi, kula
        this=FOC   water   COND=2SG.S drink-FUT   NEG
        murrumurru-ja-mi=n.
        sick-INCH-FUT=2SG.S
        If you drink this water, you won't become sick.
        N_D03-007868, BN, 37:14 mins

(827)   **Ali=nya**   wangani warlku-wa-   kula=rna   jarta-ka-ngu.
                                nganyu-rra
        that=FOC   dog   bark-speak-   NEG=1SG.S   sleep-be-PAST
                                PAST-IMPF
        That dog was barking, I couldn't sleep.
        wrl-20190206, DK, 33:02 mins

Interestingly, the form =*nya* is also used in Mudburra for 'question focus', in which =*nya* indicates the right edge of a tag-question clause (Osgarby 2018: 198), and similarly in Bilinarra and Gurindji, the clitic =*warlal*=*barla* 'focus' is regularly hosted by ignoratives (Meakins and Nordlinger 2014:

399; Meakins and McConvell 2021). In Warlmanpa, =*nya* is very rarely hosted by ignoratives (or by any constituent in a question). However, as shown above, =*nya* can attach to a constituent in an answer to a question.

9.4.6 Co-occurrences of =*ma* 'topic' and =*nya* 'focus'

The co-occurrence of =*ma* 'topic' and =*nya* 'focus' warrants further explanation. As seen in the respective sections describing the functions of the clitics, =*ma* corresponds primarily to hearer-old information and =*nya* corresponds to discourse-new information (discourse sensitivity to both states of information newness is established in Birner 2012: 217–19; and Prince 1981).

Table 9.3 Clitics marking information status

		Hearer status	
		New	Old
Discourse status	New	=*nya*	=*nya*=*ma*
	Old	?5	=*ma*

An example is given in (828), in which the speaker claims that he and the other interlocutors are sitting down, adding an afterthought: *yamanga mirlanyama* 'here in the shade'. This information would naturally be known to all interlocutors, hence its status as hearer-old (or 'given', under Prince's [1981] taxonomy), hence the attachment of =*ma*. Yet, this has not yet been mentioned in the discourse, so its status is discourse-new, hence the attachment of =*nya*.

(828)   *Jala=ma=lpa*   *ka-nya*   *ngulayi,*   *yama-nga*   **mirla=nya=ma.**
        now=TOP=1PL   be-PRES   PERF   shade-LOC   this.LOC=FOC=TOP
        INCL.S
        Now we've been sitting, here in the shade.
        N_D02-007850, DG, 05:15 mins

---

5   It is not clear what clitic would be compatible with discourse-old, hearer-new information. Birner (2012: 219) notes that this information is typically treated in the same way as discourse-old information, which if true of Warlmanpa, would predict the use of =*ma* for this type of information.

Further examples are given in (829)–(833). Each token of =nya=ma occurs on a demonstrative, likely due to the frequency of =nya attaching to demonstratives.

(829) **Yumpa=nya=ma** yiwirti, ngayinya-kurla kirta-kurla.
this=FOC=TOP stick 1.GEN-GEN father-GEN
This is my father's spear.
H_K01-506A, DG, 49:44 mins

(830) Paka-nja-wangu winyja-ka **yarri=nya=ma** karli!
hit-INF-PRIV leave-IMP **that=FOC=TOP** boomerang
Leave that boomerang without hitting anyone!
H_K01-505B, DG, 11:04 mins

(831) **Ali=nya=ma** witta wila ka-nya wangani-jila.
that=FOC=TOP small play be-PRES dog-PRIV
The boy is playing without a dog.
wrl-20200220, DK, 44:18 mins

(832) **Ali=nya=ma** wangani ka-nya malamarri kupuwarnu-ku.
that=FOC=TOP dog be-PRES hunter kangaroo-DAT
That dog is a kangaroo hunter.
wrl-20200221, DK, 12:11 mins

(833) **Ali=nya=ma** tajpaka wirt-ma-nja-ku.
that=FOC=TOP hard lift_up-do-INF-DAT
That's too heavy to lift.
wrl-20180616-01, DK, 02:05 mins

9.4.7 =wiyi 'first, before'

The clitic =wiyi encodes that the expression denoted by its host was true at the reference time but no longer holds at speech time, as in (834) and (835). Interestingly, in (835), the host of =wiyi, lijinpa 'sick', is under the scope of clausal negation, which suggests =wiyi has scope over the entire clausal proposition ¬SICK(1SG), which was true at the reference time, but is false at speech time.

(834) | *Ngayu=rna* | *purtu- ka-nya* | *ngula=n* | **witta=wiyi** | *ka-ngu-rra.*
| 1=1SG.S | remember be-PRES | REL=2SG.S | **small=FIRST** | be-PAST-IMPF

I remember when you were a child.
N_D02-007842, BN, 33:57 mins

(835) | *Ngayu=rna* | *purtu-ka-nya* | *kula=rna* | **lijinpa=wiyi** | *ka-ngu-rra.*
| 1=1SG.S | remember-be-PRES | NEG=1SG.S | **sick=FIRST** | be-PAST-IMPF

I remember when I was not sick.
N_D02-007842, BN, 35:54 mins

It can also be used to attenuate a command, as in (836).

(836) | **Yarnunju=wiyi** | *nga-nja!*
| **food=FIRST** | eat-IMP

[Please] eat this food!
wrl-20190123, SN, 21:23 mins

Both functions of Warlmanpa =*wiyi* are also found of Warlpiri =*wiyi* (Laughren et al. 2022).

10
Grammatical relations

This chapter introduces grammatical relations in Warlmanpa clauses. Grammatical relations determine 1) the case marking of nominal constituents, 2) the bound pronoun series used to register the argument (if any), 3) reflexivisation properties, and 4) the control properties of non-finite clauses. The grammatical relations are defined in §10.1 and the types of argument structures of predicates are catalogued in §10.2.

10.1 Grammatical relations

Six types of grammatical relations can be identified in Warlmanpa, though not all criteria are relevant or exclusive to each type. I have labelled these five relations 'subjects' (§10.1.1), 'objects' (§10.1.2), 'indirect objects' (§10.1.3), 'external objects' (§10.1.4) and 'adjuncts' (§10.1.5). I situate the argument/adjunct distinction in Warlmanpa compared with other Ngumpin-Yapa languages in §10.1.6.

Across Australian languages, there is a split between whether languages mark grammatical relations on the dependants or the head. To some extent, this difference reflects whether a language is Pama-Nyungan or non-Pama-Nyungan (for a general overview, see Nichols 1986; and for an overview in Australian languages, see Nordlinger 2014). Warlmanpa, and Ngumpin-Yapa languages more generally, present somewhat of a hybrid system: grammatical relations are marked on dependants via case morphology as well as on the auxiliary via bound pronouns. The following subsections defining the different groups of grammatical relations make use of 'converging criteria' (in the spirit of canonical typology, following Corbett 2005, 2007). The criteria are given in Table 10.1 and each grammatical relation is discussed in further detail in the following sections.

Table 10.1 Criteria for distinguishing grammatical relations in Warlmanpa

Criteria	Subject	Object	Ind. obj.	Ext. obj.	Adjunct
	§10.1.1	§10.1.2	§10.1.3	§10.1.4	§10.1.5
Bound pronoun series	Subject	Non-subject	Non-subject	Non-subject	None
Case morphology	ERG/ABS	ABS	DAT/ALL	DAT	Any
Subcategorised for	Yes	Yes	Yes	Optionally	No

Note that the object and oblique series of bound pronouns are entirely syncretic except in third-person singular (see §5.4).

Throughout §§10.1.1–10.1.4, when defining grammatical relations, the evidence presented often refers to the series used to cross-reference the grammatical relation. For example, for the grammatical relation 'subject', one criterion used is that 'they are cross-referenced by the subject bound pronoun series'. However, note that there are some other factors that result in a referent not being cross-referenced (for example, inanimacy; see §5.4.3.4 for factors influencing whether referents are cross-referenced).

10.1.1 Subjects

Subjects are defined by the criteria listed in Table 10.2 and exemplified in (837)–(841).

Table 10.2 Morphosyntactic criteria for subjects

Criteria	Exemplified in
They are cross-referenced by the subject bound pronoun series.	(837), (838) (839)
The nominal(s) receives either absolutive or ergative case.	(840), (841)
They can bind reflexive/reciprocal arguments.	(839)

(837) *Ngayu=**rna***   *wa-ngami.*
       1=1SG.S   speak-FUT
       I will speak.
       H_K01-505B, DG, 01:38 mins

(838)　*Wawirri=**rna***　　*nya-ngu.*
　　　　kangaroo=1SG.S　see-PAST
　　　　I saw a kangaroo.
　　　　H_K01-505B, DG, 09:25 mins

(839)　*Nyuntu=**nyanu-n***　*kuma-rnu.*
　　　　2=RR-2SG.S　　　cut-PAST
　　　　You cut yourself.
　　　　H_K01-506A, DG, 08:26 mins

(840)　**Maliki-rlu**　　*nga=ngu=nga*　　*pi-nya!*
　　　　dog-ERG　　　POST=2SG.NS=DUB　act_on-POT
　　　　The dog might bite you!
　　　　H_K01-505B, DG, 02:16 mins

(841)　**Maliki**　　　*jutpu-ngunya.*
　　　　dog.ABS　　　run-PRES
　　　　The dog is running.
　　　　H_K01-505B, DG, 02:39 mins

10.1.2 Objects

Objects are defined by the criteria listed in Table 10.3 and exemplified in (842)–(844).

Table 10.3 Morphosyntactic criteria for objects

Criteria	Exemplified in
They are cross-referenced by the non-subject bound pronoun series.	(842), (843)
The nominal(s) is in absolutive case (phonologically null).	(842)
The anaphoric bound pronoun is used instead of the object-bound pronoun series in reflexive/reciprocal constructions.	(844)

(842)　**Wawirri**-*ja=rna-**palangu***　　*nya-ngu.*
　　　　kangaroo.ABS-DUAL=1SG.S=3DU.NS　see-PAST
　　　　I saw two kangaroos.
　　　　H_K01-505B, DG, 20:24 mins

(843) *Parra-ngu=**ju**   purtku-ma-nnya.*
       sun-ERG=1SG.NS   heat-CAUSE-PRES
       The sun is warming me.
       wrl-20190205, DK, 27:25 mins

(844) *Ali=nya=lu-**nyanu**   wangani-rlu   piya-nnya.*
       that=FOC=3PL.S-RR   dog-ERG   cut-PRES
       Those dogs are biting each other.[1]
       wrl-20180610-01, DK, 16:54 mins

Objects might not be expressed at all if the object is third-person singular and no overt nominal is used to refer to it, as in (845).

(845) *Karnta-ngu=ju   ngayu-ku   yu-ngu.*
       woman-ERG=1SG.NS   1-DAT   give-PAST
       The woman gave it to me.
       N_D02-007841, BN, 23:40 mins

Furthermore, as discussed in §5.4, the object-bound pronoun series criterion is not always useful: the bound pronoun to register a third-person singular is null for both subjects and objects (with =*rla* used for dative referents). Thus, for a predicate requiring a subject and an object, the entire bound pronoun sequence can be phonologically null, if it is a third-person singular subject and object.

10.1.3 Indirect objects

Indirect objects are defined with the criteria listed in Table 10.4 and exemplified in (846)–(849).

Table 10.4 Morphosyntactic criteria for indirect objects

Criteria	Exemplified in
They are cross-referenced by the non-subject bound pronoun series (=*rla* if third-person singular).	(846), (847), (848)
The nominals are marked with dative case.	(846), (848)
The anaphoric bound pronoun is used instead of the object-bound pronoun series in reflexive/reciprocal constructions.	(849)

---

1   I am unsure why the demonstrative *ali* does not receive ergative marking in this utterance.

(846) **Nyuntu-ku**   kapi=rna-**ngu**   Warlmanpa   wa-ngami.
       2-DAT   FUT=1SG.S-**2SG.NS** Warlmanpa   speak-PRES
       I will speak Warlmanpa <u>to/for you</u>.
       H_K01-505B, DG, 16:35 mins

(847) Yiwirti=rna-**rla**   yu-ngunya.
       stick=1SG.S-**3.OBL**   give-PRES
       I'm giving a stick <u>to him</u>.
       wrl-20170403-01, SN, 00:19 secs

(848) Maliki-rlu=**rla**   **kuyu-ku**   wayi-nnya.
       dog-ERG=**3.OBL**   **meat-DAT**   search-PRES
       The dog is searching <u>for meat/game</u>.
       H_K01-505B, DG, 07:51 mins

(849) Wa-nganya=pala-**nyanu**   witta-jarra.
       speak-PRES=3DU.S-RR   small-DUAL
       Two children are talking <u>to each other</u>.
       wrl-20190117, SN, 17:46 mins

One predicate, *ya-* 'put', selects for an indirect object that is case-marked with the allative, as in (850). Arguments marked with spatial cases are more common in Ngumpin languages, often warranting a distinct grammatical relation labelled 'subjunct' (Ennever 2021; Tsunoda 1981a: 112–15).

(850) Yali=nya-rna-**ngu**   pirntija   ya-rnu   **nyuntunya-ka**.
       that=FOC=1SG.S-**2SG.NS** beside   put-PAST   **2-ALL**
       I put that beside **you**.
       N_D02-007841, BN, 09:07 mins

(851) Jakamarra-rlu=**nyanu**   ya-rnu   pirntija   kularda,   yulu-ka.
       Jakamarra-ERG=RR   put-PAST   beside   spear   ground-ALL
       Jakamarra put the spear beside **himself**, on the ground.
       N_D02-007841, BN, 08:26 mins

10.1.4 External objects

External objects are morphosyntactically identical to indirect objects. The need for a separate grammatical relation is warranted due to the co-occurrence of external objects with indirect objects, as in (852), where the matrix predicate *wayi-* 'search' requires a subject and indirect object, and an external object is introduced as a benefactive.

(852)   *Wayi-rnu-rra=rna-ngu-rla*   *nyuntu-ku.*
        search-PAST=1SG.S-2SG.NS-3SG.OBL   2-DAT
        I was searching for him$_{IO}$ for you$_{EO}$.
        (Alternative interpretation: I was searching for you$_{IO}$ for him$_{EO}$.)
        wrl-20190213-01, DK, 10:14 mins

External objects in Warlpiri can be distinguished from indirect objects based on subordinate clause control properties, however, Simpson (1991: 385) notes that even this has exceptions. There are no clear cases in the Warlmanpa corpus of an external object controlling a non-finite subordinate clause.

External objects exhibit features of indirect objects and of adjuncts. Like indirect objects, external objects are cross-referenced in the bound pronouns (unlike adjuncts) and overt nominals receive dative case marking. Like adjuncts, they are not obligatorily selected for by predicates (unlike indirect objects).

Table 10.5 The distinctions between indirect objects, benefactive adjuncts and non-benefactive adjuncts

Criteria	Indirect objects	External objects	Adjuncts
Cross-referenced by bound pronouns	Yes (non-subject series)		No
Case suffix	Dative case		Various cases
Subcategorised for by predicate	Yes	No	

External objects can be introduced into a clause in two ways: through an optional applicative rule (§10.1.4.1) or optionally by certain coverbs (§10.1.4.2). The morphosyntactic criteria used to identify external objects are given in Table 10.6.

10. GRAMMATICAL RELATIONS

Table 10.6 Morphosyntactic criteria for external objects

Criteria	Exemplified in
They are cross-referenced by the oblique bound pronoun series.	(854), (855), (856)
The head nominal receives dative case.	(854), (856)
The anaphoric bound pronoun is used instead of the object-bound pronoun series in reflexive/reciprocal constructions.	(857)

External objects in Warlpiri and Warlmanpa are discussed in further detail in Browne (2021b).

10.1.4.1 Applicative constructions

A given argument structure can be extended to include an external object, which can be interpreted as a benefactive, a malefactive or a possessor. Interestingly, this phenomenon is found elsewhere in Australia—for example, Dench (1995: 226) notes that benefactives in Martuthunira behave more similarly to objects than adjuncts, and states they 'might best be handled by a general lexical rule which adds a benefactive object to a verb's "basic" argument structure'. And within Ngumpin-Yapa languages, the same phenomenon is found, in Ngardi (Ennever 2018: 277), Warlpiri (Hale 1982: 235–36), Bilinarra (Meakins and Nordlinger 2014), Mudburra (Osgarby 2018: 148), Wanyjirra (Senge 2015: 539 ff.), Jaru (Tsunoda 1981a: 151–52) and Gurindji (Meakins and McConvell 2021: 283–84).

Example applicative constructions are given in (853)–(857).

(853) *Maliki=ju*   **ngayu-ku**   *palu-ngu.*
dog=1SG.NS   1-DAT   die-PAST
The dog died on me. (Malefactive interpretation.)
My dog died. (Possessive interpretation.)
N_D02-007841, BN, 27:20 mins

(854) *Ali=nya=ma*   *wangani*   *pa-nji-na=ju*   **ngayu-ku.**
that=FOC=TOP   dog   go-TWD-PRES=1SG.NS   1-DAT
That dog is coming <u>for me</u>.
wrl-20180614-01, DK, 34:30 mins

(855) *Puta*   *nga-nja=ju.*
incompletely   eat-IMP=1SG.NS
Eat a little bit <u>on me</u>.
N_D03-007868, BN, 10:49 mins

(856) ***Ngarrka-ku=rla***   *ma-nu.*
       man-DAT=3.OBL   get-PAST
       She got it for the man.
       N_D02-007841, BN, 23:47 mins

(857) *Karnta-ngu=**nyanu**   kupa-nnya.*
       woman-ERG=RR   cook-PRES
       The woman is cooking it for herself.
       wrl-20190213-02, DK, 26:32 mins

10.1.4.2 External object coverbs

Some coverbs referred to as 'external object preverbs' in Warlpiri (Simpson 1991) may introduce an external object. In Warlmanpa, the set of external object coverbs includes at least *jurnta* 'away', *wuruly* 'conceal' and *yirrkin* 'with'. An example is given in (858), where the coverb *jurnta* 'away' introduced an external object to indicate the entity for which the situation was moved 'away'.

(858) *Japaljarri-rlu=**rla***   *maliki*   ***jurnta**-karikari-ma-nu.*
       Japaljarri-ERG=3SG.OBL   dog   **away**-chase_away-do-PAST
       Jungurrayi-ku.
       Jungarrayi-DAT
       Japaljarri chased the dog away from Jungarrayi.
       N_D02-007841, BN, 08:09 mins

External object coverbs are discussed in further detail in §7.4.3.

10.1.5 Adjuncts

Nominal expressions that modify the event (that is, are predicated of the main predicate) are referred to as 'adjuncts'. Adjuncts are marked with an argument-taking predicate use of case (§4.1.1.2), which relates the nominal to the main predicate, but are not cross-referenced by the bound pronouns (which distinguishes them from all other grammatical relations in Warlmanpa).

Adjuncts are defined with the criteria in Table 10.7 and exemplified in (859) and (860). These adjuncts receive their relation to the predicate by the case used to introduce the nominal. All non-core cases can be used to mark adjuncts. Naturally, some types of events will be strongly associated with some types of adjuncts: motion events will collocate with allative adjuncts, non-motion events will collocate with locative adjuncts, and so on. See §10.1.6 for further discussion of the argument/adjunct distinction.

Table 10.7 Morphosyntactic criteria for adjuncts

Criteria	Exemplified in
They are not cross-referenced by the bound pronoun series	(859), (860)
The head nominal receives an argument-taking use of case	(859), (860)
They cannot be reflexivised or reciprocated	—

(859) **Nyintinya-ka**=rna   pa-nangu-rnu.
       2-ALL=1SG.S   go-PAST-TWD
       I came to you.
       H_K01-505B, DG, 32:59 mins

(860) Pa-nka-rti   **wangani-jarra-kuma!**
       go-IMP-TWD   **dog-DUAL-AVER**
       Come here, for fear of the two dogs!
       wrl-20190213-01, DK, 38:02 mins

10.1.6 On the argument/adjunct distinction

As discussed throughout §10.1, the division between arguments and adjuncts is based on whether a given constituent is subcategorised for by the predicate, which is best reflected in the morphosyntax by the ability for the referent(s) to be cross-referenced by the bound pronouns—except for benefactives, which are a type of external object (§10.1.4). This use of morphosyntactic criteria (head-marking in particular) results in an analytical difference as to what is (and what is not) considered an 'argument' in Warlmanpa and 'arguments' in other Ngumpin-Yapa languages.

Almost all uses of semantic case (locative, allative, etcetera; see §4.1) in Warlmanpa are treated as adjuncts—that is, they are all either argument-taking predicates or attributives, in Simpson's (1991) terms—because the referents of the marked nominals can never be cross-referenced by the bound pronouns. This is particularly evident when the referent is animate, as in (861), where the locative adjunct is the second person, yet it is not registered in the bound pronouns. Its lack of bound pronoun registration is a morphosyntactic reflection of its adjunct status and, similarly in (862), the first-person free pronoun is marked for allative case but is not registered in the bound pronouns.

(861) Witta   ka-nya   **nyintinya-rla.**
       small   be-PRES   2-LOC
       The child is sitting **on you**.
       H_K01-505B, DG, 32:52 mins

(862) **Ngayinya-ka**   pa-nka-rti!
       1GEN.ALL   go-IMP-TWD
       Come to me!
       H_K01-505B, DG, 33:06 mins

Other analyses of related languages, such as Simpson (1991) for Warlpiri, treat spatial case relating to certain intransitive predicates (such as *wilypi-pardi-* 'emerge' and *yuka-* 'enter' in Warlpiri) as having spatial arguments, whereas for other intransitive predicates (such as *parnka-* 'run') and transitive predicates (such as *ka-* 'carry'), the same case-marked nominals (for example, locative-marked nominals) are treated as adjuncts. In Warlmanpa morphosyntax, there is no apparent distinction between these two groups and, as such, I have opted to treat both presupposed groups as a single category of 'adjunct'.

The exception is for a single predicate, *ya-* 'put', which seems to allow an allative-marked constituent to be cross-referenced in the bound pronouns by the oblique series, as in (863).

(863) Yali=nya=rna-**ngu**   pirntija   ya-rnu   **nyuntunya-ka.**
       that=FOC=1SG.S-**2SG.NS**   beside   put-PAST   **2-ALL**
       I put that beside **you**.
       N_D02-007841, BN, 09:07 mins

This demonstrates the contrast between nominals with spatial case that are adjuncts, as in (861) and (862), and those which are arguments, as in (863). The argument status of the last two examples is clearly demonstrated by: 1) their restriction to a certain predicate, and 2) their ability to be cross-referenced by the bound pronouns.[2]

---

2   An alternative analysis is that the bound pronoun is registering a benefactive meaning—that is, 'he put it beside himself for himself' (applicable to both examples).

This contrasts with some Ngumpin languages in which the grammatical function of the locative (and some other cases, predominantly 'spatial') is considerably less restricted (see Browne et al. 2024: 8–10; Ennever and Browne 2023). These Ngumpin languages include Gurindji (McConvell 1996b: 55), Ngardi (Ennever 2021), Jaru (Tsunoda 1981a: 127), Walmajarri (Hudson 1978: 62–63) and Wanyjirra (Senge 2015: 318). An example from Wanyjirra is given in (864), in which the comitative-marked nominal is cross-referenced by the bound pronouns with the oblique series. Similarly, the Ngardi example in (865) demonstrates the ability for an allative-marked constituent to be cross-referenced by the locational bound pronoun series for the predicate *yaparti-* 'run'—clearly contrasting with the Warlmanpa example in (862).

(864) *Nganinga   warlagu   ngu=**lanyanda**   lulu   garriny-ana*
       1MIN.OBLI   dog.ABS   REAL=**3MIN.OBL**   sit   STAY-PRES
       yangi-wunyja.
       one-COMIT
       My dog is sitting **with/by one man**.
       (Wanyjirra [Senge 2015: 318])

(865) *Yaparti-nya=**rlanyanta**   Nakarra-kuny-kurra   ngati-kurra.*
       RUN-PST=**3SG.LCT**   skin_name-GEN-ALL   M-ALL
       He ran **to Nakarra's mother**.
       (Ngardi [Ennever 2021])

Thus, the argument/adjunct distinction (in particular, the grammatical status of spatial cases) is situated differently across the Ngumpin-Yapa languages. This phenomenon has been shown elsewhere: Bantu languages also differ in the extent to which the locative case can be used as an argument-relator, with Riedel and Marten (2012: 290) concluding that 'locative object marking may be related to more or less object-like grammatical functions' *across* the languages. Furthermore, Bilinarra seems to represent a middle-ground in the ongoing fluctuation; Meakins and Nordlinger (2014: 233) note that the oblique bound pronoun series can mark 'spatial oblique arguments and adjuncts' but does not do so obligatorily.

Some authors treat semantic cases as having grammatical roles in marking arguments without being cross-referenced by bound pronouns. For example, Simpson (1991: 195) treats some non-spatial uses of the locative case in Warlpiri as marking the object of a predicate, with particular reference to cases such as that in (866), where the nominal *karti* 'cards' is marked with a locative suffix, which is taken to be the object of the predicate PLAY, in part because of the independent meaning of the locative (that is, here the locative-marked nominal does not denote a location).

(866) *Ngarrka-patu ka=lu   **karti-ngka**   manyu-karri-mi   karru-ngka.*
       man-PL   PRES=3PL.S **cards-LOC**   play-stand-NPST   creek-LOC
       The men are playing **cards** in the creek.
       (Warlpiri [Simpson 1991: 195])

There are no entirely analogous examples found in the Warlmanpa corpus, though there are some similar examples where a nominal, *wila*, is marked with the locative case, as in (867).

(867) *Ngayu=ma=rna   **wila-nga**   pa-nangu-rra   wilpa-nga.*
       1=TOP=1SG.S   **play-LOC**   go-PAST-IMPF   creek-LOC
       I was **playing** going around the creek.
       (Lit.: I was going around the creek at/in play.)
       wrl-20180614-01, DK, 19:10 mins

In §4.1.5, I treat such uses of the locative case as introducing a state during the main predicate—a metaphorical extension of the spatial use of the locative case; feasibly, *karti-ngka* 'at cards' or similar uses of the locative could also be treated as a stative use, though there are no such examples in the corpus to investigate. Regardless, these locative-marked nominals are not treated any differently by the grammar, just like the spatial examples discussed above, and any claims to grammatical status are based on semantic intuition rather than morphosyntactic exponents.

In sum, grammatical uses of non-core case in Warlmanpa are extremely limited (assuming the cross-referencing in the bound pronouns indeed reflects a distinction between core and non-core cases). Grammatical uses of non-core cases are restricted only to *ya-* 'put, place', where the allative-marked argument of the predicate is treated differently to allative-marked modifiers of other predicates by the morphosyntax of the language. Some types of events are naturally associated with some types of non-core case—for example, *pa-* 'go' is much more readily modified by an allative-marked constituent than is, say, *piya-* 'bite, cut', though these reflect semantic compatibility between the *event* and semantic cases rather than restrictions between the *predicate* and semantic cases (see, for example, Yoon 2013).

10.2 Verbal clauses

With the different groups of grammatical relations defined in §10.1, we can now categorise predicates according to the grammatical relations for which they select (henceforth, the 'case frame' of a predicate refers to the set of grammatical relations for which it selects). The set of identified case frames is given in Table 10.8.

Table 10.8 Types of case frames selected for by predicates in Warlmanpa

Valency	Subclass	Argument(s)		
Avalent	Impersonal (not instantiated) §10.2.1	—		
Monovalent	Intransitive §10.2.2	Subject ABS		
Bivalent	Transitive §10.2.3	Subject, ERG	Object ABS	
	Quasi-transitive §10.2.4	Subject, ABS	Object ABS	
	Semi-transitive §10.2.5	Subject, ABS	Indirect object DAT	
	Conative §10.2.6	Subject, ERG	Indirect object DAT	
Trivalent	Ditransitive §10.2.7	Subject, ERG	Object, ABS	Indirect object DAT/ALL
	Extended transitive §10.2.8	Subject, ERG	Object, ABS	Object ABS

Each case frame is now discussed in turn. Almost all predicates are associated with a single case frame. The main exceptions to this are:

- *Wa-* 'speak' can have a wide variety of argument structures (§A.1.7).
- The inflecting verb *la-* 'shoot' and the complex predicate *karta-pu-* 'spear' are typically transitive but can instead have a conative argument structure (§10.2.6) to indicate an unsuccessful attempt at shooting/spearing.
- Some coverbs form complex predicates that optionally alter the argument structure (§7.3).
- The inflecting verb *ji-* 'burn' has an intransitive use ('x burns/melts') and a transitive use ('x burns/melts y').

10.2.1 Impersonal clauses

There are no impersonal inflecting verbs. Classic examples of impersonal verbs in other languages, if expressed with an inflecting verb, are often intransitive or even transitive in Warlmanpa. For example, 'to rain' is expressed in Warlmanpa using the intransitive verb *wa-* 'to fall', taking *ngappa* 'water' as its subject:

(868)   *Ngappa   wa-nnya.*
        water   fall-PRES
        It's raining.
        (Lit.: Water is falling.)
        H_K01-506A, DG, 38:59 mins

A predicate of 'lightning' is transitive, also taking *ngappa* 'water' as its subject:

(869)   *Ngappa-ngu=rla   talan   ma-nu-rnu.*
        water-ERG=3.OBL   lightning   get-PAST-TWD
        Lightning was coming.
        wrl-20190201, DK, 56:04 mins

Similarly, other weather predicates in the corpus, such as *jawu-wa-* 'cold', all have a subject:

(870)   *Jawu-wa-nnya=lku=rna.*
        cold-fall-PRES=THEN=1SG.S
        I am cold now.
        wrl-20170825-01, SN, 04:08 mins

(871)   *Ngappa   jawu-wa-nu.*
        water   cold-fall-PAST
        The water was cold.
        H_K01-506A, DG, 42:08 mins

Interestingly, the cognate verb in Ngardi *wanti-* 'fall' does occur in impersonal clauses with weather coverbs:

(872)   *Kuru=wanti-nya.*
        dark=FALL-PAST
        It became overcast/fell dark.
        (Ngardi [Ennever 2021])

In Warlmanpa, certain nominals derived into verbs with *-ja-* 'become' may represent possible impersonal verbs. For example, the predicate *yakarlurlaja-* 'become night' in (873) has no clear arguments.

(873)   *Ngayu=ma=rna*   *pa-nyinga*   *ngurra-ka,*   **kala=nga**   **yakarlu-rla-ja-nmi.**

1=TOP=1SG.S   go-PATH   camp-ALL   APPR=DUB   **night-LOC-INCH-FUT**

I'm going home, lest it become night-time.
wrl-20180615-02, DK, 24:42 mins

Hale (1982: 231) presents similar examples in Warlpiri, as in (874), with the caveat that 'it is sometimes suggested by Warlpiri speakers that the "understood" subject is /ngurra/ "camp, home, country", or else /nguru/ "sky, country, area"'.

(874)   *Munga-jarri-mi=lki*   *ka.*

dark-INCHOATIVE-NPAST=NOW   PRES

It is getting dark now.
(Warlpiri [Hale 1982: 231])

However, some semantically similar predicates in Warlpiri have subjects, as in (875), where the demonstrative *yali* is the subject of *wuuly-wa-* 'become dark'.

(875)   *Wurra*   *ka=rla*   **wuuly-wanti**   *yali=jiki.*

momentarily   PRES=3.OBL   **dark-fall.NPAST**   that=STILL

It is still getting dark on him there.
(Lit.: That is still getting dark on him.)
(Warlpiri [Laughren et al. 2022: 1028])

Accepting that meteorological predicates derived by *-ja-* in Warlmanpa are truly avalent would violate two generalisations:[3] the first, that there are no avalent predicates, and the second, that there are very few predicates that allow multiple grammatical frames (as detailed in the introduction to §10.2). That is, there are numerous examples where *-ja-* is clearly intransitive, and

---

3   For English, Stanley (2000) similarly argues that meteorological verbs such as 'to rain' must have a location argument—usually implicit. Conversely, Recanati (2007) argues that meteorological predicates in English can be supplied truth conditions without a narrow location (that is, these predicates are truly 'impersonal').

inflecting verbs tend to only have one grammatical frame, so positing that examples such as (873) are avalent causes a discrepancy.[4] However, further investigation is needed.

10.2.2 Intransitive clauses (ABS)

Monovalent clauses in Warlmanpa are intransitive activities such as *pa-* 'go' or states such as *kiit-wa-* 'be broken'. Table 10.10 catalogues the inflecting verbs with intransitive case frames.

Table 10.9 Marking of the argument in an intransitive clause

	Nominals	Bound Pronoun
Subject	Absolutive	Subject

Table 10.10 Inflecting verbs with intransitive case frames

Verb class	Verb root	Gloss
1	-ja-	'become'
	ji-	'burn'
	ka-	'sit, be'
	pa-	'go'
	pali-	'die'
	parti-	'rise, leave'
	wa-	'speak'
2	waka-	'climb'
3	jutpu-	'run'
	lu-	'cry'
5	wa-	'fall'
	-ya-	'go'

---

[4] A plausible way of avoiding this discrepancy is that -*ja*- is not technically an inflecting verb. It is a derivational suffix (§6.5.2.1), which derives a nominal into a verb, so each verb derived this way represents its own 'inflecting verb'. That is, *yakarlu-rla-ja-* 'become night' is a distinct verb from, for example, *pawarrayi-ja-* 'become finished', so the generalisation is not infringed; if all cases of *yakarlu-rla-ja-* are avalent, all cases of *pawarrayi-ja-* are intransitive, and so on. Of course, the generalisation that there are no avalent predicates in Warlmanpa is still infringed. Furthermore, the generalisation that predicates are only compatible with one argument structure appears to be violated by a small number of other verbs (specifically, *wa-* 'speak' and *ji-* 'burn').

Two of the catalogued verbs in the table, *ji-* 'burn' and *wa-* 'speak', have other case frames. As discussed in §7.4.2, coverbs combining with inflecting verbs form a new predicate, so several intransitive clauses occur with inflecting verbs not catalogued here.

Motion verbs are the most common type of intransitive inflecting verb: six of the 12 intransitive inflecting verbs are motion verbs (and one further, *ka-*, is a posture verb). Examples of intransitive clauses are given in (876)–(881).

(876) *Maliki   jutpu-ngunya.*
      dog   run-PRES
      The dog is running.
      H_K01-505B, DG, 02:39 mins

(877) *Maliki   wa-nu.*
      dog   fall-PAST
      The dog fell.
      H_K01-505B, DG, 02:04 mins

(878) *Tartu=rnalu   ka-nya.*
      many=1PL.EXCL   sit-PRES
      We are sitting.
      N_D01-007836, JJN, 15:46 mins

(879) *Yimpa   Japanangka   jaru-kupa   pa-nangu-rra.*
      this   Japanangka   language-DESIRE   go-PAST-AWAY
      This Japanangka went for language.
      H_K01-506A, DG, 33:10 mins

(880) *Kurtu   kutij   partu-ngu   wa-nja-warnu.*
      child   stand   leave-PAST   fall-INF-RSLT
      The child stood up, having fallen.
      wrl-20190205, DK, 24:43 mins

(881) *Kurtu   lu-ngunya   ngampurlu-kupa.*
      child   cry-PRES   milk-DESIRE
      The child is crying for milk.
      H_K01-505B, DG, 47:47 mins

The verb *wa-* 'speak' is somewhat difficult to characterise, though (882) is most likely an intransitive use. See §A.1.7 for further discussion of this predicate.

(882)   *Karnta*   *wa-nganyu.*
woman   speak-PAST
The woman spoke.
H_K01-505B, DG, 01:33 mins

Intransitive motion predicates with an agent subject regularly co-occur with a path nominal (in the autohyponomous sense, following Kearns 2011: 210–11) or location, as exemplified in (883)–(886).

Path adjunct—Goal:

(883)   *Nyintinya-ka=rna*   *papulu-ka*   *pa-nama.*
2-ALL=1SG.S   house-ALL   go-POT
I'll go to your house.
H_K01-506A, DG, 54:50 mins

Path adjunct—Source:

(884)   *Ali=ma*   *pa-nji-nya*   *kurlarra-ngurlu.*
that=TOP   go-MOT.TWD-PRES   south-ELA
That one's coming from the south.
wrl-20190212-02, DK, 05:46 mins

Path adjunct—Path:

(885)   *Jutpu-ngunya=lu*   *wantayi-rla.*
run-PRES=3PL.S   road-LOC
They're running along the road.
wrl-20170321-02, SN, 20:38 mins

Location adjunct:

(886)   **Mirla**=*nya*=*li*   *ka-nya.*
this.LOC=FOC=1DU.INCL.S   sit-PRES
We two are sitting here.
H_K01-505B, DG, 23:01 mins

These are distinguished from arguments on the basis that the path or location is never cross-referenced by the bound pronoun series, even if it is animate, as shown in (887) and discussed in §10.1.6.

(887) **Nyintinya-ka**=rna(*-**ngu**)   pa-nangu-rnu.
2-ALL=1SG.S(-2SG.NS)   go-PAST-TWD

I came to you.
H_K01-505B, DG, 32:59 mins

10.2.3 Transitive clauses (ERG–ABS)

Transitive clauses require one ergative subject and one absolutive object.

Table 10.11 Marking of arguments in a transitive clause

	Nominal	Bound pronoun
Subject	Ergative	Subject
Object	Absolutive	Object

Inflecting verbs that are subcategorised for a transitive pattern are catalogued in Table 10.12.

Table 10.12 Inflecting verbs that permit transitive patterns

Verb class	Verb root	Gloss
1	ji-	'burn'
2	jama-	'grind'
	-jiya-	'cook'
	karla-	'poke, spear'
	kinja-	'wet'
	kiya-	'throw'
	kuma-	'cut'
	kupa-	'cook'
	la-	'shoot'
	lamarta-	'hold'
	marta-	'have'
	murla-	'copulate'
	nama-	'crush'
	ngarta-	'trim'
	ngaya	'void'*
	nguka-	'drink'
	nyurla-	'knead'
	paka-	'hit, chop'
	pangi-	'scratch, dig'
	piya-	'break, bite, cut'
	winja-	'leave alone'
	yila-	'drip, leak, melt'

Verb class	Verb root	Gloss
3	*kapi-*	'chase'
	ka-	'take'
	nya-	'see'
	pi-	'kill'
4	*nga-*	'eat'
5	*ma-*	'get'

Prototypical examples of transitive clauses are given in (888)–(894).

(888) *Maliki-rlu   kuyu   nga-rninya.*
dog-ERG   meat   eat-PRES
The dog is eating meat.
H_K01-505B, DG, 16:42 mins

(889) *Tartu-ngu=lu-ju   paka-rnu.*
many-ERG=3PL.S-1SG.NS   hit-PAST
Lots of them hit me.
H_K01-506A, DG, 28:42 mins

(890) *Japanangka-rlu   nya-nganya   yawirri.*
Japanangka-ERG   see-PRES   kangaroo
Japanangka sees the kangaroo.
wrl-20180616-01, DK, 05:11 mins

(891) *Ngarrka-ngu   warlu   ma-nnya.*
man-ERG   firewood   get-PRES
The man is getting firewood.
H_K01-505B, DG, 08:11 mins

(892) *Maliki-rlu   piya-rnu   kurtu.*
dog-ERG   bite-PAST   child
The dog bit the child.
wrl-20190201, DK, 06:31 mins

(893) *Ngarrka-ngu=lu-nyanu   karta-pu-ngu.*
man-ERG=3PL.S-RR   spear-act_on-PAST
The men speared each other.
H_K01-505B, DG, 37:53 mins

(894) *Jilyi   tuyu   ka-nya,   wangapa-rlu   ka-nganya   jilyi.*
dust   waft   be-PRES   wind-ERG   carry-PRES   dust
The dust is wafting, the wind is blowing the dust.
H_K01-505B, DG, 34:36 mins

Transitive clauses can have an instrument also marked for ergative, as in (895), and see §4.1.3 for further discussion.

(895) *Kuyu=rna   kuma-nmi   **japirru-rlu.***
meat=1SG.S   cut-FUT   **knife-ERG**
I'll cut the meat **with a knife**.
H_K01-505B, DG, 42:20 mins

Transitive clauses may have numerous types of modifiers, including spatial, as in (896) and (897), temporal, as in (898), and benefactives, as in (899).

(896) *Yapa=nya   witta   ka-ngu   hospital-   ngula   pirnti-   wa-nu.*
                                      ka   *ngurlu*
person=FOC   small   take-PAST hospital-   REL   tree-ELA   fall-PAST
                                      ALL
He took the child who had fallen out of the tree to hospital.
N_D02-007842, BN, 45:02 mins

(897) *Kankarlarra-ngurlu=lu   kiya-rnu-rnu   karrarlarla.*
above-ELA=3PLS   throw-PAST-TWD   Spear
They threw their spears from above.
wrl-20190213-01, DK, 34:26 mins

(898) *ka-nyi-nya=rna-ngu   jawarti.*
take-MOT.TWD-PRES=1SG.S-2SG.NS   tomorrow
I'll take you tomorrow.
wrl-20180531-02, DF, 15:54 mins

(899) *Yarnunju=rla   kurtu-ku   kupa-nnya.*
food=3.OBL   child-DAT   cook-PRES
He's cooking food for the child.
wrl-20190205, DK, 14:22 mins

10.2.4 Quasi-transitive clauses (ABS–ABS)

There are two predicates that allow a quasi-transitive argument structure, both of which also allow another structure. The marking patterns of quasi-transitive arguments are given in Table 10.13.

Table 10.13 Marking of quasi-transitive arguments

	Nominal	Bound pronoun
Subject	Absolutive	Subject
Object[5]	Absolutive	Object

First is *wa-* 'speak', in which there is a subject, who is speaking, and an object denoting something about their manner of speaking, such as the language being spoken, as in (900), or the quality of their speech, as in (901) and (902). Both arguments take an absolutive case.

(900)   *Tartu=lu*   *wa-nganya*   *Warlmanpa.*
        many=3PL.S   speak-PRES   Warlmanpa
        Lots [of them] speak Warlmanpa.
        H_K01-505B, DG, 43:25 mins

(901)   *Witta=rna*   *wa-nganya*   *jaru.*
        little=1SG.S   speak-PRES   language
        I speak a little bit of language.[6]
        wrl-20190123, SN, 23:15 mins

(902)   *Wa-nganya=lu*   *Warlmanpa*   *Warumungu,*   *jintangayi.*[7]
        speak-PRES=3PL.S   Warlmanpa   Warumungu   Same
        Warlmanpa and Warumungu speak the same [language].
        N_D02-007841, BN, 13:28 mins

Second, the copula use of *ka-* 'be' selects a quasi-transitive clause (see §11.2 for discussion of *ka-* 'be, sit'), as in (903), where the arguments of *ka-* are the second-person singular (only cross-referenced by the bound pronouns) and *witta* 'small'.

---

5   These are often labelled 'cognate objects' (Austin 1982). The term 'quasi-transitive' to refer to this argument-marking structure follows Ennever (2021).

6   I analyse *witta* here as a secondary predicate, taking *jaru* 'message/language' as its argument, rather than *witta* being an argument of the inflecting verb *wa-* 'speak'—that is, 'I speak language and that language is little'.

7   *Jintangayi* may be analysed as *jinta-nga=yi* 'one-LOC=STILL'.

(903) Ngayu=rna   purtu-ka-nya   ngula=n   witta=wiyi   ka-ngu-rra.
      1=1SG.S   remember-be-   REL=2SG.S   small=FIRST   be-PAST-IMPF
                   PRES
      I remember when you were a child.
      N_D02-007842, BN, 33:57 mins

(904) Ali=nya   wangani   malamarri   ka-nya.
      that=FOC   dog   hunter   be-PRES
      That dog is a hunter.
      wrl-20200221, DK, 11:05 mins

Complex predicates such as *purtu-ka-* 'listen' are quasi-transitive, as evidenced by the absolutive subject in (905) and the absolutive object in (906). However, for other speakers, the subject of *purtu-ka-* is marked with ergative case.

(905) Lanku=rna   ka-nya   kala=ji   yawirri   purtu-ka-mi.
      quiet=1SG.S   be-PRES   APPR=1SG.NS   kangaroo   listen-BE-FUT
      I'm being quiet, lest the kangaroo hear me.
      wrl-20180608-01, JK, 20:49 mins

(906) Karnta=rna   purtu-ka-ngu   wa-nganja-ka.
      woman=1SG.S   listen-be-PAST   speak-INF-ALL
      I'm listening to the woman speaking.
      H_K01-505B, DG, 09:47 mins

10.2.5 Semi-transitive clauses (ABS–DAT)

Semi-transitive argument marking is given in Table 10.14.

Table 10.14 Marking of semi-transitive arguments

	Nominal	Bound pronoun
Subject	Absolutive	Subject
Indirect object	Dative	Oblique

Predicates that permit a semi-transitive frame are rare. Notably, it seems all predicates that allow this case frame also allow a simple intransitive frame. The only inflecting verb that allows a semi-transitive without any coverbs is *wa-* 'speak':

(907) *Yumpa=ju   wa-nganya   **ngayu-ku.***
this=1SG.NS   speak-PRES   **1-DAT**
This one is speaking to me.
H_K01-506A, DG, 01:45 mins

Some nominals have a semi-transitive frame, such as *ngampurr* 'want' and *partakurru* 'good':

(908) *Ngayu=ma=rna   **ngampurr,   ngappa-ku   nguka-nja-ku.***
1=TOP=1SG.S   **desire   water-DAT   drink-DAT-INF**
I want to drink water.
wrl-20191207-01, DK, 07:54 mins

(909) *Yimpa=nya   karrarlarla   **partakurru   wirlinyi-ku.***
this=FOC   spear   **good   hunting-DAT**
This spear is good for hunting.
wrl-20200220, DK, 40:28 mins

Some complex predicates require a semi-transitive frame. For example, *walku-ka-* 'be lacking' requires a dative argument that refers to the entity or attribute that the subject lacks:

(910) *Walku=rna   ka-nya   **kuyu-ku,**   nga-rninja-jila.*
NEG-1SG.S   be-PRES   **meat-DAT**   eat-INF-PRIV
I'm without food [lit.: I am nothing for meat], I can't eat.
H_K01-506B, DG, 06:46 mins

The complex predicate *wila-ka-* 'play' also allows a dative argument that signals an animate theme of playing—that is, the person with whom the subject is playing. This is not a semantically expected use of the dative case and it is registered in the bound pronouns, so I analyse this as a permissible alternative case frame of the verb rather than an adjunct.

(911) *Kurtu   purt-pu-ka   nga=rla=nga   pulka-ku   wila-ka-ma.*
child   send-act_on-IMP   POST=3.OBL=DUB   old_man-DAT   play-be-POT
Send the child so that she might play with the old man.
H_K01-505B, DG, 41:27 mins

(912) *Kurtu-ja=ju-pala*   *wila-ka-nya.*
       child-DUAL=1SG.NS-3DU.S   play-be-PRES

   The two kids are playing with me.
   H_K01-505B, DG, 41:16 mins

However, there are numerous examples where *wila-ka-* does not require a dative argument and it is a simple intransitive predicate (so *wila-ka-* is treated as a predicate that allows two argument structures: simple intransitive and semi-transitive).

(913) *Yarnunju=rla*   *kurtu-ku*   *kupa-nya*   *ngula*   *wila-ka-nya.*
       food=3.OBL   child-DAT   cook-PRES   REL   play-be-PRES

   He's cooking vegetables for the child who is playing.
   wrl-20190205, DK, 14:40 mins

10.2.6 Conative (ERG–DAT)

There is only one inflecting verb that requires a conative frame: *wayi-ka* 'to search'. There are some inflecting verbs that seem to allow a conative frame in some circumstances. The frame is given in Table 10.15 and examples of *wayi-* are given in (914) and (915).

Table 10.15 Marking of conative arguments

	Nominal	Bound pronoun
Subject	Ergative	Subject
Indirect object	Dative	Oblique

(914) *Maliki-rlu=rla*   *kuyu-ku*   *wayi-nnya.*
       dog-ERG=3.OBL   meat-DAT   search-PRES

   The dog is searching for meat.
   H_K01-505B, DG, 07:51 mins

(915) *Karnta-ngu=rla*   *ngappa-ku*   *wayi-nnya.*
       woman-ERG=3.OBL   water-DAT   search-PRES

   The woman is searching for water.
   H_K01-505B, DG, 08:05 mins

These dative arguments differ semantically from the 'benefactive' datives discussed in §10.2.1 (which I analyse as adjuncts), as the indirect object of these predicates does not benefit from the state of affairs referred to and is semantically more akin to a theme, as in a canonical transitive clause. The dative marking of the theme likely contrasts with the (canonical) absolutive marking of the theme in that the dative-marked theme is not inherently affected by the agent, whereas in all the transitive predicates, the theme is inherently affected in some way.

Relating to this, some verbs may allow their object to be dative marked, to indicate an attempted action. In this construction, the indirect object is less affected, as the agent failed to successfully carry out the event. Compare (916), which has a typical absolutive argument to indicate the referent was affected, with (917), where the use of the dative indicates the event was attempted but was unsuccessful; the same type of contrast is shown between (918) and (919). This alternation is particularly salient for verbs of impact.

(916) *Jarrawarti=rna   karta   pu-ngu   Japanangka.*
leg=1SG.S   spear   act_on-PAST   Japanangka
I speared Japanangka's leg [successfully].
N_D02-007842, BN, 15:48 mins

(917) *Jarrawarti-**ku**=rna-**rla**   karta   pu-ngu   Japanangka-**ku**.*
leg-DAT=1SG.S-DAT   spear   act_on-PAST   Japanangka-DAT
I speared at Japanangka's leg [unsuccessfully].
N_D02-007842, BN, 15:19 mins

(918) *Karnta-ngu   la-rnu   yawirri.*
woman-ERG   shoot-PAST   kangaroo
The woman shot the kangaroo [successfully].
wrl-20190201, DK, 01:13 mins

(919) *Karnta-ngu=**rla**   la-rnu   yawirri-**ku**.*
woman-ERG=3.OBL   shoot-PAST   kangaroo-DAT
The woman shot at the kangaroo [unsuccessfully].
wrl-20190201, DK, 02:02 mins

All Ngumpin-Yapa languages have this kind of alternation (Ennever 2021; Hudson 1978: 20; Laughren 2017b: 955; Meakins and McConvell 2021; Meakins and Nordlinger 2014: 371; Senge 2015; Tsunoda 1981a), which is usually restricted to verbs of perception or force (and not necessarily extending to the full set). In Warlpiri, for verbs of impact, the dative bound pronoun clitic is doubled (sequences of the double dative are replaced with *-rla-jinta* in Warlpiri), as exemplified in (920). This clitic doubling is not evident in Warlmanpa.

(920) *Ngarrka-ngku   ka=**rla-jinta**   marlu-ku   luwa-rni.*
      man-ERG   IMPF=3S.DAT-3S.DAT   kangaroo-DAT   shoot-NPST
      The man is shooting at the kangaroo.
      (Warlpiri [Hale et al. 2015: 1690])

Finally, *wa-* 'speak' allows this argument structure, as in (921) (and see §A.1.7 for further examples), where the subject *alirlunya ngarrkangu* 'that man' is marked with ergative case and the indirect object is realised with the non-subject bound pronoun series.

(921) *Ali-rlu=nya   ngarrka-ngu   wa-nganyu=ju   'yiwirti   paka-ka'.*
      that-ERG=FOC   man-ERG   speak-PRES=1SG.NS   tree   hit-IMP
      That man told me 'cut the tree'.
      wrl-20190201, DK, 34:22 mins

10.2.7 Ditransitive clauses (ERG–ABS–DAT)

Canonical trivalent predicates in Warlmanpa have an ergative-marked subject, an absolutive object and a dative indirect object. There is one predicate, *ya-* 'put, place', which instead has an allative indirect object.

Table 10.16 Marking of ditransitive arguments

	Nominals	**Bound pronouns**
Subject	Ergative	Subject
Object	Absolutive	Object
Indirect object	Dative/allative	Oblique

The only inflecting verb that allows this argument structure is *yi-* 'give', as exemplified in (922)–(924).

(922) *Ali-ngu=nya   ngarrka-ngu   kuyu=rla   yu-ngu   kurtu-ku.*
      that-ERG=FOC   man-ERG   meat=3.OBL   give-PAST   child-DAT
      The man gave meat to the child.
      wrl-20190211-02, DK, 09:06 mins

(923) | Ali-ngu=nya=rla | wayi-nnya | nyaninya-ku | wangani-ku | nga=rla
that-ERG=FOC=3.OBL | search-PRES | 3.GEN-DAT | dog-DAT | POST=3.OBL

yi-nyi | yarnunju.
give-FUT | food

That one's looking for his dog so that he can give food to it.
wrl-20190131-02, DK, 11:16 mins

(924) | Karnta-ngu=ju | ngayu-ku | yu-ngu.
woman-ERG=1SG.NS | 1-DAT | give-PAST

The woman gave it to me.
N_D02-007841, BN, 24:01 mins

The complex predicate *purt-pi* 'send' also has a ditransitive frame, as in (925), as evidenced by the ability of the dative-marked argument to be cross-referenced by the bound pronouns.

(925) | Ngayu=ma=rna-rla | purt-pu-nga | kurtu | nyaninya-ku
1=TOP=1SG.S-3.OBL | send-act_on-PAST.AWAY | child | 3.GEN-DAT

ngartina-ku.
mother-DAT

I sent the child to her mother.
wrl-20190205, DK, 44:22 mins

It is much more frequent for the indirect object argument of *purt-pu* to be replaced with a non-finite clause (still dative marked), as in (926)–(928), which may suggest the dative phrase is a modifier rather than an argument, however, it is worth noting there are no cases of *purt-pu* in the corpus without an overt dative phrase expressing the recipient/purpose of the sending event.[8]

---

8 Alternatively, these dative-marked phrases may be modifiers, if the predicate *purt-pu-* is treated as allowing a transitive frame 'SUBJ causes OBJ to move'. This is evidenced by the dative-marked phrase not denoting a recipient (as in the ditransitive examples above); rather, they denote a purpose.

(926) Ngayu=rna   purt-pu-ngu   wangani [wirlinyi-ku   pa-nja-ku].
       1=1SG.S   send-act_on-PAST   dog   hunting-DAT   go-INF-DAT
       I sent the dog to go hunting.
       wrl-20190211-02, DK, 10:51 mins

(927) Purt-pu-ngu=rna   Jinarinji-ka   ngayinya   ngalapi
       send-act_on-PAST=1SG.S   Jinarinji-ALL   1.GEN   son
       [puliki-ku   ka-nja-ku   ngurrurla-ku].
       bull-DAT   carry-INF-DAT   return-DAT
       I sent my son to Jinarinji to bring back a bull.
       N_D02-009887, DG, 07:10 mins

(928) Jaru=ju   purt-pu-ngu-rnu   pulka-ngu   pa-nja-ku
       message=1SG.NS   send-act_on-PAST-TWD   old_man-ERG   go-INF-DAT
       nya-nja-ku.
       see-INF-DAT
       The old man told me to come see him.
       (Lit.: The old man sent me language to come see him.)
       N_D02-009887, DG, 05:11 mins

There is one known predicate that marks its indirect object with allative rather than dative case: *ya-* 'put, place', as exemplified in (929)–(931).

(929) Ngarrka-ngu   karli   ya-nnya   yulu-ka.
       man-ERG   boomerang   put-PRES   ground-ALL
       The man is putting a boomerang on the ground.
       H_K01-505B, DG, 40:43 mins

(930) Wanji-ka=npala   ya-rnu?
       where-ALL=2DU.S   put-PAST
       Where did you two put it?
       H_K06-004555, LOF, 51:51 mins

(931) Yali=nya-rna-ngu   pirntija   ya-rnu   nyuntunya-ka.
       that=FOC=1SG.S-2SG.NS   beside   put-PAST   2GEN.ALL
       I put that beside you.
       N_D02-007841, BN, 09:07 mins

10.2.8 Extended transitive (ERG–ABS–ABS)

Extended transitive clauses have an ergative subject and two absolutive objects that are in some kind of equivalent state. For all cases in the corpus, the registration of grammatical relations in the bound pronouns is unclear or irrelevant, as all the arguments are non-sentient so would not be expected to be cross-referenced in the bound pronouns. For most cases, it is the latter: the referents would not be expected to be marked by the bound pronouns, as they are generics ([932] and [933]). In one case, (934), one of the objects is marked, however, it is the first-person singular non-subject, which could be either the object or the dative series, and there is no overt free pronoun to dispel the ambiguity. This is summarised in Table 10.17.

Table 10.17 Marking of extended transitive arguments

	Nominal	Bound pronoun
Subject	Ergative	Subject
Object	Absolutive	?
Object	Absolutive	?

(932) *Yali-ngu=lu*   *nga-nnya*   *warlu,*   *Warnmanpa-rlu*   *nga-nnya.*
      that-ERG=3PL.S   call-PRES   fire   Warlmanpa-ERG   call-PRES
      They call it *warlu*, those Warlmanpa people do.
      H_K06-004548: 09, JW, 01:25 mins

(933) *Karntirri=rnalu*   *nga-nnya*   *yarnunju,*   *karntirri=rnalu*
      veg_food=1PL.EXCL.S   call-PRES   veg_food   veg_food=1PL.EXCL.S
      nga-nnya   *Warlmanpa-rlu.*
      call-PRES   Warlmanpa-ERG
      We call *yarnunju* '*karntirri*', we Warlmanpa we call it '*karntirri*'.
      H_K01-505B, DG, 31:02 mins

Alternatively, the same verb can allow a non-finite dative-marked purpose clause to denote what was told, as in (934).

(934) *Ngarrka-ngu=ju*   *nga-rnu*   [*muka=nya*   *ya-nja-ku*].
      man-ERG=1SG.NS   call-PAST   this.ALL=FOC   put-INF-DAT
      The man told me [to put it there].
      H_K01-505B, DG, 25:12 mins

In some Ngumpin-Yapa languages, 'give' verbs allow an extended transitive case frame (that is, ERG–ABS–ABS, varying in the label used to refer to the structure) and, in these cases, the secondary object (that is, the recipient of the 'give' event) is cross-referenced by the bound pronouns (Meakins and Nordlinger 2014: 376–77). However, there are no tokens of *yi-* 'give' with this case frame in Warlmanpa.

11
Syntax of simple clauses

This chapter primarily discusses the syntax of Warlmanpa matrix clauses. It is organised as follows. The core elements of clauses are introduced in §11.1—specifically, free word order (§11.1.1), discontinuous expressions (§11.1.2), null anaphora (§11.1.3) and whether there is evidence to support an analysis of noun phrases (§11.1.4).

The remainder of the chapter describes types of syntactic constructions. Copula clauses are discussed in §11.2, followed by verbless clauses (§11.3), which include equative clauses (§11.3.1), identification clauses (§11.3.2) and ascriptive clauses (§11.3.3). Interrogative clauses are discussed in §11.4, with content questions in §11.4.1 and polar questions in §11.4.2. Negation is discussed in §11.5, with different clause types requiring different strategies for negation: negative declarative clauses are analysed in §11.5.1 and negative imperative clauses in §11.5.2. After this, an analysis of secondary predication is presented—that is, nominal predicates that share an argument with the matrix verb of the clause (§11.6). Their semantics are presented in §11.6.1, followed by a discussion of the distinction (if any) to be found between secondary predicates and other modifying nominals (§11.6.2). Finally, the chapter concludes with a discussion of dislocated constituents, in §11.7.

11.1 Phrase structure and non-configurationality

Like many Australian languages, Warlmanpa is 'non-configurational', exhibiting the following syntactic patterns (following the criteria used by Hale [1983] for Warlpiri):

i. free word order (§11.1.1)
ii. discontinuous expressions (§11.1.2)
iii. null anaphora (§11.1.3).

The status of noun phrases is also discussed in this section (§11.1.4), with regards to non-configurationality.

11.1.1 Clausal constituent order

This section presents a preliminary analysis of the order of the subject, verb and object in simple declarative clauses. The results of this section are preliminary for several reasons. First, it is a rather small sample: three narratives were coded for and several clauses were excluded, specifically any with discontinuous phrases, as well as subordinate clauses (subordinate clauses in other languages have been shown to have different word-order tendencies—for example, Panyjima [Dench 1991]). Thus, only 52 clauses in all were coded. Second, arguments are extremely prone to null anaphora, so it is rare to have a clause in which the subject and object both surface (and, in some cases, neither one surfaces), particularly in narratives, as the bound pronouns carry the functional load of reference tracking, rather than nominals.

Some generalisations can be made from this small dataset. First, the overall tendency is for the subject to precede the verb and object: the subject precedes the verb in 91 per cent of the coded clauses and the subject precedes the object in 86 per cent of coded clauses (although this latter statistic is based on a count of just seven clauses in which both the subject and the object were overt). The relative ordering between the object and the verb is evenly split. Interestingly, the same is not true of adjuncts of the main predicate, especially locational modifiers. If present, locational modifiers occurred in clause-final position in 89 per cent of the tokens. In sum, the tendency for word order in basic clauses in Warlmanpa is S-V-O-L. While

I have included this brief analysis for comprehensiveness, it is extremely likely this is representative of an information structure–based word order (this analysis is briefly pursued in §5.2).

Vollmer (2021) analysed word-order tendencies in Warlpiri, which generally align with the Warlmanpa word-order tendencies suggested above. In the clauses analysed by Vollmer, SVO is the predominant word order, followed by SOV. These word orders could (preliminarily) be correlated to information structure—for example, a given object is more likely to occur in VO order than OV.

11.1.2 Discontinuous expressions

Discontinuous expressions involve multiple nominals that are coreferential but are not adjacent. Examples are given in (935)–(938). Note that in each case given, one nominal (or set of nominals) is in some position in the clause and the discontinuous nominal is on the right periphery of the clause; a similar effect has been noted for Kunbarlang (Kapitonov 2019: 90–91), although further investigation of the Warlmanpa corpus would reveal how strong a tendency this is. Note that none of these examples is prosodically detached from the rest of the clause, which would be indicative of an afterthought (§11.7.2). These are generally considered a separate phenomenon from discontinuous expressions (Schultze-Berndt and Simard 2012: 1026). I have not attempted to quantify the extent to which nominal expressions can be discontinuous, largely due to the extent of null anaphora and other possible biasing effects (such as whether the utterance is prompted). Observationally, though, discontinuous expressions are rare.

(935) *Nga=rna-ngu* **yiwirti-rlu** *karta-pi-nyi* **ngayinya-kurla-rlu**
POST=1SG.S-2SG.NS **stick-ERG** spear-act_on-FUT **1GEN-GEN-ERG**
kirtana-kurla-rlu.
father-GEN-ERG
I will spear you **with my father's spear**.
H_K01-506A, DG, 49:56 mins

(936) **Ngarrka,** **tartu** **yumpa**=**nya**=rnalu pa-nnya **kartji.**
man many this=FOC=1PL.S.EXCL go-PRES warrior
We warrior mob are going.
H_K01-506A, DG, 53:06 mins

(937) **Wawirri**=rna-palangu nya-ngu **jirrama,** wuruly-jutpu-ngu=pala.
kangaroo=1SG.S-3DU.NS see-PAST two conceal-run-PAST=3DU.S
I saw two kangaroos, they ran out of sight.
H_K01-506A, DG, 55:20 mins

(938) **Yapa** wa-nganya **witta.**
person speak-PRES small
A child is speaking.
H_K01-505B, DG, 00:49 mins

11.1.3 Null anaphora

Null anaphora can be readily demonstrated by minimal clauses, which consist of a predicate and bound pronouns. Bound pronouns themselves can be formally null if they are cross-referencing non-oblique third-person arguments, as in (939), which comprises an inflecting verb, *wanganya* 'speaking', and a third-person-singular bound pronoun, which has no overt form.

(939) Wa-nganya=∅.
speak-PRES=3SG.S
He's speaking.
H_K01-506A, DG, 44:31 mins

Further examples of minimal clauses consisting of a predicate and bound pronouns are given in (940)–(942).

(940) Nya-nyi=rna-ngu.
see-FUT=1SG.S-2SG.NS
I will see you.
H_K01-506A, DG, 44:34 mins

(941) *Lijinpa=n.*
sick=2SG.S
Are you sick?
H_K01-506A, DG, 46:14 mins

(942) *Pa-nangu-rnu=rna-ngu.*
go-PAST-TWD=1SG.S-2SG.NS
I came to you.
H_K01-505B, DG, 34:10 mins

11.1.4 Noun phrases

The status of noun (or nominal) phrases (NPs) in Australian languages has been a topic of great interest due to the varying evidence (and extent) across languages (for an overview, see Nordlinger 2014: 237–41). Some languages are analysed as entirely lacking NPs (Heath 1978, 1984; Blake 1983). This section discusses evidence for noun phrases in Warlmanpa, largely based on the typology of Louagie and Verstraete (2016): diagnostic slots (§11.1.4.1), word order (§11.1.4.2) and locus of case marking (§11.1.4.3). A fourth parameter, contiguity, was discussed in §11.1.2, which showed that nominal expressions can be discontinuous. The section concludes with a summary of the evidence for NPs, based on these criteria (§11.1.4.4). Another potential criterion for analysing NPs is intonation (Merlan 1994: 226; Schultze-Berndt 2000: 43; Schultze-Berndt and Simard 2012), however, I have not investigated prosody in Warlmanpa to a sufficient extent to utilise this criterion.

11.1.4.1 Diagnostic slots

The best syntactic evidence for noun phrases in Warlmanpa comes from the possibility for the auxiliary to follow the nominal expression, rather than intervene (that is, the auxiliary acts as a diagnostic slot). This is crucial evidence for NPs in analyses of Warlpiri (Hale 1983; Simpson 1991). As noted in §5.2, the auxiliary complex is typically found following the first constituent in the clause and, in (943)–(948), the auxiliary occurs following two nominal words, which is the key evidence that the two nominals form a syntactic constituent. However, as noted in Louagie and Verstraete (2016: 32), auxiliary placement provides evidence for NPs only in this position.

(943) [Ngarrka-ngu   tartu-ngu]$_{NP?}$=lpangu-lu   nya-nganya   ngayu.
      man-ERG   many-ERG=1PL.INCL.   see-PRES   1
                        NS-3PL.S

Lots of men are looking at us.
H_K01-505B, DG, 50:41 mins

(944) [Ngarrka   jinta]$_{NP?}$=rnalu   nya-nganga   jirrima-jinta-rlu.
      man   one=1PL.EXCL.S   see-PRES   two-one-ERG

We three are looking at one man.
H_K01-505B, DG, 54:20 mins

(945) [Ali-ngu=nya   karnta-   wayi-nnya   nyaninya-ku   wangani-ki.
                        ngu]$_{NP?}$=rla
      that-ERG=FOC   woman-   search-PRES   3GEN-DAT   dog-DAT
                        ERG=3.OBL

That woman is searching for her dog.
wrl-20190131-02, DK, 07:34 mins

(946) [Karli   yumpa]$_{NP?}$=rna-ngu   yi-nyi.
      boomerang   this=1SG.S-2SG.NS   give-FUT

I'll give you this boomerang.
H_K01-505B, DG, 28:34 mins

(947) [Karli-ngu   murlu]$_{NP?}$ nga=rna-ngu   la-nmi.
      boomerang-ERG   this.ERG   POST=1SG.S-2SG.NS   shoot-FUT

I'll hit you with this boomerang.
H_K01-505B, DG, 29:06 mins

(948) [Ngayinya-jarra   wiri-jarra   Cornelius   kapi   Cynthia]$_{NP?}$=pala
      1GEN-DU   big-DU   Cornelius   CONJ   Cynthia=3DU.S
      ka-ngu-rra   Alekarengei-rla.
      sit-PAST-IMPF   Alekarenge-LOC

My eldest son and eldest daughter were still living in Alekarenge.
wrl-20190208, DK, 24:02 mins

The auxiliary can also occur following a word-level constituent, even when two nominals would belong to an NP, as in (949). It is unclear what conditions the variation.

(949)   ***Ngarrka**=rla*   ***ali**=nya*   *wa-nganya*   *nyaninya-ku*   *ngartina-ku.*
       man=3.OBL   **that**=FOC   speak-PRES   3GEN-DAT   mother-DAT
       That man is speaking to his mother.
       wrl-20190131-02, DK, 03:47 mins

11.1.4.2 Word order

Within a contiguous nominal expression, there is no clear preference for the ordering of internal constituents. For lack of better criteria at this point of analysis, I take the 'head' nominal to be whichever nominal has the most specific intension,[1] and all other nominals are modifiers of this head. There are no clear cases where a modifier of the head NP is itself being modified. Assuming this definition, the head, modifier(s) and demonstrative can occur in any order. The only order not found is a modifier preceding a demonstrative. Examples (950)–(954) demonstrate: 1) the variety of permissible constituent ordering, and 2) that nominal expressions tend to be contiguous.

Head—Modifier:

(950)   ***Ngarrka-ngu**=ju*   ***wiri-ngu***   *nya-ngu.*
       man-ERG=1SG.NS   **big**-ERG   see-PAST
       The **big man** saw me.
       H_K01-506A, DG, 52:30 mins

Demonstrative—Head—Modifier:[2]

(951)   ***Yimpa**=ma*   ***kurtu***   ***witta***   *ngula*   *palka-ja-ngu.*
       this=TOP   **child**   **small**   REL   apparent-INCH-PAST
       This is the small child who was born.
       wrl-20170321-02, SN, 00:09 secs

---

1   The notion of the 'head' of an NP in Warlmanpa is problematic. Depending on context, any nominal could feasibly be the head and there is no *a priori* reason to select one over another and no clear grammatical process that would distinguish a head nominal. Elsewhere in this grammar, I avoid presupposing which nominal is the head of an 'NP'; the orderings presented here (and their labels) are merely presented for the sake of exemplification. I argue against noun phrases in §11.1.4.4 and, relatedly, discuss the status of nominals more generally in §11.6.3. I follow Bach (2017) in treating demonstratives as not having encoded reference; rather, demonstratives serve to constrain intension. As such, under this conjectural analysis of 'NPs' or 'nominal expressions', a demonstrative will always have the least-specific intension and therefore cannot be the head of an 'NP' unless there are no other candidates.

2   Note that in this clause the demonstrative *yimpama* seems to be predicative, so this sequence might not reflect an NP. There are no other known tokens of demonstrative-head-modifier in the corpus.

Head—Demonstrative—Modifier:

(952)   ***Kurtu   yarri   witta,***   *warungka*   *ka-nya.*
         child   that   small   crazy   be-PRES
         That small child, she's crazy.
         H_K01-506A, DG, 31:51 mins

Modifier—Head:

(953)   ***Witta   yapa***   *kari*   *jitpi-nyi*   *nga=nga*   *wa-nma.*
         small   person   COND   run-FUT   POST=DUB   fall-POT
         If the **child** [lit.: **small person**] runs, she might fall.
         H_K01-505B, DG, 14:53 mins

(954)   *La-karla   jala   **palka-parna-rlu=ma   lamanpa-parna-rlu.***
         shoot-IRR   now   present-PROP-ERG=TOP   gun-PROP-ERG
         He could shoot it, **had he a gun.**
         wrl-20190205, DK, 01:00:40 hrs

As discussed in §11.1.2, nominal expressions can be discontinuous, with other constituents intervening. An example is given in (955), where there is an inflecting verb and the auxiliary complex between the two constituents of the nominal expression (see also §11.1.2).

(955)   ***Karli****=ju*   *yu-ngka*   ***yarri****=nya*   *ngula=n*   *taka-ngu*
         boomerang=1SG.NS   give-IMP   that=FOC   REL=2SG.S   hand-ERG
         marta-nnya.
         hold-PRES
         Give me **that boomerang** that you're holding with your hand.
         H_K01-505B, DG, 28:43 mins

Notably, the head-initial orderings presented above do not have explicit information structure markers (such as =*nya* 'focus' or =*ma* 'topic'), yet the non-head-initial instances both have =*ma* and the discontinuous expression involves a focus marker, =*nya* 'focus', on the demonstrative. This suggests that the 'default' ordering may be head-modifier but may have different word orders if the modifier is somehow prominent in the information structure (Reinöhl [2020] suggests that a reversal of default ordering is indeed cross-linguistically associated with information structure). However, the interrelation between word order and information structure requires significantly more research (see §5.3.6 for a preliminary analysis).

Further investigation may reveal differences based on the type of modifier. For example, in Kuuk Thaayorre, quantifiers occur after the head nominal (Gaby 2017: 195), with some other types of intervening constituents. An inspection of *jinta* 'one' and *jirrima* 'two' in Warlmanpa yields different findings: these nominals can precede or follow a head nominal.

11.1.4.3 Locus of case marking

In Warlpiri, further evidence for noun phrases comes from continuous NPs requiring case marking only on the final constituent of the phrase (Simpson 1991: 266), as in (956), where *maliki wiringki* forms an NP meaning 'big dog' and, as such, only the final constituent, *wiri*, needs to be marked for ergative.

(956) [**Maliki wiri-ngki**]$_{NP}$ *ka=ju* *(ngaju)* *wajilipi-nyi.*
dog big-ERG PRES=1SG.NS (1SG) chase-NPAST
A/the big dog is chasing me.
(Warlpiri [adapted from Bittner and Hale 1995: 84])

In Warlmanpa, this strategy is not available and each constituent must always be marked for case. As such, case marking does not provide evidence for an NP in Warlmanpa—quite distinct from Warlpiri.

11.1.4.4 Summary of evidence for NPs

Table 11.1 presents a summary of the criteria used by Louagie and Verstraete (2016) as evidence for NPs as they apply to Warlmanpa.

Table 11.1 Extent of evidence for noun phrases based on four parameters from Louagie and Verstraete (2016)

Parameter		Extent of evidence for NP
External parameters	Locus of case marking	Word marking (that is, obligatory case on each word) provides **no evidence for NPs**.
	Diagnostic slots	The auxiliary position provides **some evidence for NPs**.
Internal parameters	Contiguity	Nominal expressions tend to occur together but do not do so obligatorily, providing **some evidence for NPs**.
	Word order	Nominal expressions have no apparent internal ordering, providing **no evidence for NPs**.

The strongest evidence for nominal expressions forming a single syntactic constituent is the auxiliary placement, which occurs in the 'second position' (see §5.2), though even this is tentative; there are exceptions in which nominal expressions have the auxiliary intervening between them, and the auxiliary exhibits variation, occurring in other positions in the clause, so it is not *strictly* a 'second position' phenomenon (§5.3.6). The preference for nominal expressions to occur in a contiguous manner provides some evidence for NPs, although given there are numerous counterexamples presented in §11.1.2, the contiguity of nominal expressions is likely related to processing or information-structured constraints rather than syntactic constraints. The word order of nominal expressions and case-marking patterns in Warlmanpa provide no evidence for NPs. Another criterion used for other languages is whether nominals can occur independently: in languages without NPs, each nominal should be able to occur independently, whereas, in languages with NPs, there are expected to be some restrictions on the types of nominals that can occur independently. For example, in Kayardild, one criterion used for NPs is that semantic adjectives such as *jungarra* 'big' can only occur modifying another nominal (Evans 1995: 233–34). However, this is not the case in Warlmanpa, in which any nominal can be the only word in a nominal expression, including *wiri* 'big'.

Based on the sparsity of the evidence, I do not analyse NPs in this grammar. Instead, I analyse 'NP construal' (Louagie and Verstraete 2016; Louagie 2019), which is a syntactic process in which contiguous nominal expressions form a syntactic constituent. Crucially, this syntactic process operates optionally (though the factors conditioning whether it operates are unclear). The analysis of NP construal allows an explanation of why the auxiliary may occur after the first word in a clause or after a contiguous nominal expression. In the case of the former, NP construal has not taken place and, in the case of the latter, NP construal has taken place. To exemplify, consider (957) and (958). Both sentences have two co-referring nominals at the start of the clause, so feasibly, NP construal may or may not operate in either clause. In (957), NP construal has not taken place, as evidenced by the auxiliary complex attaching to the first word. In (958), NP construal has taken place, as evidenced by the auxiliary complex attaching to the right edge of the syntactic constituent (in this case, after the first two words).

No NP construal—Auxiliary complex attaches to first constituent (which is a word):

(957) **Ngayinya**=*ju*   **nguru,**   *yimpa*=*ma.*
       1GEN=1SG.NS   **country**   this=TOP
       My country, this one.
       wrl-20170321-02, SN, 08:42 mins

NP construal—Auxiliary complex attaches to first constituent (which is an NP):

(958) *[Ngarrka   jinta]*=*rnalu*   *nyanganga*   *jirrima-jinta-rlu.*
       man   one=1PL.EXCL.S   see-PRES   two-one-ERG
       We three see one man.
       H_K01-505B, DG, 54:20 mins

11.2 Copula constructions

The verb *ka-* 'sit, be' forms a continuum between a lexical verb meaning 'sit' and a copula verb. At the lexical end of the continuum, its function is to denote a simple intransitive event where an ABS subject is said to be in a sitting posture, as in (959) and (960).

(959) *Karnta*=*rla*   *wa-nganya*   *ngula*   *kurtu*   *ka-nya.*
       woman=3.OBL   speak-PRES   REL   child   sit-PRES
       The woman is speaking to the child who is sitting.
       wrl-20190206, DK, 11:39 mins

(960) *Ngarrka*   *wa-nganya*   *ka-nja-karra.*
       man   speak-PRES   sit-INF-SS
       The man is speaking while sitting.
       N_D02-007842, BN, 36:53 mins

Frequently, but not necessarily, *ka-*, when functioning as a posture verb, takes a locative modifier to denote the location of sitting, as in (961).

(961) *Yama-nga*=*rnalu*   *ka-ngu-rra*   *warlanja-rla.*
       shade-LOC=1PL.EXCL.S   be/sit-PAST-IMPF   ironwood-LOC
       We're [sitting] in the shade of an ironwood tree.
       N_D02-007850, DG, 01:07 mins

Most uses of *ka-* are ambiguous without context and may denote a location in space without encoding any form of posture (whereas the lexical usage above denotes a certain posture, rather than a location). For example, (961) and (962) are ambiguous as to whether the participants are sitting.

(962) *Maliki   ka-nya   pamarrpa-rla.*
      dog   be/sit-PRES   hill-LOC
      The dog is [sitting] on the hill.
      H_K01-505B, DG, 22:27 mins

In some cases, the posture reading is less available and, instead, only a copula-like reading is permissible, denoting existential presence, as in (963), where the subject is *martayi* 'clouds', which can only metaphorically be 'sitting' in the sky.

(963) *Wajurra=ma   partakurru,   mirla=lu   martayi   ka-ngu-rra.*
      yesterday=TOP   good   this.LOC=3PL.S   cloud   be/sit-PAST-IMPF
      Yesterday was good, there were clouds [?sitting] here.
      wrl-20190205, DK, 49:37 mins

Finally, there are uses where only the copula reading is clearly available. This copula usage is bivalent. Both arguments are absolutive, which is an uncommon case-marking pattern in Warlmanpa (see §10.2.4 for other 'quasi-transitive' predicates). Examples are given in (964) and (965).

(964) **Witta**   *ngula=rna*   **ka-ngu-rra,**   *wawirri=rna*   *karta-pu-ngu-rra.*
      small   REL=1SG.S   **be-PAST-IMPF** kangaroo=1SG.S spear-act_on-PAST-IMPF
      I was spearing kangaroos when **I was small**.
      H_K01-506A, DG, 01:02:57 hrs

(965) *Yumpa=ju*   *ka-nya*   *kirtana.*
      this=1SG.NS   be-PRES   father
      This is my father.
      H_K01-505B, DG, 45:39 mins

A copula usage of a 'sit' or 'stand' verb is common in Ngumpin-Yapa languages. Most Ngumpin languages use *karri-* 'sit' as the copula (for example, Gurindji [Meakins and McConvell 2021: 391–92]). The extent to which either reading is possible varies greatly across languages: in Ngardi, karri- is analysed as a 'neutral positional verb' (that is, unspecified for posture), but can be specified with preverbs (Ennever 2021: 448–50). Interestingly, in Warlpiri, *karri-* means 'stand', whereas the inflecting verb *nyina-* refers to sitting (Nash 1986), yet it is still the 'sit' verb *nyina-* that is used as the copula. A sit/copula polysemy is also found in Western Desert (Pintupi [Hansen and Hansen 1978] and Ngaanyatjarra [Douglas 2001]) and Arandic (Arrernte [Henderson 2013] and Kaytetye [Turpin and Ross 2012]) languages, with forms likely cognate with Warlpiri *nyina-*.

11.3 Verbless clauses

Verbless clauses in Warlmanpa comprise a nominal predicate and a nominal subject. As noted in §3.1 (see also §11.6), most nominals can be used predicatively. In some cases, both the nominal predicate and its argument take absolutive case. Because of this, there is no morphosyntactic difference between the predicate and the argument, and my interpretation is based largely on my own intuition.

Unlike other Ngumpin-Yapa languages, there is no evidence that coverbs can act as predicates (for example, Meakins and Nordlinger 2014: 353). Infinitive verbs can function as the main predicate in subordinate clauses, but they cannot be the main predicate of a matrix clause.

In many verbless clauses, the predicate is an argument-taking predicate use of case (§4.1.1.2), as in (966), where the locative case is the main predicate, relating the subject 1SG to the location, *wilpa* 'creek'.

(966) *Ngayu=ma=rna*   *wilpa-**nga**.*
1=TOP=1SG.S   creek-LOC
I'm at the creek.
LOC(1SG, *wilpa*)
wrl-20180614-01, DK, 05:02 mins

Some nominals specify that their argument takes dative case (when used as a predicate). This is established for *ngampurr(pa)* 'desire', as in (967).

(967) *Ngayu=ma=rna*   **ngampurr**   [*ngappa-ku*   *nguka-nja-ku*].
1=TOP-1SG.S   **desire**   water-DAT   drink-INF-DAT
I **want** [to drink water].
wrl-20191207-01, DK, 07:54 mins

Following Simpson (1991: 121) for Warlpiri, I identify three types of verbless clauses, differentiated by their semantics: equative clauses (§6.5.1), identification clauses (§6.5.2) and ascriptive clauses (§6.5.3). In each verbless clause, the temporal reference minimally captures the present reference time and, in almost all cases, extends to a generic time reference—that is, true at any given time. Furthermore, each known case is of an atelic situation—that is, activities and states. I am not aware of any cases where the nominal predicate denotes a telic event.

11.3.1 Equative clauses

Equative clauses establish equivalence between two nominal expressions. In all known cases, one nominal is a demonstrative. Examples are given in (968) and (969).

(968) *Yali=ma   Japaljarri.*
       that=TOP   Japaljarri
       That's Japaljarri.
       wrl-20180609-01, DK, 10:14 mins

(969) *Yumpa=nya=ma   ngayinya   yiwirti.*
       this=FOC=TOP   1GEN   tree
       This is my tree.
       H_K01-506A, DG, 49:31 mins

11.3.2 Identification clauses

Identification clauses denote the subject nominal referent as being a token of a type represented by the predicate. For example, in (970), the subject demonstrative *yali* refers to a particular entity belonging to the set of *kurrinykurriny* 'rock pigeon'.

(970) *Kurrinykurriny   yali=ma.*
       Rock_pigeon   that=TOP
       That's a rock pigeon.
       wrl-20160914-02, SN, 02:40 mins

11.3.3 Ascriptive clauses

Ascriptive clauses denote some property of their subject. In (971), the predicate *pirtaparna* 'full' is applied to the first-person-singular subject. Further examples are given in (972)–(974). Unlike other types of nominal predicates, the predicate in an ascriptive clause is often (but not necessarily) a semantic case that relates two nominals.

(971) *Pirtaparna=lku=rna.*
full=THEN=1SG.S
I'm full now.
H_K06-004555, LOF, 37:34 mins

(972) *Ngayu=ma=rna   Brisbane-ngurlu.*
1=TOP=1SG.S   Brisbane-ELA
I'm from Brisbane.
wrl-20190213-01, DK, 24:24 mins

(973) *Jurlaka=ma=lu   kunturru-rla   kankarlarra.*
birds=TOP=3PL.S   sky-LOC   above
There are birds in the sky.
wrl-20190212-02, DK, 14:47 mins

(974) *Junma   yumpa   jalkarra.*
knife   this   sharp
This knife is sharp.
H_K01-506A, DG, 30:08 mins

11.4 Interrogative clauses

Interrogative clauses request information from an addressee. There are two distinct types in Warlmanpa: content questions (sometimes labelled '*wh*-questions'), discussed in §11.4.1, and polar questions (sometimes labelled 'yes/no questions'), discussed in §11.4.2.

11.4.1 Content questions

Content questions contain a proposition with a variable that the speaker is interrogating. In Warlmanpa, the following rules generally apply for content questions:

i. there is an ignorative nominal in the first position
ii. the ignorative nominal hosts the bound pronouns
iii. the ignorative nominal is inflected for the case of the variable if there is an inflecting verb
iv. the clause must have positive polarity.

The semantics of the ignorative nominals are discussed in §4.6; this section discusses the syntax of content question constructions, which obligatorily include one ignorative nominal. Each rule and its exception(s) are now discussed in turn.

Under typical circumstances, content question constructions have an ignorative nominal in first position:

(975) *Ngana=n*   *nya-ngu?*
what=2SG.S   see-PAST
What did you see?
H_K01-505B, DG, 42:42 mins

(976) *Wanjila=rna-ngu*   *ya-nma?*
where=1SG.S-2SG.NS   put-POT
Where will I drop you off?
wrl-20180614-02, DK, 17:36 mins

With regards to rule (ii), the bound pronouns will be hosted by the ignorative nominal unless there is an auxiliary base in the clause. If there is an auxiliary base in the clause, it will occur in the expected second position and host the bound pronouns. However, it should be noted that this is very rare and occurs only three times in the corpus, with an auxiliary *kapi* 'FUT' that is of marginal status in Warlmanpa (see §5.3.3). Regardless, examples (977)–(979) demonstrate the hierarchy, in which bound pronouns attach to the auxiliary rather than the ignorative nominal.

(977) *Ngana-rla*   *kapi=n*   *ka-mi?*
what-LOC   FUT=2SG.S   be-FUT
What will you sit on?
H_K01-505B, DG, 40:19 mins

(978) *Nyangurla kapi=n pa-nami?*
when FUT=2SG.S go-FUT
When will you go?
H_K01-505B, DG, 40:25 mins

(979) *Ngana kapi=n jawarti-ma partakurru-ma-n?*
what FUT=2SG.S tomorrow=TOP good-CAUSE-FUT
What will you make tomorrow?
H_K01-505B, DG, 24:03 mins

Rule (iii) is perhaps the one with the most exceptions. Generally, if there is an inflecting verb, the ignorative is obligatorily case marked as would be the corresponding nominal in a declarative clause. This can be exemplified by the following instances of *ngana* taking various case suffixes, depending on what the corresponding nominal would be marked as (note that ignoratives take the polysyllabic-stem allomorphs of case suffixes; see §4.6).

Absolutive case:

(980) *Ngana yali=ma kurtij ka-nya?*
what that=TOP stand be-PRES
Who's that standing?
(Subject of *kurtij ka-* 'stand' takes absolutive case.)
H_K06-004555, LOF, 45:28 mins

Ergative case:

(981) *Ngana-rlu yarri wawirri karta-pu-ngu?*
what-ERG that kangaroo spear-act_on-PAST
Who speared that kangaroo?
(Subject of *karta-pi-* 'spear' takes ergative case.)
H_K01-506A, DG, 51:10 mins

Dative case:

(982) *Ngana-ku=n wirliny kapu-ngunya?*
what-DAT=2SG.S follow chase-PRES
What are you following?
(The complement introduced by *wirliny* takes a dative suffix.)
H_K06-004555, LOF, 48:31 mins

Elative case:

(983) *Ngana-ngurlu=n   partu-ngunya?*
      what-ELA=2SG.S   leave-PRES
      What caused you to leave?
      (Reasons can be marked using the elative suffix.)
      wrl-20191208-01, DK, 29:29 mins

In addition to allowing cases, the ignorative can also be marked with a derivational suffix:

(984) *Nyapa-purta=rna   pa-nama   Mangalawurru-ka?*
      how-FACING=1SG.S   go-FUT.AWAY Mangalawurru-ALL
      Which way to Mangalawurru?
      wrl-20200221, DK, 23:15 mins

(985) *Nyapa-piya=rna-ngu   ma-nmi?*
      how-LIKE$_2$=1SG.S-2SG.NS   get-FUT
      What kind should I get you?
      wrl-20200219, DK, 03:13 mins

When there is no inflecting verb, the content question may optionally be unmarked, as in (986), where the speaker is interrogating the location of a dog, which would be marked using the locative case in a declarative clause.

(986) *Wanji   maliki   yarru-kurla?*
      where   dog   that-BELONG
      Where's that one's dog?
      H_K01-505B, DG, 01:03:36 hrs

The exception to rule (iii) is *wanjila*, which appears to be a locative form of *wanji* except with an alveolar lateral instead of the expected retroflex lateral, and it can occur where an allative is expected, as in (987).

(987) *Wanjila   pa-nangu   pulka?*
      where.LOC   go-PAST   old_man
      Where did the old man go?
      (*Pa-* usually takes an allative modifier to mark the destination of travel.)
      wrl-20190212-02, DK, 00:46 secs

This form of *wanjila* is so consistently used by speakers that Nash (1979, 2022) includes it as a variant form of *wanji*, rather than necessarily considering it a compositional inflected form, which is the analysis I follow here. It is possible *wanjila* is inherently marked for a motion component. A similar phenomenon is found in Bilinarra (Meakins and Nordlinger 2014: 193), in which the locative form *wanyji-ga* 'which-LOC' is used to question destinations, which would be marked as allative in other clause types (a locative–allative alternation is common across Australia, however, not in this context [McConvell and Simpson 2012; Meakins et al. 2020]).

Finally, rule (iv) stipulates that a content question must have positive polarity. Combining the clausal negator *kula* with an ignorative nominal results in an indefinite reading of the ignorative nominal, which refers to an empty set, as exemplified in (988).

(988)   *Ngana   kula   pa-nangu-rnu.*
       what   NEG   go-PAST-TWD
       Nobody came.
       N_D03-007868, BN, 39:05 mins

There are two available constructions for negative-polarity content questions. First, a stative verb may be used with a subordinate privative clause. Second, the ignorative can precede the negative-polarity particle, which is structurally identical with the indefinite reading given in (988), so for the speakers who have this construction available, (995) could be interpreted as 'who did not come?' (for these speakers, rule [iv] does not apply). Negative interrogatives are discussed in §11.5.3.

11.4.2 Polar questions

Polar questions appear to have no morphosyntactic characteristics, other than a rare particle *wayi*, which occurs clause-initially and hosts bound pronouns, as an ignorative does in content questions (this particle is discussed in §9.1.6). In polar questions lacking *wayi* (which form the majority of polar question constructions in the corpus), the distinction is made by prosody (see §2.6.2), in which the final syllable of the utterance is marked for extra high pitch. Polar questions are not restricted to any verb inflection; examples from different tenses are given below: past in (989) and (990), present in (991) and future in (992). By asking a polar question, the speaker is interrogating the truth value of the proposition of the clause, so the expected response is typically (minimally) *yuwayi* 'yes' or *walku* 'no, nothing'.

(989)   *Nya-ngu=ju-n*   *ngayinya*   *ngarnki?*
see-PAST=1SG.NS-2SG.S   1GEN   partner
[Have] you seen my partner?
wrl-20190213-01, DK, 16:02 mins

(990)   *Nyuntu=nku-ju-lu*   *nya-ngu*   *wajjurra?*
2=2.S-1SG.NS-S.PL   see-PAST   yesterday
[Did] you mob see me yesterday?
wrl-20190213-02, DK, 21:51 mins

(991)   *Purtu-ka-nya=n*   *wa-nganji-ka=ma?*
listen-be=PRES=2SG.S   speak-INF-ALL=TOP
[Can] you hear him speaking?
H_K06-004555, LOF, 44:21 mins

Polar questions may also be requesting permission, as in (992), although this can be seen as an extension of questioning the proposition of the clause. That is, the question is asking the addressee whether the proposition is true or false, and it is within the addressee's authority to deliberate on the truth value of the proposition.

(992)   *Wangani=li*   *ka-nyi*   *muju?*
dog=1DU.INCL.S   take-FUT   also
[Can] we bring the dog as well?
wrl-20190213-01, DK, 03:04 mins

11.5 Negation

Warlmanpa has numerous strategies for negation and often different clause types will be negated using different strategies. This section focuses on the negation of clausal propositions. Declarative clauses (§11.5.1) are typically negated by *kula* 'negative', which has clausal scope (§11.5.1.1) to signal that the proposition is false. *Walku* can be used, often either with a narrower scope (for example, signalling the non-existence of some entity) or as a predicate (§11.5.1.2). Negating imperative constructions has a wider range of strategies (§11.5.2): *kula* can be used by younger speakers (§11.5.2.1) and, for other speakers, there is *puta* 'incompletely', which combines with some types of situations to denote negation (§11.5.2.4) or, more commonly, *-wangu* (§11.5.2.1) or *-jila* (§11.5.2.2) can be used—interestingly, either insubordinated as a matrix predicate or subordinated to a positive-polarity imperative clause with a stative verb, for what seems to be the same meaning.

In this section, I attempt an overview of the morphosyntactic properties of each strategy. However, there is significant variation across speakers as to which strategies are used. Table 11.2 attempts to categorise negation strategies according to grammatical exponents and clause types, based on the current state of the corpora. Some preliminary observations can be made:

- The negation of a clausal proposition in a declarative clause requires a particle (nominal suffixes cannot be used, even in insubordination uses).
- The negation of an entity's existence is, unsurprisingly, restricted to nominal suffixes, though alternatively, the particle *walku* can allow a dative-marked argument.
- Negative imperatives exhibit a range of different constructions.
- Negation in interrogatives is rare and reflects a gap in the corpus.

Table 11.2 Negation strategies across speakers and clause types

	Declarative—negating clausal proposition	Declarative—negating entity	Imperative	Interrogative
kula 'not'	All speakers	No known speakers	Some speakers	Some speakers
numu 'no more'	Some speakers (both corpora)	No known speakers	Some speakers	No known speakers
walku 'nothing'	All speakers (requires *kula* in same clause, unless used as interjection)	Some speakers (present corpus)	No known speakers	No known speakers
-wangu 'privative'	No known speakers	All speakers	All speakers	Some speakers (present corpus; requires finite matrix verb)
-jila 'without'	No known speakers	Some speakers (present corpus)	All speakers (requires finite matrix verb)	No known speakers

11.5.1 Negative declarative clauses

Declarative clauses can be negated using the particle *kula* 'negative', which indicates the clause has negative polarity (§11.5.1.1). A particle, *walku* 'nothing', can be used as an object to denote an empty set of referents or as a predicate with a dative complement (§11.5.1.2).

11.5.1.1 *Kula* 'negative'

Kula is a clausal negator that indicates that the proposition denoted by the clause is not true at reference time. For example, in (993), the event of listening, situated in the past, is claimed to have not happened (located at some specific time in the past, due to the PAST inflection). This is a narrow reading, in that the temporal scope extends only to the duration of the situation and not beyond it—that is, the addressee could have been listening to the speaker at some other time and this would not violate the truthfulness of the utterance.

(993)   *Kula=ji-n   purta   ka-ngu   pala=rna-ngu   wa-nganyu.*
        NEG=1SG.NS-2SG.S   hear   be-PAST   WHILE=1SG.S-2SG.NS   speak-PAST
        You weren't listening to me while I was speaking.
        H_K06-004547, JW, 27:33 mins

However, *kula* can be interpreted with a wider scope, which extends beyond reference time, as in (994). The narrow reading is always available, whereas the wide reading is available only in certain contexts.

(994)   *Kula=rna   pama   nguka-nnya.*
        NEG=1SG.S   alcohol   drink-PRES
        Narrow reading: I'm not drinking alcohol.
        Wide reading: I don't drink alcohol.
        wrl-20190121, SN, 41:57 mins

Kula typically occurs clause-initially (distinguishing *kula* from the set of auxiliary bases [§5.3]), as in (995)–(998). Furthermore, *kula* is incompatible with any other auxiliary base and obligatorily hosts the bound pronouns. There are some noted exceptions to *kula* occurring clause-initially. First, when a relative clause headed by *ngula* (§12.1.1.1) is negated, the *ngula* can precede the *kula*, as in (999). Second, a left-dislocated nominal expression may precede *kula*, as in (1,000), though this is particularly rare (see §11.7.1 for a discussion of left dislocation).

(995) ***Kula**=rna   jama-rnu.*
NEG=1SG.S   grind-PAST
I wasn't grinding it.
H_K06-004555, LOF, 57:39 mins

(996) ***Kula**   ngappa   wa-nmi,   wirliya=rna   pa-nama.*
NEG   water   fall-FUT   foot=1SG.S   go-POT
It won't rain, I should walk.
wrl-20190201, DK, 29:40 mins

(997) ***Kula**=rna-ngu   purtu   ka-nya.*
NEG=1SG.S-2SG.NS   hear   be-PRES
I can't hear you.
H_K06-004555, LOF, 42:51 mins

(998) ***Kula**=rna   ngayu=ma   pa-nama,   ngayu=ma=rna   ka-mi*
NEG=1SG.S 1=TOP   go-POT   1=TOP=1SG.S   be-FUT
yarti.
stay_in_camp
I won't go, I'll stay in camp.
wrl-20180616-01, DK, 25:03 mins

(999) ***Kula**=rna   ma-nma   **ngula**   kula   **lu-ngunya**.*
NEG=1SG.S get-POT   REL   NEG   cry-PRES
I won't get the dog who isn't crying.
N_D03-007868, BN, 40:10 mins

(1,000) *Kurtu   yumpa   **kula**   lu-nganya.*
child   this   NEG   cry-PRES
This child isn't crying.
H_K01-505B, DG, 26:38 mins

Under the scope of negation (and other embedded contexts) ignorative nominals become indefinites:

(1,001) ***Kula**=rna   ngana   purtu   ka-ngu.*
NEG=1SG.S   who   listen   be-PAST
I didn't hear anything/anyone.
H_K01-505B, DG, 42:35 mins

11.5.1.2 *Walku* 'nothing'

Walku is commonly used as a propositional particle preposed to an utterance that is negated by *kula*.

(1,002) *Walku,   kula=rna   karta-pu-ngu.*
         nothing   NEG=1SG.S   spear-act_on-PAST
         No, I didn't spear him.
         H_K01-505B, DG, 34:54 mins

(1,003) *Walku,   kula   ngappa   wa-nmi.*
         nothing   NEG   water   fall-FUT
         No, it won't rain.
         H_K01-505B, DG, 47:32 mins

(1,004) *Walku,   kula=rna-ngu   nya-ngu   partakurru-ma-nji-ka*
         nothing   NEG=1SG.S-2SG.NS   see-PAST   good-CAUSE-INF-ALL
         karli-ka.
         boomerang-ALL
         No, I didn't see you fixing the boomerang.
         H_K01-505B, DG, 24:22 mins

In some rare instances, it can also be used as a nominal, as in (1,005), where it is the object of *nya-* 'see' (and compare with [1,006], where the event of 'seeing' is negated by *kula*, indicating the event did not happen).[3] When used as a predicative nominal, it takes a dative argument, as in (1,008).

Walku used as argument (nominal) of *nya-* 'see':

(1,005) *Kayi=rna   pa-nkarla-rra   nyintinya-ka,*
         WHEN=1SG.S   go-IRR-AWAY   2.GEN-ALL
         *nga=rna-ngu-rla   **walku**   nya-ngkarla.*
         POST=1SG.S-2SG.NS-3.OBL   **nothing**   see-IRR
         When I would go to you, I would see that you weren't there.
         (Lit.: I would see [nothing for you].)[4]
         wrl-20190206, DK, 18:50 mins

---

3   A similar use of *walku* is found in Warlpiri, for which the construction is only available with the predicate *nya-* 'see' (Laughren et al. 2022), though it is analysed as a complex predicate, *walku-nya-* 'see nothing for', where the unseen referent is treated as indirect object.

4   I am not sure what the *=rla* dative pronoun clitic is doing in this utterance. David Nash (p.c.) suggests it may be related to conative constructions that 'demote' an object to an indirect object, which expresses that the event was not completed successfully.

Negated event of *nya-* 'see' uses *kula* as clausal negator:

(1,006) **Kula** pulka-ngu nya-nganya milpa-parna-rlu.
NEG old_man-ERG see-PRES eye-PROP-ERG
The old man can't see without his glasses.
wrl-20190201, DK, 07:40 mins

Walku as predicate (nominal) taking dative argument (with optional copula verb):

(1,007) Maliki=rna nya-ngu, **minija-ku=ma=rla walku.**
dog=1SG.S see-PAST cat-DAT=TOP=3.OBL nothing
I saw the dog, not the cat [lit.: nothing for the cat].
wrl-20170328-01, SN, 04:56 mins

(1,008) **Walku**=rna ka-nya **wawirri-ku**, karta-pi-nja-jila.[5]
nothing=1SG.S be-PRES **kangaroo-DAT** spear-act_on-INF-WITHOUT
I haven't speared any kangaroos.
(Lit.: I am nothing for spearing kangaroos.)
H_K01-506B, DG, 06:36 mins

11.5.2 Negative imperatives

There is a wide range of strategies available to speakers for negative imperative constructions. Two common strategies are non-finite verb forms (or nominals) hosting either *-wangu* 'privative' (§11.5.2.1) or *-jila* 'lacking' (§11.5.2.2), with or without a positive-polarity imperative verb. Some younger speakers can instead negate an imperative clause using *kula* (§11.5.2.1), just as *kula* negates a declarative clause. Some speakers can use *puta* with certain event types (§11.5.2.4), which is likely to be a polite negative imperative given its usual meaning of 'incompletely'.

---

5   I am unsure how this non-finite verb is syntactically situated in this utterance. It may be a case of insubordination, acting as an afterthought, however, this constituency appears to be somewhat constructionalised (see [910]). It may also be the argument of *walku* (and taking *wawirri* as its own argument). This sentence was prompted by the following Warlpiri utterance:

Lawa ka=rna nyina wawirri-ki, panti-rninja-wangu.
nothing PRES=1SG.S sit.NPAST kangaroo-DAT spear-INF-PRIV.

Other Ngumpin-Yapa languages that utilise non-finite verb forms with privative suffixes to form negative imperatives require a positive-polarity main clause for the non-finite verb to modify (Mudburra being an exception [Osgarby 2018: 230]). For example, (1,009) and (1,010) represent the standard negation of imperative clauses in Warlpiri and Ngardi, respectively: a positive-polarity imperative verb with a privative subordinate clause that denotes the action that the addressee(s) should not perform—and moreover, these demonstrate the general structure of the strategies used in these languages.

Intransitive subordinate clause—SIT/BE-IMP V<small>INF</small>-PRIV:

(1,009) *Warlpiri wangka-nja-wangu=pala nyina-ya!*
Warlpiri speak-INF-PRIV=DU.S sit-IMP
Don't you two speak Warlpiri!
(Warlpiri [Laughren 2017a: 4])

Transitive subordinate clause—LEAVE-IMP V<small>INF</small>-PRIV-ERG:

(1,010) *Wanja-ka nuku=paja-rnu-wangu-rlu*
LEAVE-IMP kiss=BITE-INF-PRIV-ERG
Don't you kiss him.
(Ngardi [Ennever 2018: 124])

In Warlmanpa, both these constructions are available. Furthermore, the finite verb is not required, resulting in an insubordinate structure (Evans 2007), as in (1,011).

(1,011) *Pirtij-wa-nja-wangu!*
Climb-fall-INF-PRIV
Don't climb!
H_K06-004555, LOF, 47:45 mins

In these insubordinate constructions, the bound pronouns pattern just like in regular imperative constructions, marking only numbers (see §5.4.3.4), suggesting these clauses are truly negative imperatives, rather than an indirect alternative to other negation strategies for imperatives.

This insubordinate construction is also found in Mudburra (Laughren 2017a: 8). Similar structures are found in other Ngumpin languages, such as Gurindji (McConvell 1996b: 46) and Bilinarra (Meakins and Nordlinger 2014: 155), however, this construction is only available to nominals, coverbs and adverbs, rather than inflecting verbs in their non-finite form.

Table 11.3 summarises the strategies for prohibitive constructions in Warlmanpa and compares these with other Ngumpin-Yapa languages, which shows that each strategy in Warlmanpa is instantiated in other related languages, though no other Ngumpin-Yapa language has these three strategies ('P' is a particle and 'V' is a verb). Some related languages use strategies not found in Warlmanpa, such as Jaru, which combines *wagura* 'not' with a purposive sentence (Tsunoda 1981b: 88). An additional strategy in some languages is to mark a coverb with the privative suffix (Meakins and McConvell 2021; Meakins and Nordlinger 2014: 155–56), which is not found in Warlmanpa.

Table 11.3 Strategies for prohibition in Warlmanpa compared with other Ngumpin-Yapa languages

Strategy	Insubordination V-INF-PRIV §11.5.2.1	Subordination V-IMP V-INF-PRIV §11.5.2.1, §11.5.2.2	Negative imperative P(NEG) V-IMP §11.5.2.3
Warlmanpa	✓	✓	✓
Bilinarra			✓
Mudburra	✓	✓	
Ngardi		✓	
Wanyjirra			✓[6]
Warlpiri		✓	

Sources: Ennever (2018: 124); Laughren (2017a: 4, 7); Meakins and Nordlinger (2014: 303).

11.5.2.1 -*wangu* 'privative'

The most common negative imperative construction for most Warlmanpa speakers involves -*wangu*, though again there is variation in how the construction is formed. In both constructions, -*wangu* attaches to a non-finite verb form, however, there may be an accompanying imperative verb form. Where there is a finite imperative verb, it is usually bleached of its semantic content and the non-finite verb hosting -*wangu* bears the main

---

6   Wanyjirra uses *wagurra* 'NEG', which is more like *walku* in Warlmanpa than *kula*.

semantic load, as in (1,012). Cases without a finite imperative verb form represent instances of insubordination (imperatives are a cross-linguistically common source of insubordination [Evans 2007: 387–88]), as in (1,013).

(1,012) *Ka-rra   nga-rninja-wangu!*
          be-IMP   eat-INF-NEG
         Don't eat anything!
         wrl-20190117, SN, 20:22 mins

(1,013) *Nga-rninja-wangu!*
         eat-INF-PRIV
         Don't drink it!
         H_K06-004555, LOF, 38:25 mins

As noted earlier, negative commands formed via insubordinate constructions take only pronoun clitics indexing number features—a feature observed of true imperative clauses (see §5.4.3.4):

(1,014) *Yi-nja-wangu=**pala**-rla!*
         give-INF-NEG=DU.S-DAT
         Don't you two give it to him!
         H_K01-506A, DG, 01:00:51 hrs

11.5.2.2 -*jila* 'without'

The suffix -*jila* is infrequently used as part of a negative imperative construction (its more common use is to negate the existence of some referent; see §4.2.1). In (1,015) and (1,016), it attaches to a non-finite verb. In the former, it is subordinate to a positive-polarity imperative clause and in the latter it is not.

(1,015) *Winja-ka   karnta   **paka-nja-jila-rlu!***
          leave-IMP   woman   **hit-INF-WITHOUT-ERG**
         Leave the woman **without hitting** [her]!
         wrl-20190201, DK, 27:33 mins

(1,016) *Nyuyu   win   **kiya-nja-jila!***
          spit   chuck   **throw-INF-WITHOUT**
         Don't chuck spit!
         H_K06-004555, LOF, 31:14 mins

11.5.2.3 *Kula* 'negative'

For most speakers, imperative clauses cannot be negated by *kula*. Instead, either *puta* 'incompletely' or a verbal suffix, *-jila* 'privative', is used. *Kula* being unable to combine with imperative verbs is common in Ngumpin-Yapa languages—with the only previously noted exceptions being Bilinarra and Gurindji (Laughren 2017a), in which *kula* can combine with imperative verbs. However, some younger speakers of Warlmanpa are able to express negative imperatives using *kula*:

(1,017)   *Kula=rla*   *pa-nka*   *kala=ngu*   *pi-nyi.*
               NEG=3.   go-IMP   APPR=   act_on-FUT
               OBL   2SG.NS
            Don't go to him, he might bite you!
            wrl-20180605-01, JK, 06:37 mins

(1,018)   *Kula*   *karli*   *yali=nya*   *kiya-ka.*
               NEG   boomerang   that=FOC   throw-IMP
            Don't throw that boomerang!
            wrl-20180610-01, DK, 02:38 mins

(1,019)   *Kula*   *ma-nta*   *yarri=nya*   *karli*   *kala=n*   *kiya-nma.*
               NEG   take-IMP   that=FOC   boomerang   APPR=   throw-POT
                                                                                                 2SG.S
            Don't pick up that boomerang, you might throw it!
            wrl-20180610-01, DK, 03:58 mins

11.5.2.4 *Puta* 'incompletely'

The particle *puta* is used to indicate a lack of completion (see §9.1.5) and regularly co-occurs with imperatives. If the event can be done partially—typically an activity or accomplishment, in the sense of Vendler (1957) and Comrie (1976)—it retains the core meaning of 'incompletely':

(1,020)   *Puta*   *nga-nja=ju.*
               incompletely   eat-IMP=1SG.NS
            Drink some on me.
            N_D03-007868, BN, 10:50 mins

Puta can have the illocutionary force of cessation. If the durative event is ongoing, the use of *puta* is to signal to the addressee to cease the action:

(1,021)   *Puta*   *wa-ngka,*   *yangku*   *ka-rra!*
          incompletely   speak-IMP,   cessation   sit-IMP
          Stop speaking, sit there quietly!
          N_D02-007842, BN, 56:22 mins

If an event cannot be done partially (corresponding to [-durative] lexical aspect) then the use of *puta* indicates an instruction to not do the event at all:

(1,022)   *Puta*   *ya-ka!*
          incompletely   put-IMP
          Do not put it down!
          H_K06-004555, LOF, 52:07 mins

(1,023)   *Puta=ju*   *paka-ka!*
          incompletely=1SG.NS   hit-IMP
          Don't hit me!
          N_D02-007842: BN, 27:56 mins

Interestingly, the interpretation of *puta* in Warlpiri is also dependent on the predicate with which it combines (Bowler 2017: 14).

11.5.3 Negative interrogatives

There are few tokens of negative-polarity interrogatives in the corpus. From the limited tokens, there are two constructions (both from the same speaker). First, there is a finite-polarity matrix clause with a stative verb and a non-finite subordinate verb that contains the primary semantic content. This is exemplified in (1,024) and is the common construction for negative-polarity interrogatives in many other Ngumpin-Yapa languages.

(1,024)   *Ngana*   *ka-ngu*   *karta-pi-nja-wangu?*
          who   be-PAST   spear-act_on-INF-PRIV
          Who didn't spear anything?
          [Lit.: 'Who is without spearing?']
          wrl-20200219, DK, 39:11 mins

Alternatively, another construction has a clause-initial ignorative and the negative particle *kula* in the second position, as exemplified in (1,025) and (1,026). This strategy is structurally identical to negative declaratives for some speakers (§11.5.1.1).

(1,025) *Ngana-ngurlu   kula=n   jarta=ma   ka-nya?*
        what-ELA   NEG=2SG.S   sleep=TOP   be-PRES
        Why aren't you sleeping?
        wrl-20200219, DK, 01:03:06 hrs

(1,026) *Ngana-rlu   kula   yarnunju=ma   nga-rnu?*
        who-ERG   NEG   food=TOP   eat-PAST
        Who didn't eat food?
        wrl-20200219, DK, 40:33 mins

11.6 Secondary predicates

Secondary predicates are nominal predicates that have an argument that is shared with the matrix predicate. Secondary predicates are thus distinguished from adverbs in that adverbs modify the situation and secondary predicates modify the event participants. The shared argument can be any argument of the matrix predicate: in (1,027) the subject of the secondary predicate is the subject of the matrix verb and, in (1028), the subject of the secondary predicate is the indirect object of the matrix verb.[7]

(1,027) *Jarta-wangu   ali=nya   wangani   warlku   wa-nganyu-rra.*
        sleep-PRIV   that=FOC   dog   bark   speak-PAST-IMPF
        That sleepless dog was barking.
        (*Jartawangu* 'without sleep' is predicated of *wangani* 'dog'.)
        H_K01-505B, DG, 02:31 mins

---

[7] Formally, it is the case marker that acts as the predicate (see §4.1.1.2), taking a main-clause nominal expression as its subject and the case-marked nominal as its object. For example, in the case of 'the boomerang on the rock', the locative case on *pamarrpa* 'rock' signals the semantic relation between *karli* 'boomerang' and *pamarrpa* 'rock', denoting ON(*karli*, *pamarrpa*), where *karli* is shared by the matrix clause predicate.

(1,028) Wayi-rnu-rra=rla   karli-ku   pamarrpa-rla
         search-PAST-IMPF=3.OBL   boomerang-DAT   rock-LOC
         kankarlija.
         on_top
         He was searching for the boomerang [which was] on top of the rock.
         (*Pamarrparla kankarlija* 'on top of the rock' is predicated of *karli* 'boomerang'.)
         wrl-20191207-02, DK, 36:09 mins

I now discuss two topics pertinent to the analysis of secondary predicates in Warlmanpa. First, there are two types of secondary predicates noted, depictives and resultatives, which specify truth values for different ranges of time in relation to the matrix predicate (§11.6.1). Second, the evidence presented in the previous section is utilised to argue for an analysis under which there is no fruitful distinction to be made between secondary predicates and other 'modifying' nominals in Warlmanpa (§11.6.2), and I suggest this analysis may extend to all nominals (§11.6.3).

11.6.1 Semantic interpretations of secondary predicates

Secondary predicates in Warlmanpa may be either depictives or resultatives: depictives denote a property that the entity has during the situation denoted by the matrix verb and resultatives denote a property that the entity has as a result of the situation denoted by the matrix verb (Rothstein 2011: 1442–43; see also Simpson 2005 for a comparison of depictives in Warlpiri and English). Typically, but not necessarily, secondary predicates construed of the matrix subject are depictives and those construed of non-subjects are resultatives. Further examples of depictives are given in (1,029) and (1,030), all of which correspond to the subject of the matrix predicate.

(1,029) **Ali**=ma=nyanu   **yangarlu**   wa-nganya.
         that=TOP=RR   **alone**   speak-PRES
         That one is speaking to himself alone.
         wrl-20180614-01, DK, 29:18 mins

(1,030) **Kurtu**   ayi=nya   pirraku   **ngappa-jila**.
         child   the=FOC   thirsty   **water-WITHOUT**
         The child is thirsty, without water.
         wrl-20200220, DK, 13:18 mins

Resultative secondary predicates are most commonly marked with the translative suffix if the subject referent is transformed by the process (see §4.1.12 for further examples):

(1,031)	*Kupa-ka*	*kuyu*	*kula*	***lijji-karta!***
	cook-IMP	meat	NEG	**dry-TRANS**

Cook the meat, but don't let it turn dry!
wrl-20180610-01, DK, 05:41 mins

However, the translative is not always used, so in these cases, the interpretation of the secondary predicate must be inferred from world knowledge, as in (1,032), where *wuppa* 'ash' is in absolute form, and therefore construed of the object of the transitive clause, and the 'resultative' meaning is inferred from context.

(1,032)	*Wajurra-kanyanu=rnalu*	*pa-nanga*	*parntapi-ku*	*ma-nja-ku*
	yesterday-ANOTHER=1PL.S.EXCL	go-PAST.IMPF	bark-DAT	get-INF-DAT
	kayi=rnalu	*kupa-nmi*	***wuppa***.	
	WHEN=1PL.EXCL.S	cook-FUT	**ash**	

Two days ago, we went to get bark, which we will cook [**into**] **ash**.
wrl-20190131-03, DK, 02:23 mins

11.6.2 The distinction between secondary predicates and adjectivals

As noted by Hale (1983: 32) and Bittner and Hale (1995: 95), in most circumstances, any noun phrase in Warlpiri (and this is applicable to 'nominal expressions' in Warlmanpa) has three readings available: a 'weak' reading (indefinite), a 'strong' reading (definite) and a predicative reading (that is, a secondary predicate), as exemplified in (1,033).

(1,033) *Kurdu*   *ka=rna*   *nya-nyi.*
         child   PRES=1SG.S   see-NPAST
         (i)   I see a child.   (weak)
         (ii) I see the child.   (strong)
         (iii) I see him/her, who is a child.   (predicative)
         (Warlpiri [Bittner and Hale 1995: 95])[8]

The 'weak' and 'strong' readings, on the one hand, have been referred to as the 'merged' readings and the 'predicative' reading, on the other, has been referred to as the 'unmerged' reading (Hale 1981, 1983; Nash 1986). Ultimately, the distinction between the merged and unmerged readings in Warlpiri and Warlmanpa does not appear to be reflected morphosyntactically (unlike, for example, in English, in which the semantic distinction is reflected by syntax).

This problem of distinguishing between merged and unmerged readings is most apparent where there are multiple nominals: assuming, as discussed earlier, the nominal with the most specific intension is the head nominal (which functions as an argument to the matrix predicate), there is the issue of *how* nominal modifiers are related to the head noun. This is exemplified in (1,034), in which there are at least two interpretations under Hale's analysis.[9]

(1,034) *Ngarrka-ngu* *piya-rnu*   *kuyu* *ngula=rla* *knife* **yapa-ngu**
        man-ERG   break-PAST   meat   REL=3.OBL   **child-ERG**
        witta-ngu *yu-ngu.*
        small-ERG give-PAST

The man cut the meat after **the small child/the child who is small** gave a knife to him.
N_D02-007842, BN, 44:33 mins

Analyses of Ngumpin-Yapa languages note that it is difficult to come up with criteria to distinguish merged and unmerged readings (Osgarby 2018: 214; Bittner and Hale 1995; Simpson 2005), with the analyses typically

---

8 Mary Laughren (p.c.) notes that (iii) also has the reading 'I see that he is a child'. Furthermore, nominals in the pre-auxiliary slot lend themselves to more likely interpretations; however, it seems Bittner and Hale's central idea still holds (all these interpretations are still *available*).

9 Of course, under the Hale and Bittner analyses, the nominal that I am assuming is the 'head' could also be a secondary predicate of some unexpressed NP that is in fact the 'head nominal'. This is the analysis taken up by Speas (1990) for Warlpiri.

concluding that context determines the appropriate reading. Hale (1983: 31) notes: 'I enter into this discussion with some trepidation. My claim that the argumental and predicative uses of PS [phrase structure] nominal expressions are real and must be distinguished rests on my own intuitions about Warlpiri.'

These complications seem to stem from assuming *a priori* that there is some distinction between predicative nominals and non-predicative nominal modifiers. I believe the data in Warlmanpa lend themselves to treating all modifying phrases as secondary predicates (or at least, there is not some morphosyntactic distinction to be found, regardless of the label given). All 'merged' readings are compatible with the semantics of secondary predicates, given that secondary predicates do not encode whether the state/attribute is true of its subject outside the temporal scope of the matrix predicate (depictives with resultatives have a particular semantic relation to the matrix predicate and a specific suffix to indicate this relation). Attributive readings (or 'merged' readings) are, then, the result of pragmatic enrichment. This analysis is somewhat similar to Speas's (1990) argument that all nominals in Warlpiri are secondary predicates (see also Pensalfini 2004).

To exemplify this analysis, consider (1,035), where I take *wiri karlawurru* 'big goanna' to be the argument of the matrix predicate *kapungu* 'found'.

(1,035) *Partan   kapu-ngu   **wiri   karlawurru,**   paka-rnu=lku.*
         find   chase-PAST   **big   goanna**   hit-PAST=THEN
         He found a **big goanna**, then killed it.
         wrl-20190207-02, DK, 00:32 mins

Treating *wiri* as a secondary predicate encodes that during the event, the goanna was big, and leaves this proposition unspecified for any time outside this scope. It is likely that nominals have preferred 'default' interpretations, depending on their predicate status—for example, *wiri* is an individual-level predicate (referring to an inherent property), so the lexeme itself likely encodes (or is associated with) some temporal permanence, whereas a nominal such as *yangku* 'quiet' seems to lean towards being interpreted as a stage-level predicate, so it is unlikely to be interpreted with temporal permanence (without further contextual clues).

Resultative secondary predicates specify a change in truth values: false during the matrix event and true posterior to it (with a conventional implicature that the matrix event caused this change). The semantics of the two identified types of secondary predicates are summarised in Table 11.4.

Table 11.4 Truth value of the proposition denoted by types of secondary predicates relative to time of matrix event

Type of secondary predicate	Temporal relation to matrix event		
	Anterior	During	Posterior
Truth value of depictive predicate	Unspecified	True	Unspecified
Truth value of resultative predicate	Unspecified	False	True

Further temporal information can be specified with the use of temporal clitics—namely, =*lku* 'now, then' and =*wiyi* 'still', which combine predictably based on their meanings analysed in §9.4.1 and §9.4.7, respectively: =*lku* encodes a change of state, such that the predicate was false prior to reference time, and =*wiyi* encodes an unchanged state, such that the predicate was true prior to reference time. These interpretations are categorised in Table 11.5. Noticeably, depictive secondary predicates always leave the truth value unspecified posterior to event time, as resultative secondary predicates specify truth values for this temporal reference. Interestingly, this schema corresponds to the truth values of verbless clauses (discussed in §11.3), which are also syntactically identical to secondary predicates, thus providing a unified analysis of the data (the difference is purely terminological: the predicative nominal is performing the same function regardless of whether there is also an inflecting verb in the clause).

Table 11.5 Encoded information by a depictive secondary predicate with temporal clitics

Time	Anterior to event	During event	Posterior to event
Truth value (no clitics)	Unspecified	True	Unspecified
Truth value (=*lku*)	False	True	Unspecified
Truth value (=*wiyi*)	True	True	Unspecified

Further evidence that all modifying nominals in Warlmanpa should be treated under a single analysis is case marking. As discussed in §4.1.1.3, case concord is blocked by any other case attaching to the modifier, suggesting the two nominals do not truly form a syntactic unit (see also §11.1.4.4), much like secondary predicates cross-linguistically, which are often syntactically detached from the nominal they modify (Himmelmann and Schultze-Berndt 2005: 26–27).

This analysis also neatly accounts for part-whole and possessive constructions, which can be analysed as secondary predicate constructions as well. In part-whole constructions, under this analysis, the 'whole' part is the argument and the 'part' is a secondary predicate, predicated of the 'whole' (Simpson 2005: 81; Hale 1981). This is exemplified in (1,036), where *lirrangu* 'teeth' is treated as a secondary predicate of *wanganirlu* 'dog' (Laughren 1992 argues the semantic relation of part-whole obtains at the lexical level, unlike depictive and resultative secondary predicates).

(1,036) **Wangani-rlu**   *lirra-ngu*   *pu-ngu.*
         dog-ERG   **teeth-ERG** act_on-PAST
         The dog bit him with its teeth.
         wrl-20180605-01, DK, 05:17 mins

Similarly, possessive constructions can be seen as secondary predicates, as in (1,037), where the possessor *ngayinya* 'my' is a depictive secondary predicate of *ngartina* 'mother'.

(1,037) **Ngayinya-ku**=*rla*   **ngartina-ku**   *wa-nganya.*
         1GEN-DAT=3.OBL   **mother-DAT**   speak-PRES
         He's talking **to my mother**.
         wrl-20190131-02, DK, 06:15 mins

11.6.3 On the status of nominals

In §11.6.2, I argued that multiple nominals construed of the same grammatical relation are in a secondary predication relation. Specifically, I argued that in situations where there are multiple nominals construed of the same entity, the nominal with the most specific intension is the 'head' nominal and all others are secondary predicates of it (rather than drawing a distinction between 'adjectival' and 'secondary predicate' uses of nominals). One consequence of this analysis is that in the uses of nominal expressions with just a single nominal, that nominal should always be the 'head'.

This analysis has a significant shortcoming—exemplified in utterances such as (1,038), where the subject argument of the predicate has only one overt nominal, *yangku* 'quiet'. The bound pronoun =*rna* shows that the subject of the predicate is first-person singular, so ideally, an analysis of the sentence would allow *yangku* 'quiet' to be a secondary predicate of a first-person-singular constituent.

(1,038)　**Yangku-ngu**=rna　jama-nnya　ngurlu.
　　　　　quiet-ERG=1SG.S　grind-PRES　seed
　　　　　I'm grinding seeds [being] quiet.
　　　　　wrl-20190205, DK, 10:13 mins

This problem can be resolved by treating all nominals as secondary predicates, predicated of unexpressed constituents specified only for grammatical relation, person and number (similar ideas are pursued in Baker 1996a; and Pensalfini 2004). This solution is further supported by the lack of morphosyntactic distinctions between 'head' nominals (as I have been referring to them) and 'secondary predicates' (and 'adjectival' nominals, if analysed) in Warlmanpa. To exemplify, in (1,039), the nominal *kari* 'far' takes ergative, as it is construed of the subject—and it is the only nominal so construed. Under this analysis, *kari* is analysed as a depictive secondary predicate on an unexpressed third-person-singular subject constituent, which is also encoded by a null bound pronoun.

(1,039)　Ngapij　nya-nya　**kari-ngu**=lku　ngarra.
　　　　　smell　see-POT　**far-ERG**=THEN　maybe
　　　　　He might be smelling [goannas] **from afar** now.
　　　　　wrl-20180610-01, DK, 23:01 mins

11.7 Dislocation

Constituents may be 'dislocated' from the matrix clause. Dislocation involves a constituent that is not prosodically integrated into a clause. Each noted case of dislocation involves a single nominal, coverb or interjection on the left or right edge of the clause (even to the edge of any subordinate clauses), including case marking of the word, if appropriate. Left dislocation is discussed in §11.7.1 and right dislocation in §11.7.2. Dislocation is the only known environment in which a coverb can constitute a phonological word (that is, occurring without an inflecting verb).

11.7.1 Left dislocation

Left dislocation involves a nominal or a particle occurring on the left edge of the main clause. The syntactic disattachment to the main clause is evidenced by the auxiliary complex, which occurs after the first constituent of the main clause, demonstrating that the dislocated constituent is not considered a constituent of the main clause. This is exemplified in (1,040), where the interjection *ngulayi* is on the left edge of the clause, but not integrated into it, as the bound pronouns attach to the demonstrative *yarrinya*, signalling that *yarrinya* is the first constituent of the clause.

(1,040) *Ngulayi,*   *yarri=nya=rna-ngu*   *wa-nganya.*
         okay   that=FOC=1SG.S-2SG.NS   speak-PRES
         Okay, I've told that story for you.
         H_K01-506A, DG, 33:20 mins

The most common functions of left dislocation involve attention-getting, as in (1,041), or explicating the discourse relation to the ongoing discourse, as in (1,042), where the dislocated constituent is *alingurluma* 'from there'—that is, the destination referred to in the previous clause and this new clause signals movement from there to Tennant Creek. Left dislocation seems to be less frequent than right dislocation.

(1,041) ***Jungurrayi,***   *wanjila=n*   *pa-nya-nya?*
         Jungarrayi   where=2SG.S   go-MOT.AWAY-PRES
         Jungarrayi, where are you heading off to?
         wrl-20190201, DK, 45:56 mins

(1,042) ***Ali-ngurlu=ma,***   *partu-ngu-rnu=rnalu*   *Tennant Creek-a=lku.*
         that-ELA=TOP   leave-PAST-TWD=1PL.EXCL   Tennant Creek-EP=THEN
         From there, we left to Tennant Creek.
         wrl-20190208, DK, 24:35 mins

11.7.2 Right dislocation

Right-dislocated constituents, also referred to as 'afterthoughts', are defined as a single constituent that is prosodically separated on the right edge of the clause. Figure 11.1 provides a visual representation of the audio signal of (1,043), which shows a 0.8-second break between the main clause and the afterthought *palapala*, where the constituents in the main clause have no obvious breaks between them. As this example also shows, the afterthought does not host any bound pronouns, indicating it is syntactically related to the matrix clause.

(1,043) Jamarlamarla   ka-nya=rna,   **palapala.**
         yawn   be-PRES=1SG.S   **tired**
         I'm yawning—[I'm] tired.
         wrl-20190205, DK, 09:05 mins

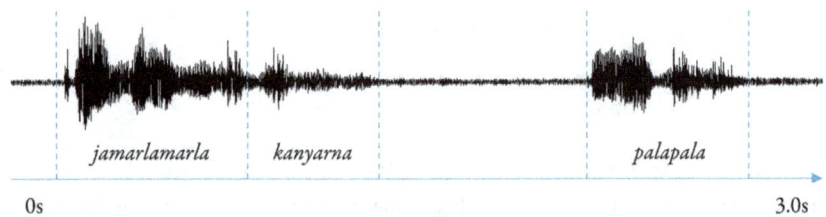

Figure 11.1 Prosodic separation of afterthoughts from the other constituents in the clause

In Warlmanpa, afterthought constructions appear to emphasise the telic point of the situation denoted by the main predicate (particularly in terms of cause, whether purposeful or not). For example, in (1,044), the afterthought provides the reasoning of the participants going to the hills and the event will be completed when they have gathered enough *kupuwarnu* 'hill wallaby'. Similarly, the afterthought in (1,045) stipulates the situation denoted by the main clause is only completed if it is done *tajpaka* 'properly'. Conversely though, (1,043) provides the cause of the main clause event.

(1,044) Wirlinyi=li   parti,   nga=li   pana~pana,
         hunting=1DU.   leave.FUT   POST=1DU.   go~RDP
         INCL.S   INCL.S

         pamarrpa-rla   kankarlarra   —   **kupuwarnu-ku.**
         hill-LOC   up   **hill_wallaby-DAT**

         We'll leave to hunt, we'll go up around the hills—[for] wallabies.
         N_D02-009887, DG, 26:18 mins

(1,045) Kalpa=nyanu   ya-ka,   —   **tajpaka.**
         tight=RR   put-IMP   **properly**
         Tie it up—properly.
         N_D03-007868, BN, 11:23 mins

(1,046) | *Ngula=ja* | *ka-ngu-rra* | *Darwin-nga* | **kurtu=lku**
| REL=1DU.EXCL | sit-BE-IMPF | Darwin-LOC | **child=THEN**

palka-ja-ngu, — **karnta.**
born-INCH-PAST **woman**

I had a child while we were living in Darwin—a girl.
wrl-20190211-01, DK, 05:10 mins

(1,047) | *Ngarrka=ju* | *muka=nya* | *pa-nangu-rnu* | *wa-nganja-ku* | — | **ngayu-ku.**
| man=1SG.NS | this.ALL=FOC | go-PAST-TWD | speak-INF-DAT | | **1-DAT**

That man came here to me to talk—to me.
N_D02-007842, BN, 47:01 mins

Meakins and Nordlinger (2014: 313–14) describe afterthought constructions in Bilinarra as providing 'the hearer with more information about the action referred to in the main clause, such as the manner of motion, the type of implement used or the position on the body where the action occurred'. More generally, afterthought constructions in these languages seem to provide clarifications regarding the main clause event.

12
Syntax of complex clauses

The discussion of the syntax of complex clauses covers complementisers, afterthoughts and coordination—all grouped in this chapter due to their ability to link two or more clauses.

Complementisers overtly specify a relation between the clause they head and a matrix clause (§12.1). Complementisers are categorised according to whether they head a finite clause (§12.1.1) or a non-finite clause (§12.1.2). Finite subordinate clauses share many aspects of Hale's (1976) 'adjoined relative clauses' (that is, not truly syntactically embedded), although see §12.1.1.1.1 for further discussion. On the other hand, non-finite subordinate clauses appear truly embedded—best evidenced by their ability to be flanked by material from the matrix clause.

Coordinators link two constituents of the same syntactic status, including clauses (§12.2). Finally, I present a tentative analysis of discourse relations between pairs of syntactically independent clauses (§12.3).

12.1 Complementisers

Complementisers serve to specify the relation between the subordinate clause headed by the complementiser and its controlling clause. There are two categories of complementiser: those that head finite clauses and those that head non-finite clauses.

Complementisers in finite subordinate clauses have word status—best exemplified by their ability to occur at the left edge of the subordinate clause, as in (1,048), and to host the bound pronouns, as in (1,049).[1]

(1,048)   *Kurtu*   *lu-ngunya*   *[ngula*   *wa-nu].*
child   cry-PRES   **REL**   fall-PAST
The child who fell is crying.
H_K01-505B, DG, 26:23 mins

(1,049)   *[Yumpa=nya*   *ngappa*   **kari**=*n*   *ngukanmi],*   *murrumurru-ja-mi=n.*
this=FOC   water   COND=2SG.S   drink-FUT   sich-INCH-FUT=2SG.S
If you drink this water, you will become sick.
H_K01-506A, DG, 03:04 mins

This contrasts with non-finite subordinate clauses that have complementisers suffixed to each constituent, as in (1,050), where the allative case is functioning as a complementising suffix; the case and complementising suffixes share large overlap, which is common to numerous languages (Austin 1981).

(1,050)   *Maliki=rna*   *nya-ngu*   **[kuyu-ka**   **nga-rninja-ka].**
dog=1SG.S   see-PAST   meat-ALL   eat-INF-ALL
I saw the dog eating meat.
H_K01-505B, DG, 21:00 mins

A finite subordinate clause can be distinguished from a non-finite clause by several criteria. Primarily, verbs in finite subordinate clauses are inflected for TAM, as they are in matrix clauses, whereas verbs in non-finite subordinate clauses obligatorily take the infinitive inflection, followed by a complementising suffix (although a subordinate clause does not necessarily require an inflecting verb). In (1,051), the inflecting verb in the finite subordinate clause has a past imperfective TAM suffix, whereas in (1,052) the inflecting verb in the non-finite subordinate clauses takes an infinitive suffix, then obligatorily takes a complementising case suffix relating it to the matrix clause. In its complementising function, the allative case

---

[1] In this section, I use square brackets to indicate the boundaries of subordinate clauses.

suffix indicates that a non-subject referent in the main clause (either object or indirect object) is the same as the understood subject of the subordinate clause. Furthermore, it also indicates that there is temporal overlap between the events denoted by the two clauses.

(1,051) [*Jurnkurakurru-rla* **ngula**=*rna* **ka-ngu-rra**] *yarri=ma=rna*
Jurnkuraku-LOC REL=1SG.S be-PAST-IMPF that=TOP=1SG.S
Warlmanpa *wa-nganyu-rra.*
Warlmanpa speak-PAST-IMPF
I spoke that Warlmanpa when I was living in Jurnkuraku.
H_K01-505B, DG, 44:27 mins

(1,052) *Nya-ngu=rna* [***waka-nji-ka***].
see-PAST=1SG.S **climb**-INF-ALL
I saw him climbing.
H_K01-506A, DG, 43:00 mins

The second grammatical distinction between finite and non-finite clauses is that finite clauses may have auxiliaries and bound pronouns, whereas non-finite clauses cannot. In (1,053) and (1,054), the subordinate clause subject is second-person singular. In the finite subordinate clause in (1,053), there is an overt bound pronoun registering the subject (=*n*), whereas this bound pronoun is not found in the non-finite subordinate clause in (1,054), and the arguments of the predicate are resolved through the complementising suffix.

(1,053) *Karli=ju* *yu-ngka* *yarri=nya* [*ngula=n* *taka-ngu* *marta-nnya*].
boomerang= give-IMP that=FOC REL= hand- have-PRES
1SG.NS 2SG.S ERG
Give me the boomerang that you're holding with your hand.
H_K01-505B, DG, 28:46 mins

(1,054) *Walku* *kula=rna=ngu* *nya-ngu* [*partakurru-ma-nji-ka* *karli-ka*].
nothing NEG=1SG.S- see-PAST good-CAUSE-INF- boomerang-
2SG.NS ALL ALL
I didn't see you fixing the boomerang.
H_K01-505B, DG, 24:22 mins

Third, finite subordinate clauses cannot be flanked by constituents of the matrix clause: these clauses must occur on either the left or the right edge of the matrix clause, regardless of the constituent they are modifying. Non-finite subordinate clauses may occur anywhere in the matrix clause, although there does seem to be a preference for the right edge. The position of the subordinate clause in relation to the main clause is discussed in further detail for commonly occurring complementisers.

When the matrix clause and subordinate clause share arguments, if the argument is overt, it will only be overt for whichever clause is leftmost, regardless of syntactic status. For example, in (1,055), the matrix clause object is coreferential with the subordinate clause object. The nominal *maliki* only surfaces in the left-most clause, which in this case is the matrix clause. Conversely, in (1,056), the subordinate clause shares its subject with the subject of the matrix clause, which is *warlaku* 'dog'. This nominal here surfaces in the subordinate clause rather than the matrix clause because the subordinate clause is to the left of the matrix clause.

(1,055) **Maliki**=rna purtu ka-ngu [ngula warlkurr wa-nganyu-rra].
dog=1SG.S hear be-PAST REL bark speak-PAST-IMPF
I heard the dog who was barking.
H_K01-505B, DG, 10:04 mins

(1,056) [**Warlaku** ngula warlku wa-nganya] lani-ma-nnya=jana
dog REL bark speak-PRES afraid-CAUSE-PRES=3PL.NS
yawirri.
kangaroo
The dog which is barking is scaring the kangaroos.[2]
wrl-20180608-01, DK, 29:31 mins

A similar effect is found in Martuthunira, for which Dench (1995: 240) notes that 'where the subordinate clause and the main clause share a noun phrase argument, this noun phrase is omitted from either the subordinate clause or the main clause, usually from whichever of the two clauses follows the other'.

---

2 The nominal *warlaku* 'dog' cannot be considered part of the matrix clause for two reasons: first, *ngula* clauses cannot be flanked by constituents from a matrix clause, and second, *warlaku* would require an ergative suffix to be the subject of the transitive matrix clause.

Table 12.1 provides an overview of each known complementiser, to be discussed in turn.

Table 12.1 Overview of Warlmanpa complementisers

Form	Function	Finiteness	Section
ngula	Relative	Finite	§12.1.1.1
kari	Logical conditional	Finite	§12.1.1.2
kayi	Temporal conditional	Finite	§12.1.1.3
nga=	Consequence	Finite	§12.1.1.4
-karra	Subject control	Non-finite	§12.1.2.1
-pa-	Ergative control	Non-finite	§12.1.2.2
-ngarnu	Source	Non-finite	§12.1.2.3
-rla	Sequential	Non-finite	§12.1.2.4
-ka	Object control	Non-finite	§12.1.2.5
-ku	Purposive	Non-finite	§12.1.2.6
-jila	Without	Non-finite	§12.1.2.7
-wangu	Privative, negative	Non-finite	§12.1.2.8
-kuma	Aversive	Non-finite	§12.1.2.9
-kupa	Desiderative	Non-finite	§12.1.2.10

12.1.1 Finite subordinate clauses

There are three clear finite complementisers: *ngula*, which introduces a relative clause (§12.1.1.1); *kari*, which is a logical conditional (§12.1.1.2); and *kayi*, which is a temporal conditional (§12.1.1.3). I also analyse *nga=* as a complementiser, introducing a clause denoting a situation that occurs because of the situation denoted by the matrix clause (§12.1.1.4). Finite subordinate clauses may also be introduced by predicates of represented speech (§12.1.1.5). Finite subordinate clauses always have a verb as the matrix predicate (that is, there are no verbless finite subordinate clauses).

12.1.1.1 *Ngula* 'relative'

Ngula introduces a finite clause to a matrix clause with numerous possible relations. These relations are introduced in §12.1.1.1.1. The more common relations are then discussed: adverbial clauses in §12.1.1.1.2 and relative clauses in §12.1.1.1.3. The discussion of *ngula* concludes with syntactic aspects of the subordinate clauses: their positioning with respect to the matrix clause (§12.1.1.1.4) and the interaction with negation (§12.1.1.1.5).

Interestingly, in Warlpiri, *ngula* is a demonstrative, 'that', except in Hanson River Warlpiri (spoken in the eastern area of where Warlpiri is spoken), where *ngula* is a complementiser, as in Warlmanpa (Nash 1986: 60). In other dialects of Warlpiri, the general complementiser is *kuja* (Hale 1976), which is likely cognate with Warlmanpa *kuya* 'thus' (an adverb). The correspondence of *ngula* as a demonstrative in Warlmanpa and a complementiser in most Warlpiri dialects was one of many similar correspondences noted by McConvell (2006), who suggests that demonstrative > complementiser is a regular grammaticalisation path in Ngumpin-Yapa languages.

12.1.1.1.1 Syntactic interpretation of *ngula* clauses: Adjoined or embedded?

Finite subordinate clauses headed by *ngula* are structurally very similar to Hale's (1976) 'adjoined clause'. Hale recognises two types of adjoined clause: T-relative and NP-relative. T-relative interpretations are available when there is an overlap of temporal reference between the two clauses, and NP-relative interpretations are available when there is coreference between an argument in each clause. Regardless of interpretation, Hale argues the subordinate clause is not syntactically embedded in the main sentence, rather, the matrix clause and relative clause would be sister nodes; any coreferentiality between referents (that is, in the NP-relative interpretation) is resolved via a semantic rule. This analysis best accounts for why the 'adjoined' clause is never flanked by the material of the matrix clause. Hale's analysis is based primarily on data from Warlpiri and Kaytetye. Nordlinger (2006) uses evidence primarily from Wambaya to demonstrate that 'adjoined' clauses across Australia are heterogeneous. Several criteria for which 'adjoined' clauses may vary across languages are suggested, the most pertinent to Warlmanpa being that an 'adjoined' clause may be an argument of a predicate, and thus must be syntactically embedded. An example of this is given in (1,057), and compare this with the Warlmanpa utterance given in (1,058). In these two examples, the clause headed by the complementiser is best analysed as an argument of a 'remember' predicate.

(1,057) *Guyala   ng-udi   ilinga   [injani   g-a   yarru].*
        NEG   1SG.A-IRR.PRES   remember   **where**   3.SG.S-PAST   **go**
        I can't remember where he went.
        (Wambaya [Nordlinger 2006: 18])

(1,058) *Ngayu=rna   purtu   ka-nya   [ngula=lu   wittawitta=wiyi*
        1=1SG.S   remember   be-PRES   REL=3PL.S   small=STILL
        ka-ngu-rra].
        be-PAST-IMPF
        I remember [when they were still small].
        N_D02-007842, BN, 34:14 mins

These are particularly interesting, as Warlpiri does not permit finite clauses as complements at all (Hale et al. 1995: 1445). However, similar constructions are reported in the Ngumpin languages Wanyjirra and Jaru (Senge 2015: 607; Tsunoda 1981a: 167–68).

In what follows, I assume that a clause headed by *ngula* in Warlmanpa can, under the appropriate conditions, be:

- a modifier of a nominal expression (Hale's 'NP-relative'; Nordlinger's 'relative')
- a modifier of a clause (Hale's 'T-relative'; Nordlinger's 'adverbial')
- a complement of a matrix predicate (Nordlinger's 'clausal argument').

Examples are given in (1,059)–(1,063).

Clausal argument:

(1,059) *Ngayu=rna-ngu   wa-nganya   [larrpalarrpa   ngula=rnalu*
        1=1SG.S-2SG.NS   speak-PRES   **long_time**   REL=1PL.EXCL
        pa-nangu-rra   wijara-ku].
        go-PAST-IMPF   yam-DAT
        I'm telling you we used to go for yams a long time ago.
        N_D02-007842, BN, 34:57 mins

T-relative/adverbial:

(1,060) *Yapa-ngu=nyanu   kupa-rnu   [ngula   jarta   ka-ngu-rra].*
        person-ERG=RR   cook-PAST   REL   **sleep**   be-PAST-IMPF
        The child burnt herself while she was sleeping.
        N_D02-007842, BN, 43:41 mins

(1,061) Ngayu=ma=rna   jarta   ka-ngu-rra   *[ngula=n   pa-nangu-rnu]*.
        1=TOP=1SG.S   sleep   be-PAST-IMPF   REL=2SG.S   go-PAST-TWD
        I was sleeping while you were coming.
        wrl-20191207-01, DK, 39:47 mins

NP-relative/relative:

(1,062) Ol'   Kurrpa   *[ngula   la-nnya   palyupalyu-ku]*.
        Name   [REL   shoot-PRES blue-tongued_skink-DAT]
        Old Kurrpa, who shoots blue-tongued lizards.
        N_D09-013557, DG, 00:55 secs

(1,063) Yimpa=ma   kurtu   witta   *[ngula   palka-ja-ngu]*.
        this=TOP   child   small   REL   apparent-INCH-PAST
        This is the small child who was born.
        wrl-20170321-02, SN, 00:09 secs

As noted by Hale (1976) for Warlpiri, the subordinate clause can be ambiguous between relative and adverbial interpretations.[3] The criterion for a relative reading is coreferentiality between clauses and the criterion for an adverbial reading being available is an overlap in temporal reference between clauses. If both criteria are met, the relation of the *ngula* clause to the matrix clause is ambiguous. An example of an ambiguous relation is given in (1,064), where the matrix clause subject is *karnta* 'woman', who can be coreferential with the unexpressed subject of the subordinate *ngula* clause, which allows a relative reading, where the subordinate clause is supplying further information about the woman. The TAM inflection on both the matrix and the subordinate verbs is PRES, which allows an adverbial reading, where the subordinate clause is supplying an event with some overlap in temporal reference. In the T-relative reading for this utterance, the subject of the subordinate clause is not necessarily the woman (though it is expected to be).

---

3 The NP-relative and T-relative interpretations are unified at the level of syntax by Larson (1982) by treating tense as a variable analogous to nominals.

(1,064)   *Karnta-ngu*   *kurtu*   *lamarta-nnya*   **[*ngula*   *nya-nganya*   *maliki*]**.
woman-ERG   child   hold-PRES   **REL**   **see-PRES**   **dog**

NP-relative$_{(S=S)}$: The woman [who is watching the dog] is holding the child.

NP-relative$_{(O=S)}$: The woman is holding the child [who is watching the dog].

T-relative: The woman is holding the child [while she's watching the dog].

wrl-20190206, DK, 08:52 mins

One complicating example is given in (1,065) since the clauses appear to have independent temporal reference and no referents are shared. One analysis is to allow NP-relative interpretations with part-whole shared arguments: in this case, the subject of the matrix clause is a subset of the subordinate clause (1SG ⊂ 1PL.EXCL). An alternative analysis is that the 'overlapping temporal reference' of the T-relative interpretation includes an overlap of the post-state of one event with another event. In this case, the situation denoted in the matrix clause overlaps with the post-state of the situation denoted in the subordinate clause, rather than the situation itself.

(1,065)   **[*Ngula=ja*   *pina*   *pa-nangu*   *Alekarengei-ka*]**   *marta-rnu=rna*
REL=1PL.EXCL.S   **return**   **go-PAST**   **Alekarenge-ALL**   have-PAST=1SG.S

kurtu   *jirrima=kanyanu=lku*.
child   two=ANOTHER=THEN

I had two more kids [**after** we returned to Alekarenge].

wrl-20190211-01, DK, 06:00 mins

Regardless of its function, the *ngula* clause must always be adjacent to the matrix clause at the surface structure; this syntactic constraint also applies to other finite complementisers; however, their semantic interpretation is considerably more restricted (and they only function as modifiers at a clausal level).

All noted examples of *ngula* involve an event concurrent with or prior to speech time. This includes verbs marked with the POTENTIAL inflection, as part of a posterior past construction, as in (1,066). For events following speech time, one of the other subordinators is used. The grammaticality of *ngula* clauses with future events remains an area for further investigation.

(1,066) **[Ngula**=rna **pa-nama** ngurra-ka], Jungarrayi-rlu=ma kupa-rnu
REL=1SG.S go-POT camp-ALL Jungarrayi-ERG=TOP cook-PAST
kampangarli.
ahead
Jungarrayi cooked dinner first, [before I had come home].
wrl-20180608-01, DK, 32:40 mins

12.1.1.1.2 Adverbial *ngula* clauses

When functioning as an adverbial, *ngula* clauses indicate that the situation denoted by the subordinate predicate shares some overlapping time reference with the situation denoted by the matrix predicate, translated as 'while' or 'when'. This interpretation is only available when the *ngula* clause has identical TAM marking to the matrix clause, as in (1,067), where both inflecting verbs are inflected for present tense.

(1,067) Ngarrka-ngu karli <u>ngarta-nnya</u> **[ngula yapa-ngu**
man-ERG boomerang <u>trim-PRES</u> REL **child-ERG**
nyaninya maliki <u>kapu-ngunya]</u>.
3GEN dog <u>chase-PRES</u>
The man is trimming the boomerang while the child is chasing her dog.
N_D02-007842, BN, 39:34 mins

Adverbial interpretations of *ngula* clauses are prohibited when the temporal reference is future; this function is performed by *kayi* (§12.1.1.3). Sæbø (2011: 1423) notes it is 'not uncommon' cross-linguistically to have different morphosyntactic exponents of what is essentially the same function but differing by whether it has future or non-future temporal reference.

12.1.1.1.3 Relative *ngula* clauses

Relative interpretations of *ngula* clauses indicate that the subordinate clause is supplying further information about the referent denoted by a nominal in the matrix clause, as in (1,068).

(1,068) Kurtu yarri ka-ngka **[ngula lu-ngunya]**.
child that take-IMP REL **cry-PRES**
Take the child who is crying.
H_K01-505B, DG, 47:39 mins

12. SYNTAX OF COMPLEX CLAUSES

There appear to be no restrictions on the type of argument in the main clause to which the *ngula* can refer, as demonstrated in examples (1,069)–(1,073).

Matrix subject = subordinate subject (S=S):

(1,069) **[*Yali-ngu=nya*   *ngula*   *karta*   *pu-ngu*]**   *yarnunju=lpangu*
         that-ERG=FOC   REL   spear   act_on-PAST food=1PL.INCL.NS
         kupa-nnya.
         cook-PRES
         That one who dug the ground is cooking us dinner.
         wrl-20180616-01, DK, 14:20 mins

Matrix subject = subordinate object (S=O):

(1,070) *Pulka-ngu*   *pirrka-ma-nnya*   *karli*   **[*ngula=rla***
         old_man-ERG   trim-do-PRES   boomerang   **REL=3.OBL**
         karnta=ma   ***wa-nganya].***
         woman=TOP   **speak-PRES**
         The old man who the woman is talking to is trimming a boomerang.
         (Also a T-relative interpretation: The man is trimming a boomerang while the woman is speaking to him.)
         wrl-20191207-01, DK, 44:39 mins

Matrix object = subordinate subject (O=S):

(1,071) *Maliki=n*   *nya-ngu*   *[ngula=ju*   *pu-ngu].*
         dog=2SG.S   see-PAST   REL=1SG.NS   act_on-PAST
         You saw the dog [that bit me]?
         H_K01-505B, DG, 13:40 mins

Matrix object = subordinate object (O=O):

(1,072) *Wawirri=rna*   *kupa-n*   *[ngula=n*   *karta*   *pu-ngu].*
         kangaroo=1SG.S   cook-FUT   REL=2SG.S   spear   act_on-PAST
         I'll cook the kangaroo [which you speared].
         H_K01-505B, DG, 21:56 mins

Matrix external object = subordinate subject:

(1,073) *Ngayu=ma=rna-rla   yarnunju   marta-nnya   kurtu-ku   [**ngula***
        1=TOP=1SG.S-3.OBL   food   have-PRES   child-DAT   REL
        lu-ngunya].
        cry-PRES
        I have food for the child [who is crying].
        wrl-20190205, DK, 42:53 mins

12.1.1.1.4 Positioning of *ngula* clauses

The *ngula* clause obligatorily occurs on the left or right edge of the matrix clause, regardless of semantic interpretation. Clearly, then, the *ngula* clause does not have to be adjacent to the nominal expression it is modifying. The ordering of the *ngula* clause and the matrix clause is usually (but not necessarily) iconic, in that the event that occurs (or begins) first is denoted by the left clause, as in (1,065)–(1,075). If there is no temporal ordering, the *ngula* clause tends to occur on the right edge, as in (1,076).

Within the subordinate clause, *ngula* typically takes the auxiliary position (that is, second position; see §5.3.6). Notably, however, the verb of the subordinate clause can never precede *ngula*, which overrides the preference for second position (just as an inflecting verb can never precede an auxiliary base in a matrix clause). Regardless of whether it is in second or first position, *ngula* always hosts the bound pronouns.

Second-position *ngula*:

(1,074) *[Ngarrka-ngu   **ngula***=ju   paka-rnu,]   nga=ngu=nga*
        man-ERG   REL=1.SG.NS   hit-PAST   POST=2SG.NS=DUB
        paka-nma=yijala.
        hit-POT=ALSO
        The man who hit me might hit you, too.
        H_K01-506B, DG, 08:22 mins

(1,075) *Ka-ngu-rra=rna   [wangani-rlu   **ngula***=ju   pu-ngu].*
        sit-past-IMPF=1SG.S   dog-ERG   REL=1SG.NS   bite-PAST
        I was sitting down when a dog bit me.
        wrl-20180528-03, JK, 4:15 mins

First-position *ngula*:

(1,076) Ngarrka-ngu   karla-nnya   karli   [***ngula***=jana   karnta-ngu
man-ERG   trim-PRES   boomerang   REL=3PL.NS   woman-ERG
yarnunju-ku[4]   kurtu~kurtu-ku   yu-ngunya].
food-DAT   child-PL-DAT   give-PRES

The man is trimming the boomerang [while the woman is giving food to the children].

N_D02-007842, BN, 40:29 mins

There is evidence for recursion of *ngula* in (1,077), where the right-most *ngula* clause is a relative clause modifier of the indirect object of the left-most *ngula* clause.

(1,077) Nya-ngu=rna   karnta   [ngula=rla   yarnunju   kupa-rnu-rra
see-PAST=1SG.S   woman   REL=3.OBL   food   cook-PAST-IMPF
kurtu-ku   witta-ku   [ngula   jarta   ka-ngu-rra]].
child-DAT   small-DAT   REL   sleep   be-PAST-IMPF

I saw a woman [who was cooking food for the small child [who was sleeping]].

wrl-20191209, DK, 01:37 mins

12.1.1.1.5 Negation

Like other finite clauses, *ngula* clauses can be negated with *kula*. As discussed in §11.5.1.1, *kula* is typically found clause-initially, however, *ngula* precedes *kula* when they co-occur. This appears to reflect the general constraint that when the *ngula* clause follows the matrix clause, *ngula* must be found clause-initially (in each case, the *ngula* clause is found following the matrix clause).

(1,078) Kula=rna   ma-nma   **ngula**   **kula**   lu-ngunya
NEG=1SG.S   get-POT   REL   NEG   cry-PRES

I won't get the dog who isn't crying.

N_D03-007868, BN, 40:10 mins

---

4   I am unsure why there is a dative suffix on *yarnunju* 'food'; the expected case frame of *yi-* 'give' is ERG–ABS–DAT, but the indirect object (which takes dative marking) is *kurtukurtu-ku* 'to/for the children'. In the lexicon, *yarnunjuku* is a well-formed nominal meaning 'hungry', but it cannot be construed of the indirect object in this clause because it lacks dative marking (that is, 'for the hungry children' would be *yarnunjuku-ku kurtukurtu-ku*).

(1,079) Yapa=rna   witta   ka-nganya,   or   ma-nma
       person=1SG.S   small   take-PRES   get-POT
       ngula   **kula** lu-ngunya.
       REL   NEG   cry-PRES
       I am taking [or getting] the child who isn't crying.
       N_D03-007868, BN, 40:26 mins

A matrix clause can be negated without affecting the polarity of the subordinate clause, as in (1,080).

(1,080) Walku, kula=rna   maliki nya-ngu   ngula=ngu   pu-ngu.
       no   NEG=1SG.S   dog   see-PAST   REL=2SG.NS   act_on-PAST
       No, I didn't see the dog which bit you.
       (This still presupposes that 'the dog bit you' is true.)
       H_K01-505B, DG, 13:49 mins

12.1.1.2 Kari 'conditional'

12.1.1.2.1 Function of kari

Kari indicates the subordinate clause is the condition of the main clause.

(1,081) [**Kari**=n   karli   kiya-nmi,]   kapi=rna-ngu   paka-nmi.
       COND=2SG.S   boomerang   throw-FUT,   FUT=1SG.S-2SG.NS hit-FUT
       I will hit you if you throw that boomerang.
       H_K01-505B, DG, 14:18 mins

(1,082) Ngarrka=rla   wa-nganyu   karnta-ku,   'Yapa-ku   kula=rla
       man=3.OBL   speak-PAST   woman-DAT,   child-DAT   NEG=3.OBL
       yi-nyi   yarnunju,   [**kari** **lirra** **patti**   **wiri-ja-nya**].'
       give-FUT   food   COND   teeth   hard   big-INCH-PRES
       The man told the woman, 'You won't give the child any food until her teeth get better.'
       N_D02-007842, BN, 53:14 mins

Kari has slightly different functions depending on whether it combines with the counterfactual inflection. When occurring with any other verb inflection, the cooperative truth conditions of *kari* are p ⇔ q—that is, the sentence is true if and only if both clauses are true or both are false.[5] This is exemplified in Table 12.2 using (1,083) as an example. The table shows that the sentence is only felicitous in outcomes 1 and 4, and that no appeal to 'possible worlds' is necessary for *kari* in most circumstances.[6]

(1,083) [**p**] [**q**]
[*Kari=n   nyuyu   kiya-nma*]   [*nga=rna-ngu=nga   paka-nma*].
cond=2sg.s   spit   throw-POT   PURP=1SG.S-2SG.NS=DUB   hit-POT
If you spit, I'll hit you!
H_K01-506A, DG, 11:06 mins

Table 12.2 Cooperative truth conditions of kari when not combining with a counterfactual protasis

Outcomes		p	q	p ⇔ q
1	**You spit and I hit you**	T	T	T
2	You spit and I don't hit you	T	F	F
3	You chuck spit and I hit you	F	T	F
4	**You chuck spit and I don't hit you**	F	F	T

Kari has different truth conditions when it co-occurs with a COUNTERFACTUAL condition. These sentences are true if and only if for all possible worlds (which are relevantly similar to the real world) where *p* is true, *q* is true, following Lewis (1973) and Kearns (2011: 83).

This analysis can be exemplified with (1,084), where the use of the counterfactual inflection conveys that *p* is false in the real world, so the addressee must consider the (relevant) possible worlds where *p* is true, and in each of these worlds (that is, where the addressee has walked a long distance), *q* must be true (the addressee becomes tired).[7]

---

5   I assume *p* being false and *q* being true would be an uncooperative use of *kari* and should be ruled out as a reasonable interpretation by implicature. However, I have not tested this.
6   This is an oversimplified analysis of the semantics of conditionals, in that all conditionals necessarily refer to possible worlds, however, the connection between the possible worlds relevant to strict conditionals such as in (1,083) is much smaller than for counterfactual conditions, as in (1,084). My key assumption is that the former seem to be conceptualised as referring to the real world at their core, whereas the latter seem to have a wider range of possible worlds that are often quite unlike the real world. Lewis (1973: 4–13) and Hilpinen (1981) discuss this problem in more detail.
7   See Kearns (2011: 88–92) and McCawley (1993: Ch. 12) for a discussion of 'relevant' possible worlds. For our sake, 'relevant possible worlds' are ones in which travelling long distances makes people tired, etcetera—that is: $S \Leftrightarrow \forall w((p \text{ in } w \ \& \ w \text{ otherwise relevantly similar to } w_0) \rightarrow q \text{ in } w)$.

	[	p	]	[	q	]
(1,084)	*[Kari=n*	*kari-ma*	*panja-kurla,]*	*[nga=n=nga*	*palapala-ja-ma].*	
	COND=2SG.S	far-EXT	go-CFACT,	ADM=2SG.S =ADM	tired-become-POT	

You might become tired if you were to go that far.
H_K01-506A, DG, 04:56 mins

The use of *kari* can be summarised as:

a. If considering situations in the real world (actualised or expected to be actualised), non-counterfactual inflections are used with *kari*, to express p ⇔ q.
b. If considering situations not actualised in the real world, the counterfactual inflection is used to convey that: 1) *p* is false, and 2) in all relevant possible worlds where *p* is true, *q* is true.[8]

12.1.1.2.2 Syntactic constraints

Kari typically occurs in first position of the subordinate clause, as in (1,085).

(1,085) *[**Kari**=n   mirla   ka-njakurla,]   nga=rna-ngu=nga   paka-nma.*
COND=2SG.S this.LOC be-CFACT POST=1SG.S-2SG. hit-POT
NS=DUB

If you were to sit there, I might hit you.
H_K01-506A, DG, 05:36 mins

It may also occur in second position—that is, where the auxiliary base occurs in matrix clauses—as in (1,086).

(1,086) *[Karnta-panji **kari**=lu   jitpi-nyi,]   nga=lu=nga   wa-nma.*
woman-PAUC COND=3PL.S run-FUT POST=3PL.S=DUB fall-POT

If the few women will run, they might fall.
H_K01-506A, DG, 03:04 mins

---

8   The example has the potential inflection in the main clause, so the proposition *q* can still *contain* an uncertain event while being true.

(1,087) [yapa   **kari**   wa-njakurla]   nga=nga   li-nya.
         child   COND   fall-CFACT   POST=DUB   cry-POT
         If the child were to fall, she might cry.
         H_K01-506A, DG, 05:10 mins

Regardless of whether *kari* surfaces in first or second position, it hosts the bound pronouns. Unlike *ngula*, there are no instances of *kari* clauses occurring on the right edge of the matrix clause, other than (1,082).

12.1.1.3 *Kayi* 'when'

The usage of *kayi* encodes that during the time that its clausal proposition is true, another proposition (denoted in the matrix clause) will also be true. Furthermore, *kayi* presupposes that the protasis will become true at some point. In example (1,088), the meaning of *kayi* is similar to that of *kari*, with *kayi* emphasising that the consequence 'the dog not biting you' will only hold while the condition 'you sit next to me' is also true, so once the condition no longer holds, nor will the consequence. This contrasts with *kari*, which expresses that if the condition is true, the consequence will be true, with no temporal component encoded.

(1,088) [*Kayi=n*   *ngayinya-rla*   *ka-nya*]   *wangani*   *kula=ngu*   *pi-nyi*.
         WHEN=   1-LOC   sit-PRES   dog   NEG=2SG.   bite-FUT
         2SG.S   NS
         While you sit next to me, the dog won't bite you.
         wrl-20180605-01, DK, 13:35 mins

(1,089) *Ngayu=ma*   *pa-nnya*   *ngurra-*   [*kayi=ju*   *parra*   *puruly*
         =rna   *ka=lku,*
         1=TOP=   go-PRES   camp-   WHEN=   sun   set
         1SG.S   ALL=THEN   1SG.NS
         wa-nmi].
         fall-FUT
         I'll go home when the sun sets on me.
         wrl-20180605-01, DK, 22:53 mins

The contrast between *kayi* and *kari* is clearer in (1,090), where the speaker expects the addressee to return later, so the use of *kari* would be infelicitous.

(1,090) [Kayi=n   pa-nami-rni   pina]   ngayu=ma=rna   jarta.
         WHEN=2SG.S   go-FUT-HITH   return   1=TOP=1SG.S   asleep
         When you come back, I will be asleep.
         (#If you come back, I will be asleep.)
         wrl-20190201, DK, 32:06 mins

Kari and *kayi* also exhibit differing syntactic properties, in that *kayi* clauses regularly occur on the right edge of the matrix clause, as in (1,091), whereas *kari* clauses are generally restricted to the left edge of the matrix clause.

(1,091) Kala=rnalu-nyanu   paka-nmi   [kayi=rna   pa-nama].
         APPR=1PL.EXCL.S-RR   hit-FUT   WHEN=1SG.S   go-FUT.AWAY
         We'll fight each other/ourselves when I go.
         wrl-20190213-02, DK, 33:31 mins

Only one speaker has been recorded using *kayi* (this speaker contributes to the 'present' corpus). For other speakers, it appears these uses are subsumed by *kari*. There also are no instances of *kayi* occurring in the second position in the clause that it heads, unlike the other finite complementisers.

Kayi may be cognate with *kaji* in Warlpiri and Ngardi. In these languages, *kaji* signals temporal or logical conditionality (Ennever 2021; Nash 1986: 240), whereas Warlmanpa *kayi* signals only temporal conditionality.

12.1.1.4 *Nga=* 'purposive'

Nga= heads a subordinate clause related to the matrix clause with a relation of 'purpose', as in (1,092)–(1,094).

(1,092) Ngayu=ma=rna   wayi-nnya   ngayinya-ku   wangani-ku
         1=TOP=1SG.S   search-PRES   1GEN-DAT   dog-DAT
         [nga=rna-rla   yarnunju   yi-nyi].
         PURP=1SG.S-DAT   food   give-FUT
         I'm searching for my dog so I can give food to him.
         wrl-20190131-02, DK, 11:57 mins

(1,093) Pingka   wa-ngka,   **[nga=rna   purtu   ka-mi]**.
         slowly   speak-IMP   **PURP=1SG.S   hear   be-FUT**
         Speak slowly, so that I can hear.
         H_K01-506A, DG, 32:09 mins

(1,094) *Jangala   ma-nta   [nga=rna-rla   wanga-mi].*
         Jangala   get-IMP   PURP=1SG.S-3.OBL   speak-FUT
         Get Jangala so I can speak to him.
         wrl-20200219, DK, 01:00:57 hrs

This complementiser may be related to the auxiliary base *nga* 'FUT', however, I analyse them as distinct, both synchronically and diachronically. Historically, they are very likely to have been two distinct lexemes, with cognates in Warlpiri shown in Table 12.3 (Warlpiri data from Nash 1986: 59–60).

Table 12.3 Warlpiri cognates of Warlmanpa *nga=*

Warlpiri gloss	Warlpiri form	Warlmanpa form
PURPOSIVE	*yinga*	*nga*
FUTURE	*ngarra*	*nga(rra)*

Synchronic evidence of Warlpiri *yinga* corresponding to Warlmanpa *nga* can be seen in Warlpiri prompts including *yinga*, which are then translated into Warlmanpa with *nga*, as shown in (1,095).

(1,095) a. *Ngampurrpa   ka=rna   nyina   **yinga**=rna   yama-kurra*
           desire   PRES=1SG.S   sit.NPAST   CAUSAL=   shade-ALL
                                                      1SG.S

   ya-ni.
   go-NPAST
   I want to go to the shade.
   (Warlpiri [Ken Hale prompt, H_K01-505B: 25:52 mins])

b. *Ngampurrpa=rna   ka-nya   **nga**=rna   yama-ka*
   desire=1SG.S   be-PRES   PURP=1SG.S   shade-ALL

   pa-nama.
   go-FUT.AWAY
   I want to go to the shade.
   (Warlmanpa translation of a.)
   H_K01-505B, DG, 25:58 mins

These examples of *nga=* as a complementiser also demonstrate further iconic ordering, in which the subordinate clauses headed by *nga=* always occur on the right edge of the matrix clause, as the event denoted by the matrix clause must occur for the causal effect, denoted by the *nga=* clause.

12.1.1.5 Direct speech

Direct speech is typically introduced as the object of a predicate of speech, such as *wa-* 'speak' or *jili ka-* 'ask', as in (1,096), where the speaker is reporting on a command given to them:

(1,096) *Ayi=nya=ju   wa-nganyu 'Kula kataj   paka-ka   yiwirti.'*
        that=FOC=1SG.NS speak-PAST NEG   cut_down   strike-IMP tree
        That one said to me, 'Don't cut down the tree!'
        wrl-20191208-02, DK, 30:42 mins

The deictic centre switches to that of the quoted speakers, overtly marked by the verb inflections and bound pronouns in the represented speech. For example, in (1,097), the verb takes a future inflection for an event that occurred after the reported speech, but before the retelling. Similarly, the bound pronoun registering is from the perspective of the referent, hence the use of the inclusive bound pronoun, despite the addressee of the narrative not taking part in the event.

(1,097) *Still=rna   purtu ka-nya   ngula=nganpa-lu   ngayinya yapa*
        still=1SG.S   hear   be-PRES   REL=1EXCL.   1.GEN   person
                                         PL.NS-3PL.S

 wa-nganyu-rra   'Army-kuma=lpa   kantukantu   ka-nji-nmi,
 speak-PAST-IMPF   army-AVER=1INC.PL.S   hide   be-INC-FUT

 kala=lpangu   la-nma.'
 APPR=1INC.PL.NS   shoot-POT

I still remember our old people used to tell us, 'We're going and hiding in case the army shoots us.'
N_D02-007844, BN, 27:05 mins

Because the deictic centre is overtly marked (flagged by the auxiliary and the verb inflection), there appear to be no strict lexical restrictions on which verbs can introduce direct speech.

In sequences of reported speech, there is often no overt verb to denote the consequent deictic centre switches. In (1,098), the first deictic centre switch is explicitly introduced by the coverb *jilij* 'ask', but the next switch (the answer to the reported question) is not overtly introduced.

(1,098) a. *Kala=rna-*   *ngayu=ma*   **jilij ka-ngu**   *'ngana-*
jana   *ngurlu=lpangu*
HAB=1SG.S-   1=TOP   **ask be-PAST**   what-ELA=1INC.
3PL.NS   PL.NS

la-nmi,   *kala=lpangu*   *la-nmi?'*
shoot-FUT   HAB=1INC.   shoot-FUT
            PL.NS

I would ask my old people, 'What are they going to shoot us for? Why will they shoot us?'

b. *'Kula=nkulu*   *nya-nganya*   *kurtukurtu-rlu*   *ngula=lu*   a̠r̠m̠y̠
NEG=2PL.S   see-PRES   children-ERG   REL=3PL.S

jaala   *jutpu-ngunya*   b̠i̠t̠u̠m̠e̠n̠-nga.'
up_and_down   run-PRES   bitumen-LOC

'You kids can't see that the army is running on the bitumen.'
N_D02-007844, BN, 26:27 mins

12.1.2 Non-finite subordinate clauses

Non-finite subordinate clauses in Warlmanpa lack an auxiliary (including bound pronouns) and any TAM inflections and each constituent obligatorily hosts a complementiser suffix. The main predicate of a non-finite subordinate clause tends to be an infinitive hosting a complementising suffix (given in Table 12.4), although it can be a nominal (hosting a complementising suffix). The subordinate clause is typically on the right edge of the matrix clause.

Complementising suffixes can be categorised according to their function: some are more grammatical, in that they signal only temporal and argument control relations, and some are more semantic, in that they specify a semantic relation (to the matrix clause). The grammatical complementising suffixes (which overlap with the case system) signal at least one of the following:

i.   Argument control—that is, a grammatical relation of the subordinate clause matrix predicate is coreferential with an argument of the matrix clause (for example, the complementising suffix *-karra* indicates coreferentiality between the subjects of the matrix clause and subordinate clause; and the allative case *-ka* signals that the subject of the subordinate clause is coreferential with the object of the matrix clause). This is also referred to as 'switch-reference' (Austin 1981), although, unlike other languages such as Martuthunira (Dench 1988) and Mparntwe Arrernte (Wilkins 1988), there is no finite tense switch-reference mechanism in Warlmanpa, only non-finite complementising suffixes.

ii. Temporal relation—the temporal reference of the subordinate clause is specified in relation to the event of the matrix clause: posterior, simultaneous or anterior.

Conversely, some complementising suffixes specify a semantic relation between the subordinate clause and matrix clause, with a less clear specification for argument control and temporal relation (if any).

Table 12.4 Non-finite complementisers

Form	Case/function	Complementising function		Section
		Argument control	Temporal relation	
-karra	Same subject	Subject	Simultaneous	§12.1.2.1
-pa-	Ergative subject	Subject	–	§12.1.2.2
-ngarnu	Source*	Subject	Anterior	§12.1.2.3
-rla	Locative*	Subject	Posterior	§12.1.2.4
-ka	Allative*	Object	Simultaneous	§12.1.2.5
-ku	Dative*	–	Posterior	§12.1.2.6
-jila	Without*	–	–	§12.1.2.7
-wangu	Privative*	–	–	§12.1.2.8
-kuma	Aversive*	–	–	§12.1.2.9
-kupa	Desiderative*	–	–	§12.1.2.10

Note: Subordinators marked with an asterisk also have a case function.

An example of a non-finite clause is given in (1,099). Each constituent in the subordinate clause hosts an allative suffix, indicating that: 1) the object of the matrix clause is coreferential with the subject of the subordinate clause, and 2) the temporal reference of the non-finite clause overlaps with that of the matrix clause.

(1,099) *Nya-ngu=ju-n*   *[partakurru-ma-nji-ka   karli-ka].*
         see-PAST=1SG.NS-2SG.S   **good-CAUSE-INF-ALL   boomerang-ALL**
         You saw me fixing a boomerang.
         You saw me$_i$ e_i fixing a boomerang.[9]
         N_D03-007868, BN, 41:40 mins

Non-finite subordinate clauses modify either clauses (for example, the dative that relates a PURPOSE subordinate clause) or nominal expressions—the latter evidenced by the fact that non-finite subordinate clauses obligatorily share at least one argument with the main clause. Furthermore, constituents of some non-finite clauses take ergative case, if the understood subject of the non-finite clause is coreferential with an ergative-marked subject in the matrix clause, as in (1,100) and (1,101). However, some complementising suffixes block further case, such as *-wangu* 'privative'. Note that the subordinate clauses in these two examples have different temporal relations to the matrix clause: *-karra* indicates simultaneity between the situations in the two clauses and *-rla* indicates that the subordinate clause situations precede the matrix clause situation.

(1,100) ***Ngarrka-ngu***   *karli*   *ngartannya*   *[wa-nganja-karra-rlu].*
         man-ERG   boomerang   trim-PRES   **speak-INF-SS-ERG**
         The man is trimming the boomerang while speaking.
         The man$_i$ is trimming the boomerang while e_i speaking.
         N_D02-007842, BN, 38:10 mins

(1,101) *Kuyu=rna*   *nga-rnu*   *[kupa-nji-jila-rlu].*
         meat=1SG.S   eat-PAST   **cook-INF-WITHOUT-ERG**
         I ate the meat, having cooked it.
         I$_i$ ate the meat$_j$, e_i having cooked it$_j$.
         wrl-20190205, DK, 04:13 mins

Non-finite complementisers derive an infinitive from an inflecting verb (§6.2.3.8). Infinitives are much like nominals in that they are subject to case agreement (see §3.1.6), but unlike most nominals, infinitives cannot function as arguments of predicates. The only type of case agreement that is possible, as far as I can tell, is a subordinate clause where constituents

---

[9] In this section I will include a second translation line that will include *e* for unexpressed arguments and subscripts to make coreferentiality explicit. The subscript $_i$ is reserved for grammatically obligatory coreferentiality and $_{j/k}$ are used for non-obligatory coreferentiality.

are marked with an ergative suffix in addition to their complementising suffix, where the subordinate clause is modifying an ergative argument, as in (1,100) and (1,101).[10] In these cases, the matrix clause has an ergative-absolutive case frame and the subordinate predicate is construed with the ergative argument of the matrix clause, so it hosts an ergative suffix.

Generally, all words in the subordinate clause obligatorily bear the complementiser suffix:

(1,102)   *Purt*   *pu-ngu=rna*   *Jinarinji-ka*   *ngayinya*   *ngalapi*
          send   act_on-PAST=1SG.S   Jinarinji-ALL   1.GEN   son
          *[puliki-**ku**   ka-nja-**ku**   ngurrurla-**ku**].*
          cow-DAT   carry-INF-DAT   return-DAT
          I sent my son to Jinarinji to bring back a bullock.
          I sent my son$_j$ to Jinarinji to e_j bring back a bullock.
          N_D02-009887, DG, 07:10 mins

However, there are a few cases where, like Warlpiri, only the final constituent of the subordinate clause hosts a suffix, as in (1,103), where in the subordinate clause *Warlmanpa wanganjika* 'speaking Warlmanpa', only the right-most constituent takes the allative case (in its subordinating function).

(1,103)   *Tartu=rna-jana*   *purtu-ka-ngu*   *[Warlmanpa*   *wa-nganji-ka].*
          many=1SG.S-3PL.NS   listen-be-PAST   Warlmanpa   speak-INF-ALL
          I heard lots of them speaking Warlmanpa.
          I heard lots of them$_i$ e_i speaking Warlmanpa.
          H_K01-505B, DG, 43:32 mins

Non-finite subordinate clauses typically occur on the right edge of the matrix clause. There are only a few instances of the subordinate clause occurring on the left edge (see [1,110], [1,111] and [1,115]) or, even more rarely, intervening between matrix clause constituents, as in (1,104), where *kupanjaku* 'to cook' intervenes between two main clause constituents.

---

10   Many complementising suffixes are case suffixes, thereby preventing any further case agreement, hence the sparsity of case agreement processes possible for subordinate clauses.

12. SYNTAX OF COMPLEX CLAUSES

(1,104)   *Ka-nganya=rna*   **[*kupa-nja-ku*]**   *ngurra-ka.*
take-PRES=1SG.S   **cook-INF-DAT**   camp-ALL
I'm taking it home to cook.
I^j am taking it$_k$ home to e_j cook e_k.
wrl-20190211-02, DK, 13:48 mins

Grammatical relations between the subordinate predicate and its dependants are not morphologically encoded. For example, the predicate of the subordinate clause in (1,105) is *nya-* 'see' and the object argument is *papulu* 'house'. In a matrix clause, this relation would be realised with *papulu* being in its absolutive form (that is, morphologically unmarked), but in the non-finite subordinate clause it hosts a dative suffix. Then, Wuppa, the name of a camp in Tennant Creek, is itself a modifier of the nominal *papulu* ('the house in Wuppa'), but the exponent of this morphosyntactic distinction—that *Wuppa* would be expected to host a locative suffix—is not realised, as each constituent in the subordinate clause can only host the complementising suffix.

(1,105)   *Pa-nyinga=lku*   **[*Wuppa-ku*   *nya-nja-ku*   *papulu-ku*].**
go-PATH=THEN   **Wuppa-DAT**   **see-INF-DAT**   **house-DAT**
Now he's going [to see (the house [in Wuppa camp]$_{LOCATION}$)$_{ARGUMENT}$].
Now he$_j$'s going to e_j see the house in Wuppa camp.
wrl-20190213-01, DK, 17:11 mins

However, there is one example where this appears to not be the case. In (1,106), the purposive subordinate clause is marked with the dative case (evidenced by the dative case on the infinitive), but the adjunct *muka* 'there' (in its allative form) does not take dative marking. Both (1,105) and (1,106) adhere to the restriction of only allowing one case suffix on a word, yet in (1,105) the complementising agreement seems to take priority, whereas the semantic case in (1,106) seems to take priority.

(1,106)   *Ngarrka-ngu=ju*   *nga-rnu*   *[muka(*-ku)=nya*   *ya-nja-ku].*
man-ERG=1SG.NS   tell-PAST   this.ALL(*-DAT)=FOC   put-INF-DAT
The man told me to put it there.
The man told me$_j$ to e_j put it there.
H_K01-505B, DG, 25:12 mins

It is not clear whether subordinate clauses are recursive; based on the case-marking rules of the language, nominals are unable to take more than one case, so there would be no mechanism to create recursive subordinate clauses (given that most complementising suffixes *are* case suffixes and it is quite likely that the complementising suffixes that have no corresponding case function still have the same morphological status as case). To exemplify, consider (1,107). The main predicate of the left-most subordinate clause is *pa-* 'go', which denotes the purpose of the matrix clause sending event. A second subordinate clause, *nyanjaku* 'to see him', could reasonably be interpreted as a purposive modifier of the 'go' event. If this is the case, it would take a dative case to indicate its purposive relation and that it is a modifier of the dative-marked *panjaku* 'to go', but only one dative suffix would surface due to the inability for case suffix stacking. Thus, the surface constituent *nyanjaku* 'for seeing (him)' could also be a second subordinate clause to the matrix clause.

(1,107) *Jaru=ju*   *purt pu-ngu-rnu*   *pulka-ngu*   **[pa-nja-ku]**
         message=1SG.NS   send act_on-PAST-TWD   old_man-ERG   **go-INF-DAT**

[nya-nja-ku].
see-INF-DAT

?That old man told me [to go (to see him)].
?That old man told me [to go] [to see him].
N_D02-009887, DG, 05:11 mins

Similarly, in (1,108), there are two subordinate clauses, both dative marked. The left-most subordinate clause denotes 'to get his gun' and the right-most denotes 'to go hunting'. In this case, the semantic interpretation of two subordinate clauses related to the matrix clause is somewhat more difficult: the event of getting his gun (the left-most subordinate clause) has the purpose of hunting (the right-most subordinate clause). It is semantically unintuitive to directly relate the matrix clause predicate, *pananga* 'went', and the subordinate clause, *wirlinyiku panjaku* 'to go hunting', by purpose.

(1,108) *Ngarrka=ma=nya*   *pa-nanga*   **[lamanpa-ku**   **ma-nja-ku]**
         man=TOP=FOC   go-PAST.AWAY   **gun-DAT**   **get-INF-DAT**

[wirlinyi-ku   *pa-nja-ku].*
hunting-DAT   go-INF-DAT

?The man went [for his gun (to go hunting)].
?The man went [for his gun] [to go hunting].
wrl-20190205, DK, 53:28 mins

While these examples are semantically appealing evidence for an analysis of syntactic recursion, there is no apparent morphosyntactic exponent of recursion and, as such, I assume each subordinate clause in these examples is construed of the matrix clause.

Finally, it should also be noted that non-finite clauses are often heavily reduced, usually containing just a predicate and any appropriate arguments. There are no examples in the corpus of discontinuous subordinate clauses. Modifiers are extremely rare in non-finite subordinate clauses. Each complementising suffix is now discussed in turn.

12.1.2.1 -*karra* 'subject-controlled relative'

A subordinate clause marked with -*karra* indicates the situation denoted in the subordinate clause has overlapping temporal reference with that of the matrix clause, as well as a coreferential subject.

(1,109) Ngarrka   wa-nganya   [**ka-nja-karra**].
         man   speak-PRES   **sit-INF-SS**
         The man is talking while sitting.
         The man$_i$ is talking while e_i sitting.
         N_D02-007842, BN, 36:53 mins

If the matrix subject is ergative, the subordinate -*karra* clause may also be marked with ergative, as in (1,110)–(1,112), although this appears to be optional, as shown in (1,113), where the matrix subject noun phrase has ergative marking, yet the subordinate clause does not host any ergative marking.

Subordinate -*karra* takes ERG suffix:

(1,110) [***Luyu-karra-rlu***]=*ju*   *karta*   *pu-ngu*.
         crying-SS-ERG=1SG.NS   hit   act_on-PAST
         He hit me while [he was] crying.
         He hit me while e_i crying.
         H_K01-505B, DG, 36:28 mins

(1,111) **[Yina nga-rninja-karra-rlu]** karta pungunya karli.
  sing eat-INF-SSCOMP-ERG trim act_on-PRES boomerang
  He is trimming the boomerang while singing.
  He$_i$ is trimming the boomerang while e_i singing.
  H_K01-505B, DG, 36:12 mins

(1,112) Ngarrka-ngu karli ngarta-nnya **[wa-nganja-karra-rlu]**.
  man-ERG boomerang trim-PRES **speak-INF-SS-ERG**
  The man is trimming the boomerang while talking.
  The man$_i$ is trimming the boomerang while e_i talking.
  N_D02-007842, BN, 38:10 mins

Subordinate -*karra* lacks ERG suffix:

(1,113) Karnta-ngu nya-ngu wangani **[kurtu-karra lamarta-nja-karra]**.
  woman-ERG see-PAST dog **child-SS hold-INF-SS**
  The woman saw the dog while holding the child.
  The woman$_i$ saw the dog while e_i holding the child.
  wrl-20190206, DK, 07:48 mins

Similar to -*ka*, it appears the temporal relationship between the matrix clause and the -*karra* subordinate clause is one in which the situation denoted in the subordinate clause provides a wider temporal context in which the situation denoted by the matrix clause occurs—that is, $T_{MATRIX} \subseteq T_{SUB}$.

12.1.2.2 -*pa*- 'ergative control'

A subordinate clause marked with -*pa*- is obligatorily controlled by the ergative argument of the matrix clause. In most cases, the temporal relation is one of overlap (as with -*ka* and -*karra*), as in (1,114)–(1,116).

(1,114) Ngurlu=rna ma-nyanya **[pa-nji-pa-rlu]**.
  seeds=1SG.S get-PRES.AWAY **go-INF-SS-ERG**
  I'm collecting seeds going [around].
  I$_i$'m collecting seeds e_i going [around].
  wrl-20190205, DK, 07:55 mins

(1,115) *[Pa-nji-pa-rlu]*=lu   yulu   karta   pu-ngunya.
        go-INF-SS-ERG=3PL.S   ground   spear   act_on-PRES
        They're digging holes in the ground going [around].
        They$_i$'re digging holes in the ground e_i going [around].
        H_K01-505B, DG, 36:21 mins

(1,116) *Karnta-ngu*   *ngurlu*   *jama-nnya*   *kantu*   *papulu-rla*   **[ka-nji-pa-rlu]**.
        woman-ERG   seed   grind-PRES   inside   house-LOC   **sit**-INF-SS-ERG
        The woman is inside the house grinding the seeds while sitting.
        The woman$_i$ is inside the house grinding the seeds while e_i sitting.
        N_D02-007842, BN, 38:31 mins

There is one token where it has a 'prior' meaning, in which the situation denoted by the subordinate clause occurs prior to that of the matrix clause, seen in (1,117b.), which is a translation of a., where the Warlpiri prompt uses *-rla* 'sequential'.

(1,117) a. *Kuyu=rna*   *nga-rnu*   **purra-nja-rla.**
            meat=1SG.S   eat-PAST   **cook**-INF-SEQ
            I ate the meat having cooked it.
            I$_i$ ate the meat$_j$ e_i having cooked it$_j$.
            (Warlpiri [Ken Hale prompt, H_K01-505B: 21:23 mins])

        b. *Kuyu=rna*   *nga-rnu*   **kupa-nji-pa-rlu.**
            meat=1SG.S   eat-PAST   **cook**-INF-SS-ERG
            I ate the meat having cooked it.
            I$_i$ ate the meat$_j$ e_i having cooked it$_j$.
            (Translation of a.)
            H_K01-505B, DG, 21:24 mins

This suggests the encoded function of *-pa-* is ergative control and the temporal relation is inferred, rather than encoded by *-pa-*.

Given the ergative cannot attach directly onto non-finite verb forms (unlike in other Ngumpin-Yapa languages such as Warlpiri), it is possible that *-pa-* is simply a link allowing an ergative subordinator to be hosted by a verb. Thus, perhaps (1,118) is a reanalysis of (1,116). However, it is not clear why an epenthetic would be used, given there is no phonological motivation.

(1,118) *Karnta-ngu   ngurlu   jama-nnya   kantu   papulu-rla   [ka-nji-**pa-rlu**]*.

woman-ERG   seed   grind-PRES   inside   house-LOC   sit-INF-LINK-ERG

The woman is inside the house grinding the seeds while sitting.
N_D02-007842, BN, 38:31 mins

In terms of its function, *-pa-* has significant overlap with *-karra* (§12.1.2.1): both have subject control and, other than the one exception shown in (1,117), both have simultaneous relative tense. A primary distinction is that *-pa-* can only be controlled by transitive subjects, whereas *-karra* can be controlled by intransitive or transitive subjects. It is not clear what conditions the use of *-karra* or *-pa-* for subordinate clauses controlled by transitive subjects.

12.1.2.3 -*ngarnu* 'source'

A subordinate clause can be marked to signal that the situation it denotes causes the situation denoted by the matrix clause to occur—that is, the subordinate clause is related to the matrix clause by CAUSE. For example, in (1,119), the event of running caused the speaker to be tired and, in (1,120), the speaker is sick from speaking. This complementising suffix is also used as a derivational suffix on nominals (§4.4.2) with the same semantic function.

(1,119) *Palapala=rna*   ***[jitpi-nji-ngarnu]***.

tired=1SG.S   **run-INF-SOURCE**

I'm tired from running.
I$_j$'m tired from e_j running.
H_K01-505B, DG, 23:27 mins

(1,120) *Maju-ja-nya=rna*   ***[wa-nganji-ngarnu]***.

bad-INCH-PRES=1SG.S   **speak-INF-SOURCE**

I'm sick from speaking.
I$_j$'m sick from e_j speaking.
H_K01-505B, DG, 41:08 mins

There is allomorphy conditioned by whether the suffix is attaching to a nominal host or an infinitive: *-ngarnu* is used for infinitives (that is, inflecting verbs with the infinitive inflection) and *-warnu* is used for other nominals.

12. SYNTAX OF COMPLEX CLAUSES

This is exemplified in (1,121), where the subordinate clause is marked with the source complementiser: the nominal *karli* 'boomerang' hosts the *-warnu* allomorph and the non-finite verb *pakanji-* hosts the *-ngarnu* allomorph.

(1,121) *Palapala=rna* **[*karli-warnu*** *paka-nji-ngarnu]*.
tired=1SG.S **boomerang-SOURCE** **hit-INF-SOURCE**
I'm tired from trimming a boomerang.
I$_j$'m tired from e_j trimming a boomerang.
H_K01-505B, DG, 23:36 mins

12.1.2.4 -rla 'prior'

The 'prior' complementiser indicates the event or action described in the subordinate clause temporally precedes that of the main clause, with coreferentiality between the subjects of the clauses.

The locative suffix in many Ngumpin-Yapa languages functions as a complementiser (Ennever 2018: 131; Meakins and Nordlinger 2014: 427; Senge 2015: 615) and, indeed, this *-rla* resembles the locative in Warlmanpa and is not subject to the same allomorphy. For example, in (1,122), the disyllabic stem *manja* takes *-rla*, where *-nga* would be expected if it were the locative morpheme (§4.1.1.3), since *-nga* is the locative allomorph for disyllabic stems.[11]

(1,122) *Kuyu=rna* *nga-rnu* *[ma-nja-rla]*.
meat=1SG.S eat-PAST **get-INF-PRIOR**
I ate the meat after getting it.
I$_i$ ate the meat$_j$ after e_i getting (it$_j$).
H_K01-505B, DG, 21:20 mins

Like *-karra* (simultaneous subject control [§12.1.2.1]), the use of ergative marking on the subordinate clause appears to be optional, as demonstrated by the pair of utterances in (1,123), differing only in the use/non-use of the ergative case on the infinitive verb.

---

11 The same *lack* of allomorphy is found in Warlpiri (Hale 1982), though Mary Laughren (p.c.) notes that at least one speaker exhibits variation between *-nga ~ -rla* on disyllabic infinitivised verbs.

(1,123) a. *Kuyu=rna*   *nga-rnu*   *[kupa-nji-rla].*
meat=1SG.S   eat-PAST   cook-INF-PRIOR
I ate the meat after cooking it.
I$_i$ ate the meat$_j$ after e_i cooking (it$_j$).
wrl-20190205, DK, 03:52 mins

b. *Kuyu=rna*   *nga-rnu*   *[kupa-nji-rla-rlu].*
meat=1SG.S   eat-PAST   cook-INF-PRIOR-ERG
I ate the meat after cooking it.
I$_i$ ate the meat$_j$ after e_i cooking (it$_j$).
wrl-20190205, DK, 04:13 mins

12.1.2.5 -*ka* 'allative'

The allative case can function as a complementising suffix to indicate that the subject of the non-finite predicate is coreferential with a non-subject argument of the main verb and that there is temporal overlap between the situations denoted in the clauses. Examples (1,124) and (1,125) show the subordinate clause being coreferent with an object of the main clause and (1,126) provides an example of coreference with an indirect object. As can be seen from the examples, the argument control cannot be specified to a single grammatical relation of the matrix clause as, in (1,124) and (1,125), it is the object of the matrix clause that is coreferential with the subject of the subordinate clause and in (1,126) it is the indirect object.

(1,124) *Karnta=rna*   *purtu-ka-ngu*   *[wanga-nja-ka].*
woman=1SG.S   listen-be-PAST   speak-INF-ALL
I heard the woman speaking.
I heard the woman$_i$ e_i speaking.
H_K01-505B, DG, 09:47 mins

(1,125) *Ngarrka-ngu*   *karla-rnu*   *wawirri*   *[warnpaka-ka*   *nga-rninja-ka].*
man-ERG   spear-PAST   kangaroo   grass-ALL   eat-INF-ALL
The man speared the kangaroo while it was eating grass.
The man speared the kangaroo$_i$ while e_i was eating grass.
N_D02-007842, BN, 38:45 mins

(1,126)   *Yu-ngu=rla   kurtu-ku   [li-nja-**ka**].*
         give-PAST=3DAT   child-DAT   cry-INF-**ALL**
         He gave it to the child (who was) crying.
         He gave it to the child$_i$ e$_i$ crying.
         wrl-20200219, DK, 06:55 mins

The temporal overlap relationship is necessarily $T_{MATRIX} \subseteq T_{SUB}$ —that is, the situation denoted in the matrix clause is a subset of the temporal duration of the subordinate clause. There are no cases where the subordinate clause marked with *-ka* denotes an event that is a temporal subset of the situation denoted by the matrix clause. Thus, the subordinate clause can be seen specifying a wider temporal context in which the situation denoted by the matrix occurs.

12.1.2.6 *-ku* 'dative'

A subordinate clause marked with the dative case *-ku* relates to the matrix clause with the PURPOSE relation, indicating why an agent undertook some course of action. There is no encoded argument control from the matrix clause because the subject of the subordinate clause can be the same, as in (1,127) and (1,128), or different, as in (1,129).

Same subject:

(1,127)   *Ngarrka=ju   pa-nangu-rnu   mu-ka=nya   [ngayu-ku   wa-nganja-ku].*
          man=1SG.NS   go-PAST-HITH   this-ALL=FOC   1-DAT   speak-INF-DAT
          The man came to me here to talk to me.
          The man$_j$ came to me$_k$ here to e$_j$ talk to me$_k$.
          N_D02-007842, BN, 47:05 mins

(1,128)   *Jawarti=rna   pa-nami-rni   [ngappa-ku   ma-nja-ku].*
          tomorrow=1SG.S   go-FUT-TWD   water-DAT   get-INF-DAT
          Tomorrow I will go to get water.
          Tomorrow I$_j$ will go to e$_j$ get water.
          H_K01-506A, DG, 01:02:01 hrs

Different subject:

(1,129) *Nungarrayi=jana   wa-nganyu   kurtukurtu-ku   [kupa-nja-ku]*.
Nungarrayi=3PL.NS   speak-PAST   children-DAT   **cook-INF-DAT**
Nungarrayi told the children to cook.
Nungarrayi told the children_j to e_j cook.
wrl-20200224, DK, 33:44 mins

The dative case in its complementising function can be seen as semantically underspecified in comparison with *-kupa* 'desire' and *-kuma* 'aversive', which denote a positive and negative purpose, respectively. Interestingly, the 'desire' and 'aversive' suffixes are clearly built off the dative suffix, suggesting that they both indeed represent subsets of *-ku*, represented in Figure 12.1.

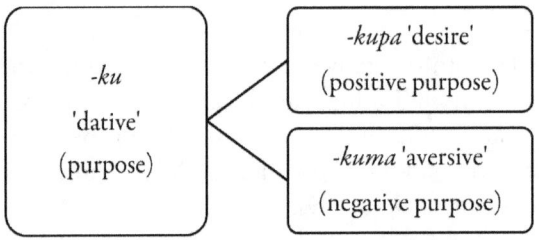

Figure 12.1 Semantic hierarchy of suffixes related to *-ku* 'dative'

Many predicates of represented speech, such as *wa-* 'speak' or *jilij ka-* 'ask', express the message of speaking using the dative case, as in (1,129) and (1,130).

(1,130) *Jilij   ka-ngka   [yarnunju-ku   yi-nja-ku]*.
ask   take-IMP   **food-DAT**   **give-INF-DAT**
Ask him to give food.
Ask him_j to e_j give food [to e_x].
N_D02-009887, DG, 11:01 mins

12.1.2.7 *-jila* 'privative'

The suffix *-jila* is used as a complementising suffix in negative imperative constructions (§11.5.2.2) and as a derivational suffix on nominals or subordinate clauses indicating a lack of an entity (§4.2.1). As a complementising suffix, it has no coreferentiality requirements, though it does seem to require temporal overlap between the *-jila* clause and the matrix clause.

(1,131) Kuyu   kapi=rna-rla   yi-nyi,   **nga-rninja-jila-ku.**
        meat   FUT=1SG.S-3.OBL   give-FUT   **eat-INF-WITHOUT-DAT**

I'll give meat to him, (who is) not eating.

I'll give meat to him$_j$, e_j not eating.

H_K01-506B, DG, 06:54 mins

12.1.2.8 -*wangu* 'privative'

The suffix -*wangu* is used as a complementising suffix in negative imperative constructions (§11.5.2.1) and as a privative case on nominals (§4.2.1). Unlike -*jila*, -*wangu* requires the subject to be coreferential with the subject of the matrix clause. Like -*jila*, -*wangu* requires temporal overlap between the -*wangu* clause and the matrix clause.

(1,132) Ngana   ka-ngu   **karta-pi-nja-wangu?**
        what   be-PAST   **spear-act_on-INF-PRIV**

Who didn't spear it?

Who$_i$ is e_i without spearing it?

wrl-20200219, DK, 39:11 mins

12.1.2.9 -*kuma* 'aversive'

Subordinate clauses denoting situations that are a) undesirable and b) avoidable can be marked with -*kuma* 'aversive'. In (1,133), the speaker orders the addressee to go slowly to avoid falling. In (1,134), the speaker is attempting to avoid a situation in which someone hits them with a boomerang. In (1,133), the subordinate clause subject is coreferential with the matrix clause subject, whereas in (1,134) the subject of the subordinate clause is coreferential with the object of the matrix clause (-*kuma* does not encode any argument control).

(1,133) Pingka   pa-nka   **[wa-nja-kuma].**
        slowly   go-IMP   **fall-INF-AVER**

Go slowly in case you fall!

(You$_j$) go slowly in case e_j fall!

H_K01-505B, DG, 43:41 mins

(1,134)　*Kapakapa-ja-nya=rna*　　**[*karli-kuma*　　*paka-nja-kuma*].**
　　　　prevent-INCH-PRES=1SG.S　**boomerang-AVER　hit-INF-AVER**
　　　　I'm stopping him, lest he hit me with a boomerang!
　　　　I$_j$'m stopping him$_k$, lest he$_k$ hit me$_j$ with a boomerang!
　　　　N_D02-009887, DG, 02:28 mins

The meaning of *-kuma* as an apprehensive marker is discussed further in Browne et al. (2024).

There is one use of *-kuma* that does not seem to denote an apprehensive situation, as in (1,135).[12]

(1,135)　*Jungarrayi=ma*　　*pawarrayi-ja-ngu=lku*　　**[*pangi-nja-kuma***
　　　　Jungarrayi-TOP　　completely-INCH-PAST=THEN　**dig-INF-AVER**
　　　　***yulu-kuma*].**
　　　　ground-AVER
　　　　Jungarrayi has now finished digging the ground.
　　　　Jungarrayi$_j$ has now finished e_j digging the ground.
　　　　wrl-20180616-01, DK, 25:19 mins

This usage of *-kuma* is much like the evitative suffix *-kujaku* in Warlpiri, which can mark apprehensional situations, just as *-kuma* does in Warlmanpa, but it can also mark situations that are desirable but somehow prevented from happening. An example is given in (1,136), in which *warrki* 'work' is marked with the evitative case, denoting that the work was prevented. It is possible the speaker of (1,135) interpreted the digging as being prevented somehow and used *-kuma* to indicate this (which would also require *-kuma* to have a broader denotation than simply 'aversive').

(1,136)　*Janjanypa-rlu*　*ka*　*kurdu-ngku*　*warla-paji-rni*　*jaji-nyanu*
　　　　pestering-ERG　AUX　child-ERG　　stop-cut-NPST　father-ANAPH
　　　　warrki-kijaku.
　　　　work-EVIT
　　　　The demanding child is stopping his father **from working**.
　　　　(Warlpiri [Laughren 2015: 4])

12　Alternatively, this may be the dative case followed by the topic marker =*ma*. However, there are no other instances in the corpus of =*ma* attaching to an infinitive verb.

12.1.2.10 -*kupa* 'desiderative'

The use of -*kupa* encodes that the main clause situation was undertaken because the subject desired the situation denoted in the subordinate -*kupa* clause. For example, in (1,137), the speaker claims that the addressees undertook the 'go' event because they desired seeing the speaker.

(1,137) *Pa-nangu-rnu=ju-npala*   **[*nya-nja-kupa*]**.
go-PAST-TWD=1SG.NS=2DU.S   see-INF-DESIRE
You two came **wanting to see me**.
You two$_i$ came wanting to e_i see me.
H_K01-506A, DG, 56:49 mins

(1,138) *Nyuntu=ja-ngu*   *pa-nangu-rnu*   **[*wa-nganyja-kupa*]**.
2=1DU.EXCL.S-2SG.NS   go-PAST-TWD   **speak**-INF-DESIRE
We two came to you **to talk**.
We two$_i$ came to you to e_i talk.
H_K01-506, DG, 56:42 mins

The above examples of -*kupa* are both Warlmanpa translations of Warumungu -*kuwarta* 'wanting something' (Simpson 2002).

12.2 Coordination

There are two overt coordinators that link phrases, which are identical in form to two auxiliary bases, catalogued in Table 12.5. It is unclear whether there is any relationship between the coordinators and the auxiliaries. Both coordinators are now discussed in turn: *kapi* 'and/or' in §12.2.1 and *kala* 'but' in §12.2.2.

Table 12.5 Shared forms between conjunctions and auxiliary bases

Form	Coordinator	Auxiliary base
kapi	'and/or'	'future'
kala	'but'	'habitual'

However, phrases and clauses do not require an overt coordinator. For example, in (1,139), the speaker states they used to eat meat and lists three animals that are a subset of the nominal *kuyu* 'meat', but there is no overt morpheme linking these constituents as part of a larger phrase (this is construed through their identical case marking).

(1,139) Kuyu=rnalu   nga-rnu-rra   **wawirri**   **kupuwarnu**   **nyinawurtu.**
         meat=1PL.   eat-PAST-IMPF **kangaroo** **hill_wallaby** **echidna**
         EXCL.S

We used to eat meat: **kangaroo, hill wallaby**, [and] **echidna**.
N_D18-013596, LN, 19:50 mins

12.2.1 *Kapi* 'and/or'

The use of *kapi* coordinates two phrases into one constituent, which results in a conjoined phrase, denoting 'P ∧ Q' in unembedded contexts and 'P ∨ Q' in embedded contexts.

12.2.1.1 Unembedded contexts

In unembedded contexts—that is, not under the scope of negation, ignoratives or conditionals—*kapi* serves as a logical conjunction between two phrases, such as the two nominals in (1,140), where *ngarrka* 'man' and *kurtu* 'child' behave as one phrase, denoting that both referents were being spoken to. Example (1,140) also demonstrates that the individual constituents are still case-marked, so both nominals host a dative suffix.

(1,140) Ali=nya=rla – karnta=   wa-nganya   **ngarrka-ku** **kapi** **kurtu-ku.**
                         palangu
         that=FOC=   woman=   speak-PRES   **man-DAT**   CONJ   **child-DAT**
         3OBL   3DU.NS

That—the woman is talking to the man and to the child.
wrl-20190131-02, DK, 01:34 mins

Entire sentences can be coordinated, as in (1,141), likely contributing to the 'then' meaning (primarily encoded by =*lku* [see §9.4.1]).

(1,141) Wawirri[13]=rna   karta   pu-ngu   **kapi** lani=lku   jutu-ngu-rra.
         kangaroo=1SG.S   spear   act_on-   **and**   afraid=THEN   run-PAST-AWAY
                                    PAST

I speared the kangaroo, and then it ran away, afraid.
wrl-20180528-03, DK, 6:35 mins

---

13 *Wawirri* in this utterance is pronounced without the initial syllable: *wiri*. It is unclear whether this is a phonetic elision of the syllable or a lexical variant (compare with *yawirri* 'kangaroo').

The two phrases being coordinated must have the same syntactic status. For example, in (1,140), the two phrases being coordinated are dative-marked nominals. In (1,150), they are two ergative-marked nominals. In (1,141), it is two entire sentences. Similarly, (1,142) provides an example of two nominals marked with *-parna* 'proprietive' being coordinated.

(1,142) Wajurrajurra=pala   pina   pa-nangu   ngurra-ka=lku
         evening=3DU.S   return   go-PAST   home-ALL=THEN
         karrarlarla-parna   **kapi   wangani-parna,**   ngurra-ka=lku.
         spear-PROP   **CONJ   dog-PROP**   home-ALL=THEN

In the evening, they two returned home, with a spear and with a dog, to home, then.

wrl-20190207-01, DK, 55:09 mins

12.2.1.2 Embedded contexts

The Warlpiri coordinator *manu* has been analysed as denoting inclusive 'or', based on its functions in embedded contexts—specifically negation, conditionals and ignoratives (Bowler 2014). For example, when embedded within a conditional, *manu* can be interpreted either conjunctively or disjunctively, as in (1,143) and (1,144), respectively. In this environment, it seems the clusivity is determined by context.

(1,143) Kaji=npa   kuyu   manu   mangarri   nga-rni   ngula
         COND=2SG.S   meat   manu   food   eat-NPAST   that
         kapu=npa   pirrjirdi-jarrimi.
         FUT=2SG.S   strong-become.NPAST

If you eat meat and vegetables, you will become strong.

(P ∧ Q)

(Warlpiri [Bowler 2014: 140])

(1,144) Kaji=npa   jarntu   paka-rni   manu   window   luwa-rni,
         COND=2SG.S   dog   hit-NPAST   manu   shoot-NPAST
         ngula=ju   Nungarrayi-rli   kapi=ngki   jirnawangu-ma-ni.
         that=TOP   Nungarrayi-ERG   FUT=2SG.NS   scold-do-NPAST

If you hit the dog or break the window, then that Nungarrayi will scold you.

(P ∨ Q)

(Warlpiri [Bowler 2014: 140])

Bowler uses this evidence to argue that *manu* encodes only inclusive 'or' and can undergo pragmatic strengthening to allow a strengthened 'and' meaning.

Turning back to Warlmanpa, in embedded contexts, *kapi* also denotes 'or', which is analogous to Warlpiri *manu*.

Negation:

(1,145) *Jala=ma   kula=rna-palangu   nya-ngu* **Jungarrayi** *kapi* **Japaja.**
today=TOP   NEG=1SG.S-3DU.NS   see-PAST **Jungarrayi** CONJ **Japaja**
I haven't seen **Jungarrayi or Japaja** today.
wrl-20191207-01, DK, 36:08 mins
(P ∨ Q)

Conditional:

(1,146) *Kayi=n*   **murtika**   *kapi*   **wangani**   *la-nmi,*
WHEN=2SG.S   **car**   CONJ   **dog**   shoot-FUT
nga=ngu   Nungarrayi-rlu   jinawangu-ma-nmi.
POST=2SG.NS   Nungarrayi-ERG   scold-do-FUT
If you shoot the **dog or the car**, then Nungarrayi will scold you.
wrl-20191207-01, DK, 23:55 mins
(P ∨ Q) → R

Ignorative:

(1,147) a. *Nya-ngu=n-palangu*   **Japaja**   *kapi*   **Jungarrayi?**
see-PAST=2SG.S-3DU.NS **Japaja**   CONJ   **Jungarrayi**
Have you seen **Japaja or Jungarrayi?**
wrl-20191207-01, DK, 02:22 mins
P ∨ Q

b. *Yuwayi   jinta=yi,   jinta=yi=rna   nya-ngu   Japaja.*
yes   one=STILL   one=STILL=1SG.S   see-PAST   Japaja
Yes, just one, I've just seen Japaja.
wrl-20191209, DK, 03:16 mins

When *kapi* conjoins a clause to another clause that has negative polarity, the *kapi* clause inherits negative polarity (and maintains its basic 'or' meaning), despite not having any overt negative morphemes, as in (1,148) and (1,149).

The fact that *kapi* clauses inherit polarity from the matrix clause suggests *kapi* may behave as a subordinator, rather than a coordinator. Alternatively, apposed clauses (see §12.3) may allow a single *kula* to have scope over both clauses.

(1,148)   *Kula=rna-rla   jilij   ka-ngu   Gladys-ku   kapi=rna-rla*
NEG=1SG.S-3.OBL   ask   be-PAST   Gladys-DAT CONJ=1SG.S-3.OBL
wa-nganyu.
speak-PAST
I haven't asked Gladys or spoken to her.
wrl-20191207-01, DK, 12:09 mins
(P ∨ Q)

(1,149)   *Kula   wangani   lungunya kapi   warlku   wanganya,   walku.*
NEG   dog   cry-PRES   CONJ   bark   speak-PRES   nothing
The dog isn't crying or barking, nothing.
wrl-20191207-01, DK, 14:30 mins
(P ∨ Q)

The two phrases being coordinated can be syntactically removed from each other, although *kapi* must precede the second phrase being coordinated, as in (1,150), where the two noun phrases being coordinated as subjects of the predicate are on either edge of the sentence. An alternative analysis would be that *kapi* is coordinating two sentences, where *Japanangka-rlu* is the subject of a sentence with verb phrase (VP) ellipsis, which could be translated as 'Jungarrayi isn't digging, and [neither is] Japanangka'. However, I am not aware of any cases of VP ellipsis elsewhere, though there is a similar case found for the other coordinator in Warlmanpa—namely, *kala*, as in example (1,153).

(1,150)   **Jungarrayi-rlu**   *kula   karta   pu-ngunya*   **kapi   Japanangka-rlu.**
Jungarrayi-ERG   NEG   spear   act_on-PRES   CONJ   **Japanangka-ERG**
Jungarrayi and Japanangka are not digging.
(P ∨ Q)
wrl-20180616-01, DK, 22:10 mins

12.2.2 *Kala* 'but'

Unlike *kapi*, *kala* 'but' is poorly attested. The few tokens of it in the corpus are provided in this section. *Kala* is used to introduce a contrastive phrase, as in (1,151), where the speaker is comparing the length of two spears.

(1,151) Karrarlarla yumpa kirrirti, kala yumpa karrarlarla jinta
spear this long but this spear one
yarri=ma parlka.
that=TOP short
This spear is long, but this spear, it's short.
H_K01-506A, DG, 29:23 mins

Kala has some interesting and unexpected interactions with syntax. First, when used clause-initially, it is not eligible to host the bound pronouns (syntactically equivalent to a left-dislocated constituent [discussed in §11.7.1]), as exemplified in (1,152), where the ignorative nominal *wanjila* hosts the bound pronoun =*n* 'you'.

(1,152) Kala wanjila=n witta=ma yarti ya-rnu, ngayinya=ma=ngali?
but where=2SG.S small=TOP leave put-PAST 1GEN=TOP=1DU.INCL.NS
But where did you leave the child, our child?
N_D02-007850, DG, 03:20 mins

Additionally, (1,153) provides an example of *kala* coordinating a heavily reduced clause containing only *walku* 'nothing' to contrast with the apposed clause.

(1,153) [Japanangka-rlu=ma karta pu-ngkarla] [kala walku].
Japanangka-ERG=TOP spear act_on-IRR but nothing
Japanangka should be digging, but nothing [he's not digging].
wrl-20180616-01, DK, 19:34 mins

Kala as a contrastive coordinator is also found in Warlpiri and Ngardi (Laughren et al. 2022; Ennever 2021).

12.3 Discourse relations between independent clauses

Sequences of two clauses are often apposed to one another; despite being syntactically independent, these clauses are strongly integrated in discourse (however, the distinction between independent and subordinate clauses in Ngumpin-Yapa languages is not always straightforward [Browne et al. 2024]). Specifically, in these constructions, the first clause typically describes a situation and the second provides an EXPLANATION or ELABORATION of the situation. These terms follow the formal definitions of Asher and Lascarides (2003: 459–64). Informally, EXPLANATION provides a reason or justification for an action and ELABORATION describes a situation that is part of a previously described situation (that is, A ⊂ B). To exemplify, in (1,154), the first clause describes the speaker's current actions and the second provides the reasoning behind the action.

(1,154) *Ngayu=rna   kutij-ka-nya   parra-nga,   purtku-ja-nya=rna.*
         1=1SG.S   stand-be-PRES   sun-LOC   warm-INCH-PRES=1SG.S
         I'm standing in the sun, warming up.
         wrl-20190205, DK, 28:16 mins

Similarly, in (1,155), the first clause describes the actions of a dog (which is barking) and the second elaborates on what is being barked at. There is no overt shared referent, but the discourse relation of ELABORATION forces the interpretation that the entity who climbed the tree is related to the barking.

(1,155) *Warlku-wanganya,   yiwirti-ka   waka-rnu.*
         bark-speak-PRES   tree-ALL   climb-PAST
         He's barking, [at the one who] climbed a tree.
         wrl-20180610-01, DK, 24:02 mins

A similar example is given in (1,156), where the second clause elaborates on the first.

(1,156) *Yulu=ma   lijji,   kula   ngappa   wa-nu.*
         ground=TOP   dry   NEG   water   fall-PAST
         The ground is dry, [because there has been] no rain.
         wrl-20200220, DK, 14:23 mins

The discourse relation holding between these apposed clauses can be contrasted with the right dislocation of single constituents (§11.7.2). Whereas right dislocation usually emphasises the telic point or result of a clause, these apposed clauses never have a resultative relation—that is, the second clause always occurs prior to or simultaneously with the first clause. Apposition is also used for comparative constructions (§4.7.2), which may be seen as a more general process of apposition signalling elaboration.

To generalise these patterns, I suggest a primary division between constituent types, summarised in Table 12.6. Right dislocation involves just a single word, whereas apposed clauses and new clauses are well-formed independent clauses. Right dislocation involves a clause-internal relation, whereas full clauses involve a discourse relation. This contrasts with apposed and new clauses, which are syntactically independent. An apposed clause has a subordinating discourse relation[14]—typically, ELABORATION or EXPLANATION, as discussed above. Other independent clauses will typically have a discourse relation of NARRATION (in the strict sense of Asher and Lascarides [2003], roughly meaning that the second situation temporally follows the first), though of course there are various adverbs and temporal clitics that can specify the discourse and temporal relation to the preceding clause.

Table 12.6 Relations beyond the clause

Syntactic relation	Constituent	Typical semantic/discourse relation	Example
Right dislocation	Single word	Emphasise/clarify telic point of main clause	(1,157)
Apposed clause	Full clause	ELABORATION, EXPLANATION	(1,158)
New clause	Full clause	NARRATIVE	(1,159)

---

14 Constituency of discourse structure (for example, subordinate at the level of discourse) does not relate to clause-internal syntactic constituency. Generally, the entire syntactic clause (including any syntactically subordinate structures) map to one node at the level of discourse, which itself can be subordinate, superordinate or a sister node to another node at the level of discourse. Elaboration and explanation are subordinating relations, such that a relation of ELABORATION(A, B) says that B is subordinate to A in discourse structure, whereas other relations such as NARRATION(A, B) are non-subordinating—that is, B is a sister node to A in discourse structure.

12. SYNTAX OF COMPLEX CLAUSES

Right dislocation:

(1,157)   *Ngayu=ma=rna*   *warrikngali-ja-ngu-rra*   *Land Council-nga=lku,*
1=TOP=1SG.S   work-INCH-PAST-IMPF   Land Council-LOC=THEN
tarnnga=yi=lku.
long_time=STILL=THEN
I was working at the Central Land Council, [for a] long time.
wrl-20190208, DK, 25:51 mins

Apposed clause—EXPLANATION(a, b):

(1,158)   a.   *Kurtu*   *ali=nya*   *yirri-kapu-ka,*
child   that=FOC   watch_over-chase-IMP
Watch over that child,

         b.   *Kala=nga*   *wa-nma.*
APPR=POT   fall-POT
lest she fall.
wrl-20190205, DK, 56:51 mins

New clause—NARRATIVE(a, b):

(1,159)   a.   *Ngarrka=nganpa*   *missionary=lku*   *pa-nangu-rnu.*
man=1EXL.PL.NS   missionary=THEN   go-past-TWD
The missionary came to us.

         b.   *Turnu-ma-nu-rra=nganpa*   *yapa=ma.*
assemble-get-PAST-IMPF=1PL.EXCL.O   people=TOP
He gathered up all the people.
N_D02-007844, BN, 00:27 secs

Appendix A: Inflecting verb finder list

Table A.1 is an alphabetical finder list that gives the gloss and class of each known Warlmanpa verb root.

Appendix Table A.1 Complete alphabetical verb list

Word	Gloss	Class
-ja-	become	1d
jama-	grind	2
ji-	burn	1c
-jiya-	cook	2
jumpa-	kiss	2
jitpi-[1]	run	3
ka-	take	3
ka-	sit, be	1d
kapi-[1]	chase	3
karla-	poke, spear	2
kinja-	wet	2
kipa-	twist together	2
kiya-	throw	2
kuma-	cut	2
kupa-	cook	2
la-	shoot	2
lamarta-	hold	2
li-[1]	cry	3
-ma-	cause	5
ma-	get	5
marta-	have	2
murla-	copulate	2

A GRAMMAR OF WARLMANPA

Word	Gloss	Class
nama-	crush	2
nga-	tell	2
nga-	eat	4
ngarta-	trim	2
ngaya	void	2
nguka-	drink	2
nya-	see	3
nyurla-	knead	2
pa-	go	1c
paka-	hit, chop	2
pali-[1]	die	1b
pangi-[1]	scratch, dig	2
parti-[1]	rise	1b
piya-	break, bite, cut	2
pi-[1]	kill	3
wa-	speak	1a
wa-	fall	5
waka-	climb	2
wayi-[1]	search for	2
winja-	leave alone	2
ya-	put	2
-ya-	go	5
yila-	drip, leak, melt	2
yu-[1]	give	3
Subgrouped by verb class		
wa-	speak	1a
pali-[1]	die	1b
parti-[1]	rise	1b
ji-	burn	1c
pa-	go	1c
-ja-	become	1d
ka-	sit, be	1d
jama-	grind	2
-jiya-	cook	2
jumpa-	kiss	2
karla-	poke, spear	2
kinja-	wet	2

Word	Gloss	Class
kipa-	twist together	2
kiya-	throw	2
kuma-	cut	2
kupa-	cook	2
la-	shoot	2
lamarta-	hold	2
marta-	have	2
murla-	copulate	2
nama-	crush	2
nga-	tell	2
ngarta-	trim	2
ngaya	void	2
nguka-	drink	2
nyurla-	knead	2
paka-	hit, chop	2
pangu-[1]	scratch, dig	2
piya-	break, bite, cut	2
waka-	climb	2
wayu-[1]	search for	2
winja-	leave alone	2
ya-	put	2
yila-	drip, leak, melt	2
jitpi-[1]	run	3
ka-	take	3
kapi-[1]	chase	3
li-[1]	cry	3
nya-	see	3
pi-[1]	kill	3
yi-[1]	give	3
nga-	eat	4
-ma-	cause	5
ma-	get	5
wa-	fall	5
-ya-	go	5

[1] The high vowel(s) are subject to alternations (see §6.2.2.2).

The following sections briefly describe each inflecting verb found in the corpus. For those not found in the corpus, their source is Nash (2022).

A.1 Class 1 verbs

A.1.1 -*ja*- INCH

The inchoative -*ja*- is discussed in further detail in §6.5.2.1. It attaches to a nominal to derive a verb that denotes the inception of a state.

(1,160)   *Wiri-ja-ngu-rra=rna*   *purtu*   *ka-ngu-rra=yi=rna.*
big-INCH-PAST-IMPF=1SG.S   remember   be-PAST-IMPF=STILL=1SG.S
When I was growing up, I was still remembering.
N_D02-007844, BN, 26:59 mins

The inchoative is also used to incorporate borrowings into verbs.

(1,161)   *Everything=rnalu*   *kurtukurtu*   *now*   *ma-nnya,*
everything=1PL.EXCL.S   children   get-PRES
learn-ja-nya=lu   *partakurru,*   *ngarra*   *book-na*   *read-ja-nya.*
learn-INCH-PRES=3PL.S   good   FUT   book-FOC   read-INCH-PRES
The children are getting everything now, they're learning, reading books.
N_D02-007844, BN, 29:50 mins

A.1.2 *Ji*- 'burn'

The verb *ji*- 'burn' is one of the few inflecting verbs that exhibit valency alternations (excluding coverbs, which can manipulate the case frame of a predicate). It has an intransitive use, 'ABS burns', and a transitive use, 'ERG burns ABS'.

Intransitive:

(1,162)   *Warlu*   *ji-nangu.*
fire   burn-PAST
The fire burnt.
H_K01-505B, DG, 07:00 mins

Transitive:

(1,163) *Warlu-ngu=ju*   *ji-nangu.*
         fire-ERG=1SG.NS   burn-PAST
         The fire burnt me.
         H_K01-505B, DG, 07:08 mins

This inflecting verb is only known to combine with one coverb, *milily*, which is not found combining with any other inflecting verb. The combination *milily-ji-* means 'shine (as sun)' (Nash 2022).

A.1.3 *Ka-* 'be, sit'

Ka- lexically means 'sit', however, it is also used as a copula (see §11.2). It also combines with many coverbs (82 combinations are documented in Nash [2022]).

A.1.4 *Pa-* 'go'

Pa- is an intransitive motion verb, typically signalling movement towards some intentional goal (regardless of whether the allative-marked adjunct is overt). Minimally, it encodes controlled motion by an agent.

(1,164) *Ngurra-ka=rna*   *pa-nanga.*
         home-ALL=1SG.S   go-PAST.AWAY
         I went off home.
         wrl-20180614-02, DK, 11:48 mins

This verb has an inflection form seemingly not used by any other speaker (nor found for any other verb), *pantinya*, which Nash (1979) glosses as 'present centripetal'. Other speakers use the form *panjinya* for this function (where *-nji-* is the regular 'motion towards' AM suffix).

(1,165) *Yanjarra-ngurlu=rna*   *pa-nti-nya.*
         north-ELA=1SG.S   go-TWD-PRES
         I'm coming from the north.
         H_K01-505B, DG, 01:02:19 hrs

(1,166) *Kuyu-ku*   *pa-nji-nya.*
         meat-DAT   go-MOT.TWD-PRES
         It's coming here for meat.
         wrl-20160914-02, SN, 11:43 mins

This inflecting verb generally combines with coverbs that specify manners of movement. For example, the coverb *wirriri* 'in a circle' combines with *pa-* to denote curved motion.

(1,167) Ngayu=ma=rna   wirriri~wirriri   pa-nama.
        1=TOP=1SG.S   in_a_circle~RDP   go-FUT.AWAY
        I will go around.
        wrl-20180608-01, DK, 17:44 mins

(1,168) Yimpa=ma   jarrwan~jarrwan   pa-nnya.
        this=TOP   go_past~RDP   go-PRES
        This one's going past.
        wrl-20170321, SN, 09:28 mins

A.1.5 *Pali-* 'die'

The inflecting verb *pali-* encompasses an entity ceasing to operate. Prototypically, this involves the death of an entity, hence the gloss of 'die', as in (1,169).

(1,169) Maliki=ju   ngayu-ku   palu-ngu.
        dog=1SG.NS   1-DAT   die-PAST
        The dog died on me.
        N_D02-007841, BN, 27:13 mins

This also encompasses other meanings such as eyes closing, as in (1,170), and a waterhole drying up, as in (1,171).

(1,170) Milpa   palu-ngka!
        eye   close-IMP
        Close [your] eyes!
        N_D02-007842, BN, 08:01 mins

(1,171) Ngappa   pawurrayi   palu-ngu.
        water   completely   die-PAST
        The water completely dried up.
        N_D02-007842, BN, 05:08 mins

This inflecting verb is not known to combine with any coverbs.

A.1.6 *Parti-* 'leave'

Parti- refers to movement away from or out of a salient source. It can be used for motion along a generally flat trajectory or motion upwards (especially in combination with coverbs). It cannot be used for motion downwards.

(1,172)   *Nyangurla=n*   *parti-ma?*
when=2SG.S   leave-FUT.AWAY
When will you leave?
H_K01-506A, DG, 49:07 mins

(1,173)   *Ngurra-ngurlu*   *partu-nga.*
camp-ELA   leave-PAST.AWAY
He's leaving camp.
H_K01-506A, DG, 53:42 mins

(1,174)   *Partu-ka!*
leave-IMP
Get up! (English prompt)
H_K06-004555, LOF, 49:24 mins

It combines with several coverbs, especially those that force an upward motion direction. These combinations include *yurrkuly-parti-* 'vomit', *kutuj-parti-* 'stand up', *ting-parti-* 'fly' and *palyal-parti-* 'rise, emerge' (Nash 2022).

(1,175)   *Wari*   *palyal-partu-ngu*   *witta-ngurlu*   *ngulya-ngurlu.*
snake   emerge-leave-PAST   small-ELA   hole-ELA
The snake emerged from the small hole.
wrl-20200219, DK, 10:14 mins

Finally, *parti-* also combines with coverbs to describe rises in temperature, such as *ngarrak-parti-* 'get hot' (which can be contrasted with *wa-* 'fall', which combines with coverbs to describe a drop in temperature).

A.1.7 Wa- 'speak'

The inflecting verb *wa-* signals a vocalisation by an agent. It has a wide range of case frames, as exemplified in (1,176)–(1,183).

Intransitive—ABS speaks:

(1,176) *Yapa wanganya witta.*
person speak-PRES small
The child is speaking.
H_K01-505B, DG, 00:49 mins

Semi-transitive—ABS speaks to DAT:

(1,177) *Karnta=rla wa-nganya ngarrka-ku karli-ka ngarta-nja-ka.*
woman=3.OBL speak-PRES man-DAT boomerang-ALL trim-INF-ALL
The woman is speaking to the man trimming the boomerang.
N_D02-007842, BN, 38:57 mins

(1,178) *Ngarrka=rla wa-nganyu karnta-ku yarnunju-ku kupa-nja-ku.*
man=3.OBL speak-PAST woman-DAT food-DAT cook-INF-DAT
The man told the woman to cook food.
wrl-20190201, DK, 14:33 mins

Quasi-transitive—ABS speaks ABS:

(1,179) *Warlmanpa=rna jaru wa-nganya.*
Warlmanpa=1SG.S language speak-PRES
I'm speaking Warlmanpa language.
wrl-20190123, SN, 22:53 mins

Semi-ditransitive—ABS speaks ABS to DAT:

(1,180) *Nyuntu-ku kapi=rna-ngu Warlmanpa wa-ngami.*
2-DAT FUT=1SG.S-2SG.NS Warlmanpa speak-FUT
I'll speak Warlmanpa to you.
H_K01-505B, DG, 16:35 mins

APPENDIX A

Transitive complement—ERG tells DAT 'REPORTED SPEECH'$_{\text{MATRIX CLAUSE}}$:

(1,181) *Ali-rlu=nya   ngarrka-ngu   wa-nganyu=ju   'yiwirti paka-ka'.*
       that-ERG=FOC   man-ERG   speak-PRES=1SG.NS   tree   hit-IMP
       That man told me 'cut the tree'.[1]
       wrl-20190201, DK, 34:22 mins

Transitive complement—ERG tells DAT to DAT:

(1,182) *Japangarti-rlu   wa-nganyu=rla   Jakamarra-ku   la-nja-ku*
       Japangarti-ERG   speak-PAST=3.OBL   Jakamarra-DAT   shoot-INF-DAT
       Jampijinpa-ku.
       Jampijinpa-DAT
       Japangarti told Jakamarra to shoot Jampijinpa.
       N_D02-009887, DG, 09:27 mins

This use of *wa-* may be an extension replacing meaning previously denoted by *nga-* 'tell'.

Transitive complement—ERG says X$_{\text{MATRIX CLAUSE}}$:

(1,183) *But,   ngayu=ma=rnalu   Warlmanpa-rlu   wa-   'kuyu=rnalu*
                                                        nganya
              1=TOP=1PL.EXCL.S   Warlmanpa-ERG   speak-   meat=1PL.EXCL.S
                                                        PRES
       kuma-nnya   karnta²=yi=rnalu   kuma-   japirti-parna-rlu'.
                                                    nnya
       cut-PRES   woman=STILL=1PL.EXCL.S   cut-   knife-PROP-ERG
                                                    PRES
       But, we Warlmanpa say 'we cut the meat, only women cut it with knives'.
       wrl-20190201, DK, 06:38 mins

Wa- also combines with several coverbs, with the resulting combination signalling various types of noise production. The known exceptions to this are *marlal-wa-* 'twinkle' and *kiit-wa-* 'break down, give up'.

---

1   This may be an apposed clause (§12.3), where the reported speech is an ELABORATION of the first clause.
2   I am unsure why *karnta* 'woman' does not have an ergative suffix, given it is the subject of *kuma-* 'cut', and the instrumental nominal *japirti-parna* 'with knives' is marked for ergative.

(1,184) Karli=ji   kiit-wa-nganya   yimpa   ngayu.
        boomerang=1SG.NS broken-speak-PRES   this   1
        This boomerang is broken on me.
        N_D02-007841, BN, 25:10 mins

A.2 Class 2 verbs

A.2.1 *Jama-* 'grind'

Jama- refers to grinding objects (in all cases in the corpus, the object is *ngurlu* 'seeds'), with a transitive case frame. It is not known to combine with any coverbs.

(1,185) Yangku-ngu=rna   jama-nnya   ngurlu.
        quiet-ERG=1SG.S   grind-PRES   seed
        I'm quietly grinding seeds.
        wrl-20190205, DK, 10:13 mins

A2.2 *-jiya-* 'cook'

-Jiya- is not found in the corpus. Nash (1979) notes that it is found only in combination with coverbs: *lakurt-jiya-* 'roast in earth oven' and *purt-jiya-* 'burn'. Speakers in the corpus use *kupa-* 'cook' (§A.2.9) for similar meanings or, alternatively, *ji-* 'burn' (§A.1.2).

A.2.3 *Jumpa-* 'kiss'

Jumpa- 'kiss' is not found in the corpus.

A2.4 *Karla-* 'spear'

Karla- 'spear' is a transitive verb involving the puncture of an entity (in proximity to a handheld instrument, prototypically a spear). The nominal used to refer to a spear is *karrarlarla*.

APPENDIX A

(1,186) *Ngarrka-ngu karla-rnu wawirri warnpaka-ka nga-rninja-ka.*
man-ERG spear-PAST kangaroo grass-ALL eat-INF-ALL
A man speared a kangaroo eating grass.
N_D02-007842, BN, 38:45 mins

(1,187) *Ngayinya ngartina papirta karla-nji-ni.*
1GEN mother yam spear-INF-NOM
My mother hunts yams.
H_K01-506B, DG, 07:25 mins

Several combinations with coverbs do not involve a puncture: *wurluk-karla-* 'wash', *lirrlirr-karla-* 'punch' and *nyaru-karla-* 'howl'. These coverbs are not known to combine with any other inflecting verbs.

(1,188) *Kurtu-ngu maliki wirri-ya-nnya karnta-ngu=ma=nyanu yuku*
child-ERG dog chase-go-PRES woman-ERG=TOP=RR face
wurluk-karlanya.
wash-spear-PRES
The child is chasing a dog, the woman is washing her face.
N_D02-007842, BN, 41:10 mins

A.2.5 *Kinja-* 'wet'

Kinja- is a transitive verb involving an entity causing something else to be wet (the subject entity is usually *ngappa* 'water').

(1,189) *Ngappa-ngu=ju kinja-nnya.*
water-ERG=1SG.NS wet-PRES
The water wet me.
H_K01-505B, DG, 35:17 mins

(1,190) *Papulu-ka=rna purlun-ya-nmi ngappa-warnu kinja-nji-ngarnu.*
house-ALL=1SG.S enter-go-FUT water-SOURCE wet-INF-SOURCE
I'm going into the house because of the rain wetting [me].
H_K01-505B, DG, 35:49 mins

Kinja- is only known to combine with one coverb, *waramarn*, together meaning 'splash', and *waramarn* is not known to combine with any other inflecting verbs (Nash 2022).

A.2.6 *Kipa-* 'twist together'

There are no tokens of *kipa-* 'twist together' in the corpus.

A.2.7 *Kiya-* 'throw'

Kiya- 'throw' is a transitive verb indicating an agent causing a theme to be airborne. It combines with various coverbs specifying the manner of throwing, such as *win-kiya-* 'throw away' and *ngart-kiya-* 'breathe in'.

(1,191) *Nyuyu   kapi=rna   kiya-nmi.*
         spit   FUT=1SG.S   throw-FUT
         I'll chuck spit.
         H_K01-506A, DG, 10:47 mins

(1,192) *Wayi=nkulu   win-kiya-karla?*
         POLAR=2PL.S   throw_away-throw-SUBJ
         Would you mob throw it away?
         H_K06-004555, LOF, 52:39 mins

Kiya- can combine with several coverbs whose combinatorial meaning cannot be predicted from its use of 'fill' in isolation, nor do these combinations form a cohesive group (that is, suggesting a second sense of *kiya-* to accommodate these combinations does not seem fruitful). Many of these combinations involve controlled motion (not necessarily airborne). For example, the coverb *timpak* 'fill' combining with *kiya-* indicates a container filled to its limit by an agent. *Timpak* also combines with *wa-* 'fall', where *timpak-wa-* means 'overflow' (so *kiya-* 'throw' is used for containment up to the limit and *wa-* 'fall' is used for containment beyond the limit). Other members of this group include *kipirrij-kiya-* 'flip', *payang-kiya-* 'scare away', *purlin-kiya-* 'put inside', *timpak-kiya-* 'fill up' and *wijja-kiya-* 'take leave of'.

(1,193) *Ngulayi   yayi=nya   timpak-kiya-rnu.*
         PERF   the=FOC   fill-throw-PAST
         He had filled the [container].
         wrl-20190205, DK, 30:12 mins

(1,194) *Ngarrka=rla   wa-nganyu   karnta-ku,   wijja-kiya-rnu.*
         man=3.OBL   speak-PAST   woman-DAT   leave-throw-PAST
         The man spoke to the woman, [and then] he took his leave of her.
         N_D02-007842, BN, 50:14 mins

However, other combinations do not neatly correspond to motion of any kind, such as *mampaly-kiya-* 'refuse' and *tuurl-kiya-* 'burn'.

A.2.8 *Kuma-* 'cut'

Kuma- 'cut' is a transitive verb indicating an agent making an incision with a sharp surface into a theme (following the intension of *yak-* in Kuuk Thayorre, as defined in Gaby [2007: 266–67]). The incision is always performed with a sharp surface, though this entity does not constitute a grammatical relation of this predicate (the agent performing the action is the subject and the theme being incised is the object). Of course, the instrument may be realised as a secondary predicate of the subject.

(1,195) *Kurtu-ngu=nyanu   kuma-rnu   takka.*
        child-ERG=RR   cut-PAST   hand
        The child cut her hand.
        H_K01-505B, DG, 38:05 mins

(1,196) *Kuyu   kuma-nnya   karnta-ngu   japirri-parna-rlu.*
        meat   cut-PRES   woman-ERG   knife-PROP-ERG
        The woman is cutting the meat with her knife.
        wrl-20190201, DK, 05:39 mins

Kuma- is not known to combine with any coverbs other than *tiirl* 'split' (and its reduplicated form, *tirl-tiirl*), which encodes that, as part of the event, the theme was split into at least two parts.

(1,197) *Knife-ngu=lu   piya-nya,   or   mayingka-rlu=lu   tiirltiirl-kuma-nnya.*
        knife-ERG=3PL.S   break-PRES   axe-ERG=3PL.S   split-cut-PRES
        They cut it with a knife, or they split it with an axe.
        H_K06-004548, JW, 02:38 mins

A.2.9 *Kupa-* 'cook'

Kupa- 'cook' is a transitive verb that involves an agent applying heat to a theme. Prototypically, this is used to signal an agent cooking food.

(1,198)   *Yarnunju=lpangu*   *kupa-nmi*
food=1PL.EXCL.NS   cook-FUT
He'll cook food for us.
wrl-20180616-01, DK, 14:26 mins

(1,199)   *Yapa-ngu=nyanu*   *kupa-rnu*   *ngula*   *jarta*   *ka-ngu-rra.*
child-ERG=RR   cook-PAST   REL   sleep   be-PAST-IMPF
The child burnt herself while sleeping.
N_D02-007842, BN, 43:41 mins

The agent restriction on the subject of *kupa-* entails that non-sentient entities such as *warlu* 'fire' cannot be the subject of *kupa-*; however, non-sentient entities can be realised as instrumental secondary predicates, controlled by the agent.

(1,200)   *Nga=rna-ngu*   *warlu-ngu*   *kupa-n.*
FUT=1SG.S-2SG.NS   fire-ERG   cook-FUT
I'll burn you with fire.
H_K01-506A, DG, 36:43 mins

Kupa- is only reported to combine with one coverb, *ngarrak*, to mean 'heat (of/as sun)' (Nash 2022).

A.2.10 *La-* 'shoot'

La- 'shoot' involves an agent hitting a theme with an airborne projectile. Like other verbs of impact, only the agent and the theme bear grammatical relations to *la-*, and the projectile itself can be realised as an instrument secondary predicate of the subject.

(1,201)   *Pamarrpa-rlu=ju*   *la-rnu.*
stone-ERG=1SG.NS   shoot-PAST
He hit me with a rock.
H_K01-506A, DG, 41:55 mins

(1,202) Wanjila maliki ngula=nkulu nyuntu la-rnu?
where dog REL=2PL.S 2 shoot-PAST
Where's the dog that you mob shot?
H_K01-505B, DG, 47:08 mins

This inflecting verb is only reported to combine with a small number of coverbs: *tiirl* 'throw and hit', *japa* 'miss hitting', *wirrpiny* 'hit all of them' and *wuruly* 'ambush' (these glosses are based on the meaning of the coverb combining with the inflecting verb, from Nash [2022]).

A.2.11 *Lamarta-* 'hold'

Lamarta- is a transitive verb involving an entity embracing another entity. Typically, this is an agent holding a theme, though non-sentient entities can also be the subject of *lamarta-*, such as *walyparri* 'sand'.

(1,203) Yeah, walyparri-rlu=ju lamarta-rnu.
sand-ERG=1SG.NS hold-PAST
Yeah, the sand held my feet.
wrl-20190201, DK, 53:25 mins

(1,204) Yimpa=nya=ju lamarta-ka, kurtu.
this=FOC=1SG.NS hold-IMP child
Hold this child for me.
wrl-20180610-01, DK, 07:54 mins

This verb can also describe the subject coming to hold another entity (that is, 'catch').

(1,205) Wangani-rlu=ma lamarta-rnu yipakarli, nga-rnu=lku
dog-ERG=TOP hold-PAST lizard eat-PAST=THEN
The dog caught a lizard, and ate it.

It is not known to combine with any coverbs and is likely related to *marta-* 'have'.

A.2.12 Marta- 'have'

Marta- is a transitive verb that specifies a relation of possession between a possessor subject and possessum object. This need not be permanent or inherent possession—for example, it can be used to describe having an illness or the event of looking after someone else's child.

(1,206)   *Ngulayi=rna-rla*   *marta-nnya*   *yarnunju*   *kurtu-ku.*
PERF=1SG.S-3.OBL   hold-PRES   food   child-DAT
I have got food for the child.
wrl-20180608-01, DK, 07:03 mins

(1,207)   *Ngayu=ma=rna*   *jinjirla*   *paka-rnu,*   *ngarra=rna*
1=TOP=1SG.S   sneeze   hit-PAST   POT=1SG.S
kulykulypa   *marta-nnya.*
fever   have-PRES
I sneezed, I might have a fever.
wrl-20180614-02, DK, 03:25 mins

(1,208)   *Jinta-ngu*   *marta-nnya*   *mukarti*   *wiri.*
one-ERG   have-PRES   hat   big
[That] one has a big hat.
H_K01-505B, DG, 01:01:56 hrs

Marta- combines with the coverbs *jina* (historically a nominal meaning 'foot') to mean 'wait for' and *pijak* to mean 'squeeze (through/into)' (Nash 2022). Neither coverb is reported to occur with any other inflecting verb.

A.2.13 Murla- 'intercourse'

Murla- 'intercourse' is found once in the corpus. It is transitive and describes the act of copulation.

(1,209)   *Maliki-ja-rlu=pala-nyanu*   *murla-nnya.*
dog-DU-ERG=3DU.S-RR   intercourse-PRES
The two dogs are having sex with each other.
H_K01-506A, DG, 15:03 mins

A.2.14 *Nama-* 'crush'

Nama- is a transitive verb describing an entity exerting weight on another entity. There is no specification of agency of the crushing, nor of duration. Non-durative uses of *nama-* are translated as 'stomp'.

(1,210) *Yulu   nama-ka!*
         ground   crush-IMP
         Stomp the ground!
         H_K01-506A, DG, 22:18 mins

(1,211) *Murlu=ju   pamarrpa-rlu   nama-nnya.*
         this.ERG=1SG.NS   stone-ERG   crush-PRES
         This rock is weighing on me.
         H_K01-506A, DG, 30:31 mins

(1,212) *Wirliya-rlu   nama-nnya   parraja.*
         foot-ERG   crush-PRES   coolamon
         He crushed the coolamon with his foot.
         His foot crushed the coolamon.
         wrl-20200220, DK, 39:46 mins

Nama- is not known to combine with any coverbs.

A.2.15 *Nga-* 'tell'

Nga- is an extended transitive verb, requiring an ergative subject entity and two absolutive objects, where the objects are perceived to be equivalent words: one object is the word used by another entity and the other object is the word used by the subject entity.[3]

(1,213) *Kala=lu   nga-rnu   Warlmanpa-rlu=ma   'lamanpa'.*
         HAB=3PL.S   tell-PAST   Warlmanpa-ERG=TOP   gun
         Those Warlmanpa called it *'lamanpa'*.
         wrl-20190205, DK, 59:55 mins

---

3 An alternative analysis is that the two absolutive nominals are in a secondary predication relationship—that is, 'X says Y, of Z', where Z is predicated of Y rather than *nga-*.

(1,214) *Ngana=nkulu   nga-nnya   ngula=rna   marta-nnya?*
        what=2PL.S   tell-PRES   REL=1SG.S   have-PRES
        What do you mob call this thing that I have?
        H_K01-506A, DG, 25:38 mins

Nga- may be used to convey a message (though *wa-* 'speak' tends to be used for this function).

(1,215) *Ngayu=ma=lpa   nga-nnya   wirliya-rlu   nama-nnya   parraja.*
        1=TOP=1PL.INCL.S   tell-PRES   foot-ERG   crush-PRES   coolamon
        We told him to crush it with his foot.
        wrl-20200220, DK, 39:24 mins

Nga- can also be used to mean 'scold', as in a dog growling at someone.

(1,216) *Yali=ma   ngarra   Japaja   nga-nnya.*
        that=TOP   MIGHT   Japaja   tell-PRES
        [The dog] might be growling at that Japaja.
        wrl-20180615-02, DK, 10:46 mins

Nga- combines with two coverbs: *jiily* (and its reduplicated form, *jilyjily*) to mean 'show, point out' and *yurt* (and its reduplicated form, *yurtyurt*) to mean 'show, point at' (Nash 2022).

A.2.16 *Ngarta-* 'trim'

Ngarta- 'trim' is a transitive verb that refers to the act of shaving an object. In the corpus, it is found only with *karli* 'boomerang' as the object. It is not known to combine with any coverbs.

(1,217) *Ngarrka-ngu   karli   ngarta-nnya   wa-nganja-karra-rlu.*
        man-ERG   boomerang   trim-PRES   speak-INF-SS-ERG
        The man is trimming the boomerang while speaking.
        N_D02-007842, BN, 38:10 mins

A.2.17 *Ngaya-* 'excrete'

Ngaya- is a transitive verb in which an agent expels a theme from their body through their anus, such as laying an egg or defecating. It is not known to combine with any coverbs.

(1,218) *Kuna=rna*   *ngaya-nmi*
         excrement=1SG.S void-FUT
         I'll shit.
         H_K01-506A, DG, 12:27 mins

A.2.18 *Nguka-* 'drink'

Nguka- is a transitive verb signalling an agent ingesting a theme that is liquid (in all cases, the object is *ngappa* 'water'). It combines with the coverb *wirrpin* 'all' to encode that the liquid was entirely consumed.

(1,219) *Ngappa=rna*   *nguka-rnu.*
         water=1SG.S   drink-PAST
         I drank water.
         H_K01-506A, DG, 47:33 mins

(1,220) *Puliki-rli=lu* *pawarrayi* *wirrpin-nguka-rnu.*
         bull-ERG=3PL.S   completely   all-drink-PAST
         The bulls completely drank up all of it [the water].
         N_D02-007842, BN, 05:23 mins

A.2.19 *Nyurla-* 'knead'

There are no tokens of *nyurla-* 'knead' in the corpus.

A.2.20 *Paka-* 'hit'

Paka- is a transitive verb referring to an entity striking another entity, though the manner of striking seems highly unspecified. It encompasses acts of killing, hitting (for example, with the fist), chopping (for example, of boomerangs) and illnesses.

(1,221) *Paka-nmi=rna-ngu.*
         kill-FUT=1SG.S-2SG.NS
         I will kill you.
         H_K06-004555, LOF, 54:03 mins

(1,222) *Murlu=nya*   *nga=ju=nga*   *paka-nma.*
         this.ERG=FOC   POST=1SG.NS=DUB   hit-POT
         This one might hit me.
         H_K01-506A, DG, 15:31 mins

(1,223) *Karli=ju*   *paka!*
         boomerang=1SG.NS   hit.IMP
         Chop a boomerang for me!
         H_K01-506A, DG, 57:11 mins

(1,224) *Kulykulypa-rlu*   *ngayu=ju*   *paka-nnya.*
         fever-ERG   1=1SG.NS   hit-PRES
         I have a flu [lit.: the fever is hitting me].
         wrl-20180614-02, DK, 03:32 mins

Paka- combines with many coverbs, which generally specify the manner of striking, though some combinations fit less clearly into this category.

(1,225) *Waak-paka!*
         block-hit.IMP
         Block him!
         H_K01-505B, DG, 29:19 mins

(1,226) *Yurt-paka*   *ayi=nya* *maliki,* *nga=jana=*   *wittawitta* *pi-nya!*
                                             nga
         chase-hit.IMP the=FOC   dog   POST=3PL.   children   act_on-POT
                                            NS=DUB
         Hunt the dog away, lest he bite the children!
         N_D02-009887, DG, 12:13 mins

(1,227) *Jinjirla=n*   *paka-nya-nya.*
         sneeze=2SG.S   hit-MOT-PRES
         You're going around sneezing.
         wrl-20180614-02, DK, 5:34 mins

(1,228) *Kawaj-paka-*   *kula=rna-rla*   *yu-ngu*   *yarnunju.*
         rnu=rna
         forget-hit-   NEG=1SG.S-3.OBL   give-PAST   food
         PAST=1SG.S
         I forgot, I didn't give food to him.
         wrl-20191208-02, DK, 11:46 mins

Kawaj also combines with *wa-* 'speak' to mean 'warn'; *jinjirla* is not known to combine with any other inflecting verb.

A.2.21 *Pangi-* 'dig'

Pangi- is a transitive verb that involves scraping a surface—prototypically digging the ground, but it extends to other similar event structures such as scratching. The object can refer to the surface being scraped (such as the ground) or the resulting structure (such as a hole, dug in the ground). It is possible this latter object type is better treated as a secondary predication on a null argument denoting the scraped surface (I tentatively resist this analysis because I have never seen the two co-occur, which would be expected to be permissible if there were a secondary predication relation).

(1,229) *Ngayu=ma=rna-rla   pangi-nmi   wawirri-ku   ngulya.*
         1=TOP=1SG.S-3.OBL   dig-FUT   kangaroo-DAT   hole
         I'll dig a hole for a kangaroo.
         wrl-20191208-03, DK, 19:07 mins

(1,230) *Yapa   jinta   ngulya   pangu-rnu.*
         child   one   hole   dig-?
         One child is a hole digger.[4]
         H_K01-506A, DG, 23:58 mins

(1,231) *Jungarrayi=ma   pawarrayi-ja-ngu=lku   pangi-nja-   yulu-kuma.*
                                                      kuma
         Jungarrayi=TOP   completely-INCH-   dig-INF-   ground-AVER
                            PAST=THEN   AVER
         Jungarrayi has now finished digging the ground.
         wrl-20180616-01, DK, 25:19 mins

It is not known to combine with any coverbs.

---

4   This clause seems to have a nominal predicate, *pangu-rnu*, where *-rnu* is a nominaliser, rather than the past-tense inflection (which is also *pangu-rnu*). This mirrors a construction in Warlpiri where the past-tense inflection is homophonous with a nomic derivation (except Class 1 verbs). See Nash (1986: 29–30) for the details in Warlpiri. My thanks to Harold Koch for highlighting an earlier incongruity in my analysis and to David Nash for suggesting this revised analysis. This is the only known example in Warlmanpa where a verb is nominalised in this manner—typically *-nji-ni* is used (§4.4.7).

A.2.22 *Piya-* 'break'

Piya- 'break' is a transitive verb that seems to semantically intersect with *kuma-* 'cut'—other than *piya-* not encoding an action done with a sharp blade. At the most general level, *piya-* refers to either puncture(s) of an object or causing an object to stop being able to perform its intended function. Commonly, it refers to acts of biting, cutting or (physically) breaking.

(1,232) *Ngarrka-ngu   piya-rnu   kuyu   ngula=rla   knife   yapa-ngu*
man-ERG   break-PAST   meat   REL=3.OBL   child-ERG
witta-ngu   yu-ngu.
small-ERG   give-PAST
The man cut the meat after the small child gave him a knife.
N_D02-007842, BN, 44:33 mins

(1,233) *Maliku-rlu   piya-rnu   kurtu.*
dog-ERG   break-PAST   child
The dog bit the child.
wrl-20190201, DK, 06:31 mins

(1,234) *Karli=rna-rla   marlaja-piya-rnu   Japanangka-ku.*
boomerang=1SG.S-3.OBL   reason_for-break-PAST   Japanangka-DAT
Because I broke the boomerang on Japanangka.
N_D02-007841, BN, 30:41 mins

It combines with several coverbs, all of which combine with other verbs of impact, such as *tirl-piya-* 'break, crack, slice' and *kiit-piya-* 'break' (where *kiit* specifies the object must be non-functional as a result of the event).

(1,235) *Karli=ju   Japanangka-rlu   jurnta   kiit-piya-rnu.*
boomerang=1SG.NS   Japanangka-ERG   away   break-break-PAST
Japanangka broke the boomerang on me.
N_D02-007841, BN, 29:19 mins

A.2.23 *Waka-* 'climb'

Waka- is an intransitive verb involving an entity using both arms and legs to move. This verb encodes a manner of motion that can be contrasted with path-of-motion verbs such as *wa-* 'fall', which encodes vertical motion regardless of manner. Typically, *waka-* refers to climbing, but also extends to crawling.

(1,236) *Kurtu   yiwirtika   waka-nnya.*
child   tree-ALL   climb-PRES
The child climbed up the tree.
H_K01-505B, DG, 31:32 mins

(1,237) *Kula   waka-ka   yayi=nya   yiwirti-nga   kala=n   wa-nmi!*
NEG   climb-IMP the=FOC   tree-LOC   APPR=2SG.S   fall-FUT
Don't climb the tree, you might fall!
wrl-20180605-01, DK, 14:58 mins

Upwards climbing is specified by the coverb *pirtij* 'upward' combining with *waka-*.

(1,238) *Ngana-ku=n   pirtij-waka-nya?*
what-DAT=2SG.S   upward-climb-PRES
Why did you climb up?
H_K06-004555, LOF, 47:59 mins

A.2.24 *Wayi-* 'search for'

Wayi- is a conative verb taking an ergative subject and dative indirect object. The subject is an entity aiming to locate an indirect object entity. It does not encode that the indirect object is successfully located as part of the situation.

(1,239) *Maliki-rlu=rla   kuyu-ku   wayi-nnya.*
dog-ERG=3.OBL   meat-DAT   search-PRES
The dog is searching for meat.
H_K01-505B, DG, 07:51 mins

It is only reported to combine with one coverb, *maly* 'spread out, where *maly-wayi-* means 'spread out seeking' (Nash 2022).

A.2.25 *Winja-* 'leave alone'

Winja- is a transitive verb involving an agent leaving a theme and ceasing to interact with it (regardless of whether any interaction was taking place prior).

(1,240) *Nakamarra-rlu winja-rnu, ayi=nya=ma tajpaka, kula nga-rnu.*
Nakamarra-ERG leave-PAST the=FOC=TOP hard NEG eat-PAST
Nakamarra left it alone, the [cookie] was stale, she didn't eat it.
wrl-20191207-01, DK, 28:42 mins

(1,241) *Pulkapulka-rlu=ju-lu winja-rnu.*
old_men-ERG=1SG.NS-3PL.S leave-PAST
The old men left me [for work].
N_D18-013596, LN, 17:51 mins

It is not known to combine with any coverbs.

A.2.26 Ya- 'put'

Ya- is a difficult verb to classify. Its semantics refer to an agent moving a theme to a goal (location), though the grammatical status of the goal is dubious. In the grammar, I have analysed it as an argument on its ability to be cross-referenced when it is an animate, though there are only two cases of this, and this is an area that I would like to further investigate, particularly as these are the only cases of allative-marked referents being registered in the bound pronouns.

(1,242) *Yali=nya-rna-ngu pirntija ya-rnu nyuntunya-ka.*
that=FOC=1SG.S-2SG.NS beside put-PAST 2-ALL
I put that beside you.
N_D02-007841, BN, 09:07 mins

(1,243) *Puta ya-ka!*
incompletely put-IMP
Don't put it down!
H_K06-004555, LOF, 52:07 mins

(1,244) *Ya-rnu=ja.*
put-PAST=1PL.EXCL.S
We left it there.
H_K06-004555, LOF, 52:00 mins

A.2.27 *Yila-* 'drip'

There is only one token of *yila-* in the corpus. It seems to be an intransitive inflecting verb referring to a liquid coming out from a source along or on an entity, where the liquid is the subject. It may involve a dative-marked affected entity though it is unclear whether this reflects a benefactive (malefactive) adjunct or an indirect object.

(1,245) *Ngarrka-ku=rla   kulykulypa   yila-nnya.*
         man-DAT=3.OBL   fever   drip-PRES
         The fever is leaking on the man.
         N_D02-007842, BN, 22:54 mins

A.3 Class 3 verbs

A.3.1 *Jitpi-* 'run'

Jitpi- (alternatively, *jiti-* for some speakers) is an intransitive verb that denotes an agent running. It refers specifically to movement at a high pace (rather than the physical movements of the body involved in running) and, as such, can be applied to machines.

(1,246) *Train   jutpu-ngunya.*
                    run-PRES
         The train is running.
         wrl-20170321-02, SN, 20:57 mins

It combines with some coverbs to specify the manner of running. For example, combining with *wuruly-* 'out of sight' means 'run out of sight, escape'.

(1,247) *Wawirri=rna-palangu   nya-ngu   jirrama,   wuruly-jutpu-ngu=pala.*
         kangaroo=1SG.S-3DU.NS   see-PAST   two   conceal-run-PAST=3DU.S
         I saw two kangaroos, [who] ran out of sight.
         H_K01-506A, DG, 55:20 mins

As discussed in §6.2.1.3, *jitpi-* may alternatively be analysed as a coverb + inflecting verb combination—that is, *jit-pi-* (where *pi-* is a transitive impact verb broadly meaning 'act on'). I do not follow this analysis because coverbs are not subject to vowel alternations, unlike inflecting verb roots. That is, if *jitpi-* comprised a coverb and inflecting verb, the coverb form, *jit*, would not be affected by high vowel alternations, so the past form, for example, would be **jit-pu-ngu*, rather than *jutpu-ngu*. This can be contrasted with coverbs combining with *pi-*, such as *miti* 'go [mother-in-law speech]', which is unaffected by the vowel alternations (hence the form *miti-pu-ngu* 'ran'), and *pali* 'extinguish' (hence the form *pali-pu-ngu* 'extinguished').

An additional argument against a complex verb analysis of *jitpi-* is that for at least one speaker, the form of the verb is *jiti-*, without a stop cluster, as in (1,248). In the analysis of *jitpi-* as a monomorphemic root, the alternative form, *jiti-*, does not violate any phonotactic constraints, unlike the analysis in which *pi-* has an alternative form, *i-*, violating the constraint that all words begin with a consonant.

(1,248) Wawirri=rna   karta pu-ngu,   kapi lani=lku,   **jutu-ngu.**
         kangaroo=1SG.S   spear act_on-PAST   and   afraid=THEN   **run-PAST**
         I speared the kangaroo, and then afraid, it ran off.
         wrl-20180528-03, DK, 18:39 mins

A.3.2 *Ka-* 'take'

Ka- is a transitive verb in which an agent moves a theme to a different location.

(1,249) Wajurrajurra=ma   Elliott-ka=lku=palangu   ka-nganya   kapurlu-nginta.
         afternoon=TOP   Elliott-ALL=THEN=   take-PRES   sister-RECP
                           3DU.NS
         He's taking the two sisters to Elliott this afternoon.
         N_D02-007850, DG, 01:52 mins

(1,250) Wangani=li   ka-nyi   muju?
         dog=1DU.INCL.S   take-FUT   too
         Can we take the dog with us too?
         wrl-20190213-01, DK, 02:52 mins

It combines with path-of-motion coverbs such as *pina* 'return' and manner-of-motion coverbs such as *rarra* 'drag' and *wuruly* 'conceal'.

(1,251) Pina=rna   ka-nganya   wangani   ngurra-ka.
        return=1SG.S   take-PRES   dog   camp-ALL
        I'll take the dog back home.
        wrl-20200219, DK, 29:58 mins

Furthermore, it combines with several coverbs without clear 'take' semantics, such as *yirri* 'tickle, itch', *jilij* 'ask' and *ngurl* 'squeeze'.

(1,252) Kapi=rna-ngu   jilij-ka-nyi.
        FUT=1SG.S-2SG.NS   ask-take-FUT
        I'll ask you.
        H_K01-506A, DG, 18:37 mins

A.3.3 *Li-* 'cry'

Li- is an intransitive verb involving the subject crying (including animals, in which case it is better translated as 'howling'). It is not reported to occur with any coverbs.

(1,253) Kurtu   lu-ngunya,   murrumurru   ka-nya.
        child   cry-PRES   sick   be-PRES
        The child is crying, she's sick.
        H_K01-505B, DG, 26:12 mins

(1,254) Kula=rna   wangani=ma   purtu-kangu   li-nja-ka.
        NEG=1SG.S   dog=TOP   listen-be-PAST   cry-INF-ALL
        I didn't hear the dog howling.
        wrl-20191207-01, DK, 14:07 mins

A.3.4 *Kapi-* 'chase'

Kapi- is a transitive verb typically involving a subject following an object, especially in pursuit. The object does not need to be within vision—for example, tracking the trail of a kangaroo, in which case the tracks or the kangaroo itself could be the grammatical object.

(1,255) Wirliya   kapi=rna   kapu-nyi.
        foot   FUT=1SG.S   chase-FUT
        I'll follow the tracks.
        H_K01-505B, DG, 07:20 mins

It is also offered as the translation of English 'drag', in which case the entity 'following' is the object, rather than the subject, as in the examples above, so perhaps there is a more general 'follow' relation between the two grammatical roles and the more agentive referent takes the subject slot.

(1,256) *Ngana=n   kapu-ngunya?*
         what=2SG.S drag-PRES
         What are you dragging?
         H_K06-004555, LOF, 53:19 mins

Kapi- combines with several path-of-motion verbs, resulting in combinations such as *timirl-kapi-* 'follow through narrow path' and *payang-kapi-* 'intercept'. It also combines with non-motion coverbs such as *yirri-kapi-* 'watch over'.

(1,257) *Warlu=rna   payang-kapu-ngu.*
         fire=1SG.S   intercept-chase-PAST
         I found firewood.
         H_K01-505B, DG, 35:12 mins

A.3.5 *Nya-* 'see'

Nya- is a transitive verb in which an experiencer or agent (depending on the level of control) visually perceives a theme.

(1,258) *Ka-ngu-rra=rnalu   nguru=ma   nguru-nga,*
         be-PAST-IMPF=1PL.EXLC.S   bush=TOP   bush-LOC
         nya-ngu-rra=rnalu   parra.
         see-PAST-IMPF=1PL.EXCL.S   sun
         We would sit [out in] the bush, and watch the sun.
         wrl-20190211-01, DK, 06:54 mins

(1,259) *Kari=ju   wangani-rlu   nya-nyi,   kula   warlku-wa-ngami.*
         COND=1SG.NS dog-ERG   see-FUT   NEG   bark-speak-FUT
         If the dog sees me, it won't bark.
         wrl-20180601-01, DK, 24:30 mins

It combines with *ngapiny* (and its reduplicated form, *ngapinyngapiny*) to mean 'smell'—that is, perceive by smell.

(1,260)　*Maliki-rlu*　*wirliya*　*ngapiny-nya-nganya.*
　　　　　dog-ERG　　foot　　smell-see-PRES
　　　　　The dog is smelling the tracks.
　　　　　H_K01-506A, DG, 16:09 mins

A.3.6 *Pi-* 'act on'

Pi- 'act on' is a generic verb of impact (with a transitive case frame)—possibly the inflecting verb least specified for event structure. It denotes a transitive event, in which one entity acts on another entity. Prototypically, this involves hitting, biting or killing.

(1,261)　*Murlu=ju*　　　　　*pu-ngu.*
　　　　　this.ERG=1SG.NS　　act_on-PAST
　　　　　This one hit me.
　　　　　H_K01-505B, DG, 06:18 mins

(1,262)　*Kuyu=ju-lu*　　　　　*pu-ngu.*
　　　　　meat=1SG.NS-3PL.S　　act_on-PAST
　　　　　They killed game for me.
　　　　　N_D02-007841, 21:23 mins

(1,263)　*Kurtu*　*kanya*　　*wana-warnu*　　*pi-nji-ngarnu.*
　　　　　child　　be-PRES　　snake-SOURCE　　act_on-INF-SOURCE
　　　　　The child is sitting after being bitten by a snake.
　　　　　H_K01-505B, DG, 28:18 mins

(1,264)　*Maliki-ja-rlu=pala-nyanu*　　*kili-ngu*　　*pu-ngunya.*
　　　　　dog-DUAL-ERG=3DU.S-RR　　angry-ERG　　act_on-PRES
　　　　　The two aggressive dogs are biting each other.
　　　　　H_K01-505B, DG, 29:51 mins

It combines with a wide range of coverbs, most of which seem to fall into two semantic groups: first, some result in intransitive movement meanings, such as *jarra-pi-* 'dance (women's dance)' and *marntiwa-pi-* 'hover'; second, are various manners of impact such as *muut-pi-* 'detach', *tingkirr-pi-* 'tie up' and *karta-pi-* 'spear, wash, dig'. A few other combinations do not seem to neatly fall into either semantic group, such as *jangart-pi-* 'echo back' and *jura-pi-* 'pour, fill'.

(1,265) *Jarra-pu-ngka!*
dance-act_on-IMP
Dance!
N_D02-007844, BN, 15:16 mins

(1,266) *Yukulyarri   wawirri=rna-palangu   karta-pu-ngu.*
wallaby   kangaroo=1SG.S-3DU.NS   spear-act_on-PAST
I speared a wallaby and a kangaroo.
H_K01-505B, DG, 46:24 mins

(1,267) *Witta-ngu   yapa-ngu   wila-pungunya   nganinya   wangani.*
small-ERG   person-ERG play-act_on-PRES   3GEN   dog
The child is playing with her dog.
wrl-20200220, DK, 43:02 mins

A.3.7 Yi- 'give'

Yi- 'give' is a ditransitive transfer-of-possession verb, in which an agent gives a theme to a recipient. In related languages, the cognate verb allows alternations in the case-marking pattern (for example, both the theme and the recipient taking absolutive case). This is not evident in Warlmanpa: in all tokens, the agent takes ergative marking (as the subject), the theme takes absolutive marking (as the object) and the recipient takes dative marking (as the indirect object). Thus, compare the case marking of the recipient *(w)ita* in Warlmanpa (1,268) and in Ngardi (1,269).

(1,268) *Ngayu=rna-rla   ngappa   yu-ngunya   **witta-ku**.*
1=1SG.S-3.OBL   water   give-PRES   **small-DAT**
I'm giving water to the child.
H_K01-505B, DG, 17:59 mins

(1,269) ***Ita**$_{ABS}$=rla   mangarri$_{ABS}$ yi-nya   ngati-ngku.*
small=3.OBL   veg_food   GIVE-PST   mother-ERG
Then the mother gave the kid the food.
(Ngardi [Ennever 2021])

Yi- is only reported to combine with one coverb, *palyarr* (which is not known to combine with any other inflecting verbs), to mean 'rub' (Nash 2022).

A.4 Class 4 verbs

A.4.1 *Nga-* 'eat'

Class 4 has one inflecting verb, *nga-* 'eat'. In isolation, it is a transitive verb referring to an agent ingesting a theme. As far as I am aware, it is used specifically for ingestion of solids (ingestion of liquids is covered by *nguka-* 'drink').

(1,270)   Bush tucker   *nga-rnu=rna*   *papirta,*   *wijara,*   *yakajirri,*
                             eat-PAST=1SG.S   yam   yam   desert_raisin

         nganjawarli.
         bush_tomato

         I ate different sorts of bush tucker: different types of yams, desert raisins and bush tomatoes.
         N_D18-013596, LN, 19:44 mins

In combination with coverbs, the resulting meaning is usually within the domain of motion, such as *jirti-nga-* 'sneak up on' and *purlpaj-nga-* 'jump', though one non-motion combination is also found: *yina-nga-* 'sing'. *Yina* is not known to combine with any other coverb and, interestingly, it is likely cognate with an inflecting verb in Warlpiri, *yunpa-rni* 'sing' (historical/cognate nasal + stop clusters were reduced to just nasals in Warlmanpa verb roots).

(1,271)   *Jirti-nga-rnu-rnu*   *kalkirni*   *ngayinya-kapina.*
                   sneak-eat-PAST-TWD   towards   1-PREP

         It was about to sneak up towards me.
         wrl-20180528-03, JK, 08:39 mins

(1,272)   *Yawirri-piya*   *purlpaj*   *nga-rninya.*
                   kangaroo-LIKE$_2$ jump   eat-PRES

         He's jumping like a kangaroo.
         wrl-20191208-02, DK, 26:01 mins

(1,273)   *Ali-ngu=nya*   *jurlaka-rlu*   *yina-nga-rninya*   *pirnti-nga*
                   that-ERG=FOC   bird-ERG   sing-eat-PRES   tree_top-LOC

         kankarlarra,   *yiwirti-rla.*
         above   tree-LOC

         The bird in the treetop above is singing.
         wrl-20191208-01, DK, 09:16 mins

A.5 Class 5 verbs

A.5.1 -*Ma*- 'cause'

The derivational suffix -*ma*- derives a nominal into a transitive inflecting verb, generally with the meaning 'cause to be X'. See §6.5.2.2.

A.5.2 *Ma*- 'get'

In isolation, *ma*- is a transitive verb involving an agent obtaining a theme.

(1,274)   *Jawarti=rna*   *pa-nami-rni*   *ngappa-ku*   *ma-nja-ku.*
tomorrow=1SG.S   go-FUT-TWD   water-DAT   get-INF-DAT
Tomorrow I will come to get water.
H_K01-506A, DG, 01:02:01 hrs

(1,275)   *Ma-nta-rti*   *ngami*   *ka-ngka-pa!*
get-IMP-TWD   coolamon   carry-IMP-AWAY
Come get this coolamon and take it away!
wrl-20180601-01, DK, 32:48 mins

It combines with many coverbs, with a general 'do' meaning in relation to the meaning of the coverb (especially when referring to vocalisations, Warlmanpa seems to have collapsed a historical distinction between a do verb and a say verb both of which have the root *maN-*, which is still evident in some Ngumpin languages, such as Walmajarri [Hudson 1978: 43]).

(1,276)   *Maliki*   *payi-ma-nu.*
dog   bark-get-PST
The dog barked.
H_K01-505B, DG, 02:11 mins

(1,277)   *Jalal-ma-nu=lku=rna.*
lift-get-PAST=THEN=1SG.S
Then I lifted it.
H_K01-506B, DG, 01:12 mins

(1,278) Parti-ma=lpa   yali=nya=lu   yapa   ka-nya
         leave-FUT.AWAY=1PL.EXCL.S that=FOC=3PL.S   person   be-PRES
         kawaj~kawaj-ma-nnya=lpangu-lu.
         forget~RDP-get-PRES=1PL.EXCL.S-3PL.S
         We left, those people sitting have forgotten us.
         wrl-20191208-02, DK, 29:20 mins

Analytical problems arise with whether some of the coverb combinations would be better treated as instances of *-ma-* 'cause' rather than the lexical verb root *ma-* 'get'.

(1,279) Lurrija~lurrija-rlu   warlu   jarra~jarra-ma-nta!
         quickly~RDP-ERG   fire   flame~RDP-CAUSE?-IMP
         Quickly build a fire!
         ('Cause there to be a fire.')
         H_K01-506B, DG, 08:39 mins

This would allow for a more compositional analysis, though would require extending the syntactic scope of *-ma-*, allowing it to derive coverbs (rather than just nominals). In this grammar, I have opted against this analysis, largely on the basis that coverb + inflecting verb combinations do not need to be compositional, so it seems more parsimonious to restrict the scope of *-ma-* based on the clear usages, though there is justification for either analysis.

A.5.3 *Wa-* 'fall'

Wa- is an intransitive inflecting verb indicating a subject moving along a vertical axis. It is prototypically used for downward uncontrolled motion.

(1,280) Waka-rnu   wa-nu=lku.
         climb-PAST   fall-PAST=THEN
         He climbed then fell.
         H_K01-506A, DG, 43:07 mins

(1,281) Walku   kula   ngappa   wa-nmi.
         nothing   NEG   water   fall-FUT
         No, it won't rain.
         H_K01-505B, DG, 47:32 mins

(1,282)   *Partu-ka!*   *Ngayi*   *yiwirti*   *wa-nmi,*   *kala=ngu*   *nama-nmi!*
leave-IMP   oh   tree   fall-FUT   APPR=2SG.NS   crush-FUT
Get away! That tree really will fall, it might crush you!
wrl-20200225, DK, 07:23 mins

Several coverbs can specify the manner or path of motion.

(1,283)   *Pirtij-wa-nja-wangu!*
upward-fall-INF-PRIV
Don't climb up!
H_K06-004555, LOF, 47:45 mins

(1,284)   *Kurtu*   *wali-wa-nu.*
child   trip-fall-PAST
The child tripped over.
wrl-20190205, DK, 20:06 mins

Some coverb combinations do not necessitate motion as part of their event structure, though they still seem related to the event of falling.

(1,285)   *Ngappa-nga*   *kangkurr-wa-nnya.*
water-LOC   submerge-fall-PRES
He's bathing in the water.
(Vertical movement is required to be submerged.)
wrl-20170321-02, SN, 02:17 mins

(1,286)   *Jawu-wa-nnya=lku=rna.*
cold-fall-PRES=THEN=1SG.S
I am cold now.
(May be considered a metaphorical 'fall'.)
wrl-20170825-01, SN, 04:08 mins

(1,287)   *Jarta-wa-nta!*
sleep-fall-IMP
Go to sleep!
(Vertical movement to get to sleeping position?)
H_K01-506A, DG, 18:57 mins

A.5.4 -Ya- 'go'

The inflecting verb -*ya*- only occurs with a small number of coverbs and these only occur with -*ya*-. It cannot be used other than in combination with these coverbs. The regular 'go' verb in Warlmanpa is *pa*- (§A.1.4). The known coverb combinations are *purluny-ya*- 'enter', *laki-ya*- 'howl' and *wuruly-purluny-ya*- 'disappear' (Nash 2022).

(1,288)   *Takka*   *purluny-ya-nta*   *ngulya-ka!*
hand   enter-go-IMP   ground-IMP
Put your hand in the hole!
N_D02-009887, DG, 13:39 mins

In combination with the coverb *marrarla*, -*ya*- is also used as a generic verb for a man addressing his wife's brother.

(1,289)   *Marrarla-ya-nta-rti=ju*   *yuranypa!*
R_generic-go-IMP-TWD=1SG.NS   R_vegetable_food
Give the food to me!
H_K01-506B, DG, 05:51 mins

Appendix B: Narrative collection

B.1 Biography

Speaker: Doris Kelly
Source: wrl-20190211-01 and wrl-20190208

1. *Ngayu=ma=rna   palka-ja-ngu   Mankamarntangi.*
   1=TOP=1SG.S   born-INCH-PAST   Phillip Creek
   I was born in Phillip Creek.

2. *Ngayu=ma=rnalu   partu-ngu-rnu   Mangkamarntangi   ngurra-ka*
   1=TOP=1PL.EXCL   leave-PAST-HITH   Phillip Creek   camp-ALL
   Warrabri-ka.
   Warrabri-ALL
   We moved from Phillip Creek to Warrabri.

3. *Jala=ma=lu   yirti   ma-nnya   'Alekarengei'=lki.*
   now=TOP=3PL.S   name   get-PRES   Alekarenge=THEN
   Now they call it Alekarenge.

4. *Ngayu=ma=rna   pa-nangu-rra   school-ka   Alekarengei-rla.*
   1=TOP=1SG.S   go-PAST-IMPF   school-ALL   Alekarenge-LOC
   I went to school in Alekarenge.

5. *Ngula=rna   wiri-ja-ngu   ma̱rry-ja-ngu=lku=rna.*
   REL=1SG.S   big-INCH-PAST   marry-INCH-PAST=THEN=1SG.S
   I got married when I was older.

6. | *Ngayu=ma=rna* | *palka* | *ma-nu* | *kurtu=lku.*
   | 1=TOP=1SG.S | born | get-PAST | child=THEN

   I had a son there.

7. | *Yali-ngurlu=ma* | *ngayu=ma=jarra* | *kangkuya-jarra* | *partu-nga*
   | that-ELA=TOP | 1=TOP=DUAL | old_man-DUAL | leave-PAST.AWAY

   Darwin-ka=lku.
   Darwin-ALL=THEN

   Then me and the old man moved to Darwin.

8. | *Ngula=ja* | *ka-ngu-rra* | *Darwin-nga* | *kurtu=lku*
   | REL=1DU.EXCL | sit-BE-IMPF | Darwin-LOC | child=THEN

   palka-ja-ngu— *karnta.*
   born-INCH-PAST woman

   I had a child while we were living in Darwin—a girl.

9. | *Yali-ngurlu=ma* | *pina* | *pa-nangu=ja* | *Alekarengei-ka*
   | that-ELA=TOP | return | go-PAST=1DU.EXCL.S | Alekarenge-ALL

   tarnnga=yi.
   long_time=STILL

   Then we moved back to Alekarenge.

10. | *Ngula=ja* | *pina* | *pa-nangu* | *Alekarengei-ka* | *marta-rnu=rna*
    | REL=1DU.EXCL.S | return | go-PAST | Alekarenge-ALL | have-PAST=1SG.S

    kurtu *jirrima-kanyanu=lku.*
    child two-ANOTHER=THEN

    Then I had two more sons when we returned to Alekarenge.

11. | *Ka-ngu-rra=rnalu* | *nguru-nga,* | *nya-ngu-rra=rnalu* | *parra.*
    | sit-PAST-IMPF=1PL.EXCL.S | bush-LOC | see-PAST-IMPF=1PL.EXCL.S | sun

    We were living in the bush, watching the sun.

12. | *Ali-ngurlu=ma* | *partu-ngu=rnalu* | *Kunuyungku-ka,*
    | that-ELA=TOP | leave-PAST=1PL.EXCL.S | Kunuyungku-ALL

    tarnnga=yi=rnalu *ka-ngu-rra.*
    long_time=STILL=1PL.EXCL.S sit-PAST-IMPF

    Then we moved to Kunuyungku, and stayed there for a long time.

APPENDIX B

13. | *Ngaka=ma=rnalu* | *partu-nga* | *Mangalawurru-ka.* |
    | SOON=TOP=1PL.EXCL.S | leave-PAST.IMPF | Mangalawurru-ALL |

    Later on we moved to Mangalawurru.

14. | *Manfred=ma* | *palka-ja-ngu* | *Tennant Creek-nga.* |
    | Manfred=TOP | born-INCH-PAST | Tennant Creek-LOC |

    Manfred was born in Tennant Creek.

15. | *Ali-ngurlu=ma=rna* | *pina* | *ka-ngu* | *Mangalawurru-ka=lku* |
    | that-ELA=TOP=1SG.S | return | take-PAST | Mangalawurru-ALL=THEN |

    witta-nga.
    small-LOC

    After that I then brought him back to Mangalawurru while he was small.

16. | *Kala=rna-jana* | *kurtukurtu* | *ka-nja-nu-rnu* | *school-ka=ma* |
    | HAB=1SG.S-3PL.NS | children | take-MOT-PAST-HITH | school-ALL=TOP |

    Warrego Mine-ka.
    Warrego Mine-ALL

    I used to bring the kids to school at the Warrego Mine.

17. | *Kala=rna-jana* | *pina* | *yu-ngu* | *school-ku.* |
    | HAB=1SG.S-3PL.NS | knowledge | give-PAST | school-DAT |

    I would teach them school.

18. | *Ngayu=ma=rna* | *ka-ngu-rra* | *jirrima-jinta-parna.* |
    | 1=TOP=1SG.S | sit-PAST-IMPF | two-one-PROP |

    I was living with three others at Mangalawurru.

19. | *Ngayinya-jarra* | *wiri-jarra* | *Cornelius* | *kapi* | *Cynthia=pala* |
    | 1GEN-DU | big-DU | Cornelius | CONJ | Cynthia=3DU.S |

    ka-ngu-rra *Alekarenge-rla.*
    sit-PAST-IMPF Alekarenge-LOC

    My eldest son and eldest daughter were still living in Alekarenge.

20. *Ali-ngurlu=ma   partu-ngu-rnu=rnalu   Tennant Creek-ka=lku.*
    that-ELA=TOP   leave-PAST-HITH=1PL.EXCL.O   Tennant Creek-ALL=THEN
    Then we moved to Tennant Creek.

21. *Ngayu=ma=rna   warrikngali-ja-ngu-rra   Land Council-nga=lku,*
    1=TOP=1SG.S   work-INCH-PAST-IMPF   Land Council-LOC=THEN
    tarnnga=yi=lku.
    long_time=STILL=THEN
    I was working at the Central Land Council.

22. *Jala=ma=rna   ka-nya   Tennant Creek-nga,   tarnnga=yi.*
    now=TOP=1SG.S   sit-PRES   Tennant Creek-LOC   long_time=STILL
    I live here in Tennant Creek now, still.

B.2 A boy and his dog

Speaker: Doris Kelly
Source: wrl-20190207-01

1. *Kurtu   ka-ngu-rra   Kunayungku-rla   nyaninya-parna   panpiya-parna.*
   child   sit-PAST-IMPF   Kunayungku-LOC   3.GEN-PROP   family-PROP
   There was a little boy living at Kunayungku with his family.

2. *Parungarla   jawujawu,   kula   ngappa   wa-nu-rra.*
   cool_season   cold   NEG   water   fall-PAST-IMPF
   It was autumn, it was cold, it wasn't raining.

3. *Parra-kanyanu   wirlinyi   partu-nga   kurtu   wangani-parna*
   sun-OTHER   hunting   leave-PAST.AWAY   child   dog-PROP
   wayi-nja-ku   yipakarli-ku   kapi   jurlaka-ku.
   search-INF-DAT   lizard-DAT   CONJ   bird-DAT
   One day he went away hunting with a dog, to search for lizards or birds.

4. *Partan   kapu-ngu   jinta   yipakarli.*
   find   intercept-PAST   one   lizard
   He found just one lizard.

5. | *Tartu=jana* | *nya-ngu* | *jurlaka* | *ngula=lu* | *wirriri~wirriri* |
   |---|---|---|---|---|
   | many=3PL.S | see-PAST | bird | REL=3PL.S | in_a_circle~RDP |
   | *pa-nangu-rra* | *kankalarra* | | *kurnturru-rla.* | |
   | go-PAST-IMPF | above | | sky-LOC | |

   Those two saw lots of birds going around up in the sky.

6. | *Jurlaka-rlu=lu-rla* | *wirriri* | *nya-ngu-rra* | *yipakarli-ku.* |
   |---|---|---|---|
   | bird-ERG=3PL.S-DAT | in_a_circle | see-PAST-IMPF | lizard-DAT |

   The birds were looking around for a lizard.

7. | *Wangani-rlu* | *wirriri~wirriri* | *wirri* | *ya-nu-rra,* |
   |---|---|---|---|
   | dog-ERG | in_a_circle~RDP | chase | put-PAST-IMPF |
   | *nyanungu=ma=lu* | | *putjanarra* | *partu-ngu-rra.* |
   | aforementioned=TOP=3PL.S | | cause_to_scatter | leave-PAST-AWAY |

   The dog was chasing the birds, but they would fly away.

8. | *Wangani-rlu=ma* | *lamarta-rnu* | *yipakarli,* | *nga-rnu=lku.* |
   |---|---|---|---|
   | dog-ERG=TOP | catch-PAST | lizard | eat-PAST=THEN |

   The dog caught a lizard, then ate it.

9. | *Wajurrajurra=pala* | *pina* | *pa-nangu* | *nyaninya-parna* | *yiwirti-parna* |
   |---|---|---|---|---|
   | afternoon=3DU.S | return | go-PAST | 3.GEN-PROP | stick-PROP |
   | *kapi* | *Wangani-parna* | *ngurra-ka=lku* | | *yipakarli-wangu.* |
   | CONJ | dog-PROP | home-ALL=THEN | | lizard-PRIV |

   In the afternoon the child with his dog and spear went home, without any lizards.

10. | *Takkajarra=pala* | *pa-nangu* | *ngurra-ka=lku.* |
    |---|---|---|
    | empty_handed=3DU.S | go-PAST | home-ALL=THEN |

    The two of them went home empty handed [lit.: with two hands].

B.3 Reminiscences of youth

Speaker: Bunny Napurrula
Source: NASH_D02-007844
Transcribed by David Nash and Mitchell Browne

1. Well   larrpalarrpa   ngula=rnalu   ka-ngu-rra   army,   war-nga, time.
   long_time   that=1PL.EXCL   be-PAST-IMPF   war-LOC
   Well, long ago, when we were in the war, army time, war time.

2. Still=rna   purtu   ka-nya   ngula=nganpa-lu   ngayinya
   still=1SG   hear   be-PRES   REL=1EXCL.PL.O-3PL.S   1.GEN
   yapa   wa-nganyu-rra:
   person   speak-PAST-IMPF
   I still remember that our old people, they used to tell us:

3. 'Army-kuma=lpa   kantukantu   ka-nji-nmi,   kala=lpangu   la-nma.'
   army-AVER=1INC.PL.S   hide   be-INC-FUT   HAB=1INC.PL.NS   shoot-POT
   'We hide from the army, otherwise they might shoot us.'

4. But   kula=rna-jana   ngayu=ma   nyaninya   jaru   purtu
   NEG=1SG.S-3PL.O   1=TOP   3.GEN   talk   listen
   ka-ngu-rra.
   be-PAST-IMPF
   But I wasn't listening to their language.

5. Kula=rna-jana   nganayi   ma-nu-rra   ngula=ju=lu
   NEG=1SG.S-3PL.O   DUMMY   do-PAST-IMPF   REL=1SG.O-3PL.S
   nyaninya-rlu   pulkapulka-rlu   lani   ma-nu-rra:
   1.GEN-ERG   old_men-ERG   frighten   cause-PAST-IMPF
   I didn't get that those old men were frightening me:

APPENDIX B

6. *'Kantukantu=lpa   yapayapa   ka-nji-nmi.'*
   hide=1INC.PL.S   people   be-INC-FUT
   'We people have to hide ourselves.'

7. *'Kala=lpa=nya   kartipa-rlu   la-nma   papulanyi-rlu*
   HAB=1EXCL.PL.S=FOC   white_people-ERG   shoot-POT   white_people-ERG
   military-rlu.'
   military-ERG
   'Those white military men might shoot us.'

8. *Kala=rna-jana   ngayu=ma   jilij   ka-ngu:*
   HAB=1SG.S-3PL.NS   1=TOP   ask   be-PAST
   I would ask the old people:

9. *'Ngana-ngurlu=lpangu   la-nmi,   kala=lpangu   la-nmi?'*
   what-ELA=1INC.PL.NS   shoot-FUT   HAB=1INC.PL.O   shoot-FUT
   'What are they going to shoot us for? Why will they shoot us?'

10. *'Kula=nkulu   nya-nganya   kurtukurtu-rlu   ngula=lu   army   Jaala*
    NEG=2PL.S   see-PRES   children-ERG   REL=3PL.S   army   up_and_
                                                                                   down
    jutpu-ngunya   bitumen-nga.'
    run-PRES   bitumen-LOC
    'You kids can't see that the army is running up and down on the bitumen.'

11. *Ngayu=ma=rna-jana   wa-nganya-rra   'kula=lpangu   ngana-ngurlu*
    1=TOP=1SG.S=3PL.NS   speak-PRES-IMPF   NEG=1INC.PL.O   what-ELA
    la-nmi.'
    shoot-FUT
    I'm telling them, 'They won't shoot us from anything [without reason].'

12. *'Kula=lpa=jana   nyapa   ma-nu.'*
    NEG=1INC.PL=3PL.NS   how   get-PAST
    'We didn't do anything to them.'

13. | *Yi!* | *Maju=lu* | *papulanyi=ma* | *wa-nganya* | *'nga=lpa=ngu-lu* |
    | yes | bad=3PL.S | white_people=TOP | speak-PRES | POST=1.S=2SG.O-1PL.S |

   | *wumpurrani=ma* | *wirrpin* | *la-nmi.'* |
   | black_people=TOP | all | shoot-FUT |

   Yes! The bad white people are saying, 'We will shoot all you black people.'

14. | *Kula=rna* | *ngayu=ma* | *kawaj* | *wa-nganyu-rra.* |
    | NEG=1SG.S | 1=TOP | warn | speak-PAST-IMPF |

   I never used to listen to the warnings.

15. | *Purtu* | *ka-ngu-rra=rna* | *still.* |
    | listen | be-PAST-IMPF=1SG.S | |

   I still remember.

16. | *Tarnnga* | *purtu* | *ka-ngu-rra.* |
    | always | listen | be-PAST-IMPF |

   I always remembered.

17. | *Wiri-ja-ngu-rra=rna* | *purtu* | *ka-ngu-rra=yi=rna,* |
    | big-INCH-PAST-IMPF=1SG.S | listen | be-PAST-IMPF=STILL=1SG.S |

   When I was growing up, I kept remembering.

18. | *Ngayinya* | *ngula=ju-lu* | *pulkapulka-rlu* | *turu* | *ma-nu-rra:* |
    | 1SG.GEN | REL=1SG.NS=3PL.S | old_men-ERG | tell | get-PAST-IMPF |

   | *'kala=lpangu* | *la-nma* | *kayi=lpa* | *kita-nga=ma* |
   | APPR=1INC.PL.NS | shoot-POT | COND=1INC.PL.S | bare-LOC=TOP |

   | *pana~pana,* | *wartawarta-rla=lpa* | *pana~pana,* | *kantu* | *yimirna=rla.'* |
   | go~RDP | scrub-LOC=1INC.PL.S | go~RDP | under | scrub=LOC |

   My old people were telling me: 'They might shoot us if we go about in the open, we'll go about in the scrub.'

19. *Ngarrka=nganpa   missionary=lku   pa-nangu-rnu.*
    man=1EXL.PL.NS   missionary=THEN   go-past-TWD
    The missionary man came to us.

20. *Turnu   ma-nu-rra=nganpa   yapa=ma.*
    assemble   get-PAST-IMPF=1PL.EXCL.NS   people=TOP
    He gathered up all the people.

21. *Kampa-warnu   ma-nu   missionary   pa-nangu-rnu   Mr West.*
    ahead-RSLT   get-PAST   go-PAST-TWD
    The first missionary to come to us was Mr West.

22. *Yapa=nganpa   ngayinya   Warlmanpa   Warumungu   turnu*
    people=1PL.EXCL.NS   1.GEN   assemble
    ma-nu-rra.
    get-PAST-IMPF
    He got my people together, the Warlmanpa and Warumungu people.

23. *Wa-nganyu-rra   make   ma-nu-rra   friend.*
    speak-PAST-IMPF   get-PAST-IMPF
    He was speaking and getting us to be friendly.

24. *Kutu   ka-nja-ku   partakurru   yapa   paka-nja-wangu.*
    close   be-INF-PURP   good   people   hit-INF-PRIV
    People lived close to each other, it was good, without fighting.

25. *Ka-ngu-rra   tarnnga   missionary-rlu=lku   yapayapa*
    be-PAST-IMPF   always   missionary-ERG=THEN   people
    turnu   ma-nu-rra   Warlpiri   Warlmanpa   Warumungu.
    assemble   get-PAST-IMPF
    They came to stay at the mission, the missionary got the Warlpiri, Warlmanpa and Warumungu people together.

26. *Jinta   ngayinya   marta-nnya.*
    one   1.GEN   have-PRES
    They were as one mob.

27. *Ngayu=ma=rnalu   wiri-ja-ngu-rra   purtu   ka-nya=rna*
    1=TOP=1PL.S   big-INCH-PAST-IMPF   remember   be-PRES=1SG.S
    tarnnga=yi.
    always=STILL
    As I was growing up, I always remembered.

28. *Jirrima-ku, Christmas-ku.*
    two-DAT, Christmas-DAT
    For two Christmases.

29. *Jirrimajinta,   jirrimajinta   wa-nganyu=nganpa   nyuntu   ma-nta*
    three   three   speak-PAST=1EXCL.   2   get-IMP
                                              PL.O
    wittawitta   school-nga=lku   pa-nka-rti.
    children   school-LOC=THEN   go-IMP-TWD
    We three say you kids have to come to school.

30. *Ngayu=ma=rnalu   lani-ja-ngu-rra   kanu   yapayapa=ma*
    1=TOP=1PL.EXCL.S   frighten-INCH-PAST-IMPF   sorrow   people=TOP
    jalya   wittawitta   too much   pa-nangu-rra.
    bare   small   EMPH   go-PAST-IMPF
    Us and our kids were going around, naked and scared.

31. *Missionary-rlu=nganpa   wawarta   yu-ngu-rra*
    missionary-ERG=1PL.EXCL.S   clothes   give-PAST-IMPF
    ration=nganpa   yu-ngu-rra.
    ration=1PL.EXCL.S   give-PAST-IMPF
    The missionary used to give us clothes and give us rations.

32. *Papulanyi-ku=rla   brains   ma-nu   kumpumpu,   partakurru.*
    white_people-DAT=3.OBL   brains   have-PAST   brains   good
    We needed to have smart brains for white people.

APPENDIX B

33. *Wiri-ja-ngu=rnalu   1945   school-ka=lku=rnalu*
    big-INCH-PAST=1PL.EXCL.S   school-ALL=THEN=1PL.EXCL.S
    pa-nangu-rra   tartu   kurtukurdu.
    go-PAST-IMPF   Many   children
    When we were growing up, in 1945, we children were all going to school.

34. *Ngurra-nga=lku=rnalu   papula-rla   ka-ngu-rra.*
    home-LOC=THEN=1PL.EXCL.S   building-LOC   sit-PAST-IMPF
    We were living in houses.

35. *Learn-ja-ngu-rra=rnalu   papulanyi   way   partakurru.*
    learn-INCH-PAST-IMPF=1PL.EXCL.S   white_people   Good
    We were learning white people way, good.

36. *Ngayu=ma   still   purtu   ka-nya.*
    1=TOP   remember   be-PRES
    I still remember.

37. *Still=rna   ngurrarla   purtu   ka-nya,   ngula=rnalu*
    still=1SG.S   return   remember   be-PRES,   REL=1PL.EXCL.S
    larrpalarrpa   ka-ngu-rra.
    long_time   be-past-IMPF
    I still remember way back, that was a long time ago.

38. *Ngula=rna-jana   nya-nganya,   well,   ngayinya   yapa   wittawitta*
    that=1SG.S-3PL.O   see-PRES   1.GEN   people   children
    school-ka.
    school-ALL
    When I see them, well, my kids at school.

523

39. | *Ngayinya* | *ma-nu* | *kumpumpu* | *still* | *turn back-ja-nnya* | *purtu* |
    | 1.GEN | get-PAST | brains | | turn_back-INCH-PRES | remember |

   | *ka-nya=rna* | *ngurrarla.* |
   | be-PRES=1SG.S | return |

   I had to get smart, I still remember.

40. | *Jalajala=ma=lu* | *partakurru,* | *kurtukurtu=ma* | *pa-nnya* |
    | nowadays=TOP=3pl.S | good | children=TOP | go-PRES |
    | *school-ka=ma,* | *learn-ja-nja-ku* | *partakurru* | *too papulanyi* |
    | school-ALL=TOP | learn-INCH-INF-PURP | good | white_people |

   way.

   Nowadays it's good, children go to school to learn, white people way.

41. | *Larrpalarrpa=ma=rnalu* | *majukarra* | *pa-nangu-rra* | *lani-ja-ngu-rra.* |
    | old_days=TOP=1PL.EXCL | very_bad | go-PAST-IMPF | afraid-INCH-PAST-IMPF |

   Olden days were very bad, we were going around afraid.

42. | *Kala=rnalu* | *jikirri* | *lani-ja-ngu-rra.* |
    | HAB=1PL.EXCL.S | goosebumps | afraid-INCH-PAST-IMPF |

   We used to be scared, with goosebumps.

43. | *Kula=rnalu-rla* | *wa-nganyu-rra* | *papulanyi* | *ngula=nganpa* |
    | NEG=1PL.EXCL.S=3.OBL | speak-PAST-IMPF | white_people | REL=1PL.EXCL.S |

   wa-nganyu-rra.
   speak-PAST-IMPF

   We never used to talk to white people, we spoke our way.

44. | *Kula* | *too much=rnalu* | *majju* | *ka-ngu-rra* | *myall.* |
    | NEG | EMPH=1PL.EXCL.S | bad | be-PAST-IMPF | ignorant |

   We never understood that English.

45. | Kula=rnalu | understand ... | purtu | ka-ngu-rra | English. |
|---|---|---|---|---|
| NEG=1PL.EXCL.S | | understand | be-PAST-IMPF | English |

We used to not understand English.

46. *We never understood that their English, you know?*

47. | Kula=rnalu | purtu | ka-ngu-rra | jaru=ma |
|---|---|---|---|
| NEG=1PL.EXCL.S | understand | be-PAST-IMPF | talk=TOP |
| papulanyi-kurla=ma | kawarr | ka-ngu-rra. | |
| European-GEN=TOP | lost | be-PAST-IMPF | |

We weren't understanding white people's language.

48. | But | jalajala=ma | partakurru | now. |
|---|---|---|---|
| | nowadays=TOP | good | |

But it's better nowadays.

49. | Everything=rnalu | kurtukurtu | now | ma-nnya |
|---|---|---|---|
| everything=1PL.EXCL.S | children | | get-PRES |
| learn-ja-nya=lu | partakurru, | ngarra | book-na | read-ja-nnya. |
| learn-INCH-PRES=3PL.S | good | FUT | book-FOC | read-INCH-PRES |

The children are getting everything now, they're learning, reading books.

50. *Everything they're coming on real well, I can't say anymore.*

B.4 Palyupalyu dreaming story

Below is a dreaming story given in Capell's (1952) account of the Warlpiri people, though the story itself is told in Warlmanpa. No source is named, other than that the story was given at Banka Banka Station. I first give the story exactly as it was transcribed by Capell and then attempt a rendering.

Capell's transcription and glossing:

1. | Walu | lanu | guru | djagbaduŋubala. |
|---|---|---|---|
| Fire | in | the | bush they-two-made |

2. | *Djibuŋu* | *Banaŋura,* | *guju* | *ŋanura* | *ŋurambimba.*
   | Feared-it | B. | meat | having-eaten | he-came-out

3. | *Ṇabaŋu* | *baṇinjaŋu* | *bulgama* | *lanilgu* | *djudbuŋu.*
   | Lightning | smelled the | old-man [who] | was-afraid | [and] ran

4. | *Guraŋu* | *landjanu* | *waraga* | *djilubaliga* | *guraŋu* | *wadili*
   | It was | killing him | pursued
   | *mandjanu* | *njimidj* | *wanura*
   | he came along | [old man] | lying down
   | *wajunu alula* | *garilgu* | *badjalbaduŋura.*
   | they-were-looking-for-him, | he came out a long way | from-the-ground.

5. | *Djaridjala* | *wiri janu alu* | *Gululuŋuwa* | *lanu alula;*
   | It-found-him-out | chased-him-along, | at Gululuŋu [?] | tried to kill him;

6. | *aruŋuluma* | *Djimamalguwa;*
   | he went to | Djimamalgu;

7. | *aruŋuluma* | *Mawidju,*
   | he went to | M,

8. | *aruŋuluma* | *Baralandji*
   | he went to | B,

9. | *guraŋu* | *djidjilala.*
   | lightning | tried again.

10. | *Aruŋulu amu.*
    | It came after him.

11. | *Wamur* | *mandjiŋi* | *bulga* | *ŋuramula.*
    | At W.? | lived | | old man at a spring.

12. | *Aɲura* | *milgari* | | *eiganu* | *malu* | *wirialu* |
    | he-was | blind-in-one-eye | | lightning | chased him | |

   | *bulgama* | *Djaŋala,* | *djambuɲu* | *mandulga* | *dil* | *lanu* |
   | the old man | Djangala, | struck him | in the heart | he | fell |

   | *ɲuraga* | *Bu'naraban.* |
   | in the spring at | Rennie's Springs. |

Source: Capell (1952: 129).

Author's rendering and glossing (with Capell's transcription):

<u>Underlines</u> represent particularly uncertain renderings. This rendering benefited from the assistance of David Nash, particularly with regard to placenames.

1. | *Warlu* | *la-rnu* | <u>*kurra*</u> | <u>*partu</u>-ngu=pala* |
   | *Waḻu* | *lanu* | *guṙu* | *djagbaduŋubala.* |
   | Fire | hit-PAST | lightning | leave-PAST=3DU.S |

   He made fire ... They two set off.

2. | *Jutpu-ngu,* | *pa-nangu-rra* | *kuyu* | *nga-rnu-rra* | *ngurra-<u>mimpa</u>* |
   | *Djibuɲu* | *Banaŋuṙa,* | *guju* | *ɲanuṙa* | *ŋurambimba.* |
   | run-PAST | go-PAST-IMPF | meat | eat-PAST-IMPF | camp-ONLY |

   He ran, he went and ate meat just at camp.

3. | *Ngappa-ngu* | *parni-nya-ngu* | *pulka-na* | *lani=lku* | *jutpu-ngu* |
   | *ŋabaɲu* | *baṇinjaŋu* | *bulgama* | *lanilgu* | *djudbuɲu.* |
   | water-ERG | smell-see-PAST | old_man=TOP | afraid=THEN | run-PAST |

   The storm smelled the old man.

A GRAMMAR OF WARLMANPA

4. | *Kurra-ngu* | *la-nja-nu* | *warraka* | *Jurlaparli-ka* |
    |---|---|---|---|
    | Guraŋu | landjanu | waṟaga | djilubaliga |
    | lightning-ERG | shoot-MOT-PAST | lancewood | Jurlaparli-ALL |
    | *Kurra-ngu* | *wajili* | *ma-nja-nu* | *nyimij-wa-nu-rra* |
    | guraŋu | wadili | mandjanu | njimidj wanuṟa |
    | lightning-ERG | chase | do-MOT-PAST | dive-fall-PAST-IMPF |
    | *wayu-rnu=lu-rla* | *kari=lku* | *palyal-partu-ngu-rra* | |
    | wayu-rnu alula | kari-lgu | badjalbaduŋura. | |
    | search-PAST=3PL.S-3OBL | far=THEN | emerge-rise-PAST-IMPF | |

    Lightning struck the lancewood, going along to Jurlaparli. Lightning chased him, he dived in, they went looking for him, he came out far away.

5. | *Yarri=yijala* | *wirriri-ya-nu=lu* | *Kululungu-rla* |
    |---|---|---|
    | Djaridjala | wiri janu alu | Gululuŋuwa |
    | that=ALSO | chase-go-PAST=3PL.S | Kululungu-LOC |
    | *la-rnu=lu-rla* | | |
    | lanu alula. | | |
    | shoot-PAST=3PL.S=3.OBL | | |

    That lightning chased him again at Kululungu and shot at him.

6. | *Yalu-ngurlu=ma* | *Jimamalku-ka.* |
    |---|---|
    | Aruŋuluma | Djimamalguwa. |
    | that-ELA=TOP | Jimamalku-ALL. |

    From there, to Jimamalku.

7. | *Yalu-ngurlu=ma* | *Mawuriju.* |
    |---|---|
    | Aruŋuluma | Mawidju. |
    | that-ELA=TOP | Mawuriju. |

    From there, to Mawuriju.

8. | *Alu-ngurlu=ma* | *Pararlanji.* |
    |---|---|
    | Aruŋuluma | Baralandji. |
    | that-ELA=TOP | Pararlanji. |

    From there, to Pararlanji.

9. | Kurra-ngu | ? |
   | Guraŋu | djidjilala. |
   | lightning-ERG | ? |

10. | Yarru-ngurlu=ma | Wamurumarntingi | | pulka | ngurra |
    | Aruŋulu amu. | Wamur | mandjiŋi | bulga | ŋuramula. |
    | that-ELA=TOP | Wamurumarntingi | | old_man | camp |

    | ngula | ka-ngu-rra | milkari. |
    | ŋuramula | Aŋura | milgari. |
    | REL | be-PAST-IMPF | blind |

    From that, the old man at Wamurumarntingi camp was blind.

11. | Yajka-ngu=ma=lu | wirriri-ya-rnu | | | |
    | Eiganu | malu | wirialu | | |
    | travel-ERG=TOP =3PL.S | in_a_circle-put-PAST | | | |

    | pulka=ma | Jangala | jampu-ngu | marnturlka | tiirl-la-rnu |
    | bulgama | Djaŋala, | djambuŋu | mandulga | dil lanu |
    | the old man | Djangala, | left_hand-ERG | heart | split-shoot-PAST |

    | ngurra-ka | Punarrapan |
    | ŋuraga | Bu'naraban. |
    | camp-ALL | Renner Springs. |

    Those lightning chased old man Jangala, it shot him in the heart, which scattered into the ground at Renner Springs. [Author's note: I am not sure how *jampu-ngu* fits into this sentence.]

Appendix C: Alternative verb analysis

Warlmanpa verbs are extremely difficult to capture according to a morphemic model that presupposes that speakers memorise a high degree of allomorphy that is lexically conditioned. Under the current analysis in §6.2, the implicative relations between members of the paradigm are opaque, for the sake of lumping all the allomorphy into the inflectional suffix paradigm, leaving the verb roots with only phonologically conditioned allomorphy (§6.2.2.2). In this appendix, I present an analysis that attempts to 'organise' the allomorphy into more analogical chunks. Specifically, the analysis presented in this appendix instead attributes far more allomorphy to the verb root, focusing on how the allomorphy is structurally similar across verb classes. The verb root paradigms are given in Table C.1 and the verb inflections in Table C.2.

Appendix Table C.1 Alternative verb root paradigm

Class	Unaugmented	Augmented C/V	Augmented CV	Example members
1a	X	X*a*		*wang-* 'speak'
	IMP	elsewhere		
1b	X	X*ng*	X*ngu*	*parti-* 'rise'
	elsewhere	IMP	PRES	*pali-* 'die'
1c	X	X*n*	X*na*	*pa-* 'go'
	INF, INC, MOT	elsewhere	PAST, FUT, POT	*ji-* 'melt'
1d	X			*ka-* 'be'
				-ja- 'become'
2	X	X*n*		*la-* 'shoot'
	elsewhere	PRES, FUT, POT		*kuma* 'cut'
3	X	X*ng*	X*ngu*	*ka-* 'take'
	elsewhere	IMP	PRES	*li-* 'cry'

Class	Unaugmented	Augmented C/V	Augmented CV	Example members
4	X	X*n*	X*rni*	*nga-* 'eat'
	PAST	IMP, FUT, POT	elsewhere	
5	X	X*n*		*ma-* 'get, take'
	elsewhere	imp, fut, pot, pres		*wa-* 'fall'

Appendix Table C.2 Alternative verb inflection paradigm

	1a	1b	1c	1d	2	3	4	5a	5b
IMP	*-ka*			*-rra*	*-ka*		*-ja*	*-ta*	*-rra*
PAST	*-nyu*	*-ngu*			*-rnu*	*-ngu*	*-rnu*	*-nu*	
PRES	*-nya*								
FUT	*-mi*					*-nyi*	*-mi*		
POT	*-ma*					*-nya*	*-ma*	—	
INF	*-nja-*							—	
INC	*-nji-*							—	
MOT	*-nja-*							—	
MOT.AWAY	*-nya-*							—	
MOT.TWD	*-nji-*							—	
PATH	*-nyinga*							—	
PATH.AWAY	POT.*ma*							—	
SUBJ	IMP.*rla*							—	
CFACT	INF.*kurla*							—	

Under this analysis, the verb root is conditioned by the inflection and the inflectional form is conditioned by verb class (that is, lexical conditioning). Each verb root has an 'unaugmented' minimal form. Most verb roots also have an unaugmented form with one segment on the right edge of the root (typically a nasal consonant), labelled 'Augmented C/V' form. Most forms that have an 'augmented C/V' have a form comprising a nasal plus a vowel, labelled 'augmented CV'. To exemplify, the 'eat' verb, *nga-*, has an augmented form, *ngan-*, and a further augmented form, *ngarni*:

'eat'	Form	Example	
Unaugmented	*nga-*	*nga-rnu*	'eat-PAST'
Augmented C/V	*ngan-*	*ngan-mi*	'eat-FUT'
Augmented CV	*ngarni-*	*ngarni-nya*	'eat-PRES'

APPENDIX C

This analysis captures the structural similarity between augmented forms (which is not captured by the analysis presented in §6.2), in that the 'variation' can be classified into either 'augmented C/V' or 'augmented CV' across the entire verb paradigm. Furthermore, it also highlights the similarities across the verb inflections: there is now very little allomorphy in the inflection forms (since it has been shifted to the root in a generally structured manner).

The implicative relations (in the sense used by Ackerman et al. 2009) between cells are now more transparent—for example:

- A verb root without an augmented C/V form cannot have an augmented CV form.
- If a verb root has an augmented C/V form and an augmented CV form, the augmented CV form is always the augmented C/V form plus a vowel on the right edge, except in the case of *nga-* 'eat'. For verbs other than 'eat', if the C is [+dorsal] then the V is /u/, and if the C is [–dorsal] then the V is /a/.
- Augmented C/V forms tend to be used for irrealis moods—in particular: FUTURE, POTENTIAL, IMPERATIVE and, by extension, SUBJUNCTIVE. The PRESENT tense also tends to require an augmented form, though this seems to have a historical explanation in *na~nga* likely being markers of imperfective aspect (see, for example, the Yankunytjatjara verb paradigm [Goddard 1985: 90]).

Bibliography

Aboriginal Land Commission (ALC). 1982a. *Kaytej, Warlpiri and Warlmanpa Land Claim*. Canberra: AGPS.

Aboriginal Land Commission (ALC). 1982b. *Warlmanpa, Warlpiri, Mudburra and Warumungu Land Claim*. Canberra: AGPS.

Aboriginal Land Commission (ALC). 1997. *Warlmanpa (Muckaty Pastoral Lease) Land Claim No. 135*. Canberra: AGPS.

Ackerman, F., J.P. Blevins, and R. Malouf. 2009. 'Parts and Wholes: Implicative Patterns in Inflectional Paradigms.' In *Analogy in Grammar: Form and Acquisition*, edited by J.P. Blevins and J. Blevins, 54–82. Oxford: Oxford University Press. doi.org/10.1093/acprof:oso/9780199547548.003.0003.

Aikhenvald, A.Y. 2010. *Imperatives and Commands*. Oxford: Oxford University Press.

Ameka, F.K. 1992. 'Interjections: The Universal Yet Neglected Part of Speech.' *Journal of Pragmatics* 18, nos 2–3 (September): 101–18. doi.org/10.1016/0378-2166(92)90048-G.

Ariel, M. 1988. 'Referring and Accessibility.' *Journal of Linguistics* 24, no. 1 (November): 65–87. doi.org/10.1017/S0022226700011567.

Asher, N., and A. Lascarides. 2003. *Logics of Conversation*. Cambridge: Cambridge University Press.

Austin, P.K. 1981. 'Switch-Reference in Australia.' *Language* 57: 309–34. doi.org/10.2307/413693.

Austin, P.K. 1982. 'Transitivity and Cognate Objects in Australian Languages.' In *Studies in Transitivity. Syntax and Semantics, Volume 15*, edited by P.J. Hopper and S.A. Thompson, 37–47. New York: Academic Press. doi.org/10.1163/9789004368903_004.

Australian Associated Press (AAP). 2014. 'Indigenous Elder Speaks Out at NT Nuclear Waste Dump Trial.' *The Guardian*, 9 June. www.theguardian.com/world/2014/jun/09/indigenous-elder-speaks-out-nuclear-waste-dump-trial.

Australian Research Council (ARC) Centre of Excellence for the Dynamics of Language. 2017. *Annual Report 2016*. Canberra: ARC Centre of Excellence for the Dynamics of Language. legacy.dynamicsoflanguage.edu.au/pages/selected-highlights.php#annual_report [page discontinued].

Bach, K. 2017. 'Reference, Intention, and Context: Do Demonstratives Really Refer?' In *Reference and Representation in Thought and Language*, edited by M. de Ponte and K. Korta, 57–72. Oxford: Oxford University Press.

Baker, B., and M. Harvey. 2010. 'Complex Predicate Formation.' In *Complex Predicates: Cross-Linguistic Perspectives on Event Structure*, edited by M. Amberber, M.C. Baker, and M. Harvey, 13–47. Cambridge: Cambridge University Press. doi.org/10.1017/CBO9780511712234.003.

Baker, M.C. 1991. 'On Some Subject/Object Non-Asymmetries in Mohawk.' *Natural Language and Linguistic Theory* 9: 537–75. doi.org/10.1007/BF00134750.

Baker, M.C. 1996a. 'Notes on Dependent-Marking-Style Nonconfigurationality in Australian Languages.' Unpublished manuscript, McGill University, Montreal.

Baker, M.C. 1996b. *The Polysynthesis Parameter*. Oxford: Oxford University Press.

Baker, M.C. 2001. 'The Natures of Nonconfigurationality.' In *The Handbook of Contemporary Syntactic Theory*, edited by M. Baltin and C. Collins, 407–38. Malden: Blackwell. doi.org/10.1002/9780470756416.ch13.

Battin, J. 2019. 'Topics in Nyiyaparli Morphosyntax.' BA (Hons) subthesis. The Australian National University, Canberra. hdl.handle.net/1885/209187.

Bavin, E., and T. Shopen. 1985. 'Warlpiri and English: Language in Contact.' In *Australia, Meeting Place of Languages*, edited by M. Clyne, 81–94. Canberra: Pacific Linguistics.

Bell, D. 2002. *Daughters of the Dreaming*. Melbourne: Spinifex Press.

Birner, B. 2012. *Introduction to Pragmatics*. Hoboken: Wiley-Blackwell.

Bittner, M., and K. Hale. 1995. 'Remarks on Definiteness in Warlpiri.' In *Quantification in Natural Languages*, edited by E. Bach, E. Jelinek, A. Kratzer, and B.H. Partee, 81–105. Dordrecht: Springer. doi.org/10.1007/978-94-017-2817-1_5.

Blake, B.J. 1983. 'Structure and Word Order in Kalkatungu: The Anatomy of a Flat Language.' *Australian Journal of Linguistics* 3, no. 2: 143–75. doi.org/10.1080/07268608308599307.

Blake, B.J. 1987a. *Australian Aboriginal Grammar*. London: Croom Helm.

Blake, B.J. 1987b. 'The Grammatical Development of Australian Languages.' *Lingua* 71, nos 1–4 (April): 179–201. doi.org/10.1016/0024-3841(87)90071-4.

Blythe, J. 2018. 'Genesis of the Trinity: The Convergent Evolution of Trirelational Kinterms.' In *Skin, Kin and Clan: The Dynamics of Social Categories in Indigenous Australia*, edited by P. McConvell, P. Kelly, and S. Lacrampe, 431–71. Canberra: ANU Press. doi.org/10.22459/SKC.04.2018.13.

Boersma, P. 2001. 'Praat, a System for Doing Phonetics by Computer.' *Glot International* 5: 341–47.

Bond, O., F. Meakins, and R. Nordlinger. 2019. 'Prominent Possessor Indexing in Gurindji.' In *Prominent Internal Possessors*, edited by A. Bárány, O. Bond, and I. Nikolaeva, 80–106. Oxford: Oxford University Press. doi.org/10.1093/oso/9780198812142.003.0003.

Bowern, C. 2014. 'Complex Predicates in Australian Languages.' In *The Languages and Linguistics of Australia*, edited by H. Koch and R. Nordlinger, 263–94. Berlin: De Gruyter Mouton. doi.org/10.1515/9783110279771.263.

Bowern, C., and Q. Atkinson. 2012. 'Computational Phylogenetics and the Internal Structure of Pama-Nyungan.' *Language* 88, no. 4 (December): 817–45. doi.org/10.1353/lan.2012.0081.

Bowler, M. 2014. 'Conjunction and Disjunction in a Language without "And".' In *Semantics and Linguistic Theory* 24: 137–55. journals.linguisticsociety.org/proceedings/index.php/SALT/article/view/24.137. doi.org/10.3765/salt.v24i0.2422.

Bowler, M. 2016. 'The Status of Degrees in Warlpiri.' In *The Semantics of African, Asian and Austronesian Languages 2*, edited by M. Grubic and A. Mucha, 1–17. Potsdam: Universitätsverlag Potsdam.

Bowler, M. 2017. 'Quantification in Warlpiri.' In *Handbook of Quantifiers in Natural Language. Volume 2*, edited by D. Paperno and E. Keenan, 1–37. Dordrecht: Springer Verlag. doi.org/10.1007/978-3-319-44330-0_19.

Brato, T. 2015. 'TB-Basic Vowel Analysis V2.2.' *Praat Scripts* [Online.] Universität Regensburg, Germany. www.uni-regensburg.de/language-literature-culture/english-linguistics/staff/brato/praat-scripts/index.html.

Browne, E., and F.G. Napaljarri. 2021. 'Communities of Practice in the Warlpiri Triangle: Four Decades of Crafting Ideological and Implementational Spaces for Teaching in and of Warlpiri Language.' *Languages* 6, no. 2: 68. doi.org/10.3390/languages6020068.

Browne, M. (collector). 2016. *Warlmanpa Corpus*. Collection WRL1 at catalog.paradisec.org.au [Open Access]. catalog.paradisec.org.au/collections/WRL1.

Browne, M. 2017. 'Warlmanpa Nasal Clusters.' Presented to Ngumpin-Yapa workshop, Brisbane, 10–11 August.

Browne, M. 2019. 'A Description of Tense in Warlmanpa (Ngumpin-Yapa).' Presented to Australian Languages Workshop, Marysville, Vic., 15–17 March.

Browne, M. 2020a. 'Contrast and Retroactive Implicatures: An Analysis of =lku "Now, Then" in Warlpiri and Warlmanpa.' *Australian Journal of Linguistics* 40, no. 2: 218–45. doi.org/10.1080/07268602.2020.1753651.

Browne, M. 2020b. 'Distinguishing Complementisers, Auxiliaries, and Particles in Warlmanpa.' Presented to Australian Languages Workshop, Minjerribah, Qld, 28 February – 1 March.

Browne, M. 2021a. 'A Grammatical Description of Warlmanpa: A Ngumpin-Yapa Language Spoken around Tennant Creek (Northern Territory).' PhD thesis, University of Queensland, Brisbane. doi.org/10.14264/d0fcbc2.

Browne, M. 2021b. 'On the Integration of Dative Adjuncts into Event Structures in Yapa Languages.' *Languages* 6, no. 3 (August): 136. doi.org/10.3390/languages6030136.

Browne, M., T.B. Ennever, and D.J. Osgarby. 2024. 'Apprehension as a Grammatical Category in Ngumpin-Yapa Languages (Australia).' In *Apprehensional Constructions in a Cross-Linguistic Perspective*, edited by E. Schultze-Berndt, M. Vuillermet, and M. Faller. Berlin: Language Science Press.

Bundgaard-Nielsen, R.L., and C. O'Shannessy. 2019. 'Voice Onset Time and Constriction Duration in Warlpiri Stops (Australia).' In *Proceedings of the 19th International Congress of Phonetic Sciences, Melbourne, Australia 2019*, edited by S. Calhoun, P. Escudero, M. Tabain, and P. Warren, 3612–16. Canberra: Australasian Speech Science and Technology Association Inc. assta.org/proceedings/ICPhS2019/papers/ICPhS_3661.pdf.

Butcher, A. 1994. 'On the Phonetics of Small Vowel Systems: Evidence from Australian Languages.' In *Proceedings of the 5th Australian International Conference on Speech Science and Technology*, 28–33. Canberra: Australian Speech Science and Technology Association.

Butt, M. 1998. 'Constraining Argument Merger through Aspect.' In *Complex Predicates in Nonderivational Syntax*, edited by E. Hinrichs, A. Kathol, and T. Nakazawa, 73–113. New York: Academic Press. doi.org/10.1163/9780585492223_004.

Bybee, J. 1998. '"Irrealis" as a Grammatical Category.' *Anthropological Linguistics* 40, no. 2 (Summer): 257–71. www.jstor.org/stable/30028628.

Bybee, J., R. Perkins, and W. Pagliuca. 1994. *The Evolution of Grammar*. Chicago: University of Chicago Press.

Capell, A. 1952. 'The Wailbri through Their Own Eyes.' *Oceania* 23, no. 2 (December): 110–32. www.jstor.org/stable/40328381. doi.org/10.1002/j.1834-4461.1952.tb00193.x.

Carrington, V.G. 1946. *Report on the Administration of the Northern Territory for the Year Ending 30th June, 1946*. Canberra: AIATSIS.

Caudal, P., and R. Mailhammer. 2022. 'Linear Lengthening in Iwaidja: An Event-Quantifying Intonation at the Phonology to Semantics/Pragmatics Interface.' *Languages* 7, no. 3: 1–23. doi.org/10.3390/languages7030209.

Central Land Council (CLC). 2015. *Every Hill Got a Story*. Edited by Marg Bowman. Melbourne: Hardie Grant Books (Australia).

Chappell, H., and W.B. McGregor. 1996. 'Prolegomena to a Theory of Inalienability.' In *The Grammar of Inalienability*, edited by H. Chappell and W. McGregor, 3–30. Berlin: De Gruyter Mouton. doi.org/10.1515/9783110822137.3.

Chappell, H., and J. Verstraete. 2019. 'Optional and Alternating Case Marking: Typology and Diachrony.' *Language and Linguistics Compass* 13, no. 3 (March): e12311. doi.org/10.1111/lnc3.12311.

Comrie, B. 1976. *Aspect: An Introduction to the Study of Verbal Aspect and Related Problems*. Cambridge: Cambridge University Press.

Comrie, B. 1978. 'Syntactic Typology: Studies in the Phenomenology of Language.' In *Ergativity*, edited by W.P. Lehmann, 329–94. Austin: University of Texas Press.

Corbett, G.G. 2000. *Number*. Cambridge: Cambridge University Press.

Corbett, G.G. 2005. 'The Canonical Approach in Typology.' In *Linguistic Diversity and Language Theories (Studies in Language Companion Series 72)*, edited by Z. Frajzyngier, A. Hodges, and D.S. Rood, 25–49. Amsterdam: John Benjamins Publishing Company. doi.org/10.1075/slcs.72.03cor.

Corbett, G.G. 2007. 'Canonical Typology, Suppletion, and Possible Words.' *Language* 83, no. 1 (March): 8–42. doi.org/10.1353/lan.2007.0006.

Dench, A. 1988. 'Complex Sentences in Martuthunira.' In *Complex Sentence Constructions in Australian Languages*, edited by P.K. Austin, 97–140. Amsterdam: John Benjamins Publishing Company. doi.org/10.1075/tsl.15.06den.

Dench, A. 1991. 'Panyjima.' In *Handbook of Australian Languages*, edited by R.M.W. Dixon and B.J. Blake, 4: 124–243. Sydney: Oxford University Press.

Dench, A. 1995. *Martuthunira: A Language of the Pilbara Region of Western Australia*. Canberra: Pacific Linguistics.

Dench, A., and N. Evans. 1988. 'Multiple Case-Marking in Australian Languages.' *Australian Journal of Linguistics* 8, no. 1: 1–47. doi.org/10.1080/07268608808599390.

Disbray, S., R. Plummer, and B. Martin. 2020. 'Languages Ideologies and Practice from the Land and the Classroom.' *The Modern Language Journal* 104, no. 2 (Summer): 519–25. doi.org/10.1111/modl.12658.

Disbray, S., and Warumungu Speakers from the Tennant Creek Community. 2005. *Warumungu Picture Dictionary*. Alice Springs: IAD Press.

Dixon, R.M.W. 1980. *The Languages of Australia*. Cambridge: Cambridge University Press.

Dixon, R.M.W. 2002. *Australian Languages: Their Nature and Development*. New York: Cambridge University Press. www.cambridge.org/us/universitypress/subjects/languages-linguistics/other-languages-and-linguistics/australian-languages-their-nature-and-development?format=HB&isbn=9780521473781.

Dixon, R.M.W. 2009. *Basic Linguistic Theory. Volume 1: Methodology*. Oxford: Oxford University Press.

Douglas, W. 2001. *Illustrated Topical Dictionary of the Western Desert Language: Based on the Ngaanyatjarra Dialect*. Perth: Edith Cowan University.

Dowty, D.R. 1989. 'On the Semantic Content of the Notion of "Thematic Role".' In *Properties, Types and Meaning. Volume II: Semantic Issues*, edited by G. Chierchia, B.H. Partee, and R. Turner, 69–129. Dordrecht: Springer. doi.org/10.1007/978-94-009-2723-0_3.

Ennever, T.B. 2018. 'Nominal and Pronominal Morphology of Ngardi: A Ngumpin-Yapa Language of Western Australia.' MPhil. diss., University of Queensland, Brisbane.

Ennever, T.B. 2021. *A Grammar of Ngardi*. Berlin: De Gruyter Mouton.

Ennever, T.B., and M. Browne. 2023. 'Cross-Referencing of Non-Subject Arguments in Pama-Nyungan Languages.' *Australian Journal of Linguistics* 43, no. 1: 1–32. doi.org/10.1080/07268602.2023.2217412.

Ennever, T.B., F. Meakins, and E. Round. 2017. 'A Replicable Acoustic Measure of Lenition and the Nature of Variability in Gurindji Stops.' *Laboratory Phonology: Journal of the Association for Laboratory Phonology* 8, no. 1: 1–32. doi.org/10.5334/labphon.18.

Evans, N. 1995. *A Grammar of Kayardild: With Historical-Comparative Notes on Tangkic*. Berlin: De Gruyter Mouton. doi.org/10.1515/9783110873733.

Evans, N. 2003. 'Context, Culture, and Structuration in the Languages of Australia.' *Annual Review of Anthropology* 32 (October): 13–40. doi.org/10.1146/annurev.anthro.32.061002.093137.

Evans, N. 2006. 'Dyadic Constructions.' In *Encyclopedia of Language & Linguistics*, edited by K. Brown, 24–28. Oxford: Elsevier. doi.org/10.1016/B0-08-044854-2/00188-7.

Evans, N. 2007. 'Insubordination and Its Uses.' In *Finiteness: Theoretical and Empirical Foundations*, edited by I. Nikolaeva, 366–431. New York: Oxford University Press.

Evans, N. 2008. 'How to Write a Grammar of an Undescribed Language: Introductory Issues.' Handouts presented to the grammar-writing group, The Australian National University, Canberra.

Fletcher, J., and A. Butcher. 2014. 'Sound Patterns of Australian Languages.' In *The Languages and Linguistics of Australia*, edited by H. Koch and R. Nordlinger, 91–138. Berlin: De Gruyter Mouton. doi.org/10.1515/9783110279771.91.

Gaby, A. 2007. 'Describing Cutting and Breaking Events in Kuuk Thaayorre.' *Cognitive Linguistics* 18, no. 2: 263–72. doi.org/10.1515/COG.2007.014.

Gaby, A. 2017. *A Grammar of Kuuk Thaayorre*. Berlin: De Gruyter Mouton. doi.org/10.1515/9783110459067.

Gaby, A., and R. Singer. 2014. 'Semantics of Australian Languages.' In *The Languages and Linguistics of Australia*, edited by H. Koch and R. Nordlinger, 295–328. Berlin: De Gruyter Mouton. doi.org/10.1515/9783110279771.295.

Givon, T. 1978. 'Definiteness and Referentiality.' In *Universals of Human Language*, edited by J.H. Greenberg, 291–330. Stanford: Stanford University Press.

Goddard, C. 1982. 'Case Systems and Case Marking in Australian Languages: A New Interpretation.' *Australian Journal of Linguistics* 2, no. 2: 167–96. doi.org/10.1080/07268608208599290.

Goddard, C. 1985. *A Grammar of Yankunytjatjara*. Alice Springs: Institute for Aboriginal Development.

Guillaume, A. 2016. 'Associated Motion in South America: Typological and Areal Perspectives.' *Linguistic Typology* 20, no. 1: 81–177. doi.org/10.1515/lingty-2016-0003.

Hale, K. 1973. 'Person Marking in Walbiri.' In *A Festschrift for Morris Halle*, edited by S.R. Anderson and P. Kiparsky, 308–44. New York: Holt, Rinehart & Winston, Inc.

Hale, K. 1976. 'The Adjoined Relative Clause in Australia.' In *Grammatical Categories in Australian Languages*, edited by R.M.W. Dixon, 78–105. Canberra: AIAS.

Hale, K. 1977. 'Elementary Remarks on Walbiri Orthography, Phonology, and Allomorphy.' Unpublished manuscript, University of Cambridge.

Hale, K. 1981. 'Preliminary Remarks on the Grammar of Part-Whole Relations in Warlpiri.' In *Studies in Pacific Languages & Cultures in Honour of Bruce Biggs*, edited by J. Hollyman and A. Pawley, 333–44. Auckland: Linguistic Society of New Zealand.

Hale, K. 1982. 'Some Essential Features of Warlpiri Verbal Clauses.' In *Papers in Warlpiri Grammar: In Memory of Lothar Jagst*, edited by S.M. Swartz, 217–315. Darwin: Summer Institute of Linguistics.

Hale, K. 1983. 'Warlpiri and the Grammar of Non-Configurational Languages.' *Natural Language and Linguistic Theory* 1: 5–47. doi.org/10.1007/BF00210374.

Hale, K., M. Laughren, and J. Simpson. 1995. 'Warlpiri.' In *Handbücher zur Sprach- und Kommunikations-wissenschaft* [*Handbooks of Linguistics and Communication Science*]. *Syntax: Ein Internationales Handbuch Zeitgenössischer Forschung. Volume 2* [*An International Handbook of Contemporary Research*], edited by J. Jacobs, A. von Stechow, W. Sternefeld, and T. Vennemann, 1430–51. Berlin: Walter De Gruyter. doi.org/10.1515/9783110142631.2.21.1430.

Hale, K., M. Laughren, and J. Simpson. 2015. 'Warlpiri.' In *Syntax: Theory and Analysis*, edited by T. Kiss and A. Alexiadou, vol. 3, 1677–1709. Berlin: De Gruyter. doi.org/10.1515/9783110363685-008.

Hansen, K.C., and L.E. Hansen. 1978. *The Core of Pintupi Grammar*. Alice Springs: Institute for Aboriginal Development.

Harvey, M., and B. Baker. 2005. 'Vowel Harmony, Directionality and Morpheme Structure Constraints in Warlpiri.' *Lingua* 115, no. 10 (October): 1457–74. doi.org/10.1016/j.lingua.2004.06.007.

Haspelmath, M. 1993. 'The Diachronic Externalization of Inflection.' *Linguistics* 31: 279–309. doi.org/10.1515/ling.1993.31.2.279.

Haspelmath, M. 1996. 'Word-Class-Changing Inflection and Morphological Theory.' In *Yearbook of Morphology 1995*, edited by G. Booij and J. van Marle, 43–66. Dortrecht, The Netherlands: Springer. doi.org/10.1007/978-94-017-3716-6_3.

Heath, J. 1978. *Ngandi Grammar, Texts and Dictionary*. Canberra: Australian Institute of Aboriginal Studies.

Heath, J. 1984. *Functional Grammar of Nunggubuyu*. Canberra: Australian Institute of Aboriginal Studies.

Henderson, J. 2013. *Topics in Eastern and Central Arrernte Grammar*. Munich: Lincom.

Hilpinen, R. 1981. 'Conditionals and Possible Worlds.' In *Tome 1: Philosophie Du Langage, Logique Philosophique [Volume 1: Philosophy of Language, Philosophical Logic]*, edited by G. Fløistad and G.H. von Wright, 299–335. Dordrecht: Springer. doi.org/10.1007/978-94-009-8356-4_12.

Himmelmann, N.P., and E. Schultze-Berndt. 2005. 'Issues in the Syntax and Semantics of Participant-Oriented Adjuncts: An Introduction.' In *Secondary Predication and Adverbial Modification: The Typology of Depictives*, edited by N.P. Himmelmann and E. Schultze-Berndt. Oxford: Oxford University Press. doi.org/10.1093/acprof:oso/9780199272266.001.0001.

Hudson, J.A. 1978. *The Core of Walmatjari Grammar*. Canberra: Australian Institute of Aboriginal Studies.

Hudson, J.A., and E. Richards. 1969. 'The Phonology of Walmatjari.' *Oceanic Linguistics* 8, no. 2 (Winter): 171–89. doi.org/10.2307/3622819.

Iatridou, S. 2000. 'The Grammatical Ingredients of Counterfactuality.' *Linguistic Inquiry* 31: 231–70. doi.org/10.1162/002438900554352.

Janda, L. 2010. 'Inflectional Morphology.' In *The Oxford Handbook of Cognitive Linguistics*, edited by D. Geeraerts and H. Cuyckens, 632–48. Oxford: Oxford University Press. doi.org/10.1093/oxfordhb/9780199738632.013.0024.

Jelinek, E. 1984. 'Empty Categories, Case, and Configurationality.' *Natural Language & Linguistic Theory* 2, no. 1 (June): 39–76. www.jstor.org/stable/4047560. doi.org/10.1007/BF00233713.

Jones, B. 2011. *A Grammar of Wangkajunga: A Language of the Great Sandy Desert of North Western Australia*. Canberra: Pacific Linguistics.

Jones, C., E. Schultze-Berndt, J. Denniss, and F. Meakins. 2019. *Ngarinyman to English Dictionary*. Canberra: Aboriginal Studies Press.

Kapitonov, I. 2019. 'A Grammar of Kunbarlang.' PhD diss., University of Melbourne.

Kawahara, S. 2010. 'Get F0, F1 and Duration. 2010.' [Online.] user.keio.ac.jp/~kawahara/scripts/get_F0F1Dur.praat.

Kearns, K. 2011. *Semantics*. Basingstoke: Palgrave Macmillan.

Klein, W. 1994. *Time in Language*. London: Routledge.

Koch, H. 2014. 'The Reconstruction of Inflectional Classes in Morphology: History, Method and Pama-Nyungan (Australian) Verbs.' In *Language Description Informed by Theory*, edited by R. Pensalfini, M. Turpin, and D. Guillemin, 153–89. Amsterdam: John Benjamins Publishing Company. doi.org/10.1075/slcs.147.08koc.

Koch, H. 2020. 'Development of Aspect Markers in Arandic Languages, with Notes on Associated Motion.' *Journal of Historical Linguistics* 10, no. 2 (August): 209–50. doi.org/10.1075/jhl.18016.koc.

Koch, H. 2021. 'Associated Motion in the Pama-Nyungan Languages of Australia.' In *Associated Motion*, edited by A. Guillaume and H. Koch, 231–324. Berlin: De Gruyter Mouton. doi.org/10.1515/9783110692099-007.

Koch, H., and J. Simpson. 2020. 'Junior Skin Names in Central Australia: Function and Origin.' In *More Than Mere Words: Essays on Language and Linguistics in Honour of Peter Sutton*, edited by P. Monaghan and M. Walsh. Adelaide: Wakefield Press.

Krauße, D., and M. Harvey. 2021. 'Complex Predication and Adverbial Modification in Wagiman.' *Australian Journal of Linguistics* 41, no. 1: 96–129. doi.org/10.1080/07268602.2021.1913401.

Lakoff, R.T. 1968. *Abstract Syntax and Latin Complementation*. Cambridge: MIT Press.

Larson, R.K. 1982. 'A Note on the Interpretation of Adjoined Relative Clauses.' *Linguistics and Philosophy* 5: 473–82. doi.org/10.1007/BF00355583.

Laughren, M. 1978. 'Directional Terminology in Warlpiri.' *Working Papers in Language and Linguistics* 8: 1–16.

Laughren, M. 1982a. 'A Preliminary Description of Propositional Particles in Warlpiri.' In *Papers in Warlpiri Grammar: In Memory of Lothar Jagst*, edited by S.M. Swartz, 129–64. Darwin: Summer Institute of Linguistics.

Laughren, M. 1982b. 'Warlpiri Kinship Structure.' In *Languages of Kinship in Aboriginal Australia*, edited by J. Heath, F. Merlan, and A. Rumsey, 72–85. Sydney: University of Sydney.

Laughren, M. 1992. 'Secondary Predication as a Diagnostic of Underlying Structure in Pama-Nyungan Languages.' In *Thematic Structure: Its Role in Grammar*, edited by I.M. Roca, 199–246. Berlin: De Gruyter Mouton. doi.org/10.1515/9783110872613.199.

Laughren, M. 1999. 'Constraints on the Pre-Auxiliary Position in Warlpiri and the Nature of the Auxiliary.' *Proceedings of the 1999 Conference of the Australian Linguistic Society*, edited by J. Henderson. Melbourne: Australian Linguistic Society.

Laughren, M. 2002. 'Syntactic Constraints in a "Free Word Order" Language.' In *Language Universals and Variation*, edited by M. Amberber and P. Collins, 83–130. Westport: Praeger.

Laughren, M. 2010. 'Warlpiri Verbs of Change and Causation: The Thematic Core.' In *Complex Predicates: Cross-Linguistic Perspectives on Event Structure*, edited by M. Amberber, B. Baker, and M. Harvey, 167–236. Cambridge: Cambridge University Press. doi.org/10.1017/CBO9780511712234.008.

Laughren, M. 2015. 'Expressing Unwanted Outcomes: The Warlpiri Evitative Construction.' Presented to Australian Linguistics Society 2015 Conference, University of Western Sydney, Parramatta, 9–11 December.

Laughren, M. 2017a. 'A Comparative Study of Clausal Negation in Ngumbin-Yapa Languages.' Presented to Ngumpin-Yapa workshop, Brisbane, 10–11 August.

Laughren, M. 2017b. 'The Ergative in Warlpiri: A Case Study.' In *The Oxford Handbook of Ergativity*, edited by J. Coon, D. Massam, and L.D. Travis. Oxford: Oxford University Press. doi.org/10.1093/oxfordhb/9780198739371.013.39.

Laughren, M., K. Hale, J.E. Nungarrayi, M.P.P. Jangala, R. Hoogenraad, D.G. Nash, and J. Simpson. 2022. *Warlpiri Encyclopaedic Dictionary: Warlpiri Yimi-Kirli Manu Jaru-Kurlu*. Canberra: Aboriginal Studies Press.

Laughren, M., and P. McConvell. 2004. 'The Ngumpin-Yapa Subgroup.' In *Australian Languages: Classification and the Comparative Method*, edited by C. Bowern and H. Koch, 151–77. Amsterdam: John Benjamins Publishing Company. doi.org/10.1075/cilt.249.11mcc.

Lausberg, H., and H. Sloetjes. 2009. 'Coding Gestural Behavior with the NEUROGES-ELAN System.' *Behavior Research Methods* 41: 841–49. doi.org/10.3758/BRM.41.3.841.

Lea, J.P. 1989. *Government and the Community in Tennant Creek, 1947–78*. Darwin: The Australian National University, North Australia Research Unit.

Lee, E., and J. Choi. 2009. 'Two Nows in Korean.' *Journal of Semantics* 26, no. 1 (February): 87–107. doi.org/10.1093/jos/ffn012.

Legate, J.A. 2002. 'Warlpiri: Theoretical Implications.' PhD thesis, Massachusetts Institute of Technology, Cambridge, MA. doi.org/10.1162/ling.2003.34.1.155.

Legate, J.A. 2003. 'The Morpho-Semantics of Warlpiri Counterfactual Conditionals.' *Linguistic Inquiry* 34: 155–62.

Lewis, D. 1973. *Counterfactuals*. Oxford: Blackwell.

Louagie, D. 2019. *Noun Phrases in Australian Languages: A Typological Study*. Berlin: De Gruyter Mouton. doi.org/10.1515/9781501512933.

Louagie, D., and J.-C. Verstraete. 2016. 'Noun Phrase Constituency in Australian Languages: A Typological Study.' *Linguistic Typology* 20, no. 1: 25–80. doi.org/10.1515/lingty-2016-0002.

Mansfield, J. 2015. 'Consonant Lenition as a Sociophonetic Variable in Murrinh Patha (Australia).' *Language Variation and Change* 27, no. 2: 203–25. doi.org/10.1017/S0954394515000046.

Matthews, P.H. 1972. *Inflectional Morphology: A Theoretical Study Based on Aspects of Latin Verb Conjugation*. Cambridge: Cambridge University Press.

McCawley. 1993. *Everything That Linguists Have Always Wanted to Know about Logic ... But Were Ashamed to Ask*. Chicago: University of Chicago Press.

McCloy, D.R. 2016. 'Normalizing and Plotting Vowels with phonR 1.0.7.' [Online]. [Last updated 26 August 2016.] drammock.github.io/phonR/.

McConnell-Ginet, S. 1982. 'Adverbs and Logical Form: A Linguistically Realistic Theory.' *Language* 58, no. 1 (March): 144–84. doi.org/10.2307/413534.

McConvell, P. 1980. 'Hierarchical Variation in Pronominal Clitic Attachment in the Eastern Ngumbin Languages.' In *Papers in Australian Linguistics No. 13: Contributions to Australian Linguistics*, edited by B. Rigsby and P. Sutton, 31–117. Canberra: Australian National University Press.

McConvell, P. 1982. 'Neutralisation and Degrees of Respect in Gurindji.' In *Languages of Kinship in Aboriginal Australia*, edited by J. Heath, F. Merlan, and A. Rumsey, 86–106. Sydney: University of Sydney.

McConvell, P. 1983. '"Only" and Related Concepts in Gurindji.' Unpublished manuscript, Batchelor, NT.

McConvell, P. 1985. 'Time Perspective in Aboriginal Australian Culture: Two Approaches to the Origin of Subsections.' *Aboriginal History* 9, no. 1: 53–80. doi.org/10.22459/AH.09.2011.04.

McConvell, P. 1996a. 'The Functions of Split-Wackernagel Clitic Systems: Pronominal Clitics in the Ngumpin Languages (Pama-Nyungan Family, Northern Australia).' In *Approaching Second: Second Position Clitics and Related Phenomena*, edited by A.L. Halpern and A.M. Zwicky, 299–331. Stanford: CSLI Publications.

McConvell, P. 1996b. 'Gurindji Grammar.' Unpublished manuscript, AIATSIS, Canberra.

McConvell, P. 2006. 'Grammaticalization of Demonstratives as Subordinate Complementizers in Ngumpin-Yapa.' *Australian Journal of Linguistics* 26, no. 1: 107–37. doi.org/10.1080/07268600500531669.

McConvell, P. 2009. 'Loanwords in Gurindji, a Pama-Nyungan Language of Australia.' In *Loanwords in the World's Languages: A Comparative Handbook*, edited by M. Haspelmath and U. Tadmor, 790–822. Berlin: De Gruyter. doi.org/10.1515/9783110218442.790.

McConvell, P. 2010. 'Mood Swings: Imperative Verbs Attract Pronominal Enclitics in Ngumpin-Yapa (Australian) and Southern European Languages.' In *Grammatical Change: Theory and Description*, edited by R. Hendery and J. Hendriks, 123–56. Canberra: Pacific Linguistics.

McConvell, P., and J. Simpson. 2012. 'Fictive Motion Down Under: The Locative–Allative Case Alternation in Some Australian Indigenous Languages.' In *Shall We Play the Festschrift Game?*, edited by D. Santos, K. Lindén, and W. Ng'ang'a. Berlin: Springer. doi.org/10.1007/978-3-642-30773-7_11.

McGregor, W.B. 1990. *A Functional Grammar of Gooniyandi*. Amsterdam: John Benjamins Publishing Company. doi.org/10.1075/slcs.22.

Meakins, F. 2010. 'The Development of Asymmetrical Serial Verb Constructions in an Australian Mixed Language.' *Linguistic Typology* 14, no. 1 (June): 1–38. doi.org/10.1515/lity.2010.001.

Meakins, F., S. Disbray, and J. Simpson. 2020. 'Which MATter Matters in PATtern Borrowing? The Direction of Case Syncretisms.' *Morphology* 30: 373–93. doi.org/10.1007/s11525-020-09357-3.

Meakins, F., T.B. Ennever, D.J. Osgarby, M. Browne, and A. Hamilton. 2023. 'Ngumpin-Yapa Languages.' In *The Oxford Guide to Australian Languages*, edited by C. Bowern, 918–32. Oxford: Oxford University Press. doi.org/10.1093/oso/9780198824978.003.0076.

Meakins, F., and P. McConvell. 2021. *A Grammar of Gurindji: As spoken by Violet Wadrill, Ronnie Wavehill, Dandy Danbayarri, Biddy Wavehill, Topsy Dodd Ngarnjal, Long Johnny Kijngayarri, Banjo Ryan, Pincher Nyurrmiari and Blanche Bulngari*. Berlin: De Gruyter Mouton. doi.org/10.1515/9783110746884.

Meakins, F., P. McConvell, E. Charola, N. McNair, H. McNair, and L. Campbell. 2013. *Gurindji to English Dictionary*. Batchelor: Batchelor Press. gurindjidictionary.org.au/.

Meakins, F., and R. Nordlinger. 2014. *A Grammar of Bilinarra: An Australian Aboriginal Language of the Northern Territory*. Berlin: De Gruyter Mouton. doi.org/10.1515/9781614512745.

Meakins, F., and R. Nordlinger. 2017. 'Possessor Dissension: Agreement Mismatch in Ngumpin-Yapa Possessive Constructions.' *Linguistic Typology* 21, no. 1: 143–88. doi.org/10.1515/lingty-2017-0004.

Meakins, F., and C. O'Shannessy. 2012. 'Typological Constraints on Verb Integration in Two Australian Mixed Languages.' *Journal of Language Contact* 5: 216–46. doi.org/10.1163/19552629-006001001.

Merlan, F. 1994. *A Grammar of Wardaman: A Language of the Northern Territory of Australia*. Berlin: De Gruyter Mouton. doi.org/10.1515/9783110871371.

Moens, M., and M. Steedman. 1988. 'Temporal Ontology and Temporal Reference.' *Computational Linguistics* 14: 15–28.

Moravcsik, E.A. 1978. 'On the Distribution of Ergative and Accusative Patterns.' *Lingua* 45, nos 3–4 (August): 233–79. doi.org/10.1016/0024-3841(78)90026-8.

Mosel, U. 2006. 'Grammaticography: The Art and Craft of Writing Grammars.' In *Catching Language: The Standing Challenge of Grammar Writing*, edited by F.K. Ameka, A. Dench, and N. Evans, 41–68. Berlin: De Gruyter Mouton. doi.org/10.1515/9783110197693.41.

Mushin, I. 1995. 'Epistememes in Australian Languages.' *Australian Journal of Linguistics* 15, no. 1: 1–31. doi.org/10.1080/07268609508599514.

Mushin, I. 2013. *A Grammar of (Western) Garrwa*. Berlin: De Gruyter Mouton. doi.org/10.1515/9781614512417.

Nabarula, B., J.N. Cooper, D.J. Graham, N.N. Graham, J.J. Newcastle, S.N. Nelson, B.N. Graham, D.N. Weston, C.J. Freddie, L.N. Freddie, L.N. Morrison, L.N. Benson, P.N. Kelly, E. Newcastle, P.N. Williams, W.J. Graham, L.N. Martin, G.N. Brown, S.N. Grant, V.N. Williams, J.N. Foster, D.J. Foster, D.G. Nash, and G. Wightman. 2022. *Warlmanpa Plants and Animals: Aboriginal Biocultural Knowledge from Tanami Desert Country, Central Australia*. Tennant Creek & Palmerston: Papulu Apparr-Kari Aboriginal Corporation & NT Department of Environment, Parks and Water Security.

Nash, D.G. 1979. 'Grammatical Preface to Vocabulary of the Warlmanpa Language.' [Updated 16 September 2020.] www0.anu.edu.au/linguistics/nash/aust/wpa/wpa-vocab.intro.html.

Nash, D.G. 1980. *A Traditional Land Claim by Warlmanpa, Warlpiri, Mudbura and Warumungu Traditional Owners*. Alice Springs: Central Land Council.

Nash, D.G. 1982. 'Warlpiri Verb Roots and Preverbs.' In *Papers in Warlpiri Grammar: In Memory of Lothar Jagst*, edited by S.M. Swartz, 165–216. Darwin: Summer Institute of Linguistics.

Nash, D.G. 1986. *Topics in Warlpiri Grammar*. New York: Garland.

Nash, D.G. 1989. 'Donald Graham Jupurrula [Obituary].' *Australian Aboriginal Studies*, no. 1: 68–69.

Nash, D.G. 1990. 'Patrilects of the Warumungu and Warlmanpa and Their Neighbours.' In *Language and History: Essays in Honour of Luise A. Hercus*, edited by P.K. Austin, R.M. Dixon, T. Dutton, and I. White, 209–20. Canberra: Pacific Linguistics. doi.org/10.15144/PL-C116.209.

Nash, D.G. 1992. 'Warlmanpa Language & Country.' Unpublished manuscript. www0.anu.edu.au/linguistics/nash/papers/lgshift.pdf.

Nash, D.G. 1996. 'Pronominal Clitic Variation in the Yapa Languages: Some Historical Speculations.' In *Studies in Kimberley Languages in Honour of Howard Coate*, edited by W.B. McGregor, 117–38. Munich: Lincom Europa.

Nash, D.G. 1997. 'Brief Chronology of the Central Northern Territory.' [Online.] www0.anu.edu.au/linguistics/nash/aust/chrono.html.

Nash, D.G. 2000a. 'Warlmanpa Language.' [Online.] [Last updated 1 August 2001.] www0.anu.edu.au/linguistics/nash/aust/wpa/.

Nash, D.G. 2000b. 'Warlpiri Subsection ("Skin") Names.' [Online.] [Last updated 13 May 2016.] www0.anu.edu.au/linguistics/nash/aust/wlp/skins.html.

Nash, D.G. 2018. *Warlmanpa Dictionary*. DN1-Warlmanpa at Catalog.Paradisec. Org.Au. [Online.] catalog.paradisec.org.au/repository/DN1/Warlmanpa.

Nash, D.G. 2022. 'Warlmanpa Lexicon in LexiquePro (2018–2022).' Unpublished work in progress. mbrowne94.github.io/Warlmanpa2022.exe.

Nichols, J. 1986. 'Head-Marking and Dependent-Marking Grammar.' *Language* 62: 56–119. doi.org/10.1353/lan.1986.0014.

Nordlinger, R. 1998. *A Grammar of Wambaya, Northern Territory (Australia)*. Canberra: Pacific Linguistics. doi.org/10.15144/PL-C140.

Nordlinger, R. 2002. 'Non-Finite Subordinate Verbs in Australian Aboriginal Languages: Are Nominalised Verbs Really Nominalised?' In *Proceedings of the 2001 Conference of the Australian Linguistic Society*, 1–10. Melbourne: Australian Linguistic Society. www.als.asn.au/proceedings/als2001/nordlinger.pdf.

Nordlinger, R. 2006. 'Spearing the Emu Drinking: Subordination and the Adjoined Relative Clause in Wambaya.' *Australian Journal of Linguistics* 26, no. 1: 5–29. doi.org/10.1080/07268600500531610.

Nordlinger, R. 2010. 'Verbal Morphology in Murrinh-Patha: Evidence for Templates.' *Morphology* 20: 321–41. doi.org/10.1007/s11525-010-9184-z.

Nordlinger, R. 2014. 'Constituency and Grammatical Relations in Australian Languages.' In *The Languages and Linguistics of Australia*, edited by H. Koch and R. Nordlinger, 215–61. Berlin: De Gruyter Mouton. doi.org/10.1515/9783110279771.215.

O'Grady, G.N., C.F. Voegelin, and F.M. Voegelin. 1966. 'Languages of the World: Indo-Pacific Fascicle Six.' *Anthropological Linguistics* 8: 1–197.

Osgarby, D.J. 2018. 'Verbal Morphology and Syntax of Mudburra: An Australian Aboriginal Language of the Northern Territory.' MPhil. diss., University of Queensland, Brisbane.

Osgarby, D.J. 2021. 'Mudburra Associated Motion in an Areal Perspective.' In *Associated Motion*, edited by A. Guillaume and H. Koch, 325–56. Berlin: De Gruyter Mouton. doi.org/10.1515/9783110692099-008.

Osgarby, D.J., and C. Bowern. 2023. 'Complex Predication and Serialization.' In *Oxford Handbook of Australian Languages*, edited by C. Bowern. Oxford: Oxford University Press. doi.org/10.1093/oso/9780198824978.003.0026.

Palmer, F.R. 2001. *Mood and Modality*. 2nd edn. Cambridge: Cambridge University Press. doi.org/10.1017/CBO9781139167178.

Panther, F., and M. Harvey. 2020. 'Associated Path in Kaytetye.' *Australian Journal of Linguistics* 40, no. 1: 74–105. doi.org/10.1080/07268602.2019.1703644.

Pensalfini, R. 2004. 'Towards a Typology of Configurationality.' *Natural Language & Linguistic Theory* 22: 359–408. doi.org/10.1023/B:NALA.0000015794.02583.00.

Pentland, C., and M. Laughren. 2004. 'Distinguishing Prosodic Word and Phonological Word in Warlpiri: Prosodic Constituency in Morphologically Complex Words.' In *Proceedings of the 2004 Conference of the Australian Linguistic Society*, edited by I. Mushin. Melbourne: Australian Linguistic Society. hdl.handle.net/2123/107.

Prince, E. 1981. 'Toward a Taxonomy of Given-New Information.' In *Radical Pragmatics*, edited by P. Cole, 223–56. New York: Academic Press.

Pullum, G.K., and R. Huddleston. 2002. 'Adjectives and Adverbs.' In *The Cambridge Grammar of the English Language*, edited by R. Huddleston and G.K. Pullum, 525–96. Cambridge: Cambridge University Press. doi.org/10.1017/9781316423530.007.

Recanati, F. 2007. 'It Is Raining (Somewhere).' *Linguistics and Philosophy* 30: 123–46. doi.org/10.1007/s10988-006-9007-1.

Reichenbach, H. 1947. *Elements of Symbolic Logic*. New York: Macmillan.

Reinöhl, U. 2020. 'Continuous and Discontinuous Nominal Expressions in Flexible (or "Free") Word Order Languages: Patterns and Correlates.' *Linguistic Typology* 24, no. 1: 71–111. doi.org/10.1515/lingty-2019-0029.

Rice, K. 2005. 'A Typology of Good Grammars.' *Studies in Language* 30: 385–415. doi.org/10.1075/sl.30.2.10ric.

Riedel, K., and L. Marten. 2012. 'Locative Object Marking and the Argument-Adjunct Distinction.' *Southern African Linguistics and Applied Language Studies* 30, no. 2: 277–92. doi.org/10.2989/16073614.2012.737606.

Ritz, M.-E.A., A. Dench, and P. Caudal. 2012. 'Now or Then? The Clitic -rru in Panyjima: Temporal Properties in Discourse.' *Australian Journal of Linguistics* 32: 41–72. doi.org/10.1080/07268602.2012.657753.

Ritz, M.-E.A., and E. Schultze-Berndt. 2015. 'Time for a Change? The Semantics and Pragmatics of Marking Temporal Progression in an Australian Language.' *Lingua* 166, part A: 1–21. doi.org/10.1016/j.lingua.2015.07.007.

Rochemont, M. 2019. 'Topics and Givenness.' In *Architecture of Topic*, edited by V. Egerland, V. Molnár, and S. Winkler, 47–66. Berlin: De Gruyter Mouton. doi.org/10.1515/9781501504488-002.

Romero, M. 2014. '"Fake Tense" in Counterfactuals: A Temporal Remoteness Approach.' In *The Art and Craft of Semantics: A Festschrift for Irene Heim*, edited by L. Crnič and U. Sauerland, vol. 2, 47–63. Cambridge: MIT Working Papers in Linguistics.

Rothstein, S. 2011. 'Secondary Predicates.' In *Semantics: An International Handbook of Natural Language Meaning. Volume 2*, edited by K. von Heusinger, C. Maienborn, and P. Portner, 1442–62. Berlin: De Gruyter.

RStudio-Team. 2020. *RStudio: Integrated Development for R*. [Online.] Boston: RStudio, PBC. www.rstudio.com/.

Sæbø, K.J. 2011. 'Adverbial Clauses.' In *Semantics: An International Handbook of Natural Language Meaning. Volume 2*, edited by K. von Heusinger, C. Maienborn, and P. Portner, 1420–41. Berlin: De Gruyter.

Sandefur, J.R. 1986. *Kriol of North Australia: A Language Coming of Age*. Darwin: Summer Institute of Linguistics.

Santorini, B., and A. Kroch. 2007. *The Syntax of Natural Language: An Online Introduction*. [Online.] www.ling.upenn.edu/~beatrice/syntax-textbook/index.html.

Schiffrin, D. 1996. 'Narrative as Self-Portrait: Sociolinguistic Constructions of Identity.' *Language in Society* 25: 167–203. doi.org/10.1017/S0047404500020601.

Schultze-Berndt, E. 2000. 'Simple and Complex Verbs in Jaminjung: A Study of Event Categorisation in an Australian Language.' PhD diss., Radboud University, Nijmegen, The Netherlands.

Schultze-Berndt, E. 2003. 'Preverbs as an Open Word Class in Northern Australian Languages: Synchronic and Diachronic Correlates.' In *Yearbook of Morphology 2003*, edited by G. Booij and J. van Marle, 145–77. Dordrecht: Kluwer. doi.org/10.1007/978-1-4020-1513-7_7.

Schultze-Berndt, E. 2008. 'Recent Grammatical Borrowing into an Australian Aboriginal Language: The Case of Jaminjung and Kriol.' In *Grammatical Borrowing in Cross-Linguistic Perspective*, edited by J. Sakel and Y. Matras, 363–86. Berlin: De Gruyter Mouton. doi.org/10.1515/9783110199192.363.

Schultze-Berndt, E., and C. Simard. 2012. 'Constraints on Noun Phrase Discontinuity in an Australian Language: The Role of Prosody and Information Structure.' *Linguistics* 50, no. 5: 1015–58. doi.org/10.1515/ling-2012-0032.

Senge, C. 2015. 'A Grammar of Wanyjirra, a Language of Northern Australia.' PhD diss., The Australian National University, Canberra. doi.org/10.25911/5d77867908aac.

Silverstein, M. 1976. 'Hierarchy of Features and Ergativity.' In *Grammatical Categories in Australian Languages*, edited by R.M.W. Dixon, 112–71. Canberra: Australian National University Press.

Simpson, J. 1983. 'Aspects of Warlpiri Morphology and Syntax.' PhD diss., Massachusetts Institute of Technology, Cambridge, MA.

Simpson, J. 1988. 'Case and Complementiser Suffixes in Warlpiri.' In *Complex Sentence Constructions in Australian Languages*, edited by P.K. Austin, 205–18. Amsterdam: John Benjamins Publishing Company. doi.org/10.1075/tsl.15.10sim.

Simpson, J. 1991. *Warlpiri Morpho-Syntax: A Lexicalist Approach*. Dordrecht: Kluwer. doi.org/10.1007/978-94-011-3204-6.

Simpson, J. 2002. *A Learner's Guide to Warumungu*. Alice Springs: IAD Press.

Simpson, J. 2005. 'Depictives in English and Warlpiri.' In *Secondary Predication and Adverbial Modification: The Typology of Depictives*, edited by N.P. Himmelmann and E. Schultze-Berndt, 69–106. Oxford: Oxford University Press. doi.org/10.1093/acprof:oso/9780199272266.003.0002.

Simpson, J. 2007. 'Expressing Pragmatic Constraints on Word Order in Warlpiri.' In *Architectures, Rules, and Preferences: Variations on Themes by Joan Bresnan*, edited by A. Zaenen, J. Simpson, and T. Holloway King, 403–27. Stanford: Center for the Study of Language and Information.

Simpson, J. 2017. 'Warumungu (Australian–Pama-Nyungan).' In *The Handbook of Morphology*, edited by A.M. Zwicky and A. Spencer, 707–36. Hoboken: John Wiley & Sons. doi.org/10.1002/9781405166348.ch32.

Simpson, J. 2023. 'Warumungu Vocabulary.' Unpublished draft.

Simpson, J., and J. Heath. 1982. 'Warumungu Sketch Grammar.' Unpublished manuscript.

Simpson, J., and M. Withgott. 1986. 'Pronominal Clitic Clusters and Templates.' In *The Syntax of Pronominal Clitics*, edited by H. Borer, 149–74. New York: Academic Press. doi.org/10.1163/9789004373150_008.

Singer, R. 2001. 'The Inclusory Construction in Australian Languages.' *Melbourne Papers in Linguistics and Applied Linguistics* 1: 81–96.

Speas, M.J. 1990. *Phrase Structure in Natural Language*. Dordrecht: Kluwer. doi.org/10.1007/978-94-009-2045-3.

Spencer, B., and F.J. Gillen. 1904. *The Northern Tribes of Central Australia*. London: Macmillan & Co. Ltd.

Stanley, J. 2000. 'Context and Logical Form.' *Linguistics and Philosophy* 23: 391–434. doi.org/10.1023/A:1005599312747.

Stanner, W.E. 1979. *Report on Field Work in North Central and North Australia 1934–5*. Canberra: AIAS.

Stump, G. 2015. *Inflectional Paradigms: Content and Form at the Syntax–Morphology Interface*. Cambridge: Cambridge University Press. doi.org/10.1017/CBO9781316105290.

Tennant & District Times. 2015. 'Mrs B. Nabarula.' *Tennant & District Times*, [Tennant Creek, NT], 21 August.

The Northern Territory of Australia. 1977. 'Welfare Ordinance 1953–1960.' In *Ordinances*, 2307–38. Canberra: Commonwealth Government Printer.

Traugott, E.C., and R.B. Dasher. 2004. *Regularity in Semantic Change*. Cambridge: Cambridge University Press.

Tsunoda, T. 1981a. *The Djaru Language of Kimberley, Western Australia*. Canberra: Pacific Linguistics.

Tsunoda, T. 1981b. 'Split Case-Marking Patterns in Verb-Types and Tense/Aspect/Mood.' *Linguistics* 19: 389–438. doi.org/10.1515/ling.1981.19.5-6.389.

Turpin, M., and A. Ross. 2012. *Kaytetye to English Dictionary*. Alice Springs: IAD Press.

Vendler, Z. 1957. 'Verbs and Times.' *The Philosophical Review* 66, no. 2 (April): 143. doi.org/10.2307/2182371.

Vollmer, M. 2021. 'Understanding Morphosyntactic Variation in a Temporally and Spatially Representative Warlpiri Corpus: A Preliminary Report on Word Order in Clauses.' Presented to First Global Australian Languages Workshop, Yale University, New Haven, CT, 17–20 May.

von Prince, K. 2019. 'Counterfactuality and Past.' *Linguistics and Philosophy* 42: 577–615. doi.org/10.1007/s10988-019-09259-6.

Wilkins, D.P. 1988. 'Switch-Reference in Mparntwe Arrernte (Aranda): Form, Function, and Problems of Identity.' In *Complex Sentence Constructions in Australian Languages*, edited by P.K. Austin, 141. Amsterdam: John Benjamins Publishing Company. doi.org/10.1075/tsl.15.07wil.

Wilmoth, S., R. Defina, and D. Loakes. 2021. 'They Talk Mutumutu: Variable Elision of Tense Suffixes in Contemporary Pitjantjatjara.' *Languages* 6, no. 2: 69. doi.org/10.3390/languages6020069.

Witzlack-Makarevich, A. 2019. 'Introduction.' In *Argument Selectors: A New Perspective on Grammatical Relations*, edited by A. Witzlack-Makarevich and B. Bickel, 1–38. Amsterdam: John Benjamins Publishing Company. doi.org/10.1075/tsl.123.01wit.

Yoon, S. 2013. 'Correlation between Semantic Compatibility and Frequency: A Usage-Based Approach.' *Linguistic Research* 30, no. 2: 243–72. doi.org/10.17250/khisli.30.2.201308.005.

Zester, L. 2010. 'The Semantics of Avoidance and Its Morphosyntactic Expression: Australian Languages vs. English.' MPhil. thesis, Heinrich Heine Universität Düsseldorf, Germany.

www.ingramcontent.com/pod-product-compliance
Lightning Source LLC
Chambersburg PA
CBHW070754300426
44111CB00014B/2402